The University of Kansas
A History

THE
UNIVERSITY OF
KANSAS

A History

by Clifford S. Griffin

THE UNIVERSITY PRESS OF KANSAS

Lawrence/Manhattan/Wichita

© Copyright 1974 by The University Press of Kansas
Library of Congress Cataloging in Publication Data

Griffin, Clifford Stephen, 1929–
    The University of Kansas; a history.

    Includes bibliographical references.
    1. Kansas. University—History. I. Title.
LD2688.G74   378.781'65   73–12349
ISBN 0–7006–0106–6

Printed in the United States of America
Designed by Gary Gore

Publication of this history of the University of Kansas was made possible by a grant from the Kansas University Endowment Association.

*This book is dedicated to
the Graduate Faculty
of the University of Kansas*

Acknowledgments

THE size and complexity of the University's history compelled me to ask many people for very considerable aid. All of them gave generously of their expertise and time. My greatest intellectual debt—for services, advice, and criticism—is to my research assistants: a long line of able students extending in order of appointment from David C. Skaggs through Leonard F. Parkinson, John E. Brown, Thad H. Billingsley, Stanley K. Schultz, Edward A. Purcell, Jr., John R. Finger, Lee M. Peters, Kenneth L. Smock, and John D. Unruh, Jr., to Vernon E. Mattson. Every scholar should be blessed with such assistants. Their burdens and mine, though, were lightened by the eager helpfulness of several librarians and archivists. As head of the former Kansas Collection in Watson Library, Laura E. Neiswanger did me innumerable favors far beyond the call of duty and—although she did not know it at the time—helped sustain my sometimes flagging enthusiasm for the project. She was a marvel. Her successor in the Kansas Collection, Michael J. Brodhead, was also wondrously hospitable. After the Kansas Collection metamorphosed into the Regional History Collection in Spencer Library, Jane Riis and Frank L. Aydelotte and their staffs went out of their way to hasten the history along. And as the University Archives took on substance and shape, John M. Nugent and his crew were, I should say, even more helpful than possible.

I could not have completed the first two chapters, and parts of several others, without the help of Nyle H. Miller, Executive Secretary of the Kansas State Historical Society, and his staff, whose friendliness was as important as their holdings. I am also indebted to Miller and the *Kansas Historical Quarterly* for permission to publish "The University of Kansas and the Years of Frustration, 1854–

1864" (*KHQ*, 32, Spring, 1966, pp. 1–32) as parts of the present chapters 1 and 2.

Without financial aid from the University's General Research Fund and its administering Research Committee I could have neither undertaken nor completed this history. And thanks to arrangements made by then Vice-Chancellor James R. Surface, moreover, I was able to have a full semester free of teaching duties in which to write.

Other University officers and former officers were remarkably magnanimous. When he was Executive Secretary of the University, Chancellor Emeritus Raymond Nichols guided me through the scattered University records, remnants, and remains before they became the University Archives. At least as important was his reading of and comments on volume 1 of this history when it was in a two-volume manuscript form, and then his similar—and even more perspicacious—treatment of the one-volume edition, which saved me from numerous errors. Former Graduate School Dean John H. Nelson also read the former volume 1 and commented on it. Francis H. Heller, former Vice-Chancellor, read the current version and in doing so corrected mistakes and prevented several aesthetic lapses. He also found money for typing the final draft. I also appreciate very much the reading that Irvin E. Youngberg, Executive Secretary of the Kansas University Endowment Association, gave the work, as well as his granting me access to the Association's archives.

Deans Martin B. Dickinson, Jr., of the School of Law and George R. Waggoner of the College of Liberal Arts and Sciences generously opened the records of their schools to me, as did former Deans William P. Albrecht of the Graduate School, Kenneth E. Anderson of the School of Education, and Clifford D. Clark of the School of Business. Former Athletic Director Wade R. Stinson helped me locate the files of his division and answered my questions about athletic scholarships.

Several of my professorial colleagues in the University have been extremely charitable. The late George L. Anderson, Chairman of the Department of History when I began this project, encouraged me from the start, offered good advice at every turn, and incisively commented on parts of the manuscript. His successor, W. Stitt Robinson, similarly gave me every encouragement. James C. Malin, in conversations, helped me develop my ideas about univer-

sities in general and the University of Kansas in particular. John
G. Clark read the manuscript in its various versions and stages and
commented on it in his usual trenchant way. The departmental
Hatchet Club offered suggestions for the improvement of the introduction and chapter 21. Other men gave me access to important
sources: James O. Maloney to his speech to the University Senate
in 1958; Milton Steinhardt to the minutes and files of the University
chapter of the American Association of University Professors; Robert P. Hudson to materials at the Medical Center; and G. Baley
Price to his manuscript history of the Department of Mathematics.

For access to the personal manuscripts of Chancellor Ernest H.
Lindley I thank his sons Stanley B. Lindley of Salisbury, North
Carolina, and Ernest K. Lindley of Washington, D.C. Dr. Monti L.
Belot of Lawrence kindly talked with me about the Sudler affair at
the Medical School.

No editor could possibly have been more gracious, perceptive,
imaginative, tough-minded, and in all ways helpful than Donna
Martin of the University Press of Kansas.

My great thanks to Lois E. Clark, who typed the manuscript—
again and again—with steady good humor and steady perfection.

I know only one way adequately to thank my family—Marianne,
Stephen, Anne, and Angela—for their gifts of love, freedom, peace,
and long-suffering listening that I found necessary to complete this
book. That is by promising never—ever—to mention the University
of Kansas to them again.

Contents

List of Illustrations

Introduction

$\mathcal{W}$HEN the University of Kansas opened on September 12, 1866, the only things it had in common with the genuine universities of the time were a name, a charter, and a quarrelsome faculty. Two of the three professors thought the other, who was also the acting president, both intellectually incompetent and personally uncongenial, and were conniving with several regents to unseat him. But in all the ways that mattered the so-called University of 1866 was merely a preparatory school for a nonexistent college, and an undernourished one at that. It had no college students, for no high-school graduates or students with equivalent preparation had applied for admission. It had no school other than a preparatory school. It had no research scholars on the faculty, no library worthy of the name, and only one building—and that a jerry-built three-story structure, fifty feet square, set high on a windswept, treeless hill in Lawrence once called Hogback Ridge but now named, more elegantly, Mount Oread. The charter of 1864 had absolved the legislature of all financial responsibility for creating the institution and made no promises of future support. In 1865 and 1866 the regents had only some $21,000 to spend, and despite the faith that University spokesmen professed in the enlightened generosity of the citizens, they had no guarantee of getting any more.

During the next hundred years, however, the University rose above the poverty of its beginnings to become a university in fact. It became, that is, an institution of learning with aspects so diverse, often so antagonistic, as to beggar description. Its nature, indeed, often seemed to lie in its contradictions. Through the research of its faculty, for example, the University fostered the highest learning: the pursuit of truths yet unknown. Yet many of its undergraduates

1

—and even many faculty members—cared nothing for research and publication, and actively opposed it in the name of better classroom teaching. While spokesmen of the College of Liberal Arts and Sciences argued for the liberal education of every undergraduate, leaders of several of the undergraduate professional schools, whatever the deference they paid to the liberal arts, gave their students a severely technical training. Although the modern University was always searching for an elusive something called "excellence" in higher education, many of its citizens measured excellence in part by the successes of a mammoth intercollegiate athletic program complete with highly paid professional coaches and quasi-professional athletes. Among the faculty and students were idealists who believed that man's greatest dignity lay in his quest for truth for its own sake alone and relativists who asserted that only socially useful truths had value. If the University was a place where students learned, it was also a place where students played—sometimes at innocent diversions sanctioned by the authorities; sometimes not. In the institution's mixed bag of possessions were a contract with the Peace Corps, an outstanding art collection, the only United States Cavalry survivor of Custer's Last Stand (a horse named Comanche displayed, stuffed, in a glass case), the oldest chapters of Phi Beta Kappa and Sigma Xi west of the Mississippi, a university press, an alumni association, vast tracts of vacant land, a traffic problem, and sizable amounts of intellectualism, aestheticism, and the crasser forms of pragmatism.

All of which meant that the University of the 1960s was a modern American state university that had outrun its founders' rosiest dreams. It had nine professional schools and an undergraduate college, a library of 1,100,000 volumes, impressive laboratories, over 100 buildings, 15,000 students, and almost 1,000 faculty members, many of them professionally eminent. It had great sums of money— though never enough—acquired from the state legislature, private gifts, the federal government, prudent investments, and levies on the students and their parents. Taken altogether, it was one of the greater glories of the Sunflower State.

Despite the differences between the modern and the early University, however, there was an all-important similarity, a likeness that both explained and gave meaning to the institution's history. For a century both the University's members and the people of

Kansas had remained perplexed and confused about the proper nature of American universities in general and their own university in particular. The University's development during its first hundred years, indeed, was the result of a continuing argument among bemused Kansans about what the school should do and what it should be. Nor was the argument only between those atop and those beneath Mount Oread. Within the University itself the faculty, students, deans, chancellors, and regents continually clashed over functions, structure, and goals. If they could not agree, Kansans generally could not be expected to agree either. Inside and outside the University, men of different inclinations naturally offered different ideas. At the century's close, moreover, it was clear that disagreement and conflict would continue to shape the school in the decades lying ahead. The past and future of the University of Kansas, like those of every other American university, were the past and future of an institution seeking its own identity.

The uncertainty and arguments were inevitable. They arose from three uncontrollable forces: confusion among the nation's academicians about the proper character of universities; the inability of Kansans, like Americans generally, to agree on anything at all, but especially on the nature of their state institutions; and a national disagreement about the ideals and goals of America itself.

"We may as well state frankly," said Kansas Chancellor Joshua A. Lippincott in 1883, "that the position of the university as distinguished from the college is, as yet, quite unsettled in the American educational system." Lippincott was correct. During the latter half of the nineteenth century, when many American colleges were rapidly evolving into universities and when new institutions were appearing, there was no agreement among higher educators about what a university was. To be sure, there was a consensus that a university should have both a liberal arts college and several professional schools, that it should teach both undergraduates and graduate students, and that its faculty members should perform research as well as teach. But these were general guidelines only. Within them a great variety of combinations and emphases was possible, and there was no telling which was the more correct or desirable. Ideas that were exciting at Harvard were unpopular at Yale and anathema at Princeton. To reach the ideal university the leaders of

Johns Hopkins and those of Cornell took diverging paths. There was no standard university for later comers to take as their guide.

For a century the results were both happy and unhappy. Lack of agreement meant freedom and flexibility, plurality of form and function, all sorts of public services. In making and implementing decisions, universities could be autocratic or democratic or anarchistic; in supervising students, strict or lenient; in determining curricula, reactionary or avant-garde. Yet at Kansas and elsewhere freedom inevitably yielded awkwardness and friction as well as opportunity. The key processes in building a university were balancing its parts and expanding its activities in an environment of economic scarcity. These in turn demanded the pondering of the imponderable, the measuring of the immeasurable. There were, for example, no objective or agreed-upon standards by which to assess the relative values of the Departments of Philosophy and Home Economics, or the Schools of Fine Arts and Education, or the humanities and the natural sciences, or research and teaching, or any other of the University's clashing interests. Neither were there clear standards for determining the relative power of faculty and regents, or how the chancellor should relate to the faculty, or what authority the students should have. Yet decisions about such matters had to be made, and their making inevitably yielded confusion, animosity, resentment, tension.

Complicating the internal argument was the fact that as the University grew, it became increasingly difficult for the hundreds and then thousands of its citizens to discuss its nature in any coherent or meaningful way. Even the faculty—let alone the students —found it all but impossible. In the school's early years—a sort of golden age that ended in 1893—the entire faculty met together, the chancellor presiding, to pass on important questions and to make to the regents recommendations affecting the University as a whole. Such plenary meetings gave every faculty member the opportunity to join with all his colleagues in defining the University's character. In 1893, however, the faculties of the various schools began meeting separately, and a University Council was organized, composed of school representatives. Although the membership of this body had been broadened by 1914 to include all the full and associate professors—its name had been changed to Senate—an era of dispersed discussion, fragmentation, and even ignorance had clearly arrived.

The problem was one of faculty inertia, however, as much as one of size. Assuming that the University Senate was the best place to carry on such a discussion and that junior faculty members should not be allowed to participate in it, however interesting the ideas they might have, any general inquiry into what the University should be would still require great effort. A full investigation would have demanded very frequent meetings and, academicians being what they are, almost interminable talk. It would have required of Senate members detailed knowledge about the University as then constituted, familiarity with the various views on the American university then circulating in the national academic community, and a good deal of creative thought. It would have demanded an enormous amount of time and effort, a sacrifice of both research and leisure.

For various reasons, during most of the University's history after 1893 the Council and Senate members were not ready to make such sacrifices. There were only two discussions of any significance. One culminated in the writing of a short-lived University constitution in 1913. The other lasted from 1932 to 1937 as a University Senate Survey Committee and then the Senate itself attempted to pierce to the heart of the mystery of the institution's definition. The final report explained the Senate's position on a host of matters: from the purpose of the American state university in general to the functions of the deans, from academic freedom to extracurricular activities, from faculty tenure to the question of course duplication. It was a bold new step to resolve past and present confusion—but its importance was ultimately slight, for it established no precedents.

In the late 1940s and throughout the 1950s the closest the Senate came to considering the University's proper nature was a discussion of its own structure and power—an important part of the problem, but only a part. Chiding his colleagues in 1958 for their inattention to the real question, the chairman of the Senate Advisory Committee said that across Mount Oread there was a "lack of concern for developing an understanding of the nature and ideals which must exist in order to form a great university." At Kansas there was very little discussion of the "essential nature of a university. . . . It is hard to comprehend in any definite and vivid way what we are trying to do here." The reasons?: "our preoccupations, our lack of tradition, the absence of a ready model and our own ignorance—all these conspire against the initiation of a conscious effort toward greatness."

The citizens of Kansas also had difficulties deciding what they wanted of their state university. If the state legislature expressed their ideas, most of them believed most of the time that the University should grow less rapidly than its officers and faculty wished: that is, that it should be something other than they desired. Yet within that apparent majority consensus were all sorts of diversity, and there was always a significant minority who believed and acted as the University asked. To balance them, though, there was another minority who suspected that the University required drastic redefinition. This led to investigations and new laws that University employees and supporters deemed unwise, to inquisitions about the political and moral opinions of its faculty and students, to damaging changes in its structure. More important, it led to a feeling on the Hill that the legislature and the people did not understand the university idea as they should.

But how could they? Immersed in their daily concerns, divided among themselves about what the state itself should be, attacked too frequently by grasshoppers, drought, floods, and hard times, Kansans had precious little time to give to a proper understanding of institutions of higher education. And those Kansans who were interested in the matter had divided loyalties, for in an agricultural state the Agricultural College was not part of the University— thanks to the foolishness and greed of numerous men in the 1860s— and there were several other state colleges and a cluster of small denominational schools. University authorities, of course, did their best to enlighten the people about their institution's worth and work. In words by the million they spoke of such things as the values of the search for truth and of the freely inquiring mind, the relation of knowledge to material prosperity, the success of democratic government, and moral progress. They spoke of well-balanced minds in well-balanced people, and of the natural connection between the lower schools and the University. Lacking a University, they contended, Kansas would be forever a wasteland.

In most of the propaganda, however, lay evasions and half-truths about the University's character, which actually prevented a full public understanding of the school. Because of the problems that University publicists faced, their explanation of what the institution was and what it ought to be had to be a practical, dollars-and-cents, simple explanation. It had to appeal to sentiments easily aroused and offer ideas easily grasped. It could not overly tax the mind or trouble the spirit. It had to present the University in an exclusively favorable—that is, a less than wholly honest—way. What was the point, for example, of telling the people that the University faculty was always divided against itself about the proper character of its own institution, yet also less than eager to discuss the subject intelligently? What was the point in telling the people about confusions and doubts, of rivalries and feuds between schools, departments, and individuals, or of faculty-administration rancors? What, in other words, was the point of trying to explain the University's complex reality?

From the publicity of partiality came both fortunate and unfortunate results. Because of the ceaseless propaganda, and also the growth in the number of alumni, successive generations of Kansans favored the University more and gave it more of the things it said it needed. New buildings appeared, new faculty members were hired, new schools, divisions, and departments began, statistics that were meant to rise, rose. Although it was impossible to say just where the University of Kansas ranked at any given time in the hierarchy of American universities, it came to include much that was excellent.

At the same time, because Kansans were unaccustomed to hearing the full truth about the University, many of them came to assume that the things they heard actually described it. This, in turn, made them overreact when they discovered facts that had existed all along but had been wholly or partially concealed. Thus Kansans have customarily heard that the University's faculty and students were generally united and harmonious in their desire to help Americans find a better life within the traditional institutions of American democratic society. In fact the University always contained a significant number of freely inquiring minds speculating wildly on such fundamental problems as the nature of God, man, human destiny, social institutions—minds that reached decisions very much at odds with popular ideas. Their speculations and conclusions, of course, were never part of the University's official publicity. When the citizens more or less accidentally found out what was going on, then, they called for investigations and purges, called upon the University's leaders to make the school what its publicity said it had been all along: one which served society according to society's own needs and dominant ideas.

Again, because several generations of Kansans heard and read too much about simple and practical things, they became less interested than they might have been otherwise in such things as the requirements and characteristics of the free and creative mind, the lofty flights of intellect and spirit that the University encouraged, or the ever present and ever vexing question of what a university should be. The nearest that most people on Mount Oread came to a discussion of such things with the people was to offer elegant platitudes on great ceremonial occasions. Those platitudes, of course, were always briefly presented, rather than carefully explained, analyzed, justified, and refined. They were easily uttered and—although they were often true—they were just as easily forgotten.

And just as the people have had trouble understanding the University, so have the University and its citizens had trouble understanding the people. For where were the means of yesterday and where are the means of today by which Kansans generally might explain their ideas to the University? Too often the members of the University have allowed the opinions of a few Kansans to stand for those of most. Snide little newspaper editorials by snide little men, for example, have often been taken to express the views of their readers. The eccentric speeches of eccentric men have often been taken to mean that most Kansans are eccentric. Attacks upon the University by men of unsound judgment or vicious natures have been seen as attacks by the people at large. Thus they have caused University dwellers to think evil and petty thoughts and become a little vicious themselves. Up on the Hill men have not known just what Kansans have wanted of their University. Nor, above all, have they known just how much of the total truth about the University the people could absorb and deal with intelligently. The means of getting such knowledge were not there. Communications between the University and its constituency on fundamental substantive questions have been lamentably deficient.

In all the hesitancy and doubts about the University's nature, Kansans on and off Mount Oread have reflected a national uncertainty about the nature of their country. Fittingly, the University's appearance symbolizes the larger society: the architecture of its buildings is by turns beautiful, ugly, honest, deceitful, exalting, depressing, nondescript, confused—a hodgepodge of moods, styles, thoughts, and afterthoughts that could only be classified as Mount Oread eclectic. Even so was American society confused about the relation between things intellectual, spiritual, and secular, about the affinity between nebulous truth and tangible reality, about the desirable relations between education and democracy, about whether the assets of the nation and its people would ever prove adequate to their needs. Until those and related questions were answered, the University could be no different from what it was.

The feeble preparatory school of 1866, then, would develop in ways unforeseen by its founders. Yet the essence of the modern institution is like the essence of its predecessor. Still vague in nature, still arguing that nature intramurally and extramurally, still satisfying many of society's needs, still both a creator and a creation of that society, the modern University is so different from the early University because it resembles its forebear so much. Within that apparent paradox lies the institution's history.

1

The Years of Frustration

"THEY call Kansas the Sunflower State," wrote Charles F. Scott a few years after his graduation from the University of Kansas in 1881. "Not because it is overrun with the noxious weed," he explained, "but because as the Sunflower turns on its stem to catch the first beams of the morning sun, and with its broad disc and yellow rays follows the great orb of day, so Kansas turns to catch the first rays of every advancing thought or civilized agency, and with her broad prairies and golden fields welcomes and follows the light."[1]

Making allowances for the hyperbole, Scott was right. Early Kansans, struggling to humanize an often cruel wilderness, needed all the advancing thoughts and civilized agencies they could get, and they eagerly imported them from the East. Among them, inevitably, was a state university, for which there was widespread enthusiasm from the start. Yet that very enthusiasm, paradoxically, delayed the university's founding for a decade and then weakened the institution that appeared. During the territorial period of the 1850s both pro-slaveryites and Free-State men desired to create a public university, but each group sought a university of its own, and the conflict between them aborted their schemes. After Kansas became a state in 1861, a fierce competition among several towns for the university delayed its creation for two more years and then, tragically, ended in chopping what had been designed as a single institution into three starveling parts. In so doing, the legislators prepared the way for a century and more of discord, confusion, duplication, and waste.

10

In a later day many of the University's supporters would be fond of believing that the school was the product of the noble idealism of Free-Staters who came to Kansas in the mid-1850s to keep slavery out. Tradition would have it that they knew that freedom required an educated people and therefore built the institution. Kansas in the 1850s, rhapsodized a lady faculty member half a century after her graduation from the University in 1874, was settled by the pure of heart. They had emigrated not "in quest of gold, or adventure, as men have peopled many other states, but with the unconquerable purpose to keep this soil free from the curse of human slavery. . . . It was these freedom-loving men and women who, with small resources and in a scantily-populated territory, built a complete school system, which they crowned with the State University."[2]

Like many another legend, this one was both charming and childish. The university idea came to Kansas with Free-Staters and proslaveryites alike, and if the Free-Staters were first in theory the proslaveryites were the first to act. On May 30, 1854, President Franklin Pierce signed the Kansas-Nebraska Act. The law divided the vast Nebraska Territory in two and provided governments for Kansas and Nebraska, thereby making their settlement possible. For many Americans, however, the law's significance was not that it aided westward expansion but that it made possible the expansion of slavery. Repealing the Missouri Compromise of 1820, which had prohibited slavery in the Louisiana Purchase north of 36°30′ except in Missouri, the Kansas-Nebraska Act allowed the territorial legislatures to decide whether they would admit the "peculiar institution." Antislaveryites and anti-Southerners in the North and West were outraged.

Among slavery's opponents were men who saw in the opening of Kansas opportunities for both economic and moral gain. In the spring of 1854 the Massachusetts legislature chartered the New England Emigrant Aid Company. The organization had two goals: to transport to Kansas people determined to exclude slavery, and to make profits for its backers. Led by Eli Thayer and Amos A. Lawrence in Massachusetts, and represented in Kansas by Charles Robinson, Samuel C. Pomeroy, and others, the Company supplied its settlers with money, supplies, and antislavery propaganda, and helped found a number of towns, among them Lawrence, Manhattan, and Topeka. Lawrence was the strongest redoubt of the Free-State partisans. Many of the town fathers liked to think of it as a bit of New England transplanted to the prairies. Scenically and morally they had a point. Located in a green and fertile valley between the Kansas and Wakarusa rivers, Lawrence stood among lovely rolling hills and boasted a modest mount of its own, the view from which was enchanting. If there were few trees, no real mountains, and no ocean, the community at least had an unquenchable thirst for righteousness. Leading Lawrencians, determined to bar slavery from the territory, were always ready to suffer much for the cause of virtue and justice and, with the old New England spirit, to make others do the same.[3]

The Lawrence Free-Staters were also determined to supply their community with schools and a college. According to the original petition of the Emigrant Aid Company to the Massachusetts legislature, one of the organization's purposes was to provide the emigrants with the "advantages of education," and the Company's Kansas agents promised to start a college as soon as possible. But in neither New England nor Kansas was there enough money. Although the Lawrence leaders opened a school in 1855, thus showing the sincerity of their desire for educational institutions, creating a college was beyond their means.[4]

While the Free-State men dreamed, the proslaveryites acted. By order of Governor Andrew H. Reeder elections of delegates to the first territorial legislature came on March 30, 1855. Confusion and knavery accompanied them. Even though proslaveryites clearly outnumbered Free-Staters, on election day several thousand proslavery Missourians crossed the border to vote illegally, just to make sure that the legislators had the right ideas. On June 25, before the legislature had met, Free-Staters in convention at Lawrence repudiated that body and styled it the "Bogus Legislature."[5] But bogus or not, the legislature chartered a territorial university. Governor Reeder had assumed that the lawmakers would naturally furnish an educational system for the territory. "To enlarge upon the necessity of general education for producing good government," he told them, "would be at this day a work of supererogation, and I leave the matter in your hands, confident it will receive the attention it deserves."

The legislature responded as expected. It established a territorial common-school system and approved a charter for the University of the Territory of Kansas. To be located in the town of Douglas, several miles up the Kansas River from Lawrence, its main support was to be a fund derived from the sale of lands that the national government would presumably bestow. Its purpose was the "promotion of literature and of the arts and sciences." Its twenty curators, chosen by the legislature, might confer all such degrees as were "known to and usually granted by any college or university."[6] But with many Kansans repudiating the Bogus Legislature and its works, and with Congress uninterested in granting land, the territorial university never materialized.

All the Free-Staters could do now was follow suit. Surprisingly, they played a weak hand. In September, 1855, many of them gathered in Topeka under the leadership of Charles Robinson to begin the so-called Topeka Statehood Movement. Among their accomplishments was a constitution under which they hoped Congress would admit Kansas to the Union. While the Topeka Constitution required the state legislature to create a public-school system, on the establishment of a state university it was only permissive. If the legislature wished, it could charter a university "with such branches as the public convenience may hereafter demand, for the promotion of literature, the arts, sciences, medical and agricultural instruction."[7]

Nothing ever came of that university, either, for Congress did not admit Kansas under the Topeka Constitution. In supporting its creation, however, the Free-Staters, like their opponents, were expressing in a new environment an idea long familiar to thousands of Americans. As Governor Reeder said, everyone knew the importance of public education as a bulwark of democracy. By the mid-1850s, state universities had become commonplace in the South and West, though not in the Northeast. Missouri had one, chartered in 1839, and so had Wisconsin, Michigan, Iowa, Ohio, Indiana, Georgia, Alabama, South Carolina, and several other states. While the Kansans of 1855 deserved credit for thinking of a public university, their thoughts were conventional.[8]

Through years of strife, they kept the university idea alive. For the Kansas environment, alas, was anything but conventional. From the Free-State–proslavery enmity, complicated by personal feuds and the confusion and violence that always attended the settlement of

American territories, came a civil war in the summer of 1856, a distressing struggle over the proslavery Lecompton Constitution of 1857, and continuing conniving to capture the territorial legislature. Yet Kansans on both sides continued to plan for a state university.

But if there was idealism in the university movement, there was also chicanery. Both Free-Staters and proslaveryites wanted their own institution. There was no chance that a territorial legislature boycotted by Free-Staters would choose Free-State curators. Late in 1856, similarly, when several Lawrence men began a territorial university movement, it was a strictly Free-State school they had in mind. Plans laid by a committee of the town's leading citizens culminated in a mass meeting on Christmas Day under the control of Charles Robinson, George W. Deitzler, William F. M. Arny, Erastus D. Ladd, and others. The welfare of every community, they believed, depended in great part upon educational institutions. And the educational system most conducive to the public good was one providing for the education of the whole people "on an equal basis and at the public expense. The child of the honest and humblest parent ought in the eye of the State, to stand on a par with the most favored child of fortune. A system of Free Public Schools, in which the child can be received at the start, and carried forward, if he demands it, to the university with all its opportunities for preparation to fill the highest positions in society, is the greatest boon that can be conferred on any community."[9]

And especially on the town of Lawrence. With little discussion the citizens adopted a resolution stating that the time had come to create a college in Kansas, specifically in their own community. Although privately supported at first—Charles Robinson thought that $100,000 would be necessary to give it a good start and hoped to raise the money back East—the college was designed as the beneficiary of an enormous land grant for a state university which the promoters hoped to get from Congress. After Robinson explained the scheme, the citizens appointed a committee to petition the national legislature. It consisted of men adept at concealing their real purposes: Robinson, Arny, Philip P. Fowler, F. A. Hunt, and George W. Brown. Professing to be appointed by a "mass convention of the citizens of Kansas Territory," they asked Congress for a stupendous 650,000 acres of land, of which 400,000 would be divided equally among four seminaries and the other 250,000 would go to the state university. The committee reminded Congress that since 1803 every new state had received a university land grant; they neglected to mention, however, that the standard grant was only 72 sections, or 46,080 acres. The land was to be selected at once, before the Kansas lands generally were put on the market, and held for the disposal of the state legislature—which the Free-Staters hoped to control.[10]

If the trickery was obvious to proslaveryites, it was equally transparent to indignant Free-Staters in Manhattan who had their own plans. At a mass meeting in January, 1857, Manhattanites heard Albert A. Griffin claim that his Free-State colleagues in Lawrence, who had been "extolled as *martyrs*" were playing "a 'grab game' for the building up of the places they are particularly interested in." Although the Lawrence leaders had called a mass meeting of all interested Kansas citizens, he pointed out, the call had appeared only on December 20 and reached Manhattan only after the Lawrencians had acted and adjourned. Kansas needed a public university, Griffin argued, but it should be established in a central and accessible location—like Manhattan. For all the spleen of the Manhattanites, however, the second Free-State legislature, convened as an answer to the Bogus Legislature, decided in favor of Lawrence. On June 13 "Governor" Charles Robinson signed a bill establishing a university in his community.[11]

Meanwhile the territorial legislature—though still bogus to the Free-State faction—had acted again. When it met in Lecompton in January, 1857, Governor John W. Geary urged that it ask Congress for land to support a territorial university. The legislature accepted the idea without debate, and on February 19 the Governor signed a bill creating the Kansas Territorial University and locating it at Kickapoo in Leavenworth County. Its purpose was to "promote and encourage the diffusion of knowledge in all the branches of learning, including the literary, law, medical and theological departments of instruction." The twenty-two members of the governing board— they were named in the act; none was a leading Free-Stater—were given all the powers and privileges granted in the act of 1855.[12]

Throughout 1857 and 1858, while Kansans remained divided politically, they shared an interest in a public university. In May, 1857, Governor Robert J. Walker reminded them that they still lacked one and urged upon them the old idea that the success of

democracy depended on the people's enlightenment through education.[13] "A general diffusion of knowledge being essential to the
liberties of the people," said the proslavery Lecompton Constitution
the following October, "schools and the means of education shall be
forever encouraged in this state." The "Ordinance" that the Lecompton convention hoped that Congress would approve when it
admitted Kansas as a state envisioned a state college or university
supported by the sales of seventy-two sections of government land.[14]
While Congress and Kansans wrangled over the admission of the
state, in the spring of 1858 Free-Staters put the so-called Leavenworth Constitution before the people. It called for a "complete
system of public instruction, embracing the primary, normal, preparatory, collegiate, and university departments."[15] Kansans rejected the Lecompton Constitution, however, and although they
approved the Leavenworth document, the vote was so small and
interest so slight that the request that Congress approve it came
to naught.

A year later, at the call of the territorial legislature, Kansas
voters chose representatives to still another constitutional convention. It met from July 5 to July 29, 1859, and the people later approved the Wyandotte Constitution that it produced. The document required the legislature to create a state university.

That provision had nothing to do with the Free-State–proslavery
factionalism of an earlier day. As one of its regular committees the
convention appointed a Committee on Education and Public Institutions, the seven members of which were all originally from the
Ohio Valley, middle eastern, or border states from which most Kansans had come. The chairman, William R. Griffith of Bourbon
County, was from Indiana. Samuel D. Houston of Riley County
and C. B. McClellan of Jefferson County were sons of Ohio. Edward
Stokes of Douglas County, John A. Middleton of Marshall County,
and Samuel Hipple of Leavenworth County had come from Pennsylvania. The seventh member, Caleb May of Atchison County, was
a Kentuckian.[16]

On July 14 the Committee reported its proposals. The legislature was to encourage the "promotion of intellectual, moral, scientific, and agricultural improvement" by providing a uniform system
of common schools and other institutions of a "higher grade," embracing normal, preparatory, collegiate, and university departments.

More specifically the legislature was to create a state university
which would promote literature, the arts, and the sciences and
which would include both normal and agricultural divisions. The
institution was to be located at some "eligible and central point."
Its revenues were to come from the returns on an investment fund
composed of receipts from government land sales, grants from the
state legislature, and private gifts. No religious sect was to have any
right to or control of the University Fund. All the state's educational institutions were to be open to both sexes.[17]

The debate on these proposals was curious. At the start the delegates decided that the constitution should at least refer to a university when they beat down without debate an ill-tempered motion of
John P. Greer of Shawnee County to strike out the mandate on the
legislature to create the institution. Greer claimed that higher
education should be left to private enterprise, that public universities often generated "acrimonious controversy" between various
sections of the states, and that, in all, they were of "no particular
good." But the delegates dismissed Greer's objections as silly.[18]

There was a very close division, however, on whether the constitution should compel or merely permit the legislature to create a
state university. Although John W. Forman of Doniphan County,
James G. Blunt of Anderson County, and several others did not
question the usefulness of such an institution, they argued that the
lawmakers should at least have power to consider the question. But
they faced a shrewd counterattack led by education committee member Samuel D. Houston of Manhattan. Kansas required an agricultural school or college, Houston said, in order that its citizens might
discover how to get maximum yields from the dry lands in the
west. An "agricultural branch" of the state university would
assist the "highest possible development of that soil." Without research, the land would remain comparatively worthless, thus de-
laying sale and settlement. "I hope, gentlemen," Houston pleaded,
"you will consider the importance of taking some step that will thus
enhance the value of one-half the land in Kansas." By a vote of 17
to 16 the delegates let the original proposal stand.[19]

But the delegates refused to provide for the equal admission of
men and women to the university. Before considering the report of
the Committee on Education and Public Institutions, the delegates
had approved a proposal by Solon O. Thacher of Lawrence that

when the legislature provided for the formation and regulation of common schools, it should make no distinction between the rights and privileges of males and females. But an effort to extend the provision to the university had met such opposition that it was withdrawn.[20] Now the delegates supported John T. Burris of Johnson County in his motion to strike out the reference to equal admission in the Committee's report. James G. Blunt thought that Burris's motion was an effort to stem racial prejudice. If the provision for the "admission of pupils of both sexes" were stricken, Blunt said, there would be no opportunity for the Democratic delegates opposed to equal education for Negroes to insert the word "white" before the word "pupils." Burris did not explain, however, and his amendment passed.[21]

Except for the Burris amendment and a few minor changes in wording made by the Committee on Phraseology and Arrangements, the report of the Committee on Education and Public Institutions on the university became Sections 2, 7, and 8 of Article VI of the Wyandotte Constitution. The constitution also specified that a Board of Commissioners, composed of the state superintendent of public instruction, the secretary of state, and the attorney general, was to control the management and sale of school and university lands granted by the federal government. Whatever the grandiose schemes of earlier days, the "Ordinance" adopted by the convention proposed that Congress give Kansas only seventy-two sections for the university's erection and maintenance.[22]

It was one thing to write a constitution, however, and another thing to write the university into law. On January 29, 1861, Congress admitted Kansas as a state. But during the next two years a number of local and personal interests frustrated the university movement, violated the spirit, if not the letter, of the Wyandotte Constitution, and finally weakened the university that was chartered.

The Kansas legislature of 1861 was, among other things, an arena in which the towns of Kansas hotly contested for the state institutions which the lawmakers had to bestow. Chief among them was the state capital, but not far behind came the university and the penitentiary. In the running for the three institutions were four towns: Lawrence and Leavenworth in the east and Topeka and Manhattan farther west. At the start Manhattan had the best chance of winning the university, for Lawrencians and Topekans were more interested in the capital and Leavenworth boomers proved willing to settle for the penitentiary. In April Representative William H. Smyth of Manhattan introduced a bill to locate the university there. A week later the House Committee on Public Institutions, after examining the bill, recommended its careful consideration. In Manhattan, the Committee informed the House, stood a Methodist institution called Bluemont Central College. Its trustees had offered it to the state in return for its becoming the state university. A joint legislative committee should investigate the college and the proposed donation and make a report.[23]

Both the House and Senate agreed, and Representative William H. Grimes of Atchison and Senator Otis B. Gunn of Topeka went to Manhattan to look around. They found a "substantial and commodious" three-story building containing eight rooms, an "elegant hall," and a library of some twelve to fifteen hundred volumes, standing on a high piece of land which presented a "landscape to the eye not surpassed in beauty and variety of scenery by any other locality in Kansas." The college grounds included 120 acres of excellent land and a fine quarry for stone with which to build future buildings. What Grimes and Gunn did not say was that the offer of the Bluemont College trustees was a shrewd move to relieve themselves of an unbearable burden, a college that had failed. Chartered in 1858 and opened in 1860, Bluemont lacked money, college students, and prospects for the future. Unloading the school on the state, moreover, would tie in nicely with the Manhattanites' long-standing desire for the state university.[24]

On April 29, when the two men reported, Grimes offered a substitute bill for Representative Smyth's original proposal, accepting the trustees' offer and making Bluemont College the state university. Ten days later the House passed it, 43 to 19, and sent it to the Senate. But there it became embroiled in a fight between Topeka and Lawrence over the location of the capital. The Wyandotte Constitution prescribed that a popular vote should locate it, but the rivals were seeking different electoral bills to help their chances. Finally the Senate passed the Lawrence measure and at the same time approved the Manhattan university bill. The capital proposal then went to a joint committee. While its members clashed, Governor Charles Robinson of Lawrence had to decide whether to sign the Manhattan proposal. With the capital issue in doubt and Rob-

Where the University should have begun: Bluemont Central College, Manhattan, in 1861. (Courtesy Kansas State Historical Society.)

inson uncertain if Lawrence would get any state institution at all, he saw no choice but to veto it. "All portions" of the state should have the opportunity to make proposals to attract the university, Robinson said; and since the university had no endowment yet, its location was premature. The constitution required a two-thirds majority to override. Despite frantic efforts the Manhattan men in the House could muster only 38 of the 58 votes cast, 2 less than they needed.[25]

On November 15, 1861, Kansas voters chose Topeka as the state capital. The decision meant that the Lawrence boosters would have to make a great effort to capture the university. They could only wish each other luck, for to that time they had proved failures as college or university builders. All they had to show for several years of effort was the foundation of an uncompleted college building on a few acres of ground atop Mount Oread and a large number of thwarted hopes.

For a short time things had gone well. In December, 1856, when the Lawrence leaders had organized their mass meeting in support of the private college as the nucleus of the state university, Amos A. Lawrence in Boston had pledged over $10,000 to the enterprise. The gift was in the form of promissory notes for $10,000 and interest that Lawrence held on the Lawrence University of Appleton, Wisconsin, to which he had earlier loaned the sum. Amos Lawrence thought that the Kansas college would serve two purposes. On the one hand it would be a "center of learning." On the other it would be a "monument to perpetuate the memory of those martyrs of Liberty who fell during the recent struggles. Beneath it their dust shall rest"—and Lawrence meant literally that the college should rise over their graves. "In it shall burn the light of Liberty which shall never be extinguished until it illumines the whole continent. It shall be called the 'Free State College' & all the friends of Freedom shall be invited to lend it a helping hand."[26]

Unfortunately, the other friends of freedom kept their hands in their pockets. Neither Amos Lawrence nor Charles Robinson, on a swing through the East, was able to scare up funds. Thereupon the discouraged Lawrence withdrew his offer from the university in February, 1857, and, adding $1,000 in Emigrant Aid Company stock, directed that it be used to support common and Sunday schools, which he thought of more use than a college "at this early day." The amount, which was to be an endowment fund, came to $12,696.14.[27]

During the rest of 1857 and most of 1858 the cause of higher education in the town of Lawrence languished. A national financial panic in 1857 and a subsequent depression made private funds scarce, and Congress granted no land. But in the fall of 1858 the town's promoters hit upon a new scheme, which would occupy them for the next four years: to get money from churches to support a denominational school. The territorial legislatures of 1858 and 1859 granted charters for a number of sectarian institutions—for Methodist schools in Palmyra, Atchison, Manhattan, and Doniphan, a Presbyterian university in Highland, an Episcopal university in Wyandotte, and several more—and Lawrence men now jumped at the same idea. It proved a chimera. First they turned to the Presbyterian Church in the United States of America—the so-called Old School or conservative wing of Presbyterianism—for they had heard that the General Assembly's Board of Education might have money. (There was irony in the choice, for the Old School General Assembly had long refused to condemn slavery and thus had great support in the South.) At their behest, the legislature of 1859 chartered the Lawrence University, twelve of whose twenty-one trustees were to be chosen by the Old School Presbyterian Church in Kansas. Among the original group were Charles Robinson, Samuel C. Pomeroy, Timothy Dwight Thacher, and several other Lawrence leaders.[28]

But within a few months the Lawrence University trustees had begun to develop doubts about Old School Presbyterianism. Although they scraped together enough money to build a foundation for the college building—the cornerstone was laid in October, 1859—the General Assembly was unresponsive. In the spring of 1859, however, the Kansas General Association of the Congregational Church met in Lawrence, and offered a denominational college to whatever community would support it most handsomely. Lawrence men induced Amos Lawrence to contribute his fund to the project—none of the money had been spent, for the Lawrence University trustees had not paid their debt—and threw in a little more cash, 151 town lots, and almost 1,400 acres of land. But while they won the right to the college, they could find no private contributions in either West or East to support it.[29]

If Calvinists were poor, however, Episcopalians might be rich. In January, 1861, Acting Governor George M. Beebe signed a bill chartering the Lawrence University of Kansas. Half its trustees were to be chosen by the Standing Committee of the Episcopal Diocese of Kansas, on nomination by the bishop. Among the first trustees, named in the act, were Charles Robinson, the Reverend Charles E. Miner, the Reverend Charles Reynolds, and James Blood, all of whom had been trustees of the Lawrence University in its Presbyterian phase.[30] But it no longer mattered which denomination backed the college. Depression, drought—no rain fell in Kansas from June, 1860, to November, 1861—and the excitements of both the organization of a state government and the disorganization of an oncoming civil war dried up prospective donations. The state legislature was Lawrence's last hope.

In the legislature of 1862 Manhattanites renewed their Bluemont College offer and there was also a bid from Emporia, though it was only forty acres of land. To outbid both, a group of Lawrence men offered $15,000 in cash—most of the money was the Amos Lawrence fund although no one had asked Amos's permission to use it this way—twenty acres of land for the campus, and $10,000 worth of other real estate. But in February the House approved the Manhattan proposal by the comfortable majority of 45 to 16.[31]

This time in the Senate the bill ran afoul of internecine warfare in the Republican party. In a continuing contest for power James H. Lane of Lawrence and his faction were attempting to oust Governor Robinson and several other elected state officials by charging them with conspiring to defraud Kansas of thousands of dollars' worth of state bonds. In February the House voted to impeach Robinson and his cohorts, and Lane immediately began scheming to get a majority in the Senate for the trial in June. The best way seemed to be to expel four pro-Robinson senators—Lane's charge was that they held state elective office at the same time that they held federal military positions—and replace them with Lane men. All four were supporters of the Manhattan university bill, and so was Senator M. L. Essick of that city who, in a closely divided Senate, held the balance of power between the Lane and Robinson factions. Until Lane approached Essick with the obvious deal, he had been voting to keep the Robinson senators. But in return for Essick's anti-Robinson vote, Lane promised that he could supply enough votes to carry the Manhattan bill, and he apparently guaranteed Essick that the new Lane senators would also support the measure.[32]

Lane's promises were worthless. Before Essick switched his vote and the Robinson men were expelled, the Senate had defeated the Manhattan measure, 13 to 10. With the new Lane men present, however, the Senate voted, 18 to 4, to reconsider, and three of the four new senators voted with the majority. Yet immediately afterward, when the bill came up for a final vote, only one of them voted in favor and the other three opposed it. Manhattan lost, 12 to 11, in a stunning disappointment to Essick and his friends.[33]

For all that anyone could tell in the spring of 1862, the Kansas solons might go on arguing forever about the university's location. The federal government, however, along with the usual political conniving and payoffs, made it possible to satisfy all the leading contenders. On July 2, 1862, President Abraham Lincoln signed the so-called Morrill Act. It gave to each state thirty thousand acres of government land for each of the state's senators and representatives under the apportionment of 1860. The receipts of the land sales were to be an investment fund to support at least one college whose "leading object" was to teach such branches of learning as related to "agriculture and the mechanic arts" in order to "promote the liberal and practical education of the industrial classes in the several pursuits and professions in life."[34]

On January 14, 1863, Governor Thomas Carney, in his inaugural message, called the legislature's attention both to the Morrill Act and to the constitutional requirement of a university. Given the words of the constitution, Carney naturally assumed that the legislature would wish to create only one university, with an agricultural department. "A wise combination of the interests of the State, and a just application of the means which the general government should grant," he said optimistically, "will enable us to do for education all that an intelligent people could ask or desire."[35] But the legislators had other ideas. Four days after Carney signed a joint resolution accepting the terms of the Morrill Act, the House unanimously passed a bill accepting Bluemont College as a gift from its ever generous trustees, this time in return for its becoming the state agricultural college. The Senate debated the measure for a time, then also approved it unanimously.[36]

While one part of the original University of Kansas headed west to Manhattan, other parts headed east to Lawrence and south to Emporia. By the end of January the House of Representatives had bills from Lawrence and Emporia to deal with. Lawrence was still offering the $15,000 fund and the twenty-acre campus, but not the $10,000 worth of extra land. Emporia had increased its pledge from forty to eighty acres. On January 31 the House Committee on Public Institutions, probably knowing that the Lawrencians did not have the $15,000 actually in hand, recommended passage of the Emporia bill. But during the next ten days the Lawrence supporters mounted a huge lobby whose propaganda featured the $15,000 gift. After the contest was over and Lawrence was victorious, Charles Robinson told Amos Lawrence that his money was mainly responsible for the triumph. "It was with great difficulty that the location was secured here," Robinson wrote, "and nothing saved us but the inducement of your fund."[37]

Yet if several of Robinson's contemporaries were correct, Lawrence was saved by political jobbery as well. In a later year a brother of one of the Lawrence lobbyists recalled that they had bought as many votes as they could at the going rate of around five dollars apiece. William Miller asserted that his brother Josiah, the Lawrence postmaster, had actually saved the university for his hometown when he accidentally discovered two unbribed members of the House and bought their votes with four dollars that he happened to have in his pocket. According to Charles V. Eskridge of Emporia, men on the streets of Topeka were talking about the use of "corrupt means" to procure passage of the Lawrence bill. Eskridge demanded an investigation, but in the absence of specific charges the House refused to act.[38] At the same time rumors were common in Topeka that Lawrence men had struck one deal with those interested in securing the state insane asylum for Osawatomie in Miami County, and another with representatives of the northern tier of Kansas counties who desired legislative authorization for a railroad to run west from Atchison to connect with the great transcontinental line.[39]

It is impossible to say, however, exactly what factors influenced individual House members. During hours of bitter arguing in the Committee of the Whole on February 9 the Lawrence backers, led by James S. Emery, George Ford, and William Foster, managed to get the Emporia bill amended to provide for the university's location at Lawrence in return for $15,000 and forty acres of land. When the amended bill came to a vote in the Committee of the Whole, the House was tied, 33 to 33. Representative Edward Russell of Doniphan County—one of the northern tier—was speaker pro tem; he voted for Lawrence. Then the Committee of the Whole rose, the House beat down a motion to adjourn, and then voted to send the measure to third reading. The next day the House passed it, 38 to 32.[40]

The Senate was far more hospitable. On February 13 its Committee on Public Institutions and Buildings recommended the bill for passage; four days later the Senate defeated a motion by Perry B. Maxson of Lyon County to substitute the original Emporia measure; and on the eighteenth the Senate passed the bill, 19 to 4. On February 20 Governor Carney signed it. The act provided that three commissioners appointed by Carney were to locate the University at "some eligible point" in or near Lawrence on at least a forty-acre site. Within six months after the transfer of the land to the state Lawrence citizens had to deposit a $15,000 endowment fund with the state treasurer. If they failed to raise it, Emporia would get the university, providing the town gave eighty acres of land.[41]

Now that Lawrence and Manhattan had been satisfied, there seemed no reason that a generous legislature should not satisfy Emporia as well. On February 19 Representative Eskridge brought in a bill to locate and endow a state normal school there. The bill passed both houses easily, and early in March, Governor Carney obligingly signed it, too.[42] After nine years with no territorial or state institutions of higher education, Kansas suddenly had authorization for three, two of them, by the spirit of the constitution and the intent of its writers, properly parts of the university. If the new University of Kansas obeyed the constitution, moreover, the state would have two agricultural schools and two normal schools. Because Manhattan was a more "eligible and central point" than Lawrence and the gift of Bluemont College would have saved the state several thousand dollars, the university should have been located there. But local rivalries and personal jealousies had dismembered it, and the friends of public higher education could only hope that the future would be better than the past.

2

The University Comes
to Lawrence

THE next five years were not especially encouraging. Between 1863 and 1868 an institution of learning calling itself the University of Kansas did appear in Lawrence; it had a charter, a building, fifty-five students in its first semester, and three full-time faculty members. Yet its location in Lawrence meant that it was $5,000 poorer than it should have been; many of its early regents were uninterested in the school; none of its first students desired a college education; and the legislature showed little enthusiasm for building a distinguished university. During the University's early years its most remarkable characteristic was that it existed at all.

First came the pillaging of the endowment fund. Governor Carney had appointed Simeon M. Thorp and Josiah Miller of Lawrence and Isaac T. Goodnow of Manhattan as commissioners to locate the university. Thorp had just completed a year's term as state superintendent of public instruction, Goodnow was his successor, and Miller was the Lawrence postmaster.[1] The obvious site—though they inspected others—was the brow of Mount Oread, south of and above the plot where the Lawrence University foundation stood. But the brow belonged to ex-Governor Charles Robinson and his wife, Sara, who were asking $2,000 cash. After a local subscription drive failed to raise all the money, the Robinsons settled for cash and a swap: for half a block of city land, ten acres elsewhere on Mount Oread, and $600 they gave forty acres to the state.[2]

The $15,000 came harder. After the location, Lawrence resi-

dents had until November 1 to raise it. Two days after Governor
Carney had signed the Lawrence bill, Charles Robinson asked Amos
A. Lawrence for permission to use the fund earlier promised to the
Congregational college to win the university. Lawrence agreed at
once and even offered to pressure his Wisconsin debtors to pay up.
But they had no money. Neither was there money to be found in
Lawrence—especially after William Clarke Quantrill and his cut-
throats sacked the town on August 21. Robinson and his cohorts
went back to Amos Lawrence, this time with a bold request for a
$15,000 gift. Their daring almost paid off: Lawrence promised
$10,000 outright if they would raise the rest. After a frenzied search
for $5,000 the town leaders found that Governor Carney himself
would loan it from riches accumulated as a Leavenworth grocer. He
took the notes of the citizens for the money and on November 2
announced that the university was in Lawrence to stay.[3]

Immediately afterward he and the Lawrence men began scheming to get their money back from the state. In 1864 Carney asked
the legislature to reimburse the Lawrencians for the money they had
just contributed. Their gift had been "noble as well as generous,"
he said, but in the "fell hour" of Quantrill's raid, "they lost, as it
were, their all. Rebel assassins did this fatal work. Where, then,
the patriot heart in the State, that would not say promptly, 'Return
to these public-spirited men the generous gift, which, when wealthy,
they promised, and which promise, when poor, they fulfilled?' "
Patriot hearts in both houses passed the relief bill unanimously.
But unfortunately for the university, the bill, introduced by Representative James S. Emery of Lawrence, took the $5,000 from the
endowment fund itself. Before the institution opened, before it
even had a charter, for that matter, it was already a third poorer
than it had been in 1863.[4]

But at least and at last the University of Kansas had a home.
The legislature of 1864 also gave it a form. On March 1 Carney
signed an organization act.[5] Like many another college and university charter, it was precise on the nature and powers of the Board
of Regents and on financial matters, and vague and inconsistent on
the nature of the University itself. The University's purpose was
to provide Kansans with the means of acquiring a "thorough knowledge of the various branches of literature, science and the arts." It
was to consist of six "departments" or schools, the first of them a

Department of Science, Literature, and the Arts. The other five, in theory apparently special branches of the first, were a Normal Department and Departments of Law, Medicine, the Theory and Practice of Elementary Instruction, and Agriculture. The relations of the last two, and of the Normal Department, to the schools at Emporia and Manhattan were undescribed.

Another of the charter's perplexing parts stated that the University was to include both male and female branches; each year the regents were to allot enough money to "establish and maintain" the female branch. The buildings for the two branches were to be separate, and female students might be taught exclusively by women. Although the existence of the female branch meant that women could matriculate on equal terms with men—the charter did not say so directly—it was unclear whether each department and its subdivisions were to be duplicated in the two branches, or whether the female branch was to be merely an adjunct to the rest of the institution.

A Board of Regents and the faculty were to govern the University. The Board was to consist of fifteen members, twelve of them appointed by the governor with the Senate's advice and consent for staggered six-year terms to prevent political manipulation; the other three were the state superintendent of public instruction, the secretary of state, and the University chancellor, whom the other regents were to elect. To prevent sectarian control of the University, not more than three regents at one time could belong to the same church. The regents were to appoint a secretary, a treasurer, and a librarian, none of whom had to be from their own number.

To the regents went almost complete control over the University. Although the chancellor was to be president of the Board, his duties were undefined. The faculty served at the regents' discretion: they could hire such faculty members and "other officials" as they desired, determine their salaries, and remove them whenever the University's "interests" required. While the immediate government of each department resided in its faculty, the regents had general power to govern the University and specific power to regulate the courses and, with the professors' advice, to prescribe the "books and authorities" to be used. The regents might grant such degrees and diplomas as were "usually conferred and granted by other universities." Only in denying the regents the right to require certain religious tenets or opinions of the faculty was the Board's power really limited.

Generous in granting power, the charter was niggardly in granting money. Its last section specifically relieved the state of all expense for the University's organization. To start the school, the regents could spend the income of the general University Fund and the Amos A. Lawrence fund for buildings, equipment, books, and a "cabinet of natural history." Since none of the government land had been sold, however, and since the interest on $10,000 was negligible, the University would be cramped from the start. In addition the charter required the regents to have enough money on hand to complete an entire building—or at least a whole wing—before construction could start. Both the governor and the secretary of state had to approve in advance proposed building plans and equipment purchases.

Fortunately the regents could levy admission and tuition fees. The admission fee was never to exceed $10. In the Departments of Science, Literature, and the Arts and the Theory and Practice of Elementary Instruction tuition fees could not exceed $30 a year for state residents. As soon as the size of the University Fund permitted, education in the two departments was to be free to Kansas students.[6]

With the approval of the charter, the progress of the University of Kansas came to a year-long halt. The first Board of Regents never met, apparently because of the apathy of five of them and the death of another.[7] During the year of March, 1864, to March, 1865, Governor Carney and his successor, Samuel J. Crawford, had to choose six new members of the Board. Three of the holdover appointees were prominent citizens of Lawrence: ex-Governor Charles Robinson; James S. Emery, a lawyer, state legislator, and United States district attorney for Kansas; and Solon O. Thacher, another lawyer, the presiding justice of the Fourth Judicial District and the Republican Union Convention's candidate for governor in 1864. Two more were clergymen: the Reverend J. D. Liggett was editor of the official *Congregational Record,* and the Reverend Daniel P. Mitchell was minister to the First Methodist Church of Leavenworth. The sixth holdover was Charles B. Lines of Wabaunsee, a well-to-do farmer and fruit grower, and receiver of the United States Land Office at Lecompton and Topeka from 1861 to 1865.[8]

Joining them on the Board in 1865 were Cyrus K. Holliday of

Topeka, a lawyer, the Kansas adjutant general, and the dominant force behind the Santa Fe Railroad; the Reverends George W. Paddock and William A. Starrett of Lawrence, pastors respectively of the First Methodist Episcopal Church and the Lawrence Presbyterian Church; Dr. Joseph L. Wever, a Leavenworth physician; Theodore C. Sears, a prominent Baptist layman and lawyer of Ottawa; and Elijah M. Bartholow of Wyandotte, the general superintendent and land commissioner of the Union Pacific Railroad. Isaac T. Goodnow, who had once been principal of Bluemont College, was the state superintendent of public instruction, and Rinaldo A. Barker was the secretary of state.[9]

The new regents showed little more enthusiasm than their predecessors. At the Board's first meeting on March 21, 1865, only Thacher, Emery, Robinson, Paddock, and Mitchell, among the appointed regents, appeared; luckily, Goodnow and Barker were also there to make a quorum. To complete the Board, the seven men elected the Reverend Robert W. Oliver chancellor. Oliver was an Episcopalian who had been a pastor in Philadelphia and a chaplain in the Civil War and had come to Lawrence in 1863. Affable and congenial, he was a friend of most of the city's leading citizens and had been a warm supporter of the state university and its location in Lawrence.[10] The regents, exasperated by the absence of half the Board, also resolved that "in filling vacancies in the Board of Regents, the State Executive should have reference to the appointment of such persons as will attend the meetings of the Board." At the regular meeting the following December, nine of the twelve appointed regents appeared, along with Goodnow.[11]

In 1865 and 1866 the regents' most pressing problem was getting money. They proved ingenious in locating and tapping modest pools. In 1863 Charles Robinson had induced Amos A. Lawrence to give to the university cause not only $10,000 cash, but also the interest on his Lawrence University loan. Pushing the Lawrence University trustees as hard as he dared, by August, 1865, Robinson had secured $4,720. To that he added a $600 note he held against the Plymouth Congregational Church in Lawrence. Several months later the regents induced the citizens of Lawrence to give the institution some $6,700 in so-called relief bonds contributed by sympathetic people in St. Louis to aid the victims of Quantrill's raid. From ex-Governor Thomas Carney in Leavenworth came a few hundred dollars more in relief funds. The regents also sent Chancellor Oliver east to beg for money from the Boston relief fund, but he secured only $2,500 to provide a free education for children orphaned by Quantrill—and then only if the widows and families did not want for money collected in their behalf.[12]

But because such private and semipublic contributions could never be sufficient to construct a building and hire a faculty, in 1866 the regents turned to the state legislature. Despite the prohibition of the charter, their bill moved easily through both houses and in February Governor Crawford signed it. Anticipating a full-time faculty of three professors when the University opened, the regents asked and received $4,000 for salaries. They proposed to give each professor $1,200 a year and spend the rest for part-time assistance. To buy scientific apparatus, furniture, and library books, the legislature gave $3,000. Besides the appropriations, the regents had, by July, 1866, about $1,800 in income from the $10,000 Amos Lawrence gift, which had been invested in state bonds.[13]

In all by the end of 1866 the regents had almost $21,000 to spend.[14] Except for the appropriation of $7,000 all of it had gone for a building on the Lawrence University foundation which rose by fits and starts as cash on hand and the weather permitted. Although the location act of 1863 specified that the University was to be situated on a forty-acre tract, building on the Robinson land would have forced the regents to start from scratch when to the north there already stood an apparently firm foundation. The site at this time belonged to several men who were holding it in trust for the city for public purposes, including schools. In the spring of 1865 the regents talked both the trustees and the city council into giving it to the University and through Chancellor Oliver secured whatever right the Episcopal Diocese had by the Lawrence University of Kansas charter of 1861. To complete a rectangular site of 7 acres, the regents bought 2¾ acres from James H. Lane for $275, which Lane later returned as a gift.[15]

The regents also hoped to get some construction funds from the city council. Their first suggestion had been that they would accept the foundation and site for the University if the council would present it in such a condition that $5,000 would finish the building. But the council would have none of that idea and the regents were on their own.[16] In September, 1865, they violated the charter by signing contracts with two local firms for a structure to cost about $21,000, which was several thousand dollars more than they had in hand. Construction went ahead into December, when the weather grew fierce and the Board ran out of funds. It picked up again in March. From then until August the regents raised enough money to keep the building going, and thanks to constant watchfulness over the contractors and sizable errors in the original estimates, the building cost much less than expected. Three weeks before the opening in September, 1866, the regents had again run out of money, but by then the building was mostly completed.[17]

Later known as Old North College, it was fifty feet square and three stories high, and had a stone exterior. Inside were ten rooms for offices, classes, and library, laboratory, and storage purposes, together with a large assembly hall on the second floor, and a larger chapel on the third. There was no central heating; each room had its own stove. The University library contained some reports of the United States Patent Office and a few miscellaneous volumes of no importance. A museum room on the third floor had a few geological specimens collected by the faculty in their travels. But if it was a day of small things, by November the regents were planning for several additional structures. In 1866 and 1867, moreover, the Board began the transformation of the barren Mount Oread into a lovely park by grading the grounds, planting Osage hedges, and, more important, setting out some five hundred trees.[18]

While the building was going up, the regents searched for and found a faculty. On July 19, 1866, they met formally and on motion of Cyrus K. Holliday voted to establish three chairs, each so remarkable for its breadth that one of the faculty would describe them as benches. There was to be a professor of belles lettres and mental and moral philosophy, a professor of languages, and a professor of mathematics and the natural sciences. There were only three serious candidates. The first professorship went to Elial J. Rice, the second to David H. Robinson, and the third to Francis H. Snow.[19]

Robinson and Snow would serve the University long and well. Robinson was an upstate New Yorker who had graduated with high honors from the University of Rochester in 1859. Afterward he taught in academies in New York and Michigan, and then pushed west in 1865 to teach school in Leavenworth. Robinson's specialty was Latin—though he was also competent in Greek—but he was no

Where the University began. The original building (Old North College) in 1867, with the town of Lawrence and the Kansas River in the background.

The University of Kansas (Lawrence) at the end of its first century. The first building struck by a line drawn vertically upward from the farther end of the football stadium stands on the site of Old North College.

narrow linguist. For him the ancient languages were a means of introducing students to the whole of ancient culture: its society, history, and art as well as its literature. He strove to interest the student in everything that would "kindle his enthusiasm and make the old civilizations seem vital, fresh, and real to his alert mind and growing imagination." Widely read in science, philosophy, and history, he believed that every college teacher should be a moral example and guide to his students, and he gave of himself freely to both the quick and the slow.[20]

Francis H. Snow, twenty-six years old, was a native of Fitchburg, Massachusetts, where his father had known Charles Robinson in pre-Kansas days. After graduating with first honors from Williams College in 1862, he served as a volunteer with the United States Christian Commission in the Civil War and then entered Andover Theological Seminary with the idea of becoming a Congregational minister. But in November, 1865, Charles Robinson began to prod Snow to change his mind, and at last he consented to his nomination for a professorship. He seemed a more likely candidate for either of the other two chairs than for the one he finally received. Although he had taken science courses at Williams, he was especially proficient in ancient languages and in the Andover theology and philosophy. But Elial J. Rice defeated him for the chair of belles lettres and no one nominated him for the chair of languages. He was, in turn, the only candidate for the science chair.[21]

Snow would remain a professor at the University until his death in 1908 and would serve as chancellor from 1890 to 1901. As a teacher he was vigorous, gay, brisk, and congenial, always doing his best to narrow the natural gap between professor and pupil. Both his rudimentary scientific training and his personal bent dictated that he would be more the field scientist or natural historian than laboratory investigator. His greatest love was entomology, his greatest joy the collecting trips he made through Kansas and the Southwest, his greatest pride the thousands upon thousands of superb specimens that he and his students gathered and mounted. Unlike David Robinson, Snow became a publishing scholar as well as a teacher, though most of his work would be descriptive rather than analytical.[22]

In contrast to Robinson and Snow, Elial J. Rice would serve the University briefly and poorly. An Ohio native, Rice had graduated from Madison University in Hamilton, New York, in 1854 and had taken an M.A. there in 1857. During the next nine years he taught school, established his own seminary in Savannah, Ohio, and served as superintendent of schools in Evansville, Indiana. Older and more experienced as a teacher than Robinson and Snow, Rice from the start adopted such superior airs that his colleagues sniggered at him behind his back and shunned his company as much as possible. Rice proved a stern and irascible teacher who neither gave nor received classroom affection, and poor health increased his natural acerbity. Unfortunately in July, 1866, the regents rewarded Rice's seniority by making him president of the faculty; but later in the year they reduced him to acting president and began looking for a permanent president. The demotion disheartened Rice as much as it delighted Snow and Robinson, and the following August his relations with the regents entirely deteriorated when he and his wife argued bitterly with the Board over whether Mrs. Rice should be appointed the "female professor" for whom the Board was searching. Losing the contest, the Rices went to Baker University in Baldwin, Kansas, where Elial became president. In a welcome exchange ex-President John W. Horner of Baker came to the University to take Rice's place. Horner remained for only a year; he left in 1868 to start a newspaper in Chetopa.[23]

To supplement the work of the full-time faculty, the regents hired Dr. Albert Newman of Lawrence as lecturer on hygiene and "sanitary science." Newman had volunteered his services without pay as the result of a suggestion by the Kansas Medical Society. While accepting Newman's offer, however, the regents refused to make him a member of the voting faculty.[24]

Yet the selection of a faculty did not make clear what they were to teach. In December, 1865, the regents had appointed a committee to prepare a course of study. But when the group had no report to make the following July, the regents decided only to open the school on September 12, 1866, to have two terms or semesters of twenty weeks each as the academic year, and to require examinations at the end of each term, and threw the curricular problem to the faculty.[25] But since no one knew what kind of students would appear on opening day, their suggestions were in a sense irrelevant. After Chancellor Oliver had written to his new faculty members about the question, David H. Robinson had recommended an orthodox classical curriculum modeled on the one prevalent in many older institutions. When he and Snow arrived in Lawrence, however, and went to see the Chancellor about their courses, they found him jovially unconcerned. Oliver told them that the quality and training of their future students was so uncertain that they might as well go camping on the prairie as try to write a course of study. They got even less satisfaction from their president. Elial J. Rice, according to Robinson's later recollection, was far more interested in preparing a poem for the opening ceremonies than in preparing a curriculum.[26]

On September 12 Chancellor Oliver led forty students and the faculty in morning devotions, and then the students made the rounds of the faculty to show their knowledge. Not one of them had an adequate secondary education, nor were any of the fifteen additional students who showed up in the next few days ready for college work. While Snow and Robinson were disappointed that they would have only high-school students—the regents had created a Preparatory Department in 1865—they were pleased by the intellectual promise of several of them. Besides, Snow mused, "rapid growth is the character of energetic Kansas," and the Preparatory Department would surely have a short career.[27]

To prepare the preparatory students for college, Rice, Robinson, and Snow met on opening day to complete a two-year curriculum for students at least twelve years old, the minimum admission age. It demanded two years of Latin—Caesar, Cicero, and Virgil—and one year of Greek, including the usual grammar and Xenophon's *Anabasis*; females could substitute French for Greek. In addition, there were arithmetic and algebra, modern and ancient geography, physiology, English grammar, and United States, English, and French history.[28] Later in the day the Board of Regents and the faculty staged a gala celebration and reception in the chapel for the students, their parents, and all of Lawrence, and the University of Kansas was under way.[29]

It embarked upon a sea of optimism. There could be little doubt of the University's success, Regent Solon O. Thacher told his audience at the opening ceremonies. "The Regents believe," he said, "that in the character of the men they have chosen to conduct the institution, they have secured those who will fully meet the requirements of the age, and will carry the University from this humble yet broad and solid stepping stone, up to the height of an enduring and beneficent prosperity." The building, moreover, was but the "first fair edifice among many more pretentious and commodious" structures, "only visible to-day to the eye of faith," but nonetheless real for that. Twenty-five years later David H. Robinson recalled that he and his colleagues in the early period had felt the same way. Whatever the appearance of the school when it opened, it was still a real university, though in "somewhat embryonic form." "As the most perfect forms of animate life now in existence doubtless once lay dormant in the rudest germs," Robinson said, "so to us the University then lay dormant in the creative act of the legislature, scarcely yet in the first stage of its endless development."[30]

During the next two years the faculty and regents needed all the faith they could muster, for there were problems galore. In addition to the worsening relations between Elial J. Rice and the rest of the University, in 1866–1867 there was a dispiriting number of student dropouts, especially among the men. By March, 1867, there were only forty students enrolled, down fifteen from the previous fall. Later that month and early in April male students simply drifted off. After investigating, Robinson and Snow found that some had family farm chores to do and that others, "suffering from the unusual strain of head-work," as Robinson said, had spring fever. Missionary work induced a few to return, but at the semester's end the University had only twenty-two students.[31]

Although numbers rose in the next two years—105 students enrolled in 1867–1868 and 122 in 1868–1869—the faculty continually worried about whether a real public college or university would ever exist in Kansas. The additional students in 1867–1868 had come partly because a third year had been added to the preparatory course and this at the freshman level to catch elementary students. Very few preparatory students went on to college; they and their parents were using the University as a high school. In 1867 and 1868 there were only two students in the college course, a freshman and a sophomore, both girls. The freshman withdrew without finishing the four years. The sophomore was Henrietta Black. "She is quite a prodigy of scholarship," Francis H. Snow thought, "and appears to have retained her womanly nature in spite of her attention to books." Both characteristics attracted David H. Robinson: in 1869 he married her and thus deprived the college of its junior class. Not until the fall of that year did the University have its first students willing and able to work through to graduation.[32]

And then there was the annual financial problem. In 1867 the regents had perfect success with the legislature. Doubling the last year's request, they asked about $14,000. With it they proposed to hire a permanent faculty president for $3,000; raise faculty salaries from $1,200 to $1,600; employ a "female professor" for $1,000; buy equipment; and further beautify the campus. With no trouble they got all they asked.[33]

But after two successful forays to Topeka, a time of reckoning was bound to come. It arrived in 1868. While the regents held the line on annual expenses, they asked the legislature to issue $50,000 worth of 7 percent bonds for another building. A "noble university," the regents argued, would be the "crowning feature of greatness for Kansas," which the state could not properly delay. At the time the state was floating all sorts of bond issues for noneducational purposes and was in the process of spending over $500,000 to add a wing to the state capitol. Surely there was nothing excessive about spending $50,000 on the University.[34] Most legislators disagreed. Some thought the regents were asking too much. Others, scornful of Mount Oread pretensions to university status, saw no reason to help what they sneeringly called the "Lawrence high school." Still others argued for the consolidation of the schools at Lawrence, Manhattan, and Emporia, and would offer little aid to any while they were still divided. And influential Methodists inside and outside the legislature, Francis H. Snow reported, were angry about Rice's recent ouster, and annoyed by the competition for students the state university offered Baker University, fifteen miles to the south.[35] The opposition overwhelmed the regents. With the House of Representatives proving especially pugnacious, the lawmakers not only rejected the $50,000 bond proposal, but eliminated the $3,000 for the president's salary, reduced existing faculty salaries by $100 a year each, and cut the buildings and grounds request of $2,000 to $400. In all the legislature chopped an original $13,800 request to $7,200.[36]

Yet even as the University was losing much of the ground it had won, it acquired a grand asset. That was Chancellor John Fraser, who came to Kansas in 1868 despite the legislature's refusal to appropriate money for his salary. Fraser's acceptance of the chancellorship both enabled the regents to solve a peculiar administrative problem and gave the Board and the faculty renewed hope.

The administrative problem was created by the failure of the charter of 1864 to specify any duties for the chancellor except presiding at the meeting of the Board of Regents. Although Chancellor Oliver had acted as a fund raiser and had solicited the faculty about a curriculum, as late as December, 1866, he was still asking the regents to define his duties. "Nothing can be more embarrassing to an executive officer," he complained, "than to be kept in doubt regarding the duties which are required or expected of him." The regents replied that the chancellor had two main functions: to preside at the meetings of the Board and its executive committee, and to act as the University's general financial agent—which simply summed up what Oliver had been doing right along. This left the chancellor with no relation at all to the faculty or the institution's internal structure. Presumably, the president of the faculty was to be the regents' executive officer in internal matters, but the Board never defined the presidency's nature and duties.[37]

Elial J. Rice's departure gave the regents a chance to straighten things out. At first they planned to leave Oliver as chancellor and hire a president with the $3,000 they hoped to get from the legislature of 1868. On a tour through the East, Oliver visited the University of Michigan, Friends College in Indiana, the Pennsylvania Agricultural College, and Yale. Although he recommended several men to the Board as eminently qualified, the regents at two meetings in August could not agree on a choice and postponed the subject until December.[38] By that time they had dropped all of Oliver's nominees from consideration and were arguing about three others, all of whom had some interest in the job: General Oliver Otis Howard, a soldier famous for his piety and his interest in education, at that time commissioner of the Freedmen's Bureau; former Professor Adonijah S. Welch of the Michigan State Normal School, now a prominent Republican politician in Florida; and President John Fraser of the Pennsylvania Agricultural College. Since Robert W. Oliver was about to resign the chancellorship and leave Lawrence for a new church position in Kearney, Nebraska, before the regents voted they wisely combined the offices of chancellor and president of the faculty and thus made the University's chief executive a member of the Board. After a prolonged discussion in which the regents divided equally among the three candidates, the Welch supporters threw their votes to Fraser and elected him.[39]

Later that month Fraser visited Lawrence to inspect the University. He pleased everyone he met, especially Francis H. Snow. After spending an evening in Fraser's company, Snow concluded that he was an able man with wide scholarly interests. He was animated and enthusiastic about the variety of topics discussed; in all, Snow said, he was "one of the most attractive talkers I ever listened to." When Fraser formally accepted the regents' offer, Snow and Robinson were jubilant.[40]

3

John Fraser's University

IN 1890 Day Otis Kellogg, formerly professor of history and English at the University, wrote to congratulate Francis H. Snow on his election as chancellor. In the process he reminisced about John Fraser. Kellogg had no great love for Fraser: he had conspired with other faculty members to force him from the chancellorship in 1874. But with all his faults, Kellogg admitted, John Fraser was a "generous gentleman." "There was much to like in the man," Kellogg said, "but he could not retire from United Presbyterianism into Spencerian Agnosticism bravely & so he had his insincerities."[1]

Except for the charge of insincerity—Fraser was overly sincere about what he thought was right, a trait which made him enemies—Kellogg's description presented the two most important characteristics of the Chancellor's mind. In it mingled two contemporary currents: that of traditional Christian piety and morality absorbed during his youth in Presbyterian Scotland, and that of the scientific evolution of Herbert Spencer and Charles Darwin. If the effort to synthesize the two made him sometimes difficult to live with, it also proved advantageous to the University. Fraser thought that the University should include both the old concepts and the new. The old were a number of ideas, essentially of religious origin, about the nature of God and man; the new was the nineteenth-century emphasis on and results of the scientific investigation of man and nature. His thoughts harmonized with those of other American

42

university builders who believed that a university should concern itself with all legitimate fields of learning.

Fraser acquired in the next six years faculty members as committed as he to making the University thoroughly modern. Together they began to change it from a struggling preparatory school to a thriving college, and they made Mount Oread an exciting place. Less fortunately, however, Fraser and several of his faculty were too much alike: sensitive, self-righteous, outspoken, tactless, uncompromising. The faculty and some of the regents would come to think Fraser authoritarian; the Chancellor in turn would find several faculty members impudent. By the mid-1870s the University was once again in trouble.

During most of Fraser's adult life he had been a teacher. Born in Scotland in 1827, he had graduated from the University of Aberdeen in 1844 and then gone to Bermuda to teach at the Hamilton Institute. Finding the island climate uncongenial, and later failing to make a success of his own school in New York City, Fraser started an academy in Fayette County, Pennsylvania, and in 1855 joined the faculty of Jefferson College in Canonsburg as professor of mathematics and astronomy. One of his students there remembered him as a paragon of intellect and kindness: his subject mastery was perfect, his zeal and love for teaching, unsurpassed, his sympathy for the slow student who made honest efforts, infinite. After seven years of teaching, Fraser responded to Abraham Lincoln's call for volunteers by leading his own company of college soldiers off to war in the ranks of the One Hundred and Fortieth Pennsylvania Volunteer Infantry. In September, 1862, he became the regiment's lieutenant colonel and the following July its colonel. He led it through the battles of Chancellorsville, Gettysburg, and the Wilderness, but on June 22, 1864, Confederate soldiers captured him and he spent the next nine months as a prisoner of war, mostly in camps near Columbia, South Carolina. On at least one occasion he eased the dull passage of time by lecturing to his fellow prisoners on Shakespeare.

After the war Fraser became professor of mathematics and astronomy and lecturer on military tactics at the Agricultural College of Pennsylvania and in 1866 became its president. Continually searching for excellence, he strove to introduce a number of new subjects into a reorganized curriculum and proposed a vast increase in the number of faculty members. His scheme, however, was more than the college could bear; the school suffered from falling revenues, wholesale student desertion, deepening despair, and impending disaster. Fraser was fortunate to be able to escape to the University of Kansas.[2]

Physically Fraser was short, but his military carriage and his dignity of manner, combined with his long hair and beard, made him seem taller. His head suggested the intellectual—suggested, one student thought, "the fancy that after an average head had been made there had been set upon it in addition a crown representing all the nobler parts of the brain." Fraser was also high-strung and temperamental, varying daily from dourness to amiability. Always introspective, the Chancellor often brooded about the nature of man and especially about his own nature. After his death in 1878 the state superintendent of public instruction gave him a fitting epitaph, quoting the English poet Charles Churchill:

> With curious art the brain, too finely wrought,
> Preys on herself, and is destroyed by thought.[3]

He was familiar with a wide range of writings. Like most other academicians of his day, he knew the standard moral philosophers— Sir William Hamilton, Alexander Bain, Francis Bowen, John Stuart Mill—but he was also at home in literature: the Greek and Roman classics, the works of Shakespeare, Schiller, and Goethe, and those by the Brontës, Bulwer, Coleridge, Leigh Hunt, Dickens, Thackeray, and John Ruskin. He had also read Herbert Spencer's *Social Statics* and almost certainly read his *Principles of Sociology* after the first volume appeared in 1876. While he knew less about the natural sciences—although he could talk easily of them in a general way—he was familiar with the basic principles of international law and had a strong interest in history.[4]

Fraser's educational theory began with God, but put more emphasis on man. Believing that man's ultimate purpose was to know the Creator as well as he could and to obey His will as discovered in the teachings of orthodox Christianity, the Chancellor also thought a traditional knowledge of God was not enough to create the happy and useful lives that God desired men to live on earth. Two other kinds of knowledge were also necessary: knowledge of self—both as an individual and as a social being—and knowledge of the environment.[5] Fraser knew that modern man was singularly complex: he was a creature of the imagination and emotions as well as mind and body, and all of his potentialities needed development. History showed, he said, that both *"high cultivation* of the imagination," and "large stores of knowledge, *civil, social, political, literary, intellectual & moral,"* were necessary for the "high spiritualization" of religion, morality, and life itself. "Passion & Reason in *equal proportions* form effective Energy—& Intellect & Imagination in equal proportions make history."[6]

And Fraser would have men be makers and doers rather than mere thinkers. If personal knowledge and the development of the imagination were goods in themselves, above them in a proper scale of values was the welfare of mankind; the greatness of a man or a civilization was to be measured by contributions to the general happiness.[7] The most important means to such greatness were educational institutions. "The proper education of youth," Fraser maintained, "is the highest privilege & duty & interest of an organized intelligent Christian community." By "proper" he meant institutionalized, higher as well as lower, socialized, and comprehensive. If independent study was valuable, the facts and ideas it yielded would be immeasurably more valuable when expounded by teachers with large minds and large souls. Elementary education, moreover, should be only a preface to higher education; the three R's alone were never enough to allow men to understand either themselves or the world. Education at all levels should prepare youth for the "proper performance of the duties of public and private life," for the reformation of both society and themselves. Such a reformation required an education as comprehensive and diversified as human nature itself. Fraser was as committed to literature and art as he was to science and as committed to science as he was to philosophy. Logic and mathematics would help to show how things related to each other; psychology and philosophy, how knowledge and feeling joined to produce action; biology, how organisms changed with time and circumstance; physics and chemistry, the principles of cause and effect, continuity and complexity. Literature—when properly saturated with Christianity—would diffuse moral teachings through the "little nooks [and] corners of society . . . unreachable by . . . History or Sermons"; poetry was the "blossom and the fragrance of all human knowledge, human thoughts, human passions, emotions, languages." Students should also familiarize themselves with social science, that is, the objective, dispassionate study of the *"growth, development, structure,* & *functions* of the social aggregate, as brought about by the mutual actions of individuals, whose natures are *partly like* those of *all men, partly like* those of *kindred races,* partly distinctive." To know man and to make intelligent decisions about the future, the science of society was indispensable.[8]

Only the American state university, the Chancellor thought, could provide such a diversified education for large numbers of students. The small denominational colleges, of which the nation had long had a surplus, were inadequate in resources and restricted by sectarian ideas. The larger private institutions, such as Yale and Harvard, were, because of their high costs, of benefit to the wealthy alone. Moreover, all private colleges and universities, Fraser said scornfully, were irresponsible because they did not meet the needs of modern man and his society. They held to the old theory of classical education bequeathed by the Middle Ages, keeping the ancient ideas even though their religious affiliations were now Protestant rather than Roman Catholic. This was an unfair judgment, for well before the Civil War many private college leaders were trying to lead their schools away from the traditional curriculum and make their courses more responsive to society's needs. Yet Fraser had a valid point: the state universities offered to large numbers of people opportunities that they could find nowhere else.[9]

That is, adequately supported state universities did. Chancellor Fraser arrived in Lawrence on June 12, 1868. It was immediately obvious to him that the University needed more of everything—more money, more faculty, more buildings and equipment, more college students, more books for the library. The greatest need was a new and larger building, for the swelling student body put space at a premium. There were 122 students enrolled in the 1868–1869 academic year, 152 a year later, and 227 in 1870–1871. In the 1871–1872 year the 265 students overflowed North College, and the regents had to rent rooms for classes in the Lawrence Unitarian Church.[10]

While the other regents were as enthusiastic as Fraser about getting new buildings, after their rejection by the legislature of 1868 they were in no mood to try Topeka again. On Fraser's suggestion they decided to ask the city of Lawrence to float bonds for the structure. The time seemed ripe. In the late 1860s Lawrence was riding the crest of a wave of prosperity from the top of which its citizens foresaw a metropolis of enormous size and wealth, the railroad hub of the region, greater by far than Kansas City. Already over $600,000 worth of railroad bonds had been floated, and Fraser and the Board saw no reason why they could not get another $100,000 or so for the University.[11]

Early in January, 1870, after an impassioned plea by the Chancellor, a mass meeting informally approved the bond issue. Immediately Lawrence legislators introduced a bill in the state legislature authorizing the city to issue $100,000 worth of 7 percent bonds to mature in twenty years. It passed without difficulty. On February 3 the Lawrence voters ratified the earlier informal decision. To make sure that the bonds would be sold, the Lawrencians went back to the legislature with a bill authorizing the Board of Commissioners of the School and University Funds to buy them. When that bill became law, the Board of Commissioners, moving cautiously, bought half the bonds at 90, paying $45,000 for them. A year later the commissioners bought the rest at the same price.[12]

Knowing little about construction costs, the regents thought that their $90,000 would buy three large buildings—one for "general literary and scientific purposes," a second for a chemical laboratory, and the third for the Department of Medicine that the Board had recently voted to establish. After voting to relocate the main campus on the Robinson land, they sent Fraser east to visit various colleges and universities to "obtain the most improved plans for University buildings &c. &c." But in the spring and summer of 1870 the regents discovered that the general literary and scientific building, plans for which had been drawn by Henry J. Haskell of Lawrence, was going to cost some $70,000, leaving only $20,000 for the other two.[13] Thereupon they changed their minds and decided to build one magnificent, all-purpose structure—whether or not they had the money in hand. Construction began in July, and throughout that year the Board's concept of the edifice grew more rapidly than the building itself; in January, 1871, the regents' building committee estimated the total cost at about $139,000. Since there was no further help to be had in Lawrence, the regents went back to Topeka with a bill for $50,000 from the state's general revenues. "Ought not the state to complete the work which the city of Lawrence has so nobly begun?" the regents asked. The legislature of

1871 thought not, and gave no money. Its successor, however, answered the question favorably by granting the full amount without significant opposition.[14] But even so the regents' desires were unsatisfied. On December 2, 1872, when the University's officers and faculty dedicated the gigantic structure, Chancellor Fraser pointed out that some $35,000 was urgently needed to finish and equip the interior.[15]

As Fraser also said, the new building was without peer in all the land, a testimony both to the grace of God and to the "toiling thousands" of people of "our blood-bought Kansas." Facing to the east on the crown of Mount Oread and visible for miles, it was nearly 300 feet long by 100 feet wide at its broadest point, and four stories high. With exterior walls of mortared limestone, it outwardly appeared solid and well built; its architectural effect, said an observer, was "massive and superb." Like similar structures on other campuses, it had two sizable towers with flat roofs and a center section broader than the two wings, giving it a pleasing symmetry. Within it were rooms for all the University's departments and classes. In the basement, which had large windows, were the chemistry classrooms and laboratories, the metallurgical laboratory, a workshop, the boiler room, and storage space. The first floor held the chancellor's office, classrooms, faculty offices in physics and mathematics, and a student reading room. In the center of the second floor was a large assembly and examination hall, two stories high, on either side of which were the classrooms, offices, and laboratories for the biological sciences and drawing classes, and also temporary rooms for the library. Instruction in the ancient and modern languages was consigned to the third floor. Unlike North College the new building had a central steam heating system, as well as electric clocks in the classrooms. According to one enthusiastic observer, the building would provide a "constant and pervasive atmosphere of instruction and education. Every influence will be liberalizing and refining"; the building itself would have at least as beneficial an impact upon students as the "cramming process." Until 1897 it was called the University Building or sometimes University Hall; then the regents named it Fraser Hall.[16]

While Chancellor Fraser and the Board of Regents were providing the University with a building adequate to its needs, they were also giving it a formal organization. When Fraser came to Law-

The University Building. Named Fraser Hall in 1897, it became "Old Fraser" when it was razed in 1965 and a new building was erected on its site.

rence, the University was formless: neither the regents nor the faculty had bylaws, the relations between the two bodies was unclear, the position of the chancellor was obscure. But in December, 1868, at the first full meeting of the Board after Fraser's arrival, the regents gave to their executive committee the power to organize the regents and faculty.

With Fraser making most of the suggestions, the committee adopted a set of bylaws in January, 1869. They required that the Board meet each December to decide important matters; the executive committee or any three regents could call special meetings. The executive committee included all regents living in or near Lawrence. Meeting as the members thought best, the committee could deal with all contingencies as long as they were not important enough to demand a special Board meeting. It was to report its actions to the Board for approval.

For the first time the regents clarified the chancellor's powers and duties. Besides presiding at Board meetings, he was to be the regents' chief executive, carrying out their orders, spending money as they directed, caring for the University's property and its general interests. He also chaired faculty meetings, made sure that the professors obeyed the rules, and required similar obedience from the students. Those general powers left the chancellor with a large amount of discretionary authority.

The government of the faculty grew out of a peculiar mixture of administrative practice and educational theory. In addition to their teaching duties faculty members were to enforce the rules that the regents made for the students; but the faculty could also impose such rules as were consistent with the regents' bylaws and the laws of the land. Each faculty member was to have a "free and equal voice in all deliberations regarding the internal management of the University." To introduce "such improvements in the branches taught, and in the methods of instruction and discipline, as shall have received the sanction of approved experience," toward the end of each academic year the professors were to discuss among themselves their ideas about teaching and discipline. To faculty members in the languages—including English—went a special directive: all recitations were to be "uniformly conducted in such a manner as will serve to enable the student to *speak* and *write* as well as to *read* the language with ease and propriety." In all the language and science courses students were to be trained to *"habits of independent observation, and research."*

In addition to intellectual competence, the regents sought to guarantee the faculty's good behavior. "Every member of the faculty," they said, "shall be required to conduct himself with exemplary propriety on all occasions, but especially toward the students in his classroom, and toward his colleagues in the presence of the students." Except in cases of "gross misconduct, or of flagrant breach of the laws of the University," where dismissal would be summary, the Board promised three months' notice before firing a faculty member and asked, in turn, for three months' notice of resignations.[17]

Both the new bylaws and the start of the University Building showed that Chancellor Fraser and the other regents were determined to lift the University above the poverty and confusion of its beginnings as soon as possible. The most important boost, however, had to come from the state legislature. Except for the Lawrence bonds, small amounts of money from the Amos Lawrence fund, and student fees, the institution had no other source of support. Wealthy donors were nowhere to be found in early Kansas, and the regents had no intention of selling their federal government lands at current low prices. Yet the regents had learned in 1868 to be wary of the lawmakers; and in the next four years they found them mercurial. During 1868 the regents had had only about $8,600 at their disposal, $7,100 of which had come from the legislature. By December they had spent it all and were over $1,900 in debt for faculty salaries, equipment, work on the interior of North College, and newspaper advertisements. For 1869 they projected a budget of about $13,700, with $12,500 to come from the legislature. The money would allow the Board to continue the present salaries of Fraser, Robinson, and Snow, pay their back salaries, hire part-time teachers in German, drawing, anatomy, chemistry, and singing, and buy scientific equipment and furniture.

The regents promised to run the University in the future with the "same scrupulous care which they have evidenced in the past,"[18] but the legislature was unimpressed. While granting the requests for material improvements, it cut the $7,200 salary request to $6,500 and left the Board to distribute it. In a generous gesture Fraser volunteered to take a reduction from $3,000 to $2,300 a year so that faculty salaries could stay where they were; the regents later pledged to reimburse him from student fees. Not only was the reduction disappointing; the whole appropriation bill was insulting—for the salary money was given not as a grant but as a loan which the regents were to repay as soon as they had sold enough government land.[19]

Undaunted, the Board appeared before the legislature of 1870 with a request for $14,600. Most of the increase was for expanding the faculty from four—including the Chancellor—to six. Apparently impressed by the Lawrence bond issue, the legislature granted every penny.[20] So encouraged were the regents that at once they began thinking about both a further expansion of the faculty and a general salary increase. Although Chancellor Fraser could live comfortably on his $3,000 a year, the Board told the legislature of 1871, the $1,600 paid the faculty was inadequate to reward them for their work—which was far greater than that of professors in older and larger universities—or to support their families, or to retain the "best class of instructors" at Kansas. Of a total request of close to $19,000, $14,300 was for salaries; it would have been enough to raise those of the present staff to $2,000 a year and bring in two more faculty members at lower amounts. But as in 1869 the present legislature disagreed with the regents about the worth of professors, and voted only $13,200 for eight of them. Fortunately, few of the legislators were as cynical as one of their number in the early 1870s who claimed to know a man and his wife who would teach all the University's courses for $500 a year. Yet most of them, whatever their ignorance about the nature and work of the professoriate, were often willing to overrule the regents' decisions about the faculty's value.[21]

This time, though, the regents granted raises in spite of the legislature. By careful manipulation salaries went up from $1,600 to $1,800 a year. In 1872 the legislature accepted the increase by granting enough money to maintain that level. Indeed, it proved the most generous legislature that the regents had faced. By votes of 64 to 1 in the House and 18 to 0 in the Senate it gave the full $18,290 that the regents had asked, besides approving $50,000 to complete the University Building. With additional money from the Lawrence fund, student fees, and a balance from the previous year, the University had almost $23,000 for regular expenses.[22]

Some of the money went to hire still another professor, bringing the total of full-time faculty members—including Chancellor Fraser —to nine. They were a remarkable group. Partly by careful searching and partly through sheer good luck the University acquired faculty members far more than adequate to its needs. It was not yet a faculty of scholarly renown, nor were its members eminent in the academic community. Until Frank Harris published the first volume of his salacious and delightful *Life and Loves* in 1922, for example, practically no one outside Lawrence had heard of the University's most remarkable professor, Byron Caldwell Smith. Francis H. Snow was attracting local fame as a scientist and educator but his great work lay ahead of him. Latinists were unfamiliar with David H. Robinson, historians with Day Otis Kellogg, German and French specialists with Elizabeth P. Leonard. The faculty, moreover, had to spend most of their time in the enervating teaching of high-school courses. Yet in their enthusiasm and dedication, and the notable personal flair that several of them possessed, they added excitement and distinction to the institution.

During John Fraser's first year the faculty consisted of four professors and four part-time instructors. The professors were Fraser himself, who taught mental and moral philosophy, David H. Robinson, Francis H. Snow, and Mrs. Cynthia A. Smith in French language and literature. The instructors were Dr. John Folkmann in German and drawing; Dr. Albert Newman in anatomy, physiology, and hygiene; Dr. William H. Saunders, another Lawrence physician, in chemistry; and Samuel M. Newhall, who gave special instruction in voice.[23]

In July, 1869, the Board of Regents at a special meeting took the first step in expanding the faculty and changing its ratio in favor of the professors by deciding to hire two new members. One was a professor of modern languages and drawing who would consolidate the work of Mrs. Smith and Dr. Folkmann; the other a professor of mathematics and engineering who would relieve Francis H. Snow of part of his incredible variety of subjects and courses. To the first position they appointed Miss Elizabeth P. Leonard, a native of Franklin, Connecticut, and a classmate of Sara Robinson at the Belchertown Classical School in Old Hadley, Massachusetts; at the time of her appointment she was teaching in a young ladies' seminary in Quincy, Illinois. Her students at Kansas remembered her grand manner—she had toured Europe twice—and high ideals, and her vigorous, penetrating mind. No typical schoolmarm, she had tremendous enthusiasm and was much interested in art, albeit in a genteelly stuffy way, as well as literature.[24]

The professorship of mathematics and engineering, which also included astronomy, went to Frederick W. Bardwell, then an assistant professor at the United States Naval Observatory in Washington, D.C. He would remain at the University until his death in 1878. A kind and generous man with a well-furnished mind and a wide range of interests outside the sciences, Bardwell proved both an effective teacher and a congenial colleague. He published as well as taught. An article in 1873 suggested that the apparent tails of comets were the result of their passage through a medium designated as a "luminescent field" emanating from the sun. In another article in 1874 he undertook to explain the discrepancies in published theories of eclipses by pointing out that because it took time for light to travel from point to point, the stages of eclipses occurred slightly before observers on earth perceived them. Bardwell also wrote an arithmetic textbook which he put forth as one of the very few that treated the subject systematically. Rejecting the haphazardness of past methods, he arranged the book to proceed by logical stages from the simplicities of whole and fractional numbers through compound denominations and reductions and thence to the so-called practical application of arithmetic.[25]

After the hiring of Miss Leonard and Bardwell, Fraser at once made plans to expand the faculty in other directions. On December 1, 1869, the regents accepted his suggestion to establish a chair of history and English language and literature. While the fields of knowledge covered by such a chair were astoundingly broad, available resources would not permit a greater specialization. In August, 1870, the Board elected Day Otis Kellogg. Born in Troy, New York, in 1837, Kellogg had attended Hobart College and then studied for the Episcopal ministry at the Virginia Theological Seminary; at the time of his appointment he was rector of a church in Providence, Rhode Island. Kellogg was a reflective, sensitive man, looking very much the scholar with his pallid complexion, impressive forehead, and keen blue eyes. He had a bold and trenchant wit, which he used extensively to describe both the shortcomings of his students and the idiosyncrasies of his chancellor. While Kellogg required great amounts of work in his courses, he never believed that recitations or lectures would fully educate. He constantly spurred his students to extracurricular reading and gave them free access to his own small but select library.[26]

The following year the regents added two more scientists—a professor of chemistry and physics and a professor of general and industrial drawing. The reasons for both were vocational as well as scholarly. Drawing was not only an essential part of a good general education, the regents explained to the legislature of 1871, but a necessary study for carpenters, draftsmen, mechanics, engineers, and all other "employees in the various arts and manufactures." Applied physics and chemistry were even now revolutionizing almost every branch of skilled industry and in the future would be of enormous practical importance. The present "limited number of overworked Professors" at the University, moreover, could not offer them.[27]

To the chair of general and industrial drawing the regents elected in succession two professional engineers. The first was Captain Albert J. S. Molinard, a West Point graduate then with the Army Corps of Engineers.[28] But Molinard resigned in 1872 and to replace him the regents chose S. W. Y. Schimonsky, who after emigrating to the United States from his native Prussia had worked for several railroads, among them the Leavenworth, Lawrence, and Galveston. With Frederick W. Bardwell confining himself mainly to mathematics and astronomy, Molinard and Schimonsky taught not only free-hand and mechanical drawing, but also, and more important, civil engineering, including surveying, topography, and applied mechanics.[29]

The new professor of chemistry and physics was Boston-born Frederick E. Stimpson, a graduate of the Massachusetts Institute of Technology. There he had studied the properties and manufacture of illuminating gas under Francis H. Storer and gained repute as an authority on the subject. At Kansas, unfortunately, he had little time to continue his research, for he faced a shortage of chemical equipment and a surplus of duties. Besides teaching all the physics and chemistry courses, he had to serve as his own laboratory assistant, performing the "petty and engrossing labor" of setting up and taking down apparatus. Dismissed by the regents in 1874, he would leave chemistry and physics, and later join Timothy Dwight Thacher in publishing the Lawrence *Journal*.[30]

Of all the faculty members during John Fraser's chancellorship the most remarkable individualist was Byron Caldwell Smith. He came in 1872 as assistant professor of Greek and became a full professor the next year. Although he stayed at the University only until 1875, his impact was nonetheless great. Born in 1849 at Island Creek, Ohio, Smith had graduated at nineteen from Illinois College in Jacksonville and had spent the next four years as a wandering scholar in Europe, studying at universities in Heidelberg, Berlin, Munich, Vienna, and Athens. In the spring of 1872 he returned to live with his mother in Humboldt, Kansas, where Fraser found him. Smith was a tall, lithe young man with the grace of an athlete and the looks of an aesthete: his skin was fair, his dark brown hair grew in ringlets about his face. Alert, courteous, quiet, yet exciting in address, seeking purity and beauty with childlike eagerness, he attracted people wherever he went. A philosophical idealist and a religious pantheist, he found the spirit of Absolute Being in all men and all things and before that spirit he worshiped. "Every manifestation of the divine life is divine, the horse as well as the man," he had written in 1871. "That a thing is, is cause of endless wonder, of a nameless sensation of admiration in the true poet. To him the whole universe is holy, is divine." The Greek language, then, was an introduction to the whole of Greek culture, through which, in turn, one approached the divinity of all men at all times.

Even the more loutish male students knew Smith for a rare bird; most of the females were mightily drawn to him. He fell in love with Kate Stephens of the class of 1875; but they never married, for Smith resigned from the faculty in sickness and died in 1877. When Kate herself joined the faculty in 1878 to teach Greek, she brought to her students the same ideas and ideals as had her lover.[31]

Upon this faculty Chancellor Fraser and the regents built a college. In 1869 the University enrolled its first two college freshmen who would have the stamina to complete the four-year course. They were Ralph Collins, a sixteen-year-old native of Pittsburg, Kansas, who had prepared at a private academy, and Murray Harris, three years older, born in the United States legation in Buenos Aires, where his father had been serving, and who had entered the University's senior preparatory class in 1868. The next year Lindorf Deloss Lockhart Tosh, who had completed his freshman year at Miami University in Ohio, would enter Kansas as a sophomore. And in February, 1872, the class of 1873 acquired a female member: Flora

E. Richardson, a Wisconsin native who had done her freshman work at Lombard University in Galesburg, Illinois, and had taken a few courses at Kansas during a stay in Lawrence in 1871.[32]

The faculty had arranged two four-year courses of study, either of which the students might choose. Collins, Tosh, and Miss Richardson elected the Classical Collegiate Course, which led to the Bachelor of Arts degree. It required two and a half years of Latin, two years of Greek, and a year of either German or French. Along with the languages in the freshman and sophomore years went algebra, plane and analytical geometry, trigonometry, and English grammar, composition, and elocution; in the junior year were added physics, mechanics, English literature, physical geography and geology, and logic. Seniors took a modern language, mental and moral philosophy, political economy, American Constitutional history and law, astronomy, general chemistry, and natural theology, which featured Joseph Butler's *Analogy of Religion*.[33]

There was also a Scientific Course. It eschewed the ancient languages, required but a year of French or German, and exposed students to every science represented in the University. There were algebra, geometry, human anatomy and physiology, botany, and chemistry in the first year; plane and analytical geometry, trigonometry, drawing, surveying, zoology, botany, and astronomy in the second; calculus, physics, mechanics, geography, geology, and chemistry in the third; and astronomy, mineralogy, meteorology, and chemistry in the fourth. Along with them went a smattering of humane and social studies: English grammar, composition, and rhetoric and ancient and modern history in the freshman and sophomore years and logic in the junior; scientific seniors took mental and moral philosophy, political economy, and Constitutional history and law.

In the 1870–1871 academic year there appeared a course in civil and topographical engineering. It included the first two years of the Scientific Course, while juniors and seniors took an additional year of French or German, and also logic, mental and moral philosophy, and "Lectures on History, Political Economy, and the Science of Government." Otherwise, students took a host of specialized engineering subjects, ranging from the drawing of plans, profiles, and elevations to the construction of roads, canals, railways, and buildings. Murray Harris decided to become an engineer, and moved through the special course.[34]

On June 11, 1873, the University of Kansas truly became a college. Though the graduating class was small, the significance of the first commencement was great, for until the institution awarded its first degrees it was only a preparatory school with collegiate courses. Wishing to advertise the event widely, the faculty and regents arranged several days of celebrations in the still unfinished University Building. On Sunday, June 8, the Reverend Richard Cordley of the Plymouth Congregational Church spoke at the baccalaureate exercises. Two days later came the Class Day ceremonies, complete with erudite addresses by three of the graduating seniors and an exhibition of drawings and a bridge model by Murray Harris, the planting of a class vine, and musical selections by the Fifth United States Infantry Band. To deliver the main commencement address, the University's leaders invited United States Senator John J. Ingalls, certainly the most awesome orator in Kansas, if not the entire nation. Ingalls perfectly expressed the spirit of the occasion:

The first time I stood upon this consecrated eminence, I looked southward and eastward down the enchanted valleys of the Wakarusa and the Kaw, through the vacant embrasures of a rude fortification that frowned with incongruous menace above the pastoral landscape for whose tranquil and diversified beauty, nature has no rival, art has no synonym. Clustered along its base, and mirrored in the sluggish stream, were the humble homes of those new Pilgrim Fathers of the West, impelled by
"The Unconquerable mind
And freedom's holy flame"—
to establish in solitude the germs of those institutions which in this brief interval have grown and expanded into a civilization that is one of the great wonders and marvels of the world; a civilization that would have been almost miraculous had its energies been expended in the material triumphs which have been achieved over the stubborn forces of nature, and the wild and wasteful wilderness; the railroads that have been builded, and the cities that have been strung like pearls along their iron cords; the streams that have been bridged, the commerce that has been nurtured; the vast areas that have been rendered productive; the industries that have been developed; but far more marvelous when considered in its connection with those higher attributes which today find their highest expression in the rites which we here perform, to commemorate the first annual commencement of the University of Kansas. This is the State's consummate hour.[35]

4

Starving Times

YET hours of darkness were nigh. Even as Senator Ingalls spoke, the University was entering a period of decline. Everything that could hurt the institution happened at once. In 1873 Kansas along with the rest of the nation began to suffer from an economic recession which would linger for several years. In 1874 came hordes of grasshoppers which gobbled up farm crops and made citizens' cries for economy in state expenditures more strident than usual. Along with recession and grasshoppers came drought in many areas of the state, and to them all was added the gloomy conviction that eastern financiers and rapacious railroad owners were crushing Kansans without mercy.[1] Amid the sufferings of hard times the University's government was reorganized by the state legislature without the advice or consent of the regents or the faculty, and on top of everything else, a power struggle broke out between Chancellor Fraser and his professors.

The legislature of 1873 dealt harshly with the Board of Regents' financial requests, put the University under close scrutiny, and restructured the Board itself. Remembering the generosity of 1872, the regents now asked for over $36,000, almost double the previous year's request; much of the increase reflected the regents' desire to expand the regular faculty from eight to ten and to pay off some $7,500 in debts incurred for the new building. Once more the regents praised themselves for their economical management, but this time the legislators decided to conduct their own investigation.

In February they appointed a joint committee of two—Senator Marshall M. Murdock of Wichita and Representative Isaac S. Kalloch of Lawrence. Their report was wholly favorable. The regents and the faculty, the inquisitors said, were doing fine work, and the new building was excellent in every respect. Though its total cost would be about $180,000, it would be one of the state's cheapest public buildings and one of which Kansans could be proud. In all, the University was a "credit to the State, and worthy [of] the fostering care of the Legislature."[2] A majority of the lawmakers, however, were not easily persuaded. The appropriation act threw out the requests for both the two new faculty members and the $7,500, and reduced the total to about $24,000. While this was an advance over 1872, it was still disappointing to men hoping for rapid progress.[3]

Similarly disappointing was an act reorganizing the Board of Regents. Many legislators had come to believe that all of the state institutions of higher education threatened to become too independent, too unresponsive to the people's needs, too free of legislative supervision. Most of the animus was against the Agricultural College, which had emphasized liberal arts more than the popular mechanic arts and agriculture,[4] but the solons were also concerned about the relevance of the schools in Lawrence and Emporia. The result was a law reconstituting all their governing boards and providing for their regular inspection by a state commission.

As the law affected the University, it provided for a new Board of Regents of seven members, the chancellor and six others appointed by the governor and confirmed by the Senate. The appointees were to serve staggered terms of three years rather than six, as under the charter of 1864; no two appointees, moreover, could come from the same county. Whether by accident or design the law said nothing about the regents' religious affiliations and did not repeal that section of the law of 1864 allowing up to three regents of the same denomination. Thus if three regents and the chancellor were coreligionists, they could control the Board in that respect. Meeting in regular sessions at least twice each year, the regents had to make an annual report to the governor. To the regents went "full and complete powers to adopt and enforce all necessary rules and regulations required under law" for the University's government, and, more specifically, power to appoint the officers, principals, teachers, and employees required for the institution's "practical and economic management."

Yet the legislature would not trust the regents too much. A visiting commission of three citizens, in no way connected with the state institutions, was to be appointed by the governor and confirmed by the Senate. Holding office for three years, they were to make semiannual visits to each school to investigate its financial condition and general conduct and make annual reports and recommendations to the governor.[5]

To the relief of the University community, Governor Thomas A. Osborn's appointments proved friendly. Serving one-year terms—to begin the staggering—were Charles Robinson and William Fairchild, a Leavenworth lawyer and businessman. Two-year terms went to the Reverend Archibald Beatty, an Irishman who was now rector of the Episcopal Church of the Epiphany in Independence, and the Reverend John A. Anderson, pastor of the Junction City Presbyterian Church. After Anderson resigned to become president of the Agricultural College, Governor Osborn appointed V. P. Wilson, a newspaper editor, businessman, and politician of Abilene, in 1873 one of the founders of Enterprise, and withal a Universalist minister. The three-year members of the new Board were the Reverend Frank T. Ingalls, the Senator's younger brother and a Congregational pastor in Atchison, and Noah C. McFarland, a prominent Topeka Republican lawyer and state senator.[6]

At meetings in April and June, 1873, the Board met to survey the University. Commending the previous Board for its forethought, judgment, and economy, the regents appointed a committee on finance and a committee on internal management, the latter to report on the school's general condition and consider the bylaws. On both counts the University came off well. There was general harmony in the faculty, even though several professors had to teach subjects outside their fields of interest and special training. The regents commended Chancellor Fraser for his zeal and energy in performing his "oftimes delicate & efficient work." But there were a few changes to be made. Fraser was to be free from instructing preparatory students—his classes in English, arithmetic, and geography were handed to other faculty members—to give himself fully to college teaching and his duties as chancellor. Accepting the recommendations of a faculty committee headed by Fraser, the regents ordered the faculty to add a Modern Literature Course to the scientific and classical courses of the Preparatory Department. To produce more effective teaching, the Board gave S. W. Y. Schimonsky's free-hand drawing classes to Elizabeth P. Leonard, and her German classes to Schimonsky. The regents then ordered the faculty to frame a plan of discipline for the students; made the faculty responsible for student order and for the "highest possible development of the work of the University"; and, changing only the number of meetings each year, adopted the bylaws of the former Board.[7]

Meanwhile the new Board of Commissioners for Public Institutions—J. C. Wilson, C. S. Brodbent, and Charles Puffer[8]—was making its own investigation. Less impressed than the regents with the University, they praised the past and present but were unenthusiastic about the future. The former regents, according to the commissioners, were men of "superior qualifications in education, of intellectual attainments, and financial and administrative experience," who had husbanded their funds with discretion and spent them with judgment. Within the University there was "perfect harmony" between regents and faculty. The Board of Regents' published report accurately described the institution's management, and the school was "worthy of the care of the State, and of the confidence and patronage of the people."

At the same time the commissioners urged the governor and legislature to trim expenses and appropriations to the bone. Despite the desire of some Kansans to begin all six departments authorized by the charter of 1864, the commissioners recommended no increase. Too many professors at both the University and the Agricultural College were getting fancy salaries of from $1,500 to $1,800 a year for teaching mostly preparatory students. By what the commissioners called a "wise discrimination," two or three "high-priced professors" could be dispensed with and their places in the Preparatory Department filled with lower-paid "subordinate teachers" of "less attainments." More disturbing still was the commissioners' opinion that the Agricultural College was the "peer of the University." This may have been merely farmer-pleasing rhetoric, but if the idea ever gained wide currency in the state it might mean two competing universities rather than one that was, theoretically at least, all-inclusive.[9]

During the 1873–1874 academic year, moreover, the very existence of the University was threatened. Its continuance depended on the ability of its regents, chancellor, and faculty to work with relative harmony and provide means for settling their differences. Yet no such means had been devised, and one result was a battle for control between John Fraser and his faculty.

The root of the trouble was that Fraser and the faculty came to lose whatever respect they had once had for each other. There was Byron Caldwell Smith, for example. In 1872 Fraser had much admired the young man, but on closer acquaintance Smith appeared conceited, visionary, and "passionately fond of riding logical hobbies." "Without experience in life," Fraser charged in a private account of his difficulties, "he is full of German airs and conceits, & manifests a disposition to slight American Colleges & American Education. He is disagreeably captious and critical." Small sparks detonated explosive personalities. In a faculty meeting in December, 1873, Smith accused Fraser of doctoring the University catalogue—by including for an extra year the names of departed students —to make the student body seem larger than it was. Fraser shot back that he would not go to Smith for lessons in honesty, or in "modesty or good breeding" either. The remark cut deeply. Fraser claimed that he offered an apology the next day, but that Smith refused it.

At the time, Smith was rooming with Day Otis Kellogg and his family, which did little for Fraser's peace of mind. In the fall of 1873 Fraser heard reports that while Kellogg had been serving as a temporary pastor in Leavenworth and Topeka churches, he had denigrated Fraser's capacities for the chancellorship and suggested that he himself was more fit for the position. No angry words passed between the two men, but Fraser was suspicious. In the storm that came, Kellogg was more testy than usual because he was distraught over the recent death of his small daughter.[10]

With three other faculty members Fraser found other things wrong. He thought that Frederick W. Bardwell, David H. Robinson, and Elizabeth P. Leonard were incompetent as teachers, and told them and other people so. Bardwell immediately took offense and his anger grew when Fraser denied, on the grounds of incompetence, his request to teach engineering as well as mathematics and to supervise construction of the University Building. Fraser also refused to give Bardwell brief leaves of absence in the spring and fall of 1872 to extend his summer vacation so that he could make some extra money surveying Indian lands for the government, and Bardwell neither forgave nor forgot. An additional member of the anti-Fraser group appeared when Regent Charles Robinson, who already disliked the Chancellor, told David H. Robinson of some teaching defects that Fraser had mentioned to the Board. Miss Leonard joined after Fraser gave her German classes to S. W. Y. Schimonsky and after Charles Robinson again played the tattletale with remarks about her abilities that Fraser had made to the regents. Under the "manipulation of Smith, Kellogg & Gov. Robinson," Fraser said dryly, "she didn't learn to love me." Charles Robinson's dislike was the product of two authoritarian personalities: his own and the Chancellor's. He had severely criticized aspects of the University Building's construction, and while on the subject of faults he censured Fraser for trying to run the University by himself and for making contemptuous remarks about the old Board of Regents. Fraser later admitted that he might have been too vigorous an executive, but denied the contempt charge. At any rate Fraser replied to Robinson sharply enough to make Robinson his enemy forever.[11]

By late 1873 the dissident professors were accusing Fraser of all sorts of shameful acts: of arrogating control of the University to himself and ignoring faculty rights in the process; of wishing more to appear a successful university builder than actually to be one; of obstructing student discipline. Scratching for defamatory material, they also accused him of using language unbefitting the dignity of the chancellorship—specifically of using the word "privy" on one occasion ("earth closet" was the genteel term) and "jackass" on another.[12] Though proof for the charges remained vague—except that Fraser admitted his two lapses from verbal decorum—on December 19, 1873, David Robinson, Bardwell, Kellogg, Smith, and Francis H. Snow demanded Fraser's resignation. Snow had joined the dissidents at the last minute. He and Fraser had not argued, but he bore the Chancellor no great respect; with his friends Charles and David H. Robinson standing against Fraser, his choice was an easy one. Convinced that "harmony of feeling and action" between the five professors and Fraser was no longer possible, they abruptly offered him two alternatives. If he would resign as chancellor at the close of the academic year in June, 1874, they would press the matter no further. If not, they would lay the matter before the Board of Regents.[13]

Fraser, of course, would not quit. "I did not sneak into the institution," he told the regents later, "& I could not afford to sneak out of it, leaving the construction of my conduct in the hands of persons, who, by the abrupt & uncharitable course which they had taken towards me, showed that they were animated by an implacable spirit." In January he told his accusers that he would take the dispute to the regents, whom he called his "rightful judges."[14] The reply pushed the five professors to quick action. Because the one-year terms of Regents Charles Robinson and William Fairchild would expire on April 1, 1874, and because their successors might be friendly to Fraser, the dissidents urged the Board to meet at once. Snow had heard that Fraser was trying to prevail on Governor Osborn not to reappoint Charles Robinson, expecting that without Robinson, he would have a majority. He therefore asked Frank T. Ingalls to join with Robinson and Archibald Beatty to call a meeting. Under the law of 1873 any two regents could call a special meeting, and four members were a quorum.[15]

The outcome was peculiar. In March, 1874, the Board met, listened for three days to the faculty's charges and Fraser's defense, and then voted unanimously to lay the whole subject on the table, requesting the faculty to withdraw their accusations. But after the meeting had ended and the regents were preparing to leave, they and Fraser struck an agreement which sounded suspiciously like a payoff for Fraser's vindication. Fraser mentioned that some of his friends had urged him to run in the fall for election as state superintendent of public instruction, and asked if the individual regents would support him if he resigned as chancellor to enter the contest. The entire Board, Charles Robinson included, agreed to back him. In April, at a meeting of the new Board—it included the Reverend T. F. Houts of Leavenworth, a Methodist, and former Regent James S. Emery of Lawrence—Fraser formally resigned as of the close of the academic year. The regents accepted the resignation, on condition that Fraser remain until they found a successor.[16]

Two months later at commencement John Fraser took formal leave of the University. What could have been a most unpleasant affair passed off with dignity. The Chancellor spoke briefly on the general state of the institution and offered a few remarks on the reasons for his resignation. After the awarding of degrees, students cast several bouquets onto the stage as a tribute to Fraser. Overcome by emotion, he did not see them. Day Otis Kellogg moved from the wings, picked them up, and graciously presented them to the Chancellor. At the commencement banquet that afternoon the Reverend Thomas H. Vail responded in a fitting manner to a (nonalcoholic) toast that summed up Fraser's work during the past six years: "The University under the old regime—broad were its foundations." A more sentimental comment on Fraser's tenure was part of a poem written by members of the Oread Society, a student literary group, and read by James A. Wickersham at the organization's exercises on June 8:

> Leader of our youth, farewell
> Many thoughts our bosoms swell,
> Thoughts which are too sad to tell,
>   Because thou goest.
> What indeed hast thou not been,
> As a father, brother, friend,
> Teaching us our lives to mend,
>   As thou knowest.[17]

Finding a successor proved difficult. Originally the Board of Regents hoped to hire as chancellor a distinguished academician who would add luster to the University. There were, however, only two serious candidates, and the more eminent of them turned the offer down. On June 9, 1874, Regent T. F. Houts offered the name of the Reverend James Marvin, like Houts a Methodist and then professor of mathematics at Allegheny College in Meadville, Pennsylvania. On July 15, however, the Board elected the other candidate, Stephen H. Carpenter, professor of logic and English literature at the University of Wisconsin. Carpenter was a New York native who had graduated from the University of Rochester in 1852 and had gone to Wisconsin immediately afterward. After a varied career as university tutor, newspaper editor, and assistant state superintendent of public instruction, he rejoined the Wisconsin faculty in 1868. He had already published his *English of the Fourteenth Century*, a critical study of Chaucer's English, and was close to completing *An Introduction to the Study of the Anglo-Saxon Language*, later to become a much-admired text.[18]

But in August, Carpenter went to Lawrence and disliked everything he saw and felt. Daily temperatures were a hundred degrees
and more, drought and dust overlay all, the only relief from the sun
was clouds of grasshoppers. So appalled was he that he did not visit
the University or seek out either Chancellor Fraser or any of the
regents. Noah C. McFarland and James S. Emery, appointed by the
Board to greet Carpenter and give him a tour of Lawrence, never
saw him. As soon as Carpenter got back to Wisconsin, he wrote to
decline the offer.[19]

That left John Fraser as acting chancellor. But that awkward
situation could not long continue, for in November he won election
as superintendent of public instruction and would take office in
January. There was nothing for the regents to do but choose James
Marvin, the only other candidate. On November 19 the Board
elected him, and on the twenty-seventh he accepted.[20]

Whatever Marvin would do to or for the University after he
came in 1875, he would find the institution depleted of money and
men and low in morale. In the mid-1870s economic conditions in
Kansas grew steadily worse and the University had to suffer as well.
The legislature of 1874 was less than generous. The regents had
asked for $34,000, of which over $22,000 was for regular expenses
and the rest for special payments: $7,500 to pay off the University
Building debt, $3,000 to build up the inadequate University library,
$1,000 for mothproof cases for Francis H. Snow's specimens. They
also suggested that the legislators appropriate the $35,000 necessary
to finish the University Building's interior.[21] But the lawmakers
would have none of that, and while they did grant the indebtedness
money, they cut the library appropriation in half in the process of
reducing the overall request by some $5,000. Most of the reduction
came where it hurt the most—in faculty salaries. Including the chancellor's stipend, the request had been $18,200. The appropriation
was $15,000.[22]

At the time the University had eight professors, each of whom
received $1,800 a year. The Chancellor, who was also professor of
mental and moral philosophy, received $3,000, and two part-time
instructors received $400 each. Since the reduction of $3,200 was
almost the total salary of two professors, some paring of personnel
was inevitable. The regents' first plan, adopted in April, 1874, was
to reduce the number of full professors from nine to six and hire

three assistant professors at lower salaries. Elizabeth P. Leonard's professorship of French and free-hand drawing was to be abolished, as was Frederick E. Stimpson's chair of chemistry and physics; Byron Caldwell Smith's Greek chair was to be consolidated with David H. Robinson's Latin chair. Hard upon those decisions came resignations and dismissals: Miss Leonard resigned in mid-April, and the Board fired both Stimpson and J. E. Bartlett, the singing instructor. On May 8, however, came the unexpected resignation of S. W. Y. Schimonsky, which made it possible to keep Smith. The regents transferred Schimonsky's courses in engineering and industrial drawing to Frederick W. Bardwell and gave his German classes to one of the new assistant professors. In May, Day Otis Kellogg also resigned. At first the regents refused to accept the resignation, thus showing that they were not trying to remove the anti-Fraser faculty. But Kellogg insisted: he wanted his family to be close to his ailing father and mother-in-law in the East, and the constant Kansas winds distressed Mrs. Kellogg. Besides, he had had two job offers at higher pay and there was nothing to keep him in Kansas.[23]

In May and June the Board of Regents appointed both old and new professors to their positions and added the assistant professors. The new chancellor would take over Fraser's mental and moral philosophy chair; Francis H. Snow would continue as professor of natural science; David H. Robinson and Byron Caldwell Smith would be professors of Latin and Greek; and Frederick W. Bardwell would have charge of engineering in addition to his mathematics and astronomy courses until a full-time engineering professor could be found. To replace Kellogg the regents picked William T. Gage, a Dartmouth graduate and formerly faculty president at the small Highland University in Atchison. He would remain, however, for but a year.[24]

Helping those five professors, when the University opened in the fall of 1874, were three assistant professors: Ephraim Miller in mathematics, Frances Schlegel in German, French, and drawing, and George E. Patrick in chemistry and physics. Miller, an Ohio native and Allegheny College graduate, had been superintendent of schools in Youngstown and Findlay, Ohio, and since 1870 had held the same position in Lawrence. Miss Schlegel, who was only nineteen years old, had been born in Boston; she was a normal-school graduate who had had a year of graduate study before coming to

Kansas. She was also a friend of Francis H. Snow, who apparently recommended her to the Board of Regents. Patrick was a youth of twenty-three, a native of Hopedale, Massachusetts, who had taken his Bachelor of Science degree from Cornell in 1873 and spent the next year there as an instructor in quantitative analysis and agricultural chemistry. After a year as an assistant professor, the regents gave him a chair of his own. Along with the full-time faculty went Dr. Albert Newman, who continued to teach human anatomy, physiology, and hygiene.[25]

Before the 1874–1875 academic year was half over, the University lost Byron Caldwell Smith. Never in good health, in November he asked for and received a leave of absence without pay to seek medical treatment in Philadelphia, where he rejoined the Kellogg family. While there he became interested in a position in the new Johns Hopkins University in Baltimore. In June he asked for an indefinite leave of absence from Kansas. The regents refused it, and abruptly voted to dismiss him after the obligatory three months' notice. Bitter and depressed, Smith blamed his misfortune partly on the regents' insensitivity and inhumanity, and partly on the slanders of Professor D. B. English, his replacement in the Greek chair. English had accused Smith of inflating his reputation as a scholar and of having had intercourse with a young lady of good character and family while he was a student in Athens. Smith did not get the Johns Hopkins position, his illness turned into pneumonia, and after seeking relief in Colorado he died there in 1877.[26]

By the end of 1874 the University was suffering badly, and in 1875 things got worse. With money in short supply and with a balance of some $2,300 from 1874, the regents tried to be gentle in their requests to the legislature, asking about $23,000, of which $15,500 was for salaries for ten faculty members, including the chancellor. But to get even these moderate amounts the regents knew they faced a stiff fight. Well before the legislature met, economizers were in full cry. Chancellor James Marvin's proposed salary of $3,000 was exorbitant, said William C. Tenney of Douglas County, a former regent now running for the state legislature. In a time of "unprecedented pecuniary stringency," when taxes were heavy and many Kansans starving, it was a wretched thing indeed for the regents thus to squander the people's hard-earned money. "If our legislature and the people of our state shall sanction this action of the Board of Regents," Tenney said, "let all future demands for retrenchment and economy be treated as the most impudent of all impudent humbugs."[27]

The legislature of 1875 would be full of Tenneyites—and all of them had taken heart at the report of the Board of Commissioners for Public Institutions for 1874. Appropriations—especially for salaries—should be reduced, the commissioners thought. The University's "efficiency" had not been at all impaired by the reductions of 1874 and the faculty reorganization. Preparatory students should not be taught by full professors; the annual cost of $140 per student was too high; the legislature should grant nothing for the library or commencement expenses; the chancellor was worth no more than $2,500, which was what the president of the Emporia State Normal School, who worked just as hard as his Lawrence counterpart, was getting. After all, the commissioners argued, universities were not built mainly by money. A university could be created "wherever there is scholarship to fashion it. If men love money, or fame, or ease, more than learning, *per se*, they need not attempt to build up a university, especially a university in Kansas, where many are without the actual necessities of life. Universities are made by men, not by money, and Kansas at present can do no more than give a limited financial assistance to those who have the great work in charge. The same degree of study required to prepare a man for a professorship in a university, as a professor *should* be prepared," the Board of Commissioners concluded, "would give him affluence and honor in any other calling."[28]

If professors expected to suffer in affluence and honor, the legislature of 1875 saw no reason to disappoint them. The University was hurt not only by the large number of economizers, but also by a fight between the House and Senate. Angered by the Senate's refusal to pass relief legislation for people suffering from grasshoppers, drought, and hard times generally, western representatives fought all appropriation bills, including the University's. When the House got through with a measure introduced by Dudley C. Haskell of Lawrence, the University had only $18,100, or almost $5,000 less than the regents had asked; the House then rejected Senate efforts to increase the amount. The act forbade paying the chancellor more than $2,000 a year, and appropriated only $12,000 for all salaries, $3,500 less than requested. Another $1,000 was sliced off the requested library appropriation of $1,500. Either the faculty would have to be reduced in number and reorganized once again, or their salaries would have to be cut. Either way the University was in an extremely unfortunate situation as its first decade drew to a close.[29]

The work of the legislature of 1875 made clear two troublesome facts about the University of Kansas. First, there was nothing at all certain about the institution's prosperity. Despite what men of later generations would say about the commitment of Kansans to higher education manifested in the University's creation, neither the people as a whole nor the legislature had committed themselves to anything. It was up to those who cared about higher education to convince people of the University's value to the state and, even more important, of the need to make it the genuinely excellent institution that it now was not. Second, the University was deeply involved in politics. It was not so much party politics that affected the school, for in Kansas Democrats were scarce and the great majority of regents were Republican appointees. It was factional and personal politics in which the University was involved, and the working of the state's political machinery itself. As a state institution created by and responsible to the legislature, as an institution whose representatives had to deal and plead and trade with the people's representatives, the University was in politics to stay—however much the faculty, the regents, and their allies might talk about placing it "above politics," as the phrase was.

Even before 1875 the University's supporters had realized that to create a great institution of higher learning in Lawrence, they would have to evangelize among the unconverted. After the debacle of that year they had to try harder. In the mid-1870s they renewed and expanded their propaganda campaign to explain to the public what a state university was, what it did for the general welfare of state and nation, and what it could do in the future if only Kansans would give it the means.

5

The Nature of a
State University

*E*XPLAINING the nature of the University to the people was no easy task, however, for the institution's officers and faculty were themselves uncertain about its proper character. To be sure, they had no trouble describing the benefits of public higher education. Doing so required only that they repeat to Kansans ideas long current about the pleasures enjoyed by men of awakened intellects and the dependence of democratic society on educated men who could understand and solve complex social problems. But defining a state university—describing what it was and what it ought to be—was something else again. Every definition seemed to lose itself in vagaries and contradictions. Spokesmen for the University from the mid-1870s to the early 1890s were in the strange position of attempting to win support for an institution whose blessings were allegedly obvious but whose essence was obviously obscure.

In facing the problems of definition, though, Kansans were not alone. The problem of identity and essence was a national problem, coeval with the rise and development of the American university itself. Much of the impetus for creating universities during the years from 1860 to 1900 lay in dissatisfaction with the work and scope of the older colleges. University builders believed that the colleges' restricted curricula and unfamiliarity with scholarly research did not befit a nation becoming intellectually mature. Admiring both the spirit and the structure of the eminent German universities, they sought to fashion institutions that would stress

72

research by faculty scholars and graduate students and that would contain several professional schools as well as an undergraduate college. They sought at the same time to free the undergraduate curriculum from its bondage to tradition—to make it broader and more flexible and to give students a freer choice of programs and courses.

Yet within the university movement there were different emphases. Some men were most concerned about the apparent irrelevance of many colleges to the immediate needs of an expanding society which was aggressively secular in outlook. Carrying the idea of social service to its logical extreme, they asserted that universities should be almost literally universes of learning, practical as well as impractical. "I would found an institution," said Ezra Cornell as he contemplated his future university in New York, "where any person can find instruction in any study." Others, however, followed President Daniel Coit Gilman of Johns Hopkins, who contended that the true university existed mainly to pursue scholarly research—whether or not that research had social value—and to train graduate students.[1]

Now there were assets in the lack of agreement and the uncertainty. There being no model university, each institution could develop as it would, could be innovative and free and experimental with form and function. A university might have an agricultural school as well as a graduate school, for example, because seeking improvement of crops, cows, and swine might be just as legitimate an endeavor as scholarly research in Greek, chemistry, or history. Again, the state and land-grant universities could undertake an incredible variety of direct public services—partly to improve society, partly to justify their existence to suspicious taxpayers—for there was no necessary inconsistency between the university ideal and such things as advice to farmers on how to get higher yields or to communities about improving their sanitation systems. As long as an institution had the general prerequisites for university status—several schools, an emphasis on research, a respect for both the newer science and the older liberal arts, and a certain freedom for its students—it was in fact a university.[2]

In Kansas in the 1870s and the 1880s the regents who would have to decide such matters were men—and a woman—of diverse types. By 1875 the Board of Regents and their terms were Noah C. McFarland and the Reverend Frank T. Ingalls (1873–1876), the Reverend

T. F. Houts and James S. Emery (1874–1877), and the Reverend Archibald Beatty and V. P. Wilson (1875–1878). Between then and another reorganization act of 1889 there was too little continuity. By the spring of 1877, for example, half the regents were new. Joining Ingalls, who had accepted reappointment, and Beatty and Wilson were Milton W. Reynolds, editor of the Parsons *Sun*; Brinton W. Woodward, an old Free-State leader now a prosperous Lawrence druggist and merchant and a devotee of the fine arts; and R. N. Hershfield, a wealthy Leavenworth jeweler, all appointed by Governor Osborn. That Board hung together until 1879, thanks to Beatty's and Wilson's willingness to accept reappointment in 1878 from Governor George T. Anthony. But Hershfield resigned before his term ended and Reynolds was glad to retire at the end of his. To replace Hershfield for a year Governor John P. St. John chose Dr. John W. Scott of Iola, and then gave him a full term to 1883. Reynolds's place went to Noah C. McFarland.[3]

In the next few years the Board saw many new faces. When Frank T. Ingalls resigned before his term ended, his place went to Samuel S. Benedict of Guilford, a stockman and former state legislator. After Woodward left in 1880, Governor St. John chose another Lawrencian and former Free-State leader, Timothy Dwight Thacher, who had established the Lawrence *Republican* in 1856 and had been active in politics ever since. St. John had the opportunity to appoint four more regents as well. To replace Archibald Beatty when his service ended in 1881, he selected the Reverend Eugenius Nisbet, a Leavenworth Methodist; when Nisbet resigned the same year, St. John shrewdly called upon Mrs. Cora Downs of Wyandot, who became the University's first woman regent. With her appointment the Governor at once expressed his belief that every state school which educated females should have a woman on its board of control, rewarded one of his ardent Republican supporters, and secured a regent with considerable intellectual and literary interests. The wife of a prosperous lumber dealer and Republican politician, Mrs. Downs was widely known as a writer of numerous newspaper and periodical articles on public issues and as one of the chief supporters of the *Kansas Magazine*. George R. Peck of Topeka, McFarland's replacement in 1882, was also a wise choice: a prominent lawyer and general solicitor of the Santa Fe Railroad, he was widely read, a fine orator, and much interested in improving the quality of higher education in Kansas. John W. Scott and V. P. Wilson were reappointed when their terms ended in 1880 and 1881 respectively.[4]

Thus in January, 1883, the Board included Scott, Wilson, Thacher, Peck, Benedict, and Mrs. Downs. But in the fall of 1882 Kansans had departed from the ways of the fathers to elect a Democratic governor, George W. Glick of Atchison, and as a result two-thirds of the Board changed within three months. It was Glick's fortune to be able to appoint all six regents. In 1883 the terms of John W. Scott and Timothy Dwight Thacher ended; V. P. Wilson had resigned. The other three regents were caught by the law of 1873, which stated that when a vacancy occurred when the legislature was not in session, the appointment to fill it expired three weeks after the next legislature met. Mrs. Downs was filling out Eugenius Nisbet's term, while Peck and Benedict had not yet received Senate ratification.

Glick promised even his Democratic cohorts that he would seek the best men regardless of party,[5] but inevitably some Democrats seemed best. To replace Thacher and Scott, the Governor picked two of them—Alfred G. Otis of Atchison, president of the Atchison Savings Bank and Glick's former law partner, and James H. Humphrey, a lawyer of Junction City. To one-year terms, in place of Wilson and Mrs. Downs, Glick chose William S. White, the Democratic editor of the Wichita *Beacon*, and George R. Peck. Glick had not intended to reappoint Peck, but did so when the Senate rejected James S. Emery of Lawrence. The other two places went to Frank A. Fitzpatrick, the school superintendent of Leavenworth, and Samuel S. Benedict, reappointed to fill out Peck's old term.[6]

During the next six years the Board's membership had greater stability than before. Of Governor Glick's appointees, Otis served until 1889, Fitzpatrick until 1888, and Peck until 1887. To replace W. S. White in 1884, Glick chose C. R. Mitchell, a Geuda Springs Republican lawyer, who continued for a decade. In 1885 the Board got three new members, appointed by Governor John A. Martin. Matthew P. Simpson, a McPherson lawyer and railroad promoter, took Samuel S. Benedict's place, and would serve until 1891. Charles W. Smith of Stockton of the class of 1876 was the first University alumnus to become a regent. An attorney, he had taken his law degree at the University of Michigan; he would leave the Board in 1889 to become judge of the Thirty-fourth District. Two other men completed the list of pre-1889 appointees. The first was Charles S. Gleed, a member of the class of 1881, who had also taken his LL.B. from the University's Law School. During the 1880s he had worked as chief clerk for George R. Peck in the Santa Fe Railroad's law department, edited the Denver, Colorado, *Daily Tribune*, and later opened a law office in Topeka with his brother, J. Willis Gleed. He would continue on the Board until 1893. The other appointee was J. F. Billings, a Clay Center lawyer, who served from 1888 to 1891.[7]

Although the appointed regents had more power than the chancellors or the faculty to shape the University, they said very little publicly about the institution's nature. But James Marvin, second choice for chancellor though he might be, squared off against the problem in his inaugural address. When Marvin became chancellor, he was fifty-five years old and had behind him a long career as teacher and executive. Born in Clinton County, New York, he forsook a planned career as a farmer to acquire a formal education. After graduating from Allegheny College in 1851, he taught at Alfred Academy in New York for five years, and then did an eight-year stint as superintendent of schools in Warren, Ohio. Allegheny College then called him back as professor of mathematics, and he remained there until elected chancellor of the University of Kansas. In temperament Marvin was placid, gentle, and quiet, usually wearing what one student described as a "calm, tired, patient smile." If Marvin sometimes seemed too withdrawn, even unworldly, he was nonetheless a competent judge of men who was not surprised by either their virtues or their sins.[8]

Marvin had often speculated on the nature of the American state university, and he offered his ideas in his inaugural address on June 16, 1875. After reviewing the history of the European universities and paying tribute to their greatness, Marvin argued that American universities could not and should not servilely imitate them. The European institutions, he said, were the products of undemocratic societies bound by tradition and restricted by a pervasive conservatism. America was different, and should therefore take from Europe what was good and reject the rest. "Our youth, our domains, our people all conspire to force upon us customs and institutions widely different from those across the seas."

But what was the American type of university to be? Marvin confessed that he was uncertain, for as yet in the United States there was no "approved plan of University organization." At bottom, however, a university was not a physical thing, but a set of relations between students and teachers. The distinguishing feature of the American university, Marvin said, echoing many university leaders outside Kansas, was that it satisfied the diverse interests and purposes of its students. Some of them would desire to widen their "general knowledge," others to follow some "favorite subject or class of subjects nearer the fields open for original investigation," still others to get professional training. Where students had a choice of two or more courses, there was a university. So far so good, but when Marvin tried to describe more precisely what subjects a university should include, he bogged down in generalities. A proper basic education—which he insisted that a university could provide where the lower schools were wanting, as in Kansas—included the construction and correct use of English, the citizen's duties and privileges, enough arithmetic to conduct "ordinary business," and such knowledge of "general society" as would enable people to understand the "common weekly news of the world." Growing from those and more properly within the university's sphere were the "ever widening fields of literature, science, art, with all their applications to the industries, and economies of the human family."

The Chancellor also believed that American universities should vary according to their social and physical environment. In determining the courses offered to students, the "wants of the patronizing country should be especially studied," for they would largely shape the students' tastes and determine their vocations. The immediate emphasis of the University of Kansas, then, should be on those sciences affecting "human industry," the laws of "social and political economy," and general English literature. A "fair demand for professional education" might also be anticipated as the state became more densely settled. "To provide for these just needs is the duty of the hour."

Yet Marvin's concept of human needs and interests was broad. "We desire and design radically utilitarian," he said, "but confess to little sympathy with that sort of utilitarianism which reduces all human muscle and brain to cash." While the aim of every "well adjusted system of education" was partly to provide vocational or professional training, more important was that it prepare people for "life in all its fullness," which included moral, aesthetic, and spiritual dimensions. Being a Protestant clergyman, Marvin had to assert that in the Bible were the higher laws necessary for moral conduct and eternal life—and also for national greatness. But he did so, he said, without either denominational or political dogmatism.[9]

Chancellor Marvin's ideas were as confusing as they were stimulating and attractive. The crucial question was just how inclusive or comprehensive the University of Kansas should be. Were the professions of which he spoke merely those of the charter of 1864, or were there others? When Marvin talked of the study of science in its various applications, did he mean that literally no branch of technology was foreign to the University's legitimate work? And if the laws of personal and social conduct were to be found in the Bible, where did this leave men whose ethical systems—which might well shape their teaching—came from other sources? Freedom and flexibility were surely praiseworthy, but their limits were extremely fuzzy.

Eight years after Marvin's analysis Chancellor Joshua A. Lippincott wrestled with the same problem and came off a little better. Like Marvin, he was a Methodist cleric for whom teaching and administration had proved more attractive than the ministry. Born in 1837 in Burlington County, New Jersey, Lippincott had taken his degree from Dickinson College in 1858. After graduation he had taught in an academy, served as superintendent of schools in Scranton, Pennsylvania, and then joined the faculty of the New Jersey State Normal School in Trenton. In 1865 he became a minister and for the next two years was a pastor in Hackensack. Then he returned to Dickinson College as professor of mathematics and astronomy and remained there until 1883, when he succeeded James Marvin at Kansas. Pious and moralistic, Lippincott resolutely believed that the University should train its students for Christian living as well as sharpen their intellects. Naturally dour, he always impressed people with his earnestness, but many of his faculty and students thought him far less personable than James Marvin and too grim for comfort.[10]

Like Marvin, Lippincott was perplexed about the essence of the American university. "We may as well state frankly," he said in his inaugural address, "that the position of the university as distinguished from the college is, as yet, quite unsettled in the American educational system." Some men thought of the university as a combination of colleges, each with a different sphere of work. Others conceived it as an institution offering only "professional and practical" work, which left to the college those studies that were "preparatory and disciplinary." A third group saw it as a school in which "any applicant may find competent instruction in any useful study."[11]

Lippincott thought the ideal university combined all these characteristics, save that no state university could offer work in dogmatic theology. But to those three characteristics he added another: the true university should foster original research, which was probably more important than teaching alone. In research the university "intensifies its own enthusiasm," and secures a firmer grasp on its students, for "nothing so grandly inspires the human soul as the forcing of nature's secret from her willing but reluctant hand." The process would draw professors and students together in the "oneness of their aim and enthusiasm. It is in this moment of fusion that the competent teacher finds the opportunity for his grandest work, and on a plane, too, higher than that of mere scholastic training."[12]

Within that broad framework, Lippincott made certain emphases. The University of Kansas had always to keep abreast of the latest developments in all fields of study. Then, too, it ought to be a "conservatory of knowledge," by which the Chancellor meant that it should have a superb library, one excellent enough to attract scholars from afar; similarly superb natural history collections; and a distinguished body of students and scholars in all the branches of science, literature, art, and philosophy. Last, Lippincott stressed that the American state university must be an integral part of the state's educational system. Its development should keep pace with that of the lower schools. Before trying to become the ideal university, Kansas should wait until the high schools had prepared the students.[13]

At the end of his address, however, Lippincott predicted that for two reasons his University would never achieve the ideal state. The first was that men were not perfect and therefore their creations could not be perfect. The second was that the ideal itself was not static, but was always growing: "Further still, it may be said that the ideal itself grows more rapidly toward perfection than [the workman's] actual work." Yet ideals remained necessary as models toward which to strive and by which to direct development and change.[14]

Seven years later Francis H. Snow in his own inaugural address as chancellor said much the same thing. In 1890, Snow pointed out, Kansas was in the process of evolving from a college into a university. The main difference between the two types of institutions had to do with the question of freedom. Colleges required all students to follow a prescribed curriculum, with a minimum amount of deviation in the form of elective studies. An ideal university, by contrast, offered the "best instruction in all branches of learning," and in it the student, "who presumably has reached full maturity," was allowed to choose his course of study for himself. Like Lippincott, Snow emphasized scholarly research as a necessary component of the "model University": it was incumbent on the faculty "not only to teach the old truth, but also to discover new truth." Professors with superior research abilities should be released from much of their classroom teaching, which should be given to less competent researchers. But there was a golden mean between teaching and research. A "fair amount of class instruction," Snow thought, "is a stimulus rather than a hindrance to original work"—though he did not explain why or how.[15]

Once more like Lippincott, however, Snow said that the ideal could never be realized. No university anywhere had attained the "perfect ideal of faultless instruction in all branches of knowledge"; if the great German institutions—Berlin, Heidelberg, Göttingen— had not done it, surely Kansas could not, for the state's resources would not permit it. Then, too, the youth of Kansas, like all other American students, were too immature to be trusted with the absolute freedom to choose their own courses. More important was Snow's conviction that the University of Kansas had to be a university for Kansans. "It cannot be a mere ideality, offering to Kansas youth a theoretical culture adapted to a state of society as pictured by Edward Bellamy for a far-away future time. It must be adapted to actual Kansas of the last decade of the 19th century, and not to actual Massachusetts, or Connecticut, or New Jersey, or England, or Germany." The idea was sensible, but Snow did not explain what the needs of Kansas were, except to say that the most important step

in creating a "genuine Kansas University" was to form a more intimate connection between the University and the state public-school
system.[16]

Thus did three chancellors try to explain what an American state
university in Kansas ought to be. But if their ideas were modern
and exciting, they were also vague; the practice would tell far more
than the theory. The University was to be truly a Kansas institution, but it was not clear exactly what unique conditions demanded
attention. The faculty was to engage in scholarly research—else
there would be no real university—but the relation between research
and the necessary teaching was obscure. The University would offer
work in all branches of learning, but neither Marvin, nor Lippincott, nor Snow was willing to say just how comprehensively the
word "all" should be defined. Across the nation in every university
men were discussing such questions, and there was neither agreement nor clarity among them.[17] The result was that the American
university in general and the University of Kansas in particular continued to be eminently pragmatic and experimental. Where it was
hard to see and harder to understand the ideal university, the leaders
of actual institutions watched each other, taking what seemed good,
rejecting what seemed bad, and examining their constituencies'
needs and demands to discover new opportunities for service.

Uncertain though the University's leaders might be about what
a university was, however, they were sure that it bestowed numerous
blessings upon individuals and society. What was this "individual
class of beings which we call man?" James Marvin asked, and then
answered that he was a being of mind, body, and personal uniqueness or individuality. Higher education should aid students to
realize all their potentialities, of course, but only in the university,
rather than the college, was individuality fully respected. Colleges
that required all students to follow the same course had a "factory
air" about them. Students went through the "same milling process"
and came out the "same sort of machines" with but "slight variations
in size and finish." But God had not intended man to be a machine,
and the University of Kansas should be about His work.[18] The
great goals of all education, said Joshua A. Lippincott in 1888, were
to quicken the intellectual powers and increase man's self-knowledge, and thereby gain self-mastery. Intellectual power brought joy
and contentment; self-knowledge and mastery made men more

82   THE UNIVERSITY OF KANSAS: *A History*

moral beings and better citizens.[19] Denying that it was enough for men to be merely good, Regent George R. Peck told the students at the opening convocation in 1888 that the intellectual faculties should be as highly developed as the moral faculties. "Every scholar," he said, "is the sworn foe of that mental triviality and mental indolence which hides behind a screen of presumable goodness. What you need for yourselves, and what the world needs of and from you"—and what the University would help provide—"is healthy, strong, vigorous character, capable of contact at all points with life as it is." Such a character was the product of the "due and equal proportion which we call harmony" between the intellectual and moral faculties, "which in art, in music, and in nature itself is the one sign of perfection."[20]

For reasons both personal and practical the University's spokesmen always emphasized that they were as interested in the students' moral growth as in their intellectual. John Fraser had a strong religious orientation, his two successors were Methodist divines, and Chancellor Snow had originally intended to become a clergyman. Almost every faculty member was an active member of some Lawrence church.[21] And since the University was always under suspicion and sometimes under attack from churchmen worried about its moral atmosphere or its competition with the denominational colleges, it behooved the school's propagandists to speak of moral things. While nondenominational the University was a "'Christian institution, founded by a Christian State," Lippincott wrote a doubting parent. And Francis Snow, in 1888, said, "We have daily prayers conducted for the most part by members of the Faculty of whom nearly all are Christian and several ministers of the Gospel. The 'tone' here is altogether wholesome." Although attending a nondenominational school, a student wrote publicly in 1880, "we are all seeking the truth—we are all earnest in the effort to correctly solve the great problem of a worthy and useful existence—we all recognize the wonderful features of a Christian age and a Christian country—we all hope to be true men and women—and almost all acknowledge that in accomplishing this we need an inspiration which is not of this earth nor fashioned after this world. . . ."[22]

In addition to a proper morality and the joys of an awakened intellect, the University of Kansas promised its students material happiness. As everyone knew, education helped men to succeed.

"Let it be made known that at the University of the State," Chancellor Snow proclaimed in a typical statement in 1890, "every son and daughter of the state may receive the special training which makes chemists, naturalists, entomologists, electricians, engineers, lawyers, musicians, pharmacists and artists, or the broader and more symmetrical culture which prepares those who receive it for that general, well-rounded efficiency which makes the educated man a success in any line of intellectual activity"—that is, any work that required thought—"ten years earlier in life than the uneducated man."[23]

While the University gave freely of itself, it demanded much in return. The rewards of education should extend through the educated individual to the whole of society. University graduates, said Chancellor Marvin, should strive to make the world a better, brighter, happier, more wholesome place in which to live. In an address to the graduating class of 1885 which the regents published as a pamphlet and spread around the state, Chancellor Lippincott asserted that, in the old spirit of noblesse oblige, intellectually trained men should help to redress human wrong, secure human rights, lift up the lowly, protect the defenseless, restrain the vicious, educate the ignorant, and in general elevate the masses and improve the quality of human life. "A man is worth to himself what he is capable of enjoying," James H. Canfield, professor of history, wrote in 1891, and "worth to a state what he is capable of imparting." One main purpose of the University was to make sure that its graduates lived for others as well as for themselves.[24]

Many of the remarks that University apologists made about the value of higher education to themselves and to society could apply to either private or state-supported institutions. Thus the question arose as to why public universities were necessary, why the people should not leave higher education to private initiative. In 1885 and again in 1891 James H. Canfield provided a series of answers that summed up all the responses offered in the University's early years. Canfield was the school's most vigorous and articulate faculty advocate of public education. So enthusiastic and persuasive was he that he acquired statewide and then nationwide fame. In 1886 he was president of the Kansas State Teachers Association; from 1886 to 1889 he was secretary of the National Education Association, and in 1889 he became its president.[25]

Canfield told the people of Kansas that the state supported all education from the lower to the higher because of an enlightened self-interest. The preservation of democracy and all its benefits depended on the intelligence and morality of its citizens. While a democratic government should be kept simple enough to be understood and properly managed, it was still bound to be a more complex affair than "ignorant people" could understand. "Men of wisdom and virtue," Canfield said, "are the men who make a good state; and wisdom and virtue are not qualities that come with inheritance so much as qualities that must be carefully propagated by general and wise education of youth." Education, moreover, was useful to all classes of men in strengthening the mind in the search for wisdom and wisdom's legitimate uses—to the blacksmith and the barrister, the farmer and the philosopher, the peasant's son and the president's son. Furthermore, public education was the best means of preserving "republican equality," of allowing men to compete in the "race of life" on more or less equal terms, of helping men to go as far as their abilities and training would permit, of permitting men to make their maximum contribution to social welfare.

Therefore education could simply not be allowed to depend on "individual resources or individual willingness or individual generosity, but must be by the public and of the public." To forsake public education available to all in favor of private education, moreover, would be to foster a disagreeable and dispiriting class structure, the very antithesis of democracy.[26]

While all public educational institutions had important roles to play in the effort to extend freedom and increase happiness, Canfield thought the University especially important. "The common-school work is a sort of hand-to-mouth regime," he argued. "It does not insure, as does higher education, a surplus of information and intellectual training for emergencies"—for the extraordinary duties and responsibilities that at different times every citizen had to bear. The lower schools alone could not guarantee an "intelligent, industrious, and moral citizenship at large." Neither could they create a large pool of intelligent men from which the nation might choose its leaders, nor provide those leaders with the information and training necessary to solve complex problems. The very success of the lower schools, moreover, depended on their direction by university graduates, and on the spirit of the "higher culture. A stream cannot rise higher than its fount; and common schools, under the control and inspiration of graduates from common schools only, become and remain very common schools indeed." That higher culture had always been an "instinct of civilization"; for over two centuries in America it had been blessed by the "best citizens, by communities, by the courts of law, by statute." It would be folly for Kansans to question it.[27]

With one emphasis or another, these were the ideas offered to the people of Kansas over and over again as University spokesmen sought their support.[28] Such ideas were much more than mere justifications for greater aid from the legislature or for the backing of the people themselves. As much as for money the leaders of the University asked the people for faith. Like faiths of other kinds, this one was a belief in things unseen. A real university did not yet exist; its true character was vague to the institution's leaders, and even vaguer to the citizens, most of whom had had none of the benefits of a higher education. Yet the value of a public university, according to the Mount Oread evangelists, was unquestionably great, and they could only hope that the faith of Kansans would be large enough to make the ideal ever more manifest.

6

The University as a
State Agency

*W*HEN the University's spokesmen described the benefits that their institution showered upon the commonwealth, they knew they were talking to large numbers of apathetic or hostile people. Had Kansans generally shared the enthusiasm of the regents, the faculty, and the students, most of the propaganda would have been unnecessary. Although Chancellors Marvin and Lippincott contended that the University cause could not possibly fail ("The people love their own creation," Lippincott asserted),[1] the citizens were always divided in their attitudes. From the 1870s to the 1890s Kansans offered a number of notions about their university that did not harmonize at all well with the official doctrines and that would set the standards of criticism for decades to come.

Taking the criticism altogether, it was both honest and dishonest, constructive and destructive, large and petty. Whatever its nature, however, the idea that underlay it was entirely sound. Had the University's supporters had their way, there would have been no public discussion of the University at all. Yet in a democracy no state institution was sacred. The people paid for the University, their representatives ruled it, the University's faculty and officers were all state employees. In questioning the truthfulness of the University's self-portrait, Kansans kept the school in the arena of public debate, which was exactly where it belonged.

If only they had been gracious about it! Like the little girl with the curl, when Kansans were good they were very, very good, but when they were bad they were horrid. It is difficult to account for the extreme nature of some of the anti-University statements. Hyperbole had always come easily to Americans, of course, and Kansans shared the disease. The military and verbal wars of territorial days helped explain some of the irascibility, for in the bitterness on both sides lay precedents for the future. Then there was the nature of the state itself. Roughly a rectangle four hundred by two hundred miles, Kansas contained some eighty thousand square miles of land which, when properly treated and worked, was excellent for several grain crops and pasturing. When the sun smiled and the wind gently rippled the prairie grasses and wildflowers and wheat stalks, when the rain and the rivers watered things aright, Kansas was one of the pleasantest places on earth. But too often the sun burned all beneath it, and there were either floods or droughts, and grasshoppers ate the crops and practically everything else, and the winds carried off the soil.

> Cover the Sun, O God!
> Oh! cover it with thy hand!
> For it scorcheth man, and it scorcheth beasts,
> And it burneth up the land;
> It glowers and simmers: A sun in its name,
> But a hell in its wasting, its fierceness and flame!
>
> The cattle vainly roam
> In search of spring and stream;
> But nothing they find, though fainting and blind,
> Save dust and the Sun's red gleam:
> For the springs are dry, and the streams are bare,
> And all moisture is burnt from this fiery air!

So wrote a suffering Kansan in the midst of a horrible drought in 1860,[2] but there was worse to come in the mid-1870s, the late 1880s, and much of the 1890s. Under any circumstances the suffering would have been hard to bear, but compared with the boom times and happiness of just a few years before, it was an awful burden. While the timid or the broken went back east or pushed hopefully to greener fields beyond Kansas, others stayed—but they lived in bitterness in hard times and in skepticism in good. Many of them lived, moreover, in relative isolation, for the population was never great; by 1890 Kansas had 1,428,108 people.[3] Loneliness led to brooding, and brooding to alternating extremes of happiness and despair.

When most Kansans thought about the University, moreover, they thought about a kind of institution they did not personally know, for most of them had no college or university education. To expect people whose prosperity or penury had nothing to do with the University to believe everything its spokesmen said about it was plainly foolish.

So when those men claimed that democracy itself depended on their institution, others naturally retorted that the University was in fact undemocratic because it was offering to an elite class advantages unknown to most of the people. If such charges were most frequently heard in hard times, they bespoke a preexisting bitterness made only sharper by suffering and frustration. In 1887, for example, the Jamestown *Cloud County Kansan* claimed editorially that the University served only a minority of the people. Most students lived near Lawrence, and exorbitant room and board rates kept the poor man's child away, even though tuition was free. People should support private denominational, neighborhood colleges, for the University was productive of no good at all. There were "some nabobs" whose sons were above attending the smaller private colleges, and "so the State of Kansas has built, equipped and yearly supplies the expenses of this state university. Here they learn a smattering of law and Latin, part their hair in the middle, wear tight pants and gain other emblems of greatness and the yahoos who live out in the border counties crawl out of their dugouts and haul corn 40 miles and sell it for 15 cents a bushel to help foot the bill."[4]

Two years later, with times still hard, the same ideas—they had long since become traditional—appeared in the legislature. Very few poor children ever got to the University, said T. E. Berry of Clark County, for it was the "high-toned school of the state," run for the rich alone. Most of America's famous men came from the common schools or the denominational colleges, added Carl A. Swensson of McPherson County. "The atmosphere surrounding state universities," he said, without explanation, "is not that kind which makes the best and ablest men." In an equally vague but more impassioned way, Daniel W. Poe of Butler County charged the University with trying to "run the legislature and the state." Poe wanted the regents and professors to understand that the state was not the "tail of the State University," and he proposed to show them which end of the animal was which by carving a huge amount from the requested appropriations.⁵

Solomon Miller of the Troy *Kansas Chief* felt the same way. An inveterate opponent of the University, Miller was also one of the state's foremost masters of invective. In 1895 the Kansas Supreme Court ruled that under a law of 1889 the regents could not levy an annual five-dollar library fee on the students. Miller thought the decision a triumph for the people over the arrogance prevalent on Mount Oread, and once more a Kansan's bitterness transcended the immediate issue. "The time is not far distant," Miller wrote, "when the people of the State will find themselves compelled to take the University in hand, and put it back in its proper place. It was intended to be an institution under the control of the State, for the benefit of the youth of the State; but it is already assuming the airs of an aristocratic dictator, independent of the people, above them, aspiring to rule them. The appropriations to the University each year are enormous, and constantly increasing. The well-paid faculty are constantly scheming for an increase in their salaries. They are allowed thousands of dollars every year to go on wild goose chases, pleasure outings, and to waste in humbug experiments." Arguing that the faculty's purpose was to "get the State by the throat," Miller claimed that the professors had far too much influence with the legislature: "Members of the Legislature, under the influence of the aristocracy of the University, were ready to sacrifice their party, and would have betrayed Jesus Christ, in order to gain additional favors and power for the University. It is high time the people were looking to this matter."⁶

A more serious kind of criticism than that of Miller and the Millerites came from men who believed that the University should exist and even prosper, but who would much restrict its sphere in the education of Kansas youth. By 1875 Kansas had seven private denominational colleges; by 1890 it had seventeen.⁷ Their leaders and supporters recognized the University as their greatest competitor and both condemned it as irreligious and demanded that its work be limited.

On December 26, 1872, Professor M. S. Ward of Ottawa University, a Baptist college some thirty miles south of Lawrence, discussed the matter in a typical way before the annual meeting of the Kansas

Solomon Miller of the Troy *Chief*.

State Teachers Association. Ward agreed that public colleges and universities were necessary for the general welfare, for they undergirded democratic government, increased both public and private wealth, promoted social harmony, and enlarged all sorts of secular opportunities. Ward argued, however, that the mere satisfaction of personal and social needs was not the highest goal of higher education: "If only the hand and the brain are educated, is the education complete?" He thought not. Higher education, rightly conceived, developed "equally and symmetrically the spiritual, physical, and intellectual powers of the human being." Thus the public institutions could never do the work, for they lacked consistency: their faculties changed at the whims of politicians, the taxpayers' attitudes were unstable, they lacked the national support that denominational colleges enjoyed. So eager were the leaders of the state schools to make them nonsectarian, moreover, that they had become virtually anti-Christian. "But in our denominational institutions," Ward said, "the teachers are known to be Christian men. A religious influence prevails."

All that the University had to do to establish harmony with Ottawa and the other religious schools was to abolish its undergraduate college and confine itself to professional training. Just as college work supplemented that of the high schools and academies, so should the University's work be "supplemental to the work of the denominational college." After the colleges had cultivated the mind in a "general way, by *disciplining all its faculties*," students should find in the University preparation for all the "various pursuits and callings of society, as jurists and journalists, as physicians and farmers, as citizens, tradesmen, and teachers." Ward claimed, indeed, that the provision of only such training was "doubtless . . . the ultimate aim of our own State University. . . . A liberal State, a generous Church, the highest Christian culture, an ample professional training," he concluded, "will make our civilization the highest possible on earth."[8]

For years the University would have to contend with those ideas. In 1907 President Lemuel H. Murlin of the Methodist Baker University offered a tribute before another meeting of the State Teachers Association: "Here's to our denominational colleges; may they drop the word 'university' out forever and remain colleges in the best American sense of the term. . . . Here's to the State University!

As citizens of Kansas, we shall place it in the very lead in the American educational procession; that it be a real American university, cooperating with all the educational interests of the State, and I propose as a motto, 'millions for graduates; not a cent for undergraduates.' "⁹

But there were other sectarians neither as charitable as Ward nor as genial as Murlin. Thus a Methodist magazine asserted in the late 1880s that the state institutions of learning were in the hands of men "hostile to Christianity, so that in this Christian state a generation of young men are being trained at public expense either to such disbelief in religion or such disregard of its claims as bodes no good to their future career as citizens." Thus worried parents heard rumors that University faculty members were not Christians, that there was a student-faculty association of infidels, that the moral atmosphere on Mount Oread was polluted. Thus did President Jacob A. Clutz of the Lutheran Midland College deplore at a State Teachers Association meeting in 1888 what he alleged to be a lack of reverence and religious instruction in the state institutions, and charge that they entirely neglected their students' spiritual needs.[10]

As soon as Clutz sat down, Francis H. Snow rose to refute him. The University had chapel exercises, Snow said, many students were church members, and both students and faculty did extensive "religious work." He added that many of the University's graduates had entered the ministry and commented that the "standard of morality" in the University was equal to that of any denominational college.[11]

Yet the pious remained suspicious and easily disturbed. An interesting case had arisen in 1882 and 1883 during the Reverend James Marvin's chancellorship. Late in 1882 a joint committee of the student Oread and Orophilian literary societies voted to invite Robert G. Ingersoll to speak at their public exercises the following June. Among Christian folk Ingersoll was anathema. An agnostic freethinker, he opposed all religions, described the Bible as a fraud, and denied the possibility of knowing that God existed. Ingersoll was a belligerent speaker and writer, but he was able of mind and a superb orator. Although the students desired only an address on some literary topic, the mere thought of Ingersoll's presence on campus drove many Kansas Protestants to despair. It all went to prove, said the Baldwin *Index*, published by three literary societies at Baker University and speaking for the faithful throughout the state, that University students were "constantly breathing an atmosphere tainted by his doctrines." Many Kansans seriously doubted "whether the leading institution of learning in one of the eminently Christian states of the Union should so entirely disregard the wishes of the citizens."[12]

The students also had numerous extracurricular defenders.[13] But Chancellor Marvin and several faculty members were horrified by both the Ingersoll invitation itself and the criticisms of the orthodox. Yet if they cancelled the invitation, they ran the risk of further offending students who were already extremely critical of the faculty on several counts. After an argument between pro- and antistudent professors, the faculty passed a motion designed to prevent Ingersoll's presence on campus without actually forbidding it. It said that although the faculty would not prohibit his addressing the students in June, the "impolicy . . . of inviting persons to address the literary societies of the University whose presence creates mischievous dissensions would seem to be sufficiently obvious." Before this criticism the students stood their ground, only to find that Ingersoll had a previous engagement and could not come.[14]

There was unorthodoxy of another kind within the University, however, and it troubled Kansans as much as the religious. In 1883 James H. Canfield, professor of history and political science, published a small volume called *Taxation; A Plain Talk for Plain People*. The book condemned the protective tariff, an institution dear to thousands of Kansas Republicans and to most of the party's leaders inside and outside the state. During the rest of the 1880s Canfield frequently took to the lecture platform to expound his ideas in person before plain Kansans. He did so with verve. "This Canfield, it seems, is a free trader," wrote a graduating senior in 1889, accurately portraying Canfield's spirit in a verbal caricature, "one of those wild, rampant free traders that get up in meeting and throw books at the parson when he gives out the hymn, 'Protect Me, O Lord.'" Canfield believed that the only legitimate purposes of government were to make decisions in an "apparent conflict of rights," to protect people from willful infringements on their "rightful well-being," and to secure to all who worked the fruits of their toil. Thus it should not interfere with either capital or labor as long as those involved behaved themselves. Since economic freedom was a positive good, the tariff, which interfered with that freedom, was a positive evil. Its only functions were to raise prices and make the rich richer; it was an unjust and "crooked" tax, the creature of "arbitrary rulers, commercial politicians, and self-asserting place-seekers" gathered in a Congress "hot with partisanship, and tainted with self-aggrandizement, personal rancor, and schemes for individual preferment."[15]

When Canfield addressed the people, he did so as a private citizen, not as a faculty member. Although his personal views were well known, his students affirmed that in his classes he scrupulously presented all aspects of the tariff question and left them to draw their own conclusions. Many of them rejected his free-trade ideas: in 1888 Chancellor Lippincott told a group of protectionists outside the state that most of the students favored the tariff.[16] But many Kansans were unable or unwilling to distinguish between the professor and the citizen. By 1888, the year of a presidential election in which the tariff was a controversial issue, many editors and politicians had become practically apoplectic at the thought that he was still a faculty member. "Two-thirds of the people of Kansas are in favor of protection," wrote Solomon Miller in the *Kansas Chief*, "and they do not want to employ and keep a man in the State University to preach that their doctrine is robbery. . . . We are in favor of the man for Governor who will pledge himself to appoint a Board of Regents who will promise to give Canfield his walking papers instanter." In the Hutchinson *News* Ralph M. Easley charged that the Board of Regents would be "certainly remiss in its duties if it does not find a vacancy in Canfield's chair very shortly. To retain him is a libel on Kansas. Fire him!"[17]

After Kansas went for Benjamin Harrison, Republicanism, and protection in 1888, Representative Daniel W. Poe of Butler County got the Kansas lower house to resolve that its Committee on State Affairs should determine "whether it is a fact that the British doctrine of free trade is being taught at the State University at Lawrence, and if so, by whom." When the committee discovered better ways to spend its time, Poe brought in a bill prohibiting the teaching of the "free-trade doctrine of the Cobden Club of England." The House referred it to the Committee on State Affairs, which killed it.[18]

Canfield himself was delighted and amused by the attacks upon him. Looking back on the battle some years later, he spoke of his "great pleasure and satisfaction while it was passing." His position in the University remained secure. He continued to be one of the two or three most popular teachers; the students faithfully supported him; and the regents left him to do as he would. "I always had an absolutely free hand," he said, "I was left to choose my way and given absolute right of way after it was chosen." He also won considerable support outside the University. Canfield had the same rights as any other Kansas citizen, said the Lawrence *Journal* in 1888. He had never tried to impose his ideas on his classes; outside class he could speak as he wished. Getting in its own licks, the *Journal* said that Canfield's critics were merely "howling journalistic dervishes" and "harsh voiced croakers who are just now stirring their little frog pond with their billious wails."[19] In 1890 and 1891, when the regents were seeking a replacement for Chancellor Lippincott, Canfield was the outstanding Kansas candidate. But the regents were too timid to choose him. When he resigned in 1891 to become chancellor of the University of Nebraska, many of his supporters made him a martyr to freedom in Kansas. Canfield claimed, however, that his "reputation of martyrdom" was entirely undeserved, said that he had left simply to take a better position, and gleefully quoted one newspaper editor who described him as a man "who would never have been heard of if a lot of us jackass editors had not busied ourselves for several years in kicking him up stairs when we thought we were kicking him down."[20]

Because the University of Kansas was a state agency, then, many Kansans demanded the privilege of helping to determine its nature. Dubious of its value and management and unwilling to believe all or part of what they were told, they insisted that it was accountable to them—to all the people—rather than merely to those who supported and controlled it. Their insistence upon that broader accountability raised one of the most excruciating problems that the University—like every other public agency and institution in a democracy—had to face: how much information about and explanation of decisions made did those in control owe the public? The regents of the 1870s and 1880s gave that question different answers at different times. In their annual and biennial reports and in the catalogues they reported honestly and fairly important decisions about finances, curricula, and general policies—that is, about routine matters. But in three exceptional cases the regents made decisions in secret and offered the public no explanation of their actions. Concealing the facts and concealing their motives, they refused to tell the people what was happening in the people's university. One of the cases was the argument between Chancellor Fraser and the faculty in 1873 and 1874. The other two were the firing of Chancellor Marvin in 1883 and the dismissal of Kate Stephens, professor of Greek, in 1885. Although there was nothing illegal in what the regents did—under the law of 1873 their authority over the University and its faculty was complete—their decisions and the means by which they were reached showed a certain contempt for both the public and the faculty.

The Marvin and Stephens troubles began in April, 1883, after the regents appointed by Governor Glick took office. During the next two months the Board grew dissatisfied with the Chancellor. Apparently the main reason was Marvin's desire to drive out chemistry professor George E. Patrick. Though Patrick was a good teacher and a dedicated scholar, his liberality and tolerance in political and religious affairs offended Marvin. Patrick was an Independent Republican when his chancellor was an orthodox party man—Marvin had represented Douglas County at the Republican State Convention in 1882—and he had supported the students who desired to have Robert G. Ingersoll on campus. In addition the two men simply disliked each other. When the new Board met, Marvin prevailed upon the other members to dismiss Patrick at the end of the current academic year. In June, Marvin prevented the passage of a motion to reconsider the dismissal by casting a tying vote against it in the absence of Samuel S. Benedict.[21]

But in May and June the regents had grown so disgusted by Marvin's maneuverings to oust Patrick that they in turn decided to get rid of Marvin. Rather than dismiss him outright, however—which would certainly have forced them to offer some explanation, however tortured—they put him in a position where he had to resign to keep his dignity. Without telling Marvin what they intended, they brought to Lawrence Professor Charles Kendall Adams of the University of Michigan to see if they could induce him to accept the chancellorship. Thus on June 5 Marvin resigned, saying that although he had received no information to that effect, "recent events" had convinced him that the regents wished a new chancellor. "A proper self-respect induces me now to present my resigna-tion," he said, subject to the ninety-days'-notice rule. Since Charles Kendall Adams was no more eager to go to Lawrence than Samuel H. Carpenter had been in 1874, and since the regents had found no one else, they asked Marvin to withhold it for the present. But soon they came upon Joshua A. Lippincott and on August 29 they for-mally accepted Marvin's resignation and elected him. Although the Board gave Marvin a splendid public tribute and three months' extra salary, neither the praise nor the payoff could soften the fact that the regents had acted in a dishonest and underhanded way.[22]

Marvin was not to be pitied overmuch, perhaps, for his part in the dismissal of George E. Patrick was unworthy. His successor also played an unworthy role in the dismissal of a faculty member. With-in a year after Chancellor Lippincott reached the University, he discovered that his female Greek professor was a tartar. Kate Stephens was the most tortured soul to dwell on Mount Oread dur-ing the University's early years. The daughter of Nelson T. Stephens, a prominent lawyer and judge, she had come to Lawrence from New York with her family in 1868. Entering the junior pre-paratory class, she remained at the University for the next seven years and took a B.A. in 1875. Having fallen under both the schol-arly and the personal spell of Byron Caldwell Smith, after gradua-tion she remained at the University to study Greek, receiving her M.A. in 1878. In manner and mind Miss Stephens was exactly Smith's female counterpart. Ever the intellectual, she was a free-thinker in religion who eschewed traditional Christian beliefs in favor of the transcendent verities of Spirit, Mind, and Beauty. She was also an imperious woman who thought that only her own ideas were correct, and she had no tact at all. She spoke and wrote bluntly, letting the sacred cows fall where they might. At the same time she was high-strung and sensitive. Criticism cut her deeply and she always slashed back hard. The crushing sorrow of Smith's death in 1877 made her a waspish spinster for life.[23]

In June, 1878, the regents hired Miss Stephens as assistant pro-fessor of ancient languages, and a year later elected her to the Greek chair. Her students remembered her as an excellent teacher with incredible enthusiasm for using the language, as had Smith, to intro-duce them to the entire culture of ancient Greece.[24]

During the 1882–1883 year, when Governor Glick was appoint-

Kate Stephens in 1915, at the age of 62: The high cost of outspoken idealism.

ing his new regents and they were firing both George E. Patrick and James Marvin, Kate Stephens was on leave for a much-needed physical and mental rest. She returned as irascible as ever, and especially indignant over Marvin's dismissal. She speedily developed a contempt for Chancellor Lippincott's Methodist piety, and her dislike for all the regents deepened after they turned down her request for a salary raise early in 1884. And so in her faculty report the following July, which she had carefully discussed in advance with her father,[25] and which she knew would be published as part of the Board's biennial report, she lashed out at both the regents and Chancellor Lippincott. The "study of Greek and the Greek chair," she said, "have always obtained a reluctant recognition." The reason was the "ultra-utilitarian views on 'education' which flourish in this section of our country." Ignorance of those views by the students, or their willingness to set aside the "life conceptions and life philosophy of the Philistine materialism which is about us," had fortunately caused the number of students wishing to study Greek to increase at a higher rate than the student body as a whole. In her classes, moreover, she said that she always encouraged her pupils to rise above the silly political factionalism of the day, "above minor every-day disturbances, the personalities and strife of puny newspapers, and the pettiness of social and political rival factions."

Touchy regents translated those words to mean that they were merely crass, unenlightened tools of Governor Glick. Chancellor Lippincott, moreover, who was even pricklier than his colleagues on the Board, found two special insults to him. In September, 1883, Kate Stephens reminded the regents, the Board had denied her request for an assistant instructor to teach an additional class in Greek. She received the news, she said, from "your representative in the faculty," which Lippincott took to mean that he was nothing more than the regents' agent who cared little for the faculty's interests. Later in her report she studiedly referred to Lippincott's predecessor as the "former President and honorable Chancellor, James Marvin," which was about equal to saying that Lippincott was neither honorable nor a worthy faculty president.[26]

A peculiar series of events followed. On All Fools' Day, 1885, the new Board of Regents, with Charles W. Smith, Matthew P. Simpson, and C. R. Mitchell replacing Samuel S. Benedict, William S. White, and James H. Humphrey, organized itself. The older members had no difficulty convincing the newer that they should punish Kate Stephens for her insubordination. The Board voted unanimously to "make a change in the management of the Department of Greek Language & Literature at the close of the present scholastic year," and told secretary Frank A. Fitzpatrick to inform Miss Stephens that her services would no longer be needed.[27]

At that point both the University community and interested Kansans had to begin guessing exactly why the Board had fired Kate Stephens, for the regents and the Chancellor refused to say. On April 30, 1885, an inquisitive reporter from the Lawrence *Journal* tried without much success to worm some information from Lippincott. The Chancellor said that no member of the Board had ever questioned Miss Stephens's knowledge of Greek. But he then went on to assert that if a man had written the report of the Greek Department in 1884, he would have been fired on the spot, thus suggesting that it was the report that had caused his own wrath. A few days later a *Journal* reporter cornered Regents Otis and Fitzpatrick at the Eldridge Hotel. After officially refusing to be interviewed, they claimed that the Board had no personal animosity for Kate Stephens, and no prejudice against her because of her sex or her lack of religious orthodoxy. Neither the reporter nor the regents mentioned her report. In May the St. Joseph (Missouri) *Herald* asserted that her dismissal resulted from her religious freethought, her sex, and the grudge of an unnamed regent against her father for an unfavorable decision from the bench some years before. In 1911 ex-Regent Fitzpatrick told Miss Stephens that the legal decision was all-important: Nelson T. Stephens had died in 1884, and then one of the Board members had successfully sought vengeance upon his child.[28] Miss Stephens herself believed that her sex and her religious heterodoxy were most responsible for her firing, but admitted that her insulting report might also have had something to do with it. In 1929 she said that Chancellor Lippincott from the first had disliked having a woman on the faculty and had muttered about it in public until her father told him to stop.[29]

Whatever the reasons, the Board of Regents had acted secretly, without offering Miss Stephens an opportunity to defend herself before the Board, and without explaining either to her or to the public that supported the University the motives for the action. Thus the regents were treating democratic government as well as

Miss Stephens with contempt, for free decisions by the people required free information, and where knowledge was limited, so was choice. Although the regents' conniving in the Marvin and Stephens cases was an exception to their usual procedures, such concealed and unexplained actions could persist as long as the laws permitted. Along with the natural prejudices of many Kansans, they would continue to produce reservations about the University's value and doubts about its nature.

7

"Why Shall We Delay the Superstructure?"

THE ultimate goal of efforts to assuage those reservations and doubts was hard cash, for without money in large amounts no distinguished university could appear on Mount Oread. A modern American university needed buildings for its classes, equipment for its laboratories, and thousands upon thousands of books for its libraries, as well as professors for its faculty. The research that university faculty members had to perform, moreover, demanded free time as well as tools, and free time, in turn, required more faculty members to reduce teaching loads. Whatever the desires and abilities of regents and faculty to make the University of Kansas excellent, only money could realize their hopes and fulfill their potential.

Of the four sources of money that the University could tap, only one was of much importance. Both the University Fund and student fees brought sums which, though welcome, were small. Private gifts, except for a large bequest in 1891, yielded little. The largest revenue pool was that fed by the legislature from public taxes; upon its depth and careful conservation would the University's prosperity and distinction depend.

During the halcyon days of the late 1860s some men had thought that the University Fund, accruing from the sales of the seventy-two sections of land granted by the federal government in 1861, might be enough to support the institution. In 1862, before the University existed, state officials had located them in Anderson, Woodson, Coffey, Lyon, Wabaunsee, Osage, and Allen counties, in the east-central part of the state. Although a law of 1866 authorized the regents to start selling the land for at least $1.25 an acre, Chancellor Fraser and the regents wished to delay sales until settlement around them had raised their price high enough to provide an endowment, as Fraser said, "sufficient for the maintenance and support of a University of which our ambitious young commonwealth need not be ashamed." In 1873 the Board of Commissioners for Public Institutions believed that the land should sell at from $5.50 to $6.50 an acre, and thus produce a fund of between $250,000 and $300,000. Assuming a 7 percent return on the investment, the fund would yield from $17,500 to $21,000 a year, which the commissioners called a "substantial and steady revenue" for the University's support.[1]

Although the commissioners warned against selling the land at "panic prices" during the recession of the seventies, they argued that the regents should appraise and market it as soon as conditions justified the sale. Creating the University Fund would both relieve the state of much or all of the annual cost of supporting the institution and soothe restless citizens in the counties containing the land: because the land was not taxable, county residents thought they were paying more than their just share of public expenses while at the same time increasing the value of University lands by improving their own acreage.[2] But the Board of Regents did nothing, whereupon the state legislature of 1875 passed a law—unanimously in the Senate and 75-1 in the House—ordering it to start selling. Three commissioners appointed by the governor were to appraise the lands—but at not less than $3.00 an acre. Within three months after the appraisal the regents were to put the land up for sale at no less than the minimum price. Buyers could pay 10 percent down and spread the rest over ten years at 10 percent interest a year.[3]

The next few years were disappointing. Because of the law the commissioners appraised most of the land at $3.00 an acre, but they found most of it so poor in quality that it would bring only $1.25 if sold in the open market. With Regent V. P. Wilson acting as land agent—at a 4 percent commission—the regents managed by April 1, 1878, to sell only 1,600 acres for $5,880, or about $3.60 an acre. Several factors hurt sales, the regents' Committee on Lands reported: there was no money for advertising, some of the land was overvalued, and, most important, the interest rate on deferred payments was often higher than that charged by railroads and other companies that had land for sale, and the ten-year period was too short.[4]

At the regents' solicitation the legislature of 1879 extended the time period from ten years to twenty and dropped the interest rate from 10 percent to 7. The act also lowered the minimum price by 25 percent.[5] Under that act, aided by boom times in the early eighties, the regents sold the rest of the land. By June, 1882, all of it was gone; from then on the Board was concerned only with repossessing and reselling forfeited land. Twenty years after the last of the land had been sold, the investment fund was slightly over $150,000. Including the interest payments and the sums received for forfeited and resold land, the price per acre was about $3.30. The total was disillusioning. In 1880, with the land selling rapidly for $2.80 an acre, Chancellor Marvin foresaw that the investment fund would be "but a fair beginning for a University endowment."[6] It was not even that. By acts of 1877, 1879, and 1883 the money was to be invested by a board of commissioners in city, county, state, or federal bonds. In the 1880s the commissioners put most of it into school-district bonds at 5 to 7 percent. The annual returns varied considerably, depending on the amount available for investment and the paying off of old bonds and the purchasing of new ones. From July 1, 1878, to June 30, 1892, the University Fund produced slightly over $62,000, with the greatest annual return in fiscal 1889 of about $7,100. Because of local conditions the contribution of the federal government to the University through the land grant of 1861 was far less than men of an earlier day had hoped it would be.[7]

Except for the few hundred dollars that trickled in each year from the Amos Lawrence fund, the only other regular source of nonlegislative income was student fees. Democratically the regents kept them as low as possible. Except in 1866 and 1867, when charges were $10 a year in the Preparatory Department and $30 a year in the College,* students in those schools attended the University without tuition. All students had to pay an annual matriculation or "contingent" fee of $10, but nothing more. Students in most of the

---

* I have consistently used the name "College" to refer to the undergraduate school which awarded the B.A. The charter of 1864 termed it the Department of Science, Literature, and the Arts. Often called the "Collegiate Department" by the catalogues of the 1870s and 1880s, it was named the School of Arts in 1893 and the College of Liberal Arts and Sciences in 1904.

professional schools were not so lucky. Although the Normal Department was free of tuition charges, law students paid $25 a year tuition, and pharmacy students $15 until 1888, when the amount rose to $25. For the one-year medical course, students also paid $25. Music students paid from $12 to $36 a semester for their lessons, and in 1888 the regents imposed a $30 per semester fee on art students. To pay for diplomas and commencement expenses, each graduate was assessed $5.[8]

Between 1875 and 1889 fees of all kinds amounted to between $2,000 and $8,000 a year. Until fiscal 1885 the regents put all the fee money into a general account, to be used as needed. After that time they kept the contingent fees for general expenses, but used the other moneys for salaries and equipment in the departments whence they came. In fiscal 1888, for example, contingent fees produced about $3,600. Tuition fees in the Department of Law yielded $765 for salaries; Pharmacy tuition added $630, which went for equipment; and tuitions in the Department of Music, which was almost entirely self-sustaining, provided over $3,100. Thus student fees furnished things that could have been gotten from the legislature only with difficulty, if at all.[9]

A third source of extralegislative income was private gifts. At the start gifts had made possible both the University's location in Lawrence and the construction of the University Building, but there was a falling off in later years. Small amounts of money appeared occasionally, but the most noteworthy gifts were books to the University's pitiful library: 230 miscellaneous volumes from Dr. L. Chase of Irving, Kansas, for example; the works of Alexander von Humboldt from graduate student Ellis B. Noyes; 90 volumes of assorted periodicals from the Reverend C. G. Howland; a set of the Harleian Miscellany from Frank R. Cordley of Boston; and others.[10] But there was no regularity about gifts and no systematic fund drives.

By far the greatest single donation came from William B. Spooner of Boston, who died in 1880 and remembered the University generously in his will. A wealthy leather merchant and philanthropist, Spooner was also Francis H. Snow's uncle. He had been a Free Soiler in 1848 and later a director of the New England Emigrant Aid Company. In 1878, after Spooner had retired from business, Snow visited him and waxed suitably enthusiastic about the

University's prospects. The impressed Spooner wrote into his will a provision that after certain individual bequests had been made and a charitable trust fund established, the balance of his estate should be divided equally between the University of Kansas and Oberlin College. Because of legal delays, the money did not come until 1891. With the settlement day drawing near, the Board of Regents thought they might get as much as $250,000; the actual amount was a smaller, though still appreciable, $91,618.03. Along with it came a testimonial from trustee Charles F. Coffin, who said that Francis H. Snow, in Boston to collect for the Board, should consider the money "in some degree a measure of your uncle's confidence in you, his admiration for your work in the great field of science, and his faith in the institution to which you have so nobly devoted your life." With the money the regents built a splendid hundred-thousand-volume library—though at the time there were only 21,700 books to put in it—and a residence for Chancellor Snow.[11]

For money, then, it was always the legislature that mattered most. In the years from 1876 to 1889 the University climbed out of the depression and secured money to expand the faculty, raise their salaries, and construct two new buildings. It was in this period, moreover, that the Board of Regents began to perfect fund-raising techniques that would remain standard during the rest of the school's first century. At the end of the period the legislature began a new policy of imposing a tax to raise a fixed sum—originally $75,000 a year—for the University, thus providing a certain stability.

Getting money from the legislature required three obvious steps: preparing a budget, justifying it and the resulting requests to the public, and steering the appropriation bill around the legislative shoals. The first two were elementary; it was the third that produced difficulty and anguish.

Most of the budget's preparation fell to the chancellor and faculty. During the year, Marvin, and later Lippincott, talked with the faculty about their needs and desires, their salaries, equipment, and the demands of the University as a whole. Most often the discussions were informal, though they came both inside and outside faculty meetings. After securing a general understanding of what was possible and what was not, the chancellor prepared a tentative budget for the regents.[12]

Usually the professors themselves added their voices to the chancellor's in urging the regents to be generous. Moths were eating some of the natural history specimens, the faculty told the regents in 1875; appropriate cases were needed. The Department of Chemistry also needed money for laboratory equipment and labor and the Departments of History and English Language and Literature and of Ancient Languages and Literatures had to have maps, charts, and lecture illustrations. In 1884 the faculty joined to support a whole new building for Francis H. Snow's Department of Natural History, whose encroachments of bugs, bones, and skins on space needed by other departments was such as to cause "great embarrassment and impair their efficiency." A "proper presentation" by the Board to the legislators would surely succeed.[13] Individual faculty members also made suggestions to the regents in their annual reports. By the mid-1880s Professor Ephraim Miller, who became University librarian in 1873, was getting desperate. Pointing out in 1885 that the library was growing by only 500 volumes annually, he practically demanded that the Board ask $3,000 for books for the coming year. "Is that sum too much?" he asked. "The question should rather be, Why is it so little? What is a university without a library?" In 1880 an overworked James H. Canfield urged the regents to divide his chair of history and English language and literature in two, and a worried George E. Patrick asked the Board for a separate chemistry building. The low ceilings and poor ventilation of the basement laboratories in the University Building, Patrick reported, trapped noxious gases from experiments, which sometimes made the rooms unfit for human occupancy and were a "great annoyance" if not a health hazard to those on floors above.[14]

After receiving suggestions from the chancellor and faculty, the Board of Regents passed judgment upon them, decided on the size of the request to the legislature, and published it in their annual or biennial report. While the purpose of publication was partly to inform, the main objective was to generate enthusiasm for the University as a whole and especially support for the appropriation bill that the regents intended to introduce. Hence in the reports appeared statements about the University's value and functions, faculty reports of both accomplishments and needs, and the chancellors' reports to the Board. In all the words, however, there were but two themes. One was that within the limits of present resources the

University was doing an excellent job. "In all that goes to make such an institution a living force for the good of the patronizing public," Chancellor Marvin said in a typical statement in 1878, "we have had success." Ten years later, conditions were just as happy. "In every element of the true college," Chancellor Lippincott said, "the University of Kansas has made the most gratifying progress."[15]

The other theme was that past and present attainments were but slight compared with what the school could do if it had more money. "The expenditures already made . . . are such as to force us to the conviction that the people intend the establishment and mainte-nance of a University of highest grade," said the regents, typically, in 1886. "Economy, State pride, and the wants of a rapidly increas-ing population, all seem to us to be in the line of a liberal expendi-ture. The foundations of the University rest broad and deep upon the affections of the people and the wants of the State. Why shall we delay the superstructure?"[16]

In 1884 Lippincott and the other regents began to emphasize that, compared with other American universities, their own was sadly lagging. While Kansas had total receipts of about $41,000 for fiscal 1884, for example, Missouri had $97,000, Wisconsin $115,000, and Michigan $264,000. The Kansas endowment was about $145,000, whereas Iowa had $216,000, Michigan $475,000, Minnesota $575,000, and California $1,675,000. Where Michigan spent $70,000 on in-struction alone, Wisconsin $50,000, and Missouri $44,000, Kansas spent but $24,000. Chancellor Lippincott's salary was $3,000 a year, which contrasted unfavorably with the $4,000, $5,000, and $6,000 received respectively by the presidents of Wisconsin, California, and Minnesota. Full professors at Kansas had an average salary of $1,650 a year, but their counterparts at Minnesota, Missouri, and Wiscon-sin got an average $2,000, at Michigan $2,200, and at California $3,000. Only in undesirable statistics did Kansas lead the list. In contrast to the twenty hours each week that the average Kansas faculty member taught in class, his colleagues at Wisconsin taught fifteen, at Minnesota twelve, at Michigan ten, at California nine. The student-faculty ratio was 34:1 at Kansas, 19:1 at Missouri, and 9:1 at Nebraska, California, and Wisconsin. On seventeen different points of comparison "touching matters essential to good work," the Board said, "and showing generous patronage and support, Kansas stands in nearly every respect at the foot of the list! Was there ever a better year than this, in which to make a radical reform?"[17]

Besides such arguments the University's leaders had several other techniques for winning public favor and public appropriations. The annual catalogues were a species of advertising: by 1890 the regents were distributing ten thousand each year, most of them to the general public. To keep the University in the public eye and to reach "most people in their homes," as James Marvin said in 1880, the regents advertised widely in Kansas newspapers.[18] There were also special publications for statewide distribution, such as a statistical analysis in 1884, which duplicated the material of the biennial report, and a more general compendium of 1885 called *Facts of General Interest to the People. The University of Kansas. What It Is, and What It Does.* And the Board spent money to send out hundreds of copies of student publications, which contained not only essays, fiction, and poetry, but large amounts of University boosterism as well.[19]

As valuable as the printed word were personal contacts. The University's regents, faculty, and friends spoke before various groups, lobbied with the legislature, talked up the cause generally. Rumor had it that when a train carrying Francis H. Snow killed a man on the tracks, he was asked, as the nearest thing to a minister around, to say a few words over the deceased. Snow replied that, not knowing the man, he could offer very little. But having a small audience of fellow passengers before him, he proceeded to speak on the merits of the University.[20]

One of the potentially most effective groups of public advocates was the alumni. Until 1882, however, they were but loosely organized. In 1876 the graduates had formed an Alumni Association, but the group met only at commencement time to reminisce and to hold musical, poetical, and literary exercises. In June, 1882, they organized themselves more tightly with Professor William H. Carruth as president and created an executive committee to function between the annual meetings. The executive committee established several subcommittees, including a correspondence committee to maintain contact among the alumni and a Committee on the Best Interests of the University. In 1884 Lippincott urged the latter group to foster support among all the people, answer criticism, spread word of the institution's "excellent character," and get all the alumni to do the same. The University's future, Lippincott said, was "closely bound up in the loyalty and zeal of its alumni." As many of them found occasion—as private citizens, newspaper editors, legislators, public officials—they followed Lippincott's advice.[21]

All the planning and propaganda reached a climax each year or two at the meeting of the state legislature. Until 1877 the legislature met annually, afterward biennially. The regents regularly prepared their own appropriation bill and gave it to some University supporter to introduce. Then they and their backers used the techniques of every other group seeking the lawmakers' favor: friendly newspapers published pro-University editorials, the chancellor and regents went to Topeka to lobby, sympathetic representatives tried to convince doubtful colleagues that the requests were just. Once the legislatures of the 1870s and 1880s had passed a bill, approval by the governor was routine. During those years no chief executive vetoed a University bill either in whole or in part.

Struggling upward from the mid-1870s' depression was a slow business. During the year from November, 1874, to November, 1875, the regents had about $20,000 to spend, slightly over $18,000 of which had come from the legislature. Determined that the financial drought should end, Chancellor Marvin and the Board asked the legislature of 1876 for the comparatively huge sum of $54,000, including $25,000 to finish the University Building, $17,000 for faculty salaries (in contrast to $12,000 from the preceding legislature), and $2,000 for library books. But the regents ran into a swarm of economizers and were badly stung. "If there ever was a time in the history of our state when retrenchment was necessary," said a House Committee on Retrenchment and Reform, "it is to-day." All the state institutions were spending too much money, and the University had probably twice as many faculty members as it needed. The House of Representatives sent the appropriation bill to the Ways and Means Committee for trimming, and other representatives secured further reductions on the floor; the Senate concurred in most of them, but made a few amendments of its own. Away went $20,000 for the University Building, the entire library fund, $3,000 from salary requests; the total reduction was over $30,000. Worse yet was that the legislature specified faculty salaries in the appropriation act. And worse than that was that the University would have to do more work. Taking the advice of the House Committee on Retrenchment and Reform, the legislature abolished state normal schools at Leavenworth and Concordia, drastically lowered the appropriation for the school at Emporia, and made the University's appropriation contingent upon its opening a Normal Department at once.[22]

For a year the University community simply marked time and hoped that both the state's financial condition and the temper of its representatives would improve. According to the Lawrence *Kansas Tribune*, the institution's prosperity depended on the choice of orthodox Republicans, rather than those of the Reform faction, who were all economizers. "Send those howlers to Topeka, and the owls will hoot where professors lecture, and the bats will inhabit the places students now occupy. . . . Be wise in time."[23]

The legislature of 1877 was less disappointing than its predecessor, which made for a measure of progress. Anticipating a continuation of the customary fiscal year from November to November, the Board asked for some $53,000 for fiscal 1877 and $29,000 for 1878; the main difference was $20,500 still needed for the University Building. Most legislators thought the sums too high. Where the regents begged $10,800 a year for the salaries of six full professors, they received only $9,600. To finish the University Building they got only $10,000. To build up the library they wanted $1,500; they received only $500. For regular expenses the appropriations were about $10,000 less per year than the regents desired, a reduction of close to a third.[24]

Some compensation for the disappointing totals, however, came in the legislature's altering the state's fiscal year to the July 1–June 30 period. During the time the November to November year was in effect, the legislature usually passed the appropriation bill in March and the University had to cover the monthly expenses from the fall to the spring by borrowing and student fees; no one could be sure, moreover, that the legislators would continue for the rest of the academic year the salaries of men already teaching. Now making a special appropriation to cover the period from November, 1876, to June, 1877, the legislature went ahead to appropriate all money in advance, which, if it made longer-range planning possible, also made the anguish last longer.

In the late 1870s it seemed doubtful that the legislature and the regents would ever see eye to eye on the University's future and nature, about just what kind of a state university Kansas should have. Yet hopes of progress revived in and after 1879, for the depression passed and the regents mastered the lesson taught by the legislatures of 1876 and 1877: if there were times to be bold, there were also times to be realistic. Thus the $70,750 they asked of the legislature of 1879 was some $11,000 less than the request of the previous biennium, and except for $16,000 in special appropriations —most of it for finishing the University Building—it would have been lower still. In 1877, for example, the regents sought $22,000 for faculty salaries; now they wished about $20,500. Having failed earlier to get the $1,500 for the library, they now asked for $1,000. The legislature pared here and there—mostly by refusing to increase the amount for faculty salaries—and the University came out with about $10,000 less than the regents needed. Though disappointing, the reduction was hardly disastrous.[25]

Again in 1881 and once more in 1883 the regents held the line and got most of what they wished for regular appropriations and even a new—if small—building. The proposals for fiscal 1882 and 1883 were $28,350 each year, an increase of only $1,200 over the requests of 1879. The legislature cut the amounts by only $2,000 for 1882 and $3,000 for 1883. Better yet was the absence of significant opposition to the appropriation bill on the floor.[26] Heartened by the favor the regents decided to try for a chemistry building. By the early 1880s the Department of Chemistry was the University's greatest nuisance. "The Chemical Laboratory, under three stories of recitation-rooms," said the student *Kansas Review* in 1882, "sends its noxious gases into the Department of Physics, corroding the delicate instruments there, into the Library, damaging the bindings of the books, into the Natural History Department, attacking the colors of the innumerable fine specimens, and in all these rooms bringing great discomfort and perhaps actual injury to the human occupants." And always there was the danger of fire. The faculty agreed with the students, and the regents determined to seek $12,000 for a separate structure from the legislature of 1883. With that request went one for almost $31,000 for general expenses for each of the next two years, with most of the increase being for an expansion of the faculty.[27]

The legislature cut slightly over $5,000 from the total biennial request, and made a peculiar appropriation for the chemistry building. Because the Senate unanimously wished the University to get the full $12,000 while the House wished to grant but $8,000, a conference committee and then the whole legislature agreed to appropriate $8,000—out of the accumulated interest on the University Fund—and to make the extra $4,000 available only if the governor certified in writing to the state auditor that it was necessary to complete the structure.[28] Getting the extra money proved relatively easy. Chancellor Marvin himself had designed a building to cost the full amount, and in the spring of 1883 the regents convinced Governor Glick that the University could do with nothing less. Glick warned the Board, however, that he would not tolerate an expense of one penny more than $12,000, whereupon the Board let a construction contract for $10,500, and spent to the last cent $1,500 to equip the interior. In January, 1884, the Chemistry Department moved in and everyone else breathed more easily.[29]

Located about fifty feet southwest of the main building, the new structure was a T-shaped, architecturally nondescript affair of native limestone with brick and stone trimmings. On the ground floor were two assay rooms, a metallurgical and blowpipe laboratory, and a storeroom. On the floor above were a lecture amphitheater seating a hundred students, an office and laboratory for Edgar H. S. Bailey, who succeeded George E. Patrick in 1883, a laboratory for special students, and a large qualitative chemistry laboratory, forty feet square with room for fifty-four undergraduates and equipment. The ceilings were high and the lighting and ventilation excellent; there was a water tank in the attic. Though it would take several years to equip the laboratories completely, Bailey boasted in 1884 that the Department of Chemistry was now "as amply provided with facilities for instruction as any institution west of the Mississippi."[30]

Success in 1883 led to a bold effort in 1885 which paid off handsomely. Prodded by the faculty and Chancellor Lippincott, the regents determined to ask the legislature of 1885 for $50,000 for a building for Francis H. Snow's Department of Natural History. To that amount they added almost $77,000 in regular requests for the 1885–1887 biennium, to permit raises in faculty salaries and growth in faculty numbers, to buy a refracting telescope for the observatory, and to purchase other equipment. In support of the request the regents organized a sizable campaign. For men impressed by statistics there was the report of 1884 and the special pamphlet showing how Kansas lagged. For Kansans who saw no particular good in the University the regents circulated the results of a questionnaire asking the alumni to list the advantages of attending the institution. The replies that the Board saw fit to print were gratifying: "My success in business is due to University work," for example, or "As a citizen, I have been changed from a narrow seeker of local interests to a lover of my whole country," or "The University ... made a *man* of me"; to another the University gave "respect for learning, contempt for frivolity, love of virtue." And for Kansans who wondered why Natural History needed its own building, Chancellor Lippincott praised its professors in his published report to the regents. Francis H. Snow had given to the University specimen collections in botany, zoology, and geology that in number and value were second nationally only to those at Harvard. Lewis L. Dyche's collections of stuffed birds and mammals were growing rapidly. To make the collections usable and display them properly, the new structure was the University's "most pressing and immediate" building need.[31]

While the general appropriation lost only $900 on its way to unanimous passage in both houses, the natural history building appropriation had tougher going. It passed the Senate with only one dissenting vote, but many House members thought $50,000 too much; only after frantic work by the University's supporters did the House pass it, 79–39. It appropriated $25,000 for each of the next two fiscal years.[32] When Governor Martin signed both bills, the University erupted. On the night of March 6 some two hundred singing, cheering students, faculty, and alumni, carrying torches and led by a drum corps, marched around the streets east of Mount Oread, visiting homes of the Chancellor and faculty. Four undergraduates carried Francis H. Snow on their shoulders to a platform downtown, and there a crowd roared approval of addresses by Lippincott, faculty members, alumni, and townspeople. The Chancellor believed that the large appropriations had begun a new era in the University's history and replied to the familiar gibes that his school was at best merely a local "Lawrence University" or at worst only a "Lawrence high school." There was now "no such thing as a Lawrence University," Lippincott said. "It is now the University of Kansas, and we are proud of it."[33]

Well they might be. With the $50,000 the regents in 1885 and

1886 built the Snow Hall of Natural History, named even before its completion for Francis H. Snow. It was a Romanesque, T-shaped structure about 110 by 90 feet at its wider end, located west of the University Building. In its two main stories, plus basement and attic, were a large lecture hall, laboratories and work rooms for subjects biological, taxidermical, geological, botanical, zoological, anatomical, and osteological, and four museums: for geology on the first floor, for zoology and entomology on the second, and for anatomy near the roof. For its time Snow Hall was well lighted and ventilated. It would serve the University's natural scientists for over forty years.[34]

When next the regents faced the legislature, they were not merely bold, but brash—and they both suffered and prospered as a result. Joining several special requests—equipment for Snow Hall, foundation repairs on the University Building, an enlarged power plant, and a chancellor's residence—to increased regular appropriations, the Board came up with pleas for almost $108,000 in fiscal 1888 and another $54,000 for fiscal 1889. At stake, the regents said in their report, was the "establishment and maintenance of a University of highest grade." But the legislature saw things differently. The total amount was $35,000 more than the University had obtained in 1885, which from the legislators' viewpoint was too much. Out went the whole $10,000 for the chancellor's house, $13,000 of a requested $18,000 for building repairs, half the $2,000 for the library, and several other items. In all, the legislature took some $30,000 from the request for fiscal 1888 and $2,000 from that for 1889, and then approved the bill unanimously. Despite the reduction, however, the University had over $78,000 to spend in 1888 and $52,000 the next year.[35]

If the regents and faculty had paused in 1889 to review the University's material progress since 1876, they could only have been gratified. During the year ending November 30, 1876, the institution had had just over $26,000 to spend for all purposes, about $23,000 of which had come from the legislature. In the year ending June 30, 1889, the regents had over $71,000, including a balance from the previous year.[36] Besides the money, the University had two new buildings, which eased the strain on the old one and made Mount Oread look more like a real college campus. In the later 1870s and the 1880s there were also growing numbers of trees and shrubs to please the eye and ease the heat. In November, 1876, Chancellor Marvin had told the regents that the University site "lies without fence to protect or tree to adorn," and suggested that if the grounds were fenced and graded, the students and Lawrence citizens might join in planting trees. Getting $1,200 from the legislature of 1877, the regents decided to enclose the campus with a hedge fence on the west and south, and a post board and wire fence on parts of the north and east. At the main entrance to the campus was to be a mortared stone wall with iron gates across the drive. During the next five years Marvin found great support for his beautification plan. From Lawrence citizens came 300 trees in 1877, planted mostly by the students; the Douglas County Horticultural Society and N. N. Osburn, a local nurseryman, added 650 more in 1878. That fall Marvin induced N. P. Deming, a farmer living on the slope west of the University to give two bushels of walnuts for a grove the regents named for Marvin. The most attractive planting was a lilac hedge east of the main building, given in 1878 by Joseph Savage, a local farmer; others added to it, and its annual flowering attracted thousands of visitors. Marvin relentlessly pressed for ever more beautiful grounds. "This campus," he told the other regents in 1882, "is susceptible of rapid transformation from a rough common to a beautiful park." Time proved him correct.[37]

Also pleasant to contemplate was the growth of the student body and faculty. There were 237 students who matriculated in 1875–1876, and 505 in 1888–1889; the increase was 113 percent. The faculty grew even more rapidly: during the 1875–1876 year it had eleven members, whereas thirteen years later there were thirty-two.[38]

During the 1880s most of them rejoiced in higher salaries. After the disappointments of the legislature of 1875 the regents lowered the full professors' annual stipends from $1,800 to $1,500—and then praised them for their willingness to suffer for the cause of higher education in Kansas. "Some of the men now employed are so interested for the future of the University, and so identified with it," said the Board, "that they are willing to starve in the temporary depression. . . ." The legislature kept them lean a few more years. Though the law of 1873 empowered the regents to set faculty salaries, the legislature of 1876 specified $1,600 amounts for the male professors and gave Chancellor Marvin $2,000; except for

Francis H. Snow, whose eminence won him $1,800 in 1879, the legislatures of 1877 and 1879 refused to grant money enough to return to the $1,800 amount. After 1881 conditions slowly improved. In that year Snow went up to $2,000 and in 1887 to $2,500. Larger appropriations allowed raises for a few professors to $1,800 in 1881 and $2,000 in 1885; the average in 1884, however, was only $1,650. From 1881 to 1885 Chancellors Marvin and Lippincott got $2,500; starting in 1885 Lippincott received $3,000. In the same year the legislature awarded Dean James W. Green of the Department of Law $2,500 a year.[39]

While the regents protested that salaries were too low,[40] they were more disturbed that the legislature limited their power to set them. The lawmakers of the 1870s and 1880s appropriated funds specifically for salaries of the chancellor, Snow, and the deans of the Normal and Law Departments and then gave lump amounts for a specified number of faculty members. In 1885, moreover, the legislature specified that the $5,000 granted for the salaries of five assistant professors had to come from the interest on the University Fund and forbade the regents using any more of the fund for salaries. The regents chafed against such restrictions and pleaded for discretionary power over appropriations, but in vain. But in 1886, at least, they secured from Attorney General Simeon B. Bradford an opinion that the use of contingent fees to supplement what the legislature gave was legal.[41]

Behind the desire for control over salaries and over the University Fund lay a wish for the appropriation of a lump sum every year or two which the regents could spend as they desired. Yet at no time was the Board ready to propose this publicly. From the legislature of 1889, then, the regents asked specific sums for specific purposes. The amounts, however, were astounding: $138,000 for fiscal 1890 and $102,000 for 1891. The $240,000 total was about 85 percent more than the $130,000 received for the 1887–1889 biennium. With the money the Board proposed to raise the full professors' average salary to $2,400, increase Snow's stipend from $2,500 to $3,000 and Lippincott's from $3,000 to $5,000, and spend $26,000 to repair the foundations of the University Building, $10,000 for physics and electrical engineering equipment, and $25,000 for the library. Each item, the regents assured the astonished legislators, was justified by the University's "helpful influence . . . upon the educational interests of the state."[42]

Under the best of conditions the huge request would have met opposition, and in 1889 conditions were anything but good. After 1886 boom times ended in drought, hard winters, and falling prices for grain and livestock which cost Kansans their profits, farms, and peace of mind. Governor John A. Martin, friend of higher education though he was, told the legislators that its needs had to be considered in light of the citizens' misfortunes. The past two years had not been "seasons of prosperity. Crop failure, epidemic diseases among stock, and other calamities of nature, have impoverished many of our people." The legislature should be on special guard against unnecessary appropriations. "Increased salaries, at such a time," Martin said, "are especially obnoxious, and should not be allowed."[43]

In order to get some first-hand information about the University's needs, the House Ways and Means Committee, which had first crack at the appropriation bill, sent a subcommittee to Lawrence. The group inspected every room in every building, talked with the faculty, and concluded that the institution could continue to function very well indeed without much extra money. With considerable foresight, it was true, the subcommittee left the library appropriation intact, for Professor Arthur Richmond Marsh of the English Department and Dean Green of the Law Department had impressed the members with the utter inadequacy of both the University Library and the Law Library. The former had but ten thousand volumes, of which four thousand were public documents of limited usefulness and another two thousand were "either obsolete or worthless for University use." Law students had to use Dean Green's personal library of twelve hundred volumes and that of Judge Solon O. Thacher. Yet the subcommittee excised the salary raises, reduced the building repair fund by $18,000, and made cuts in a number of lesser items.[44]

The recommended library appropriation infuriated the University's opponents. In the Committee of the Whole, Representative Joseph R. Burton of Abilene led the attack by claiming that great numbers of books were irrelevant to a good education. Look at Abraham Lincoln, Burton urged: he had a very small library yet learned much. For that matter look at Burton himself. His college had had only a $70,000 library building—and Burton had never been inside it. Yet he was not an ignoramus, for he had read the Bible, Shakespeare, and Bulwer, and if students would do the same, they would know more than if they read thousands of library books. Daniel W. Poe of Butler County joined Burton in demanding the elimination of the library appropriation and went on to assert that all appropriations, especially for faculty salaries, should be reduced. The University's defenders counterattacked as expected—Kansas needed a great university, they said, which in turn required at least an adequate library—but the most they could get was $10,000 instead of $25,000. Yet it was fortunate that the representatives spent so much time arguing over the library appropriation, for they had no time to make great reductions in the other recommendations of the Ways and Means Committee. The amended bill, which passed the House 84–3, cut about $41,000 from the request.[45]

In the Senate the House bill became entangled with another measure, sponsored by Senator Joel Moody of Mound City. Educated at Oberlin College and the University of Michigan, Moody was a man of many parts. Lawyer, lumberyard owner, politician, and author, an intellectual disciple of Tom Paine, he was also so interested in the cause of education in Kansas that the Topeka *Capital-Commonwealth* dubbed him the "watch-dog of the state's educational interests" in the legislature. On January 10 he introduced a bill to reorganize the University and its government. It provided for a tax of three-tenths of a mill on the state's taxable property, the proceeds of which would go to the University. Although the Board of Regents had never been brave enough to ask the legislature for a mill tax, the idea was not new. Friends of the University had long believed it a way out of all financial difficulties —particularly that of relying on the legislature—and in 1878 the regents themselves had pronounced it desirable.[46]

The so-called Moody Bill came out of the Senate Ways and Means Committee in a restricted version. Instead of authorizing a general tax, it limited the amount to be raised to $75,000 for fiscal 1891 and every year thereafter. While far below the $102,000 that the regents sought for 1891, this was a few thousand dollars more than the House had granted in its appropriation measure. On February 22, after a conference committee had settled minor differences, both houses passed the Moody Bill without opposition.[47]

Then the Senate Ways and Means Committee reported out a drastically cut—by $20,000—version of the House appropriation bill for 1890. After the Senate passed it, a conference committee restored some of the amount, but the final measure gave the University only about $70,000 instead of the requested $138,000. In all, for the coming biennium the regents got about $95,000 less than they said they needed.[48]

Besides the reduction and the failure of the mill tax, the University community found in the work of the legislature other reasons to despair. Neither the appropriation law nor the Moody Act appropriated the interest on the University Fund, as was necessary for the University to get it; the Moody Act, moreover, stated that the $75,000 was to be "in lieu of all other appropriations," which apparently forbade appropriating the interest forever. In addition the act repealed the charter of 1864, which had permitted both matriculation and tuition fees, and either accidentally or by design did not give the regents power to charge such fees in the future.[49] Added to everything else was the certainty that if legislatures to come believed that $75,000 a year was all that the University needed, all hopes for a distinguished institution were dead.

But at least the regents could spent the $75,000 as they pleased. In the future, they saw, their main problems would be to retain that power, get the lump sum appropriation increased and add to it special grants for buildings, and recover student fees and the University Fund interest. Along with efforts at solving those problems would go prayers that the new depression would lift and the state as a whole grow prosperous once more.

8

Curricular Activities

*A*T the same time that the University's leaders were seeking an adequate—or even more than adequate—income, they were also questing after the nature and meaning of the University itself. For if money was necessary to create a university, it was not always clear what kind of institution money should build. As the search applied to the character of the curriculum in the 1870s and the 1880s, it went along three main paths: toward the abolition of the Preparatory Department, the introduction and development of the elective-major-minor system, and the establishment of new schools in addition to the College.

If the University of the 1870s lacked things that a true university needed, it also had things that no true university wished, and chief among them was the Preparatory Department. No one desired to keep it a year longer than necessary. Though Chancellor Marvin justified its presence in the University in 1875, he also looked forward to the time when secondary schools would do its work. Eight years later Chancellor Lippincott said bluntly that just as the high schools could not do the University's work, neither should the University have to offer preparatory instruction.[1]

But inducing Kansans to support enough high schools to supplant the Preparatory Department was hard work. In 1878 Chancellor Marvin surveyed the state's schools and came away gloomy. The common schools provided nothing approaching adequate preparation for college. Most teachers were unqualified; those who were

121

trained had to spend too much time with preadolescents; little apparatus and few reference books were available for the higher classes. There were a few city high schools with separate grades, but the training they offered was usually poor and they refused to admit students from the countryside. Agrarian Kansans, Marvin said, had yet to learn the advantages of education beyond the common schools, and he attacked the "false theory" that "farming requires but very little brain, and less learning; that only the learned professions require these higher conditions and provisions for education." Kansas should have a high school in every county, or at least one for every four counties—so that no child would be farther than a day's journey from one—and the high schools should offer courses that the University could accept for admission.[2]

The University could do little about increasing the number of schools except urge Kansans to act. Until well past 1891, when the Preparatory Department closed, state law did not require high schools in cities or counties, provide state aid for them, or demand any part of a high-school education for Kansas youth. Statutes of 1861 and 1863 had authorized schools in the high-school districts into which the state was divided and in first- and second-class cities, but they continued to be few. Between 1864 and 1880 high schools appeared in Leavenworth, Lawrence, Wichita, Atchison, Topeka, Wellington, Winfield, Junction City, and several other places, and there were several private academies. After years of agitation by interested citizens the legislature of 1886 passed a law requiring county commissioners to levy a tax whenever voters approved building a high school. But there was no state money provided, and the law forbade any city high school from also being the county school, thus demanding duplication. Very few schools resulted from the law.[3]

The existing high schools, moreover, had no common curriculum, for the state did not require it.[4] But rather than waste time trying to get the legislature to impose one, the University faculty decided to attempt to persuade the high schools to prepare students. In the effort they were following other universities, for Michigan had begun in 1870 to admit automatically graduates of certified high schools, and by 1874 Minnesota, Iowa, Wisconsin, Indiana, Illinois, and Ohio were developing their own certification systems.[5] After a convention of high-school teachers and officers had recommended a uniform course in 1872, the regents and faculty met with school authorities and by February, 1874, had prepared a course acceptable to a number of schools. But the University's internal strife prevented action on the scheme. Not until the spring of 1876 did the regents issue a formal statement about the proposed high-school curriculum. It was, naturally, practically a duplicate of the University's own preparatory curriculum. At the time, the Preparatory Department had three separate courses to parallel those of the College: a Classical Course, a Scientific Course, and a Modern Literature Course. The main differences between the first two were that French and German replaced Latin and Greek in the second and third years of the Scientific Course and that natural philosophy and drawing appeared in the Scientific Course but not the Classical Course. French, German, and drawing, but no natural philosophy, characterized the Modern Literature Course. The regents and faculty urged the Classical Course on the high schools. It included three years of Latin and two of Greek, along with arithmetic, algebra, geometry, geography, English grammar, composition, and elocution. But French, German, and natural philosophy might replace Greek to prepare students for the Scientific and Modern Literature courses. Students from high schools adopting the curriculum would be admitted to the University if they passed a final written examination over the work—the questions were to be prepared by the principal, but approved by the University faculty—and were so certified by the principal. Over the years, of course, the recommendations changed with the University's own curriculum.[6]

In 1876 there were four accredited schools—at Lawrence, Atchison, Winchester, and Emporia. By 1883 seventeen were accredited among the state's forty-eight public schools offering secondary courses. While the growth was encouraging, the faculty found the accreditation process vexing. Once the University had accredited a school and published the fact in the catalogue, there was no certainty that the school would continue to meet the requirements. By October, 1883, it was obvious that some sort of continuing supervision would be necessary, and even a lowering of standards. At that time the faculty decided to require school officials to submit their actual curricula every January and to allow up to a year's deficiency in any one subject. Students would make up the deficiency at the University. In April, 1884, the faculty recommended to the regents that a University officer regularly investigate each accredited school, but nothing came of the proposal.[7]

Even amid uncertainty, however, in the spring of 1883 the faculty took the first step in abolishing the Preparatory Department by ending the first year, effective the following fall. In October, 1884, the regents, with the faculty's approval, voted to end the second year of preparatory work with the end of that academic year. Claiming that the state's high schools were "steadily advancing in efficiency," the Board said that as soon as possible the faculty should be offering only "University work, proper." But that time was five years in coming. Only in August, 1888, did the regents, on Chancellor Lippincott's recommendation, decide to accept no more preparatory students—after June, 1889. The Department would end when all enrolled students had passed out of it. To guarantee the Department's demise, the regents had it written into law: the Moody Act specified that all "elementary courses and instruction to prepare students for the admission to the University" should cease in the spring of 1891, and that henceforth admission was to rest on either examination or certification of graduation from an accredited high school.[8]

But as the death of the Preparatory Department drew near, the old problem of certification remained very much alive. In 1888 a faculty investigating committee reported discouragingly that most of the accredited schools did not report their courses regularly, did not hold the required final examinations, and, where they were held, did not present the questions to the faculty for approval. Instead of appropriate certificates, students seeking admission often presented only general diplomas of graduation which failed to list the courses taken. Worse yet, of the thirty-two students who failed two or more final examinations at the end of the first semester in January, 1888, eighteen were from "our supposed best preparatory schools," and in several cases the cause was insufficient preparation.[9]

During the next two years, therefore, the faculty investigated what other state universities were doing to keep school authorities in line and then drew up a new system which the regents approved. It called for precise reporting of the work done in preparatory subjects and required that unless visited in person by a professor or the chancellor, each school had to submit final-examination questions for faculty approval. In the catalogues, approved schools would be divided into two groups: those fulfilling all the preparatory requirements for one or more College courses, and those whose work fell short by not more than three semesters' work in one subject. While graduates of the first group would be admitted routinely, those from the second could enter only "with conditions," which had to be made up either in the Preparatory Department—while it lasted—or the Lawrence High School. Delinquent schools would be dropped from the lists at once.[10]

One more problem remained. By the spring of 1890 many Kansas educators were disturbed by the fact that all four of the University's approved admissions courses—a Latin Scientific Course was added in 1883—required two languages, whether ancient or modern. The high-school men argued that the language demands prevented the admission of students otherwise prepared, and that a course asking only one language should be created. Lest the opposition ruin the experiment of dropping the Preparatory Department, faculty representatives met with several educators in April, 1890, to draw up a preparatory Latin English Course, whose only foreign language requirement was Latin through parts of Caesar and Virgil. A convention of high-school superintendents approved it, with a few changes, in May, and so did the University's faculty and regents. The new preparatory course required the creation of a similar course in the College.[11]

When the University shed in 1891 what Francis H. Snow, now chancellor, called its "high school posterior appendage," the signs for the future augured well. During the 1889–1890 academic year there were but nineteen high schools completely preparing students for admission in one or more courses, and thirty-six which were deficient in no more than three terms' work in one subject. In the following year the numbers were respectively forty-one and thirty; the Latin English course had eased things considerably. In the 1891–1892 year fifty-three schools were fully accredited in one or more courses and Chancellor Snow reported that the University, "standing at the head of the public school system," was now "reached from the high schools by simple and natural gradation as the high school is reached from the grammar school. . . ."[12]

At the same time University authorities eased the process of administering entrance examinations for students who had attended nonaccredited schools. Until 1880 such examinations were held only at the University, but in that year the faculty started giving them at various points around the state—to which the professors traveled as University evangelists as well as examiners. Beginning in 1890 the regents allowed high-school principals to examine their students and certify them as ready for college. In defense of the policy the regents argued that the principals would use great caution lest students whom they passed do poorly at the University; furthermore, they pointed out, the University was not obliged to keep every student admitted.[13]

In trying to decide what undergraduates should do, the faculty and the regents faced an amazingly complex task. But they began with the idea, reflected in the curricula of the mid-1870s, that the University should be a variegated institution committed to neither classical nor scientific nor practical education alone; rather, it should offer elements of all three. In 1876 the College curriculum had a Classical Course, a Scientific Course, and a Modern Literature Course. The Scientific Course led to a Bachelor of Science degree, the other two to the Bachelor of Arts. Students were free to choose their own course, but in each course the requirements were the same for all students. Each gave some attention to all the fields of knowledge. Students in the Classical Course, for example, studied not only Latin, Greek, and Greek history in the freshman year, but algebra, geometry, botany, and English composition as well. In the sophomore year, continuing with Latin and Greek, they added trigonometry, analytical geometry, physics, and zoology. The junior year had Latin in the first semester and Greek in the second, together with chemistry, logic, physiology, English literature, and astronomy. And the senior year was equally varied: in the first semester it demanded Greek, English rhetorical and historical criticism, mental and moral science, meteorology, and geology; in the second semester students took only political economy and medieval and modern history.

In the Scientific Course, which substituted German and French for Latin and Greek, freshmen took both languages and in addition studied drawing, chemistry, botany, and English composition. With German, French, and drawing in the second year went trigonometry, surveying, physics, zoology, and analytical geometry. The junior year held another semester of German and calculus, logic, physiology, medieval history, English literature, and astronomy. Seniors finished the four years with mental and moral science, mineralogy, geology, meteorology, English rhetorical and historical criticism, and medieval and modern history.

Like the Scientific Course, the Modern Literature Course required three semesters of German and two of French during the first three years. In addition to the two languages freshmen took ancient history, drawing, algebra, geometry, and English. The next year there was still more ancient history, and also trigonometry, analytical geometry, physics, and zoology. The junior year comprised German, logic, chemistry, and physiology in the first semester, and medieval history, mineralogy, geology, meteorology, and English in the second. Seniors duplicated the Scientific Course.[14]

Further curricular variety was offered through three other programs, then also called courses, but corresponding to what later years would know as majors. After completing the freshman and sophomore years of the Scientific Course, a student could elect to spend his last two years in the Civil Engineering Course, the Natural History Course, or the Chemistry Course, each of which demanded the same work of all its students.[15]

In the idea of the special courses was the elective system in embryo, the birth and growth of which were the most important characteristics of the University's curriculum in the late 1870s and the 1880s. "The elective system is fast becoming a reality in our leading schools and colleges, and with remarkable success," an editor of the student *Kansas Review* correctly stated in 1879, in urging that he and his fellow students be allowed more freedom to choose their own curriculum. Since no one could know everything, why not let the students decide what they would learn? Minds, personalities, and life goals differed from student to student, and the curriculum should express that fact. Like other faculty and student supporters of the elective system across the nation, the editor attacked the "mental discipline humbug." Known more formally as faculty psychology, it held that each mind was composed of certain faculties —memory, reason, and will, for example, or the mathematical, the mechanical, and the poetical—each of which needed due attention. But faculty psychology had begun to crumble under the attacks of scholars who knew man to be far more complex and less compartmentalized than their predecessors suspected. In the light of man's nature, the *Kansas Review* editor complained, the existing curricular requirements were foolish. "Our catalogues comprise a course of a little mathematics, more Latin, a smattering of aesthetics, a taste of modern languages, and a mere glance at the sciences. Four long, weary years, we spend at our universities, wasting hour after hour, over some extremely complicated example in calculus, or higher astronomy, or mayhap in committing to memory some formula in physics, which in later life will be of no earthly use to any student thus spending his time. It savors too much of drudgery." At the end of it all the student had gained only a "paltry sheepskin: the certificate that the previous four years course had been wasted for all time."

A widening of the elective principle would quicken the University's intellectual life. Students taking courses of their own choosing would pursue them with unprecedented zeal. Faculty members would now be free to offer the courses that they desired and were best qualified by training and research to teach. The elective system would produce more enthusiastic professors, improved academic departments, and better research. From it would come a real university—an institution offering instruction in all sorts of subjects. More students would be drawn to it and, with them, more financial support. Withal, the elective system's specialization would better prepare students for service to a society itself becoming ever more complex and specialized.[16]

Though briefly stated, here were the main arguments that opponents of the fixed curriculum everywhere were using. The idea of choice itself, however, was nothing new—even if proponents often talked as if it were; it was the extent and form of the choice that presented problems, and as usual, there was no agreement on these matters among American university leaders. Under President Charles W. Eliot, Harvard after 1869 indulged in an orgy of freedom: by the early 1890s the only formal demand was a freshman course in English composition. Other authorities, most notably President James McCosh at Princeton, thought that education was too noble an undertaking to be left to adolescents and held their elective courses to a minimum. Yet Princeton did not dictate all courses; here and there upperclassmen had some choice.[17]

With the elective system growing in national popularity and with many Kansas students in full cry for it, the faculty in December, 1879, appointed Francis H. Snow and James H. Canfield to investigate the curricula of other universities and colleges. They studied the two extremes of Harvard and Princeton. After hearing their report, the faculty voted two months later to take a position midway between complete freedom and complete prescription. Freshmen and sophomores still had to work within one of the three main courses. But juniors and seniors could choose two of the three subjects of each semester—and they continued free to choose one of the three special courses. They had to take a half-semester each of logic and physiology and a full semester of history in the junior year, and a semester each of mental and moral science and political economy in the senior year, but otherwise they were free to choose their courses from a wide range of subjects. The faculty hampered them a little, however, by providing a list of approved classes for each of the four semesters; a first-semester junior, for example, had to select his electives from among Latin, Greek, calculus, German, and physics. In April the Board of Regents approved the plan. As the faculty expanded and the number of electives grew, Chancellor Marvin thought the new curriculum a great success. It met the students' needs, he said in 1882, and at the same time provided a nice balance between what they desired and what the faculty thought they needed.[18]

The elective movement at Kansas reached a climax in 1887. During the fall semester the faculty appointed a committee to review the courses of study in the College and make recommendations. It consisted of three scientists—Edgar H. S. Bailey of Chemistry, Ephraim Miller of Mathematics, and Edward L. Nichols of Physics —and three nonscientists—Chancellor Lippincott, Arthur Richmond Marsh of English, and William H. Carruth of German. Early in February the committee recommended and the faculty agreed that all juniors and seniors should be entirely free to shape their own curricula. In order to focus their choices, however, the faculty instituted majors and minors—that is, groups of related subjects within particular fields of study. There were local precedents for the idea in the special courses of the 1870s, and for several years higher educators, most notably President David Starr Jordan of Indiana University, had been discussing the concept.[19]

Starting in the fall of 1887, then, juniors and seniors, having passed through the general course requirements of the underclass years, were free to elect majors and minors. At the time there were fifteen majors, corresponding with the existing professorships: biology, chemistry, mineralogy, physics, mathematics, philosophy, history, political science, Greek, Latin, Greek and Latin in combination, German, French, German and French combined, and English literature. A major consisted of four courses—one each semester, subject to faculty approval. In addition students were to have two minors of two courses each. One of them was to be within the major field, consisting of two courses over and above those for the major, and the other was to be in a different field.[20] The whole plan was a compromise between absolute rigidity and absolute freedom. Students were free, but not too free; the courses were fixed, but not too fixed. In 1888 Chancellor Lippincott pronounced the elective-major-minor system a success. Students were more eager learners than before, and the teaching was more enthusiastic, partly because the major departments had to compete for students. Under the required curriculum the professor had been his students' "master and dictator," but now he was their "friend and companion."[21] Future generations of University faculty members would share Lippincott's enthusiasm. During the rest of the University's first century, the College curriculum would continue to express a medial position between liberty and autocracy.

Lippincott and his faculty, however, were unwilling to have electives throughout the University. By the late 1880s the University included "departments" or schools, other than that of Science, Literature, and the Arts, whose requirements were narrowly professional or vocational. Although the professional schools helped the institution toward the modern university ideal, their relatively rigid curricula fostered certain inconsistencies in the theory of undergraduate education.

According to the charter of 1864 the University was to have six departments: a Department of Science, Literature, and the Arts, a Normal Department, and Departments of Medicine, Law, the Theory and Practice of Elementary Instruction, and Agriculture. Although the charter enabled the University to escape entirely the arguments at many other institutions about whether the main purpose of higher education was liberal or professional,[22] it also produced practical difficulties. An Agricultural Department would compete with the Agricultural College in Manhattan, a Normal Department, with state normal schools in Emporia, Concordia, and

Leavenworth. And it was hard to say what a Department of the Theory and Practice of Elementary Instruction was. That left the Departments of Law and Medicine for consideration. At first the Board of Regents had been reluctant to establish either; creating a Department of Medicine, the Board of 1866 told an overenthusiastic State Medical Society, would be "premature, inexpedient, and fatal to the first great object of a State University," which was giving the undergraduate college a firm foundation. In 1869, upon John Fraser's urging, the regents voted to establish both departments as soon as practicable,[23] but that committed the Board to nothing, and nothing was what the regents had done by the time Chancellor Marvin arrived.

But the legislature of 1876 pushed the University into professional training, much against the will of the regents and faculty, by requiring it to create a Normal Department. On March 10 the regents voted to establish it as of April 1. At the opening ceremonies Chancellor Marvin promised that although the legislature had imposed on the University "labors it is fair to characterize as extraordinary," he and his faculty would do their best to make the Normal Department a success.[24]

During the eight years of its existence the Normal Department passed through a strange metamorphosis. Until 1881 it had no permanent dean; four different persons served for short periods. But in that year Philo J. Williams, who had been dean in 1876–1877 and then had become president of Ottawa University, returned to Mount Oread to stay for seven years. It was a pity he could not have stayed forever. A Connecticut native, he reached the University by way of Dartmouth College, the superintendency of schools in Leavenworth, and Ottawa. Charitable, forthright, and tolerant, a sloppy dresser but a keen thinker, Williams cared for nothing—reputation, fortune, environment, comfort—except the idea of social salvation through education. His earnestness and devotion inspired his students. His mind was a "veritable Damascus blade," one of them recalled. "In coordinating and presenting facts and truths, he was to me a modern combination of Socrates and Aristotle. . . . He was a very prince of teachers."[25]

Originally the Normal Department had a Common School Course and a Higher Course for Grammar School Teachers, but after a year the regents dropped the first. The remaining "Higher

Normal Course" stood somewhere between the Preparatory Department and the College. Students who had attained sufficient skill in reading, spelling, arithmetic, American history, and other subjects could enter it without having a high-school diploma or completing the University's preparatory course. Normal students at first took a standard three-year course requiring Latin for five semesters along with the various sciences, English, mathematics, and English history. The course also provided lectures on teaching theory and twenty weeks of practice teaching in the Preparatory Department. Completing the course won a diploma entitling the graduate to all privileges that the state gave to the graduates of its normal schools.[26]

This was something more than a high-school education—for the Higher Normal students took regular undergraduate classes—but less than a college education. But in 1879 the regents, with faculty approval, created three college-like courses for the Normal Department: a Classical Course, a Modern Language Course, and an English Course. The first required Latin, the second German, and the third no foreign language at all. In 1884 the Normal Department became an integral part of the College when the faculty and regents created a Collegiate Normal Course for juniors and seniors which corresponded to the special courses in natural history, chemistry and physics, and engineering. Allowing but one elective each semester, it required varying amounts of logic, physiology, history, mental and moral science, and political economy. At graduation, students received either a B.A. or a B.S., depending on which course they had followed in their underclass years, and a Bachelor of Pedagogy, the customary normal degree.[27]

Though the name changed, the course survived the abolition of the Normal Department by the legislature of 1885. The regents had asked $1,650 a year for Philo J. Williams's salary as dean, but received nothing. They therefore abolished his department and made him professor of didactics, paying him from the general fee fund. The new Course in Didactics was essentially the same as its predecessor, except that graduates now received a Bachelor of Didactics degree besides the B.A. or the B.S.[28]

Hard upon the Normal Department's creation came a Department of Law. In 1875 and 1876 the regents received a number of urgent pleas to open one. They appointed a committee to investigate the matter, and in August, 1878, decided to go ahead. If their

Committee on Instruction could find a dean willing to take as salary only the fees that students paid, which meant that he would have to continue his own law practice, the Department's first session was to start the following fall and run through March, 1879. The logical choice as dean—at first to be the entire faculty—was Judge Nelson T. Stephens of Lawrence, father of the outspoken Kate. Stephens was a native of Genoa, New York, who had established a lucrative practice in Moravia, given it up to fight for the Union, and emigrated to Kansas for his health in 1865. There he prospered once again, brought out his family in 1868, gained a substantial reputation, and championed a law school at the University; it was natural for the regents to invite him to become its first dean. But both his modesty and his position on the bench made him decline.[29]

As it happened, however, Judge Stephens's son-in-law, James W. Green, was very much available. Green was then thirty-six. Born in Cambridge, New York, he had taken a B.A. at Williams in 1866 and four years later began to practice law in Olathe, Kansas. From 1878 to 1880 he served as county attorney of Douglas County. Although Judge Stephens declined to nominate Green for the deanship, he had another contact for the position in Regent Frank T. Ingalls, a fellow undergraduate at Williams. When Ingalls asked him if he would accept the position, Green assented at once, and the Department opened on November 6, 1878.[30]

For the next decade and more it held an ambiguous place in the University. One reason was that the Department's small number of students—from 1878 to 1885 an average of fifteen a year and never more than twenty-four—made the regents unwilling to hire Green full time. In 1880 the Dean described his Department as an "unparalleled success" from the start and predicted that its future growth would be "steady and healthy." The regents were not much impressed. By requesting only $500 a year for his salary in 1881, $1,000 in 1883, and $1,200 in 1885, they manifested their desire to keep Green on a part-time basis. The Dean, however, was always busy in his own behalf. "In my opinion," he told the Board in 1884, "one person should be sufficiently paid so that he may devote his entire time to the Law department," for it was of "vital importance" that Kansas lawyers be properly educated. Going around the regents, he induced his friends in the legislature of 1885 to appropriate $2,500 a year for his salary, providing he gave all his time to the deanship. No longer having a choice, on April 1 the regents put the school on a more permanent basis by making Green dean and professor of constitutional and criminal law, evidence, equity, and jurisprudence; two other professors, Marcus Summerfield and J. Willis Gleed, shared the other subjects. From time to time prominent Kansas lawyers served as lecturers.[31]

Even after the change, however, the Department of Law was peculiar. However well it prepared students for the bar, its standards of admission and therefore its standards of teaching were lower than those of the College. While Green recommended that matriculants take a course of "liberal studies" before entrance, not even a high-school diploma was required. Students eligible for admission to the College were welcome, but so was everyone else who could pass simple examinations in the English language and American and general history. The lower demands meant not only a lack of reasonable uniformity in University admission standards, but also that some students were receiving a lower rather than a higher education.[32]

Throughout the 1880s the Department's curriculum remained fairly consistent, and so did its teaching methods. During the two-year course the fledgling barristers studied the appropriate subjects from standard textbooks—Edwards on bills and notes, Schouler on domestic relations, Stephen and Gould on pleading, and so on. Experience had proved, according to Dean Green, that the best teaching method was by the "approved modes of teaching the fundamental principles of the sciences." Thus there were daily recitations on the texts, supplemented by class lectures and addresses by members of the Kansas bar. A moot court met once a week to give the students practice, and there was a Blackstone Club—later the Kent Club—in which papers were read and cases argued. In the 1889–1890 year the Department had fifty-six students.[33]

Shortly after the regents created the Law Department, they started to build a Department of Medicine. Here they had to move slowly, for high-quality medical study demanded not only classroom instruction but extensive clinical work in large hospitals under the supervision of experienced physicians and surgeons. Chancellor Marvin was enthusiastic about introducing a first-year medical course into the University, but he urged caution about a complete medical program, for neither the University nor the city of Lawrence had suitable facilities for clinical work. "To attempt to furnish this finishing part of a physician's education in a rural district, however complete the outfit of manikins and skeletons," Marvin warned, "is to trifle with the dearest interests of civilized life. The results of such charlatanry are seen in the awkward empiricism which fills our cemeteries with the prematurely dead and the foul suspicion of laws broken in premature resurrections. Let the University for the present be content with laying well the foundations, though others may exult in setting the cap-stones." On March 25, 1880, the faculty passed and sent to the regents a proposal for a preparatory or first-year medical course which would be a combination of existing classes in chemistry, anatomy, physiology, zoology, toxicology, and materia medica. The regents approved the plan and stipulated that only students eligible to enter the College as freshmen might enroll in it.[34]

It would be twenty years before the University would offer the second year of the medical course. In 1885, though, the legislature enabled the regents to establish a chair of pharmacy, which had a close relation to medicine. Five years earlier a convention of physicians and druggists had urged the Board to offer a special course to serve both doctors and pharmacists. The regents were originally enthusiastic about the idea, but soured when they failed to get a requested $1,000 a year from the legislature of 1881, and when they failed to find a lecturer for a series they hoped to sponsor on pharmaceutical subjects. But after a long battle between groups of druggists and physicians the legislature of 1885 passed a law creating a state Board of Pharmacy to examine and license pharmacists. A supplemental law established a chair of pharmacy in the University to be supported by surplus funds of the Pharmacy Board. The regents were to fill the chair without delay and also appoint a committee of registered pharmacists to examine the graduates and sign their certificates.[35]

Lucius E. Sayre became the new professor. New Jersey born, he was a graduate and now a faculty member of the Philadelphia College of Pharmacy and also a faculty member of the Woman's Medical College. No cloistered scientist, Sayre had already begun a personal campaign for pure food and drugs laws and other public-health legislation. In future years he would gain a considerable national reputation for his monographs and textbooks and would

serve on the Committee of Revision of the United States Pharma-
copoeia. Before 1885 was out, the regents discovered that the resources of the Board of Pharmacy were inadequate to pay Sayre's
$1,800 annual salary, and after considerable lobbying, they got a
special session of the legislature in 1886 to assume it. Since the legislators refused money to equip a laboratory, however, the regents
scraped up $700 from the general fee fund and special pharmacy fees
and voted to outfit the basement of the Chemistry Building for
Sayre and his students.[36]

Like those in law, the pharmacy students were special students
rather than regular college undergraduates. Although graduates of
accredited high schools were admitted without examination, a minimum age of sixteen and the passing of examinations in arithmetic,
American history and the Constitution, geography, and English
grammar and composition would gain acceptance for anyone else.
The two-year course was severely practical and rigidly prescribed.
In addition to completing it, students seeking both the degree of
Graduate in Pharmacy and certification had to finish a two-year
apprenticeship in the "actual drug business" and then pass the test
of the regents' pharmacy examiners. The Department of Pharmacy
was a success from the start. Twenty-three students enrolled the
first year; three years later there were forty-three, of whom four
were women. In 1888 the regents gave Sayre an assistant professor,
George Weida, whose salary came from student fees. The regents
were so favorably disposed to the Department that in 1890 they
approved the idea of a separate pharmacy building for it—for the
Chemistry Building basement was never adequate—but the Department remained where it was for another decade.[37]

While the Departments of Pharmacy and Law were being established in short order, Engineering and Fine Arts, two departments in
the College, were passing through a lengthy evolution toward separate status. The Civil Engineering Course was one of the three
special courses for juniors and seniors established in the College in
1873. Upperclassmen who completed the first two years of the Scientific Course took four full semesters of civil engineering, engineering mechanics, drawing, and field practice in addition to several
more generally required courses on their way to a Bachelor of Science degree. But that amount of engineering was insufficient and
remained so until 1883, when Professor Frank O. Marvin decided

that the time had come to expand the course. The son of the University's third chancellor, he had been born in 1852 and was an engineering graduate of Allegheny College. He spent the 1875–1876 year as assistant professor of German, French, and free-hand drawing at the University, leaving to become principal of Lawrence High School. After Frederick W. Bardwell's death Frank joined the faculty in 1879, now as assistant professor of mathematics, physics, and civil engineering under Herbert S. S. Smith. In September, 1882, the regents introduced a chair of civil engineering and elected Marvin a full professor to fill it.[38]

Within a year Professors Marvin and Smith were asking the faculty to expand the offerings of the two-year course to include mechanics, analytical mechanics, the construction of roofs and bridges, and specifications and contracts, as well as an engineering thesis. While neither man apparently wished to work outside the College, the request contained a harbinger of a separate four-year engineering course in additional work in drawing in the freshman year and the substitution of railroad field work for French in the sophomore year. After the faculty and regents approved the changes,[39] Marvin continued to work to give the engineering course a separate existence within the College. By 1885 he had effected a peculiar marriage between the Latin Scientific and General Scientific courses which required German in the underclass years but allowed either Latin or French as the other language. The catalogue of that year listed a separate four-year Civil Engineering Course, dropping the statement that two years of one of the other courses should precede it. In his report Marvin said that he wanted the civil engineering work to be equal to that of the "better schools of engineering elsewhere," asked for another faculty member, and suggested that the "University ought ere long to so advance the work of this department, as to be able to grant the degree of Civil Engineer to its graduates."[40]

In 1887 Marvin's desires drew closer to realization when Edward C. Murphy became assistant professor of civil engineering and Lucien I. Blake, who was peculiarly qualified to offer a course in electrical engineering, became professor of physics. Like the civil engineering course, that in electrical engineering appeared in the catalogue as a separate four-year one; the freshman year duplicated that of the civil engineering course, but the second year provided more work in physics and chemistry. Its purpose was entirely vocational. "This course," said the catalogue statement, "is designed to give students as complete preparation for the profession of electrical engineering as is possible within the limits of a college course." Whatever the cultural value of the foreign languages, for example, it was now subordinate to professional ends, for students were to have enough French or German to allow them to read scientific works in the languages. By the end of the 1880s, then, the engineering courses were something more than majors though less than those of an entirely separate school, and it was clear that they were parting company with the rest of the College. The divorce came in 1891 with the creation of the School of Engineering.[41]

The development of the work in engineering was paralleled by the offerings in music and art, which in the 1880s moved from an inferior position to one of eminence and then to inclusion in a separate school. In the University's early years none of the regular courses required art or music and there were no full-time faculty members in either subject. After the faculty reorganization of 1875 Alice G. Boughton, a graduate of that year, taught instrumental music for her students' fees, and a year later the regents rehired J. E. Bartlett of Lawrence at $125 a semester to teach singing to the Normal students. Chancellor Marvin hoped to make instrumental music a more integrated and permanent part of the University's curriculum. "No one attainment, above the merest rudiments of learning," Marvin believed, "carries into the home and the neighborhood more pleasure than music. Argument is not needed to enforce a conviction of its value." But the legislature of 1879 turned a deaf ear to the regents' request for $1,200 a year to pay a musical instructor. The Board was able only to buy one piano and rent another, and between 1877 and 1881 Clara L. Morris taught the instrument for student fees. By 1880 she had worked out a four-year course.[42]

Three years later the regents appointed Professors James H. Canfield and Frank O. Marvin and Regent W. S. White, all of them music lovers, as a committee to investigate the possibility of introducing music study as a regular part of the University curriculum. After they reported favorably, in 1884 the regents accepted the resignation of Richard A. Lehman, then instructor in music, and hired William J. MacDonald as professor of piano, harmony, and theory and as dean of a new Department of Music. His annual salary of $1,500 was to come from his students' tuition fees, supplemented by money from the general fee fund.[43] MacDonald proved an excellent choice. The son of a Methodist divine in Providence, Rhode Island, he had graduated from the New England Conservatory of Music in 1884 just before going to Kansas. An enthusiastic and friendly person as well as an accomplished pianist and a fine teacher, he was a powerful evangelist for more music in both the University and the state. He traveled widely to give concerts and speak and arranged many concerts and addresses on musical subjects for the University and Lawrence communities.[44]

But MacDonald's greatest contributions to the University were well-planned courses integrated with the College curriculum. By the end of his first year he had prepared a five-year course in piano and one of equal length in vocal culture, and stood ready to offer courses in harmony, musical theory, and various instruments. A year later he introduced a six-year combined College-Music course which allowed College students to add enough music to one of the regular courses to secure both a bachelor's degree and the Graduate in Music degree that the Department offered. MacDonald also sought continually to improve the Department's physical accommodations. When he resigned in 1890 to continue his studies in the East, he had the satisfaction of knowing that his department would soon be moving from the top floor of the University Building, where the rooms were anything but soundproof, to the renovated North College, where it would join the Departments of Art and, strangely, Law. Because of his ceaseless activity and personal warmth the Department had an average of eighty students a year.[45]

The Department of Art was not so fortunate. Throughout the 1870s free-hand drawing passed from professor to professor. In 1877 Frederick W. Bardwell received it from Frances Schlegel, and when he died the next year, it went to physics professor Herbert S. S. Smith. But Smith was also professor of astronomy and civil engineering, and drawing was of minor importance. Painting was not offered. After 1885 things improved somewhat. Free-hand drawing was then offered by Alice Litchfield, who was a general assistant to Frank O. Marvin; she received $250 a year out of interest on the University Fund. When Miss Litchfield resigned, the regents replaced her with Mary Louise Simpson at the same salary. Except for a year's study in Europe she remained an instructor in oil painting past the end of the decade, and in 1888 the regents added Cora Parker as a drawing instructor. The two of them prepared a four-year course in drawing and perspective and a three-year course in painting; by 1890 they had forty students. But their classes remained merely adjuncts of the regular curriculum until the School of Music and Fine Arts was organized in 1891.[46]

If a university was a collection of vocational or professional schools surrounding an undergraduate college, by the end of the 1880s a real university had begun to appear on Mount Oread. With the disappearance of the Preparatory Department and the introduction of the elective system and majors and minors, the University became steadily more mature. But the ultimate test of a true university, and of an institution in the process of becoming one, was its faculty. The University of Kansas needed not merely courses and teachers, but research scholars. Fortunately it had them.

Gentlemen and Scholars

SEVERAL years after James H. Canfield left the University of Kansas, he recalled that his colleagues had been a remarkably stimulating group. Himself an able and outspoken man, Canfield had worked hard during his fourteen years in Lawrence (1877–1891) to make the institution more of a real university, and he had come to know his fellow faculty members well. "In the faculty meetings," he remembered, "there was constant discussion of ways and means and methods—in fact, those early faculty meetings seem to me to have been more overflowing with energy and enthusiasm and determination and hope and scheming than any other faculty meetings I have ever attended."[1]

As usual Canfield's memory was accurate. During the fifteen years after the rebellion against Chancellor Fraser the University collected a number of interesting professors who not only seasoned their enthusiasm with idiosyncrasies, but gave the school an emphasis on scholarly research and familiarity with ideas current in the nation's intellectual and academic communities as well as good teaching.

One of the more attractive definitions of the American university in the late nineteenth century held it to be a community of scholars. Although the presence of a sizable number of scholars was more important to a university's welfare than the presence of a community spirit among them, Mount Oread had both. The environment promoted close contacts among the faculty, sparked a continuing intellectual interchange, and allowed a far better understanding of each other than would be possible at a later day. Into the early 1890s the number of faculty members remained small: there were ten in 1875–1876, and forty-two, including several parttime lecturers, in 1891–1892.[2] While the percentage increase was impressive, the latter number was not large and communion among them was easy. Then, too, the University's limited number of buildings brought most faculty members into contact every day.

But more important in producing a sense of faculty community was the nature of their regular meetings. Until the University's division into separate schools, which occurred between 1890 and 1892, the entire faculty met together to hold discussions and make decisions affecting the University as a whole. Until 1884 the faculty rules called for a meeting each week with every faculty member expected to attend; in practice the faculty met less often, though more than once a month, and in 1884 voted to meet semimonthly. The gatherings were more than routine. Both the reorganization law of 1873 and the regents' bylaws gave the faculty large powers to shape the University—to determine its curriculum and its internal rules and regulations, and, together with the regents, to create new departments and divisions. It was the entire faculty, then, which debated the merits and form of the elective system and decided the relations between the University and the high schools. The regents' bylaws, moreover, required faculty members to discuss their teaching methods in the meetings. Such discussions held some risk of public embarrassment, but they seemed to go off fairly well and certainly enlightened the members about each other's activities. As part of the continuing discussion during the 1877–1878 year, for example, during the spring semester the faculty heard Frederick W. Bardwell on the work of his classes in astronomy, engineering, and drawing, David H. Robinson on the problems of teaching Latin and Greek to Kansas youth, and Ephraim Miller on the best means of teaching mathematics. Nor was the Chancellor exempt: in March James Marvin explained what he was trying to do for his students in mental and moral philosophy.[3]

Still another means of fostering mutual understanding was the faculty's reports, which until 1888 appeared regularly as parts of the regents' published biennial report to the governor, and thus were available to one's colleagues. While some of the reports were merely formal and routine, others were lively and informative statements of both successes and problems. It was in Kate Stephens's report of 1884, for example, that she lambasted the Board of Regents. Through James H. Canfield's report of 1880 the faculty members who did not already know discovered how overworked he was. "This chair," he said bluntly, "needs relief," for as professor of history and English language and literature he was teaching grammar, composition, etymology, rhetoric, and early and modern literature, along with American, Greek, Roman, and medieval and modern European history, to students from the first preparatory year to the senior year of college. Canfield felt himself in danger of becoming only a teaching machine, hearing recitations in a mechanical way. He also told his readers that the University should have a separate chair of history and political science, for the two subjects were related and were "pushing rapidly to the front as vital studies" in the academic world. Readers of other reports learned of Francis H. Snow's efforts to cultivate his students' "faculties of observation and comparison" instead of only their memories; of Frances Schlegel's experiments with the "natural method" of teaching German and French, which demanded that English not be spoken in the class-room during the early weeks of courses; and of Herbert S. S. Smith's contempt for all the outdated physics textbooks and his consequent reliance on his own lectures. The students, Smith said, seemed to have a "definite understanding" of the subjects he discussed.[4]

On the whole, the faculty believed that the days of greatness for the University were not distant. The idea was there in 1882 in James H. Canfield's conviction that few of the older colleges and universities had a better program in history and political science than Kansas, now that the regents had split English from his chair. It was there in Edgar H. S. Bailey's report of 1888, stating that in the past two years there had been a "general advancement" in all scientific departments, and that the Department of Chemistry had "kept pace with this spirit by raising the standard of scholarship as fast as the circumstances would allow." It was there, too, in Francis H. Snow's conviction in 1886 that with the completion of Snow Hall no other university in the land had a building that "so admirably combines the qualities requisite for the special instruction of college students and the general instruction of the visiting public."

For these and other faculty members the progress of the past was a harbinger of even greater progress in the future.[5]

Yet there was an inconsistency between the idea of future excellence and the preservation of faculty community, for excellence demanded the creation of distinct schools, each with its own faculty, a great increase in the number of faculty members, and a growing specialization of subjects. Specialization was necessary for several reasons: by the 1870s no man could be master of all knowledge in even one academic field; the elective system required a larger number of courses which were more restricted; concentration in one area would help to relieve heavy teaching loads. At the same time the growing importance that American university leaders were attaching to doctoral degrees, which required specialized scholarship, meant that prospective faculty members were almost certain to be specialists rather than generalists.

At Kansas as at every other American university there were two stages to specialization, though they overlapped in time. The first was the splitting of huge general areas of knowledge into their component parts and making each a separate chair or department. The second was the division of the departments among several men, each with his own interests and specialties.

During the 1875–1876 academic year the University faculty consisted of ten members who more or less divided among them the entire learning of the Euro-American world. Four men shared the sciences. George E. Patrick was professor of chemistry, physics, and mineralogy, and Ephraim Miller professor of mathematics. Frederick W. Bardwell had charge of astronomy and civil engineering, and Francis H. Snow of botany, zoology, geology, and meteorology. Outside the sciences the specialization was just as rudimentary. Because the legislature of 1876 provided for only one chair of ancient languages, the regents made David H. Robinson professor of Latin and Greek and appointed D. B. English, who had been teaching Greek, professor of history and English language and literature. Chancellor Marvin was also professor of mental and moral philosophy, which included political economy and logic as well as mental and moral science. Besides the seven professors there were two assistant professors, Frances Schlegel and Frank O. Marvin, who shared responsibility for German, French, and drawing, and a teacher of instrumental music, Alice G. Boughton.[6]

As the regents were able, they sought to expand the faculty, and with the expansion came specialization. When Frederick W. Bardwell died in 1878, the regents made George E. Patrick, who had also been teaching physics, professor of chemistry, mineralogy, and metallurgy, and hired Herbert S. S. Smith to supervise physics, astronomy, engineering, and drawing; at the same time they rehired Frank O. Marvin to assist both Smith and Ephraim Miller in mathematics. Since Smith was more a physicist than an engineer and Marvin just the opposite, the two men complemented each other. When Marvin became a full professor of civil engineering in 1882, Smith confined himself to physics and astronomy.[7]

More important, though slower of realization, was the splintering of Francis H. Snow's "bench" of natural history. In the 1870s his greatest need was for a museum assistant, and in 1881 he at last got one in Lewis L. Dyche, a member of the class of 1884. In 1883, even before Dyche took his degree, Snow gave him the classes in comparative anatomy and special natural history; and in 1884, having completed requirements for both a B.A. and a B.S., Dyche became an assistant professor of natural history. But Snow still taught botany, zoology, physiology, geology, and meteorology. In 1886 he told the regents that in "Eastern colleges of the first class" at least four professors, each with an assistant professor, taught the classes embraced by natural history at Kansas. Though he asked for three assistants, not until 1889 and 1890 could the regents ease his load. Assistants in botany and the zoological museum came in 1889. When Snow became chancellor the next year, the regents divided his professorship by making him professor of botany, entomology, and meteorology; elevating Dyche to a full professorship of zoology, anatomy, and physiology; and luring to Mount Oread Samuel W. Williston, a graduate of the Kansas Agricultural College then on the faculty of the Yale Medical School, as associate professor of geology and paleontology. Two recent graduates became assistants in entomology and zoology, and thus there were now three professors and four assistants where fifteen years before there had been only Snow.[8]

Similar developments took place in the nonscientific fields. In 1881 the Board of Regents answered James H. Canfield's plea for relief by appointing him to a newly created chair of history and political science—which also included political economy, taken from Chancellor Marvin—and establishing a professorship of English literature, rhetoric, and belles-lettres. To fill it the regents chose the Reverend Leverett W. Spring, who for the previous five years had been pastor of the Plymouth Congregational Church in Lawrence. Appreciative though Canfield was, during the 1880s he grew increasingly dissatisfied by his inability to offer more courses—especially in the history of Spain, Italy, Germany, and the Orient, and in such subjects as political theory, political institutions, and industrial society. But not until 1889 could the regents help him once more: then they made him professor of American history and civics—that is, political science—and created a chair of history and sociology. In it sat Frank W. Blackmar, with a Johns Hopkins Ph.D. and the warmest possible recommendations from Herbert Baxter Adams, the leading professional historian of his day.[9]

Specialization in foreign languages came more readily than in the social sciences, for each one seemed to demand at least one professor. The regents had consolidated Latin and Greek in 1876 because they had to, but from 1877 to 1879 the acquisition of an assistant professor of Greek allowed David H. Robinson to concentrate on Latin, and in 1879 Kate Stephens became full professor. Henceforth the two ancient languages remained divided. The same year Frances Schlegel was elected to a full professorship of French and German. She taught both languages until 1882; her successor—and her husband—William H. Carruth, continued to teach both for another year. But in 1883 the regents made Arthur G. Canfield, James Canfield's cousin, assistant professor; he took the French and Carruth kept the German. Four years later both men became full professors.[10]

Throughout the 1880s all the work in English literature was supervised by a single professor with such assistant professors as he could get. After Leverett W. Spring resigned in 1886 to accept a position at Williams, the regents intensively searched the East and found a worthy successor in Arthur Richmond Marsh of Harvard. Marsh stayed for only three years, however, and his place was taken by Associate Professor Charles G. Dunlap, who had come as an assistant professor in 1887 and was raised to a full professorship in 1890. The regents then changed his chair to that of English language and literature.[11]

Perhaps the most notable new specialization in the College appeared in 1890 with the creation of a chair in philosophy. Until the introduction of majors in 1887, logic had been required of every junior, and mental and moral philosophy of every senior. Both Chancellor Marvin and Chancellor Lippincott, who taught the courses, were Methodist clergymen who believed that the goal of philosophy was to uncover for students preexisting truths about the nature of God and man, ethics and society. While both men maintained that their courses helped students to reason more clearly, Marvin pointed out in 1880 that they were supposed to support the positions they took in their regular critical reviews by both logical argument and "reference to standard authorities." There was little in those authorities—Sir William Hamilton, for example, or James McCosh, or Francis Wayland—that might tend to subvert orthodox Christianity or even to excite the mind.[12]

After 1887, however, philosophy was a major like any other subject, no more exalted than history, chemistry, or Latin; with its passing as a requirement the University became still more a secular institution. To provide major courses, Lippincott undertook to offer advanced psychology, and the catalogue had Philo J. Williams presenting courses in ethics, metaphysics, Hamiltonian logic, and the history of philosophy. But Williams left Kansas in 1887, and only in 1890 did the University get its first professional philosopher. He was Associate Professor Olin Templin, an alumnus of the class of 1886, who had studied in both England and Germany and had been serving as Ephraim Miller's assistant in mathematics. Templin created eight new courses in ethics, the history of philosophy, logic, metaphysics, and psychology, any four of which were a major. Although Templin himself was not far removed from Marvin and Lippincott—for he was religiously devout, idealistic, and convinced that philosophy's value lay in its encouragement to students to live noble and righteous lives—the relation of his subject to the rest of the College curriculum was wholly different from what it had once been.[13]

By 1890, then, the University embraced both a community of faculty members and the growing size and specialization that would one day destroy that community. But the most important thing it possessed was the scholarly research of its faculty, for without it no university of the approved kind could exist on Mount Oread. In terms of sheer quantity of books and articles the scientists were the most impressive. Francis H. Snow provided them with an excellent example of the dedicated researcher and writer. Blessed by nature with superabundant energy, he put behind him his original hopes of teaching humanistic studies to give himself wholly to the natural history of Kansas and the Trans-Mississippi West. As Samuel W. Williston, who knew him well, pointed out in 1908, Snow was a "field naturalist," rather than a laboratory analyst—a collector, classifier, and descriptive writer. "The study of beast, bird, and insect as they live," said Williston, "was to him, as to many of us, whom some would call old-fashioned, the deepest joy of science." Snow loved it all, but he especially loved entomology. He collected and classified thousands upon thousands of bugs, beetles, and butterflies, building up a *Coleoptera* collection that he knew to be the best in the nation. As fast as he could he published his discoveries and descriptions in well over a hundred articles. His great ambition, said a contemporary newspaper editor, seemed to be to ascertain the "name, age, sex, color and previous condition of servitude of every bug, moth, and butterfly between the Mississippi and the Rocky Mountains." If he did not quite succeed, he came very close. As a field scientist, moreover, Snow offered as much assistance as he could to destroy the insects which devoured the crops of Kansas farmers. He became the state entomologist in 1882 and as such he gave advice to both the state Board of Agriculture and individual husbandmen and worked with especial zeal to rid the state of the chinch bug, a pest whose staple was Kansas grain.[14]

Snow carried his enthusiasm into the classroom, encouraging his students to make their own investigations and collections. The man who took his message most to heart was Lewis L. Dyche, successively Snow's student, assistant professor, and professorial colleague. Dyche determined to do for the zoology of North America what Snow was doing for the region's entomology. His great ambition, he told James H. Canfield, now chancellor of the University of Nebraska and trying to entice Dyche to Lincoln, was to leave behind him "in some good institution the best collection of North Am. mammals in the world." To get it Dyche became the compleat hunter and explorer, billed when he lectured as the modern Nimrod, the mightiest hunter in North America. He tracked walruses in Greenland, sea lions in California, bears in Alaska and the Canadian Arctic, all creatures in all places that promised new specimens and satisfactions for his love of the unknown. In Lawrence, busy at teaching and mounting specimens, he studied and published articles on the red crossbill, the golden eagle, a puma shot at Hays City that he rushed out to measure, three types of gophers, and the garden mole. By 1910 his Department of Systematic Zoology had almost as many items—stuffed mammals and birds, skins and skeletons, eggs, shells, and the like—as Francis Snow had bugs. Dyche's collection was not the best in the nation, but it was equal or superior to that of any other university. At the same time Dyche was a perfect publicist for himself and his university. He lectured almost as widely as he traveled; his exhibition of North American mammals was a most popular attraction at Chicago's Columbian Exposition in 1893; and his fame became so great that a number of his less colorful faculty colleagues were extremely jealous.[15]

In its chemists and physicists the University had men as noteworthy as its naturalists. George E. Patrick, who taught chemistry and several related subjects from 1874 to 1883, established precedents for his successors. Partly because of limited laboratory facilities and partly because of his own interests, Patrick was a practical rather than a theoretical chemist who applied his knowledge for the material welfare of Kansas. Thus he described and analyzed both a gas well and the mineral water of Iola, investigated soils and chalk and salt deposits around the state, and wrote of the Great Spirit Spring and the so-called alkali of western Kansas. In later years he headed the Dairy Laboratory of the United States Department of Agriculture, worked out a test for milk fat, and crusaded for the strict enforcement of pure food and drug laws. Patrick was a kindly, enthusiastic man dedicated to his profession. In the "environment of the chemical laboratory," said his successor, Edgar H. S. Bailey, "he lived unselfishly for the advancement of the science."[16]

Bailey was describing himself as well. A Connecticut native, he had graduated from the Sheffield Scientific School at Yale in 1873, spent a year in graduate work there, and then joined the faculty of Lehigh University. On leave from Lehigh, Bailey did two things typical of the newer American scholarship. In 1881 he went to Germany to study, at the Kaiser Wilhelm University in Strasbourg under Rudolph Fittig. Back in America, in 1883 he took a Ph.D., at Illinois Wesleyan University just before leaving for Kansas.[17]

Even more than George Patrick, Bailey wished to make chemistry useful to society. In his first report to the Board of Regents in 1884 he contended that his department should not only study chemistry and the allied sciences from a "theoretical standpoint," but should also use its knowledge for a "better understanding of the various industrial and domestic pursuits of life." Bailey would later boast with good reason that the Kansas Chemistry Department was among the first in the nation to offer "practical courses related to everyday life." They included such things as toxicology and materia medica, assaying, metallurgy, and domestic and sanitary chemistry. Most of the more than a hundred articles and books that Bailey wrote during the next forty years were of a practical nature. He analyzed municipal water supplies, inquired into the composition of the state's oil, coal, and gas deposits, and investigated poisons and their effects. He became especially interested in preventing the adulteration of foods and in preserving, packaging, and cooking them properly, and made himself a leader in the fight for pure food laws in the state. In 1905 he became the chemist of the state Board of Health. His work both helped to make Kansas a safer place in which to live and brought the University great fame.[18]

While Herbert S. S. Smith, professor of physics from 1879 to 1883, was a competent teacher, he was not much interested in original research. His successor was a less popular teacher with a strong research bent. Edward L. Nichols was a Cornell University graduate who like Bailey had gone to Germany—to Berlin and Göttingen —for further study, and had afterward taken his doctorate at Johns Hopkins. At Kansas from 1883 to 1887 Nichols did research in the superheating of liquids, the supersaturation of vapors, the action of acids on iron in a magnetic field, the spectrophotometry of pigments, and the sensitivity of the eye to colors of a low degree of saturation. He read papers on the last three subjects to the American Association for the Advancement of Science, and published them and several others before leaving Kansas for his alma mater.[19]

In his place the regents hired Lucien I. Blake, who quickly became the Lewis L. Dyche of the Physics Department. Another New Englander, Blake had taken a B.A. in 1877 and an M.A. in 1880 from Amherst, and then studied under Hermann von Helmholtz and Heinrich Hertz at the University of Berlin, where he took his Ph.D. in 1883. He then spent two years as a faculty member at Adelphi College on Long Island and another two at the Rose Polytechnic Institute in Terre Haute, Indiana.

Outside the classroom, one of Blake's former students wrote, he was "fundamentally an experimenter and to some extent a promoter." Blake's most important technical investigations came in the practical areas of underwater wireless telegraphy, mainly for ships in distress, and the uses of x-rays. Continuing on the Kansas River experiments begun on the Wabash in Terre Haute, Blake developed and secured patents on several signaling processes, and in 1906 joined the Submarine Signal Company of Boston, which had bought the patents. In the 1890s Blake sought to discover more about the properties of x-rays, their worth to physicians, and their possibilities as a cancer cure; he and Edward C. Franklin of the Chemistry Department devised methods of shortening considerably the time it took to develop x-ray photographs. As a promoter, Blake exuded the electricity that he delighted in studying. Shortly after his arrival he introduced new courses in electrical engineering, dynamos, thermodynamics, and electrical laboratory work, and threw himself into laboratory labors alongside his students. When not in the classroom or laboratory he was likely to be addressing various groups of Kansans, for he was a fine after-dinner speaker and a compelling propagandist for electricity's practical benefits. He was one of forty of the world's most eminent electrical scientists invited to an International Industrial Congress held in conjunction with the Chicago Columbian Exposition of 1893. So successful was he in calling attention to himself that when the regents in the 1890s asked the legislature for six new buildings, Blake's physics building was the only one approved.[20]

The University's two social scientists were similarly engaged in investigation and publication. But James H. Canfield was not a man content to investigate political and historical subjects for their own sake. His goal was not merely to inform people about institutions and how they worked, but to improve those institutions. Unfortunately the amount of his published work at Kansas was small, and he attracted little professional attention. In 1882 he produced an article on the necessity of preserving national forests; the next year his popular book on taxation appeared; and he also wrote a study of *Local Government in Kansas*. In 1894, when he was chancellor of the University of Nebraska, he brought out his *History and Government of Kansas*. The book showed that Canfield was not always perceptive, for his history of the territorial period was strongly biased in favor of the Free-State forces.[21]

Frank W. Blackmar was the professional scholar that Canfield was not. When he came to the University in 1889 to assume the chair of history and sociology, he had an undergraduate degree from the College of the Pacific, four years of experience there as a mathematics teacher, and a newly acquired Ph.D. from Johns Hopkins. His doctoral dissertation on federal and state aid to higher education had already been accepted for publication by the United States Bureau of Education. While at Johns Hopkins he had also worked on a study of Spanish institutions in the Southwest, and his research appeared in an article in 1890 and a book in 1891. Three years later he wrote an appreciation of Charles Robinson as a territorial Free-State leader; in 1902, with Sara Robinson practically guiding his pen, he finished a biography of the man. In between came *The Story of Human Progress,* a popular rather than scholarly work, containing a long series of generalizations about human history from barbarism to civilization and advancing the scarcely novel concept that progress was to be measured by the increase of human happiness.[22]

Yet Blackmar never became the scholar he might have been. There were large fields open to him in both Spanish institutions and the relations between government and higher education, but he skimmed over both. One reason was that he was always short of money and therefore had to write books that would sell. Another was that he was so eager to unite history and sociology, which in his day were growing ever farther apart, that he could never pause long enough to penetrate deeply into either one. To Blackmar sociology meant the objective study of all aspects of contemporary society. Yet modern society had its origins in the past, and here it made contact with history, though not with history as usually defined. Rejecting the idea that history was merely a "prose narrative of past events," mainly political, Blackmar argued that it had to treat social and economic themes and to make objective comparisons of societies at different stages of development. History became both the narrative of unique events and past sociology; sociology both an analysis of contemporary institutions and present history. "Just as the study of sociology finds its best results in the investigation of living institutions," Blackmar maintained, "so history will yield to the student of living institutions the best and most useful returns." It was Blackmar's misfortune to be interested in the entirety of both subjects at once and he spread himself too thinly.[23]

With Canfield's enthusiastic cooperation Blackmar helped introduce the research seminary—later seminar—to Kansas in 1889. Blackmar had discovered it at Johns Hopkins. Borrowed directly from Germany, the seminary was a group of advanced students, usually graduate students, which met regularly under a professor's supervision to hear the results of original research and criticize the papers. Original student research at Kansas was nothing new, for many faculty members had demanded it in their courses, and numerous student-faculty clubs had long been hearing and discussing formal presentations.[24] But the seminary was novel in that it asked only original research, in contrast to the ordinary courses, and because unlike the clubs it was absorbed into the curriculum.

When the Seminary of Historical and Political Science opened in October, 1889, as an outgrowth of the Political Science Club, it was an extracurricular organization of both students and nonstudents, but early in 1891 Blackmar and Canfield decreed that all students taking more than two courses in their departments had to enroll in it. It was also open to University alumni and to other persons of "known scholarly habits" who would promise to read at least one paper during the academic year. Meeting once a week, the Seminary discussed papers prepared "as far as possible from consultation of original sources and from practical investigation of existing conditions," ranging from "The Russian-Jewish Problem" and "Indian Education," to "The Status of Women" and "The Character and Object of Railroad Legislation in Kansas." In 1891 Blackmar began a monthly publication, *Seminary Notes*, in which many of the papers appeared. He and Canfield were proudly conscious of what the Seminary meant to the University. "The Seminary," they wrote in 1891, "is a natural result of the growth of the 'Lawrence High School,' (as the institution was formerly called by its detractors) into a university; with all the larger methods and broader outlook which characterizes such advanced education."[25]

Over against the natural, physical, and social scientists stood a group of men in the literatures, scholars in their own right. Because several of them were exceptionally idealistic, they gave the University a spiritual or antimaterial dimension that generated considerable friction between the humanities and the sciences.

The most important of the humanists was William H. Carruth. Born in Osawatomie, Kansas, in 1859, he graduated from the University in 1880 and immediately became a tutor, or instructor, in the Department of French and German. Two years later he became the professor, and would remain a faculty member until 1913, when he went to Stanford. As a scholar Carruth was more than a Germanicist. He wrote in his field—on Schiller's *Wallenstein,* on the relation between Wilhelm Hauff's *Lichtenstein* and various novels of Sir Walter Scott, on the *Niebelungenlied,* a Germanic epic, and other works[26]—but he was also the coauthor of a book on woman suffrage in Kansas, a student of Kansas dialects, a historian (though with the familiar Free-State prejudices) of early Kansas, and an analyst and propagandist of the state's literature.[27] These subjects bespoke the idea that a man with broad interests should follow wherever they led him; and that notion, in turn, arose from Carruth's emphasis on the whole man and man's relation to the whole of existence. Influenced alike by German idealism and American romanticism, Carruth affirmed the unity of all being, the common essence of everything from the microcosmic to the macrocosmic. He was a religious man for whom religion was the "longing of the human soul for harmony with the spirit and tendency of the universe." His most famous expression of the oneness of existence came in his oft-printed poem, "Each in His Own Tongue," which first appeared in 1895. Four stanzas elaborated the idea that four things—evolution (which stood for all science), autumn (or the natural universe), human longing, and human consecration—were both themselves and God, a belief which made Carruth virtually a pantheist:

> A fire-mist and a planet,
>   A crystal and a cell,
> A jelly-fish and a saurian,
>   And caves where the cave-men dwell,
> Then a sense of law and beauty
>   And a face turned from the clod,—
> Some call it Evolution,
>   And others call it God.
>
>   . . . .

A picket frozen on duty,
   A mother starved for her brood,
Socrates drinking the hemlock,
   And Jesus on the rood;
And millions who, humble and nameless,
   The straight, hard pathway plod,—
Some call it Consecration,
   And others call it God.[28]

The trouble was that although the University might become a center of scholarship, the high idealism that Carruth professed was possible only for individuals. No institution of higher learning could embody this kind of unity, for that learning seemed to demand precisely the kind of specialization and fragmentation—and secularism, too—that Carruth deplored. "Frustration was the bitter essence of his blood," a former student reported. He grew convinced that science and scientists had excessive fame and prestige; he fought and lost a battle against overemphasis on intercollegiate football, which embodied so much of the worldliness that he detested.[29] Yet through it all he kept his humor and his zest, and through his writing, teaching, and example he spread the gospel of idealism. A handsome, graceful man, he was the Byron Caldwell Smith of a later day.

Carruth had an intellectual counterpart in Arthur Graves Canfield, who came to the University in 1883 and four years later became professor of French language and literature. His major scholarly interest was French lyric poetry, whose artful appeal to the purest sentiments attracted Canfield both intellectually and emotionally. A poet himself, he was much concerned with what he took to be a debasement of thought, language, and morality in contemporary literature. Canfield argued that the writer should feel a moral responsibility to his public, no matter how strong the adverse pressures working on him. His own poetry was as pure as he.

Be thou a bird, my soul, and mount and soar
   Out of thy wilderness,
   Till earth grow less and less,
      Heaven, more and more.

Be thou a bird, and mount and soar and sing,
   Till all the earth shall be
   Vibrant with ecstasy
      Beneath thy wing.

With such a spirit Canfield joined Carruth in refusing to truckle to academic authority and in condemning what they saw as publicity-seeking and self-promotion by the scientists.[30]

The occupants of the chair of English language and literature during the 1880s were as high-principled as Canfield and Carruth, though not quite as ethereal. When the regents divided James H. Canfield's chair in 1881, they chose the Reverend Leverett W. Spring as the new professor of English. The appointment showed that the Board was not yet entirely committed to the idea of professional specialization, for Spring was really a gifted amateur. A native Vermonter and a graduate of both Williams College and the Hartford, Connecticut, Theological Institute, Spring had become pastor of Lawrence's Plymouth Congregational Church in 1875. Kind as well as intelligent, he labored to make his students lovers of literature rather than mere repositories of information. In 1883 he introduced American literature into the curriculum and thus became a pioneer in that important field. Yet Spring's scholarly research was historical rather than literary: while at Kansas his chief work was a territorial history called *Kansas: The Prelude to the War for the Union*, published in 1885. While Spring sympathized with the Free-State faction, he tried to present an unbiased account, and the work was a step toward objectivity.[31]

Spring was followed by Arthur Richmond Marsh, who had taken his B.A. at Harvard in 1883 and had served there as lecturer on ancient art in 1884–1885. He stayed at Kansas only three years, but during that time he was one of the University's brightest ornaments. When he resigned in 1889 to return to Harvard, the regents paid tribute to his "rare genius and power." His influence in University affairs had been remarkable, the Board said, and his future in the "educational world" promised to be "most brilliant." Marsh was a powerful teacher and an equally powerful literary nationalist. In 1888 he edited a collection of student and faculty poems called *Sunflowers*. In the introduction Marsh maintained that all the signs predicted the appearance of an American literature and poetry of excellence and sensibility. Marsh likened his America to William Shakespeare's England: it had the same bold spirit, the same practicality, the same ability and desire to combine old things into new forms. The descendants of the Teutons had poetry in their blood; whether westerners or easterners the Americans were not materialists but dreamers—the "very creatures of their eager fancies." If most of their "imaginative energy" went to political and economic affairs, the time was not far distant when it would spill over into poetry. The contents of *Sunflowers*, which Marsh confessed to be a little collection of amateurish verse, might thus be a precursor of a "great age of American poetry." *Sunflowers*, alas, was no such thing. Yet much of Marsh's popularity arose from his conviction that a new and glorious cultural age was beginning in the heart of America.[32]

With scholars such as Snow and Dyche, Patrick, Bailey, Nichols, and Blake, the two Canfields, Blackmar, Carruth, Spring, and Marsh, the University could make itself something more than an undergraduate college. In 1892 the creation of the *Kansas University Quarterly*, which served as one outlet for the growing number of faculty publications, testified to the institution's scholarly maturity. When Francis H. Snow became chancellor in 1890, he suggested to the regents that the University could now sustain a series of official university research bulletins. The faculty of a "university of high rank," he said, contributed to their institution's welfare not only through undergraduate instruction but also by their reputation in "educational, literary, and scientific circles" acquired through research and publication. Kansas should have its own publications through which its faculty's discoveries might be "first made known to the world."[33]

With support from both the faculty and regents, the first issue of the *Quarterly* came out in July, 1892. Then and later the journal included all sorts of articles. The first volume, for example, contained writings as diverse as William H. Carruth's "Foreign Settlements in Kansas," Edward C. Murphy's "Maximum Bending Movements for Moving Loads in a Parabolic Arch-Rib Hinged at the Ends," Frank W. Blackmar's "Penology in Kansas," and Vernon L. Kellogg's entomological "Notes on Melitera dentata Grote." During the ten years of its existence the *Quarterly* published 240 articles by 74 different faculty members, with far more than half of the papers coming from the natural and physical scientists. Starting in January, 1897, the *Quarterly* appeared in two parts, Series A for articles in science and mathematics, Series B for those in philology and history. By itself the *Quarterly* was ample evidence of the lively research spirit present in the University. But that publication was never large enough to contain all the articles that the faculty produced, and it could not, of course, include the books.[34]

Yet the University's faculty never consciously sacrificed good teaching for scholarly research. Most of its members agreed with Francis Snow's statement of 1890 that a "fair amount of class instruction is a stimulus rather than a hindrance to original work."[35] It is clearly impossible to measure the impact of the faculty on their students, for the relation between them was always an intimate and personal one which depended as much on the proclivities of the student as the abilities of the professor. Yet many faculty members gained substantial reputations among the students for the intellectual excitement and elevation of their classes. The best and most popular of them was James H. Canfield—at least among the men, for the women did not respond as readily to his techniques. Working on the principle that no idea was indubitably correct, that every statement was open to question, and tolerant in class of everything except sloppy thought and expression, Canfield goaded his students continually and turned his classroom into a seething center of argument, discussion, and criticism. A tireless worker with unlimited affection for his students, Canfield "set us to reading books and loving him," as William Allen White wrote later.[36]

But there were others who were just as effective in their own way: Kate Stephens, who encouraged her students to think the same noble thoughts as the Greeks of old; William H. Carruth, whose personal idealism pervaded all his teaching; Lucien I. Blake, whose students thought of him as an enthusiastic equal rather than their superior. David H. Robinson, though always depressed about the de-emphasis of Latin in the changing curriculum, labored with dignity and charm to make a dead world live once more. Francis H. Snow insisted that his students get out of the classroom and into the fields around Lawrence to collect specimens for description, and he took many interested undergraduates along on his summer collecting trips. To replace Arthur Richmond Marsh in 1889, the regents elevated Charles G. Dunlap from an assistant to an associate professor. Dunlap had a B.A. from Ohio Wesleyan, was a graduate student at Johns Hopkins when he joined the University in 1887, and would take his Litt.D. at Princeton in 1892. An immensely learned man who amassed one of the finest private libraries in the state, Dunlap delighted in sharing his knowledge with students.

Inside and outside class, William Allen White remembered, Dunlap was a "flaming spirit consecrated to the love of truth and beauty."[37]

The University naturally had men who, though able, were not so popular. Edward L. Nichols in physics was a dour, stern taskmaster who threw his students on their own resources in the laboratory as soon as he decently could. "He oriented you well at the outset," William Chase Stevens said, "jotted down the necessary references and then for you it was sink or swim." Those of physical bent swam well and respected Nichols; many another student sank. Over in the Department of Mathematics, Ephraim Miller confessed in 1882 that he had a hard time making most of his students, especially the beginners, see either value or purpose in the study of his subject. "My advice to students so situated," Miller told the regents, "always is: Go on, and rest assured that the nature of the unmeaning preliminaries will ultimately be understood and appreciated." Some students, at least, later told Miller that his advice had been good.[38]

In 1890 the quality of both the teaching and the research of the faculty was recognized by the establishing of chapters of the national honor societies of Phi Beta Kappa and Sigma Xi. Each was the first chapter in any institution west of the Mississippi. In 1889 the eight faculty Phi Beta Kappans petitioned the society's National Council for a charter. They were the two Canfields, Blake, Marsh, Robinson, Snow, Alexander M. Wilcox, professor of Greek, and Max Winkler, assistant professor of German and French. After appropriate investigation the National Council approved the application, and in April, 1890, the University had the society's twenty-ninth chapter.[39]

Just a few days later the University also acquired the nation's fourth chapter of Sigma Xi; the other three were in the East, at Cornell, Rensselaer, and Union. In January, 1885, the scientists at Kansas had organized the Science Club, whose meetings combined the presentation and discussion of original research papers with a notable conviviality. After Edward L. Nichols went to Cornell in 1886, he helped found the national Sigma Xi society. Remembering the abilities of his Kansas colleagues, he suggested the formation of a chapter and then asked for one from the national organization. In December, 1889, the request was granted and the following April the University's chief scientists—Bailey, Dyche, Snow, Marvin, Miller, and Blake—formally organized the group.[40]

By 1890, then, the University was at the beginning of a new era. Many of its faculty members were now scholars as well as teachers. Its curriculum was changing to provide more freedom for the undergraduates and more specialization for the faculty, and the research seminary had appeared. It was about to drop its Preparatory Department. The legislature had made possible two new buildings and offered reasonable assurance of a guaranteed income for the next few years. In the "departments" that existed separate from the College were the progenitors of schools that were soon to follow. The University's most glaring deficiency was its discouragingly inadequate library, but at least it was growing more rapidly than before, and a large new building for it was in the offing. Francis H. Snow described the institution precisely in 1890: "It *has been* a High School, a College, and it is now in the transition stage from College to University, with some of the best points of the college, and some of the peculiar characteristics of a University."[41] It would assume more of those peculiar characteristics in the near future.

10

The University of Kansas
Becomes a University

FRANCIS H. SNOW and his successors as chancellor were always fond of surveying the University's history. In 1890 Snow looked back over the preceding quarter-century and admired the progress that he saw. But Chancellor Frank Strong, who followed Snow, saw the recent past—that is, Snow's own administration—as years of decay. Soliciting a legislator's support for the appropriation bill of 1903, Strong claimed that the institution had been sliding downhill. "The University of Kansas long ago fell from the first rank of state universities into the second," Strong said. "It has now fallen from the second rank into the third and at the present rate unless our legislature places the University decisively back in the second class, it will fall from the third to the fourth. . . . State pride leads us to say that the University of Kansas is one of the great institutions of the country, but it is not so."[1]

It behooved every chancellor, of course, to tell the legislators that the University was not what it should be, and when Strong spoke of ranks and classes, he was talking of income levels rather than intellectual quality. Yet quality depended very much on money, and during the later 1890s the University—along with the state itself—suffered disastrously from hard times, political upheaval, and the pain of having a vision of the future more glorious than most Kansans could comprehend. The suffering was especially dispiriting because the first half of the decade had glimmered with achievement. New schools had appeared; academia's highest de-

161

gree, the doctor of philosophy, had been introduced; the faculty and
regents had devised a new government for the institution. There
was also an enthusiastic new chancellor who had been with the University from the start and who had every hope of guiding it toward
greatness.

Despite Francis H. Snow's assets, however, he had not been the
regents' first choice for chancellor; in this he was in the tradition of
James Marvin and Joshua A. Lippincott. On February 28, 1889,
Lippincott told the Board of Regents that he would resign in June
to become pastor of the First Methodist Church of Topeka. The
attacks on the University in the legislature of that year, the reduced
appropriations, and the far-reaching consequences of the Moody Act
convinced him that he should accept the church's invitation ("It
is," he wrote a friend, "a case of superior attraction").[2] It took the
Board over a year to find a replacement, and during that time the
regents argued among themselves while the newspapers and citizens
chose sides. Originally the Board hoped to lure to Kansas a leading
educator from outside the state. At the Board's behest Regents William C. Spangler and J. F. Billings canvassed the presidents of leading eastern universities and came back with a goodly list of recommendations. The two most prominent were Professor Herbert
Baxter Adams of Johns Hopkins and the Reverend Charles F.
Thwing, pastor of the Plymouth Congregational Church in Minneapolis, Minnesota. Thwing was a Harvard B.A. of 1876 whose
reputation resulted mainly from his book *American Colleges:
Their Students and Work*, published in 1878. Harvard's President
Charles W. Eliot and Professor George Herbert Palmer and Cornell's President Charles Kendall Adams gave him very strong support for the chancellorship.[3]

At the same time that the regents looked outside the state, they
also had to look to Mount Oread because of the growing support for
James H. Canfield. Anathema though he was to many protectionist
Republicans, his integrity, ability, and reputation among educators
made him a candidate from the start. The Newton *Republican* was
behind him by early May, and in the next few months he picked up
support from several dozen other journals, the most important of
them being the Topeka *Capital*. Although its editors favored a
protective tariff, they argued that Canfield's educational and administrative abilities outweighed his mistaken economic views. "An

enthusiastic Kansan, broad, cultured, and experienced as an educator, in love with his adopted state and his profession," the *Capital*'s encomium ran, "he is the best man east or west, north or south, to place the . . . University at the very head of western institutions." In August, John MacDonald, editor of the *Western School Journal*, organ of the State Teachers Association, announced his support for Canfield, claimed that 99 percent of Kansas teachers and many superintendents favored him, and praised him for his scholarship and executive abilities and his "manhood, robustness, ruggedness and strength."[4]

Less frequently other men, including Canfield himself, backed Francis H. Snow, and a few were for Lucien I. Blake. Meanwhile the regents found it impossible to reach agreement with reasonable speed. Fearful of a political reaction against the choice of Canfield and at the same time naturally differing among themselves, they became supercautious, minutely considering "every possible objection to every possible man," as Regent Charles S. Gleed said later. To their credit the regents were determined to achieve unanimity— but this guaranteed delay. Also holding things up was the fact that a chancellor hired in 1889 could receive only $3,000 a year, the amount authorized by the last legislature; one hired to start in 1890 could be paid as much as the regents wished from the Moody Act appropriation. Thus the Board hemmed and hawed, keeping the candidates on tenterhooks and exasperating many Kansans. "Does the state university have a chaplain?" asked the Abilene *Reflector* early in 1890. "If it does, why does he not pray the Lord to give the Board of Regents backbone enough to select a chancellor? The present slipshod method of running our leading institution of learning is a disgrace."[5]

On March 12, 1890, the regents at last elected Thwing over Canfield at a salary of $5,000. Predictably, Canfield supporters were angry. The University needed a "live, progressive educator," said the Topeka *Capital*; instead the regents had bowed before the will of a "handful of huckstering politicians" to choose "a minister, who, as we understand, has never had any experience whatever as an educator." Thwing thought over the offer for a few days and then declined it. Rumor had it that he had learned of the unfavorable reaction of the Canfield press and wished to save himself embarrassment; but he was also interested in the presidency of Western Reserve University in Cleveland, Ohio, which he would accept in November. The regents now extricated themselves from their awkward position with magnificent speed. Refusing to reconsider Canfield, they turned to Snow, who had been serving during the year as acting president and dean of the faculty. More than a week before his formal election on April 11 many newspaper editors knew that the choice was all but certain. When the offer came, Snow accepted it at once.[6] Letters of congratulation by the dozen showered down upon him, and the tone of many was as much one of relief that the regents had settled the matter as happiness that Snow would become chancellor. F. H. Clark, superintendent of schools in Minneapolis, Kansas, and a Canfield supporter, spoke for many other Kansans when he told Snow that his election was probably for the best. No one, he said, "can do so much to quiet all factional spirit as *you can simply in accepting* the position as well as by your liberally conservative policy." From Minnesota, Charles F. Thwing opined jocularly that the "State of Kansas owes me a debt of gratitude for declining, that it might be privileged with your services."[7] There was more truth in the remark than he probably intended, for Snow had far more popularity and support in the state than Thwing, he knew the University much better, and he was an able and vigorous administrator as well.

In his inaugural address Snow explained generally his theories of what a university was and what a university in Kansas ought to be, and then said that all that was now needed to make the University great was money. Since the institution's strength depended on the strength of its faculty, Snow intended to ask the legislature for funds sufficient to keep the present faculty and even to attract equally able men away from eastern institutions. "It may be a matter of pride to us," he said, "that our University should have furnished professors to Cornell, to Williams, and to Harvard, but such pride can be indulged in only at the expense of the mental development of our own sons and daughters. . . . The self-respect of a professor should not be too heavily sacrificed to his patriotic desire to serve the state of Kansas." Even more important than salaries were research facilities—and free time to use them. "No man with the right sort of ambition will be satisfied to remain in a college whose managers decline to furnish a generous provision in the line of apparatus, books, and properly constructed lecture-rooms and laboratories," Snow asserted. He added that the "professor whose mental energy is exhausted by from three to six hours per day in the classroom or students' laboratory, will be unable in his own laboratory and library to produce results which will make his University famous for the discovery of new truths in any branch of learning." More money would buy reduced teaching loads by buying more faculty members.[8]

Although Snow had a vision of greatness, there was no new idea in his address. "Liberally conservative" described his announced ideas and policies, for he seemed to desire that the University continue to travel along existing routes, that it do more of what it was doing and get more of the things it had already obtained. "Liberally conservative" also described his theories of the general nature and purpose of education. Rejecting the idea of higher education for an elite alone, he said in 1891 that the University's watchword was "Education for the people, of the people, and by the people," the outgrowth and counterpart of American democracy itself. He advocated a liberal education for most people and favored such training before professional education began; the ideal education broadened men "on all sides," gave them a "broad foundation and an insight into various subjects" both scientific and humanistic. Yet since man was a triune being, the good education trained the body and the spirit as well as the mind—the first through curricular physical education, the second partly through the atmosphere of the University itself. Snow knew that the school could not require courses to foster spiritual development. But he believed that students could quicken it by attending daily chapel services, by constant contact with faculty members and fellow students whose "spiritual natures are in an active condition," and by membership in churches and allied organizations such as the YMCA, the YWCA, and the Methodist Epworth League.[9]

If Snow had no new theories to offer in 1890, however, he and his faculty were even then devising a new structure for the University. The process involved the conversion of the large departments—Science, Literature, and the Arts; Law; Pharmacy; and Music—into schools, the similar elevation of the special courses in civil and electrical engineering into a school, and the writing of new rules to govern the whole institution. Complex enough in their own right, the problems were the more difficult because the legislature of 1889 had interfered with the University's internal organization in a particularly confusing way. It was by the Moody Act, which was so full of contradictions that when the University's leaders reorganized their school, they wisely disobeyed the law and followed their own, more sensible, inclinations.

In 1888 Chancellor Lippincott and the faculty had concluded that the University, now considerably larger, more complex, and more sophisticated than five years before, needed a new internal organization. Lippincott thereupon wrote letters to a number of college and university presidents to discover how their institutions were structured. When the regents met in November and the Chancellor told them of the faculty's desires for a more precise and formal organization, the Board appointed a committee of Regent Charles S. Gleed and Professors Snow, Green, MacDonald, and Sayre to investigate the subject and make a report. At the same time the Board designated another committee—Lippincott and Regents Gleed and Charles W. Smith—to draw up a proposed code of statutes for the University's government.[10] But while both groups were at work, Senator Moody brought into the legislature a reorganization scheme of his own, which made the committees' considerations superfluous. Late in 1888 Moody had conferred with several faculty members, suggested plans to them, and apparently found substantial support.[11] As his reorganization bill moved through the legislature, his bills for a guaranteed income and the abolition of the Preparatory Department were attached to it; thus the Moody Act became an omnibus University measure.[12]

Most of the law was so thoroughly confusing that it is all but certain that the faculty had never fully approved it before he submitted it. Abolishing all previous legislation dealing with the University's organization, including the original charter of 1864, the act effectively provided for a new state university. Its purposes were two: to provide the "means of acquiring a general and thorough knowledge in literature, the sciences, and the arts" and to provide students wishing to pursue "special studies" with the "most approved appliances, authorities and instruction to insure the greatest knowledge and research in any special branch of learning connected with university education." What the law meant by "special studies" was obscure, but Moody seemed more concerned with special students than with regular ones. University authorities, the act

Senator Joel Moody of Mound City. According to the Moody
Act of 1889, which remains in force, the University is still (1973)
organized in an illegal fashion. (Courtesy Kansas State Historical
Society.)

went on, were to give "due regard" to students who desired to select a course of studies outside the ordinary curricula, and were to furnish "every advantage and assistance" to those wishing "special branches of learning" which led to no regular degree, as long as there was no conflict with the University's ordinary work. For high attainments in special studies the University might award special degrees.

Henceforth the institution was to consist of three departments—one each of the literatures, the sciences, and the arts. Within each the regents, "in connection with the faculty," could establish whatever schools they desired. Atop that organization, which had no similarity whatever to that of the existing University, were to be at least four "courses," although the act did not define them, each leading to a corresponding degree. Postgraduate courses could be created in any of the departments.

The University's government, as before, was under seven regents, six appointed by the governor and confirmed by the Senate, the other to be a chancellor chosen by them. Terms of the appointees were to be four years instead of the present three, with half the Board chosen every two years on February 1. Some vague fear made Moody bar any University employee except the chancellor from being a regent. The Board had power to prescribe the faculty's bylaws, regulate the courses of instruction, and with the advice of the chancellor and faculty decide the books, authorities, and apparatus to be used. With the power to hire all faculty members the regents could increase or decrease their number "as the interests of the University may require"; all University employees held their positions at the Board's pleasure. The chancellor's own powers were largely undefined. He was to be president of the Board with the full powers of a regent, the University's "chief officer," and "head" of each of the three departments, but otherwise the regents were to determine his duties and powers. Together the chancellor and the respective faculties were to govern the departments.[13]

Only perplexity could come from the act's requirements for three wholly new departments with schools in each and four courses overlaying all. In March, 1889, Chancellor Lippincott told the Board of Regents that he did not know how to define the words "department" and "school," and that he thought he saw in the act a most confusing division of the present undergraduate college—the

Department of Science, Literature, and the Arts under the charter of 1864.[14] The regents themselves were no more knowledgeable, even though they included Joel Moody himself. Appointed by Governor Lyman U. Humphrey, four of Moody's colleagues on the new Board were holdovers: J. F. Billings, C. R. Mitchell, Charles S. Gleed, and Matthew P. Simpson. Joining Moody as a new member was William C. Spangler of Lawrence. A University graduate of 1883, Spangler had gone on to complete the law course, and in 1887 had become the Lawrence city attorney; his force, energy, and ability already were making him a prominent citizen. Billings, Mitchell, and Simpson received two-year appointments; the others were to serve full terms to 1893. In 1891 Governor Humphrey reappointed Mitchell, and in place of Billings and Simpson chose Charles F. Scott and Delbert A. Valentine. Scott was an active alumnus in the University's class of 1881, the editor of the Iola *Register*, and a young Republican politician on his way to statewide respect. Valentine had no college education, but his rise to fame and fortune had been nonetheless rapid. Thirty-four years old, he was junior member of the law firm of Campbell and Valentine in Clay Center, joint proprietor of the Clay Center *Times*, and a hotel owner and local railroad entrepreneur.[15]

To clarify the new law, the other regents asked Moody to speak at the opening convocation in September, 1889. He proceeded to muddy the waters even more. Following Aristotle, Moody said, every branch of learning needed classification. Moody's classification, adapting Aristotelianism to nineteenth-century Kansas, was that within the Department of the Literatures there should be at least three schools—of philology, history, and rhetoric. The Department of the Sciences should contain at least eight schools. Four of them—mathematics, physics, chemistry, and astronomy—pertained to what Moody called "inanimate nature"; the other four—biology, medicine, law, and psychology—had to do with "animate nature." The school of psychology would deal with metaphysics, mental and moral philosophy, and logic, "in short," Moody said, "all laws and sciences pertaining to the mind." In the Department of the Arts "we would naturally have four schools, which have been determined from time immemorial": of music, painting, sculpture, and architecture. Then he explained that those departments and schools did not yet exist because the University was still young and the state too poor to supply the "camp and garrison equipage." But there they were, as a plan for the future.[16]

Unfortunately Moody said nothing about the relations of the four courses to those three departments and fifteen schools, or about such relevant matters as the existing engineering and pharmacy courses, or those University divisions that the regents and faculty had long since named "departments." Was a student working toward a specific degree like the B.A., for example, to confine himself to one of Moody's departments, or even one of his schools, or was he to spread himself around? What was going to happen to the existing undergraduate college? Even more important, how was the University to shape itself into a form that had no precedents whatever in its previous development?

Because both the faculty and the regents thought the Moody Act a royal road to chaos, they simply ignored it, and Joel Moody acquiesced, for he remained a regent until February 1, 1893, when the reorganization was almost completed. In 1890 the Departments of Pharmacy and Law had their designations changed to schools, although the former in no way fit the Moody Act's specifications and there was no overarching "department" in which to put the lawyers. By the spring of 1890, moreover, though without a formal decision, the regents were calling both the Department of Music and the Department of Art "schools"; a year later, with George B. Penny having replaced William MacDonald as dean, they consolidated the two into a School of Music and Fine Arts. While this was about the same as Moody's Department of the Arts, the school's name confused the matter. Things became more confounded when the Board approved a faculty request to create a School of Engineering offering its own degree. Since in the Moody Act only courses led to degrees, the new school was both a school and a course in a Department of the Sciences that did not yet exist. And when the regents in 1892 approved Dean Penny's request to replace the old degree of Graduate in Music with that of Bachelor of Music, in the light of the Moody Act it meant that a mere school, with its own degree, in the Department of the Sciences was the full equivalent of one of the three departments.[17]

Most significant of all was the refusal of the regents and faculty to cleave the College. On January 6, 1893, the regents voted that the "part of the University which under the present rules of the

Board is connected with the work leading to the degree of Bachelor of Arts be organized and established as the School of Arts." The Moody Act had ordered the division of the work of the former Department among two new departments, with their various schools, but it was not to be.[18]

With the creation of new schools their faculties and the regents had to determine the relations among them and the University's government in general. In February, 1892, Chancellor Snow inquired into the organization of ten outstanding colleges and universities.[19] After an extended consideration of the replies, in January, 1893, the Board approved a new plan. It was an essentially hierarchical structure, the main elements being the faculties and deans of the schools, the chancellor, and a new University Council. Each faculty —which included all full, associate, and assistant professors, and instructors—had considerable power: it determined admission requirements, prescribed the courses of study and the rules for graduation, established its own examinations, and regulated its own government and proceedings as long as they did not contravene the "act governing the University, the Statutes, or any regulation of the Board of Regents."

The immediate chief executive and administrator of each school was to be the dean, chosen annually by the regents from among the University's full professors. His powers and duties were but generally set forth. Each dean, the regents said, "shall in a special manner undertake to advance the interests of his school." In addition to executing the faculty's will, the dean was to report to the chancellor, both annually and as occasion should require, on the conditions and needs of the departments in his unit. This was a notable innovation. In the past the professors had themselves conferred with the chancellor about departmental needs and often had gone directly to the Board of Regents. Although there was nothing in the new rules prohibiting such activities, the influence of the intermediary deans was certain to be large. The regents made logical choices to fill the deanships. James W. Green, Lucius E. Sayre, and George B. Penny continued over the Schools of Law, Pharmacy, and Music and Fine Arts; Frank O. Marvin became dean of the School of Engineering; and David H. Robinson, who with Snow had been a faculty member since 1866, dean of the College. On

Some members of the University community in 1892. From the left: Top row: Elmer F. Engel, Charles G. Dunlap, Erasmus Haworth, Lucius E. Sayre, Arthur H. Wilcox, David H. Robinson, Arthur G. Canfield, Edwin M. Hopkins. Middle row: Lucien I. Blake, A. W. Shepherd, Ephraim D. Adams, Samuel R. Boyce, William H. Carruth, Olin Templin, Edward C. Murphy, Frank O. Marvin. Front row: Samuel W. Williston, Henry B. Newson, Edgar H. S. Bailey, Hannah Oliver, Francis H. Snow, Carrie Watson, Ephraim Miller, Eugenie Galloo, Miles W. Sterling.

172

Robinson's death in 1895 the regents chose Ephraim Miller to succeed him.[20]

Above the faculties and deans was a University Council. Its members were the chancellor and deans, ex-officio, and one elected representative—only full and associate professors were eligible—from each school except the College which, by virtue of its greater size, sent five. The Council's main powers were vague: it administered student discipline, constituted an "advisory body" to the chancellor, and exercised "control in all University matters not referred by statute or delegated herein to the Chancellor or the several Faculties."

Except to make the chancellor president of both the University Council and all the faculties, the regents did not change his position. Restating the Moody Act's directive that he was to be the University's "chief officer," the Board charged him with making sure that its regulations and orders were obeyed, and exercising "such general executive powers as are necessary to the good government of the University and the protection of its interests which are not otherwise provided for."

The last of the new rules provided for a registrar to relieve the chancellor and faculty of such routine matters as making sure that entering students were duly qualified, keeping student records, and issuing catalogues.[21]

Creating the schools and dividing the faculty would bring momentous changes to the University. The most important was the growth in the chancellor's power and influence. Although he had always been more than first among equals when the entire faculty met together, the faculty itself could lay a claim to as great an understanding of University affairs as he. Now only the members of the University Council could make that claim—but since the deans reported to the chancellor rather than to the Council, he was to be the only man who could claim to understand the institution in all its parts. At the same time, although the faculty members would certainly benefit from the work of the deans and the Council, as a group they now lacked the power to vote on all-University matters. Their status was further altered by the fact that the information about them and their schools available to the chancellor and the regents would be in part refined and interpreted by men whom the school faculties had no power to select.

As significant as all these structural changes were, an even more important one came later in the decade with the start of the Graduate School. Graduate work itself was not new to the University. Since 1875 there had been programs leading to the Master of Arts and Master of Science degrees. The original rules required three years' work beyond the bachelor's degree and a thesis, but over the years the time period had been shortened; starting in the fall of 1887 it took only one year and a thesis. After granting the first two M.A.'s in 1876, during the next fifteen years the faculty awarded thirty-seven more.[22]

But the University's greatest glory would be to offer the Ph.D., for it was the highest degree known and was given both by the great German institutions and a growing number of prestigious American schools. In 1861 Yale had awarded the first earned Ph.D.'s in America, and by 1876, the year in which Johns Hopkins was organized primarily as a graduate university, twenty-five institutions offered doctoral studies. During the 1880s Columbia, Michigan, and Yale systematized their graduate work, and in 1890 both Harvard and the new University of Chicago began graduate schools. All the best institutions were offering doctoral studies, and so in June, 1893, the faculty of the College, determined to make their institution one of the best, approved a motion by Samuel W. Williston to inquire into the requirements of other universities for the Ph.D. Since the question concerned the University as a whole, however, early in 1894 the University Council appointed Williston, Frank O. Marvin, Erasmus Haworth of Geology, and William H. Carruth to investigate the feasibility of starting courses leading to the doctorate and to formulate such courses if the committee thought it wise.[23]

The committee concluded that the time for the Ph.D. had come, the Council agreed, and in April, 1894, the regents added their blessing. On the "ground of advanced scholarship and the performance of independent work in some special line" the University would henceforth grant the doctorate. A candidate had to have a baccalaureate degree either from Kansas or from an equivalent institution, or "equivalent preparation for graduate studies." He had to spend at least three academic years in graduate work, the first two of which might be at another university. Before October of the year in which he expected to take his degree, he had to demonstrate an ability to read fluently such German and French as were necessary for the "proper prosecution of his studies," and to pass both written and oral examinations in one "chief or major" study and two "allied, subsidiary or minor" studies; the oral examination was to be taken before the entire University Council. Last, the candidate had to present the results of his research in a doctoral thesis, which had to be published, with 150 copies deposited in the University library. The Council then decided that the University could offer the doctorate in Greek; Latin; French; German; English; political economy, sociology, and American and European history; entomology; paleontology; mineralogy, and stratigraphical and physical geology; and mathematics.[24]

A year later the University awarded its first Ph.D. It went to Arnold Emch, a brilliant young Swiss mathematician educated in the Solothurn gymnasium, the Zurich Polytechnicum, and the Kansas State Agricultural College, where he spent the 1893–1894 academic year. The Department of Mathematics pronounced Emch's thesis on "Continuous Groups of Collineation in the Plane" highly creditable, and mathematics professor Henry B. Newson pronounced Emch a genius. Even as a doctoral candidate he was competent to teach any course the Department offered; after receiving his degree he taught at Kansas, but left in January, 1897, for Switzerland, partly because there were so few students on Mount Oread prepared for the courses he wished to offer. There were, Newson thought, less than half a dozen men in the United States superior to Emch in his field, and no one of equal combination of ability and potential. "Barring accidents to his career," Newson said, "it is safe to venture the prediction that our University's first Ph.D. will do honor to the learned circles of Europe." Actually, he did more honor to the learned circles of the United States. Between teaching stints in Switzerland (1897–1899 and 1903–1911) he taught at the Agricultural College once again and at the University of Colorado; in 1911 he entered upon a long and distinguished career at the University of Illinois.[25]

Having awarded its first doctorate, the University Council naturally turned to creating a graduate school, both to relieve the Council of its supervisory duties and to match other institutions. On January 2, 1897, Samuel W. Williston moved and the Council passed a request that the Board of Regents establish the school with its own dean and faculty—the latter consisting of all full and associate professors offering courses "distinctively adapted for the graduates of this and other institutions of like rank." The school would set admission requirements, formulate and arrange all graduate courses, and determine the fitness of the candidates. In April the Board approved the request, and, after canvassing the faculty, elected Frank W. Blackmar dean.[26]

The requirements for the Ph.D. in the Graduate School were essentially those of 1894, except that candidates now faced an oral examination before the graduate faculty rather than the Council; at that examination they might be required to defend their theses. Originally only five departments actually offered major courses for the doctorate, but by 1900 twenty-two—including the Schools of Engineering, Pharmacy, and Music and Fine Arts—had them.[27]

Of the University's schools the Graduate School was at once the most significant and the most peculiar. It was the most important because it controlled the University's highest degree and because its standards were superior to those of the other schools, none of which asked a baccalaureate degree for admission. Its existence raised the University from a merely undergraduate school to one of the very highest learning. In structure, moreover, it could potentially give some coherence to an increasingly fragmented faculty. Yet the Graduate School was peculiar in that it did not have a faculty uniquely its own. The graduate faculty was simply the undergraduate faculty in a different guise, both because it was the only faculty available and because there were not enough graduate students to support a full-time graduate staff. In the 1899–1900 academic year, for example, there were only 57 graduate students as against almost 1,100 in the other schools; the faculty owed most of its allegiance and time to the undergraduate divisions.[28] It would be thus for the rest of the University's first century. While the ratio of graduate students to undergraduates would increase, the Graduate School, whatever its theoretical distinction and importance, would play only a secondary role in shaping the institution.

Had Chancellor Snow and the Board of Regents had their way, the University might have achieved another triumph almost as great as the introduction of the Ph.D. and the Graduate School: the creation of a school of medicine. But they lost a battle to start it, and the medical school would have to wait another decade.

Not six months after his inauguration Snow was urging a four-year medical course on his fellow regents. Here he differed sharply from Chancellor Lippincott, who believed that it would be impossible for either the University or the city of Lawrence to provide adequate hospital or clinical facilities for medical training, and that it would weaken the course and increase its cost "enormously" to divide it between Lawrence and some larger city, like Topeka or Kansas City, Kansas. In 1888 Lippincott suggested that the University should content itself with adding a second year to the medical curriculum and should raise the standards of both years by demanding two years of undergraduate work for admission. "The demand is not for more physicians," he said, "but for a more thorough preparation of those who seek to enter the profession."[29]

Snow agreed that the University should not be dismembered, for separating the medical school would deprive its students of the benefits of "participation in the scientific and literary advantages connected with the University as a whole," and increase its costs by duplicating instruction and equipment. But between his inauguration and the fall of 1890 Snow visited the University of Michigan, whose excellent medical school was attached to the rest of the institution in Ann Arbor, and returned convinced that his school could do as well. Ann Arbor was no larger than Lawrence; it was almost as far from Detroit as Lawrence was from Kansas City; yet it attracted from one thousand to fifteen hundred patients a year from all over the state, which was more than ample. All that an equivalent school at Kansas needed was money. Ignoring the Moody Act, Snow pointed out that the charter of 1864 had provided for a medical school and claimed that the time for its creation had come.[30]

But while Snow thought large, his fellow regents thought small. Believing that a school of medicine should exist "before long," they still refused to ask the legislatures of 1891 and 1893 for funds. Their coolness chilled Snow's ardor. By July, 1894, he was willing to settle for a three-year course and even to see the third—a clinical—year in Topeka or Kansas City; he had concluded that Lawrence would never draw enough patients.[31] His change of mind came in the nick of time. In August he learned of a stupendous windfall in the form of a gift of land which might support a medical school from Dr. Simeon B. Bell of Kansas City, Missouri. A native of New Jersey, Bell had practiced in Ohio, then moved to Johnson County, Kansas, just over the state line from Missouri, in 1857. There he profited, and bought land as he was able. He now proposed to give the University 108 lots of platted land in what was known as the Rosedale area of Wyandotte County, just outside Kansas City, Kansas, which could be sold for profit. With the gift, however, went a provision that within ten years the University build a hospital on a designated bloc of land in that area that Bell would also contribute. Bell's gift had come at the solicitation of Dean Sayre of the School of Pharmacy and Dr. Flavel B. Tiffany of Kansas City, a friend of both Bell and Chancellor Snow.[32] Snow was overjoyed, and he and the other regents went ahead to accept the gift and its conditions. Anticipating the regents' favorable action, the Chancellor, Sayre, and Samuel W. Williston concluded that they should locate the first two years of the medical school in Lawrence and the last two in Rosedale. Snow thought that with Bell's gift only about $10,000 a year would be necessary to maintain the school on a "creditable basis."[33]

The House of Representatives of 1895, however, failed Snow miserably. In routine fashion the Senate passed a bill authorizing the University to build a hospital and provide for its current expenses, but the House Committee on Ways and Means refused to report it out. A varied protest movement by Kansas physicians was too strong for the Committee to resist. Some Topeka doctors desired the school for their own town. Other physicians thought that a medical school so close to the Missouri line would be of more benefit to sick Missourians than ailing Kansans and under the real control of Missouri medical men. The "sooner some sound business sense is pounded into the gentlemen who are trying to force this medical department of the university on the Missouri line," said one irate doctor, "the better for our great institution at Lawrence." Filled with supporters of the recently organized Kansas City, Kansas, College of Physicians and Surgeons, the Wyandotte County Medical Society charged Simeon B. Bell with a land speculation scheme of trying to increase the value of some of his near-worthless Rosedale land by getting a hospital for the area. According to the Society, Bell's site was "isolated, inaccessible, and entirely unsuited for an institution of this kind." It lacked drainage and sewage facilities and other municipal improvements. To get to it from Kansas City, Kansas, required a roundabout journey through Kansas City, Missouri, which meant that the hospital would become only an "asylum for harboring the paupers of Missouri and treating their ailments at the expense of the whole people of Kansas." The Society sent a resolution to the legislature and appointed a correspondence committee to alert Kansas physicians, and their efforts paid off.[34]

Frustrated and disappointed, the faculty and regents did not try again to get authorization for the hospital. They contented themselves instead with adding a second year to the medical course in 1899, calling it the School of Medicine, and appointing Samuel W. Williston dean. While students with a high-school education were still eligible for admission, in 1900 the School tried to encourage would-be physicians to get more prior training by allowing seniors in the College to choose the first year of the medical course as their last undergraduate year of college. At graduation they received a Bachelor of Science in Medicine. The same year the School of Medicine got the old Chemistry Building for its own when the Department of Chemistry and the School of Pharmacy moved into a new structure provided by the legislature of 1899. That progress encouraged Snow to reopen the question of the four-year medical course in his report for 1900, but the idea was wasted on the legislature, and the regents were not willing to brave the wrath of the state's physicians.[35]

With its schools old and new, its Ph.D., and its University Council, the University of Kansas was at last living up to its name. But while the University's leaders indulged themselves in optimistic thoughts about the future, there were portents of storm and stress abroad. The last half of the Snow administration was not a happy time.

11

Thorns Along the Way

"VERILY the way of the college builder is thorny," Francis H. Snow said in 1897 after the legislature had slashed the University's appropriation requests and reduced the salaries of all its employees. The way of the University builders paralleled the path of the state itself. In the early 1880s Kansas had left behind the hard times of the 1870s and reached new plateaus of prosperity, but toward the decade's end fickle nature sent a succession of droughts, severe winters, and floods to beset the farmers. Along with the rest of the nation Kansans also suffered from the financial panic of 1893 and a drawn-out recession. Economic losses brought the usual demands for retrenchment in public expenditures and taxation and helped to create a state Populist or People's party. Tied to that society, fastened to forces beyond its control, the University was bound to suffer, too.[1]

From 1891 to 1895 the institution enjoyed relative prosperity. Snow's first campaign against the legislature was a success—though mainly because he and the Board of Regents sought no real increase in the standard appropriation of $75,000 authorized by the Moody Act of 1889. They and the faculty badly wanted more money for general expenses and buildings, but with the state financially pinched they dared not ask for it. Senator—and Regent—Joel Moody's bill called simply for $75,000 for each of the next two fiscal years, and it had no trouble passing. Snow crowed that despite an economizing spirit prevalent in the legislature, "we have succeeded in obtaining our $75,000 without a breath of opposition in either house. This is remarkable as every other state institution was seriously crippled by the false economy of the Populist Party."[2]

Materially, then, the University could not change much during the next two years. But having decently held the line in 1891, the University's leaders expected the legislature of 1893 to be more generous. This time they asked for an increase in the regular appropriation from $75,000 to $100,000 a year and for two new buildings. Actually, Snow and the Board asserted, the University needed seven new structures "at the earliest possible date": a library, a physics and electrical engineering building, a new chemistry building, a gymnasium, an astronomical observatory, an addition to Snow Hall, and a women's dormitory. But the authorization for the library from the William B. Spooner bequest and the physics building were most pressing.[3]

The legislature of 1893 showed the University's leaders that they had little to fear at the time from the Populist party as such. In the elections of 1892 the Populists had won the Senate; the House was about equally balanced between Populists and Republicans. Between January 20 and February 23 the two factions wrangled bitterly over House organization, with the Populists assembling each day after the battle in the so-called Dunsmore House to pass legislation as if they were actually the lower branch. Finally, the State Supreme Court decided that the Republicans should have control. Although the delay made University officials nervous, after peace descended, their bills moved rapidly through the House. The total appropriation for all purposes was the greatest to that time. While the House Ways and Means Committee blocked the $25,000 increase in the general appropriation, the legislature approved $21,500 for the 1893–1895 biennium as a special appropriation for library books and other equipment. More heartening still, the legislators authorized use of the Spooner money for a library building and a chancellor's residence—in recognition of the "valuable services of Chancellor F. H. Snow to the state," he was allowed to occupy it for the rest of his natural life, free of charge—and granted $50,000 for a new physics and electrical engineering building for Lucien I. Blake and his students.[4]

All the measures had notable support from Populists and Republicans alike, and Chancellor Snow rejoiced that the legislature had treated the school better than had any previous legislature. "The populist movement," he told President Benjamin I. Wheeler of Cornell, "has not affected us unfavorably. . . . This result however I do not attribute so much to the greater estimation of higher education on the part of the populist party as compared with the republican party, but to the fact that the University has become so strongly entrenched in the good opinion of men of all parties that its support has ceased to be a party question." At the time Snow's analysis seemed valid.[5]

When the three new buildings appeared in the next two years, they made the school seem far more like a true university. The Spooner Library and the chancellor's house were completed in 1894. Standing northeast of the University Building, the library was built so that its façade, which faced west, exposed fewer stories than its rear, whose foundations were lower down the steep hill. It was the first of the University's buildings to have some architectural significance, to escape from the triteness, homeliness, and merely derivative nature of the other structures. Its architect was the nationally famous Henry Van Brunt of Kansas City, Missouri, who explained at the dedication that Spooner Library was an effort to continue the process of adapting the more attractive European architectural styles to American needs, moods, and ideas. Since the United States had not yet developed its own style, Van Brunt said, American architects had to take and modify the best of the European models. Following Henry Hobson Richardson, Van Brunt had chosen Southern Romanesque, characteristic of tenth-century Auvergne, which he thought honest, unaffected, and capable of keeping its beauty through the ages. As part of the process of domesticating foreign models, Van Brunt thought, Spooner Library was part of a "patriotic experiment" which included at least a "dim prophecy of the new civilization" rising in America. But whatever the future might bring, the building would remain as an example of the efforts of American architects to give their country a "genuine style of architecture belonging to modern life and to a certain extent capable of expressing its aspirations."

Van Brunt also said that he had generally tried to let the interior divisions determine the exterior appearance without imposing either unnatural architectural effects or a "fictitious aspect of academical symmetry." On the main floor was the general reading room, with the delivery desk and the main stacks opposite the entrance. Shelves around the reading room held the library's reference works and encyclopedias. In the northeast corner was a room for the history and sociology seminary, and in the southeast corner was the newspaper and periodical room. Downstairs were two rooms for other seminaries. Large and pleasant, well lighted and well appointed, the library had a capacity of about one hundred thousand volumes, or almost five times as many as the University then had.[6]

Within the limits that Van Brunt had set, Spooner Library was honest and beautiful. The new physics building, by contrast, was meretricious in its exterior. It stood just southeast of the University Building. Designed by State Architect Seymour Davis, it was an imitation of a French chateau that Lucien I. Blake admired, a picture of which he had given Davis. Its façade of stone was a combination of Gothic and Renaissance styles that esthetically left everything to be desired; its rear, because of a shortage of money and the fact that there was no approach from the south and so no need to carry the chateau-theme around back, was merely plastered and marked off with imitation stone joints. None of the University's buildings harmonized architecturally, but Blake Hall, as it was named, was by far the most dissonant. Inside, however, Blake and his student physicists and electricians had most of their needs satisfied. In three stories and a basement Blake Hall had several lecture rooms—one holding a hundred students—a library and reading room, and many laboratories for physical and electrical research. The basement laboratories had piers going down to bedrock to free them from vibration. Heavy-duty electrical circuits ran throughout the structure. In order to prevent unwelcome magnetic fields, no iron was used below the third story except, probably by accident, in the nails and window sash weights. To pay for the extra cost of plumbing and fittings made of brass, copper, and lead, the University had to beg an additional $8,000 from the legislature of 1895, which the solons granted.[7]

Enormously encouraged by the legislature's response of 1893 and by the building boomlet, the Board of Regents urged even greater generosity on the legislators of 1895. They wanted some of the things denied them earlier: an increase in the regular appropriation to $100,000 and several buildings, the more important of

The University in 1896. From the left: the chancellor's residence, Spooner Library, Blake Hall, the University Building (with an end of the Chemistry Building appearing behind), and Snow Hall.

Architect M. P. McArdle's model of his proposed administration building (Strong Hall).

which were a chemistry and pharmacy building, engineering shops, a museum for the expanding collections of the indefatigable Lewis L. Dyche, and a gymnasium. Chancellor Snow, pointing out that in the past eight years Minnesota had paid for seventeen new buildings at its university while Kansas had paid for only one, pleaded with the legislature to make "approximately equal provision" for the state's "highest educational institution." But because economic conditions had worsened in the last two years, everyone expected a hard fight. The *Students Journal* implored undergraduates to write legislators from their home districts, and late in January, Edgar H. S. Bailey, Lucius E. Sayre, and Dyche went to Topeka to lobby for their buildings. The Joint Ways and Means Committee heard them politely enough, but with the financial outlook gloomy no one was making promises.[8]

The legislature proved willing to amend the Moody Act to increase the regular maintenance to $100,000 a year and to outfit Blake Hall, but at that point its largesse ended. Senator Solon O. Thacher and Representative Charles H. Tucker of Lawrence had introduced identical bills for a chemistry building, a museum, and engineering shops, but the respective ways and means committees kept them from the floor. As a forecast of things to come, moreover, there were attacks on the allegedly high salaries of the faculty. In January Senator Wesley B. Helm of Ellsworth brought in a bill that would have fixed the salaries of all the officers and faculty of the University, the Agricultural College, and the Emporia Normal School. Although the measure never reached a vote, it was clear that unless the economy took a turn for the better there was trouble ahead.[9]

Political difficulties complicated the economic. In 1893 Populists began to contest with Republicans for control of the Board of Regents. In 1892 Kansas elected not only a legislature full of Populists, but a Populist governor as well, in Lorenzo D. Lewelling of Wichita. He would have three regents to appoint, for the terms of Joel Moody, Charles S. Gleed, and William C. Spangler were ending. Chancellor Snow hoped to influence Lewelling on all three appointments, and asked some of his friends to persuade him to appoint ex-Governor Charles Robinson to replace Spangler, who declined reappointment, and to reappoint Charles S. Gleed. Snow was not certain whom he wanted as the third man, although he definitely did not want Joel Moody. Ultimately the Chancellor decided to support Senator William Rogers of Washington County, a Populist who had been active in state politics for years and had been chairman of the Senate Ways and Means Committee in the legislature of 1893, where he had worked hard for the University bills.[10] Lewelling was willing to appoint Rogers and Robinson, but balked at Charles S. Gleed as too much the orthodox Republican. Instead he sent to the Senate the name of James P. Sams, a Populist farmer from Centralia, and the Senate routinely approved all three.[11]

Rogers and Sams fit in well with the four Republican regents, but by the spring of 1894 Charles Robinson concluded that he could do more for the University as a private citizen than as a regent, and resigned. His decision was prompted by a fearsome attack on the University by the Lawrence *Jeffersonian*, the local Populist newspaper. The editors charged that Chancellor Snow was an incompetent administrator, that he spent too much time delivering his "fish lectures"—those on evolution—around the state, that student rowdyism was rampant on Mount Oread, and that faculty salaries were too high. In general, the *Jeffersonian* added, the University suffered from the "aristocracy and seclusiveness of the clique in power" and from professors "puffed up" with their own importance. The town of Lawrence had suffered from "toadying" to the University too long. "Just so long as we toady to the University, just so long will we be a dead University town, nothing more. . . . Don't be a toady. Set down on these snobs."[12]

Robinson wanted to set down on the *Jeffersonian*. He told Snow that he could not work to silence the editors while a regent, lest he seem to involve the University in party politics. He also wished not to offend Rogers and Sams, who had proved friendly to the institution's interests. Though sorry to see Robinson leave and apprehensive that the *Jeffersonian*'s ideas might become those of Populists generally, Snow consoled himself with the fact that Governor Lewelling let Robinson pick his own successor. Robinson chose Henry S. Clarke, a Lawrence Populist who had been president of the City Council and of the Board of Education, chief tax assessor, and sheriff of Douglas County. And he made Clarke promise that he would resign as a regent if Robinson ever found him negligent of the University's interests. Chancellor Snow was satisfied. "I am not

worrying at all," he told Regent C. R. Mitchell, "nor losing a
moment's sleep over the situation."[13]

But sleepless nights were drawing closer. In 1894 Kansans
elected Republican Edmund N. Morrill of Hiawatha as governor,
and he had three regents of his own to appoint to replace Mitchell,
Delbert A. Valentine, and Charles F. Scott. When Valentine declined reappointment, Chancellor Snow tried to convince Morrill
that he should continue Mitchell and Scott and make Scott Hopkins
his third choice. Hopkins was an alumnus of the class of 1881 and
now president of the First National Bank in Horton. It was important that a "fair proportion" of the regents be University alumni, Snow wrote Morrill, for they had "personal experience and
knowledge of the past condition and present needs of the institution" that others could not match.[14] Governor Morrill, however,
had his own ideas. Although he reappointed Charles F. Scott, instead of Hopkins he chose Frank G. Crowell, an Atchison lawyer
and zealous Republican who had graduated from the University in
1888. His selection greatly pleased Snow, or so he told Crowell.
Valentine's place went to Josephus W. Forney of Belle Plaine, like
Crowell a lawyer and a Republican.[15]

For a time there was harmony on the Board. But later in 1895
word reached Governor Morrill that William Rogers was a drunk-
ard. Rogers's Populism did nothing to increase Morrill's sympathy,
and in May the Governor removed him as a regent. In his place
Morrill put Oscar L. Moore, an Abilene lawyer. At first refusing to
yield his seat, Rogers claimed that he had done nothing to merit the
Governor's action and threatened to appeal to the State Supreme
Court. The other regents ignored him, accepted Moore, and gave
him Rogers's various committee posts. But Moore himself resigned
in the fall upon his election as judge of the eighth judicial district,
whereupon Morrill reappointed Charles S. Gleed.[16]

Thus a Board of five Republicans—Snow himself was strictly
orthodox—and two lone Populists went to beg before the Populist
legislature of 1897. The party controlled both houses, and Governor John W. Leedy of LeRoy was also of the faith. Immediately
after the elections of 1896 Snow told several friends that he did not
think that the Populists would do the University "serious harm."
Several party leaders had assured him that they intended to
strengthen rather than weaken the state's educational institutions.

Admittedly Kansas "went to the dogs politically" in the elections, but Snow actually believed many Populists to be more sympathetic than Republicans to the school. To make sure that they would be, the regents made their biennial report to the Governor even more vigorous than usual. After thirty years, they pointed out, the University was the greatest institution of higher learning in Kansas, but when compared with the truly distinguished American universities, it was pathetic. Consider the greatness of Princeton, which already had 150 buildings and at its recent sesquicentennial celebration had announced an addition to its endowment of $1,500,000; or of Chicago, which almost every month added from $100,000 to $1,000,000 to its capital; or of California, to which wealthy citizens had pledged $4,000,000. Consider even Nebraska: with a property valuation less than half that of Kansas, the state gave 25 percent more to its university than Kansans did to theirs. "The University of Kansas must not and will not ultimately fall behind the other states," Snow said, "yet the question is being daily asked whether it will be possible to hold the vantage ground already gained."[17]

In consideration of the people's financial plight, the regents would not ask for an increase in the regular $100,000 appropriation. But they said they had to have three buildings—for chemistry, for a museum, and for engineering shops. In the tiny Chemistry Building, built in 1883, two hundred freshmen students had to crowd into a hall seating one hundred at best, and such was the pressure on laboratory space that some of the four hundred students in all the chemistry classes together never got any laboratory work at all. Yet this was as nothing when compared with the hardships of the School of Pharmacy, which operated in two basement rooms dug out under the original building. The rooms were damp, poorly lighted, and unsanitary: green and yellow fungi stained the walls and floor, mold crept into the pharmaceutical materials, dampness ruined the instruments. Dean Sayre had frequently suffered malarial attacks. No faculty member should have to work in an "environment which seriously endangers his health," Snow said; when the Department of Chemistry left, the School of Pharmacy should get the whole building, now remodeled to conform to "some extent with the modern ideas of sanitation and of laboratory teaching."[18]

The natural history collections and the work in engineering suffered from lack of space. Every square foot of Snow Hall was now needed for classroom and laboratory work, and thus the thousands of museum specimens had to go somewhere else; besides, Snow Hall was not fireproof and the collections, whose monetary value Snow put at about $108,000, were always in danger. All the shop work of the School of Engineering took place in two small rooms under the boiler house, which were needed to expand the heating system. The absence of separate engineering shops, Snow said, meant poor training, which cheated Kansas boys out of jobs: "On account of our present inadequate facilities for this kind of education young men trained in other states are taking remunerative positions in Kansas which ought to be filled by Kansas men, and would be thus filled if the University could furnish the requisite instruction."[19]

In addition to all the pleading, the regents offered the usual figures to show that the University grossly underpaid its faculty members. Their purpose was to remind Kansans that although they asked no increase in the $100,000 appropriation, that sum was much too small.[20]

Clearly the legislature of 1897 had crucial decisions to make. Every one of them went against the University. Governor Leedy carefully said nothing in particular in telling the solons that the "conditions of the times" demanded "strict economy," but that the "economy that would take from any child the right and privilege of receiving an education is false economy, against the best interests of society and detrimental to the future of our state." Then he summarized and said he accepted the regents' arguments for new buildings and commended them to the "serious and thoughtful consideration" of the legislature.[21]

At first seriously and thoughtfully, then heatedly and wildly, the legislators proceeded to reject the requests for building funds and, far worse, to chop the University's general appropriation. The original appropriation bill was introduced in the House by Populist Edward T. Hackney of Wellington. It included $100,000 for salaries and general expenses, $100,000 for a natural history museum, $65,000 for a new chemistry building, and $25,000 for engineering shops. After the House Ways and Means Committee worked it over, all the building money had vanished and the regular annual appropriation stood at only $80,000. Chancellor Snow had argued with the committee to no avail, and when the bill reached the floor he discovered that the University had even less support than he had feared. The House Committee of the Whole dealt with the bill on January 27 in a scene that bordered on pandemonium. Supporters of the original measure—mostly Republicans, joined by a few Populists—shouted that while economizing was well and good, the state university was the wrong place to start. Populist opponents shot back that the University was no more deserving of respect than any other state institution. Amid angry confusion Republican Representative Warren W. Finney of Neosho Falls jumped to his feet to make a singularly stupid accusation against the Populists. "The reason you gentlemen of the majority oppose this measure," Finney roared, "is because the work of the University is destroying and forever destroying the power of your party." After that observation it became impossible for any University supporter to get a fair hearing, and the Committee of the Whole and then the House, by a vote of 80 to 0, passed the emasculated bill.[22]

The Senate was hardly more charitable. Its Ways and Means Committee, chaired by ex-Governor Lorenzo D. Lewelling, also rejected the building requests, but restored the $80,000 to $100,000. On the same day that the Committee reported the bill, however, Senator Horace G. Jumper of Osage County, chairman of the Committee on Fees and Salaries, proposed a measure for the general reduction of the salaries of almost all state employees. Although it was apparently a general economy measure, its opponents pointed out that almost half of the $50,000 reduction would come out of faculty salaries. As bad as the reductions was the fact that the bill would set salaries by dollar amounts, thus reviving a practice disliked and rejected by earlier regents. When the bill reached the floor on February 19, the scene was almost as tumultuous as that in the House, with the Populist majority easily beating down amendment after amendment to weaken Jumper's measure. On the final ballot only six senators cast negative votes.[23]

From a conference committee emerged an appropriation bill that set specific salaries for specific professorships and granted $8,000 a year for maintenance and supplies. It passed both houses by huge majorities and became law on March 13. Snow's salary declined from $5,000 to $4,000; Dean James W. Green's from $2,500 to $2,000; and the $2,000 full professors' stipends to $1,800 or $1,750. In all, the appropriation was $85,678 for each of the next two years.[24]

Against the Populist legislature of 1897 Snow also had to wage a campaign to hold the Board of Regents together. Unlike the financial struggle, this one was successful. In the House, Edward T. Hackney offered a bill that expanded the number of appointed regents from six to eight and forbade two regents from the same Congressional district. Because Henry S. Clarke and Charles F. Scott were from the same district and James P. Sams and Frank G. Crowell were both from another, the measure's clear intent was to displace the Republicans Scott and Crowell. According to the bill the chancellor was no longer to be a regent. With the expansion of the Board and the ousting of Scott and Crowell, Governor Leedy would have four places to fill. If he chose along strict party lines, the Populists would outnumber the Republicans, six to two. But while the bill got through the Judiciary Committee, which Hackney chaired, it never reached a vote in the House.[25]

Late in the session, however, the Senate approved a bill that would have accomplished about the same results as Hackney's. Moses A. Householder of Columbus introduced it, but it was actually the creation of Henry S. Clarke of Lawrence, now freed from his obligation to Robinson by Robinson's death in 1894. Snow thought Clarke's action disgraceful, but was still gratified that the man had "unmasked himself in public," where his "real character and intentions are universally understood." By devious maneuvering Householder got the bill through the Senate within a half-hour of its introduction by a vote of 25 to 10; the bill was not printed, however, and Snow thought that most senators did not know what they had done. As soon as Snow learned of the Senate's action, he rushed to Topeka to plan a House fight against it and rallied enough support to defeat it. Clarke was "frantic with rage," Snow reported happily.[26]

Both Snow and the Populists took some satisfaction from Governor Leedy's reappointment of William Rogers, whose original term had ended in 1897, and of James P. Sams; yet Henry S. Clarke was also reappointed. The Senate routinely approved Sams and Clarke, but balked at Rogers. A group of Populists in his own Washington County had protested that he was unfit to be a regent because his tastes and habits were "low, degrading, and groveling," because he was addicted to liquor, and because he was a "blasphemer and an infidel," "loud mouthed, indecent and vulgar in his conversation," "an object of derision and disgust at home, where he is regarded as a blowhard," and an "outcast socially." But Rogers also had his defenders, and after hearing them and Rogers himself, the Senate confirmed him.[27]

All of which went to show that thirty years after its founding the University could take nothing for granted. Economically it merely marked time for the next two years; the discouraged faculty, to their credit, held on. But a lucky accident brought one of the buildings that the legislature had refused to provide. On March 22, 1898, fire destroyed much of the power plant and engineering shops. Since the regents had no surplus funds with which to rebuild, they met with a group of sympathetic Lawrence citizens. Within a month after the Board promised it would ask the legislature of 1899 for money to repay, the Lawrencians secured $30,000 in private subscriptions as a loan. But meanwhile Lucien I. Blake had been soliciting on his own and in April he secured $18,000, later raised to $21,000, as a gift from George A. Fowler of Kansas City, who gave the money as a memorial to his father. With the grant went the provision that Blake be allowed to locate the building, and he put it on the top of Mount Oread's southern slope west of Fraser Hall. An oblong two-story structure with an allegedly decorative tower at the eastern end, Fowler Shops did much to help the School of Engineering and little to increase the University's architectural beauty. The loan of the Lawrence citizens went to outfit the shops with tools and machinery and to repair and equip the power plant; the legislature of 1899 duly appropriated the funds for repayment.[28]

With Fowler Shops abuilding, the regents needed to ask the legislature for only two new structures that the previous legislature had denied. Snow and the Board once more called attention to the sufferings of the Chemistry Department and the School of Pharmacy and to the needs of the natural history collection. More important than either, however, was the necessity to make up the losses sustained in 1897 and to move ahead. The sum asked for salaries and general maintenance was a whopping $135,000 a year. No other state university in the nation, Snow said in defense, had been as "seriously crippled by the withdrawal of state support" as his own. And the Board wanted the money in a lump sum once more. "Under the system of itemized appropriations," the Board explained, "the University is practically bound upon an iron bed, unable to move in any direction. . . . It is certainly not wise to put this great institution in a straight-jacket for two years, thus practically taking it out of the hands of the Board, which is charged by law with its management and control."[29]

The legislature of 1899, controlled once again by Republicans, eased the catastrophe of '97. After the Board of Regents scaled the request down to $130,000 a year, the House Ways and Means Committee pared it to $120,000, and then both the House and Senate passed the appropriation bill smoothly. But to secure Senate approval, Snow had to promise that he and the other regents would not raise salaries back to their former levels. On the whole the regents set them halfway between those before and those after the debacle.[30] The University's leaders were less successful in getting money for new buildings. Edgar H. S. Bailey and the Board originally wanted $80,000 for a chemistry building, but in deference to reality cut the figure to $60,000, from which the legislature cut $5,000 more. When the House bill for $55,000 reached the Senate, its Ways and Means Committee generously added $65,000 for the natural history museum. But the House would not go along, and the senators had to sacrifice it to get the chemistry building.[31]

Standing northwest of Snow Hall, the new structure was in every way an improvement over the old. Designed by Bailey and his colleagues in conjunction with J. G. Haskell, it was "plain and massive," four stories tall, including the basement, and 187 feet long by 70 feet wide at its broadest. Bailey had visited several of the country's largest and best chemical laboratories before drawing his plans, and boasted that although the building had little adornment, no expense had been spared to secure the "best practical conditions for chemical and pharmaceutical work, according to modern methods." He, Sayre, and their colleagues had a reasonably complete system of lecture rooms, laboratories, and offices. A large hall on the top floor seated 325 students, and the undergraduate laboratories on the three main stories could each accommodate 112 students at once. Bailey was especially proud of the ventilating system of hoods, flues, chimneys, and fans, which guaranteed the speedy elimination of noxious fumes and the constant introduction of fresh air. For all its assets, however, the building was not yet complete, for the chemists and pharmacists kept their $80,000 edifice in mind, used the $55,000 of 1899 to secure maximum floor space, and relied on future legislatures for money for such things as a complete plumbing and heating system, tables and hoods for the student laboratories, and adequate lighting. The legislature of 1901 gave $10,000 more for equipment, and over the years the structure came more or less to realize Bailey's original hopes.[32]

In 1901 the legislature confirmed the fact that the University's fortunes were once more on the rise by giving the institution for general maintenance the amount that the regents had thought necessary two years before. The regents had requested $160,000—$100,000 to bring salaries to pre-1897 levels, and $60,000 to expand the faculty and to buy library books, equipment for the School of Medicine, and other items. Along with that request went $100,000 more for a natural history museum. But since the mood of the legislature was not extravagant but only generous, the University got $135,000 for maintenance and $75,000 for the museum.[33]

After holding an open competition, Dyche, Snow, and the regents chose a plan submitted by the firm of Root and Siemens of Kansas City, Missouri. The architects described the exterior style as Venetian Romanesque, and the entrance was modeled upon the allegedly most beautiful portal in the world, that of the church of St. Trophime in Arles, France. In front was an impressive tower, and sitting high on pedestals on the walls were imaginative carvings of beasts, birds, and other naturalistic forms advertising the structure's use. While the effect was not beautiful, it was comfortable and pleasantly crochety. The interior, especially of the main floor, was strikingly imaginative. Dyche had designed a splendid panoramic stage for his displays of North American mammals, which extended, on several levels, around an apse at the rear. To prevent skins from fading and to offer a realistic appearance, his design provided a skylight in the roof from which natural light came down through a well to the first floor. The University's notable stuffed bird collection was on the second floor, and the fossil exhibits on the third. In the basement were classrooms and workshops.[34]

As pleased as the University's leaders were by the increased appropriations of 1899 and 1901, those very increases symbolized the fact that at the end of the nineteenth century the institution was not where Francis H. Snow and the regents of the 1890s had hoped it would be. It was exciting to have a new chemistry building, for example, but it had been badly needed for years, during which time instruction had suffered and morale had declined. The assault on faculty salaries of 1897 and the failure of the next two legislatures to give the institution what the regents thought it needed once again illustrated the wide differences of opinion among Kansans about what their state university should be. No one could claim now that the University of Kansas was not a university in fact. Nor could anyone claim that the institution was entirely inadequate or that its faculty was inferior. But it was obvious to those who knew something of what Chancellor Snow, the regents, and the faculty wished the University to be that it fell far short of their hopes. Kansans had not yet subscribed—partly because they were economically unable, mainly because they were intellectually or emotionally unable to do so—to a determined and vigorous pursuit of the ideal university.

Thus it was that Chancellor Frank Strong concluded in 1902 and 1903 that he was presiding over a third-rate university on the verge of becoming fourth-rate.

12

Students and Other Undergraduates: The Nineteenth Century

Neither prince nor peasant leads a life so pleasant
As the student's life at K.S.U.

wrote William H. Carruth in a poem describing late nineteenth-
and early twentieth-century undergraduate life. Carruth had a
point. While not all students led better than a prince's life, most of
them found at the University opportunities for far more joyful lives
than existed on farms and in the state's towns and cities. Mount
Oread offered a host of new experiences, the means of broadening
both intellectual and social horizons, and considerable freedom from
parental and societal restraints. Although the University inevitably
slowed the maturation process by postponing the time that youths
would start to play adult roles, it helped to make both adolescence
and adulthood mentally and emotionally richer. While preparing
some students for specific professions and vocations, it gave almost
all of them more requisites of worldly success than they would have
had otherwise.

As individuals the preparatory and undergraduate students were
a notably varied lot, and the variety increased as the student body
grew in number. Most years showed an increase over the previous
one. In the 1866–1867 year 55 students enrolled, although most of
them did not stay for the full nine months. Except for drops in
1873–1874 and 1881–1882 the figures climbed steadily to 1882–1883,
when 582 matriculated; during the rest of the 1880s the abolition of
the Preparatory Department and the onset of economic hardship

196

brought considerable fluctuation. In 1891–1892, with the Preparatory Department gone, 630 students enrolled; the number jumped by a hundred the next year. Two years later the University had 875 students and after that growth was steadily upward, reaching 1,000 in 1896–1897, almost 1,500 in 1904–1905, and 2,000 in 1907–1908.[1]

The School of Arts—the College—drew far more students than any other school. Of the 630 students in 1891–1892, 283 were in the College, while Fine Arts had 112, Engineering 88, Law 78, Pharmacy 41, and the Graduate School 29. Ten years later 619 of 1,233 students were in the College, and in future years it kept about the same ratio. Enrollments in the other schools grew erratically, but still impressively. By 1907–1908 the College had 899, Engineering 479, Law 186, Fine Arts 183, the Graduate School 102, Medicine 101, and Pharmacy 94. There were 289 in the Summer Session, which had begun in 1903. Although more women than men enrolled in the 1860s and early 1870s, starting in 1872–1873 there were almost always more males than females. Both sexes enrolled in all the departments and schools, but there were few women in the professional schools and comparatively few men in the School of Fine Arts.[2]

Especially while the Preparatory Department existed, the students' ages varied considerably. In 1879–1880, when 251 of 440 students were in that division, the average age was 18.4 years. But eleven years later, when only 38 of 474 were preparatory students, the average age was 22, that of seniors being about 23 and of freshmen 19.5. The high average was the result of delays in earlier schooling and of the necessity of many students' working during their teens on family farms. According to the regents, maturity was a blessing. "This age indicates," they said in 1890, "that the young men and women in attendance . . . are of an age at which the most favorable results in the way of thorough scholastic attainment can be expected."[3]

Most students naturally came from the eastern third of the state, both because those counties were most heavily populated and because the University was comparatively close to home. To refute the charge that the institution was only a local Lawrence school, the officers pointed out that students represented an increasing number of counties—sixteen in 1869–1870, forty in 1875–1876, and fifty-five in 1881–1882—but they could never deny that far more than half of their students were eastern Kansans or that Douglas and contiguous counties furnished most of them.[4]

A more serious accusation was that the University's students were the offspring of an economic aristocracy. The regents consistently denied the charge, and in 1890 provided statistics to disprove it. While their categories were not precise, they said that the parents of 38 percent of the students were farmers, 21 percent, professional men of various kinds, 19 percent, merchants and tradesmen, 5 percent, bankers and "capitalists," and 5 percent, artisans; the parents of the remaining 12 percent had a variety of occupations—railroad agents, commercial travelers, hotel and boardinghouse keepers, county officials, and hack-drivers. Almost 34 percent of the students supported themselves entirely and another 11 percent did so in part. Fifteen years later, more students still came from farm backgrounds than any other kind, with children of merchants, lawyers, physicians, and real-estate dealers following in order; sixty occupations and professions were represented. Now 56 percent were wholly or partially self-supporting.[5]

The great variety of unique student personalities combined with the diversity of backgrounds to make it practically impossible to portray the student body as a whole. Florence Finch Kelly of the class of 1881 recalled some fifty years later that the students of her day had been a sincere and earnest group. No faculty could have had better "student material," she said, "at least so far as go desire for learning, zeal in its acquisition, pleasure in mental activity and something better than average intellectual capacity, than was offered by the student body of my alma mater during my day." Another alumna said that the students of the 1880s were humble, religious youths trying to make the best of their academic opportunities so that they could better serve society. In portraying the ideal student, a writer in the *Kansas Collegiate* bespoke the high ideals of many undergraduates. That student was a combination of Socrates, Cato, Newton, and Descartes, who questioned "heaven, earth, air, laws, humanity, everything," yet never lost his humanitarian attachment to his fellow men or his ability to forget himself in the "grandeur of meditation inspired by what God has made." Ideal students "listen to the songs of nature, and drink in gladness; they watch great political changes, and are solicitous for the good of mankind; they honor and rejoice in all true forms of religion, for in these they see the upbuilding of their fellows."[6]

But the characteristics of the ideal scholar were not necessarily those of actual undergraduates. There should be more to student life than acquiring knowledge and meditating on it, said an editorial in the *Kansas Review* of 1882. Undergraduates from Kansas villages and farms generally lacked the "advantages of good society." At the University they could find them: "in the culture, ease of manners and expression that society affords, and in its refining influence" were sources of lifelong pleasure and satisfaction. For some mysterious reason, said a student in 1888, after a few months on Mount Oread many undergraduates lost their intellectual zeal. At first they displayed "energetic resolution," but as time passed they became languid and slipshod, "passive receptacles of unwelcome truths," interested only in getting a degree. Four years later another observer claimed that the personal wealth of many students made them indifferent to learning. Those who did not have to work their way through college were often unconcerned about getting the maximum possible intellectual return on their dollar investment. And because knowledge was not something that could be worn or eaten, the materially minded usually dismissed it as unimportant. "It is only the student who hungers and thirsts after knowledge that takes in and enjoys the nourishment of books and lectures"; the others did not consider their "failure to learn . . . any particular loss."[7]

In 1896 the editors of the *Kansas University Weekly* tried to characterize the student body. Making allowances for individual differences, they found two main types each of men and women. One group among the men included the flashy, conceited sort: during the winter he wore "an immaculate white shirt, an expensive suit of clothes, a high collar, and tooth-pick shoes," while in the spring his plumage was louder and breezier. "He is proud, excessively proud, and thinks that if the world does not revolve around him it ought to do so." Yet despite his egotism he was a fairly good student who would outgrow his self-centeredness and "no doubt develop into a good man as many of his type have done before." In contrast was the wholesome majority who had less money and self-esteem and were more earnest, sincere, and candid. If the typical member of this group lacked some of the social graces and had a coarser mind than his opposite number, he had both more brains and "that steadfastness of purpose which insures success. He is building a firm foundation upon which rests his future career and in later years composite number one will be one of his clerks."

Among the females was a type whose only redeeming quality was that she was a fairly good student. She was pretty of face, but with beauty went vanity, and so she passed "present, precious moments basking in the sunshine, while those about her are making serious preparation for their life work. . . . She is alas! a butter-fly of fashion." She shunned girls outside her own social set. "This girl composite is disliked by the majority of people who know her, envied or tolerated by those of her own social clique, and admired perhaps by passing strangers and a few 'cholly' boys who let their hearts rule them—body and soul." Yet there was still time for her to repent her folly and make a noble woman of herself—like her opposite, who had all the womanly graces and brains besides. "She is quiet and reserved, but has opinions of her own upon all subjects of importance," and if she lacked the other's "broad culture" she was her scholarly equal or superior. "She is polite, kind, congenial and ever ready to assist those who need assistance if the means is within her power. She has the purity of Puritan Priscilla and greater tact and independence. She is altogether a typical Kansas girl of whom the state and perhaps some day the nation will be proud."[8]

Whether or not the categories were correct, the editors had grasped the central point about the student body. It was Kansas in microcosm with its seriousness and frivolity, nobility and pettiness, falsity and truth. The University had scholars and time-servers, the dedicated and the indifferent, those with narrowly professional aims and, at least by 1896, a band of aesthetes who called themselves Bohemians and met secretly to read poetry and talk philosophy.[9]

It also had a number of outspoken students who belabored the faculty for its insensitivity to the students' needs. In January, 1873, for example, an article in the *Oread Gazette* attacked both Chancellor Fraser and Francis H. Snow for neglecting their classes. Fraser had been traveling on University business, with the result that the College senior course in logic was uncompleted and the Preparatory Department, never very good anyway, had become "something of a swindle." Fraser and Snow were not the only culprits, either, said the article. A teacher's place, the author said, was in front of his classes; the delinquent professors still owed the students an "adequate return on their time and money."[10]

Most of the criticism, however, was a less personal dissent from existing academic rules and teaching methods. Change everything, urged an enthusiastic reformer in 1879. Open the University to "all comers and all goers," eliminate formal classes and let every student move at his own speed, abolish commencements, which were only a "useless advertising medium" anyway, abolish grades in favor of certificates for passing examinations in various subjects and the present degree requirements in favor of degrees given to students who passed those examinations the faculty prescribed. Let education become informal, flexible, and free. "Will our regents try this?" the rebel asked. The regents, of course, would not, and the members of successive classes continued to hold no academic requirement sacred. Lectures were a waste of time, said the *University Courier* in 1882, for the students themselves could read and master the appropriate books. Required attendance at lectures was asinine, said other students: abolish it and the incompetent teachers facing empty seats would be weeded out in no time. Still others continued to attack final examinations and grades: "We should learn to study for its own sake," said the *University Review* in 1889, "and not for a prize that may be offered." Even when students supported existing requirements, they did so believing that they had both a right and a duty to offer their ideas on any subject that moved them. "Of all despicable things a toady is the worst," said an editorial in the *Review* in 1885, and of toadies the student body had a surfeit. They flattered and always agreed with the faculty, laughed at all their teachers' little jokes, and hardly dared call their souls their own. "It is right and proper that we should follow the advice and instructions of men who are our elders and superiors in so many ways," the editorial said. "But it is refreshing to see a man who has ideas of his own and courage enough to advance them; who when he doesn't think a joke funny doesn't laugh, who speaks out frankly when he differs from some statement or opinion advanced. By all means follow good advice, but don't be a faculty jumping-jack, don't double your arms and flop your legs and grin and bow whenever the string is pulled. Be frank and manly."[11]

Whether the academic requirements were good or bad, many students thought the curriculum less stimulating than it should be.

Thus like semibored students in other institutions they began extra-curricular literary societies and then various special-interest groups. The godfather of them all was the Acropolis Society, founded in 1866 by the preparatory students to afford "facilities for literary advancement" and also social conviviality. Meeting every Friday afternoon, the members heard readings, declamations, and musical selections, and debated topics moral, philosophical, social, economic, and political: "Resolved, that there is more pleasure in pursuit than possession," for example, or "That the sewing machine is of more benefit to mankind than the locomotive."[12] In 1870 the male students seized control of the organization, excluded women, and changed its name to the Orophilian Society. The rejected females formed the Oread Society, but before long both groups were welcoming both sexes to membership, and the two were competing for members, prestige, and literary and oratorical supremacy.[13]

By the early 1880s, however, the days of the all-purpose literary societies were numbered; though they continued into the early twentieth century, their importance steadily declined. One reason was that they became the prey of prestige-seeking students, especially fraternity and sorority members. The first of the fraternities was the Alpha Mu chapter of Beta Theta Pi, organized early in 1873 by a semisecret group within the Oread Society. Not to be outdone, later in the year several Oread Society women secured a charter for the Kappa chapter of the I. C. Sorosis, which in 1888 became Pi Beta Phi. In 1876 a second fraternity, Phi Kappa Psi, appeared, and between 1881 and 1884 six more fraternities and sororities were begun. When Greek met Greek, there was inevitably a contest for fame and power and the literary societies became prizes in the interfraternity struggle. The fraternities and sororities also provided arenas for discussion and fun that tended to make the literary organizations superfluous.[14]

Special interest groups or clubs contributed even more to the decline of the literary societies. Unlike their predecessors, which were run by the students alone, the new groups had faculty sponsors and directors. They reflected the University's increasing specialization and fragmentation. With the encouragement of Francis H. Snow, in 1873 several students formed the Natural History Society to discuss scientific subjects alone. At its meetings the members talked of such things as the nightshade family of plants, insects' antennae, snakes, and the nature of the scientific method. From 1874 to 1876 the society published a newspaper called the *Observer of Nature,* which carried articles on "Three Days among the Grasshoppers," "The Baltimore Oriole," "Mammals of the Kansas Plains," and the like. In October, 1875, other special-interest groups appeared when Frances Schlegel began French and German conversational societies; the members met in Lawrence homes.[15]

The heyday of such organizations was the 1880s. James W. Green and his law students formed the Kent Club in 1880; Philo J. Williams and his normal students followed with a Normal Literary Society in 1881; and a year later came a reorganized Deutscher Studenten-Verein under Frances Schlegel and a Young Men's Political Science Club headed by James H. Canfield. Then came an Engineering Society in 1883; a group for first-year medical students called Iatrikos in 1884; a Science Club in 1885—a combination of the Engineering Society and Iatrikos, but including all the faculty scientists and many students; a Philosophical Club in 1886; a Pharmacy Association in 1887; and a Modern Language Club in 1890.[16] Weakened by factional struggles and superseded by the specialized clubs, the Oread Society dissolved itself in 1886, and the Orophilian disappeared in 1889. New societies—the X.Y.Z. and the Adelphic among them—appeared to take their places, but they were sickly from the start and of little consequence. Students in the modern American university, said the yearbook *Helianthus* in 1889, were expected to do research in a special field, and "not so much the how as the what is said secures praise." The literary societies belonged to the days when the University of Kansas was merely an undergraduate college.[17]

Students who wished to express themselves for the sake of expression alone, the *Helianthus* said unkindly, could write for one of the three college papers. Just as the specialized clubs proliferated in the 1880s, so did student publications. Until the mid-1870s, they had found little success; both the *Meteor,* begun in 1867 by the Acropolis Society, and the *Oread Gazette,* issued a few years later by the Oread Society, were inconsequential.[18] But on April 1, 1874, the Natural History Society published the first number of the *Observer of Nature,* which contained articles by both students and faculty members, attracted 270 subscribers—a number considerably larger than the student-faculty total—and lasted for two years. In-

evitably there was a reaction by the nonscientists. In 1875 Charles
S. Gleed and several friends in the Oread Society induced the
Observer's editors to add their *Kansas Collegiate* as a supplement
to the former publication. The *Observer* printed articles such as
"An Hour among the Birds," "Hyponomeuta Wakarusa," and "The
Power of Observation," while the new sheet carried in its first num-
ber essays on "Greatness" and "The Mind's Plasticity," fiction, and
a poem.[19]

From then on rivalry, knavery, and high- and low-mindedness
brought forth a succession of periodicals and newspapers. Since the
Oread Society put out the *Kansas Collegiate*, during the 1878–1879
year the Orophilians started their own sheet, the *Courier*. Both of
them being filled with noble or sententious thoughts, for relief
there appeared an independent venture called the *University Pastime*, dedicated, its editors said, to stimulating greater interest in
the "various amusements and recreations which tend to rest the
brains and invigorate the bodies of the University students."[20] It
floundered and failed, but meanwhile a faction of the *Courier* staff
deserted their colleagues to join the *Collegiate*, which in 1879 became the *Kansas Review*, a general magazine with something for
everyone. The first issue included articles on "Our Indian Policy,"
"The Comets Observed This Year," "The College Curriculum and
the Health of College Girls," "Cruelty to Animals," and "Republicanism in Spain," as well as a "Prayer to Zeus," exchanges from
other college publications, news items, and an editorial. But the
Kansas Review company was factionalized between the Beta Theta
Pi and Phi Kappa Psi fraternities, which led to a revival of the
Courier in 1882 and then to a consolidation of the two publications
into a new *University Review* in 1884, whereupon the minority of
the *Courier* staff that opposed amalgamation founded a new, anti-
fraternity *Courier*. Charging that the political conniving of fraternity leaders was corrupting the "youthful, pure, innocent, fresh
minds" of the rank and file, the *Courier* appeared under the motto,
"Fraternity rule must be broken."[21] The natural result was that
several fraternities advanced on and captured the *Courier*. During
the next decade it and the *University Review* continued to report
campus news and provide outlets for student littérateurs, and they
were joined by other, though short-lived, journals: the *University*

Times in 1888–1889, the *University Kansan* in 1889–1890, and the *Students Journal* in 1892.

Until 1895 the faculty kept out of the journalistic wars. But by that year there were four independent student publications, each of them slandering the others and all of them serving mainly as objects of political intrigue. In February the University Council's Committee on University Journalism, disgusted with the pettiness and backbiting, recommended a new paper which was to have the "official approval and support of the University"—that is, the faculty and administration—and was to be free of existing student factions. After both the Council and a student mass meeting approved the idea, a student-faculty joint stock company was organized and on June 3 the first issue of the *Kansas University Weekly* appeared on campus. William H. Carruth, chairman of the Advisory Committee, claimed that "All factions and interests are or may be represented, and the plan of organization guarantees a clean, creditable and representative K.U. journal." With the faculty discouraging the other publications, they disappeared in 1895 and 1896. Yet the hopes for a high-toned newspaper came to nothing, for by the end of the nineties the struggle for control of the *Weekly* was as fierce as the contests of an earlier day, and its contents—biased and inaccurate campus news, sports, gossip, and social tidbits—were so poor that Professor of Greek Alexander M. Wilcox attacked it severely in a chapel address. The sheet became so wretched, indeed, that in 1902 the University Council withdrew its official recognition.[22]

The *Weekly*'s circulation and its advertising revenues declined with its quality, and in 1904 it died. On September 17 the *Semi-Weekly Kansan*, with the official support of Chancellor Strong and the faculty, took its place. After pleas by Strong and Wilcox, a mass meeting endorsed the new paper and promised to patronize its advertisers. "The University of Kansas was ashamed of the paper," a *Kansan* editorial said of the old *Weekly* in pledging better things. Though never perfect, the *Kansan* easily outclassed its predecessor and would continue in existence—becoming a triweekly in 1908 and a daily in 1912—for the rest of the University's first century and beyond.[23]

The disappearance of the *University Review* in 1896 created a mild demand for new magazines offering essays, fiction, and poetry, but the demand was too slight to make any one of them a success.

In 1895 and 1896 Hilliard Johnson, Clarence T. Southwick, and Professor of Drawing and Painting Alfred H. Clark published in Kansas City two issues of the *Lotus*, which they hoped would attract contributions from students in western colleges generally. Finding little interest in their "pure literary efforts," they sold out to Walter Blackburn Harte. In November and December, 1897, a few students published the *K.U. Idler*—a local *Lotus*—but apathy killed it. Then from February, 1901, until March, 1902, Charles L. Edson issued a humor magazine called the *Automobile*—so named, Edson said, "because there is no horse about it and it is bound to go." Lively, facetious, antitraditional, dedicated to the new, fast-moving age, the *Automobile* nevertheless broke down. Edson sold it to the *Jayhawk Quill*, published by the literary Quill Club, whose editors hoped that it would become the official campus literary magazine and win a national reputation like that of the Princeton *Tiger* or the *Yale Literary Magazine*. But Kansas was neither Princeton nor Yale, and the *Jayhawk Quill* lasted but two months. Still another magazine, the *Oread*, which contained alumni notes as well as essays, fiction, and University news, expired in the spring of 1901 after only a year of publication.[24]

Except for the *Kansan* the only student periodical with any longevity during the two decades after 1895 was the *Kansas University Lawyer*, which lasted until 1911. Containing Law School news, essays and editorials dealing with the law and its study, and comments on University matters, it was a highly specialized magazine, catering to and supported by lawyers only. "We consider that as representing the Law School we are entirely in another field," wrote the editors in their first issue in 1895, "and the trials and tribulations incident to the ordinary University student interest us only as any matter of outside news might, and that is very little."[25]

Both growing specialization-professionalization and dispersion of interest helped to explain why the literary magazines after 1895 came to nothing. Another, and probably more important, reason was that by the 1890s the students were far more interested in social activities than in extracurricular literary or intellectual matters. The undergraduates were growing both more worldly and more fractious than they used to be, and they shaped the University accordingly. So troublesome, so opposed to the University's apparent purposes, did they become that the faculty had to reverse a policy of hands-off student affairs in favor of closer control.

For the first thirty years of the University's history, faculty policy was to allow students to be generally their own masters outside of class. There were, of course, certain rules. No student, for example, could leave Lawrence without the chancellor's permission. From 1867 to 1870 attendance at daily morning chapel services was mandatory; but faced with loud grumblings and numerous truants, the requirement was dropped in 1870–1871 for all except students with first-hour recitations and three years later for everyone—though the exercises continued. In the 1870s the faculty added other regulations. Students had to be in a specific room, rather than loitering about the halls, when not in class or chapel; usually this meant the library, which became a noisy detention cell. If students frequented Lawrence liquor or billiard saloons, the faculty would notify their parents.[26]

During the 1870s, however, the faculty forsook specific directives in favor of a general policy of "unexceptionable deportment and strict observance of University rules." The University's purpose, said the catalogue of 1877–1878, was to "promote the welfare of the State by securing an intelligent, industrious and moral citizenship. The State cannot countenance habits of idleness, dissipation, or any acts of insubordination. Hence the Faculty are fully authorized to refuse admission to those of known vicious habits, and to remove by suspension those who do not prove worthy members of the institution. . . . The fewest rules possible are promulgated, and the good conduct of students is deemed sufficiently guarded under the general statement: *'Unexceptionable deportment and strict observance of University regulations are required.'* "[27]

Yet the burden of enforcing even that general rule irked the faculty. Chancellor Lippincott prowled the corridors of the University Building, nabbing loiterers, but most professors took little interest in such work. In March, 1884, the faculty decided to keep its disciplinary duties to an absolute minimum. Henceforth the only rule would be "unexceptional deportment, and strict attention to University duties." The University was not a disciplinary institution, they said, and the faculty "cannot and does not occupy the place of parents." Their overseeing extended to the students' classroom work and their general behavior as it came under public observation, but in keeping with the rationale of the elective system and the accompanying student responsibility the idea of faculty coercion of students had to be a "thoroughly subordinate one." According to James H. Canfield the "no government" system worked very well. The students acted responsibly, the faculty no longer had to serve as "detectives" and "moral police," and as a result the University prospered.[28]

Whether or not the faculty had few or many rules, however, the students were on their own most of the time, anyway, for the University lacked all of the agencies of control which would be common to a later age and the faculty took little extracurricular interest in them. There were no dormitories, no student union, no deans of men and women, no supervisory paraphernalia to regulate and stimulate student life in approved ways. Some professors often entertained students in their homes—Francis H. Snow was especially hospitable—and there were faculty-student contacts in the clubs and societies. But in 1891 Professor Arthur G. Canfield said that the faculty had done little to influence the students' social life, and faculty seclusiveness was a source of continuing undergraduate complaint. "We do not advocate a protecting supervision by the faculty," said a *University Review* writer in 1885, "but we would be glad to see them on the ball ground, in the literary societies, and other places besides the class room. Let them meet with us as sharers and not supervisors of our pleasures and duties. It will keep off from them the fossilizing touches of age, and benefit and assist us." Accusing the faculty of self-centeredness, a *Kansas University Weekly* editorial of 1901 said that the "whole company of professors and students are all dropped down here in one confused mess, with no logical and vital connection, and no effort toward attaining it, save a blind struggle for some kind of an advancement, they know not why nor where."[29]

In the nature of things the students and the faculty could not constitute a true University community, for their interests were as inevitably at odds as those of teachers and pupils everywhere. Another reason was that the students themselves were not a community; divided by courses, majors, and schools, they were also separated spatially, socially, economically, and racially.

The spatial dispersion arose in part from a lack of dormitories, which forced out-of-town students to find their own quarters and meals. Some of them lived in the growing cluster of boardinghouses near the campus. Others, living in rented rooms, formed boarding clubs or ate in groups with their fraternity brothers and sorority sisters. Among the non-Greeks the usual procedure was for several enterprising students to gather in a larger group, which elected a member to buy the food and keep the accounts and found a woman to do the cooking and provide a dining room. By 1906 there were ten independent eating clubs with 210 men and 114 women; from 1877 to 1906 the average cost varied from $1.50 to $3.00 a week. Still other students set up housekeeping for themselves. Thus when Florence Finch and her brother Charles came to the University from Louisburg in Miami County, they rented a two-room cottage and used furniture loaned by their parents. Florence had busily canned fruit, jellies, and jams during the previous summer and, with them and food bought with a small parental allowance, they fed themselves the first year. In 1886 William Allen White's mother came to Lawrence along with him to cook and keep house—and also to help him with his lessons. Many students who did not wish to join the boarding clubs got together to rent rooms and cottages and share the expenses and chores.[30]

Living costs varied widely, depending on how much the students had and were willing to spend. Florence Finch Kelly thought that in the late 1870s and early 1880s a thrifty student could get through all four years for $500 or less. Probably the figure was too low. In 1891 a survey of men students from outside Lawrence reported the average annual expense of the first three years to be about $295. Major expenses were for board ($101.34), room ($36.24), clothes ($49.32), books ($23.28), washing ($12.97), and sundries—including University fees—($65.24). Expenses tended to rise with each succeeding year.[31]

Because the University drew students from all economic and social classes, the student body was stratified accordingly. Presumably all students were equal before their professors—although there was an occasional claim that the faculty was partial to the "society crowd"—but among themselves they were anything but equal. At the bottom of the social order were the Negroes. Unlike benighted Missourians and Oklahomans, whose laws forbade the admission of Negroes to their state universities, Kansans welcomed Negro students from the start. The first black student enrolled in 1870 in the freshman preparatory class, and during the next forty years more than two hundred Negroes matriculated and sixty received degrees. But having admitted them, the officers and faculty let them find their own social level, which was usually a low one. Although the literary societies occasionally admitted a black to membership, and although one or two blacks represented the University in intercollegiate debates, as a group the Negroes suffered from consistent discrimination of which the faculty as a group took no notice. The fraternities and sororities barred them, most white students ignored them, and they associated only with each other and the Lawrence black community. Student prejudice and faculty supineness in face of it were reflections of the ideas and attitudes of most Kansans and most Americans. While "every Negro—provided he has like endowments—is just as good as a white man, and is equal to him," said the *Weekly University Courier* in 1886, equality did not demand community. Between the two races were differences in "temperament" and in "mental qualities"; between them was an "impassable gulf." "For this reason we do not desire to associate with the negroes; neither do the negroes as a social class desire to associate with us. It seems a matter of mutual pleasure that the two societies should be separate and independent."[32]

Among the whites the rich scorned the poor and the fraternity and sorority members scorned the rest as "Barbarians," or "Barbs" for short. Some poorer students found discrimination hard to bear. Whatever the rosy recollections of other alumni, said a graduate of 1886, he had suffered. "The slights endured by the 'country boys' and the feeling impressed that they were of a 'cheap' class," he said, "came to us at a period when impressions sank deep."[33]

The fraternities and sororities also manifested economic distinctions, for the poor were less likely than the rich to be invited to join or to be able to meet the expenses of membership. The societies' existence bespoke as well a widespread desire for social exclusiveness: a desire to be—or at least feel oneself to be—one of the powerful elite, to dominate other students by controlling the literary societies and publications and, later, campus politics, to share secrets known only to a few. From two in 1873 the number of Greek organizations grew to nine in 1889, thirteen in 1903, and seventeen in 1909. During the 1881–1882 academic year about one-fifth of the students belonged to the five chapters on campus; by 1913–1914, when there were thirty-one societies on campus, about 30 percent of the students belonged. At first the chapters rented rooms in downtown Lawrence, but in the 1890s they began to rent or buy their own houses as the members and alumni were able. The brothers' and sisters' activities were as varied as those of the students generally. Throughout the year they held dances, parties, and outings. Like the Barbs the Greeks drank liquor, smoked, played cards and dice and practical jokes, and fornicated as they found compliant partners. In the rooms and houses were heard literary discussions, debates, mock trials, plans for seizing control of this or that publication or organization, and descriptions of the virtues and vices of faculty members, rival fraternities, and women.[34]

Whether or not fraternities and sororities benefited the University depended on one's point of view. From the start opponents attacked them with arguments that quickly became trite. Being clannish and scornful of nonmembers, the secret societies were said to be undemocratic, un-University, and practically un-American; the desire for secrecy was also described as a characteristic of childish minds. The members were too much interested in power and eminence within the student body and too little concerned with the welfare of the whole University. Just as bad, they stunted their members' scholarship by overnourishing their social lives.[35]

Defenders of the societies countered such charges by emphasizing their value to both the members and the University at large. All fraternities had the same object, said one spokesman: "to lead to a higher, purer life; to urge excellence in all efforts; to place honor, honesty, and fidelity as the basis of all action." Fraternities strengthened the University by urging on their members exemplary conduct, good scholarship, and an interest in University affairs both before and after graduation; and they bound the alumni more closely to the school. They were, moreover, necessary for the students' welfare. "Social and literary organizations of some kind seem to be as essential to the life of the student as tea parties to old maids, or the various clubs for old bachelors, or the many social organizations of the several churches," said a fraternity supporter in 1888. "It is written that, 'Man cannot live by bread alone.' Neither can he live upon a continual diet of languages, mathematics, and philosophy."[36]

Officially the faculty took no notice of the Greek societies and simply held the members to the general standard of "unexceptional deportment." By the mid-1890s, however, that deportment was not as much in evidence as the professors thought it should be. To be sure, most student recreation was innocent. In their leisure time boys and girls played together, held public and private parties and dances, made their first, tentative approaches to love. They attended the Lawrence theaters to watch the traveling players and variety shows, and often followed the theater with refreshments in one of the city's several ice cream parlors. They attended fairs and exhibitions at Lawrence's Bismarck Grove, joined in the 1880s in the new sport of outdoor rink roller skating, rowed the Kansas River and had picnics on the banks. They took walking trips, played tennis and croquet, and when bicycling became fashionable in the 1890s, began to pedal around Lawrence and the countryside. The boys separately played informal baseball and football games, organized a company of cadets in 1878, or simply loafed. It was also common to take the train to the Kansas City metropolis for an evening or weekend. Most of the students most of the time did not transgress the limits of innocence or good taste.[37]

Yet the raffish students were always there. In the early days they took gates off townspeople's fences, tied cans to dogs' tails, and tipped over outhouses. There appeared a secret society of Turkey Catchers, whose members wore badges with a mysterious "T. C." on them and ate roast stolen turkey with some regularity until Judge Nelson T. Stephens caught them at it and shamed them into reforming. Sometimes student daring was merely senseless, such as the time in the late 1870s when someone entered the basement of the University Building through a broken window, and left a faucet on to cause a flood; but at other times there was more ingenuity. At the commencement ceremonies of 1873, for example, wags lowered a skeleton on a rope through a hole in the unfinished roof of the University Building. From a toe hung a sign reading "Prex." For a few minutes, while the band played, the bones jiggled and danced over the heads of the audience. Campus tradition had it that after a measure of order was restored, Mrs. Fraser innocently asked her husband what "Prex." meant. "The faculty," Chancellor Fraser allegedly replied, which, if true, suggested that his relations with the professors were already strained.[38]

While the dancing skeleton harmed no one, an event seven years later showed that some students could be extremely cruel. On December 3, 1879, the faculty held memorial services for the recently deceased Benjamin F. Mudge, a famous Kansas geologist who had been a University lecturer. With the chapel lectern draped in black, appropriate songs were sung, prayers offered, and addresses given on Mudge's character and work. Struck by the solemnity, William M. Thacher and Edward C. Meservey decided to trick the faculty into holding similar services for a man still alive. They picked on a regent, the Reverend Frank T. Ingalls of Atchison, and a telegram from that city reporting Ingalls's death soon reached Chancellor Marvin. On January 16, 1880, the faculty held an impressive memorial service for Ingalls, and only after it was over did word reach the University that the regent was still alive. Calling the offense a "wanton outrage of both public and private feeling," the faculty suggested that the regents expel Thacher and Meservey and, until the Board could act, suspended them for a year. But on May 1, after profuse apologies from the two, the faculty decided that since both of them had led exemplary lives both before and after the incident, the suspensions should be lifted.[39]

Even though a sizable number of students marched through downtown Lawrence to the beat of a drum to cheer Thacher and Meservey for their boldness, most of their contemporaries had better taste. But by the early 1890s the number of offenses among the men against good morals and manners—lounging in the local billiard parlors, drinking liquor, gambling, wenching—was on the rise.[40] Increasing too was the amount of campus violence which stemmed from an awakening pride in one's class. On May 1, 1891, the sophomores found atop Mount Oread a totem pole erected by the freshmen and juniors before which they were directed to bow. The sophomores interpreted the challenge as an invitation to a brawl, during which the pole was chopped down with an ax and the flag at its apex was hoisted above the University Building; in the late afternoon there was another bloody, bruising scrimmage. In 1892 the seniors were allied with the sophomores against the other two classes in a battle that lasted all morning and ended from weariness and pain as much as from faculty decree. Every May 1 for the next dozen years was riot day. And since fighting was fun, there were also class brawls on other occasions. When the seniors held an evening reception in Spooner Library on February 16, 1895, other students raided the party and tried to batter down the front doors, force locked windows, scale the porch, and seize the University powerhouse. During the ensuing battle one of the attackers chopped through the electrical power lines. By the early twentieth century the classes were liable to fight on any occasion; at least once there was a freshman-sophomore clash in chapel in which the faculty members who tried to intervene got black eyes for their efforts; and there was a regular fall riot. A sophomore circular of 1904 ran:

> Ye Odorous offal of the barn yards of Kansas,
> baffling mysteries of the Odorless Companies, known
> only by your vile stink and hence called
> FRESHMEN
> TO HELL WITH YOU
> How came you thus to sneak and crawl on the Campus;
> God! the gall, of a lot of sniveling, wild-eyed,
> asinine and wallowing hybrid, dirty swine.
> Get ye back into your bottles,
> With your hides of many mottles,
> Your advent upon the campus
> Is against K.U. a crime

and went on to challenge the newcomers to a battle royal later in September at which they promised to kill them.[41]

Such activities were scarcely the unexceptional deportment the faculty had spoken of in 1884, and because the students could not be trusted, the professors had to intervene to restore peace and order. During the 1890s, however, they moved slowly and carefully. Class spirit had value, after all, and strict regulations suddenly imposed might produce a reaction that the faculty could not control. The first step was to increase the amount of nonfaculty or indirect supervision and to put more emphasis on agencies that fostered a decorous student life, such as the YMCA and the YWCA. The second was to negotiate with the students, and this led to the introduction of student government.

Although the men were more troublesome, the women's welfare, their guidance and protection, came first. Chancellor Lippincott had hoped to secure a preceptress who might teach a few classes, but whose main duty would be to provide such "consultation, advice, and oversight of the young ladies as might be found needful in a coeducational institution." But neither he nor Chancellor Snow could find a suitable foster mother, nor could they find funds for the women's dormitories they hoped to build. In 1892 faculty wives, led by Mrs. Snow, formed the Women's League. Modeled after an organization at the University of Michigan, it was an association of all the women of the University community which held social, cultural, and religious meetings and offered the female undergraduates both friendship and advice.[42]

In the early twentieth century University authorities extended organized moral guidance to the men as well. Chancellor Snow and his faculty had done little more than exhort them to be good, but his successor, Frank Strong, while continuing Snow's pleas—"I . . . urge upon you the deepest and strongest kind of spiritual life and activity," he told students in a typical statement at the opening convocation in 1905—knew that he had to do more. With the cooperation of interested faculty members, Lawrence ministers, and the campus YMCA and YWCA there appeared a comprehensive blueprint for orientation and social order that students could use if they felt the need. Older students met arriving freshmen at the depot and advised them where they could find room and board in clean, Christian homes. Strong and his colleagues put new vigor into the daily volunteer chapel services, imported more interesting speakers, and urged attendance. Names of students who had denominational preferences were sent to the Lawrence churches, which then invited students to worship services. Although the YMCA had had a chapter on campus since 1882 and the YWCA since 1886, they had lacked members and influence. But with Strong's support the associations vivified themselves, and by 1912 were sponsoring regular Bible study and discussion groups throughout the year and importing speakers on subjects ranging from the dangers of premarital sexual activity to the application of Christian ethics in business. A growing number of students took advantage of the opportunities.[43]

Yet moral suasion and aids to Christian living were never enough. In September, 1905, with the fall freshman-sophomore scrap under way, Strong started along the path of negotiation with the students. By executive decree and general consent there had been no May Day riot that year, and now Strong called representatives of both classes together and used his considerable moral force and personal charm to secure a pledge of peace. In later years sophomores would continue to taunt the freshmen and force them to wear distinguishing caps, but the days of mass violence were over. Strong thought the result a "distinct and noteworthy advance . . . in the spirit of the University and in the desire for law and order."[44]

Negotiating with students and letting them negotiate with each other before the battle was joined, rather than merely forbidding the conflict or letting it occur and then punishing the worst offenders, was a new way of treating them. During the next three years both Strong and the undergraduates grew increasingly enthusiastic about the idea that students had a legitimate role to play in their own government. Actually, the student government movement had begun among the sororities on campus in 1905. In response to the urgings in 1902 and 1903 of national intersorority meetings, whose delegates sought ways to eliminate criticism, especially of undignified rushing and pledging, Kansas sororities formed a Pan-Hellenic Association to bind the members to common rushing and pledging practices and to make rules and regulations for the group. Chancellor Strong gave the Association full support.[45]

Two years later he helped organize a similar group for the fraternities. Himself a member of Psi Upsilon, Strong thought that fraternities and sororities were already or might become a disintegrating force in college life, that they did little to elevate the University's cultural and moral tone, and that they tended to discourage loyalty to the institution as a whole. His chance to improve them came in the spring of 1907 after a wild party by the members of the local chapter of Theta Nu Epsilon. Organized on campus in the 1892–1893 year, TNE was an interfraternity fraternity whose members were given even more than most brethren to booze, sex, and general jollity. An investigation of the party led to a meeting between fraternity leaders and the regents in April, at which the Board members told the students to be less clannish and more active in campus affairs, and the leaders promised that they and their members would withdraw from TNE. Strong took up the regents' theme in his convocation address the following fall,[46] and the fraternity men got the message. In October and November two representatives from each of the eight houses met to form a Pan-Hellenic Council, whose announced purposes were to regulate the fraternities and incorporate them more fully into University life; its unannounced purpose was to stave off administrative wrath, to reform from within to forestall reformation from without. The fraternities' good faith, however, remained to be proved. After the Board of Regents refused a petition to reinstate TNE on campus even though its members promised to behave, the organization returned clandestinely, and by January, 1910, it was common knowledge that the brothers were planning a large party, which would have been outright defiance of Strong and the other regents. Strong warned them against it and in March the Board formally barred TNE "or substantially the same society under any other name" from the University.[47] But the prohibition had no lasting effect; TNE was on campus to stay.

If the fraternities and sororities could have their Pan-Hellenic groups, perhaps the whole student body could have a self-government organization. The first attempt to provide one, however, failed for want of interest. Early in 1908 the University Council inquired into practices at other universities while conferring with campus leaders. Then the students wrote a constitution to submit to a mass meeting of the student body in May. Very few undergraduates voted, however, and the movement languished for a year.[48]

Chancellor Strong, supported by most of the faculty, revived it in the spring of 1909 by appointing two committees—of men and women—to prepare constitutions. The men students approved theirs in April and the women followed suit in May. Manifesting as much the desires of Chancellor Strong and the regents as those of the students, the men's Student Council hopefully would "draw the men of the University into closer relationship," promote unity among the schools, foster closer "relations and acquaintances" between students and faculty, further the cause of a student union, conduct campaigns for the University's support, and in general reflect student sentiment in "all matters whatsoever of concern to the students and the University." Each school had at least one representative on the Council, and one additional representative for each hundred students; the students at large elected the officers. At its semimonthly meetings the Council had power to enact conduct regulations, voice student opinion to the University's faculty and officers, and act as a board of arbitration and settlement in case of trouble between groups of students. It could organize a student union and solicit funds, call mass meetings to consider subjects of concern, and consider and settle all matters referred to it by any of the University's governing bodies. Yet because the Student Council existed by executive permission rather than by any inherent right of student self-government, it could do nothing that would conflict with rules passed by the faculties of the schools, the University Council, the chancellor, or the regents.[49]

The Women's Student Government Association was organized somewhat differently. Its purposes were more limited: to foster among the women a "feeling of mutual responsibility, and a high regard for both liberty and order," to maintain "high standards of living and scholarship," and to promote loyalty to the University. Within those boundaries the Association had about the same powers as the Council. But all of the women students in plenary session, rather than representatives, were to pass legislation. Executive power was in the hands of an Executive Council consisting of a president, a vice-president from each school with at least fifty women students, a secretary, a treasurer, and two representatives from each class.[50]

While the Board of Regents routinely approved the WSGA constitution that summer, it was more suspicious of the men and delayed authorization for two years. But both groups were in operation in the 1911–1912 academic year. Publicly the regents were well pleased, telling the governor in their biennial report for 1912 that the entire University was grappling with the "difficulties and dangers" of student social life "in a genuine and effective fashion." But not everyone was as happy as they. "What's the matter with K.U.?" grumbled an alumnus of the class of 1896 as he contemplated the student body in 1910. "The May Pole scrap is gone, or emasculated into 'Ring around the Rosy'; the junior prom and the senior reception are as tame as a pink tea in an Old Ladies Home; even our old yell is sung instead of shouted. The student body seems to be composed of the most lady-like and Lord Fauntleroyed individuals in the world. . . . The authorities seem to think that the University is a school for namby-pambies and Lizzie boys, whereas all should know it is the youth of strength and originality, the youth who is full of life, who sometimes gets into mischief or more trouble, who is really worthwhile in this vigorous world. K.U. has not grown as it should; we do not change the fact by shutting our eyes. The chief reason is that young men of talent and energy will not go to a school which bears so close a resemblance to a 'female seminary.' "[51]

Although the student body was changing, it was not merely because of efforts of the authorities and their student allies. By 1909 or 1910 students were tending to eschew violence for more sophisticated recreations. A new extravagance was apparent at Kansas, as at every other American college and university, Chancellor Strong told State Senator Charles Huffman in 1909. During the past six years personal wealth had increased greatly and people were eagerly spending it. "That tendency is sure to be reflected in the University, because what the parents do the children do." But Strong and other authorities, and many students, too, had been making every possible effort to restrain overindulgence, and the Chancellor claimed that student social life was basically "sound and wholesome." It was significant, however, that by that time the use of liquor and tobacco among the students was on the rise, that when the University Council sought to get the Junior Prom of 1911 to end at a seemly hour, they set three o'clock in the morning (otherwise it would have gone on till dawn), that in 1911 the regents were so concerned about licentiousness among the men that they asked for a full report on their physical condition, especially with reference to venereal disease.[52] Unlike the alumni of the nineteenth century, the graduates of more recent classes did not romanticize their college days as those of innocence, for their extracurricular activities were more likely to be those of society at large rather than peculiar college stunts or fights.

Yet variety was still the student body's most important characteristic. Intellectuals and aesthetes joined playboys and playgirls; the rich and poor met in class, if not socially; the University had both its mindless girls and its girl-less minds. If there were students with average grades, there were no average students. And spokesmen of the University felt this was as it should be. For when they talked of the benefits of the school to its students, the burden of their message was that the institution was there to serve the students as individuals according to the unique needs and desires of each.

13

Frank Strong and the Years of Growth

*A*LTHOUGH the University of Kansas was a university in fact when Frank Strong became chancellor in 1902, it had all sorts of inadequacies. Faculty salaries were too low, faculty members too few, buildings, equipment, and library books too scarce. The proper relation of the University to the state was still to be determined, especially in terms of the state-service work that so many other public universities were doing. While the University grew and prospered, many professors became disturbed by a lack of democracy in its internal government, and meanwhile its supporters both inside and outside the institution quarreled with their counterparts at the Agricultural College in Manhattan about the schools' legitimate spheres of work. Such problems meant that the University's nature was still to be determined.

The search for its essence would have to go forward without Chancellor Snow. By the spring of 1900 Snow was a tired, troubled man. The labors of a decade had depleted even his great store of energy and zest. In October, 1899, moreover, his only son, Will, a San Francisco newspaper reporter, had been swept off the deck of a transport ship, where he had been interviewing members of the Twentieth Kansas Regiment just returned from the Philippines, and had drowned. An extended summer vacation in 1900 failed to cure Snow's depression and ill health, and he had to extend his leave until June, 1901. Well before then, both he and the regents knew

220

this his years as chancellor were over; on May 20 he formally resigned to accept a new appointment as professor of natural history.[1]

Once more the regents had to face the difficult choice between elevating a faculty member and importing someone from outside. Had the faculty been united behind one man, the Board would probably have chosen him. The professors, however, were badly divided. The two leading candidates were William H. Carruth and Frank W. Blackmar. But Carruth and Snow had long led factions at odds about the relative position of the sciences and humanities in the University,[2] and without Snow's acquiescence at least, Carruth had no chance. Blackmar had made many enemies. According to a former student he believed the University during the Snow administration to be poorly organized and administered, thought many of his colleagues incompetent, and used class time to make mocking comments about both them and the Chancellor. Arthur G. Canfield believed that Blackmar's election would be a calamity, for either he would have to work against the "heavy odds of a faculty largely distrustful and lacking confidence, consequently lukewarm in support and discontented, if not positively antagonistic," or he would have to reconstruct the entire faculty.[3]

In August, 1901, the regents decided to look elsewhere, but the search at first was in vain. Several possible candidates declined as soon as they discovered they were under consideration: Vernon L. Kellogg, an alumnus and former Kansas faculty member, now professor of entomology at Stanford; James H. Canfield, now president of the Ohio State University; President Charles F. Thwing of Western Reserve University, who had rejected the chancellorship in 1890. Inside Kansas, Acting Chancellor William C. Spangler had some support, but not enough. As had been the case in 1889–1890, the regents' inability to find an able and willing man made many Kansans nervous; by February, 1902, they were writing to the regents to urge them to end the hiatus. "The subject of procuring a chancellor," Regent John W. Forney told Spangler, "seems to be the uppermost thought in the minds of the people."[4]

But in the nick of time the regents discovered two excellent candidates who were much interested in the Kansas position. One was President Joseph Swain of Indiana University, and the other President Frank Strong of the University of Oregon. Strong had the edge, both because he was more eager to leave Oregon than Swain to leave Indiana and because of superlative references from men at Yale, where Strong had taken a B.A. in 1884, an M.A. in history in 1893, and a Ph.D. in 1897, and had then taught history there for two years. Dean Andrew W. Phillips of the Yale Graduate School described Strong as a man of "remarkable scholarship, of almost superhuman energy and force," said that he was "most honorable and aboveboard in all his transactions," and that the university that secured him as president would "grow and thrive whether it wants to or not." Regent Scott Hopkins came away from a Yale visit very much impressed. "It would have done your soul good to have heard the emphatic statements about Strong of Oregon," he told Spangler. "*The Yale sentiment in his favor at New Haven was simply conclusive.*"[5]

In April the regents interviewed Strong, found that the recommendations seemed true and that his interest continued high, and offered him the position. When Strong accepted, it was hard to tell whether he or the Board was the more pleased. At Oregon since 1899 he had been a human dynamo whose currents of reform created powerful resistance. He had tried to give greater autonomy to schools and divisions, and conservative faculty members criticized the scheme as too elaborate and pretentious. He had tried to circumvent faculty factions by ignoring contending groups, refusing to call faculty meetings, and substituting for faculty decisions those of a hand-picked academic council, and the result was outrage. He had chafed against the regents' stringent financial management, which made him little more than a clerk, and in 1901 and 1902 he was arguing with them in behalf of a summer school for teachers. The Kansas salary of $4,500 a year, $1,000 more than he was getting at Oregon, made the position even more attractive. Kansans were as happy as he. The regents, students, faculty, alumni, newspaper editors, and citizens generally, Scott Hopkins wrote, were solidly behind him. Rejoicing that the "new regime" was starting under such favorable circumstances, Hopkins told him that he would "find everything ripe for the harvest."[6]

The reaper was a tall man of dignified bearing and distinguished mien. Born in Venice, New York, Strong was forty-three when he became chancellor. Interspersed with his career at Yale, he had taught school in Auburn, New York, read law with Sereno E. Payne, and joined the New York bar in 1886. For the next two years he practiced in Kansas City, Missouri, but gave it up to become principal of the St. Joseph high school from 1888 to 1892 and school superintendent in Lincoln, Nebraska, from 1892 to 1895. After taking his Ph.D. and teaching at Yale, he went to Oregon in 1899. Had Strong not become a university executive, he would certainly have had a productive career as a historian. Interested in the American colonial period, he had published a substantial article in 1898 in the American Historical Association's *Annual Report* on Oliver Cromwell's unsuccessful efforts to resettle many New Englanders in the Massachusetts Bay and New Haven colonies in Ireland and Jamaica. Less than a year later he published in the *American Historical Review* a vigorously written article on Cromwell's expedition to the West Indies in the mid-1650s. In 1898, too, Strong turned popular historian by writing a generally laudatory short biography of Benjamin Franklin as a volume in the American Character Study series, designed for schools, reading circles, and cultural uplift societies. During his brief career as a historian Strong also published numerous reviews of historical works, most of them in the *Yale Review*, and in 1902 he and Joseph Schafer, assistant professor of history at the University of Oregon, completed a high-school textbook, *The Government of the American People.*[7]

As chancellor of the University of Kansas for eighteen years Strong never deviated from the ideas expressed in his inaugural address in October, 1902. The ceremonies, occupying the University for four days, were on a grand scale. They included the dedication of the new Chemistry Building, a public address by Dean Le Baron R. Briggs of Harvard, concerts by the Kansas City Philharmonic Orchestra and members of the School of Fine Arts, a football game between the University and the Kansas City Medical College, and other ahtletic contests. The regents had even thought of inviting President Theodore Roosevelt, but scotched the idea lest his presence seem to convert an academic occasion into a political one. At the inauguration itself on Friday, October 17, in the hall of the unfinished Natural History Museum, Yale President Arthur T. Hadley delivered the main address, and there were speeches by Governor William E. Stanley, former Chancellor Snow, William H. Carruth for the faculty, and alumni and students. After a reception for Chancellor and Mrs. Strong that afternoon in Spooner Library, over a thousand people sat down to a "luncheon" in the evening.

After the meal two dozen speakers responded to as many nonalcoholic toasts.[8]

Frank Strong's ideas about education, described in his own address, were the result of his ideas about the worth of the individual human being and the proper connection between the individual and his society. A devout Baptist, Strong believed that the concept of human worth, though known to some of the ancient Greeks and Romans, really derived from the teachings of Jesus Christ. "When He proclaimed that man partook of the divine, that the whole world was a small price to pay for one soul, that men were on an equality before the judgment seat of God," Strong said, "He proclaimed the truth that makes men free." But the medieval Catholic Church, especially its schools and universities, he felt, had stifled individualism; and despite the emphasis on individualism in the Renaissance, the Reformation, and the Enlightenment, a true appreciation of the individual's inherent value had to await the birth and expansion of the United States. After 1830, with the rise of Jacksonian Democracy, the great migrations into the Mississippi Valley, and the renewed emphasis on the idea of natural rights, individualism at last became a reality.[9]

Yet the 1830s were also the start of an era of incredible material expansion—of such invention, technological change, and industrial-commercial activity as to "awaken the world." Darwinian-Spencerian ideas of competition and the survival of the fittest combined with that materialism to produce the unwholesome form of individualism that exalted the person at the expense of his social obligations. Educational institutions had experienced the shock: "Commercialism became rampant and the purely utilitarian idea in education was strongly felt." Fortunately, however, there had been a reaction against excessive individualism. "The whole modern movement," Strong asserted, "is away from extreme individualism and toward social unity." Educational institutions had to further it: the philosophy of education that regarded the "individual first of all in his social relations" had to be the "fundamental idea of our university training."[10]

From those ideas and Strong's own piety came the notion—the first that Strong offered about Kansas directly—that the University should inculcate the Christian virtues. No public institution, of course, could be sectarian or could engage in doctrinal controversy.

But by its "very atmosphere, by the purity of life of its Faculty, by the moral and religious wholesomeness of its entire . . . influence," the University should encourage the "deepest spiritual life and growth." The nation needed "educated Christian men" to solve its social problems; the University was the place to train men to a "sense of moral responsibility in government; for unselfish collective action for the good of the community; for self-denial for the collective honor of the State. . . ."[11]

In explaining what the University needed to lift up the mind and spirit, Strong was shrewdly honest. Rather than maintaining that the institution was great, he viewed it as beset with problems. First the school needed freedom from meddling and dictation by party politicians and religious sectarians in order that its faculty might teach the truth—even though truth, he confessed, was hard to define. Next it needed money in large amounts and from the proper source. That source was not the legislature, to which the University then had to turn every two years. Instead it was a percentage tax upon property in the state that would automatically increase with the state's wealth and the University's needs. Calling his audience's attention to the University's greatest deficiencies, Strong bluntly declared that the library was entirely inadequate for graduate and "advanced undergraduate work in its highest sense," and said that unless it became adequate, Kansas would simply have to give up its hopes of "filling the real university field" and ranking among the nation's great universities. The same was true of the faculty. Keenly aware of the importance of graduate study and faculty research, Strong asserted that the University's best interests required the professors to do far less undergraduate teaching in order to work at the higher intellectual level—which would require a tremendous increase in funds.[12]

In return for freedom and more money Strong promised that the University would give much to the state. The Chancellor desired that the University affect the life of Kansas at "every vital point," that it be the servant of the commonwealth. It would help the high schools by training teachers, carefully refrain from intruding on the work of the State Normal School at Emporia and the Agricultural College at Manhattan, and cooperate with the private denominational colleges to provide Kansans with an integrated educational system. Because many of the "pressing problems of the future" were economic and industrial, the University should both prepare students to solve them and, through faculty research and the dissemination of information, attack them directly. And Strong also argued that from the University would radiate influences that would help to purify the state's political life. "Men and women of Kansas," he concluded, "do you love this State? Do you love its broad prairies where in the springtime the wandering breath of God stirs the perfume in a million flowers? Do you love the memory of its pioneers, their struggles, their hardships, their tears? Do you love your children? Then do not allow the University of Kansas to miss its destiny."[13]

The inaugural address was the man himself: a mixture of idealism and practicality, he was obsessed with the idea of democracy, committed to Christianity as a means of both personal and social salvation, and intent on developing the University to the maximum. Strong never believed, moreover, in a circuitous approach to the institution's problems. At one point he drew up a list of qualities of the perfect "university administrator," and he always attempted to manifest them. Their essence was that he should never waver from the right. In all his dealings he should have no friends and no enemies. He should be open and frank in all his decisions, loyal to both superiors and inferiors, ready to fight for his faculty and employees at the drop of a hat, and immovable when faced with threats to his school's freedom and independence. He should also be a true democrat who considered both the full professor and the janitor his equals and a good Christian who did nothing from motives of personal advantage and never spared himself work.[14]

Strong should have added that a good administrator was also a man who kept himself and his institution favorably in the public eye, for from the start he was intent on expanding the University's publicity and improving its image. In 1899 Chancellor Snow had begun the *University News-Bulletin*, a monthly publication describing and praising the University sent free to Kansas newspaper editors with full permission to print its items without crediting the source. At Strong's urging the *News-Bulletin* became more direct, more vigorous. "Chancellor Frank Strong, of the State University, seems to be the right man for the place," ran a typical story in December, 1902. "Under his administration the University has taken on new life, and the Alumni are manifesting great interest in the welfare of their *Alma Mater*. . . . Friends of the University are more than pleased with the new administration and confidently expect an attendance of 2,000 in the next five years." In February, 1904, Strong interested himself in the University catalogue, which he thought inaccurate, sloppy, and incommensurate with the school's size and dignity, and over the years its physical appearance, prose style, and accuracy all improved.[15]

Potentially more important than the *News-Bulletin* or the catalogues was a reinvigorated Alumni Association laboring for the University's prosperity and informed by an alumni magazine. Even after the reorganization of the 1880s the Alumni Association was torpid; its meetings transacted no important business and the organized alumni were not active in the University's support. But in June, 1902, with the new chancellor chosen and a certain excitement in the air, the executive committee, led by chairman Olin Templin, got alumni approval to begin a publication. Edited by Professor R. D. O'Leary of the English Department and the class of 1893, the first issue of the *Graduate Magazine* appeared in October, 1902. In it and later numbers the alumni found articles on the University's contemporary development, historical features, and notes on alumni activities and achievements. Then, in 1905, the executive committee won support for a new constitution, aimed at making the Association both more permanent and more active. Henceforth the Association would have a permanent, paid secretary—Leon N. Flint was the first—who would also oversee the *Graduate Magazine*. In his first message to the alumni the following fall, Flint tried to prod them from their apathy by reminding them of the loyalty they owed the University which had "helped them to be capable men and women; which has helped them to *live*." But the alumni's desire to cooperate continued to be weak, and strengthening it would take time.[16]

In the years between 1907 and 1911 the University systematized its all-important newspaper propaganda. The University Council formed a Committee on Publicity in the fall of 1907, and the following January its members recommended that the *News-Bulletin* be continued, that engravings of Mount Oread's scenes and people be sent to newspapers, and that free stereotype plates be sent to the small weekly newspapers which could not afford to set into type the lengthy articles that the *News-Bulletin* carried.[17] A year later the

University organized a Department of Journalism, one of whose main tasks was to be the preparation and dissemination of publicity. Since 1903 students heading for newspaper work after graduation had taken recommended courses from existing departments and also attended special lectures by editors and journalists on "The Ethics of Journalism," "Newspaper Organization and Administration," "What a Newspaper Man Should Be," and similar subjects; now the major became a separate department. Charles M. Harger, editor of the Abilene *Reflector*, was its chairman, but Leon N. Flint, assistant professor of journalism, was really in charge of the local work.[18]

But with Flint busy with the *Graduate Magazine*, the Department needed a full-time resident chairman. In June, 1911, the regents approved a plan whereby the Department would be the University's publicity bureau, and in the summer hired as its head Merle Thorpe, who for several years had been in charge of the Department of Journalism at the University of Washington. Thorpe proved to be just the man the University needed. The purpose of University publicity, he thought, was to interpret the institution to the taxpayers and squash news that would hurt it: to "prevent . . . the circulation of sensational and foolish stories reflecting on the good name of the University." In his efforts during his first year Thorpe left no Kansas editor unturned. He and his students divided the state's 690 newspapers into four categories ranging from consistently friendly to consistently unfriendly to the University. To each of the editors went a letter explaining the Department's work, and to the unfriendly newspapermen went Thorpe himself to enlighten and plead. As part of its regular work the Department of Journalism sent out a daily newsletter to the state's seventy dailies, a six-column news bulletin to the weeklies, and from forty to fifty special articles each week to papers that were indifferent to the University's welfare but would print material about hometown students. The news stories exploited every department of the University; there were special articles by faculty members, and features about the administration, regents, students, alumni, and even the registrar. At the same time Thorpe got the Lawrence commercial clubs to bring pressure on the often critical city papers. He induced students in 102 high schools to submit news to the *Kansan*, changed it from a triweekly to a daily, spread 1,300 copies of each issue to editors, high schools, and friends around the state, and began a *Summer Session Kansan*. He also brought the 1912 annual meeting of the State Editorial Association to the University. Between September, 1911, and October, 1912, the state's newspapers published 3,250 columns of official University publicity, at the average rate of $10 a column, Thorpe said, the school had received over $32,000 worth of free news, all of it favorable. Every paper in the state had printed at least one item about the University. At the end of his first year, moreover, Thorpe was projecting a great expansion in the work.[19]

Whatever the favorable effects of such propaganda, there was one considerable problem that general publicity could not solve: the improvement of relations between the University and the private denominational colleges. Although sectarians and moralists continued to argue that godlessness, infidelity, and corrupting immorality reigned on Mount Oread,[20] the main trouble between the University and the colleges was competition for students and the kind of sympathy from which money flowed. Over and again the Chancellor did his best to allay the fears and win the support of the college presidents . He and his University, he said, valued the private schools, and hoped that the relation between them would always be one of "helpfulness and cooperation." If Kansans could be made to realize the importance of higher education, he believed, they would help all the institutions in the state. "The moment the University . . . is advanced to a right condition of income and equipment," he told President Nathan J. Morrison of Fairmount College in Wichita in 1904, "that moment the friends and alumni of the other institutions that are upon a secure footing will demand and get a larger income and a more adequate equipment." Were it within his power, he told President Lemuel H. Murlin of Baker University in Baldwin in 1904, "I would increase many times over the endowment of every college in Kansas, and whenever I get a chance to assist in such a matter I always do so."[21]

Such assurances pleased the college presidents. While they all retained their own ideas about the proper relations between their schools and the University, they remained generally cordial. "Anything I can do, either personally or officially in advancing the interest of the institution over which you preside," President John D. S. Riggs of Ottawa University told Strong in 1904, "will be cheerfully done. I see no reason why your interests and ours should in any way conflict." Riggs spoke for most of his colleagues at the time that Strong was preparing to go before the legislature of 1905, and thus Strong had reason to feel that his assurances had produced good results.[22]

For all his solicitude, however, Strong still seemed at times to wish to reduce the denominational schools to junior colleges feeding upperclassmen and graduate students to the University. Although he dared not press openly, he sometimes suggested that the ideal relation between the colleges and the University would be to have college students take only the general, introductory education of the freshman and sophomore years. "Our young men must have the best and highest training in science, history, economics and sociology that the largest resources of the state can give," he told a correspondent in 1903, and the colleges were not equal to the task. Juniors and seniors should probably forsake the colleges for the University, there to take their "more advanced and specialized work." The arrangement would enable the University to decrease or perhaps end the work of the first two years and swell the size of the colleges. But, knowing that it would also reduce their stature, Strong did not try to implement the idea.[23]

To be even more cooperative he and the University Council created an accrediting system for the colleges. Its purposes were to ease the transfer of college students to the University and to express Strong's own conviction that the University's standards should prevail throughout the state. In 1907 the Council established a Committee on Visitation and Affiliation and another on Advanced Standing. They first inspected the colleges and their courses and then recommended to the Council that their work either be accepted at face value or be penalized by a certain percentage of hours as inadequate; the Advanced Standing Committee implemented the Council's decisions when students applied for admission. Most colleges received full accreditation and thus became—on paper at least— the equals of the University's own College. As a result relations continued to improve.[24]

But for all the idealism, propaganda, and happier college relations, the real test of a successful chancellor was his ability to squeeze money from the legislature. Here Strong proved himself both able and lucky. He came along at a good time. During his first decade economic conditions in the state, on the upswing since 1897, continued to improve. In 1909 the value of all farm products in Kansas soared for the first time over $500,000,000; as prices rose, so did profits. The growing manufacturing and extractive industries gave the economy a healthy diversity. Between 1909 and 1914, moreover, the relation between prices received and retail costs proved almost ideal. Prospects for the future seemed excellent.[25]

Between 1903 and 1911 Strong and the Board of Regents confronted five legislatures, and the other regents proved as eager as the Chancellor to get an ever larger share of the state's wealth. Late in the Snow administration the University at last got rid of its Populist regents—William Rogers, James P. Sams, and Henry S. Clarke— and passed back into purely Republican hands. In 1901 Governor William E. Stanley appointed Scott Hopkins, a University alumnus (1881) and now president of the Horton First National Bank, to complete the term of Charles F. Scott, who had resigned, and chose William C. Spangler, Ernest L. Ackley, and Thomas M. Potter to regular three-year terms. Spangler had served before, Ackley was also an alumnus (1897) and a partner in a prosperous Concordia law firm, and Potter, a graduate of Michigan State College in 1867, was a farmer and stockman of Peabody. With them served Frank G. Crowell and Josephus W. Forney, whose terms would expire in 1903.[26]

Unfortunately for continuity Ackley died in 1901 and Spangler in 1902. Their replacements, who served out the full terms to 1905, were Charles N. Converse, a Burlington banker, and Alexander C. Mitchell, a well-known Lawrence lawyer and an alumnus (1889) of the Law School. In 1903 Governor Willis J. Bailey gave Hopkins a full term of his own, reappointed Crowell, and added Thomas W. Butcher, an alumnus in the class of 1889, now principal of the Sumner County High School and one of the state's more notable secondary educators. To that group—Potter and Mitchell were reappointed in 1905—Governor Edward W. Hoch added William Allen White, editor of the Emporia *Gazette*, who would become one of the most famous of all Kansans. Though White did not graduate from the University, he was on Mount Oread from 1886 to 1889 and he ever after championed the University's welfare as he understood it. "Of course I am grateful," he told Governor Hoch. "It is the only job in Kansas I ever wanted, and the only one that I would take."[27]

All of these regents pleased Strong, for they were men much like himself—sensible, progressive, honest, and plain spoken. Nor was he disappointed in the regents appointed by Hoch in 1907 and by Governor Walter Roscoe Stubbs in 1909. With Butcher and Crowell resigning, Hoch chose J. Willis Gleed—the most loyal of all loyal alumni (1879), a partner in the large Topeka law firm of Gleed and Gleed, and an influential Republican politician—and William Y. Morgan, class of 1885 and editor of the Hutchinson *News*. Politically active, Morgan represented Reno County in the lower house of the state legislature from 1903 to 1910. Reappointing White, Stubbs also chose Leon S. Cambern, an Erie banker and Republican politician, and Charles F. Foley, a Law School graduate of 1884 now practicing in Lyons.[28]

Joining White, Foley, Cambern, and Hopkins, who was reappointed in 1911, were two more Stubbs appointees: James A. Kimball of Salina, a man with no college education who had become the wealthy president of the Salina Candy Company and was active in all sorts of civic enterprises, and Rodney A. Elward of Castleton. Elward had an LL.B. from the University of Wisconsin and was a farmer and stockman, an independent scholar with a huge personal library, and an amateur poet.[29]

Frank Strong not only told the legislature of 1903 that his University was in danger of sliding from the third rank of state universities—where stood the likes of Virginia, Washington, Colorado, and Utah—into the fourth, but claimed that it was on the brink of total disaster. Unless the legislators were generous, he wrote, "the doom of the university is sealed." To save it, the regents asked a fantastic $619,000 for the biennium, up $264,000 over the grant of 1901. To $205,000 a year for salaries and maintenance, they added $80,000 for a gymnasium (though, returning to reality, they later dropped it), $70,000—later increased to $80,000—for a law building, and another $25,000 for completing the Chemistry Building. But the measure suffered from a Republican factional struggle between long-time Boss Cyrus Leland of Troy and an anti-Leland group calling themselves the "Boss-busters" and advocating a more efficient, honest, and responsive government. Anti-Leland men controlled the Senate, which passed the University bill in two days without amendment,[30] but in the House the Boss's faction was still supreme. Leland cared little for the University. In 1902 and again in 1903 Strong had commended the school to him, but the Boss replied that it mattered little to him whether the institution went up or down. "I do not care to take any active interest for the University," he said curtly, "and there is no good reason why I should." The only thing the two men could agree on was that, to reduce the charge upon the state, students should pay a reasonable tuition fee, which would require amending the Moody Act of 1889.[31]

Faced by such opposition, the University's officers and supporters worked mightily. They wrote personal letters to the legislators, lobbied in Topeka, filled the newspapers with propaganda. By special invitation the Joint Ways and Means Committee toured Mount Oread on February 6. They received a dinner at the Eldridge Hotel and the benefits of a pep rally in Fraser Hall. With the auditorium jammed with students and faculty and the walls shaking with songs and yells, it would have been a foolish lawmaker who did not promise to do his best for the University.[32]

But back in Topeka things were less promising. The House scrapped the Senate bill and substituted a measure of its own, which the Senate then approved. Instead of $205,000 a year for maintenance, there was $150,000; instead of $80,000 for a law building there was but $50,000, which would be available only after July 1, 1904. In the act, however, the legislature directed the University to charge a matriculation fee of $5 for Kansans and $10 for non-Kansans, and "incidental"—really tuition—fees in the schools. For in-staters and out-of-staters the respective yearly incidental fees were $10 and $40 for both the College and the Engineering School; $25 and $50 for the Law School; $30 and $50 for the Pharmacy and Medical schools; and $10 and $20 in the Summer Session. The fees in the School of Fine Arts remained the same, although the University had the power to raise them. Such incidental fees were to be in lieu of all others.[33]

During the coming year the fees would yield the University some $20,000,[34] but the legislature had been disappointing nonetheless. Strong wrote obligatory letters to thank key legislators for their help, but his comments were as much reproof as compliment. "It is of great assistance to us," he told Cyrus Leland, "to know that men of influence and power in the state are desirous of doing for the University whatever may appear to them as necessary." What Strong wanted, though, was that the legislators accept the University leaders' own view of what was necessary, and his statement was an admission of failure.[35]

In his biennial report for 1904 Strong said as bluntly as he could without being offensive that the legislators really had no right to decide for themselves what amounts the University should get. The Chancellor and the regents "alone know the conditions in a large and complex university," and everyone else should follow their lead. Now was the time for Kansas to do "large things" for the University, he said, for the state was prosperous—its wealth had reached $2,000,000,000—and the needed appropriations would not be felt. What was necessary was about $217,000 a year in general maintenance, $44,000 more for completing and equipping various buildings and buying more land for a cramped campus, and two new buildings. One was a gymnasium-auditorium, which would both give the University community a place to meet *en bloc*, and improve student health; under the strain of "severe mental work," Strong said, many students, especially girls, were becoming "physically weak and nerveless." The other was an engineering structure to house the School's separate departments and care for its increasing number of students. "Competent judges," Strong said, had declared the School among the five most efficient in the nation, and "we want to keep it up to its past standard." The Chancellor also urged the legislature to commit itself to an accelerated rate of physical growth. The two buildings were long overdue to place the University in "condition for efficient work. The erection of one building in a biennium no longer suffices to keep pace with the rapid growth of the institution."[36]

Despite the numerous successes of anti-Leland Boss-busters at the polls in 1904, the legislature exacted a price—the engineering building—for giving the University most of what it wanted. The lawmakers were simply not ready to give the University more than one building every two years. They appropriated the requested maintenance funds, $100,000 for the gymnasium-auditorium, $15,000 for completing and equipping the Law Building, and $12,000 to buy more land. The act also continued the incidental fees for students, though it reduced some of those required of non-Kansans. On March 7, three days after Governor Hoch signed it, the University staged an afternoon victory celebration complete with band music, speeches, and shouts of joy.[37]

If the events of 1905 were a triumph, those of 1907 were amazing, and those of 1909 all but incredible. Never satisfied, Strong wrote in his report for 1906 that even the generosity of the previous legislature had not enabled the University to regain its former position of eminence. "We labor under the handicap all the time," he said in words that should at once have become the University's motto, "of having to make up for lost time." From 1902 to 1906 the student body had grown by a third to almost 1,700, and there would probably be about 2,250 by the end of the 1908–1909 year. Already classes were too large, the faculty too small, the buildings too cramped. Now for the first time Strong and the other regents asked —in addition to $245,000 a year for general maintenance—that the legislature commit itself to a planned program of physical expansion. While he knew that no legislature could bind another, he still asserted that the University's building needs demanded $100,000 a year for the next five years. A faculty investigating committee had determined that four structures were necessary in the immediate future—one for the Engineering School generally; another for mining engineering, mineralogy, and geology; a third for the Medical School; and the last for administrative offices and classrooms. The legislature of 1907 should grant $200,000 for the first two. "We are living in the twentieth century," the Chancellor said, "and cannot do things on the basis of the first half of the nineteenth century. There are only two ways of dealing with the emergency—either to do away with the institution and hand it over to some other agency, which is unthinkable, or else adequately provide for its present and future needs."[38]

Governor Hoch agreed, and the legislature proved as cooperative as one could ask. Condemning what he described as the politically inspired cries for economy of the past fifteen years, Hoch said that the time had come for an educational "catch up"; he knew of "no higher mission of an administration," he said, "than to keep public money out of the unholy hands of grafters and boodlers and to put it into the clean hands of honest and conscientious custodians of state interests." In a strikingly routine fashion the appropriation bill went through both houses without a change. It granted over $780,000 for the coming biennium, including $245,000 a year for general maintenance and the $200,000 for the two engineering buildings.[39]

But with the state ever more prosperous and the University's needs still pressing, the regents had just begun to ask. The major theoretical emphasis of Strong's 1908 report was that the school required a permanent income derived from a regular property tax. At present, he said, the institution's leaders had to act "largely as if the state of Kansas and its University would be wiped off the map every two years," making plans impossible. Given no guarantees of future support, it was a "matter of wonder" that the University existed at all.[40]

A mill tax, however, would require an amendment to the state constitution, and in the meantime Strong upped the earlier building sum of $100,000 a year for five years to $125,000 a year for ten. With that kind of money the University could procure a second chemistry building, a domestic-science structure, a second Medical School building, a new library, an athletic stadium, and new edifices for the social sciences and for ancient and modern languages. For the biennium immediately ahead the Board wanted $311,000 for buildings— including the first wing of an administration-classroom structure, a hospital and a dispensary for the Medical School, a women's dormitory, and an electrical engineering laboratory. Added to that sum was almost $718,000 for general maintenance and about $80,000 for repairs and improvements. The precise request was $1,108,859, an increase of $328,025, or 42 percent, over the appropriation of 1907. Such was the jump that it introduced a new order of magnitude into the appropriation question. To get the amount, the whole University community worked heroically. In addition to an expanded letter-writing and lobbying campaign, on February 12, 1909, the University played host to the entire legislature at ceremonies commemorating the centennial of Abraham Lincoln's birth. The University's officers had also invited all state officers, the faculty and student body of the Agricultural College, friends of the school from all over the state, and all the citizens of Lawrence. Before and after the speeches and ceremonies, held in the new Robinson Gymnasium, the legislators toured the campus and talked with the faculty and students, and there was a great banquet served by the coeds. Special trains bore the legislators from Topeka to Lawrence and back; voluntary subscriptions from virtually every faculty member and officer covered the cost.[41]

The result was an appropriation bill which, if it fell short of the

University's requests, was nevertheless impressive. It granted the general maintenance requests down to the last dollar, $125,000 for the first wing of the classroom-administration building, $50,000 for the Medical School hospital, and $10,000 for electrical engineering equipment. In all the amount was $982,000 for the biennium.[42]

Yet the institution was still not what Strong and the Board of Regents wished it to be. "Expansion is the law of life and growth in an institution like the University of Kansas," Strong wrote relentlessly in 1910. A university that "does not feel in its veins the rising of the sap of vigorous life that leads to a true enlargement is on the way to decay and death." The sap of life allegedly required an infusion of slightly over $1,225,000 for the next two years—$870,000 for general maintenance, $135,000 for long-needed building and wiring repairs, $42,500 to start the central section of the administration building, $100,000 for a Medical School hospital, and $75,000 for a women's dormitory. Instead of having campus ceremonies and pep rallies to influence the legislature, Strong told the students that it was "entirely right and proper" for them to make the University's needs known to both their parents and their county legislators.[43] But both the House and Senate Ways and Means committees were eager to reduce the requests, and after they and the other legislators had haggled their way to a compromise, the University had about $1,020,000, a very slight advance over the 1909 figure. Gone was the hospital, the dormitory, and about a third of the repairs and improvements requests. On March 14 the bill went to Governor Stubbs, who was already worried about the legislature's generosity to all state agencies and also was hoping for election to the United States Senate when his gubernatorial term ended. It pleased him to champion economy. He therefore vetoed a $40,000 item for repairs and improvements for fiscal 1913.[44]

Whatever Frank Strong's frustrations and disappointments, by the end of his first decade as chancellor the University was in a far stronger material position than in 1902. Total income rose from some $219,000 in fiscal 1903 to over $606,000 in fiscal 1912,[45] and in area and buildings the Lawrence campus practically doubled in size. The Strong administration added about ninety-five acres to the original site as the campus expanded in the logical direction along the crest of Mount Oread to the west and down the slopes. Ten acres came by gift and forty by purchase from Frank B. Lawrence, a nephew of Charles and Sara Robinson, and the rest through other buys. In addition the University held some thirteen hundred acres of farmland northeast of the city on the far side of the Kansas River, bequeathed by Charles Robinson; about five acres in Rosedale, the gift of Simeon B. Bell; and a twelve-acre athletic field given in 1891 by Colonel John J. McCook.[46]

In the ten years after 1902, moreover, seven new structures rose on Mount Oread, in addition to the Natural History Museum which was under construction when Strong arrived. The legislature provided six, all of which fit in well with the rest of the crazy-quilt campus architecture. First came the Law Building, an "American Renaissance" structure north of Fraser Hall, designed by State Architect John F. Stanton after consultation with Dean Green. For its façade the building had the portico of a Grecian Ionic temple, complete with steps leading up to the entrance and four large pillars. A two-story structure—three counting the windowed basement—120 by 60 feet, it had offices, classrooms, a moot-court room, and the large library that the Law School had lacked for so long. "The dream of twenty years has become a reality," Green said in his address at the dedication. "The hope of every law instructor and every law student has been consummated. We meet today to celebrate the fulfillment of the dream and the achievement of our hopes."[47]

Green Hall, as it was later named, was also the first step in the fulfillment of a comprehensive plan for the University's physical development prepared by Kansas City landscape architect George E. Kessler at the commission of the Board of Regents in 1904. Kessler drew up a most impressive design, in which Mount Oread would be crowned with buildings, at whose center would be a massive classroom and administration structure facing north. Up the slope in front of it, as the main approach to the University, would be lovely lawns, groves, drives, and walks. Kessler's original plan had the athletic field on the McCook land to the right of the main entrance and the gymnasium on the left. But he and the regents changed their minds: if the gymnasium were on the crest of the bowl-shaped hill to the south, the playing fields could be located below it.[48]

Even before construction of the gymnasium began, the regents decided to name it for Charles and Sara Robinson, partly to commemorate their past services, and partly to soothe Sara's indignation at what she conceived to be undue pressure by Chancellor Strong on Frank B. Lawrence to sell his land cheaply. Sara was thrilled. All the "simplicity and humility born in me, comes to the front," she told Strong, and she thought her husband was at last getting from the regents a "fitting acknowledgement for his work for Kansas,—for the great school as well,—for his bravery, patience, calm endurance, courtesy and unselfishness." Indeed, the building, with an exterior like a squat castle, complete with crenellated roofline, required only a little imagination to be seen as the stronghold of the embattled Robinsons. In the basement were a swimming pool and men's and women's locker rooms; the first floor was the gymnasium itself, 107 by 70 feet, complete with folding doors in the center to separate the sexes; and the main part of the second floor was an auditorium-with-stage seating twenty-five hundred people. Surrounding the open spaces on both floors were office, class, and special game and exercise rooms.[49]

Three more buildings appeared in the next three years, all west of Robinson Gymnasium, and all for the benefit of the School of Engineering. In designing them, State Architect John F. Stanton, together with Dean Frank O. Marvin and Professor Erasmus Haworth, followed, more or less, the architectural style of the gymnasium, something called Collegiate Gothic, which was suggested by English Tudor architecture and was popular at the time in colleges and universities across the nation. In the fall of 1908 came a new power plant and mechanical engineering laboratory. Northeast of it was Haworth Hall, completed in 1909, a three-story structure, 110 by 60 feet, with an annex for mining and ore-dressing laboratories and facilities for faculty and students in mining engineering, geology, and mineralogy. And, most important, in 1910 there was Marvin Hall—named for the Dean—which was a splendid four-story building, 187 by 64 feet, with ample space for offices, classrooms, drafting rooms, a spacious library on the first floor and a commodious auditorium on the second. With considerable ingenuity Dean Marvin had planned the building so that the floors were supported mainly by load-bearing walls on both sides of the main corridor, making it possible to shift the room partitions to meet the School of Engineering's changing needs.[50]

According to George Kessler's plan, the center of the campus

The Kessler plan for the University (1904), looking south up the campus's northern hill. At the upper center is the proposed administration building; Spooner Library is at the extreme left.

was to be a huge central administration building. Strong and the other regents envisioned a "monumental affair," "one of the largest and most beautiful buildings in the state," which would "stand for a hundred years as the center of the University architecture as well as the University life" and would cost over $500,000. Believing the state architect incapable of doing their vision justice, they elected M. P. McArdle, a prominent St. Louis architect, professor of architecture at $2,400 a year, and gave him the design as his main duty. He planned a grand Classical-Renaissance structure to stand west of the Chemistry Building. The center section, to contain administrative offices, was four stories tall, with elegant pillars on the façade; through a magnificent dome in the center, light would fall on a rotunda sixty feet in diameter. On either side of the central section would be smaller sections, two stories high, holding an art gallery and the classical museum; and beyond them would be two three-story wings, 170 by 70 feet, for classrooms.[51]

From the start, however, economic difficulties stalked the project. The legislature of 1909 appropriated only $125,000 for the east wing, which was too little for the structure McArdle and the regents had in mind and thus forced an immediate scaling down. Then the regents could get only $42,500 from the 1911 legislature to build the foundation of the central section, and during the next six years there was no work at all on the superstructure. But finally the legislature of 1917 made the west wing possible, and that of 1921 appropriated $250,000 to finish the main portion. During the Christmas vacation of 1923 the University's administrators moved their offices from Fraser Hall. Although the building had the general form that McArdle had proposed, it lacked everything that gave proportion and beauty to the original plan: the dome, the pillars, the impressive northern façade, the harmonious connecting sections between the main part and the wings; and while the original plan called for stone facing, the actual facing was an unappealing terra cotta. Yet two things about it were fortunate; it provided badly needed classroom and office space, and it did not set an architectural precedent.[52]

During the years of growth under Frank Strong, one other structure appeared—Myers Hall, housing the work of the Bible Chair. In 1901 the Women's Board of Missions of the Christian Church had established the chair entirely outside the University to offer courses in religious history and the Bible to interested students; its occupant was Dr. Wallace C. Payne. In addition to giving courses, Dr. and Mrs. Payne advised the students about their personal problems. Frank Strong thought the Bible Chair a nearly ideal solution to the question of religion in connection with state educational institutions. When the Women's Board of Missions proved unable to provide money for a building, Strong and the other regents sought private donors, the most generous of whom was Mrs. Mary Myers of Philadelphia, who gave $10,000; another $6,000 came from Mr. and Mrs. Charles A. Beurgan of Moline, Kansas. Completed in 1906, Myers Hall was a commodious modern structure north of Spooner Library, which provided living quarters for the Paynes as well as class, conference, and recreation rooms.[53]

In the buildings of the growing University a steadily increasing number of students and faculty worked. There were some thirteen hundred students in Strong's first year, over two thousand in 1907–1908, and twenty-five hundred in 1912–1913. The growth of the faculty kept pace, increasing from 89 in 1902–1903 to 179 ten years later.[54] Yet the University's physical growth, remarkable as it was, was matched by another impressive kind of expansion. Chancellor Strong, his fellow regents, and many faculty members were most enthusiastic about making the University as responsive as possible to the problems of the citizens. During Strong's first decade an increased amount of state-service work gave the institution a new dimension.

14

Society's Servant

IN 1910 Frank Strong pointed out in his biennial report that a new concept of the American state university was emerging. Formerly, he said, the public university's main purposes had been to teach students and foster faculty research. But now the state university was to be described by the "universality of its activities. A university like the University of Kansas," he said, "must be a universal institution, to contain in its plan of life all of the activities known to the civilization that it serves, and there is no man so humble that the University ought to disregard him, and no community within the confines of the commonwealth so far removed that the University should not send its men and women to serve it."[1]

In itself the idea of service was nothing new. Every spokesman of the University in the nineteenth century had emphasized that the school existed for the benefit of the society that sustained it. But Chancellor Strong desired to extend the idea and practice of state-service work to their outermost limits, wherever they might be. He and the men who worked with him wished both to enlarge on earlier precedents and to follow the example of other universities—especially Wisconsin—which were doing far more than Kansas. There was, of course, self-interest as well as altruism in the effort, for if the University did all it conceivably could for the people's welfare, the people might well reciprocate. When preparing financial requests for the legislature of 1911, Strong asked every faculty member for an "itemized, accurate and inclusive" list of what he had done for the state during the past year. "I want to stop forever the cry that the University does nothing for the State," by preparing an "overwhelming answer to the charge always made" that the institution was practically useless.[2] Yet here the interests of the University and those of the commonwealth were the same, and no one could doubt the Chancellor's sincere attachment to the idea of the broadened institution.

The emphasis on state-service work appeared in two kinds of activities, neither of which was entirely novel: extending education and information to people beyond the campus and performing direct services, mainly of a technical nature, which the citizens could not perform themselves.

During the 1890s the University had tried and failed to establish a popular and continuing "extension" service to educate the larger public. For years faculty members had given off-campus public lectures—Francis H. Snow, Lucien I. Blake, and James H. Canfield had been especially active—and by 1890 the demand for them had grown so great that the faculty published a list of twenty-six speakers from which interested groups might choose: William H. Carruth on "Goethe's *Faust*," for example, or Lewis L. Dyche on "Wild North American Mammals and Their Haunts," or "Hypnotism," by Olin Templin (who promised not to conduct public experiments). There were also musical recitals by members of the School of Fine Arts. Meanwhile the faculty had also been preparing reading courses for Kansans who could not attend the University. On request, said the catalogue of 1884, the professors would prepare lists of books and authorities, answer questions from readers, and visit groups of off-campus students.[3]

At the same time, other institutions were beginning to provide extension courses. Influenced in part by an extension movement begun in England in 1867, several eastern universities and library associations began courses of their own; that work, in turn, gave vigor to the Chautauqua movement, a sort of people's university which sponsored reading circles, a school of theology, and even a liberal arts college, staffed in the summer by a number of prominent university professors. After 1887 the members of the American Library Association, along with civic clubs, YMCA branches, and interested groups of citizens, began to offer lecture courses on all sorts of subjects; and they acquired many of their speakers from nearby colleges and universities. So great did enthusiasm become in higher educational institutions that in 1891 a National Congress on University Extension met in Philadelphia.[4]

Familiar with what was happening elsewhere, in the winter of 1890–1891 Chancellor Snow and several faculty members proposed courses of several lectures each to present subjects in greater depth than was possible with individual talks. While the series carried no credit at first, the faculty from the start was considering the possibility of full-credit courses as long as there was a public demand for them. Snow thought the University would be considerably embarrassed if it initiated courses that failed for want of patronage, and said that the success of such programs depended on "considerable agitation among the educated people of the state."[5] Such agitation came quickly. In the fall of 1891 Topeka City Librarian William Burr got together a group of 125 people desiring a lecture course by Lucien I. Blake on electricity and magnetism, and in Kansas City, Missouri, University alumnus John Sullivan led several civic leaders in forming a University Extension Society with about the same number of members, which chose Frank W. Blackmar to lecture on "Economic Problems." During the 1891–1892 academic year the University began six more courses: Charles G. Dunlap on nineteenth-century English literature and William H. Carruth on modern German literature in Kansas City; Edgar H. S. Bailey on "Chemistry in Everyday Life" in Olathe; a joint course in astronomy and geology in Wichita by Ephraim Miller and Samuel W. Williston. Meanwhile, Blake and Blackmar exchanged locations for their lectures.[6]

The rules for such courses, set by the faculty and regents in October, 1891, fixed the basic extension course at twelve lectures, for which the lecturer was to get $100. Students with a B.A. who completed nine twelve-lecture courses were to receive an M.A., while those without the B.A. would receive such undergraduate credit as seemed fitting. Extension work offered by other universities could not count for more than four-ninths of the work for a degree from Kansas, and all such work was subject to examination.[7]

Chancellor Snow praised the extension courses in his report of 1892, both for the obvious benefits they brought to the students and for their not-so-obvious benefits to the faculty. The professors re-

turned to Mount Oread, Snow averred, with a "healthful appreciation" of the fact that they were "servants of the state" and with their
minds "invigorated by contact with men and women in practical
life. They are thus kept from the danger of mental stagnation,
which sometimes threatens the isolated college professor who knows
no world but that of his college classes." Believing that the courses
should continue, yet recognizing that normal faculty teaching duties
restricted their number and locations, Snow suggested that Kansas,
like other institutions, should have several special extension instructors.[8]

Yet during the next six years extension work declined and died.
Nineteen different courses were available in 1891–1892, but the
people asked for only eight full courses and one half-course, and
only six faculty members participated. Things improved in 1893–
1894, when six professors offered fourteen courses attended by some
3,000 people, of whom 541 enrolled for credit, but in 1895–1896
only seven of the thirty-four courses offered were requested, and
the next year there were no courses at all. Several reasons explained
the diminution. There had never been much of a response from the
state at large; most of the courses were offered within a fifty-mile
radius of Lawrence, and once a given group had sponsored several
courses, interest fell off. A few of the more popular professors carried most of the load, moreover—of the fifty classes offered from
1891 to 1898 thirty-three were given by four men (Blackmar, Blake,
Dunlap, and Edwin M. Hopkins)—and the various extension societies seemed to desire to have a man no more than once or twice.
And with the student body almost doubling in size from 1891 to
1895, there was a very rapid increase in faculty work at the University itself.

But the Board of Regents really killed the extension program.
With the state less prosperous in the nineties and demands for economy ever more strident, the regents sought to make the faculty confine themselves more closely to their duties on Mount Oread. Starting in 1893 the Board required them to submit written reports of
their work and to suffer visitations to their classes; in 1896 the
regents sought to discover if there was some correlation between
the amounts of money the departments asked and the amounts of
work their members did; and in 1897, with legislators complaining
that the faculty was overpaid and underworked, the regents made it

impossible for them to earn much money lecturing. They passed a motion offered by Populist William Rogers putting a limit of $5 a lecture where admission was charged, thus making the maximum amount $60 for a twelve-lecture course. Two months later the Board restricted extension lectures to Saturdays to keep the faculty on Mount Oread during the rest of the week, and in March, 1898, it required faculty members to report every three months all the extra work they did, their receipts from it, and the way they spent the money. Hedged about by such restrictions, the professors lost interest in extension work.[9]

Another reason for the public's declining interest was that most of the courses were the nonvocational, "impractical" courses regularly offered in the College. When Frank Strong and his colleagues revived extension work in 1907, by contrast, they emphasized professional rather than general education. By the spring of that year Strong had received many requests from schoolteachers for extension courses. After pleas by Professor Wilbur C. Abbott of the Department of History and by the Chancellor, who pointed out that the University of Missouri was attracting the teachers' favor through courses in Kansas City, the University Council voted to create courses of eight lectures each, primarily for teachers, which would carry one hour's credit. During the 1907–1908 year Abbott, Arvin S. Olin, and John E. Boodin gave one course each in Kansas City, Kansas, in history, education, and philosophy respectively, and Abbott offered another course in Paola. A year later sociologist Frank W. Blackmar organized a course for social workers in the two Kansas Citys, which was taught by both members and nonmembers of the University faculty.[10]

But in October, 1908, Chairman Edwin M. Hopkins of the Council's University Extension Committee told Strong that the new extension courses were already losing ground. Offering several recommendations to make the courses more attractive, the committee also reported that it had been asked to begin correspondence courses. Hopkins and his colleagues thought that the cost made correspondence work impracticable at present, but Strong and the regents did not. Speaking for the Board, the Chancellor said in his report for 1908 that since the shortage of faculty members made widespread extension work impossible, the University was preparing to undertake correspondence courses. The University's advantages should never be limited to the "comparatively few fortunate ones" able to attend it, he asserted. Instead, "the University of Kansas must be for all who strive for the higher things of life and must go to those who cannot go to it."[11]

There were many ways other than correspondence and extension courses, however, to go to the people, and Strong was eager to adopt them all. Hearing in December, 1908, that Governor-elect Walter Roscoe Stubbs might favor a greatly expanded program of state-service work, Strong sent Professor Robert Kennedy Duncan of the Department of Chemistry to survey the University of Wisconsin, which was in the midst of an exciting state-service program under the joint leadership of President Charles R. Van Hise, faculty members, and interested state officials and citizens. Duncan, whose enthusiasm for such work was as great as Strong's, rushed to Madison, investigated for two weeks, and wrote a report which Strong had printed for the enlightenment of the people generally and the legislators especially. It provided an extensive and enthusiastic description of Wisconsin's Extension Division, which had four branches: Instruction by Lectures, Correspondence Study, Debating and Public Discussion, and General Information and Welfare. As at Kansas, Instruction by Lectures was moribund. But the Correspondence School, though only three years old, had fifteen hundred students taught by seventy-four instructors; the Debating and Public Discussion branch was flourishing; and the Department of General Information and Welfare was spreading broadcast information on all sorts of subjects relating to personal and social welfare gleaned from reports of private and governmental agencies, universities, and philanthropic organizations. The Extension Division proposed to spend about $250,000 during the coming year.[12]

Whatever the impact of the Duncan report on the legislature of 1909, the representatives substantially increased the University's appropriation. Strong and the other regents thereupon established an Extension Division and hired as full-time director Richard R. Price, a University graduate of 1897 who had taken an M.A. from Harvard and at the time of his appointment was superintendent of schools in Hutchinson, Kansas.[13]

His division opened on July 1 with the same four departments as Wisconsin's. The weakest of them continued to be that offering off-campus lecture series for credit. By a decision of the College faculty in 1910, a course of six lectures was worth one hour's credit, and B.A. candidates might take up to sixty hours through extension classes and correspondence study. Originally the Engineering School allowed up to thirty hours, but from 1913 to 1920 it permitted as many as ninety, as long as there was also a substantial number of conferences with the faculty. Beginning in 1915–1916 there was a steady increase in the courses, and by 1921–1922 there were twenty-nine of them with 656 enrollments, mainly in eastern Kansas and western Missouri.[14]

Correspondence study proved much more popular. In 1909 twenty-two departments began offering eighty-seven courses, of which sixty-seven were for undergraduate credit, fourteen were non-credit, and six were high-school subjects. From fifty-seven students in the first year, enrollments climbed to over a thousand by 1916–1917 and two thousand five years later. Most students worked for undergraduate credit. At first they had to pay the standard matriculation and incidental fees plus $5 for each course, but in 1912 the University substituted a $10 blanket fee for residents and $15 for nonresidents. Students were limited to two courses at a time and had to complete them within a year, during which they could move at their own speed. Each course demanded eight assignments per credit hour. In addition to courses for college degrees the Department of Correspondence Study offered vocational courses for skilled and semiskilled workmen, would-be pharmacists, and retail merchants, as well as law classes and refresher courses for Kansas physicians; most of them were not for credit. They drew very few enrollees, however, deeply disappointing Extension enthusiasts.[15]

The third department was that of General Information and Welfare, charged with distributing materials for study, discussion, and debate. At the start it drew books and periodicals from the inadequate University library to send around the state. When the drain became too great and the people proved more interested in contemporary problems than scholarly pursuits, the Department's employees began to clip periodicals and combine the clippings into "package libraries." By 1914 there were four hundred different libraries available—on art and politics, literature and canning vegetables, the progress of women, and almost everything else—and during the teens the Department annually filled thousands of requests for them from women's clubs, high-school students, patriotic groups, and individuals. High-school plays and suitable poetic or prose recitations were also available.[16]

During its first four years the Extension Division also had a Department of Debating and Public Discussion, most of whose work was with high schools. In 1910 Richard R. Price and others organized the Kansas High School Debating League, with thirty-three school teams, whose annual winner received the Regents Cup. The Department furnished the debaters with subjects, package libraries on them, and pamphlets on the debating arts. In 1913–1914 the debating department was absorbed by the Department of General Information.[17]

The Extension Division gradually took on other functions. In 1909 and 1910 Director Price, who had energy enough, created a Municipal Reference Bureau within the Department of General Information and Welfare which used both faculty members and its own staff to answer questions about forms of government, street lighting, the drafting of ordinances, and numerous other subjects. A great success from the start, the Bureau won independent status in 1914. Price and Professor Frank G. Bates of the Department of Political Science, who was secretary of the State Conference of Mayors and Other City Officials, played the main roles in forming the League of Kansas Municipalities, with Price as secretary-treasurer and editor of the League's official publication.[18]

There were also aids for children. In 1914 the Board of Administration, which the year before had replaced the Board of Regents, ordered the Extension Division to start a Child Welfare Department. At its head was William A. McKeever, from 1902 to 1913 a professor of philosophy at the Agricultural College. The archetypal reformer, during the next seven years he sent child-welfare exhibits around the state, held contests to discover the best smaller Kansas city in which to raise children, lectured to parents on the best uses of children's leisure time, sponsored Child Welfare Institutes in various communities, and wrote pamphlets on *Training the Boy*, *Training the Girl*, and several other subjects. A zealous protector of all children and adolescents, McKeever fought cigarette smoking, tippling, immoral dancing, and gambling among the University students as well as throughout the state. After July, 1919, the University dropped McKeever's salary, but he continued for two more years as an unpaid faculty member.[19]

Beyond these activities the Extension Division also arranged for faculty lecturers and faculty and student concerts. It helped organize Extension Center Associations to sponsor lectures and concerts in Kansas communities. Starting in 1912 it assembled collections of lantern slides and, later, motion pictures, for loan. And the Division cooperated with the University's various schools and departments to organize meetings of business and professional groups at the University.[20]

But if, as Leon N. Flint said in the *Graduate Magazine* in 1908, the purpose of state-service work was to allow the University to "make the state its campus," it would take more than the Extension Division for the task. Another service was the offering of summer courses. Here again Frank Strong revived an idea that had appeared and all but died before he came. In the 1880s Professors William H. Carruth and Ephraim Miller had proposed summer classes in their subjects, primarily for teachers, but received little support. In 1893 a few faculty members had offered noncredit summer courses without pay, but scarcely a dozen students enrolled. Three years later Chancellor Snow tried to convince the Board of Regents that Kansas should emulate other notable American universities by starting a summer school, but the economy drive of 1897 and Snow's later illness downed the idea.[21]

Chancellor Strong had recognized the value of summer schools, especially for teachers, before he went to Kansas. After his arrival he received many letters favoring a summer school from teachers and superintendents, and in December, 1902, there was great enthusiasm for it at the annual meeting of the State Teachers Association. Strong asked the Board of Regents for immediate approval, so that funds for it could be asked of the legislature of 1903. The Board acted favorably and quickly: in January, 1903, they voted to establish a summer school; in February they limited its cost to $5,000; and in April they made William H. Carruth the director. As long as the money held out, full professors were to receive $200, associate professors $175, and assistant professors $150. For the first session the faculty committee in charge created both noncredit review courses open to everyone and regular credit courses that duplicated those of the regular academic year. Students could take four of the former, but only five hours' worth of credit. Thirty instructors and lecturers, including eight from other schools, offered thirty-six courses in fifteen departments to 134 students enrolled for credit, 65 of whom were teachers, principals, and superintendents. Carruth knew that the student body would have been even larger had not the Kansas River overflowed its banks at enrollment time, making Lawrence all but inaccessible to many prospective pupils. Earnestness characterized all the students, Carruth reported happily. There had been no disciplinary problems, no "society" problems, no athletic problems—in fact, no problems at all—and the school's success seemed assured.[22]

He was correct. Nearly two hundred students appeared the next year and enrollments grew thereafter. In 1905, with Professor of Latin Arthur T. Walker replacing Carruth, the College faculty regularized its summer-session classes to integrate them with those of the academic year. In 1906 Chancellor Strong described the summer session as "to all intents and purposes a regular session of the University" and noted that it both benefited teachers and kept the physical plant from lying idle for a fourth of the year, a "matter worthy of consideration." Strong urged that its work be broadened, in part by importing each year "famous men" from American and European universities, so that it might become the "center to which all Kansans may resort in the summer season for the highest work and inspiration."[23] While the summer session never became quite that glorious, it was now a permanent part of the University.

The spreading of information and the extension of education thus became the first emphasis within the idea of state-service work. The second was more practical, scientific, technical assistance in solving problems. Until the early 1890s such work was done on an individual basis, without specific support from the legislature and without much publicity. It was of little consequence to the University as a whole, however beneficial such work as that of the chemists in analyzing mineral deposits and city water supplies, or the labors of Francis H. Snow, first as meteorologist and then as entomologist of the State Board of Agriculture. After Snow became chancellor in 1890, however, there was a quickening and broadening of such work, thanks to Snow's own enthusiasm and to the greater amounts of money now available. The two outstanding examples were Snow's own efforts to eradicate the chinch bug and the work of the University-related State Geological Survey.

There was tragedy as well as fame in the chinch-bug affair,

however, for it demonstrated Snow's ineptitude as an experimenter. The chinch bug was a vicious little beast that thrived on Kansas grain, and as state entomologist Snow determined to fight it. Discovering an epidemic raging among the bugs and familiar with efforts elsewhere to destroy them through infection, Snow procured diseased bugs, found their sickness contagious in the laboratory, and in 1889 began sending out infected bugs to farmers to see if they would spread the disease in the field. Apparently they did: Snow maintained in 1894 that two of every three experiments of the previous year were successful and that many of the failures resulted from unfavorable weather conditions or the farmers' inability to follow instructions. From the start Snow received statewide publicity from his experiments, and the legislatures of 1891, 1893, and 1895 appropriated a total of $12,500 for an experimental station at the University to expand the work. During 1894, at the height of the campaign, some eight thousand boxes of diseased bugs went out from Lawrence. Snow and his assistants had to work feverishly to meet the demand.[24]

Later investigators, however, declared Snow's experiments a failure. In 1909, a year after Snow's death, chinch bugs were still afflicting the state, and Chancellor Strong recommended that University scientists investigate infecting them by the same process that Snow had used. Professors Frederick H. Billings of the Department of Botany and Bacteriology and Pressley A. Glenn of the Department of Entomology, neither of whom had been faculty members during Snow's work of the 1890s, looked carefully into the matter and concluded that whatever the successes of infection in the laboratory, it was impossible to infect healthy bugs in the field by putting diseased bugs among them. The apparent successes of the 1890s were really the results of disease naturally present before the bugs from the University arrived and of farmers' mistaking the skins of molted bugs for dead bugs. Strong quickly dropped the matter.[25]

But perhaps the spirit counted more than scientific accuracy, for through Snow's anti-chinch-bug work thousands of Kansans learned of his University's great commitment to their economic welfare. They found further evidence of it in the work of the University—later the State—Geological Survey. At first there had been no geological relation between the school and the state. In 1864 the legislature passed an act providing for a "geological and Mineralogical survey" of Kansas and a year later authorized the permanent position of state geologist. The job went to Benjamin F. Mudge, who in the same year joined the faculty of the Agricultural College. Francis H. Snow taught such geology as the University offered; though Mudge became a lecturer at the University in 1878, after the Agricultural College fired him for playing politics in the appointment of its regents, he died in 1879. The University's lack of a trained geologist precluded any relation to the Geological Survey.[26]

In the Moody Act of 1889, though, was a provision that the annual $75,000 grant was to include expenses for "any geological survey or scientific work which may be conducted under the auspices of the University for the benefit of science or the state." During the next three years the University hired two extremely able men to conduct it. One was the paleontologist Samuel W. Williston, who had taken his B.A. in 1872 and his M.A. in 1875 under Mudge in Manhattan, and then, after receiving his M.D. at Yale in 1880, stayed on to work for a Ph.D. under the famous paleontologist Othniel C. Marsh. Then in 1892 the University added Erasmus Haworth, whose interests as a geologist were somewhat more contemporary than Williston's. Haworth had graduated from the University in 1881 and gone to Johns Hopkins for his doctoral work. He came as professor in the new Department of Physical Geology and Mineralogy.[27]

Williston, Haworth, and Snow together tried to start the Moody Act's state survey, but at first failed. The $75,000 a year would not permit it, and the United States Geological Survey rejected their application for $2,000. During the summers of 1893 and 1894, nevertheless, Haworth and several students began their own survey of lead, zinc, coal, oil, and natural gas deposits in southeastern Kansas. Snow's report for 1894 argued for an appropriation to let them continue the work and, more especially, to pay for ascertaining the relative position of water-bearing rocks in the semiarid part of western Kansas. Rather than establish a separate irrigation bureau, Snow said, "the state should use the machinery it already has especially when, as in this case, it is of the most modern and effective character."

After the legislature of 1895 increased the regular appropriation to $100,000, the regents created a University Geological Survey, with Snow as ex-officio director and Haworth, Williston, and Edgar

H. S. Bailey of the Chemistry Department as "associates." The legislature also made Haworth the geologist of the Kansas Irrigation Commission, and in his dual capacity he got to work on an extensive series of investigations which yielded two large volumes by 1896 with the promise of many more to come. Snow said with pride that they had attracted "much favorable notice, not only from scientists, but also from men interested in the business and industrial development of the state." With a starting grant of $3,000 in 1897 the Populist legislature authorized the University Geological Survey to make a "complete geological survey of such portions of the state of Kansas as have any natural products of economic importance." From then on the University Geological Survey and the State Geological Survey were one. Its reports would prove of inestimable benefit.[28]

Thus Chancellor Strong's idea of state service was anything but new—but his emphasis on the concept and the varied directions that the University took after 1902 dimmed the earlier years by comparison. If his desires were in part native to him, they also resulted from his adherence to a broad national movement for reforms of various kinds that many men came to call Progressivism. The general emphasis of most of the reformers was that the people should use both national and state governments to improve the quality of American life: to regulate gigantic corporations, reduce or eliminate child labor, and provide for greater democracy through the direct primary, the initiative, and the referendum. They hoped to make government more honest and efficient through an expanded civil service, end political bossism, clean up the disgusting urban slums, and in general refurbish the tarnished American dream of national and individual happiness and prosperity.

Many reformers emphasized the role of the trained intelligence in solving the nation's problems. It was here that interested university faculties found a role for themselves, for they were full of experts: social scientists to dispassionately assess and solve social problems; natural scientists and technicians to ease the pangs of technological birth and growth; lawyers to write better laws; physicians to improve public health; and a host of others. The leader of them all was the University of Wisconsin, whose work for the state was so comprehensive and vigorous that the concept of ever closer relations between universities and society—particularly the state government—became known as the Wisconsin Idea. Robert Kennedy Duncan found so many Wisconsin faculty members advising state bureaus and commissions and working both formally and informally for the state, found the University's influence "so interwoven with the thoughts and conduct and daily lives of the people of the state," that to discover the full extent of its work—which was what Strong asked him to do—was impossible.[29]

Clearly Kansas could never equal Wisconsin. In the agrarian Sunflower State, for one thing, the University had no agricultural school, which severely limited its usefulness. Kansans were also less enthusiastic about their university than Wisconsinites about theirs, and they gave it less money. During fiscal 1907, for example, while Kansas had an income of $302,666 from all sources, Wisconsin had $1,124,731; Kansas had some 1,800 students, 109 faculty members, and buildings and equipment worth about $1,235,000, while Wisconsin had 3,659 students, 327 faculty members, and about $2,421,000 worth of physical facilities.[30]

Still, the University of Kansas could play its own role in its own sphere. Beyond its educational and general informational activities most of its state-service work was of an applied scientific nature. After 1905 it branched out in several directions. Some of its more notable work was for the State Board of Health. After numerous petitions and hearings the legislature of 1905 passed a pure food act providing that chemists at both the University and the Agricultural College should analyze foods and beverages sent them by state, county, or city health boards. If the products contained substances injurious to health, the state would publish the products' names and manufacturers as a warning to the people. Edgar H. S. Bailey of the University's Chemistry Department, who had worked hard for the law, became food analyst for the State Board and supervised the work. Two years later the legislature passed a more general pure food and drug act, and thanks to Dr. Samuel J. Crumbine, secretary of the Board, the analytical work again went to the University and the Agricultural College instead of to the Board itself. In Lawrence, Dean Lucius E. Sayre of the School of Pharmacy investigated the drugs, and Bailey, the food. In 1909, moreover, the regents appointed Crumbine a lecturer on pure food and drug regulations and on sanitation.[31]

Meanwhile Strong, Engineering School Dean Frank O. Marvin,

and several faculty members entered upon plans to survey the state's natural water supplies to determine their character, healthfulness, and industrial applicability. The original suggestion had come from the United States Geological Survey and the State Board of Health rather than from the University, but Strong was delighted with the opportunity. "In regard to all of the scientific work of the state," he told Governor Hoch, "let me say that the University stands ready without the additional expense for salaries and equipment that a separate laboratory would make to undertake all such work that is now necessary or may become necessary in the future. The laboratories here are the largest and best equipped for this kind of work to be found in this part of the southwest, and men eminently fitted by training and research are ready to assist the state in such matters. We therefore feel that it is the duty of the University to act as the agent of the state departments in the scientific work of the state." After the legislature of 1907 allowed the Board of Health to contract with the United States Geological Survey and provided part of the cost, Francis W. Bushong of the Department of Chemistry took charge of the University's work.[32]

Still another University chemist worked to make Kansans more prosperous. Before Robert Kennedy Duncan came to Kansas in 1906 from Washington and Jefferson College in Pennsylvania, he had traveled in Europe and been much impressed with the close relation in several countries between the universities and industry. Duncan believed, as he said in 1907, that "the absolute function of the University is not only the increase and diffusion of knowledge among men, but of *useful* knowledge. It must be remembered that it is only through useful knowledge that the people have gained the material blessings of our new civilization." That year he proposed creating at the University a number of industrial fellowships, paid for by industry, which would support the research of competent scholars on particular industrial problems, whose solutions would also benefit the public.[33] The fellowships called for contracts between the University and the donor—either an individual company or an industrial association—providing money to support the fellow and his work. Although the fellow did not have to have a Ph.D., he had to have demonstrated superior research abilities. Though he would spend most of his time investigating a particular problem, he would also teach in the Chemistry Department three hours a week. The donors of the fellowships were entitled to the patents on new discoveries and processes, but the fellows would get a percentage of the net profits accruing as the results of their work. Fellows were to prepare comprehensive monographs on all phases of their research, but could publish them only after three years; during the interval only the donors had access to their information.

From 1907 to 1911 Duncan and the Chemistry Department secured seventeen industrial fellowships. Their recipients investigated such things as the chemistry of laundering, bread-making, and cement and lime production, the optical properties of glass, and the uses of borax. Duncan's work attracted national publicity for the University—and for himself. In 1911 he left for the University of Pittsburgh and two years later became head of the Mellon Institute, founded to enlarge the work he had begun. Starting in 1913, however, the Kansas Chemistry Department had a separate state chemical research section to continue the investigation of the application of chemical discoveries to industry.[34]

Over in the School of Engineering Frank O. Marvin and his faculty had long been giving advice, serving as consultants, and publishing how-to-do-it articles. But in light of the new emphasis on social service something more seemed necessary. In 1908 at the urging of both Dean Marvin and Chancellor Strong the Board of Regents created an Engineering Experiment Station to carry on "investigations of various problems in engineering lines which are of interest to engineers and to those engaged in the industrial enterprises of the state." Staffed by the heads of the engineering departments, the station issued regular bulletins reporting on the values of different fuels for home and industrial use, the properties of iron, the characteristics of electricity-producing alternators, and similar subjects. While agriculture was still the state's chief source of wealth, Acting Dean George C. Shaad said in 1913, industries were of "considerable and growing" importance, and the Experiment Station existed for their direct "aid and benefit."[35]

The list of the University's state services continued to lengthen. Engineering School faculty helped the state bank commissioner prevent fraud by investigating the assets of companies offering stock for sale in Kansas; helped the Public Utilities Commission determine the physical valuation of railroads; and advised cities on the installation of light plants and sewerage systems. Members of the Department of Entomology sought means to end the horse plague and increase alfalfa yields; encouraged bee culture; shipped out thousands of boxes of green-bug parasites to destroy another threat to the wheat crop; helped eradicate the San Jose scale, so harmful to fruit crops, and destroy the still costly Kansas grasshoppers. By the terms of a state law in 1911 every crippled or deformed child whose case was curable had to be sent for treatment to the Medical School hospital in Rosedale. Frank W. Blackmar and his students worked for state boards and commissions investigating state prisons and reformatories, and Lewis L. Dyche served as state fish and game warden. According to the Board of Regents in 1912, the "value" of state-service work was then "perhaps second to no other institution except the University of Wisconsin. It is probable, also, that according to the amount of its income the volume of state service work done here is as great as that in any other university."[36]

Yet the path of social service was tortuous. For all the enthusiasm of Strong and the regents the Wisconsin Idea never became the Kansas Idea. Many of the men who the University's leaders thought would most favor an intimate relation between the school and the state government, as in Wisconsin, proved disappointments. Kansas, of course, had its share of Progressive reform politicians, but they were comparatively little interested in the University, especially in the cooperation of faculty members in writing and enforcing better state laws. Although several state agencies used University personnel, about all the impetus to make the institution a greater participant in the total life of Kansas came from Mount Oread rather than from the legislature or the governors.

A typical example of the politicians' half-heartedness was Walter Roscoe Stubbs, governor from 1909 to 1913. A well-to-do Lawrence contractor, Stubbs had early entered the Boss-buster movement, supported many Progressive reforms, and was a good friend of the University. Yet he was never willing to take a strong public stand for the Wisconsin Idea in Kansas. In December, 1908, right after his first election as governor, William Allen White told Strong that Stubbs was anxious to have the University equal the work of Wisconsin and would "get behind a proposition of that sort with all his power." Stubbs told Robert Kennedy Duncan the same thing before he left for Madison. Yet all Stubbs said in his address to the legislature of 1909 was that it was "particularly gratifying" that the

University, the Agricultural College, and the normal schools had in recent years made "phenomenal progress in practical, useful and scientific work"—which was hardly the Wisconsin Idea. Soon after, moreover, criticism of the University's huge appropriation of 1909 began to pour in, and the frightened Governor fired off a letter to the regents asking them to justify the increases so that he in turn could justify them to the people. The regents replied as if Stubbs had never heard of state-service work. "It must be borne in mind that the University of Kansas is not merely a teaching institution," they said. "It does a large amount of constructive work for the state and has already saved the state, through its practical work, much more than the total cost of the University up to the present time." Two years later in his legislative message, Stubbs took care to praise the Agricultural College far more than he did the University.[37]

Later in 1911, however, Stubbs waxed enthusiastic once again. He proposed that he and the Board of Regents themselves journey to Wisconsin to observe what its university was doing. The regents agreed, and the group visited Madison in the latter part of October. Everyone was most impressed; Strong told Stubbs that a committee from the legislature should make the same trip. Until it could, the Governor ought to explain to the citizens all the things that a well-nourished state university could do for them. Strong added with his usual bluntness that Stubbs should also come to Lawrence to see for himself what his own University was already doing.[38]

But no lasting good came from the Wisconsin visit. The only practical result was a reaffirmation by the regents of a new kind of state-service work begun before their trip. One of the more popular reforms of the day was the opening of neighborhood civic and social centers to which people might repair for recreation, discussion, and general and practical education. The Extension Division and the School of Education, also organized in 1909, had campaigned with some success to have Kansas towns and villages use schoolhouses for the purpose. Just before the Wisconsin trip the regents formally approved the progress made, and when their visit coincided with a large conference on civic and social center development they returned even more enthusiastic. In 1912 the Extension Division formed a Bureau of Civic and Social Center Development as part of its Department of General Information and Welfare. But a year later both Extension Director Price and Bureau head Ralph Spotts resigned, and thenceforth the work languished.[39]

In many ways the best manifestation of a close relation between the University and the state government would have been the establishment of a legislative reference bureau at the University, which like the one in Wisconsin would have helped the lawmakers write scientific, sensible bills. In 1908 and 1909 Frank Strong proposed it to several men inside and outside the legislature. Nothing came of the suggestion—at least for the University. Many legislators opposed it; many who favored a bureau thought the University too far away from the state capitol in Topeka to be of much use. When the legislature of 1909 set up a Legislative Reference Department, it made it part of the State Library instead of the University. In 1912 the Law School was claiming that it included a legislative reference bureau, but what existed was merely an informal service of which the legislators might avail themselves.[40]

By 1912, indeed, much of Chancellor Strong's hope that his university might become the Wisconsin of the Southwest was vanishing. In later years the school would continue and even expand much of the sort of direct service work that it was now performing. But the bloom was off the rose, and much of the old enthusiasm and expectation was gone. Factors both inside and outside the University worked to destroy the idea that the institution might become a sort of partner with the state government in Kansas's progress. With his first decade as chancellor ending, Strong himself said he was confused about the proper relations between state-service work and the other functions of the University. One day, he said, the former might outrank teaching in importance, and this would be a tragedy. He and various faculty members had rushed ahead without pausing to decide its proper place in the University structure, with the result that the work was neither "well organized nor well related to the other parts of the institution. I am even now planning to organize the state work by itself so as to avoid the other difficulty, namely, the belittling of the mere teacher."[41]

While Strong's newly found caution was a response to his own fears about where state-service work was taking the University, it was also a response to threats against both the institution's autonomy and its prosperity. One of the emphases of early twentieth-century reform was efficiency, and ironically the desire for it was turned by both friends and enemies against the University itself. The legislature of 1911, troubled by the apparent duplication of work in several fields between the University and the Agricultural College, moved to end it by abolishing their separate boards of regents and putting them both—along with other state agencies—under the control of a single board. Governor Stubbs vetoed the consolidation measure, but when the legislature of 1913 passed another such bill, Democratic Governor George H. Hodges signed it. Starting on July 1, the University had a wholly new form of government whose impact on the school no one could foresee. Like many another Kansas Democrat, Hodges also criticized past and present Republicans as spendthrifts and urged economy. There were "many duplications of work in our state educational institutions," he charged, and went on to say that "some departments are of little or no value, and . . . some cost more than they are worth to the state."[42]

Both the reorganization act and Hodges's plea made Strong waver in his desire to serve the commonwealth. In September, 1914, he took his fears before the entire University faculty. Even in Wisconsin, he pointed out, the Wisconsin Idea was in trouble, for opponents were charging that the university was trying to run the state. Strong desperately wanted to protect his own institution against any such charge. On the one hand, Strong said, to have rejected the demand that the University respond to the economic needs of the state would have meant the gradual death of the school in the people's favor. "On the other hand"—and here was the new caution—"to push this work too far, to extend its lines too greatly, brings powerful and destructive opposition. An institution must, therefore, be as wise as possible and do its duty as frankly and conservatively as possible." This was, he said, the policy of his administration as it prepared for the legislature of 1915.[43] And thus did boldness become timidity. Under Strong the University had expanded its state-service work, but the institution had never been able to do as much as he thought it should; there was never an enthusiasm in the state at large or in the legislature which matched his own.

Yet there was another kind of state-service work that endured and prospered: the preparation that the University offered for the various professions. Neither Chancellor Strong nor his fellow regents initiated the policy. But they broadened it and established such new divisions as the School of Education, the Department of

Journalism, and the four-year School of Medicine. As Frank Strong saw it, professional-vocational education was a direct state service, and he threw much of his great energy behind it.

15

Professional Education:
The Coming of the New

IN the years between 1890 and 1895 the faculty and regents had made the University's professional departments equal to the College by converting them into semiautonomous schools. But those changes, along with the addition of the Graduate School in 1897 and the second year of the Medical School in 1899, did not make plain the leaders' commitment to professional education or determine its relative importance within the University as a whole. Frank Strong and his fellow regents made that commitment a permanent one, and while they never tried to create a ratio of excellence or significance between it and the College, they gave professional education so much attention, publicity, and especially money that it seemed to many men in later years that they had overextended their resources.

All of professional education raised problems for the University's leaders, but it was the School of Medicine that most tried their souls. When Frank Strong reached Lawrence in 1902, the Medical School question was approaching a critical point. Dr. Simeon B. Bell's offer of land in Rosedale for a hospital and clinical facilities was good for ten years only and would expire in 1904. As the deadline drew nearer, Bell and his attorney, alumnus John Sullivan of Kansas City, pressed upon the regents the need for action. Bell promised them $25,000 more in land and cash to accept, while Sullivan urged the Chancellor that a "good thing like the Bell gift ought never to be allowed to escape," and expressed his "most poignant grief" that the regents had done nothing.[1]

Since the legislature would not meet until 1905, the Board prevailed on Bell to extend the gift for another year, with the understanding that they would ask the lawmakers' permission to accept it and its terms. Yet the regents were still dubious about splitting the University between Lawrence and Rosedale. Chancellor Strong desired to make the Medical School "the Johns Hopkins of the West," the best between Chicago and San Francisco. But to ease his doubts about its location, in 1904 he talked with many Kansas physicians. Most of them thought it impossible to build a "large and strong" clinical department in Lawrence. Because of their ideas and because Bell would give not a cent or an acre for a hospital or school outside Rosedale, Strong and the regents sought the legislature's approval of the present. To get it, they had to fight off opposition from three familiar sources. Jealous Kansas physicians feared that a hospital and clinical department just across the state line from the metropolis of Kansas City, Missouri, would not be Kansas institutions at all. Supporters of the Washburn University Medical School in Topeka were unhappy at the prospect of state-supported competition. Most ominously, many legislators suspected that an enlarged medical school would greatly increase the University's cost. Strong assured them that Bell's gifts would provide a clinical school and a hospital of moderate size and that the University would rely on hospitals in the two Kansas Citys for much of the students' training. "I can say to you authoritatively," he wrote, "that the Board of Regents and the present management of the University will not either now or hereafter call for appropriations from the legislature either for buildings or maintenance of the clinical school at Rosedale."[2]

Taking Strong at his word, the House amended a Senate bill permitting the regents to conduct the clinical work where they wished so that it provided that such work should be without expense to the state. Both houses passed that measure routinely, as well as a bill allowing the Board to accept Bell's real estate.[3]

"The whole problem of the medical school came so suddenly," Strong wrote in 1905, "that it was impossible for anyone to see in just what direction the development would have to take place." But if Simeon Bell and John Sullivan had forced the University into accepting a gift that it apparently could not afford to lose—without planning for the future or discussing whether the University was ready for a four-year medical course—Strong and the regents added to the confusion. Though it would take time to sell the land and build a hospital and other facilities, the regents were determined to open the clinical department in the fall of 1905—even if it had no hospital, no money, no assured future, and a sloppy organization.

After preliminary negotiations the University Medical School acquired students, faculty, and facilities in one great swoop in April, 1905, by absorbing the College of Physicians and Surgeons of Kansas City, Kansas, and the Medico-Chirurgical College and the Kansas City Medical College of Missouri. The merger increased the student body from 30 in the two-year course in 1904–1905 to 162 when the four-year course opened and gave the school a faculty of over a hundred men. Using the College of Physicians and Surgeons building for classes, the regents contracted with metropolitan hospitals on both sides of the state line for access to patients or "clinical material."[4]

Over the longer run Frank Strong thought that the University might actually divide the Medical School between Rosedale and the two Kansas Citys. Building a small hospital, together with the necessary laboratories and classrooms, would satisfy Simeon Bell's terms, while the existing larger hospitals could house most of the clinical training. When Rosedale boosters learned of the scheme, they were aghast. The Rosedale Commercial Club, professing to have only the University's welfare at heart, resolved that the plan would be "detrimental to the Medical department of the University," and that the last two years should be "entirely and inseparably located at Rosedale." The regents dealt with them in the obvious way. In the fall of 1905 they agreed to locate the clinical department in Rosedale if the local promoters would guarantee the University $60,000, including the receipts of the Bell land sales. Bell himself pledged $20,000 more in cash and a year later the regents had almost $51,000 of the amount in hand.[5]

Presiding over the Clinical Department was Dean George H. Hoxie, also professor of internal medicine. After graduating from New York's Union College, Hoxie had taken his M.D. from the University of Zurich in 1901 and come to Kansas the next year. He was too dictatorial and too blunt to be an effective dean. University Vice-President William H. Carruth observed that Hoxie wanted to be "God almighty" in Rosedale without either the Lord's omniscience or His mercy. Thinking that many of the faculty were incompetent physicians and teachers, Hoxie told them so to their faces until Strong ordered him to desist. Hoxie's testiness was the greater because he had no control over the Medical School's first two years in Lawrence, which were called the Scientific Department and headed by Dean Mervin T. Sudler. In 1905 and 1906 Hoxie angered Sudler by meddling in the management of the Scientific Department, whereupon Sudler took his case to Chancellor Strong. "It will not do for you to interfere here in any way," Strong curtly told Hoxie, "as you have no authority or responsibility for matters here."[6]

Gradually the regents gave shape to the Medical School. The curriculum included all the approved subjects; and early in 1907 the Board established five subdivisions within the Clinical Department: internal medicine, surgery, gynecology and obstetrics, clinical pathology and hygiene, and "special subjects" such as ophthalmology and dermatology. In November, 1905, the regents approved a five-week postgraduate course; the following February the School began a training course for nurses. In 1906 the University completed the Eleanor Taylor Bell Memorial Hospital, together with a laboratory and an out-patient department. To coordinate Sudler's work with Hoxie's, moreover, the regents set up a Medical School Council composed of the Chancellor, the two deans, and five elected members from each department. The Council, subject to the regents' authority, would control the course of study, admission requirements, and the promotion of students. Chancellor Strong reported in 1906 that the Medical School had had "abundant success," and prophesied a great future.[7]

A great medical school, however, needed enormous amounts of money and equipment. The Rosedale institution was starved for both. Dean Hoxie thought that the hospital should have at least 250 beds—initial cost $250,000, maintenance cost $50,000 a year—but it had only 35. The division of the clinical work between the Bell hospital and several Kansas City institutions produced an awkward fragmentation. Late in 1909 Dr. Abraham Flexner, after surveying the school as part of an investigation of medical education in the United States that he was making for the Carnegie Foundation, thought it entirely inadequate. Its best features were its well-equipped laboratory at the hospital and its rising admission standards. Starting in 1909 admission required two years of college in-

In the beginning at Rosedale: The Eleanor Taylor Bell Memorial Hospital in 1906.

The Medical Center after fifty years (1958).

stead of one. But the hospital was too small; the students did not see enough patients; the faculty was not composed of men "whose medical training has been modern," and they gave too much time to private practice rather than teaching. At a second out-patient department in Kansas City, Kansas, Flexner said, "a fair amount of material has hitherto been handled in an incredibly slipshod manner."

Flexner contended that the University's leaders had simply not realized how much money it took to build a good medical school. To create one would compel the regents to "refrain from many other projects." It would also require Kansans to systematize public higher education. Observing that the state was spending money for duplicated work in engineering and teacher training at the several institutions, Flexner said that "no comprehensive and well coordinated scheme of state educational development has been worked out." Eliminating duplication would free money for the Medical School. Flexner also deplored the School's "severed halves" and noted that "fundamental questions respecting the location, organization, and general scope" were yet to be settled. After their settlement, the creation of a comprehensive development plan, and the acquisition of adequate funds, the University could proceed step by step and year by year to create the excellent school it now lacked.[8]

Even before Flexner's investigation Dean Hoxie and Chancellor Strong had decided to ask the legislature for relief. Hoxie's $250,000 was too much to hope for, so the regents asked only $50,000 for another hospital building and $11,000 for an out-patient department in Kansas City to take advantage of the "vast amount of clinical material from the districts of the packing-houses and stock-yards" there. Fortunately the legislators had forgotten Strong's promise of 1905; he did not remind them of it. Instead he said that the hospital would help the "indigent sick from the various counties of the state in order that they may be adequately cared for and restored, if possible, to the condition of self-supporting citizens." The solons granted the full $61,000, although the hospital money was to be available only after July 1, 1910.[9]

In that year several problems reached a climax, confusing the Medical School question still more. In June Dean Hoxie resigned—distressed by the Sudler feud, annoyed because he could not control the whole School, wounded by the Flexner report, discouraged by student criticism of his alleged authoritarianism and his too lofty standards of work. While the regents searched for a successor, they also sought to end the continuing criticism of Kansas physicians that the School was more a Missouri institution than a Kansas one because so many of its faculty were Missourians. If the regents wished the backing of the State Medical Society, said an angry doctor at the annual meeting of 1910, "they had better get rid of their Missouri men and get Kansas men." It was a scandal that most faculty members, because they lived across the state line, could not belong to the Medical Society.[10]

The regents worked cleverly and rapidly to win friends. After December, 1910, the School of Medicine would cooperate with the Board of Health to prevent disease and teach "curative medicine." More important, the regents chose Dr. Samuel J. Crumbine, secretary of the Board of Health, as "administrative head" of the School, with Mervin T. Sudler becoming associate dean in charge of instructional work. Crumbine was an able administrator who had rendered great service to public health by his "Swat the Fly" campaign, his fight against the public drinking cup, and his crusade for pure food and drug laws. Then the regents put the chairmen of the Medical School's departments on a full-time basis in order to place their teaching "upon the same basis as the rest of the University."[11]

But the shrewdest move of all—if only it had worked—was a decision to relocate the Clinical Department in a new hospital in Kansas City, Kansas. There it would be farther away than Rosedale from the Missouri line, easier of access by Kansans, and altogether more of a Kansas institution. Frank Strong was careful to consult leading Kansas physicians and found that the move had great support. To ease the expense on the state, the regents sought to get Kansas City to furnish a ten-acre site and pay part of the operating costs. The new hospital itself, however, would have to come from the legislature. To win support for the desired $150,000—of which $50,000 was to be a reappropriation of the 1909 amount, not yet spent—the regents mobilized the doctors. Early in 1911 the Capitol was full of lobbying physicians praising the advantages of Kansas City, arguing that the construction of a state hospital—for such the new one would be—was long overdue, and pleading for the state's sick.[12] Their work did no good. Many Topeka physicians, never enthusiastic about the original location of the School, opposed the additional expense of relocation. Most legislators had no interest: the Senate rejected an appropriation bill, and a House measure never got out of the Ways and Means Committee. Their failure complete, the regents rushed to commit the $50,000 of 1909 before June 30 when the appropriation would expire. For it they got a new building in October with sixty-eight beds.[13]

All that the Medical School's leaders had and all that they would have for a decade was a small, inadequate, understaffed school with a poor reputation. Dean Sudler, who had much more to do with the School's administration than Crumbine, was constantly embarrassed by a want of facilities and money. In 1911, for example, having received refusals from a number of nationally distinguished physicians whom he had invited to join the faculty, Sudler asked them to give their reasons in detail. The replies were unanimous in saying that the $2,500 full professor's salary was too low, the hospital and teaching facilities ridiculous, the provisions for individual research exceptionally poor, and the medical library unsatisfactory. Considering these and other factors, said Dr. J. H. Hewitt of Chicago in a typical response, "I believe that it would be suicidal, almost, for me to give up what I have here which is secure and certain . . . for something that is small to begin with and appears rather problematic and to a degree uncertain for the future."[14]

A year and a half later Sudler was even more discouraged. In a tour of eastern medical schools he had found them getting everything that Kansas lacked: "larger funds, favorable contracts with cities for the use of their hospitals and dispensaries; and . . . the inducements which attract the best men, both in the matter of salary, and in opportunities for professional advancement." Kansas did not even compare very well with leading medical schools in the Middle West. By 1913 it had graduated eighty-four physicians and had a faculty of fifty-five. Several of the faculty were excellent men, including Sudler himself, who was professor of surgery; Don Carlos Guffey, professor of obstetrics and gynecology, who would serve for over forty years; Franklin E. Murphy, professor of clinical medicine; and Clarence Case Goddard, professor of neurology. Yet Sudler had to admit that his school's clinical training was inferior to training elsewhere. "The students who come to us to study medicine," he told Chancellor Strong, "are bright, intelligent men who mean business and who expect to get all they can for their time and money;

and with the facilities that they can obtain at other institutions there is only one way that we can hope to hold them,—and that is by giving them work of the same quality that they can get in St. Louis or Chicago, or other centers."[15]

Ultimately the University would get the money it needed to convert the School of Medicine into a first-rate institution. But for its first decade and more it suffered from careless planning and no planning, from Simeon Bell's egocentric philanthropy and Frank Strong's eagerness to have an appendage called a Medical School, whatever its quality. To start a school when it was "impossible for anyone to see in just what direction the development would have to take place," as Strong said in 1905, was irresponsible.

Conditions in the School of Education, while troublesome enough, were less distressing. Behind its creation in 1909 lay over a decade of discussion about the University's proper role in teacher training, the relation of that work to the College curriculum, and the question of how far the offerings of the University and those of the Normal School at Emporia might overlap. The School was more a solution to existing problems than the outgrowth of a firm desire for it by Strong and the regents.

The events leading to the School of Education began in 1893 when the legislature passed an act regulating the certification of public-school teachers. Henceforth the State Board of Education could exempt from examinations in academic subjects graduates who had taken them in an institution that had as "efficient" a course of study as the Emporia Normal School. This left only examinations in the "professional subjects": the history and philosophy of education, teaching methods, school laws, and school management. Chancellor Snow at once got the regents' approval for the School of Arts to offer those subjects and for Arvin S. Olin to teach them. Olin was a well-known educator who had served as a principal and school superintendent in several Kansas cities, including Lawrence. Although he occupied a grandly titled Chair of Pedagogy, the course that he offered in 1893–1894 was a single one extending throughout the year to prepare students for the state examination. But Olin rapidly expanded the number and scope of his offerings until by 1900 he had six half-semester courses in things such as school law, school management, and the comparative study of educational systems, two full-semester courses in the history of education and edu-

cational theory, and a semester seminary for the "original investigation of special subjects." Starting in 1896 the University awarded
students who took the pedagogy courses a "teacher's diploma," as
well as a B.A.[16]

Despite tremendous opposition from Normal School supporters,
in 1899 the legislature put the University on a par with the Emporia institution by allowing any college graduate who had the
teacher's diploma to receive a teaching certificate without examination. Olin thereupon revised the requirements for the diploma. By
1901 there were four semester courses in the subject that the student
intended to teach and two and a half semesters' work in the (renamed) Department of Education. Effectively this added five hours
—or one course—to the normal undergraduate load. Several academic departments also offered "teachers' courses" to train students
in the techniques of teaching particular subjects. Ideally they were
to include a half-semester of practice teaching. They were not required, however, and not every department offered one.[17]

Until 1909 the Department of Education remained in the College. But by that time both Chancellor Strong and Professor Olin
had concluded—though for different reasons—that it should become
a separate school. Strong had been concerned since 1902 about the
growing tendency of the Normal School officers to train high-school
teachers rather than only the common-school teachers for whose
benefit the Emporia institution was begun. In his inaugural address
the Chancellor had argued that it was the University's peculiar function to prepare high-school and college teachers, and he did not
welcome competition. Because of the shortage of such instructors,
he told Regent J. Willis Gleed in 1908, there was currently room
enough for both the University and the Normal School. But the
former should never forsake its "preeminent position in the field."
His university, he asserted in his biennial report the same year, "is
and must ever remain the most important place for the training of
teachers for high schools and colleges."[18] A School of Education
with the same rank as the University's other schools would give the
work more importance and show that the University intended to
expand the work rather than contract it.

Meanwhile Arvin S. Olin was concluding that both practical
problems and the theory of teacher training required the separation
of the Department of Education from the College. In the spirit of

the law of 1899 the State Board of Education had required the Kansas private colleges to offer essentially the same curriculum as the University for the teacher's diploma, including the extra five hours. After chafing for years, early in 1909 several college presidents wrote to ask Chancellor Strong to have the College faculty consider removing the extra work, claiming that it put an unnecessary burden on the students.[19] When Strong laid the request before the faculty, Olin immediately protested that the College professors were not competent to deal with it, that the "large question" of professional training involved "could better be determined by professional men on a professional basis." Only the faculty of a separate education school could decide the matter on its merits. And such a school would have several other advantages. It could teach domestic science, manual training, and agriculture without danger of criticism from the Agricultural College. It could set lower admission standards than the College and thereby accept worthy students from inferior high schools who could enter the College only with conditions. It could also experiment with lowering, or even eliminating, the foreign language admission requirement.[20]

On July 15, 1909, the regents formally organized the School of Education. It had three parts: the regular instruction that Olin now offered; a division of school supervision and appointments under Professor William H. Johnson; and originally the whole of the University's extension work under Richard R. Price. To head the School the regents sought a "man of personal power and force," as Frank Strong said, "backed by a personality that will attract and not repel men. He must be a real campaigner and by reason of his force and scholarship he must compel the admiration and following of our teachers." Whatever his abilities, Arvin Olin was not that man. It took the regents a year to find him—during which time they separated University Extension from the School. The new dean was Charles H. Johnston, then a faculty member at the University of Michigan. Thirty-five years old, Johnston had taken his doctorate at Harvard, where he did part of his work under the incomparable William James, and had published several articles on educational curricula in colleges and universities. He came to Kansas for $3,000 a year.[21]

When Johnston described his school in the catalogue, he said that it had taken separate and equal station with the professional schools of law, medicine, engineering, and pharmacy. That status was the natural result of "modern differentiation of fields within the general subject of education," requiring more courses dealing "scientifically as well as practically with various and difficult types of educational problems" and therefore more faculty members. Yet the School of Education, though Johnston did not say so, was significantly inferior to the other professional schools. In form it had their autonomy: its faculty decreed their own courses, set the requirements for the teacher's diploma, and even granted a special degree—a Bachelor of Science in Education—which demanded, after the sophomore year in the College, seventy-two hours of work, one-third of them in the School. Because the teaching profession required competence in the subjects to be taught, however, and because only the College departments could supply it, students who worked in the School of Education for the teacher's diploma took more courses outside the School than inside. Admission to the School required junior standing in the College. Juniors and seniors then took at least fifteen hours of education courses, but they also had to complete a teachers' course in one of the College departments, the prerequisites for which were from twenty to twenty-five hours in that academic subject. The School of Education offered more than the minimum fifteen hours, of course, and it trained school administrators as well as teachers. But without the College it could not have existed; almost all its early students, indeed, were working toward a College degree at the same time they sought the teacher's diploma.[22]

On another side, though, the School did not depend on the College at all. If one of its goals was to train teachers and administrators, Johnston said, another was to function as a "service bureau" that would do "all in its power to stimulate popular interest in education; to support and advocate progressive school movements, and to disseminate among teachers, pupils and patrons the highest educational ideals of the day." By 1912 the Dean and his faculty—especially Arvin S. Olin, William H. Johnson, and Raymond A. Schwegler—had created various "Departments of School Relations": to provide speakers for teachers' institutes and publish bulletins informing teachers of the latest pedagogical advances, increase public interest in primary and secondary education, improve student health and school sanitation, and organize athletic and recreation programs.[23]

Beyond instruction and service work, Johnston and his faculty had a third function: running a high school. When Johnston came, the University had no experimental school of its own in which to provide practice teaching and try new methods. Agreements with a number of city high schools gave opportunities for practice teaching, but a University high school would be even better. In June, 1911, Johnston persuaded the regents to start the Oread Training School. Located in Myers Hall and open to the extent of its limited enrollment to any student who had completed the eighth grade, it gave the work of the School of Education a most important dimension.[24]

Dean Johnston's work marked him as an enthusiastic and capable man. Unluckily for the University his efforts caught the attention of educators elsewhere. By the 1912–1913 year he had already received several tempting offers, and in the spring of 1913 he accepted the chairmanship of the Department of Secondary Education at the University of Illinois. Sad to see him go, Chancellor Strong was the sadder because no adequate successor was in sight. Arvin S. Olin made a bid for the deanship, but Strong wanted him no more now than in 1909, and so he served only as Acting Dean for two years until Strong and the Board of Administration hired Frederick J. Kelly.[25]

When Frank Strong had helped organize the School of Education, Olin had presumed that the Chancellor agreed with him that professional training in the College was anachronistic. In fact Strong had not agreed at all. Though special circumstances made the Education School desirable, there were other kinds of vocational or professional training that the College could easily accommodate. Every College department, indeed, could be a professional department for students seeking a career in a particular field. Although the College's general purpose was to provide a liberal education, undergraduates bent on scholarly careers in such "useless" subjects as Latin, Greek, or history served their apprenticeships as majors in those departments, and prospective chemists, biologists, and geologists did the same elsewhere. Just as the education courses had existed in the College, then, so could professional or vocational courses of several other kinds.

The first of the new departures was a journalism program. In the 1890s the University had experimented with courses for would-be editors and reporters, but had not found them popular. Strong believed that students would now welcome them. He found agreement from Professor Edwin Mortimer Hopkins of the Department of English. Hopkins had joined the faculty in 1889, after completing his undergraduate work at Princeton, and was responsible for composition and philology courses. To improve the quality of Kansas journalism he had begun a course in prose invention, which gave students the opportunity to study and practice "journalistic writing." Strong and Hopkins desired not a separate department or school, but an interdepartmental major. Founded "first of all upon strong, well-developed work in English composition, to be supported by courses in economics, history, sociology, and modern languages," the major would also include, they hoped, courses in newspaper writing and reporting, and noncredit lectures by eminent Kansas editors.[26]

Hopkins, Leon N. Flint of the *Graduate Magazine*, and other interested faculty members began the journalism program in 1903, and it developed about as they had planned. Besides the recommended courses in such subjects as ethics, American colonial history, economics, sociology, and newspaper writing, there were special lectures by both editors and journalists and by faculty members: Dean Green of the Law School on the law of libel, for example, and Dean Charles S. Skilton of the School of Fine Arts on music criticism. The success of the year's experiment warranted continuance, so in 1905 editor Charles Harger of the Abilene *Reflector* became the program's director. Although he visited Lawrence only once a month to supervise and lay plans with Hopkins and Flint, he took his position seriously. He made arrangements with the Kansas City, Missouri, *Star* to have large quantities of unused, unedited copy sent to the University, on which the undergraduates practiced their skills. All the members of the class in newspaper writing—fourteen in the fall of 1905—were cub reporters for either the student *Kansan* or one of the Lawrence papers, the beginners covering the University beat and the advanced students editing copy.[27]

Inevitably the men most interested in journalism wished to convert the course into a full department. Separate status would make it the equal of every other department and also permit the introduction of more specialized courses. In October, 1909, the regents agreed to the change, with Harger becoming chairman and Flint his resident agent. Merle Thorpe replaced Harger in 1911 and immediately began sharpening the professional focus, for he thought journalism a profession like any other, even if the Department was not a separate school. "Men and women intending to enter newspaper work as a profession or as a stepping-stone to higher literary endeavor," he wrote in the catalogue of 1911–1912, "are here given the opportunity for that specialized training which has long been accorded other professions." In 1910 and 1911 the Department had six courses of its own: two each in reporting and editing, and one each in advertising and the history of journalism. By 1912 there were seventeen, including additional ones in advertising and editing and new ones in the short story, the mechanics of printing, and comparative journalism. Majors, however, took three-quarters of their work in liberal arts courses and the rest in a half-dozen journalism courses. At the same time that they gained a broader cultural outlook and specialized training, they also staffed Thorpe's publicity bureau.[28]

When Thorpe and others talked about journalism as a "profession," it was hard to tell what they meant, for the definition of the word was obscure. Traditionally theology, law, and medicine were the "learned professions," but apparently there were others, like journalism, that were less learned and that therefore required a less rigorous training. If one thought of a profession as an occupation that required considerable education, whose practitioners held to certain high standards, and which had a certain dignity or moral tone about it, almost any occupation could be made a profession if men tried hard enough. This was what Harger and Thorpe were attempting to do. But if journalism was capable of such a metamorphosis, why not other subjects? Why not, for example, business? Why not homemaking?

Believing that many of the pressing problems of America's future would be "economic and industrial," Chancellor Strong desired from the start to introduce courses in "commerce and business." In the spring of 1904 he got the consent of the College faculty and the regents for a new program called Business in Its Higher Relations. Like the journalism sequence it was a series of recommended courses for students working toward the B.A. After completing the freshman-sophomore requirements—including electives in English, a foreign language, a physical and a biological science, either economics or European history, and mathematics or surveying—juniors and seniors could choose one of four course groups. One was journalism, and the others were general insurance, business, and banking. Except for journalism, the emphasis of each was on economics and law, but courses in history and even literature had their place.[29]

In explaining and justifying Business in Its Higher Relations, Strong asserted that businessmen should have the same opportunities for professional training offered other groups. "It was felt," the Chancellor said in his biennial report in 1904, "that this numerous body of men should have the advantage of just as well organized and effective a course as is offered to those intending to enter engineering or the law." The program's specific classes were "entirely of University grade"—no cheap degrees for businessmen—while the catalogue denied that the business courses constituted a school of commerce or business, in low repute with many academicians, or that one was contemplated. Nor were the business courses on-the-job training. Instead of vainly seeking to furnish "that large portion of business training which can come only from experience," said the catalogue, the University was offering "fundamental and specialized courses of study that illustrate the economic forces that control the business world. It aims at the same time to give the cultural training which is indispensable to the thoroughly enlightened citizen."[30]

Until 1909 Business in Its Higher Relations remained an interdepartmental elective program. Unlike journalism it could never become a separate department, for most of its courses would have duplicated economics courses. Yet leaving it a mere collection of other departments' courses made business seem less "professional" than it should be. The regents therefore gave the work to the Department of Sociology and Economics, where it became an emphasis within the major. The Department recommended seventeen courses "especially adapted for business training," said the catalogue of 1909–1910. "It is in such courses of economic science that the forces and laws controlling the business world are best illustrated and grasped by the future man of affairs." Most of the seventeen were in the Department itself; those outside it, such as the economic histories of England or the United States, had an obvious bias.

There was now no mention of the "cultural training" that the "thoroughly enlightened citizen" should have.[31]

At the same time that Strong urged the business courses on the College faculty, he proposed a similar program for prospective home-makers called "Household Science." Early in March, 1904, he had written to prominent Kansas women to ask their opinion of a University course for "women who wish to prepare for home-making." His hope was to establish a "broad four-years course made up in the main of general studies . . . but with such special subjects as can be taught in a scientific manner." He also thought that the woman who directed the work would act as the "advisor and friend of the girls of the University"; the program thus bore directly on the institution's moral atmosphere. Finding considerable support for the scheme, on March 21 Strong proposed to the College faculty a group of junior-senior courses in household science, which, he stressed, were all to be of "strictly University grade."

Most faculty members were not impressed. When Strong's proposal received little support, Dean Olin Templin won approval for a compromise motion that declared that the sense of the faculty was that the University should offer "additional work for females" in the form of a small number of optional courses "especially adapted to the needs of women." A committee would decide the subjects to be presented. During the next five years female undergraduates could take classes in various departments that the catalogue called "Courses in Domestic Science." They included bacteriology, the chemistry and physiology of foods, physical education, household architecture, the sociological and historical study of the family, and others.[32]

But Frank Strong never forsook the idea of a comprehensive program and in 1908 he returned to the subject. Part of his enthusiasm then was surely owing to a growing emphasis on the need for home-economics training among women across the nation. For several years enthusiasts had been holding annual conferences at Lake Placid, New York; in December, 1908, they gave way to the American Home Economics Association, the better to promote the cause. But at least as much of his support arose from an argument between the University's Board of Regents and the officers of the Agricultural College in Manhattan about the proper sphere of each institution and the question of duplicated work. The debate naturally became a contest for the citizens' favor. In his report for 1908 Strong asserted that the state should not discriminate between its daughters in Lawrence and those in Manhattan. If the University admitted girls, surely they should be able to have the "type of training that shall fit them for the sphere of life that they ought to occupy. Would anyone care to arrange it so that the girls who attend the Agricultural College should be provided with the training that best fits them for their sphere in the home, and at the same time deny that privilege to the girls who enter the University?" If so, they were expressing undemocratic ideas of class education. "Domestic science is general in its nature and is of benefit to every girl, no matter what she may desire to do."[33]

After the legislature of 1909 substantially increased the University's appropriation, Strong pressed the matter with the Board of Regents. In the spring of 1910 the Board agreed to establish a Department of Home Economics in the College, and then hired Dr. Edna Day as chairman. Miss Day had received a Ph.D. from the University of Chicago in 1906 with emphasis on home administration, sociology, and plant physiology. At the time of her appointment she was head of the Department of Home Economics at the University of Missouri. A gracious and popular lady who made many friends among the female students, she organized a department in the basement of Fraser Hall which offered classes in cooking, home sanitation, plain sewing and garment-making, home administration, and dietetics. She required of her majors an extensive program of serious study outside her department, which included chemistry, physics, biology, sociology, and several other courses. The modern American home, Miss Day believed, was a far more complicated place than it had been in decades past. Precepts "handed down from grandmother and the experience gained by the mother herself," she said, were inadequate to meet the "still rapidly changing conditions." Only an "understanding of underlying principles makes adaptation to new conditions possible."[34]

In its way the Department of Home Economics was the most important department in the University. Standing in the liberal arts College, where it had equal status with all the traditional studies, it demonstrated how far the University was prepared to go in introducing socially useful subjects into the curriculum. While homemaking had previously been neither one of the liberal arts nor a profession, the training offered by Miss Day and her colleagues had unquestionable benefits for their students and through them for society at large. Many faculty members continued to believe that preparing women to be better wives, mothers, and home managers was no fit function for a university. But Frank Strong's and Edna Day's notions about the nature of a state university were just as valid as those of the dissenting professors. With the coming of the Home Economics Department came the question of whether there were any theoretical limits at all to the University's work. To that question there was no objective answer whatever.

16

Professional Education:
The Expansion of the Old

WHILE the newer professional education grew, the older professional education flourished—though each school had its peculiar problems. In the School of Law both the main problem and the main virtue was James W. Green, dean from the opening in 1878 to his retirement and death in 1919. For forty years, in fact, Green *was* the Law School: there were other faculty members, but Green shaped the school to suit himself, and its spirit was the one he breathed upon it. He looked upon the School as his private fief, instilled in his students the idea that they belonged to an independent community having little in common with the rest of the University, and often paid his disrespects to the larger institution. Yet according to his own lights—which he never hid under a bushel —he gave himself generously to the School's interests and those of its students. Most of them liked the Dean enormously—they called him Uncle Jimmy—for Green had warmth, enthusiasm, wit, charm, and most important, the ability to perceive his students' interests, problems, aspirations, and joys, in much the same way they did themselves.

Yet Green had his enemies, among them two chancellors, several faculty members, and the Board of Regents, who saw him as an egocentric reactionary. Green first ran afoul of higher authority by trying to continue his private law practice against the regents' will. The act of 1885 awarding Green a salary of $2,500 a year required that he give his full time to the deanship, and the regents of the

1890s continued to expect full-time service. But both Green and the School's other faculty member, William B. Brownell, were practicing law on the side and neglecting the School. In 1893 the Board issued a cease and desist order, which Green and Brownell ignored. A year later Chancellor Snow was exasperated. Though professing to write in the "kindest possible spirit," Snow said that neglect was causing the School's decline. The "entire connection of the faculty with the school," he observed, "seems to be at the hour or hours of recitation. The Board expects you to devote your whole time to the work of the School, and if you are not engaged in the work of instruction there is much other work that needs to be done." Green should be out beating the state for more students, or striving to improve relations between the School and the Kansas bar. Present conditions were intolerable.[1]

The regents did not have to tell Green again. But they had ill fortune when they tried to get him to raise the quality of the Law School by raising admission standards. An ardent democrat, Green described his institution as "the people's school," and contended for thirty-five years that it should never require a college education, or even a high-school diploma, as a prerequisite for admission. Any adolescent who had a "good English education" in the common schools and competence in the English language and American history should be allowed to enter. While more education would do future lawyers no harm, they really needed only a mind capable of grasping and applying legal principles, which ability might be gained more readily from the "training of actual life" than from the classroom. "I believe the man with a good English education," Green said, "who has spent three or four years in active commercial life, where he has met his fellow men and learned their ways of doing things, and the ways of the business world, has had a better preparation, and is better fitted to enter a law school than the man who has spent the same time in acquiring a collegiate education."[2]

Neither Chancellor Snow nor Chancellor Strong agreed, but they found the Dean practically immovable. In 1891 Snow hoped to raise admission requirements during the next year. Yet until 1899 any person who could pass entrance examinations in English and American and "general" history was admitted; high-school and college graduates entered without examination. In that year Green finally yielded to the regents' pressure and agreed that admission should require previous work in geography; Greek, Roman, English, and American history; some algebra, geometry, and physics; and as much study of English as was usually given in a two-year high-school course.[3]

Frank Strong had a little more success. By 1904 Green had conceded that a high-school education should be a prerequisite—though the Law School would always make exceptions in special cases. Meanwhile several of the nation's better law schools—among them Harvard, Columbia, and the University of Chicago—were demanding college degrees for admission. Strong, who had attended the Yale Law School for a year, was with them in spirit. Without saying specifically that every lawyer should be a college graduate, he pointed out in November, 1904, that some college training was indispensable. In reply to an article by Law Professor William L. Burdick which contended that no more than a high-school education was necessary, Strong wrote in the *Kansas University Lawyer* that so many new legal questions had arisen in the past twenty-five years that "the young man will find that not only a general but a particular knowledge of many subjects is required. The practitioner who has not widely read in literature, in history, in economics, and in science will find that his foundation for his profession is essentially weak." Only seven years later did Uncle Jimmy admit that Strong might be right. In September, 1912, the Law School began requiring a year—thirty hours—of college work for admission. The requirement stayed the same until Green's death in 1919, and never did the School stipulate that the work had to be of a particular quality. Even the faculty chafed under the reactionary policy: a month after he died, they voted to require a second year of college work, which brought the School into conformity with most other members of the Association of American Law Schools. Faculty chairman William L. Burdick said that the action would certainly improve the School's national standing.[4]

Inferior preparation among the students, of course, meant inferior teaching—at least when compared to what might have been done. It also meant a faculty inferior in numbers and therefore in specialization, for Chancellor Snow, Chancellor Strong, and the regents were not much interested in pouring money into a school with a reactionary dean. The relative neglect hurt Green's pride, and he came to feel that he and his alumni cared more than the regents for the School. "It has passed through some very discouraging periods; it has had its carpers and critics, and at times it appeared that the power that created it had forgotten its offspring or had abandoned it," he said at the dedication of his new building in 1905, "but through all its trials and tribulations, through all the sunshine and shadow, it has had a noble, a loyal alumni back of it, who have loved it, who have had faith in it, who would not suffer it to die, and today it lives and is a powerful factor in the upbuilding of this great commonwealth."[5] His sense of rejection by and separation from the rest of the University made him describe the structure as "this beautiful building erected for us by the State and dedicated by it, to and for the use of its Law School forever," and it was plain that others entered only at their peril. Making it equally obvious that the Law School was virtually an independent entity was a statement in the 1903–1904 catalogue that while law students had completely free access to the main University library, the law library in the new building would be for the "exclusive use of the students of the School of Law."[6]

Although the number of law students grew from 78 to 244 between 1891 and 1911, the Law faculty never had more than five members. In the 1890s Green's main assistance came from William B. Brownell, a Law graduate of 1886. After seven years of service he resigned in 1898 to become attorney for Douglas County. To take his place came William L. Burdick, who would remain at the School long past Green's death. A graduate of Connecticut's Wesleyan University and the Yale Law School, Burdick proved to be the scholar and writer that Dean Green was not. In 1901 he published *The Elements of the Law of Sale of Personal Property*; in 1914, a textbook on the law of real property with a companion volume of illustrative cases; in 1946, his three-volume *The Law of Crime*. Burdick was a legal historian as well as a textbook writer: in 1938 he completed an excellent survey, written as much for the general reader as the professional lawyer, on *The Principles of Roman Law and Their Relation to Modern Law*. In 1899 Green managed to obtain still another regular faculty member in William E. Higgins, an alumnus of both the University's School of Arts and its School of Law. Higgins had practiced law in Kansas City, Missouri, since 1894, but gave it up to rejoin Green in Lawrence.[7]

For years Green, Burdick, and Higgins gave most of the Law

School's courses. Starting in 1896 the School had a three-year program, which meant their loads were exceptionally heavy and varied. Knowing that it was impossible to give their students all the information they should have, the faculty regularly supplemented classwork with frequent lectures on special subjects by Kansas attorneys. In class the faculty used a combination of teaching methods. From the start of his deanship Green emphasized legal education from the textbook and by recitation. As time passed, however, he was alert enough to realize that other law schools found considerable value in the lecture method of teaching and in dwelling upon the study and mastery of cases. By 1905 he and his faculty had arranged their teaching so that their emphasis upon lecturing and case-study increased each of the three years, though the dominant emphasis continued to be on textbooks and recitations.[8]

Whatever the problems that Dean Green created, he did champion the idea that the law was a profession that required a peculiar training. No longer should young men prepare for their careers by reading law in some attorney's office, for that was usually far too casual. With its greater resources the School of Law would raise professional standards. Since Green believed that his graduates were far more capable than lawyers trained elsewhere, he constantly sought for them automatic admission to the bar without examination. The School's final examinations, he reported to the regents in 1882, were "more severe and impartial, and take a wider range, than the usual bar examination"; while the state examination took only an hour or two, those of the Law School lasted three or four days.[9] Green, the alumni, and the Board of Regents regularly asked the legislature every two years for such an act, but not until 1897, with the Populists in power, did they have any success. The law allowed any Law School graduate to practice in the district and inferior courts of the state. Graduates would still have to take the bar examination before they could practice before the Supreme Court.[10]

In the great universities of the Middle Ages—Paris, Bologna, Oxford—law had been one of the three learned professions, enjoying that status with medicine and theology. In the University of Kansas several centuries later law was still a learned profession, but it was less significant to the University as a whole than one of the newer subjects. Under the genial guidance of Dean Frank O. Marvin the School of Engineering became the University's most important professional school of the early twentieth century, and through both the training given its students and the direct services its faculty performed for the people and the state, it became one of the University's chief assets.

The Engineering School appeared in 1891 as a consolidation of the Departments of Civil Engineering and Electrical Engineering. Delighted with the elevated status of the two courses of study, Marvin labored to convince the skeptical that engineering was in fact a profession with standards as high—or which should be as high—as those of any other. At the same time he prophesied an expanding social role for the engineer. In place of the isolated individual who was merely some businessman's employee, "there is growing up a profession with professional standards and an *esprit de corps,* whose members are to be retained, not hired." Engineers were to become men of "influence whose advice and services are sought, leaders whose judgments are respected, and men who can mingle with the best anywhere on a common ground of attainment and character. . . . The very nature of an engineer's qualifications, his technical knowledge, the cultivation of his judicial and critical faculty, his training in fidelity to the trusts reposed in him by private clients,— all these fit him for places of large responsibility concerned with public works, and the people, tired of political management, are beginning to find this out."[11]

Marvin's definition of engineering was the "art of directing the great sources of power in nature for the use and convenience of man." Taking the definition literally and comprehensively, he believed it included an important aesthetic dimension. Marvin himself was a man of broad cultural interests: a devotee of music, arts, and literature, he was an accomplished artist and also the organist for Lawrence's First Methodist Church. He demanded beauty as well as utility in building and a due regard by engineers for the impact of their creations upon human beings. Engineering schools had hitherto paid no attention to such matters, he said; the result was ugliness in buildings, bridges, and city design generally. What an "uplift would come to city life," he exclaimed, "if [the engineer] could put an artistic quality into his designing, and the people would learn to appreciate it!"[12]

Speaking in 1901 as president of the Society for the Promotion of Engineering Education, Marvin asserted that the preparation offered by most engineering schools was far too narrow. To provide "useful service" to society, the engineer had to be able to see the relation of his specialty to other aspects of his environment, which required a breadth of view and an ability to discriminate among relative values. Such characteristics demanded the study of history, economics, and sociology. To present his ideas effectively, the engineer needed a wide familiarity with the English language. Added to them as requirements were appreciation of beauty, agreeable personal manners, and tact. The day would come, moreover, when growing numbers of engineers would occupy executive positions in industry and public works; thus it was the more essential that their cultural training be broad and deep. "The finest result requires the most skillful labor; the noblest workman demands the most fitting training."[13]

Yet while Marvin himself, in conversation, general addresses, and class instruction, tried to get his students to share his vision, there seemed to be no place in the four-year curriculum for the kind of broad, cultural, humanistic training that he desired. Although personal example and exhortation could count for much, history, economics, or sociology could be pursued only in College courses, for which there was no time. "The School of Engineering is the scientific or technical school of the University," said a typical statement in the 1904–1905 catalogue. "It offers what is, in the main, technical training in the various departments of engineering—civil, electrical, mechanical, mining, and chemical." And technical education was all that the students received. In the civil and electrical engineering programs, which, under Marvin and Lucien I. Blake, comprised the whole School until 1895, the only nonengineering courses were English composition in the freshman and senior years, and German and French—both of the "scientific" type—in the freshman year. Even this limited amount of extra-School work, with its obviously professional application, was too much for some students: in 1894 a number of seniors objected that they did not need the advanced English composition to become good engineers, and that because of their restricted preparation they suffered when put in the same courses as College students.[14]

In 1895 the School added two more full courses of study to its curriculum—in chemical engineering and in hydraulic and irrigation engineering. The former joined Edgar H. S. Bailey and his chemistry colleagues more closely to the School; the latter established ties with Erasmus Haworth. These courses, too, allowed no time for work in the humanities or social sciences. In the hydraulic and irrigation engineering course freshmen and sophomores duplicated the curriculum of the civil engineering course, with its emphasis on mathematics, surveying, and drafting. During the next two years they studied such things as water and soil analysis, sanitary engineering, water supply, and the mechanics of fluids and hydraulic motors. The chemical engineering course was equally restricted.[15]

Had adequate amounts of money, equipment, and space been available in the mid-1890s, the School of Engineering would have introduced other professional programs. As it was, Marvin and his colleagues had to wait until 1899 to bring in courses in mechanical and mining engineering. Agreeing with Marvin's and Blake's arguments for them, Chancellor Snow told the Board of Regents that they were necessary because the number of "manufactories" in Kansas and nearby states was growing and the University should help supply them with trained personnel. The mechanical engineering course would be one of "high grade . . . which shall fit students for designing machinery, and power plants, or for managing the engineering side of manufactories." Mining engineering would allow Kansans to take advantage of their own mineral deposits, and also' train men to develop those of Missouri, Iowa, and Arkansas. The regents approved both courses, and in 1901 Snow reported that they had proved popular.[16]

Only early in 1912 did the School of Engineering begin to move near to a realization of the cultural-aesthetic vision that Dean Marvin held. For years he and the Board of Regents had been hoping to establish an architectural course. With the hiring of M. P. McArdle as designer of the administration building, lectures on architecture were possible, and in February, 1912, they were expanded into the start of a new program. When creating it the regents voted to place its work on the "broadest practicable cultural basis," and the leaders of the School of Engineering stressed in their description of the new course that architecture was "essentially a fine art." There was no telling how the course would develop in the future, but its aim was to give students the "essentials of a liberal education," and an "appreciation of the esthetic nature of the subject," along with "technical proficiency" and a "reasonable skill in expression."[17]

Then in 1912–1913—Marvin's last academic year as dean—the Engineering School added a five-year engineering course, the first year of which might be spent in the College. Urging future engineers to choose the new course, the catalogue statement of 1913–1914 said that it allowed the student a "wider range of studies" and thus a "broader education" than was previously possible. Two years later, with Perley F. Walker now dean, a new program was introduced to train engineers more for administrative positions for industry and the railroads than technical work in the old sense. Starting in the sophomore year students could substitute from twenty to twenty-five hours of work in history, economics, and sociology for some of the specialized engineering courses. Across the nation Marvin's prediction of two decades earlier that more and more engineers would occupy executive positions was coming true. New responsibilities required new training.[18]

With new courses and the post-1899 prosperity, enrollments in the School of Engineering rose substantially: in the 1898–1899 academic year there were 112 students; by 1907–1908 there were 479. In later years there was a slight falling off, with a low point of 392 students coming in 1912–1913. Those enrollments made the School of Engineering the University's second largest, next to the College. The growth of the faculty almost kept pace: in 1898–1899 there were eight faculty members, and the student-faculty ratio was fourteen to one; in 1912–1913, a total of twenty-four faculty members created a sixteen-to-one ratio.[19]

Collectively the faculty members were able and dedicated. From 1900 to 1912, for example, the School could boast of William C. Hoad, an alumnus in the class of 1898. Hoad's specialty was sanitary engineering. In addition to teaching he campaigned ceaselessly for improved public sanitation, advised more than two hundred Kansas cities and towns on the subject, served as chief engineer for the State Board of Health from 1907 to 1912, and established the administrative standards for the state water and sewage law of 1907. The University of Michigan lured him away. Among others in the School were Clinton M. Young, who taught mining engineering from 1907 to 1914 and again from 1919 to 1946 and was especially interested in developing the Kansas coal and natural gas industries;

Martin E. Rice, whom Lucien I. Blake asked to stay on in physics and electrical engineering after taking his B.S. in 1891 and his M.S. in 1893, and who succeeded to Blake's position in 1906; and George J. Hood, another alumnus (1902) who joined the faculty immediately after his graduation and spent the rest of his career at Kansas teaching mechanical drawing. Although the subject was prosaic, Hood's inventive genius was exciting. In the early 1930s he would devise and perfect the dermatome, an ingenious device for removing human skin for grafts and thus restoring the bodies of the burned and maimed.[20] In mechanical engineering starting in 1905 the School had Perley F. Walker, who had a B.M.E. from the University of Maine and an M.M.E. from Cornell. After eight years as professor, Walker succeeded Marvin as dean. Like Marvin he would emphasize the expanding social role of the engineer. During the 1920s he became most enthusiastic about the industrial potentialities of Kansas and publicized its assets both inside and outside the state.[21]

Valuable as these and other men were to the School of Engineering, its greatest figure was Erasmus Haworth, professor of geology and mineralogy. Haworth was also a member of the Department of Geology in the College, but the mining engineers took their work with him. A prodigious researcher and writer, he gave his incredible energy to investigating underground waters and searching out and analyzing the state's lead, zinc, oil, gas, coal, clay, gypsum, cement, building stone, and salt deposits. He was director of the University Geological Survey and wrote its valuable reports—Mrs. Haworth prepared the drawings and illustrative exhibits—and constantly urged Kansans to be more aggressive in pursuit of the state's mineral wealth: the reports of the University Geological Survey, he said in the first volume in 1896, were "primarily for the masses of the citizens of Kansas." Haworth also gave himself freely to his students. A fat, hale, bluff man, he was a popular teacher whose nickname, "Daddy," bespoke a genuine affection among the undergraduates.[22]

Had the University had only a number of very "practical" professional schools and a College, it would have been culturally impoverished. Happily for both the institution and the Lawrence community, the School of Fine Arts provided a welcome aesthetic dimension, especially in music. The School was fortunate in its deans. George B. Penny and Charles S. Skilton were men of great talent, enormous energy, and unquenchable evangelistic zeal—musical missionaries who knew that all of Kansas was aesthetically under-developed and strove to make the people ever more conscious of the arts. Penny, dean from 1890 to 1903, was a New York City native who had completed a scientific course at Cornell in 1885, studied music for two years at Syracuse University, and in 1888 joined the faculty of the Normal School in Emporia. Skilton, Massachusetts born and Yale educated, had studied piano in Berlin and New York and then held academic posts in North Carolina and New Jersey. He was a composer as well as a pianist. Among his works were two orchestral suites, an oratorio, an opera, and an organ fantasy; while at Kansas he also became an authority on American Indian music. Both men were alike in immersing themselves in music to the exclusion of practically everything else. Penny was notorious for his absentmindedness in practical matters. On one of his trips outside the state, for example, he ran out of money and wired his Lawrence bank for funds, only to discover that he had forgotten which bank was his. Skilton's devotion to his art made him an incompetent administrator; the Board of Administration summarily fired him from the deanship in 1915.[23]

Both men also thought the development of music within their School much more important than that of art, though they did not entirely neglect the latter. In 1890 Penny found all the School's curricula too limited. There was only a two-year piano course, leading to the degree of Graduate in Music, and several courses in drawing, perspective, and painting leading to no degree at all. In the next five years Penny induced the regents to replace the M.G. with the Bachelor of Music degree and to rename his division first the School of Music and Painting in 1892 and then the School of Fine Arts in 1894, and created four-year courses in piano, voice, violin, and organ, all of which led to the M.B. Penny also prepared a Normal Course in Pianoforte Playing and later a Normal Course in Public School Music for teachers. In the later 1890s others appeared: Artists' Courses in piano and voice, which were more highly specialized than the others, and even a graduate course in piano leading to the degree of Master of Music. Dean Skilton and his faculty made comparatively few additions. A four-year course in violincello came in 1906; a two-year course in school music for teachers in 1912; a three-year course for teachers in 1914–1915. By contrast the drawing and painting offerings suffered. Not until 1895 was there a four-year course which led to the Bachelor of Painting degree. At the end of Skilton's deanship the course was more comprehensive than two decades before, but the scope of the work in art never matched that of music, for the deans' interests lay elsewhere.[24]

Different though such courses were from those offered in the other professional schools, the Fine Arts curricula shared with them an intensive specialization. The four-year piano course that Dean Penny established in 1894–1895, for example, left room beyond the music classes for only freshman and sophomore English composition, sophomore German and junior German and Italian, a junior course in mythology and archaeology, and a senior course in aesthetics. Those nonmusical studies, moreover, were all conceived as aids to budding pianists rather than as components of a liberal education.[25]

If Penny and Skilton had had their way, their School would have offered many more of those specialized courses in many more instruments than it did. Economically the School seemed to be one of the regents' afterthoughts. Not until 1916 did the Board put the faculty on full-time salaries. Until then some received fixed stipends from the state which they supplemented with student fees, while others received only the fees. Dean Penny came in 1890 for a $500 annual salary, plus fees; by 1903 his regular salary was up to $1,500, which was also what the regents paid Skilton to start. Actually, the arrangement proved fortunate. Penny's total income when he resigned was at least $2,500 a year, and he predicted that with increasing enrollments the new dean's salary would shortly reach $3,000. When Carl A. Preyer came to head the Pianoforte Department and K. Géza-Dome to head the Violin Department in 1892, they both received only the fee income. Chancellor Snow carefully pointed out in his biennial report that their appointments cost the state nothing.[26]

If salaries improved over the years, the School's physical environment grew worse. Partly in honor of Dean Penny's coming, the regents refurbished Old North College and gave rooms in it to Fine Arts. But they also gave space to the Law School. Since James W. Green was always uncooperative about sharing space with anyone, and since it proved difficult to teach law to musical accompaniment, in 1892 the School of Fine Arts moved into the old Methodist Church in downtown Lawrence, now rechristened Music Hall. Six years later, with the lawyers back in Fraser Hall, Fine Arts moved back to Old North. It was a frustrating existence. Because there was no central heating, everyone suffered from fall to spring. Over the years the structure became dangerously unsafe: by 1915 there were huge cracks in the walls, the floors were splintered and sagging, the outside plaster was flaking off. Although Old North was not quite ready to collapse of its own accord, Chancellor Strong warned Dean Skilton not to allow large crowds in it, "especially during heavy windstorms."[27]

The cause of art in Kansas, then, demanded faculty members willing to suffer for it. Luckily the School had them—though for varying lengths of time. The most distinguished faculty member was Professor Carl A. Preyer, who before coming to the University in 1892 had studied at the Stuttgart Conservatory in his native Germany and also in Berlin and Vienna. He stayed at the University for the rest of his life, teaching, composing, and giving recitals. His colleagues in the 1890s were a diverse group: the brilliant, eccentric Hungarian Géza-Dome, allegedly the finest violinist west of the Mississippi, who headed his department in 1892–1893 and then resigned; his successor, Joseph Farrell, a Georgia native who had attended the Leipzig Conservatory, and who stayed in Lawrence until 1900; and two junior faculty members, alumna Genevieve Lichtenwalter and Martha L. Wilson. From 1903 to 1914 C. E. Hubach, a graduate of the New England Conservatory of Music, was professor of voice; he received aid from several lady teachers. For several years after 1903 Preyer had no less than five additional members of his Pianoforte Department, all women. The Violin Department, however, had no full-time instructor until 1917; the classes were taught by part-time teachers from Kansas City.[28]

Two men offered most of the work in art. Arthur H. Clark, who had studied at the Boston Museum of Fine Arts, was a faculty member from 1894 to 1899. William A. Griffith of Emporia, his successor, had attended the Jullien Art School in Paris; he remained until 1921, when he joined the artists' colony at Laguna Beach, California. In addition to teaching, Griffith was especially interested in increasing art appreciation in Lawrence.[29]

Unlike the other professional divisions the School of Fine Arts rendered its greatest rewards to both the University and society not through the professional training of its graduates but through its more direct cultural offerings. The number of graduates, indeed, bore little relation to the number of enrollments. Between 1890 and 1895, for example, the students taking courses rose from 87 to 209, but there were only 7 graduates in 1895; during the last five years of Skilton's deanship enrollments averaged 183 a year, yet in 1911 there were only 17 graduates.[30] But no matter. Like William MacDonald in the 1880s Deans Penny and Skilton and their faculty members strove to make the University and the Lawrence community ever more musically aware. Thanks to Dean Penny's enthusiasm and work there appeared a University Glee Club, a Ladies Choral Club, a Banjo Club, which usually accompanied the Glee Club, and a University Choir. Penny also helped organize the town-and-gown Lawrence Music Club and revive the defunct Handel and Haydn Society. With student groups singing in Lawrence, with Penny, his faculty, and superior students offering frequent concerts, and with the production of several light operas in the early 1890s, Mount Oread and the town had music as never before. Penny also conducted a fund campaign for a new $3,000 organ, which in 1898 went into Fraser Hall. Withal, in 1892 he composed the University alma mater, which over the years evolved into "The Crimson and the Blue."[31]

Dean Skilton continued the work, expanding the number of concerts and light operas; establishing monthly, then weekly, vesper services; creating the May Music Festival in 1904; and starting a recital course the same year. The festival and recital course brought musicians of note to Lawrence, including the violinist Albert Spaulding, the pianist Alfred Calzin, and the Zoellner String Quartet. Skilton also led the faculty-student orchestra and gave the student band, formed in 1892, more support than Dean Penny had offered. Without the enthusiasm and idealism of the two men the University would have been poorer of spirit, less attractive, and appreciably further from the University ideal.[32]

Smallest of the University's professional schools was the School of Pharmacy. Yet Lucius E. Sayre, dean from 1885 to 1925, and his faculty did find an increasing popularity for pharmacy among Kansas youths. In the School's first year in 1885–1886 it enrolled twenty-three students. During the next two decades the number doubled, trebled, and then quadrupled until in 1908–1909 the School had its highest prewar enrollment of ninety-seven.[33]

To teach pharmaceutical arcana, Sayre gradually found the

money to build up a strong faculty. During most of the 1890s the Dean had only one assistant professor—successively S. R. Boyce and George Wagner. In 1899 L. D. Havenhill came as the assistant professor. Havenhill was an Illinoisan who had studied pharmacy at the University of Michigan and afterward had had a varied career as a government chemist in Hawaii, a pharmacist back in Illinois, and an industrial chemist. Professionally and personally Havenhill and Sayre were much alike: scholars as well as teachers, supporters of every sort of public-health reform, and sympathetic friends as well as mentors of their students. Havenhill became a full professor in 1908 and succeeded to the deanship upon Sayre's death in 1925. In 1901 the two men stole Charles M. Sterling from the Department of Botany; a University alumnus of 1897, he would spend the rest of his teaching life on Mount Oread. Two years later the School acquired Herbert W. Emerson, a Michigan graduate, as an instructor, and in 1908 it picked up still another Michigan man, George N. Watson, who would give Kansas fourteen years of service.[34]

With the faculty's expansion went an improvement in the School's physical condition and a consequent improvement in its instruction. In 1900 both the Pharmacy School and the Chemistry Department left the old, smelly, fungus-and-rat-ridden Chemistry Building for the airier spaciousness of a new home. During the preceding half-dozen years the School had made notable changes in its curricula. In 1894 it began emulating other institutions by awarding the graduates of its two-year course the degree of Pharmaceutical Chemist instead of Graduate in Pharmacy. Starting in 1896 the School also provided a four-year course for College undergraduates which led to the Bachelor of Science. And in 1899 came a three-year course—really the old two-year course spaced out to reduce the annual work load. Depending on the course followed, to become registered pharmacists students had to have from one to two and a half years of practical experience. To improve the quality of its training the School gradually raised its entrance requirements. At first not even a high-school diploma was necessary; admission demanded a minimum age of sixteen and the passing of examinations in arithmetic, geography, English, American history, and the American Constitution. By 1914, however, the standards were those of the College—either graduation from an accredited high school or passing examinations in high-school subjects.[35]

It was probably inevitable that the School's curricula should be extremely rigid. There were no electives, no concessions to the liberal arts. Even the students who pursued the four-year curriculum toward the B.S. degree found that the demands on them during the first two years, which they spent in the College, left no time for optional studies. Instead their programs were filled with required courses in chemistry, physics, botany, physiology, English, French, German, and mathematics. "The object of this school," ran the catalogue statement of 1908, "is to give its students a thorough practical training in all of those branches connected with the pharmaceutical profession in its various departments." The faculty taught in the "spirit of those principles which, in the application to other classes of modern technical schools, have proved so eminently successful."[36]

Potentially, at least, the most important of the University's professional divisions was the Graduate School. It awarded all the University's higher degrees, especially its highest, the Doctor of Philosophy; it put a premium upon both faculty and student research, which was one of the requirements of the modern American university; its admission requirements—a baccalaureate degree or its equivalent—were the highest in the University; and it was the only school which, in its authority to approve or reject departmental proposals for graduate programs, had jurisdictional power over the others.

Dean Frank W. Blackmar, however, believed that neither the regents nor the people appreciated the Graduate School enough. Student statistics showed a welcome growth: from 1897, when the regents created the Graduate School, to 1911 its student body grew from 3 to 156 and in the last year it awarded 46 advanced degrees. But there were other numbers—average teaching hours, for example, or the quantity of books in the library—that told a different story. Blackmar contended that as his school went, so went the University. "A large number of bright students carrying advanced work and scientific investigation under the direction of able instructors who are themselves investigators," he told Chancellor Strong in 1902, "make the real university." Though certain that Strong understood the point, he had his doubts about the regents. The Populists of the 1890s were unsympathetic to graduate study, he maintained, because their ideal university was a "high school for the education of farm-

ers' boys in the 'practical' affairs of life,—a university where the
instructors were wise, knew it all and therefore did not need to
study and to learn, but should stand at the desk twelve hours a day
instructing youth." While the later regents were not Populists,
Blackmar thought that they had absorbed this childish idea of a
university. They were interested almost wholly in the needs of the
increasing hordes of undergraduates—and so, said the Dean with
considerable pain, were most faculty members.[37]

Writing to the Board of Regents directly in 1911 to plead for
the Graduate School, Blackmar pointed out that as long as the number of faculty members was comparatively small, undergraduate
teaching loads would remain heavy. There was little point in trying
to build up the Graduate School or advertise it widely in order to
attract the "hundreds of students" who went east for graduate study
or to create a real university, when the "teaching force . . . is so
inadequate that nearly its entire energy is devoted to undergraduate
work leaving neither time nor opportunity to instruct advanced
students." Even many of the University's more eminent faculty
members taught over twenty hours a week—at a time when those in
the nation's best institutions usually taught from six to ten—not
including office hours, private conferences, and the peculiar kind of
supervision that graduate students required. Blackmar desired that
each department have at least one faculty member who gave all his
time to graduate instruction and supervision, and he thought that
the large appropriation of 1909 and 1911 made possible the start of
a new era of growth.[38]

Yet what could the regents do? As long as the undergraduates
kept coming—there would be about twenty-three hundred of them
in the 1911–1912 academic year—the University had to teach them.
Because more students meant both more money and a broadened
opportunity for democratic service, the regents never attempted to
restrict admissions. Throughout Kansas, moreover, dozens of high
schools had arranged the curricula to meet the University's standards, and a law of 1905 required the county high schools to have a
"collegiate course" which would fully prepare graduates to enter
any institution of higher learning in the state.[39] To refuse to admit
students trained in those schools or, once admitted, to neglect them
in favor of either graduate students or individual research, whatever

the theory of the modern university, would have been a form of institutional suicide.

Along with practically every other faculty member, Blackmar also knew that the University Library was not adequate for the needs of a distinguished Graduate School—or even a distinguished undergraduate school. For decades the library was the University's greatest shame. In 1894, when the new building went up, it held fewer than 22,000 volumes; in 1907 it had only about 55,000; by 1915 it had some 100,000 volumes, and Spooner was overcrowded. The most that Chancellor Strong and the Board of Regents could squeeze from the University appropriation for the library was $15,000 a year, a sum utterly inadequate to keep up with newly published books, let alone purchase the works that the library had been unable to acquire in the past. In 1920 Professor Frank H. Hodder of the Department of History, a faculty member since 1891 and now chairman of the Division of Libraries, told Chancellor Ernest H. Lindley that "the best that can be said of the library is that its content is fairly good as far as it goes. We have a fairly good working library in most departments but we fall far short of an adequate research library in all departments." And the Spooner building itself held peculiar horrors. It was, Hodder said, not only too small—books and unbound periodicals were piling up on the shelves and floors—but "about as badly planned from the standpoint of lighting and of library administration as it possibly could have been. It is the most obviously ridiculous thing on the campus. We cannot possibly make anyone think that we have a great university as long as we are compelled to show that library." On the whole, then, the University had been "starving intellectually for a great many years for want of adequate library facilities."[40]

Many faculty members also thought that the University suffered for want of an adequate librarian. In 1887 Carrie M. Watson, who had graduated in 1877, assumed the position. Without a doubt she loved books, desired to interest students in reading more of them, and genuinely desired to be of service.[41] Also without a doubt she saw the library as her personal preserve, in whose administration the faculty should not interfere, and she lacked administrative ability. After several years of complaints and a personal conference with Chancellor Snow the University Council got her consent to a committee, of which she was a member, to help her manage the library. But she continued to follow an erratic administrative course, and by 1900 the Council thought that the faculty itself should take charge of areas where she was especially incompetent: deciding purchase priorities, periodical binding priorities, and the classification of books of value to two or more departments. In 1901 the Council created a new Library Committee to act on "questions of library administration," and pointedly kept Miss Watson off it.[42]

Frank H. Hodder later recalled that in 1903 Chancellor Strong had promised to appoint a new librarian. Nothing came of the pledge. By 1909 complaints against Miss Watson had become so ardent that the Board of Regents was searching for a man—preferably the scholar that she was not—who "had the book sense, was a good organizer and administrator, had the general capacity for handling business, and . . . the helpful missionary spirit which can make a library so useful." The search was fruitless. Then when the new University Constitution of 1915 called for a director of libraries, Strong and the regents set to work once again. The faculty and students were protesting against Miss Watson, and the editors of the *Kansan* were threatening an exposé of library mismanagement. But not until 1919 were funds available. In the fall of that year, however, Strong resigned as chancellor. In the search for his successor the Board of Administration had to forget temporarily about a successor to Miss Watson.[43]

With an inadequate librarian in an inadequate library, a faculty overwhelmed with undergraduate students, and an uninterested Board of Regents, the potentially most important of the University's schools remained for years the least important. During Frank Strong's chancellorship from 1902 to 1920 the Graduate School never exceeded the 156 students of 1910–1911; never did graduate students compose more than 6 or 7 percent of the student body. Thus was Dean Blackmar continually frustrated, and thus was the University a poorer place than it should have been.

17

The College

THE regents' failure to make Frank Blackmar's Graduate School the nucleus around which the rest of the University revolved meant that the College of Liberal Arts and Sciences would occupy the position. Of the University's divisions the College was the oldest, most prestigious, and most numerous in both faculty and students. Its sheer numerical preponderance would determine the level of excellence that the University reached. At the same time its problems were greater than those of the other schools.

Those things were obvious to Frank Strong in his first year. To give the College the vigor he thought it needed, his first wish was to replace seventy-year-old Dean Ephraim Miller, who had served since 1895. Both the Chancellor and many faculty members thought Miller overaged, incompetent, and unprogressive. It would not do, of course, to tell the Dean those things directly. Thus in April, 1903, Strong informed him that he wished to enlarge the dean's work. He suggested that the heavier burden should not "rest upon you after your long labors for the University, and should be shouldered by a younger man." To ease the pain, Strong said that he would urge the regents to continue Miller's salary of $2,300 a year. Miller, who had some difficulty taking hints, replied that he felt perfectly fit to do whatever Strong might require. The Chancellor then secured the regents' support and in August, 1903, told Miller that he would be "somewhat embarrassed" in his plans if the Dean would not quit. Miller at last got the message; he resigned at

303

once. On October 21 the regents, following Strong's wishes, made Professor Olin Templin of Philosophy dean.[1]

Strong had elevated a man much like himself. Templin always advocated the supremacy of administrators over faculty members, opposed what would be called faculty democracy, and suspected the wisdom as well as the honesty of men who disagreed with him. Despite, or perhaps because of, his philosophical reading and training, he was often moralistic and pedantic. Yet Templin was also devoted to the welfare of the College and determined to improve its quality.

Perhaps the most difficult problem that he, Strong, and the faculty faced was finding the ideal curriculum. In several ways the development of the curriculum was the most important part of the College's history from the 1890s to the First World War. The curriculum expressed the sense of the faculty about the functions of their school. It provided their definition of a liberal education. And it offered insights into their thoughts about the College's responsibility to society.

As in earlier years all curricular decisions related to the question of how much freedom students should have to choose their studies. The tendency was to enlarge that freedom but to continue to hedge it in with numerous requirements. After the development of the elective-major-minor system in the 1880s, the first overall curricular reform came in 1892. By that time there were six courses for freshmen and sophomores: the General Scientific, Latin Scientific, Classical, Modern Literature, Latin-English, and General Language. Underclassmen enrolled in one of them and pursued set requirements until the junior year. But the faculty at a special meeting in November approved Olin Templin's motion to scrap them all for a curriculum general enough to include everyone. The new plan put a heavy emphasis on languages and the natural sciences and largely neglected the social sciences. Freshmen were to study mathematics, English rhetoric and literature, hygiene, chemistry, and botany; they also had to carry a foreign language throughout the year. The maturer sophomores had a wider choice. They had to take a semester of a second foreign language and still another semester of either some foreign language or eighteenth-century English literature; write six themes; and enroll in either elocution or music. Division of the sophomore courses into two groups, however, allowed some flexibility. Group A held all the languages, including English.

Group B contained courses in mathematics, chemistry, botany, logic and psychology, surveying, zoology, and history. Of the six semester courses required of sophomores, students could choose up to four from one group and a minimum of two from the other.[2]

Two years later the faculty liberalized some of the upperclass requirements. After a warm argument between specializers and generalizers, in the fall of 1894 they doubled from two to four the number of nonmajor courses that students could take in a single department or area. The effect was to reduce from four to two the number of departments outside their majors in which juniors and seniors had to take courses and so to allow upperclassmen greater specialization in fewer subjects.[3]

Despite the emphasis on the sciences in the revised underclass curriculum, Chancellor Snow thought that the students' scientific education was weak. The "educational necessities of the first years of the twentieth century," Snow said in 1898, required that they take more biology—mainly so that they could understand the impact of the idea of evolution on modern life—and more chemistry. Snow and several of his fellow scientists wanted a requirement that students have at least a College year's work in the biological and physical sciences by the end of their sophomore year. But that was too much for most faculty members. After wrangling over the matter in February and March, the faculty decided that by the end of the sophomore year students had to have taken, either in high school or college, a year of biological science and a semester of chemistry. The only concessions to the humanities or social sciences were the languages, English history, and logic and psychology, which sophomores might take as electives. Besides the formal courses, freshmen took elocution or voice training once a week; sophomores wrote three thousand-word themes each semester; and all underclassmen took physical training three times a week.[4]

"The development of the University here," Chancellor Strong told President Arthur T. Hadley of Yale in 1902, "because of the fact that my predecessor was a man specially interested in scientific work, has been in a large degree along scientific lines, and the growth, in some ways, of the part of this University corresponding to Yale College, has not been what it might have been." To straighten things out, Strong, University Vice-President William H. Carruth, and the faculty majority held a series of meetings and in 1903 produced an underclass curriculum integrated with that of the high schools, providing for unprecedented flexibility and raising history and economics to equal importance with the languages and social sciences. Defining a "unit" as either a year's work in high school or a semester's work in the College, the faculty required that before the junior year students had to complete four units in English; six in foreign languages; three each in mathematics, the biological sciences, and the physical sciences; and two in the historical sciences (which included both history and economics)—a total of twenty-one required units. Since the normal total number of freshman-sophomore courses was twelve, those freshmen who entered with the usual fifteen units of high-school work had six semester courses as electives. There were no restrictions on their choices. All freshmen also took English rhetoric and attended hygiene lectures. Both they and the sophomores continued the thrice-weekly physical education.[5]

In keeping with the idea of increased self-determination for undergraduates, the faculty also ended the old restrictions on juniors and seniors. As long as they completed a major and did not take more than four courses from the same instructor, they could enroll in whatever classes they wished.[6]

But the more the College curriculum changed, the more it remained the same. The consistent principle was that the studies of the underclass years should provide at least an elementary acquaintance with several different fields of knowledge and that the last two years should give students both the opportunity to specialize and considerable curricular freedom. In comparison with other American colleges, Kansas was solidly midway between the prescribed curricula of many smaller schools and the freely elective curriculum prevailing in other institutions, notably Harvard.[7]

This middle position retained its popularity as the years passed. In 1908 the faculty again assessed its curriculum. A committee headed by Dean Templin investigated college curricula around the country, found enormous variety, and came away more convinced than ever of the worth of their own system. They and the rest of the faculty changed some details, but not fundamentals. The freshman-sophomore courses were divided into eight groups: English, ancient languages, modern languages, mathematics, physical sciences, biological sciences, history (which also included political science, sociology, and economics), and philosophy (which contained education, drawing, and music, as well as formal philosophical studies). Under-classmen had to take one five-hour course in six of the eight groups, together with hygiene and physical education; they also took English rhetoric if they had not had it in high school. The rest of the sixty hours required for junior standing were elective, the only prohibi-tion being that students could not take over twenty hours in one department. Juniors and seniors had before them the same eight groups, plus a ninth called "Professional" for seniors who desired courses in either the Law School or the Medical School. To gradu-ate, thirty hours in one group was necessary, twenty of which had to be in one department. Although upperclassmen could take all sixty hours in a single group, they could not take more than forty in one department. In 1914 the faculty raised those requirements by pro-hibiting upperclassmen from taking more than twenty of their sixty hours in courses open to freshmen and sophomores. And at least twelve hours of the work needed to satisfy the major requirements had to be in strictly junior-senior courses.[8]

At the same time that the curriculum was changing, so were relations between the College and the Kansas high schools. The period from 1892 to 1915 began with efforts to supervise and con-trol the high-school curricula. It ended with the passing of a state law depriving the College of authority to set its own admission standards.

In the 1890s the main problem with the high schools was how to enforce the accrediting requirements that many of them had volun-tarily accepted. When the faculty abolished the six freshman-sophomore courses in 1892, the prescribed high-school course cov-ered physical geography, general history, civil government, algebra, geometry, physics, and language—the last including a total of six years of study, including a minimum of three years of some foreign language and at least one year of English. Those requirements pre-vailed for the next decade.[9]

By 1894 there were 102 accredited high schools and 16 accredited academies, and most of the 118 institutions were cheating on the requirements. "The trouble with the majority of schools of the state," Chancellor Snow told Superintendent W. B. Hall of Chero-kee, "is that they do not follow the outline which they submit to the State University. They make these outlines to be placed upon the accredited list of high schools and then send their students here unprepared to do our work." Closer supervision was a problem as well as an answer, for neither the Chancellor nor individual faculty members nor Arvin S. Olin, whom the regents charged with the task in 1898, had enough time to do the job systematically.[10]

Early in the twentieth century the regents and faculty opened a two-pronged attack on the difficulty. After the legislature of 1903 had increased the University appropriation, the regents hired William H. Johnson as "high school visitor." Johnson had graduated from the University in 1885, had later served as principal of high schools in Lawrence and Emporia, and was most recently high-school principal in Helena, Montana. In addition to visiting, Johnson helped place University graduates as teachers, developed teaching laboratories and school libraries, and worked generally to raise the level of school instruction. The faculty and regents also eased the entrance requirements to correspond with the new College curriculum. Unconditional admission demanded certification of fifteen entrance units in six areas: English (3 units required), mathematics (2½ units), foreign languages (3 units), and physical sciences, biological sciences, and history (1 unit each). The remaining 3½ units could come in any of the six areas. In 1909 an additional area of various vocational subjects—but also including psychology—was added, and from it one unit could be elected; by 1913 students could offer three units from it.[11]

In 1905 the state legislature moved to expand the number of high schools accredited by the University by passing the so-called Barnes Law, named after its sponsor, Representative J. S. Barnes of Pratt. Because of squabbles about location, very few high schools had been created under the county high-school act of 1886. The Barnes Law slid around the location question by allowing county taxes—in counties where the voters approved school levies—to go, on a pro-rata basis, to every high school that met certain standards. The most important of these standards was that the high schools had to have courses that fully prepared students to enter the College. Chancellor Strong, calling the act "undoubtedly one of the most important educational laws in the history of the state," joined numerous other educators in urging voters to make the law operable in their counties. By January, 1910, 112 high schools were receiving Barnes Law aid; by December there were about 150 schools, with some 8,000 students.[12]

After 1905, then, the University was accrediting the new county high schools as well as those established earlier. But in 1915 it lost all its accrediting powers to the State Board of Education. A new law gave that Board power to define "official standards of excellence" in the high and primary schools. It further stipulated that every-one who completed a four-year course in a high school accredited by the Board of Education was entitled to enter the "freshman class of the State University," and also the Agricultural College and the state normal schools. The law was mainly the result of a campaign by State Superintendent of Public Instruction Wilbert D. Ross and the Kansas State Teachers Association. In 1912 and again in 1914 the Association demanded accrediting by the Board of Education, while Ross insisted that "the high school belongs to the people and not to the colleges."[13]

Although the University's chancellor was a member of the Board of Education—along with the superintendent of public instruction, the presidents of the Agricultural College and the Emporia Normal School, and three appointees of the governor—the act of 1915 was still unwelcome. Strong had no choice but to promise that the Uni-versity would obey the law "in entire good faith in every respect," but he had neither desired nor approved it. Scrabbling to preserve as much of the institution's autonomy as possible, Strong asked Attorney General S. M. Brewster for an opinion defining the act's key clause. Brewster replied that it applied to the College, perhaps to the School of Engineering, and to every other school in the Uni-versity to which graduates of unaccredited schools were admitted. It did not apply to either the Medical School or the Law School—but that was slight consolation.[14]

While grappling with curriculum and admission problems, the College faculty also had to tussle with the questions of its own organization and Dean Olin Templin's powers. In 1893 the regents had decreed that deans were to be the executive officers of their faculties and the presiding officers of faculty meetings in the chan-cellor's absence, that deans were to report to the chancellor on the "conditions and needs" of their departments, and that each dean "shall in a special manner undertake to advance the interests of his school." This last directive was vague enough, and in 1908 Chancel-lor Strong confessed himself perplexed about his deans' duties. While they had "general oversight" of their schools and advised him on various matters, much of their authority depended on each dean's "character and personal power." "It is difficult, if not impossible," Strong said, "to state in detail what a dean should or should not do. I am not able to lay my hand on any specific order creating and defining the deanship."[15]

Olin Templin desired a more formal structure that would also increase his own authority. In the spring of 1909 he and Strong executed a deft maneuver. On March 30 Templin resigned, to take effect September 1; the intent was to free him from complicity in what came next, for he knew quite well that the regents would refuse to accept his resignation. Two days later Strong talked the regents into approving a College Administrative Committee, which the faculty had not requested. It was to do "such administrative work as may be required of it by the faculty or the Chancellor or the dean acting within his authority." Strong then announced to the faculty the regents' decision, which they now belatedly authorized. Another vote made the dean chairman and still another allowed the chancellor to choose its members.[16]

Had Olin Templin had his way, the Administrative Committee would have ruled the College. In the fall of 1909, without faculty consent, the group began recommending measures for the faculty's consideration and approval. By April, 1910, Templin was asking the faculty to accept proposals it had not previously seen, much less debated, merely on the "strength of favorable consideration on the part of the Administrative Committee." Although the faculty rejected that idea, it was understood that the committee would continue to make independent suggestions and not simply execute the faculty's will.[17]

On Strong's recommendation, the Board of Regents in 1909 also gave the College dean a final veto on the appointment and promotion of all faculty members to ranks below that of full professor. Previously the chancellor alone had recommended appointments and promotions—though customarily he had consulted with the dean. Now the dean, along with the department chairman and the chancellor, had to approve them too. During the 1909–1910 year veto power on appointments and promotion was extended to the deans of the other schools.[18]

Like the entire University whose center it was, the College was always to be measured both against an ideal—however obscure it might be—and by comparison with allegedly superior institutions. Discrepancies on both counts were the result of relative poverty. "Every year it becomes more difficult to fill vacant places with capable men," said Olin Templin in his annual report of 1912. "We need a good faculty and have it. We need a better faculty. If we ever get it we will have to pay for it." Yet the salary situation was always distressing. Before the Populist legislature of 1897 cut stipends, most full professors got $2,000 a year. In 1903 Chancellor Strong induced the Board of Regents to create salary grades. Professors were to receive from $1,800 to $2,200; associate professors $1,400 to $1,800; assistant professors $1,000 to $1,400; and instructors $600 to $1,000. Six years later the University's growing income made possible another upward scaling: now professors were to get from $2,200 to $2,500; associate professors $1,700 to $2,000; and assistant professors $1,200 to $1,500; instructors' salaries stayed the same. From the minimum to the maximum in each rank, salaries were to rise by $100 a year. In 1912 and 1913 the regents had plans to raise salaries still higher, but the new Board of Administration refused.[19]

In competition with other institutions the College and the University were at a disadvantage. When Samuel W. Williston left for the University of Chicago in 1902, for example, his annual salary rose from $2,250 to $4,000. Wilbur C. Abbott in European history went to Yale in 1908 with the same increase. In 1912 zoologist Clarence E. McClung went to the University of Pennsylvania for $4,000 compared to the $2,600 he had received at Kansas, and when Robert Kennedy Duncan in industrial chemistry departed for Pittsburgh in 1911, his salary rose by 100 percent from $2,500 to $5,000. The College's most unfortunate loss was that of Vice-President William H. Carruth to Stanford in 1913 at a salary of $4,000, up from $2,500 at Kansas.[20]

"The University man," Frank Strong wrote in 1908, "must go into his life work with the expectation of relinquishing a part of the pecuniary reward that might be his if he went into business or such a profession as law or medicine." At Kansas he also had to relinquish greater amounts of time and other things than his colleagues elsewhere. The fifteen to eighteen hours a week that many Kansas faculty members spent in class, said former psychology professor Robert M. Ogden, now at Cornell, severely reduced their time and incentive for research. Many of the country's best universities had long since decided that nine or twelve hours a week in class was a reasonable maximum. McClung started at Pennsylvania by teaching only six hours a week, in contrast to twenty-three—including his laboratory supervision—at Kansas; while this was a light load even by Pennsylvania standards, still McClung would never have to teach over twelve hours. At Kansas, moreover, McClung served on ten time-consuming committees; now he served on only one outside his department. Carruth, at Stanford, got not only a lighter teaching load but also a regular sabbatical leave and a retirement policy guaranteeing him $2,200 a year in his old age, neither of which Kansas could match.[21]

The mathematics of the case was simple. Since the Kansas faculty member worked twice as hard as his counterparts elsewhere for about half their pay, even before the lack of fringe benefits was counted, the ratio of disadvantage of remaining on Mount Oread was three or four to one. In the fall of 1907 ex-Kansas chemistry professor Edward C. Franklin was wrathful about the University's salary scale. After fourteen years in Lawrence, Franklin had gone to Stanford in 1903; even before he left he was well on his way to becoming one of the nation's most distinguished physical chemists. Now he told his brother William, who was considering an offer to join the Kansas Physics Department, that Kansas was unrealistically behind the times. "They ought not to be permitted to get a good man with an established reputation . . . for the money salaries they pay there," Edward wrote. "They ought to learn sometime that good men cannot be brought there at the salaries they offer."[22]

Yet Edward, who had been an undergraduate at the University as well as a faculty member, knew very well that there were many good men at Kansas. While the College and the University alike proved unable to attract men who were already outstanding scholars, many of the College faculty acquired considerable reputations during their tenure. A peculiar strength of the faculty in the 1890s and the early twentieth century was that it continued the tradition of scholarly research established at an earlier day. On the one hand the College retained for some years several of its older scholars. Edgar H. S. Bailey in chemistry, Frank W. Blackmar in history and sociology, Lewis L. Dyche in zoology, and Francis H. Snow in entomology lived out their academic lives on the faculty. Lucien I.

Blake in physics stayed until 1906; Arthur Graves Canfield left for Michigan only in 1898; and William H. Carruth in German stayed on Mount Oread until 1913. On the other hand the College drew to itself new scholars who quickened and strengthened the research spirit.

Much of the enthusiasm for research continued to come from the natural scientists. An example to them all was the Kansan Samuel W. Williston who, after taking both an M.D. and a Ph.D. at Yale, became assistant professor of anatomy there in 1886 and full professor in 1888 and then came to the University in 1890. According to Chancellor Snow it was Williston's "great ambition . . . to develop the geologic wealth of his native State in the service of her University" that led him to return to Kansas, even at a financial sacrifice. During the next twelve years Williston did a stupendous amount of research and writing in two different fields. As a paleontologist he published dozens of articles on Cretaceous reptiles—mesosaurs, pterodactyls, and plesiosaurs; his most significant writings appeared in the *Kansas University Quarterly* and the volumes of the University Geological Survey. But Williston thought his work as a dipterist more important. Growing interested in diptera (flies, gnats, mosquitoes, and the like) at Yale, he found that no American had written much about them, and perforce became a pioneer. Basing his analyses and classifications on Ignaz R. Schiner's study of Australian diptera, Williston finished two excellent preliminary studies in 1888 and 1896. In 1908, now at Chicago, he published his great *Manual of North American Diptera*, which immediately won him recognition as one of the three or four most eminent dipterists in the world.[23]

In the Department of Chemistry there were several scholars as able and enthusiastic as Williston. First there had been George E. Patrick, then Edgar H. S. Bailey; after 1889 there was Edward C. Franklin, a former student of Bailey's. Franklin received his B.S. in 1888 and his M.S. in 1890; in 1894 he took a Ph.D. at Johns Hopkins. The stereotype of the dedicated researcher, Franklin was in his laboratory day and night. He cared nothing for committee work, scorned administration, and paid little attention to the formalities of teaching. After researching in several different areas, he came to concentrate on the nature and properties of liquid ammonia as a solvent. By 1903, when Stanford lured him away, he had become

The faculty member in his natural habitat.

Lewis L. Dyche with an anatomy class. Undated, but probably 1880s.

The author, 1970.

Hamilton P. Cady and his machine for the immediate determination of molar weight. Undated.

the nation's leading authority on the subject; he would do even more significant work in the future.[24]

In addition to his own scholarship Franklin brought that of Hamilton P. Cady to both the College faculty and the larger scientific community. Another Kansan, Cady took a B.A. from the University in 1897, studied for two years at Cornell, and then returned to Lawrence for doctoral work under Franklin. After investigating liquid ammonia for his doctoral dissertation, Cady turned his attention to the composition of natural gas and to the presence in it of rare gases—helium, argon, neon, and coronium. In 1907 he detected a large amount of helium in gas from a well in Dexter, Kansas; during the First World War he investigated the occurrence, isolation, and properties of helium for the national government. Still later his work became the foundation of the largest helium-producing plant in the world, in Liberal, Kansas.[25]

Bailey, Franklin, and Cady made the Chemistry Department outstanding. In the early twentieth century its distinction increased. Cooperating with Robert Kennedy Duncan in the famous program of industrial fellowships was Francis W. Bushong, who came to Lawrence in 1905 after graduate study in Europe. Teaching less and less as he increased his valuable research into petroleum utilization under fellowships he received, he joined Duncan at the Mellon Institute in Pittsburgh in 1913. Two years before he left, Frank B. Dains, a fine organic chemist, joined the Department. Dains, who had a doctorate from Chicago, performed pioneering research into what would become the medical "miracle drugs" of a later day. He also became one of the foremost American authorities on the history of chemistry. His combined research and historical interests made him the Department's prime library builder.[26]

The Department of Physics proved less important to the College than the Department of Chemistry. Although Lucien I. Blake continued his electrical research and publicity until his departure in 1906, physics courses were more attractive to engineering students than to College undergraduates. Finding a replacement for Blake as chairman was not easy. William C. Franklin took his brother's advice by asking a salary of $3,000 a year, plus another $100 to pay his way to meetings of scientific societies, and the University could not meet his terms. Not until 1909 did Frank Strong come across Frederick E. Kester, an Ohioan who had taken his Ph.D. at Cornell in 1905 and was now teaching at Ohio State University. A specialist in problems of specific heat, Kester was also an astronomer interested in the grouping of asteroids, and he did notable work in both fields. As chairman for over thirty years and as a faculty member for thirty-five, Kester became an outspoken advocate of more faculty power in shaping University policy. To help him in the Department he had Associate Professor Martin E. Rice, together with an assistant professor and an instructor.[27]

In Professor Henry B. Newson the Department of Mathematics from 1890 until 1910 had a scholar of international renown. An Ohio Wesleyan graduate, he had done graduate work at Johns Hopkins, Heidelberg, and Leipzig. As the result of articles on unicursal curves, continuous groups of circular transformations, projective transformations in space, and the like, both the Circolo Matematico de Palermo and the Deutsche Mathematiker Vereinigung elected him to membership; not more than a dozen other Americans shared the same honors. At the time of his death in 1910 Newson had completed the manuscript of his most significant work, *Theory of Collineations*, published posthumously in 1911.[28] Most of Newson's mathematical colleagues were also scholars, especially John N. Van der Vries, who came in 1901 just after taking his Ph.D. at Clark; Ulysses Grant Mitchell, who joined the Department in 1907 fresh from undergraduate and graduate work at Kansas. The University's most distinguished mathematician, however, was the brilliant Solomon Lefschetz, who came in 1913 with a Ph.D. from Clark University.

There were excellent men in the biological sciences, too. From 1890 until 1894 Vernon L. Kellogg, an 1889 alumnus, took over much of the work that Chancellor Snow had to relinquish. His articles on various species of *Mallophaga* (bird lice), Kansas insects, the cattle horn fly, the milkweed butterfly, and other subjects attracted the attention of Stanford scientists, and to Palo Alto he went.[30] But several excellent biological scientists stayed longer than he. The botanist William Chase Stevens received a Kansas M.S. in 1889, joined the faculty that year, and retired only in 1937. One of the University's most popular teachers, he offered the institution's first bacteriology course in 1890 and published *Plant Anatomy* in 1907. After his retirement Stevens and his wife crossed and recrossed Kansas some sixty times to study, photograph, and collect specimens for their *Kansas Wild Flowers* (1948), an attractive, learned, and immensely popular book.[31]

Joining Stevens were two other scholars, Marshall A. Barber and Samuel J. Hunter, who won great scholarly fame. After taking an M.A. at Harvard, Barber returned to his alma mater for a stay of sixteen years. His greatest achievement was the development of a method for isolating single bacteria for microscopic study, which both astounded and delighted the scientific community when he demonstrated it at an international convention in 1908. After leaving the University, Barber won even greater respect as a malariologist and as one of the world's greatest authorities in the practical work of preventive medicine.[32] Hunter, of the class of 1893, came back to Lawrence from graduate work at Cornell a year after Barber returned. When he left the University in 1924, he had been chairman of the Department of Entomology for twenty-three years and had dozens of publications to his credit, most of them on the state's injurious insects. He also helped draft a federal law of 1912 to prevent the introduction of harmful insects and plant diseases from abroad and served as state entomologist.[33]

But greatest of all the early twentieth-century biological scientists was Clarence E. McClung in zoology. After completing the University's pharmacy course in 1892, McClung matriculated in the College, where he fell under the spell of Samuel W. Williston. He received a B.A. in 1896 and a Kansas Ph.D. in 1902. Between 1890 and 1910 he published thirty papers. The most exciting of them was his doctoral dissertation, "The Accessory Chromosome: Sex Determinant?" published in the *Biological Bulletin* in 1902. Here he demonstrated for the first time that the controls for particular bodily characteristics—here primary and secondary sex characteristics in *Orthoptera, Hemiptera, Coleoptera, Neuroptera,* and *Lepidoptera*—were located in a particular chromosome or pair of chromosomes. Almost at once he became one of the world's outstanding zoologists; his later research increased both his stature and his fame, and in 1912 he went to the University of Pennsylvania.[34]

Several fine men in the humanities and social sciences saved the University from being top-heavy with natural scientists. Frank H. Hodder, who replaced James H. Canfield in 1891, was to history what Williston was to paleontology and McClung to zoology. Behind him when he came were an undergraduate education at the

University of Michigan, two years as a civil servant in Washington, D.C., five years as a faculty member at Cornell, and a year of graduate study at Göttingen and Freiburg. Ahead of him was work that would place him, as his student and colleague James C. Malin said, in the ranks of the "nation's foremost scholars and teachers." Although interested in all areas of American history, he concentrated his research on the antebellum nineteenth century. Through his writings other scholars learned of Senator Stephen A. Douglas's role in writing and passing the Compromise of 1850, of the relation between Douglas's railroad interests and the Kansas-Nebraska Act of 1854, and of the real significance of the Supreme Court's decision in the *Dred Scott* case in 1857. Though Hodder was unable to publish all the results of his research, he poured his findings into his courses. He also generously helped historians across the country—especially the younger ones—by commenting on their manuscripts and encouraging them to further research.[35]

Hodder alone made the history faculty outstanding. But had the Department been able to keep all the other men who joined it for a while but then moved on, it would have been distinguished indeed. For a decade after 1891 it included Ephraim D. Adams, who had a Michigan Ph.D. and published several articles on European and American history. He went to Stanford in 1902, however, and it was there that he wrote his noteworthy two-volume *Great Britain and the American Civil War* (1925).[36] Succeeding Adams in European history was Wilbur C. Abbott, who after graduating from Wabash College and studying at Cornell, had taken a B.Litt. from Oxford, and taught at Michigan and Dartmouth. Two extensive articles on Charles II's Long Parliament in the *English Historical Review*, and numerous book reviews in the *American Historical Review* earned him an offer from Yale that Kansas could not equal. To the East he went to teach twelve years in New Haven and seventeen more at Harvard, establishing himself as a prominent authority on Oliver Cromwell and the Puritan Revolution and increasing his scholarly output. His most widely read work was *The Expansion of Europe*, first published in 1918. Similarly Wallace Notestein came to Lawrence in 1905, but left for the University of Minnesota after finishing work for a Yale doctorate. In Minneapolis and later at Cornell and Yale he became one of the nation's reigning authorities on Tudor and Stuart England, especially parliamentary history.

Few historians would ever associate him, or Abbott or Adams either, with Kansas.[37]

Good men could be found, but they were hard to keep. In 1908 every historian at Kansas was considering an offer somewhere else. Abbott and Notestein went, but Frank Hodder and one of his colleagues stayed. This was Carl L. Becker, who after he departed Kansas in 1916 would become, because of his ideas about the nature of history, one of the most provocative, controversial, and luminous members of the history profession. Yet at Kansas Becker was something of a misfit. He had arrived in 1902 as an assistant professor before finishing his doctoral work at Wisconsin. The completion of his dissertation and its publication in 1908 as *The History of Political Parties in the Province of New York from 1760 to 1775* earned him an associate and then a full professorship. The book was an exciting interpretation of the coming of the American Revolution which argued, with considerable documentation, that the Revolution was as much the result of struggles among the colonists for political power as of a contest between the colonies and England. Except for two essays on historical relativism in 1910 and 1913, however, Becker at Kansas published nothing else of note, unless *The Beginnings of the American People* (1915), a text, is counted. At Kansas, Becker was a poor teacher—possibly because though trained in American history, he insinuated himself into Abbott's vacated European history position in 1908—and a seclusive colleague. He was also a man already well on his way toward a rejection of the hard labor of research in favor of the collation of other men's work, toward a career as a speculator unwilling to perform the research to discover the truth or falsity of his ideas.[38]

Except for Becker's leaving in 1916, the history faculty took on greater stability after 1908. In that year the American and European history chairs were joined in one department. The year before, Clarence C. Crawford, a Kansas B.A. (1903) and Wisconsin Ph.D. (1906), became assistant professor of European history. Always much more of a teacher than a writer, he would stay for forty years. In 1910 William W. Davis, an Alabaman who had done his graduate work at Columbia under William A. Dunning, arrived. He too would remain for the rest of his academic career, thirteen years of which were spent as chairman. While he published *The Civil War and Reconstruction in Florida* in 1913, he was always more interested in teaching than research. Having traveled extensively in the Far East, he taught Asian as well as American history. He was a popular lecturer, a frequent speaker on current world affairs before student and civic groups, and the greatest sports fan on the faculty.[39]

Carl Becker's replacement in 1916 was Frank E. Melvin, another Kansas graduate (B.A., 1906; M.A., 1909) who gave the University a lifetime of service. Melvin had taken his Ph.D. from the University of Pennsylvania in 1913 and was on the Cornell faculty when Hodder called him back. Melvin published comparatively little—though his doctoral dissertation came out in 1919 as *Napoleon's Navigation System*—but he was an outstanding bibliographer and collector of hundreds of important pamphlets on the French Revolution and Napoleon, his major teaching and research field. The Melvin Collection would draw dozens of scholars to Lawrence.[40]

While the Department of History was having personnel problems, the Department of Philosophy was having a personal tragedy. When Olin Templin became dean in 1903, he and Frank Strong searched cautiously for another philosopher. "We have to be very careful here, and I am glad of it, about the trend of the philosophical teaching in the University," Strong wrote, "and I would like to know whether Mr. Boodin is inclined to upset religious faith as he finds it or whether he takes [a] sound and fair view of philosophical questions as they relate to Christianity." The candidate in question, who proved satisfactory, was John E. Boodin, a Swedish immigrant who after undergraduate study at Brown University had worked for his doctorate under the great Harvard pragmatist William James. Despite being overburdened with elementary courses and undernourished by intellectual stimulation at Kansas, during the next eight years he wrote several articles and a valuable book. *Truth and Reality*, which appeared in 1911, was an important contribution to pragmatist philosophy.[41]

At the time of its publication, however, Boodin was suffering from nervous depression. Sensitive and high strung, he had suffered a tremendous shock when William James died in 1910. To Boodin, James had been confessor, father, friend, and spiritual and intellectual guide. "I retired to my room and wept as I only had wept at the death of my father when I was a boy," he wrote later. "A light and a love had gone out of my life which could not be replaced."

Growing erratic, nervous, and moody, by the summer of 1911 Boodin was in a Topeka hospital. He proved unable to resume teaching and then asked for a paid leave of absence to restore himself. When the Board refused, Boodin took to criticizing the members, whereupon the regents fired him, effective July 1, 1913. In the meantime they gave him a year's leave, with $800 of his regular $2,500 salary. With unnecessary cruelty they ordered him to spend the leave outside Lawrence. The dismissal angered so many alumni, faculty, and students that for a time there was a movement, led by campus YMCA secretary Roy Stockwell, to "expose rottenness in the administration of the University." But the regents were immovable, and still another able scholar left Mount Oread forever.[42]

Happier lives, fortunately, prevailed among most of the College humanists. Among the classicists there were more teachers than scholars. For the three decades after 1885 the outstanding members of the Department of Greek were Alexander M. Wilcox and Miles W. Sterling. Wilcox, a Baltimorean, followed a Yale B.A. with a doctorate in 1890, then spent the next five years in traveling abroad, teaching at Connecticut's Wesleyan University, and postdoctoral study at Johns Hopkins. Devoted to all good literature, art, and music, Wilcox was the complete humanist. Beyond his teaching, his most important contribution was his expansion of the small classical museum of Greek and Roman artifacts, replicas, pictures, maps, charts, plates, and slides into a collection of note. After 1929 the museum bore his name. Sterling was a Kansas alumnus of 1880. A superb teacher and a cultured gentleman, he had studied Greek and Sanskrit with Basil Gildersleeve at Johns Hopkins and journeyed to Europe; he gave generations of students a love of ancient Greek civilization.

In addition to David H. Robinson, the more important Latinists of the period were Hannah Oliver, who took a Kansas B.A. in 1874 and served on the faculty from 1890 to 1921, and Arthur T. Walker. A brilliant classicist educated at New York University, Walker arrived in Lawrence in 1897, a year shy of finishing work for his Ph.D. at the University of Chicago. He came full of fears about the wild West—at first he slept with a loaded revolver under his pillow—but he found Lawrence tamer than he expected and stayed through his retirement in 1942 and his death in 1948. Interested in Latin teaching at every level, in 1907 he published the first edition of *Caesar's*

Gallic Wars, with a new plan for teaching it, and through the Classical Association of Kansas and Missouri encouraged high-school teachers to ever better and more enthusiastic Latin instruction.[43]

Since the College faculty had never been slaves of the old classical curriculum, the development of the modern languages kept pace with that of the ancient tongues. In 1892 the regents hired assistant professors to help Arthur G. Canfield in French and William H. Carruth in German. The French teacher was Miss Eugenie Galloo, a native of France who had studied at the Sorbonne before emigrating and had taken a bachelor of letters at the University of Michigan. A popular teacher, she spent the rest of her career in Lawrence. Elmer F. Engel of the Kansas class of 1892 was her counterpart in German. Like Galloo, Engel stayed at Kansas, rising to associate professor in 1905 and full professor in 1914. Primarily a teacher, Engel published a German reading text, wrote numerous articles on improving instruction, and devised a method of his own, which required students simultaneously to master the principles and use them in writing. A decade later the University again took back one of its own, Alberta L. Corbin of the class of 1893, who had taken a Yale Ph.D. in 1902 after several years of high-school teaching. According to Olin Templin she was more eager to find a husband and have children than to teach. Frustrated in both desires, she made the female undergraduates her children, supervised them, fought for dormitories to protect them from harm, and in 1918 became officially what she had been unofficially for years—the adviser, or dean, of women.[44]

In the quarter-century after 1890 the Department of English also collected several faculty members of great ability and power. While not all of them were research scholars, the English faculty had a vigor and a flavor that few other departments could match. Charles G. Dunlap, who came in 1887, labored for forty years with great success to transplant his love for good literature—his specialty was the English novel—into the minds and hearts of Kansas youth. Dunlap was as much a moralist as a teacher who strove to get students to follow the proper conduct expressed in the literature that he loved. "He has kept his light trimmed and burning through all these four decades," said William Allen White in 1930, "a torch not merely of learning but of joy and loveliness."[45]

With Dunlap occupying Arthur Richmond Marsh's chair, the

regents sought a man to fill the junior position. In the fall of 1889 Regent Charles S. Gleed met a Princeton faculty member on a train and mentioned the vacancy. When word got back to Nassau Hall, four of the five English graduate students rejected it out of hand. But Edwin Mortimer Hopkins decided to see what the West was like. Determined to return east if Kansas proved too barbarous, he remained for fifty years. In the 1890s he had a scholarly interest in the problems of *Piers Plowman*, but as time passed he grew far more concerned with raising standards of English teaching in the public schools. Distressed by the students' ignorance of grammar and usage, Hopkins plunged into the Kansas intellectual wilderness and acquired a great reputation as a crusader. In 1913 the United States Bureau of Education appointed him to gather information on the teaching of English, and in 1921 he became chairman of the National Education Association's Committee on Elementary School English. In the classroom, where he had more to do with grammar, philology, and writing than with analyzing literature, he was insistent on high standards, good-humored and keen of wit, both highly tolerant and highly intellectual. "I always think of him," a former student said, "when I want to picture a gentleman of culture, one of Holmes's 'Brahmin caste' in intellect."[46]

Typified by Dunlap and Hopkins, the English Department developed considerable stability. In 1895 Raphael Dorman O'Leary of the class of 1893, now with a second B.A. from Harvard, returned as assistant professor. He stayed until his death in 1935. A "Celtic wisp of a man," as one of his friends described him, O'Leary was a dynamo with charm. In his first year at Kansas he edited *Agra*, a monthly literary magazine, and in later years did extensive reviewing for the Chicago *Dial*, the *Sewanee Review*, the *International Journal of Ethics*, and other publications. He also wrote *The Essay* (1928) and a teacher's handbook on essay writing. His greatest fame among the students arose from his meticulous, comprehensive criticism of their papers and his remarkably expressive readings of essays in class.[47]

In 1902 Frank Egbert Bryant joined the Department and stayed until his untimely death in 1911. A Michigan B.A. and M.A., he was an able scholar who published articles on *Beowulf* and Lessing's *Laokoon* and prepared a translation of the "Thrymskwitha," a Norse Eddic poem, even before taking his doctorate at Harvard in

1910. In 1905 the Department took Selden L. Whitcomb away from Grinnell College, his alma mater. Whitcomb had pursued graduate study at half a dozen universities. His interests were extremely broad: his English courses became world literature courses; his knowledge of ancient and modern foreign languages made him an exceptionally competent teacher. In 1918 he appropriately became professor of comparative literature. He published his *Outlines of American Literature* when he went to Grinnell and *A Study of the Novel* when he removed to Kansas; at his death in 1930 he was revising the manuscript of *The Study of a Literature*. Five years after Whitcomb reached Mount Oread, Rose Morgan, a Kansas alumna of 1894 who had received an M.A. in 1905, joined the growing department. A gentle, kindly, and sympathetic soul with a wide reputation as an antipoverty and world peace reformer, she was beloved by her students.[48]

The development of the social sciences, as both disciplines and departments, was uneven. Until 1920 political science and history were joined. Frank H. Hodder thought the union especially unfortunate. "I have repeatedly called your attention . . . to the fact that the University of Kansas lags far behind all other institutions in the development of political science," he told Chancellor Strong in 1914. "It is surely hardly creditable that Kansas, who prides herself upon her advanced position in politics, should make such a slight provision for the teaching of the subject that makes most directly for training in citizenship." Although Strong was sympathetic, Dean Templin never seemed able to find enough money to start the new department.[49]

At the time that Hodder wrote, the University's political scientist was Clarence A. Dykstra, an Ohioan with an Iowa State University B.A. and graduate training at Chicago. He taught such courses as political theory, political parties, and American, European, state, and municipal government, but he was always more interested in application than in theory, especially in improving Kansas government at all levels. In 1918 he left Lawrence for a varied and meteoric career as a faculty member at U.C.L.A., city manager of Cincinnati, president of the University of Wisconsin, and finally U.C.L.A. provost.[50]

Until 1930 psychology and philosophy were also one department. Both Olin Templin and John E. Boodin taught both subjects, with

Templin interested in experimental psychology and Boodin in social and educational psychology. But whatever the departmental arrangement, the tremendous expansion of psychological research starting in the 1890s made hiring a specialist imperative. From 1899 to 1910 Boodin and Templin got help from Archibald Hogg, who received a Kansas B.A. in 1894 and an LL.B. in 1896. But while Hogg assisted Boodin and taught courses of his own in experimental, genetic, and laboratory psychology, he was not adequately trained. In 1909 and 1910 the Department hired two men who were better qualified. David C. Rogers had a Ph.D. from Harvard and Floyd C. Dockery was a doctoral candidate at Michigan. In 1914, moreover, Robert M. Ogden came as full professor. With a doctorate from Würzburg and a decade of teaching experience at the universities of Missouri and Tennessee, he added considerable strength. By 1915 there were a dozen undergraduate psychology courses and two graduate seminars. But Ogden left for Cornell in 1916 and the real strengthening of the curriculum would await the future.[51]

Meanwhile sociology and economics moved ahead slowly—first together, then separately. The original mediator between them was Frank W. Blackmar. Blackmar came as professor of history and sociology, but after the arrival of Ephraim D. Adams in 1891 he taught practically no history. Instead he concentrated on both a variety of sociology and several economics courses—money and banking, taxation, and the history and theory of political economy. At his request the regents in 1897 created a new Department of Sociology and Political Economy.[52]

During the next six years Blackmar acquired two assistant professors to teach most of the economics courses and free him for sociology. Ralph W. Cone, a Kansas alumnus and Harvard M.A., came in 1899, but resigned because of ill health in 1910. Arthur J. Boynton, who had an M.A. from Columbia and had completed a year's work toward a Harvard doctorate, came in 1903 and remained until his death in 1928. His guide to economic theory was Adam Smith. Uninterested in research and writing, Boynton hurled himself into teaching with a force that frightened the faint-hearted. Frank W. Blackmar had a campus-wide reputation for academic leniency, but Boynton drove his students furiously. "The proverbial five-hour snap is no more," said the *Kansan* in 1910. "No longer will everybody laugh when you tell them that you flunked in economics—for now it is one of the hardest courses on the Hill."[53]

Only in 1911 did the regents feel able to separate economics from sociology by creating a Department of Economics. They, Chancellor Strong, and Blackmar all wanted a man of "marked economic ability" to head it. Boynton did not seem to be that man, but in 1912 they found him in Harry A. Millis, late of Stanford, whose main interests were public finance, labor economics, sickness and insurance, and collective bargaining. Unfortunately Lawrence was only a way-station for him; in 1916 he was off to the University of Chicago for a distinguished career.[54]

If the new Department of Sociology had been as independent of Dean Olin Templin as it now was of economics, Frank W. Blackmar would have been a happier man. The two men were not sympathetic. In 1911 Blackmar got help from Assistant Professor Victor E. Helleberg, but he wanted at least one more department member. Even though Blackmar himself was teaching five courses for thirteen hours each semester—at the same time that he was dean of the Graduate School—Templin scorned his request. Sociology was a comparatively unimportant subject, he suggested to Chancellor Strong in 1913. Kansas was already giving it more attention than any other school except the University of Chicago. "Possibly there are peculiar conditions requiring this," Templin said, "but I do not know what they are." The large number of students in Blackmar's courses, he suggested, was because they were "here required to do less work for credit received than in any other department of the College." Blackmar fought Templin to a victory, however, for Helleberg got a recommended promotion to associate professor in 1913, and then the Department got a new instructor.[55]

During the Snow and Strong administrations, then, only one generalization applied to the College: excellence was elusive. By 1916 the College—now bigger than ever before with over 1,700 students and 153 faculty members—had gained a number of fine professors, but had also lost a number of fine professors. Salaries had risen, but not high enough, and the teaching load continued to be excessive. The curriculum had changed for the better and relations with the high schools had improved, but in 1915 the legislature deprived the University of its power to set admission standards. For every problem solved, a new one seemed to appear.

Thus it was with the University as a whole—as probably it had to be. And in 1913 a problem which in the previous decade had dwarfed all others found a solution which prepared the way for even greater difficulties. It was the question of the relation of all the state's institutions of higher education to each other and to the people. Half a century after the University's founding, the legislature abolished its Board of Regents, drastically decreased its autonomy, and in so doing brought one era of its history to an end.

18

End of an Era

BY the early months of 1913 Chancellor Frank Strong had had his fill of the University of Kansas and its difficulties. Throughout that year and into 1914 he sought the presidency of the University of Washington, corresponded with officers of the University of Arkansas, and tried to get in the running for the presidency of Vassar. A normally ambitious man, Strong might have sought such positions even if conditions in Kansas had been of the best. But from his viewpoint they were of the worst. The legislature of 1913 had replaced the separate Boards of Regents of the University, the Agricultural College, and the Emporia Normal School with a single Board of Administration, whose members were salaried state officials with almost complete sovereignty over the schools. "The change was the outcome of a somewhat bitter political campaign," Strong wrote President Arthur T. Hadley of Yale. "What developments may come, nobody knows. . . ." A year later the future of public higher education was still in doubt. There was "a very uneasy feeling here and it is yet impossible to say whether or not the presidents of the institutions are to have entire administrative independence."[1]

The law creating the Board of Administration was an effort to solve several problems arising from the obvious contradiction between the organization of public higher education and the state constitution. When the founding fathers of Kansas required that a university be established, they had in mind only one institution, which would include both normal and agricultural schools. The division of that university into three parts in 1863 meant duplication, waste, and higher taxes. Kansans had no "just conceptions" of what a superior university was or what it cost, Superintendent of Public Instruction Peter McVicar said in 1869. When they found out, they would be unwilling to pay for it. Therefore the land grants to the University and the Agricultural College should be combined (the Normal School, he thought, could take care of itself). "What folly . . . to struggle to maintain two State institutions, whose avowed objects are substantially the same, within a few hours' ride of each other, with a double corps of instructors and the two sets of expensive buildings which will very soon be needed, when one State institution could do all the work and do it equally well."[2]

During the rest of the nineteenth century, McVicar's idea found only slight support. In 1872 Representative William H. Clark of Ottawa reminded the House of the constitutional provision and asserted that the state's resources were being "frittered away upon four institutions"—there was now another normal school at Leavenworth —"none of which are above mediocrity, and without State, much less national reputation." He asked the House to instruct the Judiciary Committee to report a bill by which the University would absorb the other three schools, but his resolution never got to a vote. Four years later the House Committee on Retrenchment and Reform approved a bill substituting a single Board of Education for the separate Boards of Regents, but under pressure from standpatters Chairman Samuel N. Wood withdrew it. Most Kansans who worried about the costs of public higher education thought more about cutting appropriations than consolidation. Significantly, however, in 1901 Governor William E. Stanley urged that efficiency, economy, and the constitution required a single Board of Regents for the three schools, and a bill providing for such a Board appeared in the Senate. The Committee on State Affairs recommended that it not be passed.[3]

Chancellor Strong was as intent on educational efficiency as any other man in Kansas. He thought at first, though, that efficiency required, not unified control, but restriction of each institution to its proper sphere by the voluntary consent of its regents. The Normal School, he said in his inaugural address, should confine itself to training teachers for common and rural schools, and the Agricultural College to "industrial training" for students with at least an eighth-grade education. Promising that the University would never intrude on such work, he said that its field was to offer the "highest facilities for the most specialized instruction in every line" of study, the "most advanced and specialized courses in the various lines of graduate and advanced undergraduate work." There had recently been talk of a single board of control to eliminate needless duplication, he told President David R. Boyd of the University of Oklahoma in 1905. But he opposed it as a "new departure," "very problematical in its results," and needless.[4]

Some of the talk, however, had come from Governor Edward W. Hoch. In his first message to the legislature in 1905 Hoch said the management of all state institutions needed a "complete overhauling"; some managing boards should be consolidated, others reduced in size, still others abolished. Two years later he called for a single Board of Regents for the three state schools. "These institutions are each a part of a whole educational system," Hoch maintained, "and should be considered as a unit and built up systematically." That message and the approval by the Senate Ways and Means Committee of a bill establishing a single board gave Strong a bad scare. As soon as he heard of the bill, he wrote letters to various legislators explaining why they should oppose it. "As a general principle," he told one, "it is fatal to any institution whose object is education and the development of ideals and democratic spirit, to have its government in any way outside of itself or bound up with institutions whose educational aim is different." The principle was "entirely revolutionary and untried in educational institutions," except those of South Dakota, where the results had been "unfortunate." To alert the alumni, Vice-President William H. Carruth rushed an article into print in the March issue of the *Graduate Magazine* repeating Strong's arguments. The members of the single board, he pointed out, would be full-time state employees, paid $1,200 a year. For that money no one as well qualified as the distinguished members of the present Boards of Regents could be hired. Even if the salary were higher and well-qualified men were obtained, they would probably try to meddle in the internal administration of each school, with disastrous results. Both Strong and Carruth suggested that Hoch appoint a commission to study each institution's appropriate activities and report to the legislature of 1909. After their report the lawmakers would have no trouble seeing that each school confined itself to "its own particular field of work." Neither the bill nor the commission idea was approved.[5]

Practical as well as theoretical matters troubled Strong and Carruth. In 1907 the Agricultural College seemed to be threatening the University's preeminence in engineering. By that time the College offered four-year programs in mechanical and electrical engineering and architecture, all of which required the completion of a high-school course or its equivalent and led to the Bachelor of Science. When regents of the Agricultural College asked the legislature for over $100,000 worth of engineering buildings at the same time that University officers requested $200,000, Strong grew worried. Late in 1906 he suggested to Agricultural College President Ernest R. Nichols and his regents that they should yield to the University now and wait for their appropriation until 1909. If both institutions sought money, both might fail. But the College regents barged ahead. Strong thereupon wrote several legislators to suggest that they were asking too much money generally. "The other institutions of the State seem to think that they ought to get as much as the University," he complained, "which of course is not the case, because the University necessarily must be upon a different basis of work and expenditure than the other institutions, it being the central and original institution."[6]

Despite his concern, the lawmakers gave the University its $200,000, and the Agricultural College $80,000 for an engineering building and shops. Yet Strong knew that heavy weather lay ahead. "I hope that all friends of the University are going to keep in mind the contest which is sure to come before long with the Agricultural College," he wrote former Regent Charles S. Gleed in the fall of 1907. "This is the only dark cloud that hangs over the future of the University, and it presents a very difficult problem."[7]

Competition became so fearsome, indeed, that by December, 1908, Strong was calling for his own form of consolidated control of Kansas higher education. Early in 1908 the University's leaders clashed with those of the Agricultural College over which school should receive a subsidy for the engineering experiment station which had been authorized in a bill before Congress. Introduced by Representative William B. McKinley of Illinois, the bill appropriated $30,000 to each state and territory for applied engineering research. Strong approved the principle, but was appalled by a provision that the experiment stations be located only at those institutions aided by the Morrill Act of 1862—in Kansas, the Agricultural College. He became a one-man lobby to change or kill the bill, writing to McKinley, several state university presidents, and the Kansas Congressional delegation, and calling a meeting of interested university leaders at the meeting of the National Association of State Universities in Chicago. To everyone his message was the same: the bill would be unfair to institutions which lacked an agricultural school, and especially unfair to the University of Kansas, which had the "only . . . engineering school in Kansas which is of a grade to do this higher work in experimentation." Both to serve the people and to get a jump on the Agricultural College, in February, 1908, the University regents voted to "proceed to the establishment" of an experiment station and discover its cost. In March, Chancellor Strong and Dean Marvin proposed a catalogue statement declaring that the station existed, and the regents approved it.[8]

Stung by Strong's activity, the *Industrialist*, official publication of the Agricultural College, argued that for several reasons the stations belonged in Morrill Act institutions. Their agricultural experiment stations had long since made their faculties familiar with applied research, the stations' staffs would overlap the regular faculties, with obvious economies, and the numerous engineering students would be of great assistance. The stations would have a "reflex benefit" on the colleges; they would be a most valuable "supplement to the great work which these land-grant colleges are now doing."[9]

In an effort to stave off an undignified fight between the two schools, Governor Hoch invited their Boards of Regents to confer with him and other state officials. He also invited the officers of the Normal School, who in starting to train high-school teachers also seemed to be encroaching on the University's preserve. It was "painfully evident," Hoch told them, "that we have no very clearly defined and carefully circumscribed educational system." Neither the constitution nor state laws delimited each institution's work, described the relations that should exist among them, or defined their relation to the state's school system. Hoch was frightened by the possibility that unless Kansans checked existing duplication and made interinstitutional relations precise, the state would one day have two or more "mediocre universities, and no great agricultural and industrial school and no great university."[10]

To make plans for reversing the "dangerous direction" of the three schools, Hoch appointed a committee of two men from each. The University's representatives were J. Willis Gleed and Thomas M. Potter. Along with A. M. Story and Edwin Taylor of the Agricultural College and Lyman B. Kellogg and Milton F. Amrine of the Normal School they met with Hoch in July and September. Hoch had hoped for agreement about each institution's work which might be embodied in a bill for the legislature of 1909. But while all the delegates except Story agreed that the Boards of Regents should check the tendencies to duplication, and that "professional engineering" work belonged to the University and "practical mechanical engineering" work to the College, they could not decide how to implement their ideas. They and Hoch decided that it would be best to leave the preparation of a bill to the new governor, Walter Roscoe Stubbs.[11]

Meanwhile the Agricultural College announced in April that it was adding a civil engineering course to its curriculum, leading to a Bachelor of Science degree. Outraged, Strong sent virtually identical letters to Governor Hoch and newspaper editors in Topeka and Kansas City, Missouri. The new course, he said, was needless and costly. It rested on the erroneous assumption of Manhattanites that the "mechanic arts" included all kinds of engineering, even the "professional sort." If the practice was continued, the future held only three possibilities. Either the expense of maintaining a "first class university with its normal and agricultural departments separated from it" was going to be twice what it should be, or Kansas would have to get along with "second or third rate institutions," or one institution would have to "kill off" the other. Strong did not directly advocate collegicide, but he was meditating on fundamental changes. "How the problem can be solved with two men, one at the head of the University and the other at the head of the Agricultural College, each making his own independent plans, even with one Board of Regents, is to my mind a question of very great gravity."[12]

Strong's theoretical position on the engineering question rested on a distinction between the mechanic arts and professional engineering. The former included merely the "training of the hand and the mind for the use of tools in the art of the mechanic, or in the industrial art." Professional engineering meant designing machinery, factories, bridges, and power plants, for which the University was preparing its students. Unfortunately for his argument, however, the Morrill Act of 1862 said that the "leading object" of the land-grant colleges was to teach "such branches of learning as are related to agriculture and the mechanic arts . . . in order to promote the liberal and practical education of the industrial classes in the several pursuits and professions in life."

Professor John D. Walters of the Agricultural College stressed the professional emphasis of the Morrill Act in the *Industrialist* in June, 1908; and the following October, Board of Regents President A. M. Story carried the attack to the University. The Morrill Act demanded that the Agricultural College offer engineering, he said. Not only did the University have no such obligation, but its engineering work was probably illegal, for none of the departments of science, literature, and the arts authorized by the Moody Act of 1889 comprehended it. The University bore the stigma of duplication. Having made that nice twist in the argument, Story claimed that the University was intruding in other ways into the Agricultural College's sphere. Its Department of Entomology was doing state-service work that belonged to the agricultural experiment station; and the domestic science courses were "absolutely out of harmony and out of keeping with a university." The Lawrence school was tending toward "spreading out and absorbing the work of other institutions," toward leaving "its own proper sphere or field of operation." Furthermore, Story complained, "the University has always had the big end of the appropriation in the State. It has had practically all it asked for. It has brooked no interference. It has taken everything it desired in the way of new courses and new work."[13]

To answer Story's assault and fully set forth his own ideas, Frank Strong prepared an elaborate inquiry into the management of public higher education in Kansas. Before publishing it as part of his biennial report for 1908, he submitted a draft to the Board of Regents and changed it in light of their comments. Thus while the analysis bore only his name, in the main he spoke for the whole Board.[14]

The state's system of higher education, Strong contended, was now in crisis, and it was up to the citizens to relieve it. During the past decade there has been a "wonderful growth" in the nation's state universities and agricultural colleges. Those which had prospered most, however, were those united with each other in a single institution—Wisconsin, for example, and Illinois, Minnesota, and California. With their state-service work added to their research and teaching, with all their officers acting in concert, they were becoming the "greatest type of American university" and were about to perform the "greatest work to be done by any teaching institution in the world." But Kansas, thanks to the separate administrations of the University and the Agricultural College, had no such institution and never would as long as the division lasted. As Strong read the state constitution, the University was to "take precedence of all other institutions in its sphere of work"; nothing that it did to fulfill its "rights and functions" could infringe upon the field of any other school. Separate control and administration meant the reverse—that the other schools would inevitably intrude on the University's work, with the resulting duplication, extra expense, and lack of coordination. Division inevitably meant that the agricultural and mechanic arts colleges would seek to magnify themselves, to develop into "general educational institutions," to become in fact second state universities. It also made many people think, undemocratically, that the separate schools were for the education of separate social or economic classes: the University for the elite and the Agricultural College for the commoners.[15]

Before exploring fully the question of duplication in engineering, Strong took pains to attack the Manhattan school generally. It was, he said, a most peculiar institution, for it offered three different kinds of work: elementary-school courses such as reading, writing, spelling, and arithmetic; high-school work in such subjects as algebra, bookkeeping, the English classics, and history; and proper college and university courses. It even pretended to offer graduate study, though Strong described its quality as work that "might rightfully come in a high-school course." Worse than the common and high-school courses, though, were the low entrance requirements and low standards, which admitted students who had finished only the eighth grade and graduated them four to six years later as Bachelors of Science. When poorly prepared students were thrust into difficult professional or technical courses, the courses were cheapened; the Agricultural College B.S., Strong said, was merely a "cheap degree," of especially little value when compared with the University's degrees. The College's determination to process its students through to a degree as rapidly as possible also meant that they lacked time for such subjects as English, foreign languages, history, and others that were "by general consent considered necessary for laying a good general foundation for higher study."[16]

But the burden of Strong's charges against his Manhattan foes was that they were offering engineering training that was contrary to historical precedent, out of keeping with a proper definition of "mechanic arts," and unnecessary. From the 1870s to the 1890s, he said, the Agricultural College had offered engineering training. It was small in scope and elementary in nature, designed in part for farmers who might have building or surveying to do, and in part for "mechanics"—that is, men who wished to learn the machine trades. Starting in the late 1890s, however, the College had begun to expand its offerings to duplicate the University's. The expansion was the result of a misconception of "mechanic arts." A man trained in them was trained "primarily to use tools and to execute designs and plans already made." A professional engineer, by contrast, was trained "primarily to create designs; by his higher imagination and creative powers to make plans which at first exist only in his creative mind." Against his wishes Strong had to admit that the United States Bureau of Education had ruled that schools aided by the Morrill Act could teach engineering. But immediately he noted that the correct construction of the words "mechanic arts" had never been tested in the courts, and that Senator Justin D. Morrill himself had never defined the phrase to include engineering.[17]

Under the terms of the Moody Act, Strong went on, the University certainly had authority to establish an Engineering School, for the Department of the Sciences comprehended it. Because Kansas was an agricultural and not an industrial state, one good professional engineering school could meet all its needs; because the state's agricultural needs were so great, the Agricultural College should concentrate on them. So great were the agrarian potentialities of Kansas, indeed, that it would "pay a hundred times better" for the University to duplicate the work in agriculture than for the Agricultural College to duplicate the work in engineering.[18]

The Chancellor concluded his direct attack on the Agricultural College by arguing, in effect, that the engineering part of the Morrill Act, as it applied to Kansas, was unwise. Industrial education, he asserted, belonged in the local high schools rather than in a college or university. Because Kansas was underdeveloped industrially, the Agricultural College might do the work; there was not enough industry to justify high-school courses in the mechanic arts. But as long as the Agricultural College provided such training, it would be in part a high school.[19]

With the Agricultural College and its engineering courses dispatched to some lower realm of intellect, Strong tried to down the criticism that the University was encroaching upon the work of the other state schools. His school, he reminded his readers, was a "universal institution and covers by law, as well as by implication, all of the work which an educational institution of college rank may do, except what is made impossible by the organic law of the state or the nation." Theology was the only training it could not legitimately offer. For the benefit of all Kansans it had undertaken to train high-school teachers, offer domestic science courses, establish industrial fellowships, and conduct "applied" as well as "pure" entomological investigations. Judge Story and other carpers to the contrary notwithstanding, when the University did such things it was simply expanding to fill its own proper sphere.[20]

Strong suggested five possible ways to end the difficulties. Of the suggestions, however, he thought two impossible and two others unfeasible. The two impossibilities were either to join the University and the Agricultural College at some new location or to transfer the College to Lawrence. Either would require a considerable initial outlay for new buildings and equipment, Strong admitted, but either would ultimately save the state more than the consolidation cost and at the same time give Kansas a university equal to the best in the land. Yet both suggestions were "practically impossible and unthinkable," for the "sacred memories and the life-histories that have grown up around the institutions as they now exist" forbade consolidation at a new location, and "it would wrench too many heart-strings" to pull the Agricultural College up "by the roots."[21]

A third possibility was to allow the Agricultural College to develop as it would to become a second full-scale state university. It was to Strong's credit that he mentioned this option at all, for he detested the idea. Two state universities, he believed, would result in calamitous competition—in a "pulling and hauling in a way disastrous to the best interests of the State University," and the destruction of "general efficiency." The reverse of the suggestion that the Agricultural College be left entirely free was that the legislature prescribe very precisely what it might do. Although the Chancellor thought well of the idea, he knew that President Nichols, the Agricultural College regents, and the loyal alumni would fight such restrictions to the bitter end and even beyond.[22]

Strong supported the fifth alternative: unifying the administrations of the two schools under a single Board of Regents and a single chancellor while leaving the parts of the consolidated institution in Lawrence and Manhattan. Strong insisted that only a single executive could make the united university work. Separate chancellors or presidents would mean a "quasi-independence" for each school; each man, backed by his alumni, would seek to advance the interests of his own institution and thus perpetuate present divisions and discord. But if the regents tried to resolve the differences between the University and the Agricultural College, their incompetence would inevitably cause them to fail. Only a university executive "who has made himself by years of study and training a master of his profession" could judge such questions wisely. Either the Agricultural College and the University should be entirely independent of each other, Strong contended, or they should be entirely unified by a single board and a single executive. "The conditions of development at the Agricultural College," Strong concluded, "are such as to allow now, if ever, a permanent reconstruction of educational policy. The responsibility lies with the people of the state. Let them decide."[23]

Just to make sure that they and their legislators of 1909 made the right decisions, Strong began maneuvering politically. His main desire was to get Representative Alexander C. Mitchell of Lawrence, who was also a regent, chosen Speaker of the House, and he sought the aid of several newspaper editors. Mitchell had little support, however. When Strong discovered that Governor-elect Walter Roscoe Stubbs wanted Joseph N. Dolley of Wabaunsee County as Speaker, he dropped the matter.[24] Late in December, 1908, he turned for help to Fred S. Jackson, the state attorney general and president of the Alumni Association. First he asked Jackson to lobby with individual legislators and appropriate committees to prevent abridgment of the University's rights and powers. Then at the behest of Strong and several alumni Jackson chose a special committee to guard the school's interests. Chairman was Clyde Miller of Osage City, a former representative; among the other members were Regent J. Willis Gleed of Topeka, and legislators Arthur F. Cranston of Parsons and S. C. Westcott of Galena. Finally Strong urged University sympathizers to try to get one of their number elected chairman of the Senate Ways and Means Committee. He was delighted when Charles F. Huffman of Columbus, one of his favorites, won the post.[25]

For all the Chancellor's hopes and efforts, the legislature of 1909 made no decisions about relations between the University and the Agricultural College. Strong had suggested that the regents write a bill to deal at least with the problem of duplication, but they thought such a measure unwise. By January 9, after talking with several legislators and Governor-elect Stubbs, Strong thought that the whole matter should be postponed until 1911, so that it could be thoroughly aired and so that University officers could devise some "matured plan" for the legislators' consideration.[26]

On January 20, however, Representative William L. Brown of Kingman County and Senator Anson S. Cooke of Mitchell County introduced identical bills to end duplication. The bills prohibited the University from offering courses of study in agriculture, horticulture, and related subjects, and the Agricultural College from offering most of the professional engineering work. At once a new fight was on. Students in Manhattan wrote the legislature to defend the engineering courses, stressing that the Agricultural College was for farmers' sons who lacked the preparation required for the University, and claiming that it was the Agricultural College's "diversified courses"—engineering and agriculture together—that had drawn them to the school. The alumni and the *Industrialist* weighed in with appropriate comments. And on February 3 the entire legislature visited Manhattan at the invitation and expense of the student body. There were campus tours, a dress parade by the undergraduate military battalion, a mass meeting with speeches, songs, and college yells, and a great banquet cooked and served by the domestic science classes—which showed, the *Industrialist* said, that the Agricultural College was not "simply an aggregation of class-room theory, ancient mythology, and dead languages."[27]

Meanwhile the University's officers worked at their own schemes.

On the same day that the Agricultural College was entertaining the legislators, Vice-President Carruth was sending justifications of the University's claim to preeminence in engineering to a number of Kansas newspapers. Carruth asked the editors to disguise the source of the comments, when they were printed, by making them parts of editorials or independent news items. On February 12 the University had all the solons to Lawrence, where Strong pressed upon them his institution's engineering rights, as well as its extreme financial need.[28]

If there was a victory won in 1909, it belonged to the Agricultural College. Both bills to delimit the work of the two schools died in committee.[29]

In early 1909, then, relations between the Lawrence and Manhattan institutions could not have been much worse. During the next two years, however, they improved even more rapidly than they had deteriorated. On June 30, 1909, the presidency of Ernest R. Nichols ended at the request of his Board of Regents. His successor was Henry J. Waters, previously dean of the College of Agriculture at the University of Missouri.[30] In contrast to the testy Nichols, Waters was a genial gentleman who was anxious to improve relations with his Lawrence counterpart. He asked Strong to deliver an address at his inauguration in November and saw to it that the Chancellor received an honorary LL.D. for his efforts. Strong on his part took special pains to wish the Agricultural College well and proposed that cooperation, instead of competition, between them should be "writ large in the subsequent history of higher education in Kansas."[31]

More important was a series of private talks between the two men in the early months of 1910. They liked each other immensely. Both were open, honest, and keen-minded; neither found the other overly assertive. By June they had agreed that their Boards of Regents should meet together to discuss means of eliminating duplication, "should any be found to exist," and to seek the "fullest measure of cooperation that the conditions of the two institutions will allow." It proved impossible to get all the regents assembled— Waters was more enthusiastic about cooperation than his Board— but it was the spirit that counted. The verbal wars of 1908 and 1909 had ended. While the old problems remained and while Strong was no happier about engineering in the Agricultural College than he had been earlier, the insults and malicious propaganda vanished before greater reason and mutual respect.[32]

Also helping to bring Strong and Waters together was the opinion of a growing number of Kansans that a single salaried board of control should govern all the state's institutions of higher education. On January 17, 1911, Representative Austin M. Keene, a Republican from Fort Scott, brought in a unification bill. As approved by the legislature, it abolished the Boards of Regents and substituted a Board of Administration of three members. Appointed by the governor, they were to be full-time state employees paid $2,500 a year. They would have complete power over the schools: to appoint and dismiss the officers and faculty and fix salaries, to make all needful rules for government and administration, to supervise all expenditures. Not more than two Board members could be from one political party; not more than one of them could be an alumnus of any one of the state schools.[33]

Expectedly, Strong fought the bill before the House Committee on Educational Institutions. Waters joined him. Their position was that Kansas did not need a Board of Administration, that such a Board could never serve higher education as well as the separate Boards of Regents, that the three schools were now in fine shape, requiring no change.[34]

They never came close to winning. The House passed the measure on March 3 by a vote of 97 to 15. In less than a week Senator Charles F. Huffman guided it through the upper house. Leon S. Cambern of Erie tried to head it off by proposing an amendment calling for the appointment of an Educational Institutions Committee to investigate all aspects of the three state schools, and the School for the Deaf and the School for the Blind. The group would report to the legislature of 1913 and submit such bills as it thought necessary. But the majority of senators were in no mood for delay. Voting down Cambern's proposal, 21 to 16, they at once passed the Keene bill, 22 to 16, and sent it to Governor Stubbs.[35]

The Governor was in a delicate position, for whatever he did with the measure would offend a sizable group of Kansans. While Stubbs favored some form of consolidation, he was dubious about parts of the bill. To gain support for what he did, he sent telegrams to a number of noted university presidents, among them A. Lawrence Lowell of Harvard, David Starr Jordan of Stanford, Harry

Pratt Judson of Chicago, Cyrus Northrup of Minnesota, and Charles R. Van Hise of Wisconsin, describing the bill and asking if he should sign it. Most of the presidents disapproved of it completely. "Strongly believe that plan likely to lead to mediocrity in higher education in Kansas," wired Van Hise, while Northrup described it as "most pernicious." "The joint board sacrifices the benefit of institutional authority which is the most precious asset of every institution," said William L. Bryan of Indiana University. "A university is nothing without its own soul," he added. "The University of Kansas needs to keep its own soul as much as Harvard does."[36]

Before Stubbs killed the bill, however, he made sure that the idea of educational efficiency and cooperation would stay alive. In return for his veto, he wrote Strong, Waters, and President Joseph H. Hill of Emporia Normal, he wanted a committee of three regents from each school to study ways to bring the institutions into harmony. Three subcommittees on finances, efficiency, and general scope would handle the work. The price was cheap enough, and the executives consented. On March 14, Stubbs vetoed the Keene bill, objecting that a three-man board was too small for the best interests of higher education and that the $2,500 salaries were far too low to attract "vigorous, earnest men in the prime of life, who are qualified by business and educational experience to assume such great responsibilities." If the work of the joint committee proved to be unsatisfactory, he said, the legislature of 1913 could enact appropriate laws.[37]

At meetings in March and April, 1911, Stubbs and the regents formed the State Commission of Higher Education with the Governor as chairman. The three University representatives were Leon S. Cambern on the finance subcommittee, William Allen White on the efficiency subcommittee, and Scott Hopkins on the subcommittee on the scope of the three schools. Joining them were Regents M. M. Sherman, Alfred L. Sponsler, and Arthur Capper of the Agricultural College, and John E. Junkin, Sheffield Ingalls, and George E. Tucker of the Normal School.[38]

As the Commission began its work, Chancellor Strong and his faculty were apprehensive about its impact on the University's autonomy. They gained some confidence from the fact that the group had no standing in law, from the calm and deferential way it conducted its investigations, and from William Allen White's assurance that his Subcommittee on Efficiency, at least, had its mind made up before starting. All the members intended to do, he told William H. Carruth, was to "justify the state institutions before the tax-payers"; no "serious faults would be found." While hoping that the Commission would help to solve the duplication problem, Strong yet remained uneasy lest the members undertake to interfere with the University's internal administration. In May he told former Regent William Y. Morgan, editor of the Hutchinson *News,* "We are drifting, I fear, perhaps insensibly and without voluntary action, into a position where the independence of state educational institutions is endangered." At the same time he told Regents White and Scott Hopkins that several of the University's best teachers had already accepted positions elsewhere or were seriously considering them, and that Vice-President Carruth was mulling over an offer from Ohio State.[39]

But the Chancellor need not have worried overmuch. The most important recommendation of the report of the Commission of Higher Education in 1913 was that the three separate Boards of Regents be retained. Instead of a single board of control, the Commission urged its own continuance and establishment by law, with all the regents, the governor, and the superintendent of public instruction as members. It was to have legal authority to decide the "scope and the interrelations of the State schools and the relation that each shall sustain to the people of the State." The Commission would also determine the financial needs of the schools and make all recommendations for appropriations to the legislature. Realizing that many Kansans continued to favor the Keene bill, the regents condemned the single board scheme. Wherever men had tried it, they said—in Iowa, Oklahoma, Montana, South Dakota, Florida, Georgia, Mississippi, and West Virginia—it had proved a failure. "It would be fatal, the Commission believes, to create conditions in Kansas which have so utterly destroyed the institutional efficiency of other states, militated against harmony, and in general have produced unrest amounting in most cases to demoralization in the instructional body."[40]

The Commission's recommendations impressed few legislators, and were of no consequence whatever to the new governor, George H. Hodges, a Democrat. When Hodges addressed the legislature on January 15, 1913, he noted that the schools together were asking

$2,300,000 more than they had received in 1911. Appropriating such "vast sums" was "altogether out of the question," said Hodges. "I believe," he went on, "that you will find on investigation that there are many duplications of work in our state educational institutions, that some departments are of little or no value, and that some cost more than they are worth to the state." After casting this vote of no confidence in the present Boards of Regents, he asked for the creation of a single board of control over all the state's educational institutions, including those for the deaf and blind, to consist of three full-time, salaried members.[41]

Hodges's message was the beginning of the end of the system of University government that had existed since 1864. On January 30 Representative Keene introduced the bill the legislature had passed two years before. After the Committee on Education had reported it without recommendation, the House beat down a substitute for it, prepared by the Commission of Higher Education and offered by W. E. Lyon of Lincoln County. It would have created a Board of Administration of three men—one from each Board of Regents—to determine the "scope" and "general educational policy" of each school, the relations among them, and the "relation of each to the people of the state." The new board would also have determined school budgets and requests to the legislature. But the House killed the Lyon measure without significant debate and then passed the Keene bill, 87 to 31. Democrats were to blame. Sixty of 67 Democrats voting were in favor; 25 Republicans and 2 Socialists joined them. In the opposition stood the other 7 Democrats and 24 Republicans. When the measure reached the upper house on February 6, the Democratic leaders pushed it through in a day, without even referring it to committee. After prohibiting the Board of Administration from appointing their relatives to positions in the schools, the Senate passed it, 31 (20 Democrats and 11 Republicans) to 6 (2 Democrats and 4 Republicans). Governor Hodges signed the bill on February 10.[42]

According to the law the three new rulers of the three institutions of higher education and the schools for the deaf and blind were to be chosen by the governor "solely with regard for their qualifications and fitness to discharge the duties of their positions" and confirmed by the Senate. Not more than one member could be an alumnus of any one of the schools; not more than one could come

Governor George H. Hodges, apostle of efficiency. (Courtesy Kansas State Historical Society.)

from a single Congressional district; not more than two could be of the same political party. As full-time state employees they received salaries of $3,500 a year and were ineligible for other elective or appointive office. They were to serve four-year terms.

As they were appointed, so might they be dismissed. With the Senate's consent the governor could fire any member for malfeasance in office or "any cause that renders him ineligible to said appointment, or incapable or unfit to discharge the duties of his office." When the legislature was not in session, the governor could suspend a member and appoint a replacement, both acts being subject to Senate approval when the legislature next convened.

To the Board of Administration went all the powers possessed by the regents: to appoint all officers, faculty members, and employees and set their salaries; establish regulations for grading and promotion; write rules for internal government; manage and control property; and spend appropriated funds. On July 1, the separate Boards of Regents would cease to exist. Yet the new Board would start work even before then. The law provided that within ten days after their appointment the members were to start to "lay out and determine" the work of the schools for the 1913–1914 academic year and to announce their plans in the catalogues.

Naturally the law repealed all the provisions of previous laws that were inconsistent with it. But it also directed the Board of Administration to exercise the powers of the Boards of Regents given in laws that remained in effect. For the University this meant, among other things, that the Moody Act of 1889, with its various peculiarities, was still in force—though no one seemed to notice or care.[43]

Although the passage of the Keene bill was a defeat for every principle of University government for which Frank Strong stood, he had no choice—as long as he stayed at Kansas—but to obey it. The University accepted the act in "good spirit," he wrote Hodges, "and will cooperate in every way possible to make the new law a success for all of us here are anxious to give your measures hearty support. We realize that the success of the new method of government means a great deal to you and your administration. We realize further that it means perhaps more to us for the character of the control of an institution of learning is a matter very vital to its life."[44]

Hodges replied that neither he nor his party was unfriendly to the University. "I realize that these institutions are the greatest asset that any state possesses, and we Democrats are just as much interested in seeing a successful administration of one and all of them. . . . I intend to take plenty of time in choosing a Board and expect to get the three biggest and best men that it is possible to find for these positions."[45] He chose two men and a woman. The Republican member was former Governor Edward W. Hoch, an enthusiastic supporter of the University and higher education in general. Hoch's Democratic colleagues were Edward T. Hackney of Wellington—a University alumnus of 1895, a lawyer, and a former legislator—and Mrs. Cora J. Lewis of Kinsley. She was the wife of the editor and herself the associate editor of the Kinsley *Graphic*, and a prominent clubwoman and former president of the Kansas State Federation of Women's Clubs. From 1905 to 1907 she was a visiting member of the Kansas Board of Control, which had jurisdiction over the state's charitable and correctional institutions.[46]

Strong told Hodges that the selections were "excellent choices in every respect." Encouraging him in this belief was former Regent William Y. Morgan, editor of the Hutchinson *News*. All three appointees were his friends, Morgan wrote, and he felt they would all be "fair" to the University. Mrs. Lewis, especially, would be friendly: "She believes in you and in the University. I think whatever is done," Morgan added, "will be along lines that you can influence."[47] Strong could only hope that Morgan was right. But he remained most apprehensive. For if Governor Hodges, the state legislature, and most Kansans had paid no attention whatever to his and the other regents' ideas about University government, there was no reason in 1913 to believe that their Board of Administration would do any better.

19

The Perils of Efficiency

FOR Frank Strong's peace of mind it was a pity that his search for a new position in 1913 and 1914 came to nothing. The years from 1913 until his resignation in 1920 were by far the most dispiriting in the University's history to that time. Although the members of the Board of Administration had the best of intentions, they meddled in the University's internal affairs, proved themselves naïve and ignorant—at least by Strong's standards—of what a great state university should be, and provoked the school's officers and alumni to public attacks. A law of 1917, moreover, set up a new Board of Administration with new duties, powers, and members, and because of it a number of other difficulties arose. Atop those vexations, after the University Council wrote a constitution for the University's internal government, the law of 1917 rendered it in part inoperative; where it stood in the years to follow was anybody's guess. And then came America's entry into the World War the same year, which ripped away hundreds of students and dozens of faculty members, deranged courses and curricula, converted part of the University into a military camp, practically destroyed morale, and turned the Chancellor into a tired, discouraged, careworn man.

Step by step in 1913 and 1914 the Board of Administration antagonized Strong and the faculty. One of its first official acts was to rescind the new salary scale adopted by the Board of Regents in 1912, which had provided increases of from $400 to $500 at every level. The Board even refused to continue the regular $100-a-year

349

increase approved by the regents in 1909. Although the legislature of 1913 had granted enough money to cover the raises, the Board discovered that the University's salary level was far above that of the other schools under their control. Therefore the members agreed to apply the merit system "liberally and impartially" to all of them and to treat everyone with "equal fairness." There would be merit increases for deserving faculty, but no general raise.[1]

The Board announced the decision in May, 1913, and gloom settled down on Mount Oread. Irritation and disappointment pervaded the College faculty, Olin Templin reported, with many professors feeling that their rightful earnings had been denied them. Pleading for relief, Strong told Edward T. Hackney that several prominent faculty members had resigned and that others were considering offers: "I fear that crisis is impending now." Strong was especially downcast by the coming departures of Dean Charles H. Johnston of the School of Education for Illinois and Vice-President William H. Carruth for Stanford. "I do not expect ever again to have the same intimate and confidential relation to anyone in the University," Strong told Carruth sadly. "When you go the University will miss greatly a strong personality and I shall miss one of the best friends that I have ever had."[2]

When Hackney, Hoch, and Mrs. Lewis finally fixed salary scales by rank in April, 1914, they were more generous than anyone expected, yet less so than the regents in 1912. Allowing the $100 annual increase to stand, the Board set instructors' salaries at $600 to $1,200 a year, assistant professors' at $1,200 to $1,700, associate professors' at $1,700 to $2,200, and full professors' at $2,200 to $3,000. Compared with the schedule of 1909 the minimum salaries in each rank were the same, while the maximum salaries of assistant and associate professors were up by $200 and of full professors by $500.[3]

Other Board decisions were disturbing. In the summer of 1913 the members shut down the business offices in all the institutions they controlled in favor of a central office in Manhattan, to be moved to Topeka as soon as space was available. The Board boasted that the act saved the state "thousands of dollars" in the first year alone by releasing salaries of business managers and clerks and allowing the Board to join other state agencies in buying supplies directly

The University's greatest single loss: William H. Carruth in 1914, a year after he had gone to Stanford.

from manufacturers. Yet Chancellor Strong was aggrieved because the Board had not consulted him—though he kept quiet.[4]

He became angrier, but still said nothing, when the Board in the summer of 1913 appointed two new faculty members without consulting him. They were Professors Arthur McMurray, formerly of Iowa State College, in public speaking, and William A. McKeever, late of the Agricultural College, as head of the Child Welfare Department in the Extension Division. Strong was unwilling to fight the Board on the appointments, for he had to admit that he was on vacation in Colorado at the time and unavailable for discussion and that the Board might honestly have felt that it should act at once.[5]

The following December, however, the Board made another unsolicited appointment, and at that point the Chancellor struck back. By the fall of 1913 he and numerous other moralists on Mount Oread had concluded that the female students badly needed an adviser—or dean—of women, for licentiousness seemed to be spreading. During the 1912–1913 year students held a "tag dance." According to its rules the girls tied numbered tags to an ankle and the boys, bearing duplicate markers, found their partners by inspecting ankles—and as much as possible of the legs above. It was fun; but by Strong's standards it was not wholesome fun. Worse still, in the fall of 1913 that sensuous, provocative dance, the tango, reached the University. Two fraternities and two sororities formed a tango club, and hired professional dancers from Topeka to teach the sliding, passionate steps. Strong and the Board of Administration were shocked. They prohibited the tango and "other suggestive dances," and abolished the tango club. At the same time they were worried by an increase in smoking among the men. Believing that the tobacco fumes and the sight of smokers had bad effects on the coeds —and also on the smokers—they asked the men to stop puffing on campus, and condemned it wherever "women students or visitors congregate."[6]

To save the women from further harm, in October and November Strong and the female faculty members and several faculty wives were about to start canvassing the country for an adviser of women. Strong kept the Board of Administration informed and asked the members to make no appointment until he, the appropriate deans, the University women, and the Board had agreed on a candidate. The Board ignored his request. In December the members told

Strong that the adviser was to be Mrs. Eustace Brown of Olathe, like Mrs. Lewis a former president of the Kansas State Federation of Women's Clubs and also a former member of the State Board of Charities and Correction. Angrily Strong told Board President Edward T. Hackney that while he had no objections to Mrs. Brown as a person, the method of hiring her worked against the University's "integrity and good discipline." For the "good of higher education in Kansas," Strong hoped the Board would "recede from its position and give back into the hands of the University all initiative and powers of recommendation in regard to appointments."[7]

Strong also wanted to retain the power of dismissal. The case at issue in 1914 was that of Dean Charles S. Skilton of the School of Fine Arts. By February the Board had concluded that he was too poor an administrator and too eccentric to continue as dean. Admitting that Skilton was no business manager, Strong argued that his musical knowledge and ability, scholarship, ideals, and moral standards were of the highest, and pleaded that he be allowed to continue. The plea only delayed his firing for a year. In 1915 the Board summarily replaced him with Harold L. Butler.[8]

By that time Strong was thoroughly perplexed about the extent of his powers, for in the spring of 1914 Hackney, Hoch, and Mrs. Lewis had sent out a letter saying that they had no desire to interfere in arbitrary ways with the legitimate internal affairs of the schools. The initiative in University educational policy was to remain with its leaders, and so were matters of appointments and internal administration generally.[9] But words were only words, and Dean Skilton's dismissal belied them.

While the Board members were causing consternation inside the University, they were publicly professing their zeal to improve the quality of higher education in Kansas. Their main idea was that quality depended on service to society. There were two university ideals from which to choose, the Board said in its report for 1914. One was the "cloister ideal," which would put the University on a "pedestal of lofty scholarship, but of cold exclusiveness." The other was the "democratic ideal," which would "abate no whit of its scholarship, but would make it throb with a warm humanitarianism." This was to be the University's goal. "We want our University to measure up in scholastic standing with the very best schools of its kind, and we are proud of its high standing. We would still further exalt it, but we wish to see it more and more exemplify true greatness by practical service." The same year President Hackney in an article in the *Graduate Magazine* described the University as the nation's best among those that did not have an agricultural school—he probably meant the best state university, but he did not say so—and his emphasis was almost entirely on service. "We hear much about Wisconsin University," he said, "but Wisconsin University is also Wisconsin Agricultural College and there is no gainsaying the fact that today your Alma Mater is the greatest exclusive University in numbers, in size and in ability of faculty, in touching and helping the largest number of citizens in the state, in dealing with state problems, in technical research and investigation of the people that it serves, in the United States."[10]

And the Board was acting to keep it that way. As soon as the members organized, they said, they had voted to refrain from "unnecessary internal management" of the schools and had consistently followed that policy—which was certainly news to Frank Strong. To increase efficiency the Board had consolidated the business offices and purchasing departments, instituted a uniform system of record-keeping, and joined the chief executives in a Commission on School Relations which had allegedly done much to correlate the work of the several schools and curtail the multiplication and duplication of courses. It had also formed a committee to perform the high-school visitation work that the University, Agricultural College, and State Normal School had formerly done independently. More generally the Board had completed arrangements for sharing both human and physical resources among the schools. The employees of each, the Board said, stood ready to aid the rest through personal services and the loan of books and equipment.[11]

From the Board's point of view, the University's needs were mainly for more buildings. Although there was conventional praise for the faculty members—"Modestly they toil on, often without sufficient popular appreciation, and nearly always upon salaries proverbially below the compensation of other learned professions. They are the salt of the earth. The state can not too highly value them."—there were no plans for higher salaries. But the University was "in worse shape in the matter of classrooms and office rooms than any other institution of its character in the country." It was now impossible to meet all the classroom demands, and the office situation was worse. The nineteen members of the Department of English had only two offices, each eight by fourteen feet; the dozen members of the Department of German were almost as cramped; attics and garrets housed the scattered offices of other departments. The Department of Domestic Science had quarters directly opposite the men's toilet in the "dark gloomy basement" of Fraser Hall in "rooms with floors that are beyond description." Old North College threatened to come crashing down at any moment. Even more scandalous was the unfinished state of the main administration building, a "reproach upon the state." The Board recommended that the legislature of 1915 appropriate $250,000 to finish at least part of the central section. To guarantee the health and safety of the female students, and to protect them from greedy landlords, all the schools needed dormitories. Each of the "fifteen hundred mothers who each year send their girls for the first time from their protected homes into strange cities are praying that dormitories may be erected at once and put in charge of refined, motherly women." Unwilling to ask money of the legislature, however, the Board suggested that funds should come from either private donors or bonds to be repaid by charges on the students.[12]

For many of the University's friends, however, good will was not enough. To watch over the Board and care for the University generally, the Alumni Association in 1913 had passed a motion offered by William H. Carruth to create a Board of Visitors. The visitors, six alumni who were citizens of Kansas, were to inform themselves "intimately regarding the affairs of the institution," report once a year on the University's condition and needs, and make "such other reports as they deem wise." Without a doubt the motion had Chancellor Strong's approval.[13]

On the first Board of Visitors were former Regents Charles F. Scott, the chairman, and Scott Hopkins, together with Genevieve H. Chalkley, Lizzie W. Smith, C. I. Davidson, and J. V. Humphrey. Their 1914 report was innocuous. Asserting that the Board of Administration law had created "grave apprehension" about the University's future, which had not dissipated, the visitors said there was no reason to question the Board members' "complete devotion" to the University's welfare, or their "intention to do what in them lies" to keep Kansas in the "front rank of American universities." It remained to be seen, though, whether or not the Board could implement its ideals under the existing law.[14]

A year later the visitors concluded that those ideals had gone aglimmer. On May 21, 1915, Charles F. Scott told Chancellor Strong that the visitors unanimously thought that their coming report should point out the "weaknesses and failures" of the law and the Board of Administration. Scott asked for Strong's own criticisms of the Board, promising to keep his cooperation secret, and for permission to use the Chancellor's words when they fit the visitors' purposes. Strong provided seven major objections, which the visitors incorporated into their own report.[15]

That is, three of the visitors did. For some reason half of them were absent when the report was approved; it bore only the names of Scott, Mrs. Chalkley, and Hopkins. During the past year, they said, there had been a "distinct decline in the *morale* of the faculty and students." "Restlessness," "uncertainty," and "depression" characterized the professors; among the students there was rampant a "spirit of dissatisfaction and discontent wholly incompatible with the best work and the best discipline." If part of the difficulty was the result of the Board's dismissals of Dean Skilton and Acting Dean Arvin S. Olin, both of which showed the Board's determination to meddle in the University's internal affairs, the primary reason was the very existence of the Board itself. Admittedly the members were "distinguished citizens of the state whose devotion to the welfare of the University cannot be questioned." Yet even they were not proof against the evil system they represented. Overseeing broad policy and business matters did not require all their time, so to earn their salaries they participated in internal administration. That intrusion weakened the Chancellor's initiative, deprived the faculty of its initiative and independence, and subverted student discipline. The Board also worked in secret: Chancellor Strong attended its meetings only by invitation, its records were not public, its decisions were without review.

There was also an objectionable tendency toward uniformity in the Board's decisions, a feeling that what worked well in one institution should work well in the rest. According to Strong and the visitors the "very life of any great institution of learning is its differentiation from other institutions, giving it a personality of its own, an atmosphere and a spirit that are individual and distinctive."

No great university had ever been developed on the "community plan, merely as one of a brood." And the Board, having assumed all sorts of unnecessary administrative duties, simply had too much to do to know all the schools intimately. The Board president came to exercise a "preponderating influence" over the other two members, while at the same time all the members were likely to be fooled by ambitious, conniving professors. When the Board announced that merit would determine salaries or planned to offer worthy faculty members special opportunities for study, research, and publication, "a condition is created in which the best self-advertiser is most certain of official recognition, while the modest plodder whose work, although perhaps of the highest importance, may not lend itself easily to public exploitation, is left with his modest plodding for his reward."

Allegedly the University's tragedy was known throughout the land. Educators elsewhere were telling "strong and promising men" not to accept positions at Kansas. "That such a sentiment should exist," the visitors said, "and should be justified, certainly is a humiliation that should not be endured a moment longer than necessary." They called on the alumni to appoint a special committee of five to consider the problem of the Board of Administration and report in 1916. In the report was to be the text of a bill to be submitted to the legislature.[16] Most alumni, however, saw the matter differently. Several speakers said that there was no dissatisfaction with the Board in other state institutions, that the visitors' investigation had been superficial, and that adopting and publishing their report would injure the University. By a vote of 47 to 41 the alumni tabled the report, then decided to appoint a special committee to investigate that report and make a report of its own.[17]

Although the visitors' comments did not move the Alumni Association, they moved the Board of Administration in unexpected ways. President Hackney was at the meeting in his capacity as a University alumnus. To no one's surprise he defended the Board as enthusiastically as the visitors had assailed it. Contrary to the visitors' statements, he said, conditions within the University were excellent. The Board had not interfered in internal management, had consulted as necessary with the deans and Strong, had not acted in secret, and above all had never—either by accident or by design—caused a decline in the University's individuality. All the schools under the Board constituted the "great educational family of the State of Kansas." Just as every wise father encouraged his children's individuality, so did the Board foster the uniqueness of each school. "The University has never been made part of a brood," Hackney said, "but has ever been treated and looked upon as the eldest daughter in the educational system of Kansas."[18]

Two days later Hackney and Edward W. Hoch made an unprecedented effort to strengthen the Board's position. On June 10, 1915, they summoned into special meeting the 175 faculty members who had not left Lawrence for the summer. Hackney again defended the Board and Hoch made a few remarks of his own. Then for the next three hours they compelled each faculty member to answer three questions aloud, face to face with a majority of the group that had absolute power over his salary and tenure. The first question was, "Have you thought or felt during the year that you might be removed from your position as a teacher in this institution without the recommendation of the head of your department, your Dean, and the Chancellor?" One man confessed that such an idea had flitted across his mind, but the rest said no. "Have you been depressed or restless," ran the second question, "or lacked spirit or enthusiasm this year on account of any action of the Board?" Half a dozen faculty members said they had so suffered, the rest that they had not. The third question was less personal: "Do you know of any case during the year, in which the Board has interfered with, or taken a hand in any matter of student discipline?" All the replies were negative, and Hackney was triumphant. "It was a splendid meeting," he rejoiced in a public statement—one which brought everyone into "much closer relations and a better understanding."[19]

Charles F. Scott asserted that many faculty members were not so sure. Attacking what he called the "inquisition of the University faculty" in his Iola *Register,* he said that many professors were outraged and insulted, and that several believed a purge might be starting—at least for the few who had spoken against the Board.[20] Time proved such speculations wrong, but there was no doubt that the University's faculty and administration were even more uneasy in 1915 than they had been in 1913.

For a time the problem of the University's internal government proved almost as vexing as the problem of its external government.

By 1912 the conviction was prevalent throughout the University that the institution's structure was obscure. It was not that Strong, Carruth, and the deans were running the school in a slipshod way, but that it had grown rapidly according to no intelligible or preconceived plan. From 1902 to 1912 the student body increased from 1,294 to 2,437 and the faculty from 89 to 175.[21] Two new schools—Medicine and Education—appeared, along with a host of new programs, courses, departments, and emphases. Faced with such growth and change, men worried and wondered about the University's organization. By the 1907–1908 academic year the University Council, which had expanded in 1901 to include all the full professors, had completely lost track of its internal rules and regulations and appointed a special committee to sort them out. In 1908 Strong himself said he had no very clear idea of what deans should do and that he could not locate any rule or directive creating or explaining the deanships.[22]

Even more embarrassing was that by 1910 Strong felt that he was losing touch with the University as a whole and that administrative matters were threatening to get out of hand. The institution, he wrote his deans, had grown so large and become "so scattered in all its departments as to make it much more difficult than formerly to keep in touch with its varied activities." Henceforth, he said, he would make meaningful the fact that the chancellor was president of the faculty of each school by attending faculty meetings. He required the deans to call meetings through his office and to give him advance information on subjects to be discussed. In his biennial report for 1910 he said that the American university of "even a decade ago has passed away, never to return." Its successor, with its new schools, state-service work, varied business transactions, and oversight of the students' health and morals required complicated, extensive, and growing administrative machinery.[23]

At the start of the academic year in the fall of 1911 Strong and the faculty began to clarify and regularize the University's structure. In response to the Chancellor's request the College faculty appointed a committee to consider its organization. Led by Olin Templin, the committee went beyond College matters to request a "closer definition of the relation of the various Schools of the University to one another, and of the general powers and functions of the faculties and officers of the institution," and the faculty appointed a special committee to inquire into the matter. Meanwhile the University Council had decided that it, too, should carefully define its functions and determine its procedures. Out of the discussion on that question came Council approval of a motion from Olin Templin on December 12 that the Chancellor appoint a "large and representative" faculty committee chaired by Strong on the "reorganization of the University." It was to investigate the organization of the "best American universities," and in light of its discoveries and of the "historical development and existing conditions and customs" of the University of Kansas was to prepare the "best possible constitution" for the institution and submit it to the Council.[24]

Four days later Strong announced a committee of eighteen of the University's most powerful men. Strong, Carruth, and all the deans were members, and so was Extension Director Richard R. Price. The rest of the group were full professors whose roles in University deliberations had always been great: Arthur T. Walker of Latin, William Chase Stevens of Botany, Clarence E. McClung of Zoology, Charles G. Dunlap of English, and Frank H. Hodder of History from the College; Erasmus Haworth and William C. Hoad of the School of Engineering; and William E. Higgins of the Law School.[25]

It took the Committee on Reorganization a year to complete its work. In January, 1913, the members submitted the proposed Constitution of the University of Kansas to the Council. Eager to act, the Council met twice in January, four times in February, three times in March, and twice again in April. On April 28 the Council adopted the Constitution and sent it to the Board of Administration for approval.[26]

The Constitution was an interesting combination of tradition and novelty. Article I, adopted without amendment, set forth generally the relations between the University and the Board of Administration. The Board exercised "direct jurisdiction" over the institution's financial affairs and its relations with the state government. But subject to its own authority, the Constitution said, the Board delegated to the chancellor, to a new University Senate, and to the several faculties the "immediate control of all educational affairs, together with the internal government and administration of the University."[27]

Although the Constitution's first article won easy passage, the second did not, for it dealt with the sensitive question of the chancellor's powers. There was little argument about his authority as chief executive. He was president of each faculty and of the University Senate, the "official representative" of the Board of Administration, who carried out its orders, and the medium of communication between the Board and the University. He was charged with recommending University policy to the Board and the University's governing bodies, and with securing and preserving the coordination of the University's parts. He was also responsible for the institution's "educational and business efficiency"; and, subject to state law, Board rules, and the Constitution itself, he held authority over all other University officers.

The great question at issue, however, was the extent to which the chancellor should be able to make large decisions affecting the University or its divisions without consulting faculty legislative bodies. Neither the rules of the University Council nor the regents' bylaws required that he have anyone's consent before making significant recommendations to the Board. The draft Constitution kept things that way. To check that power, which had led to such innovations as the four-year Medical School in 1905 and the Extension Division in 1909, Professor Carl L. Becker of the History Department offered a stiff amendment forbidding the adoption of any "general university policy" without the Senate's consent or the adoption of any policy "affecting a particular school" without the consent of its faculty. Becker's amendment also required the chancellor to consult with his cabinet on the appointment of all executive officers, the reorganization of schools and departments, disputes between schools, and budget apportionment.[28]

Frank Strong did his best to head off Becker's scheme. If he was to exercise his "responsibility for initiative," he told the Council, he had to have "sufficient freedom in necessary cases to act promptly, decisively and without fear that some other body may object." There was an "indefinite responsibility" as well as a definite one which a chancellor had to possess—so indefinite that Strong could not clearly describe it—and the Council should allow him to keep it. The Council disagreed. Except for "emergencies requiring immediate action," they decreed, the chancellor had to secure faculty consent—through either the Senate or the individual schools—before

taking policy matters before the Board. Becker's amended amendment left the chancellor with power to prepare budgets and to
recommend appointments, changes in rank, and salaries, subject
only to consultation with appropriate University officials.[29]

To keep the University running smoothly in cases of the chancellor's absence or "temporary disability," Article III, which was
routinely approved, gave recognition to the position of vice-president already held by Carruth. The vice-president was to perform
the chancellor's duties at appropriate times and do whatever else
the chancellor might require.[30]

Article IV, apparently routine, was potentially exciting. It
created a University Assembly, composed of all faculty members
from assistant instructors to full professors, along with division directors, those engaged in state-service work, the registrar, and other
officers at the chancellor's pleasure. At regular semiannual meetings
and at as many special meetings as the Assembly might call, it could
consider the decisions of any school's faculty and of the University
Senate, make recommendations to them, and even better, "formulate its attitude upon any matter of University concern." Although
it had no legislative power, the University Assembly might speak
to the Board of Administration, University officers, and the citizens
with an extremely powerful voice.[31]

The core of the Constitution was Article V, which established
the University's legislative bodies and defined their duties. Expanding the base of government, the Constitution replaced the
Council with a Senate, with all associate as well as full professors—
and all administrative officers—as members. The Senate, with the
chancellor presiding, was to meet monthly. There was debate over
the scope of its powers. The Committee on Reorganization had
given the Senate jurisdiction over all matters involving "general
University policy" except where power resided in the Board of Administration, the chancellor, or the faculties. But Dean Charles H.
Johnston of the School of Education moved to give the Senate, in
addition, control over "all matters" involving more than one school.
After discussion the Council rejected the motion, 19 to 3.

Besides "general University policy," several specific areas were
primarily, though not exclusively, under the Senate's jurisdiction.
They included such things as advanced standing, examinations, student life, the University calendar, and control of University divi-

sions. The Senate might also address the chancellor, the Board of Administration, and the faculties on any "educational concern" over which it did not have direct authority.[32]

Beneath the Senate in the legislative hierarchy were the faculties of the schools. The Council rejected the proposal of the Committee on Reorganization that graduate-student assistant instructors be made voting faculty members, and counted only instructors, the three ranks of professors, the dean and chancellor, and the Extension Division director for schools offering correspondence courses. The chancellor was the chairman of each faculty, the dean was the executive officer, and each faculty chose its own secretary. Each faculty had general authority to decide all matters relating primarily to itself: entrance and graduation requirements, programs of studies, standards of scholarship, meetings, committees, and administrative work delegated by the Senate.[33]

The Constitution then defined the membership and powers of the department faculties. Comprising all members of the instructional force—including assistant instructors—whom the Board of Administration had appointed to teach in the "recognized divisions of study and investigation," the departments decided matters pertaining to them alone. Among them were "aims and methods of instruction," textbooks, recommendations of new courses to the dean, and the "cultivation of proper student relations."[34]

Outside the departments and schools there were eight parts of the University which the Constitution officially called "divisions": the Summer Session, University Extension, Athletics, Libraries, the Museums, Publications, State Service Work, and University Surveys. Except for the Division of Athletics, governed by the Athletic Board as determined by the Athletic Association constitution, each was ruled by a committee of nine: the chancellor, the director, and seven members chosen by the Senate. Each committee passed on the general policies of its division, considered appeals from the director's decisions, and served as the director's advisory council.[35]

In addition to the legislative bodies, the Constitution provided for two kinds of advisory groups. One was the Chancellor's Cabinet, whose members were the vice-president, the deans, and such other administrative officers as the chancellor desired. It considered questions the chancellor laid before it, made recommendations, and addressed the chancellor and the Board of Administration whenever the University's interests seemed to demand it. Like the chancellor, each dean had an administrative committee, appointed as each faculty desired, to assist him and make independent recommendations. Unlike the Chancellor's Cabinet, however, the several administrative committees were also executive groups to transact business their faculties gave them.[36]

Most of the rest of the Constitution dealt with three sensitive matters: the powers and duties of administrative officers, faculty tenure, and faculty appointment and promotion. Besides the chancellor and vice-president the Constitution recognized four main types of administrators: deans, department chairmen, division directors, and a variety of functionaries which included the registrar, the superintendent of buildings and grounds, and the University marshal. Deans were executive officers of their schools and chairmen of their administrative committees and had immediate charge of their schools' "educational administration." Upon them rested such duties as drafting budgets, enforcing rules and regulations, reporting to the chancellor, and recommending faculty appointments.[37]

The Constitution continued the existing distinction between "head professors" and department chairmen. In practice the head professor in each department was the full professor with the most seniority. Unless otherwise provided, the Constitution said, the head professor was his department's executive officer and its official representative with extradepartmental groups and individuals. He was responsible for his department's quality of work and efficiency, preparing the budget, assigning staff duties, making personnel recommendations to his dean, and selecting a library and equipment. Where a chairman was appointed instead of a head professor, he exercised such of the head professor's normal duties as were determined at the time of his appointment.[38]

Directors of divisions also had general oversight of their domains, as they coordinated policies, budgets, and staffs and suggested new ideas. The creation of a Division of Libraries, however, was a new departure. It was an effort to supersede the meddlesome and inefficient Carrie Watson. In general the director of libraries was to administer all the University's book collections. But in caring for the parts of the collections purchased by departments from their individual allotments, the director now had to consult departmental policy. It was also the director's duty to select reference books and miscellaneous volumes not clearly within the field of existing departments. Had Carl Becker and Dean Johnston had their way, the director of libraries would have had no power at all to help decide which books the departments would buy. They moved to reject the parts of the draft Constitution which gave the director authority to examine and approve departmental selections, but the Council would not accept their amendments. Jointly with the division committee the director also recommended to the chancellor the annual department distribution of library funds.[39]

Article VIII, concerning faculty tenure, was accepted over the objections of Charles H. Johnston and five of his colleagues. As proposed and approved it stipulated that professors and associate professors were on "permanent appointment." Assistant professors were on one-year appointments for the first two years; if reappointed for a third, they were to be permanent faculty members. Instructors were on one-year, temporary appointments "unless otherwise definitely provided." The article simply ratified present practice and said nothing at all about conditions for dismissal. Because the Board of Administration law of 1913 was also silent on grounds for dismissal, Johnston tried to amend the proposed Constitution to better protect the faculty against the Board's arbitrary action. He sought to insert a statement that permanent appointment meant permanent tenure, which could be terminated only by "honorable dismissal" because of old age or "permanent disability"; by acceptance of a resignation; or by discharge for "felony, immorality, or gross neglect of duty." Johnston's amendment also said that no member of the teaching staff could be discharged before the expiration of his term of service without the filing of formal charges and a hearing before the Board of Administration. His ideas were too radical for most of his colleagues, however, and by a vote of 18 to 6 his amendment lost.[40]

Article IX, treating appointments and promotions, carried with little discussion. Its general nature was to exclude most faculty members from the right to participate in the appointment and promotion of either superiors or inferiors, with the exception of their department chairmen. Going from the top down, the Board of Administration appointed the chancellor, and the Board and chancellor together chose the vice-president, deans, division directors, adviser for women, registrar, and superintendent of buildings and grounds. The Board appointed head professors on the recommendation of the appropriate dean or deans and on approval by the chancellor. Although chairmen were designated by the Board upon the chancellor's recommendation after he had consulted with the dean and department members, the Constitution said nothing about the weight that departmental opinion should carry.

Neither did the Constitution give department members power in the appointment and promotion of men of lesser rank. Subject to the chancellor's assent the Board selected all faculty members except department heads on the joint recommendation of the head professor, the dean of the school in which the department stood, and the deans of any other schools in which the member was expected to teach. Staff members in the divisions were hired on the joint recommendation of the directors and appropriate department heads or deans. University administrators were free to consult with present faculty members in making appointments, of course, but there was no requirement that they do so.[41]

By a vote of two-thirds of the members present the University Senate could amend the Constitution at will—as long as the Board of Administration agreed.[42]

When Chancellor Strong sent the Constitution for approval to the Board of Administration early in May, he also sent his "hearty recommendation" that Hackney, Hoch, and Mrs. Lewis adopt it. The Committee on Reorganization, he said, had gone into the "very fundamentals of university administration," had relied on both the constitutions of other universities and the "experience and advice of experts in university government," and had given the document long and careful consideration. But despite the fact that the Board of Administration was designed to promote efficiency in the management of state institutions, a year went by without action. To encourage the Board to do something, on March 3, 1914, the Council asked the Board to approve its conversion into the University Senate, with the enlarged membership. The Board agreed and the first meeting of the new group came a month later. Encouraged by this progress, in May Olin Templin offered a motion to the Senate inviting the Board to consider the Constitution, but the Senate rejected it. Someone (probably Frank Strong) told the Board that the faculty was growing restless, however, and so the Board members explained that they had supposed that the Constitution was simply the "unwritten law of the University reduced to writing"; therefore they had withheld approval until they could formulate their general rules for all the institutions they controlled. Noting that the change from the Board of Regents to the Board of Administration would require alterations in the document, the Board asked that a Senate committee be appointed to confer about the matter. The Senate chose a seven-man group with Strong as chairman, but the Board, enmeshed in all sorts of administrative problems and under attack from the University, took no action for another year and a half. Not until November, 1915, was the Constitution operative.[43]

It did not remain operative very long. By 1917 Kansas politicians had become positively obsessed with the idea of efficiency. With state expenditures ballooning and the leaders of state agencies always asking for more money than the legislature thought they should have, many believed it best to group all the educational, charitable, correctional, and penal institutions under one board. Governor Arthur Capper expressed the spirit perfectly in January, 1915, in calling upon the legislature to appoint a joint efficiency and economy committee to develop a "plan of reorganization" that would "abolish needless officers, boards and commissions, concentrate and center responsibilities, eliminate duplication of authority and reduce the public business to a compact and smoothly working unit." The legislature created a state Efficiency and Economy Committee. It consisted of Senator William P. Lambertson, Representative Ellsworth L. Burton—both Republicans—and Democratic Senator James D. Joseph. They concluded that the Board of Administration had intimidated University officers. "Out of the state the idea is prevalent that three salaried individuals are running the University and that forward-looking men do not care to come to Kansas." Every school leader should be free to "run his school in the professional sense"; that being true, "three high-salaried individuals are superfluous to the extent of two in looking after the business interest of the state schools."

The committee therefore urged the appointment of a commissioner of educational institutions to supervise the schools' business affairs only. A new Board of Administration should be formed to coordinate the work of all state educational and charitable institutions, but it was to act only in the final "checking over of important matters dealing with the institutions." For the University it would be like the old Board of Regents. Its members were to be present state officials: the governor, the commissioner of educational institutions, a new commissioner of penal and charitable institutions, the state accountant, and the tax commissioner.[44]

Those recommendations were too moderate for most legislators. The legislature of 1917 dealt with a welter of bills to reorganize the government of public educational institutions, but the one that survived to become law put them all under the control of a new Board of Administration closely resembling the old one. Besides the University, the Agricultural College, and the normal schools at Emporia, Fort Hays, and Pittsburg, the Board of Administration also supervised the School for the Deaf, the School for the Blind, the Industrial School for Girls, the Industrial School for Boys, the Orphans' Home, the Industrial Reformatory, and the State Penitentiary. If the legislature created any other educational, benevolent, penal, or correctional institutions, the Board of Administration was to have jurisdiction over them, too.

The Board had four members—the governor and three gubernatorial appointees who had to have Senate approval. There was no prohibition now against all of them being of the same political party. For their full-time service the appointed members were to receive $3,500 a year. As before, the terms of office were four years, and the appointments were staggered so that normally no governor could appoint more than two members at once. Unlike the law of 1913, however, the new statute allowed the governor to remove any member without the Senate's consent whenever he thought the "public service" demanded it.

As the "board of trustees or directors" of the institutions, the Board of Administration was to "control and manage" all of them and to adopt such rules and regulations as it wished. But the act put new power into the hands of the University chancellor. The Board had authority to select the "superintendent, warden, or other executive officer" of each agency. Once appointed, however, he could appoint every one of the "officials, clerks, guards, and employees" required to manage the institution as long as he respected the number authorized by the Board and obeyed the civil-service laws. Perhaps even more important, he could dismiss any employee "for cause." The only restrictions on firing were that the chancellor and his executive counterparts elsewhere could not dismiss an employee because of his politics, and that they had to file a written statement of their reasons with the Board of Administration and the Civil Service Commission. On recommendation of the chief executive officers, the Board would fix all salaries except those set by law.

The act's main purpose, however, seemed to be to lay down rules for the financial conduct of the institutions. A business manager with "full authority to manage and control" the agencies under the Board and buy all supplies was the Board's fiscal agent. The law was as precise and detailed about how he was to function as it was general on how the Board and the executive officers were to operate: it made him primarily responsible for the preparation of biennial budgets and requests to the legislature (though only after a "full conference" with the chief executive officer and with the Board's advice and consent); required that he approve all physical repairs and additions and plans for new buildings; and hedged him about with all sorts of restrictions about inspecting the supplies of each agency, advertising for bids, and awarding contracts.

All the existing legal provisions not inconsistent with the new law respecting the "management, control and government" of the several institutions passed to the new Board when the act became effective on July 1, 1917.[45]

Frank Strong was not altogether happy with the new law, but he liked it much better than the old one. The legislature could have improved things by providing for the service of the Board "on honor and without salary," he told Governor Capper, but perhaps that could come later. In the meantime the University would do everything possible to make the new system work, and Strong professed great confidence in its success as long as Capper had two more years to put it into operation. Strong was doubtless pleased not only by the increase in his own authority, but also by the fact that the new Board would presumably be so busy with all its duties that it would have little time to meddle in the University's internal affairs.[46]

In addition to Capper the members of the new Board were Edward W. Hoch, a member of the existing Board, Wilbur N. Mason, and Charles W. Green. Mason was a prominent Methodist clergyman who had come to Kansas in 1912 as president of Baker University in Baldwin. He had proved an extremely successful fundraiser, and Strong hoped that his success would continue with the legislature. Green was a grocer and financier, and the former Democratic mayor of Kansas City, Kansas, where he had been active in politics for years and had found considerable favor with Republicans as well as members of his own party. The four men chose as business manager James A. Kimball of Salina, president of the Salina Candy Company, a man well known in the state's business, civic, and fraternal circles, and a University regent from 1911 to 1913. Of the five men only Mason had a university degree—from Ohio Wesleyan—although Green had graduated from the Eastern Business College in Poughkeepsie, New York.[47]

In September, 1917, Chancellor Strong called the Senate's attention to the fact that the new law made a "fundamental change in the University's government. In many respects," he said, "the Chancellor . . . has been placed by law in the stead of the Board of Administration," and now had "unusual authority." Yet Strong had no desire to be a dictator. "So far as [the chancellor's] responsibility under the law will permit," he continued, saying nothing specific, he was "anxious to share his responsibility and authority with the faculties of the University." He therefore suggested the appointment of a Committee on Revision of the University Constitution, consisting of from thirteen to fifteen faculty members "scattered equitably over the University," to consider necessary constitutional changes. After haggling over whether Strong or the Senate should choose the committee, the Senate decided that it would select thirteen from a list of twenty-six nominees, half to be made by the Senate and half by the Chancellor. In November the Senate chose eleven of its thirteen nominees and but two from Strong's list.[48]

But the confusion into which the University descended as a result of the World War made action impossible. Not until the spring of 1919 did the Committee turn to the Constitution. Just as the group was beginning its study, however, Chancellor Strong decided to resign. During the search for his successor there was much debate—without resolution—about the respective powers of the chancellor and the faculty, but the Constitution itself was largely in abeyance. Neither the Senate nor the new Board of Administration ever repealed it, yet the new Board never noticed it and the Senate never revised the parts that the law superseded. As a result, after 1917 the University's formal internal organization was confused and the bulk of the power lay with the chancellor.

20

The War Industry

IN 1921 Frank Strong recalled with continuing anguish the University's suffering and privation during the First World War. His school, it was true, had done much for the war effort, and Strong was proud of its work and the service of its students and alumni in the armed forces. Yet the cost had been fearful. The conflict continually portended the "possibility of an almost total paralysis and disintegration of the institution." During it, he said, "I saw what I hope no other university administrator will ever be obliged to see—a partial paralysis of the activities of the University and draining of its best life blood onto the battle fields of Europe." Mount Oread changed in many ways in 1917 and 1918, all of them for the worse.[1]

Paradoxically and cruelly, the University's tragedy in wartime arose from the ideal of service to society which had been one of its greatest virtues in time of peace. Patriotism and social service clearly demanded that the institution do its utmost to fight the foe. Yet it was unprepared for the newer kind of work. Its previous efforts had been for civilians; now it tried to train soldiers. Its previous efforts had mainly concerned the intellect; but war was largely anti-intellectual, and its pressures turned men's thoughts away from traditional academic subjects. In the past the University had tried to prepare students for lives of responsible freedom; now it asked them to regiment themselves for the duration of a war whose end no one could foresee. By the summer of 1918, Strong told the Board of Administration, the University had become al-

371

most a "war industry."[2] Unlike other war industries, however, this one yielded not greater profits to its managers and employees, but chaos, frustration, and death.

Chancellor Strong's personal tragedy was the greater because he had opposed America's entering the war. Though sympathetic to the cause of Britain and France, and properly horrified at the possibility that the "outcome of European culture is after all to be a militarism like that of Germany and a negation of democratic thought," he fought, in the prewar years, against military preparedness and mobilization. He urged the Kansas Congressional delegation to vote against both, spoke publicly against involvement, and in the fall of 1916 joined the executive committee of the Kansas Branch of the League to Enforce Peace, whose purpose was to keep the nation out of the war. Strong's pacifism had two theoretical bases. The first, as he told the University Assembly and student body in 1914 and 1915, was that it was America's destiny to preserve Western civilization, which seemed to be destroying itself abroad. While the youth of Europe were dying on its battlefields, the youth of America must seek higher education to enable them to carry on "our present standards of life." From the United States must come the "material for the leadership of the world. . . . America and its universities"—with the University of Kansas having a "big place" among them—"must become the center of the greatest intellectual life that the next generation should know." His second argument was that a war effort would require the cooperation of all universities, which would in turn subvert their true function. "I look upon all attempts toward militarism among us with great apprehension," he told President Charles R. Van Hise of Wisconsin, "and believe that colleges and universities should be the very last agencies in our civilization to further, by compulsion and official action, the military idea."[3]

But when the nation went to war, Strong went right along with it. Shortly after Congress declared war in April, 1917, he asserted before a University convocation that democracy throughout the world was at stake and that only the United States could save it. Then he notified President Woodrow Wilson that the entire University was at the disposal of the national government. "It has always been loyal to the country and the flag," he told the public in July, "and always will be."[4]

To offer advice, assist with administrative matters, and recommend policies for the "advantage of the University, the State, and the country," Strong prevailed upon the Senate to approve an advisory committee of nine. The first of the multitudinous problems that the committee and Senate faced was what to do about the academic credits of students who left school, either for the armed services or for industrial or agricultural work, as soon as Congress declared war. By commencement more than five hundred had gone. The majority asked permission to withdraw from their courses; the bolder asked full credit. Overcome by patriotism, the Senate in April, 1917, decided that students passing their courses who departed for the armed forces, for agricultural labor, or to replace an enlisted man in positions "where employment is in the interest of public service," would get full credit for the semester's work. A year later the Senate thought better of giving academic credit for civilian jobs, and cancelled it. Yet actual military service was worth a full semester's credit for graduating seniors. In December, 1917, the Senate voted that any senior in good standing who enlisted or was drafted after completing one semester should receive his degree. The action was a generous repudiation of the standards of the past.[5]

Originally Strong and the Board of Administration had hoped to show departing faculty members something of the same largesse. By June, 1917, half a dozen had left for military service; a year later forty-five had gone—into either the armed forces or war-related civilian work. The Chancellor and Board wanted to give to those in service the difference between their regular salaries and their military pay. But State Auditor F. W. Knapp declared this illegal, Attorney General S. M. Brewster upheld him, and University officials abandoned the scheme. Most departing faculty members received simply a payless leave.[6]

Those faculty and students who remained geared themselves for war. Only a little could be done by the semester's end in the spring of 1917. Faculty members with military experience organized four voluntary companies of trainees, which included over three hundred students. Lacking weapons, uniforms, and immediate purpose, they did calisthenics and drilled for an hour a day. Other faculty members started courses in subjects such as military engineering, mapping, electrical signaling and telephony, military science, and explosives. A combination of courses and military drill could gain

exemptions from up to six hours of their regular academic requirements. Men who took a special course in shop training in the
School of Engineering, to become either military or civilian mechanics, were exempt from all other academic work.[7]

In the fall, however, the University adopted a compulsory plan
of military and physical training. On motion by Olin Templin the
Senate accepted the idea of Secretary of War Newton D. Baker that
all undergraduates should strengthen themselves. Henceforth every
student, male and female, was to engage in regular exercise "suitable to his personal needs" as determined by a physical examination. Both intercollegiate and intramural athletics would be part of
the program, with the limitation that the "ultimate aim of the
physical vigor and health of the whole student body shall never be
sacrificed for financial gain or the amusement of the public." More
important was the motion's statement that the University would
provide military drill for students whom the Department of Physical Education, after the examinations, might assign to it.[8]

At that point the University went to war. Additional Senate
regulations provided that a "rising whistle" would sound at 6:30
a.m.; in theory the students would rise with it. Boardinghouse
keepers, restaurant owners, and eating club officers were asked to
start serving breakfast at 7:00. Classes ran from 8:00 to 11:50 and
1:00 till 4:00. To allow time for athletics and military drill, there
were no classes from 4:00 to 6:00; not even work in the library was
permitted. Whether they wanted to or not, some seven hundred
male undergraduates—over half the men enrolled during the regular
academic year—became members of the University regiment, organized according to plans issued by the War Department. Its
colonel was Professor E. M. Briggs of the German Department, who
had had military experience with the Army along the Mexican
border and was fresh from a summer course at the Harvard University Officers Training Camp. Dr. John Sundwall of the Medical
School was lieutenant colonel, and the battalion majors were C. C.
Williams of Engineering, W. W. Davis of History, and Dean Frederick J. Kelly of the School of Education. J. C. McCanles, director
of the University band, was the adjutant. Student officers led the
companies and squads. According to the War Department plans
the undergraduate soldiers were to study such matters as infantry
tactics, bayonet combat, trench construction and maintenance, mili-

tary map reading, and Special Western Front Conditions. At first there were no uniforms and no equipment—though five hundred dummy guns were under construction in Fowler Shops—and the University regiment presented a most unmilitary appearance.[9]

But it was the spirit that mattered, and the spirit was poor. An article in the *Graduate Magazine* in December asserted that things were proceeding smoothly and patriotically. Time was when most students took no exercise at all. "But times have changed. America is now at war, and the University has changed its course in order to fit its students to render the greatest possible service to the country during the present struggle." The trouble was that the students did not much change their attitude, and the men's physical training and military drill program went from bad to worse. Engineering and medical students protested that they were deprived of time they badly needed for study and relaxation. Students with jobs found their working hours and pay reduced. The drill classes often did not end on time, and grumbling about overtime service grew louder. Among the University regiment's rank and file, moreover, there was strong resistance to military discipline. They cut drill in large numbers—sometimes only half the troops were there—and often disobeyed orders when they showed up, for the Senate had provided no means to enforce discipline. "Military drill at the University has reached a point where it is almost a joke," said the *Kansan* in January, 1918. "In numerous cases men in the ranks have wilfully disobeyed the orders of superior officers who are powerless to demand obedience to their commands."[10]

In the winter and spring of 1918 the Senate struck a compromise with the recalcitrant soldiers. They were to be allowed one unexcused absence every two weeks, with those who exceeded the quota required to make up the lost work by extra drill or suffer suspension until they complied. Students recommended by the regimental commandant might count up to four hours of military science toward their degrees, if the faculties of their schools consented. Starting in the fall military drill would be required of every able-bodied male student, but for only three hours a week.[11]

At first the women were no more inclined toward regimentation than the men. As soon as they discovered in the fall of 1917 that they had to take physical exercise, there was a mass meeting to condemn the Senate preparedness program. But Dr. Florence B. Sherbon, director of physical education for women, gave them a pep talk about their patriotic duties, and the girls fell into line. The Senate met them half way by allowing some of them to enroll in knitting or Red Cross classes instead of the physical-training groups. Of the forms of exercise available the most popular was cross-country hiking, which had six hundred women divided into squads of thirty. Besides getting them out into the open air, hiking allegedly taught them to dress sensibly: low-heeled shoes were worn instead of the fashionable high-heeled French models, and heavy skirts instead of thin afternoon dresses. Women also had to attend weekly lectures on personal hygiene, first aid, home and community sanitation, and the like.[12]

All of this, of course, was only playing at war. In the fall of 1918 the University undertook more serious work. That summer the War Department had established the Students' Army Training Corps (SATC), designed to use colleges and universities to provide both military and academic training for enlisted men who were prospective officers. Contracting schools made their faculties and facilities available to the groups, constructed dormitories, and supplied food. The federal government ultimately paid the costs, but only after the institutions first paid and then sought compensation.[13]

The history of the SATC was chaotic. Including both former University students and soldiers from outside, it numbered about seventeen hundred. To house, feed, and comfort them, the University threw up a dozen barracks east of McCook Field and between the engineering buildings, wrote contracts with local eateries, including the Oread Cafe and the Eldridge Hotel, and turned part of Myers Hall into a "hostess house" and canteen. To provide time for drill and other military training, Captain B. F. Scher, the commandant, demanded of the Senate a rigid class schedule which set aside the hours from 10:00 a.m. until noon and 1:00 until 4:30 p.m. for courses; the men would study from 7:30 to 9:30 weekday evenings. The Senate rearranged the normal class schedule to coincide with that of the SATC, adding two class periods before 10:00. Then the whole academic year had to be rearranged, for SATC regulations required the quarter instead of the semester system, and it was too complicated to operate on one basis for civilians and another for soldiers.[14]

SATC students had a variety of courses from which to choose.

According to their interests and their intended military specialization, they could work in biology, chemistry, English, French and German, history, mathematics, military geography, physics, military map reading, psychology, sanitation, and several more. Some were regular University courses, others newly created or redesigned for the SATC. All counted toward a degree. Every soldier had to take a special "Issues of the War" course, supervised by Frank H. Hodder of the History Department. Hodder split it into fifty sections and conscripted faculty throughout the University to teach it.[15]

These arrangements were all merely a prelude to tragedy. Captain Scher swore in his troops on October 1, 1918. A few days later the national epidemic of Spanish influenza struck Lawrence. As a preliminary safety measure the State Board of Health ordered the University closed from October 8 to 15. With the SATC students jammed together in the barracks, however, the disease ran rampant. The University did not open again until November 11, by which time 32 students—10 of them from the SATC—had died and as many as 750 had been ill at once. Since the school infirmary was wholly inadequate, parts of the wooden barracks had to be used; because the Red Cross could not furnish enough assistance, faculty wives, women undergraduates, and even faculty members had to act as nurses, and many of them became infected. Except for the drilling of the healthy SATC members, the University was at a deathly standstill.[16]

And all the while it was on the edge of bankruptcy. On the eve of an "almost certain declaration of war," Frank Strong wanted the legislature of 1917 to place a "large excess of funds in the hands of the educational institutions having practically the only great scientific departments in the state, on which the government must rely, so far as Kansas is concerned." Instead the lawmakers allowed no expansion at all. Except for an appropriation for the administration building, the total amount—both appropriations and fees—that the University had for fiscal 1918 was only $2,500 more than the year before. Only a great upsurge in student fees would carry the University out of the financial doldrums in 1919. But by November 1, 1918, the SATC had cost about $173,000 and there was no money in the state treasury for other operating expenses. Under orders from the Board of Administration Strong pressed government officials as hard as he could for payment, but not until 1919 did the money arrive. To everyone's relief, the war ended as the University was reopening. In December the SATC was closed up, the barracks were torn down, and the school was no longer an army post.[17]

Yet a residue of wartime militarism would remain. Early in December, 1918, Chancellor Strong referred to the Senate a query from the War Department, asking a quick answer, about whether the University desired a permanent Reserve Officers' Training Corps. The Senate was badly divided on the matter. After defeating a motion by Frank W. Blackmar, seconded by Frank H. Hodder, that the University have nothing to do with ROTC, the Senate sent the question to the committee which had dealt with military training during the war. All the members except Hodder desired an ROTC, providing it was strictly voluntary. On December 19, however, the Senate adopted, 30 to 25, Hodder's minority report recommending postponement of a decision until the fall of 1919. But during the next two months support for the ROTC grew. Before the Senate's action about fourteen hundred male students had signed a petition favoring it, and enthusiastic undergraduates continued to badger Strong and the faculty. Several of Hodder's twenty-five opponents worked to win converts. In February, 1919, the Senate voted to reconsider its earlier action and then, 39 to 26, approved a motion by George C. Shaad of the School of Engineering to have a campus ROTC. Five days later the Board of Administration also approved it.[18]

As originally established the ROTC was elective for all male students. Under the command of Captain Harold D. Burdick of the Coast Artillery and several sergeants, ROTC members took courses in such things as military drill, tactics, topography, and military administration and law; there were special optional courses for those pointing toward the infantry, coast artillery, engineering corps, and signal corps. The basic course demanded three hours a week in the freshman year and two hours thereafter. By a decision of the College faculty in 1920 ROTC students could count up to fifteen military credits toward their degrees; the School of Engineering allowed up to thirteen.[19]

Considering the problems of the University regiment and the SATC disaster, it might have been better if the University had ignored military training. It had much better luck with nonmilitary activities. Three kinds were especially significant: the information and teaching of the Extension Division, explaining the war to students and beginning special courses for them, and volunteer work by students and faculty.

The Extension Division needed no great changes to adapt itself to war service. It had long been supplying the public with speakers and information on numerous subjects and all it had to do was introduce new topics. To explain to Kansans what the war was about and urge them to "do their bit," the Division organized many War Conferences and Community Institutes and furnished them with speakers: Lieutenant Paul Perigord, an itinerant propagandist from the French Army, for example, with his heartfelt "Message from France"; or Chancellor Strong on "Readjustments to Meet War Emergencies"; or Gertrude Lynn of the Agricultural College on "Conservation of Food and Related Problems"; or William A. McKeever on "School Gardening as Juvenile Patriotism." Other speakers—faculty members and public figures—toured the state at the Extension Division's behest to clarify war issues, exhort people to buy Liberty Bonds, and think about the problems of peace and reconstruction. There were also motion pictures on food conservation for showing in local theaters, and lantern slide collections on such patriotic subjects as the Founding Fathers, Abraham Lincoln, and the workings of democracy in Washington, D.C.

As the war continued, the Extension Division expanded its work. To educate and entertain soldiers at Camp Funston and Fort Riley, the state's major military posts, the Division sent out faculty members, arranged musical concerts, and through the Bureau of Correspondence Study offered courses in English, French, mathematics, wireless telegraphy, and telephony. The Department of General Information worked endlessly to supply a sharply increasing number of requests for package libraries on wartime subjects: "Women and the War," "Clara Barton," "Spies," "War Poetry," "American Relief Work," "Tractors on the Farm," "Profiteering," and others. Into the package libraries and all correspondence the Extension Division inserted Liberty Bond circulars and pleas from the Red Cross.[20]

Within the University, Chancellor Strong created a University Committee on Intelligence with Dean Olin Templin as chairman. One of its main tasks was to explain to the students their relation to the war effort. The committee urged them to hold to their educational goals amid the war's excitements, to become informed, intelligent citizens who could help prosecute the war and solve the problems of peace. "Educate yourself as well as you can," the committee said, "and insist on the need of more education for others both in high schools and colleges." And especially educate yourselves on the conflict's nature and meaning. "This war is the most stupendous event in history," the committee believed. To help students understand it, the committee posted bulletin boards around the campus with maps, charts, and articles to read. In Spooner Library Carrie Watson grouped together a large number of books about the war, which the committee urged students to peruse. The *Daily Kansan* published a valuable war column, and there were public lectures that students should attend.[21]

In addition students might shape their academic programs to help the war effort. The Committee on Intelligence urged undergraduates in relevant schools and departments—especially Engineering, Medicine, Home Economics, and Chemistry—to stay where they were. College students should not arbitrarily change their majors, but might well take militarily significant subjects as electives: mathematics, physics, engineering shopwork, and drafting for the men; dietetics, chemistry, and mechanical drawing for the women. Special new courses appeared as the war progressed: wireless telegraphy in the Engineering School, war relief and home service in the Sociology Department, several food conservation and home-nursing courses in Home Economics, and noncredit courses in stenography and typing. When the war ended the Department of Economics and Commerce began courses on the economic problems of war and peace, and the Department of History and Political Science started courses on war, peace, and reconstruction; governments of the warring powers; and international law and the war.[22]

Besides taking courses and becoming informed, the female students performed many nonacademic, nonintellectual tasks. They learned about first aid from Red Cross workers and knitted sweaters and socks for the troops. They sewed layettes for French babies and sold Easter cards for the Fatherless Children of France Fund. They scoured the campus for old rubber, tinfoil, paper, and general waste, and set up huge boxes in Fraser Hall and Robinson Gymnasium to collect the materials. In February, 1918, they converted a room in Fraser Hall into a surgical dressing factory where every afternoon up to forty coeds, faculty, and faculty wives donned white caps and aprons for the work. The *Graduate Magazine* reported that the war work gave the girls a "feeling of national relation" and a "serious desire for usefulness." "I don't see what we used to do with our time before we did all these things," one of the gauzefolders remarked.[23]

Students of both sexes and their social organizations also took austerity measures. There were meatless, wheatless, and dessertless meals in the fraternities and sororities. In the fall of 1917 Strong asked the students to cut expenses for social affairs to the bone and to forgo the traditional elaborate parties for "inexpensive and informal functions." They tried. The Junior Prom in January, 1918, for example, was arranged as a wartime party. Patriotic bunting and American and allied flags decorated the gymnasium, the grand march was eliminated, and the usual flaunting of student wealth and social class was taboo. There were supposed to be no taxis used, no corsages, no dress suits for the men, no punch for anyone. Most prohibitions were respected, except that many couples came in taxis, for snow covered the ground and the temperature was fourteen degrees below zero. In May, 1918, the Senate imposed its own austerity program on student social affairs. For the duration all parties and dances were to end by midnight, dance tickets were to cost no more than $1.50, and refreshments were to "conform rigidly to the rules and regulations of the United States Food Administration."[24]

The faculty as a group performed a variety of war services. They shaped the University to meet the war's demands, served on different committees, taught special classes to civilians and servicemen, delivered lectures, supplied the students with information. Colonel E. M. Briggs and Professor Goldwin Goldsmith of the Department of Architecture induced many of their colleagues to train with the students in the ranks, but when this proved unpopular with the faculty recruits, they split into a separate section, which, however, did not last for long. As individuals the faculty did the same things as other civilians throughout the nation: they bought Liberty Bonds, planted vegetable gardens, joined public committees, gave money to relief organizations such as the Red Cross and YMCA, and nursed the sick during the influenza epidemic. Chancellor Strong was the busiest of them all. By December, 1917, he was chairman of the Committee on Public Relations of the State Council on Defense; a member of the executive committees of the United States

Food Administration for Kansas and the Lawrence chapter of the Red Cross, and of the Emergency War Committee of the National Association of State Universities; and a lecturer for both the Food Administration and the Security League. He was busier than he had ever been before, and had practically no spare time.[25]

In the spring of 1917, moreover, Strong and Dean Olin Templin more or less officially made the University an agency to promote wartime prohibition. Like the great majority of Kansans, both men thought tippling was a personal sin and a social evil; their ideas meshed perfectly with the desirability of saving grain for food. On April 17 they sent from the University several thousand printed petition forms on which sympathetic Kansans were to collect signatures to send to President Wilson and Congress. The forms asked simply for legislation to forbid the "consumption of food products in the manufacture of intoxicating liquors." Three days later Strong induced a mass meeting of between a thousand and fifteen hundred students to endorse prohibition unanimously, and Strong duly telegraphed the news to the Kansas Congressional delegation and other lawmakers. Olin Templin kept after both the Kansas delegates and college deans across the country. Throughout the nation, he said in a letter to the congressmen—a copy of which went to every dean—colleges and universities were releasing students to work on farms and thus feed the fighting men. Yet even as they labored, brewers and distillers were pouring hundreds of thousands of bushels of good grain into their vats. Noting that Congress seemed to be about to accept a proposal from distillers to levy a higher tax on liquor rather than enact prohibition, Templin called the idea a "cruel wrong," a "monstrous system," an affront to the thousands of young people who were "nobly answering this call of humanity." According to Templin prohibition had widespread support among the deans.[26]

Although scientists in some American universities engaged in government research, the number was small—the government had not yet learned to mobilize them fully—and Kansans did little. One important exception, however, was Professor Hamilton P. Cady of the Chemistry Department. During the war the United States Bureau of Mines became interested in helium as a means of floating dirigibles. Cady undertook extensive research on the gas at a nominal salary of a dollar a year. In large part as the result of his work the government decided to undertake production of the gas on a large scale. The use of helium for inflating dirigibles would later become commonplace.[27]

All together the University's wartime activities brought its members both pride and sorrow. Chancellor Strong repeatedly assured the public that the institution was eager to do its part to defeat the foe, whatever the cost to itself. If the war lasted for several years, as well it might, he wrote the alumni in May, 1918, the school would make ever larger efforts to destroy the "menace to our own freedom as well as the freedom of the rest of the world," even though such efforts might require the virtual cessation of ordinary work. At commencement Strong unfurled the University's "service flag," which had a blue star for each former student now in service and eight gold stars for the men who had died. The alumni dead, Strong said, had given themselves for the freedom of "all the peoples of the world," and the University was proud of them: in the University's name he assured their friends and relations that "we shall hold their names sacred on the records of the University as long as records shall endure." All former students and the faculty members serving in the armed forces, he wrote the following summer in a document called the *War Record of the University of Kansas*, actually represented the University in the "great struggle." Their service showed the "honorable part" that the University itself played.[28]

For all the pride and accomplishment within the University, however, as the war continued there was a decline in intellectual vigor and student spirits, and this was reflected in Chancellor Strong himself. By May, 1918, Strong believed that the war had given students a "more serious" attitude toward the "important things of life." Interest in both athletics and social activities had decreased, and this was all to the good. But there had also been a "lessening . . . of interest in the class work and general intellectual life of the institution," which was not so fortunate. Yet it was the same with every American university, and how could it be helped? "Students that are of draft age and are expecting to be called become restless, and insensibly give their main attention to the great project that is before them." The women were affected almost as strongly because of their "relation to the multitudes of men who are awaiting call." Merely witnessing the "fluctuations of a great world struggle," indeed, had a disturbing impact on the minds of both teachers and students.[29]

The *Daily Kansan* made the same points. After a year of war the students had no interest in anything, social or intellectual. A "wave of apathy" had washed over the campus. Interest in intercollegiate athletics was low, interest in debating and dramatics even lower. No one seemed to care about the elections for the Men's Student Council or the Women's Student Government Association. The freshmen were not wearing the obligatory caps, the sophomores could not have cared less, and for two months not a soul had yelled "Rock Chalk, Jayhawk!" "Students appear in classes with a nonchalance which is suggestive of their having been gassed. . . . It has been a long drag for most students. Many have left for the service. The interest of many has been scattered. Studies have suffered and the student body has assumed a perpetually bored air." The *Kansan* wanted more school spirit, but even its call was listless: "There is no better time than the present for a little proof that all the ginger has not gone into the army." But until the war ended, ginger was scarce on Mount Oread.[30]

Where the students were lackadaisical, Frank Strong was physically and emotionally drained. The war was a huge burden piled on top of the vexations and uncertainty created by the Board of Administration. "I already see signs of the fact that I am nervously run down and must recuperate," he told the new Board in July, 1917. The events of the next year and a half all but broke him. "The death of so many that had been students during my administration, and the calamitous history of the Students' Army Training Corps, with the appalling list of those who succumbed to the Spanish influenza," he said later, "caused personal shock from which I found it very difficult to recover, and helped to produce an overwhelming desire to be relieved of the responsibilities attaching to the office." By the spring of 1919 weariness had made him ready to resign.[31]

Yet there was another reason for his resignation that he did not care to mention in public. In the years after 1913 rumblings of protest against Strong grew louder among the alumni—especially those who had graduated since he became chancellor in 1902. The focal point of the discontent was the Kansas City metropolitan complex on both sides of the state line. Its immediate cause was an argument between the Chancellor and many Kansas City alumni about the location and date of the annual football game with the University of Missouri. In the past the great clash had come in Kansas City, Missouri, on Thanksgiving Day. It had become a spectacle that attracted thousands and worried Frank Strong. He was no ardent advocate of football, anyway. Like many other American university leaders, and like most members of the old Board of Regents, he thought that it was too rough, that the importance attached to winning teams detracted from the University's real purpose, that football crowds—especially the Kansas-Missouri crowd—indulged too much in drinking, gambling, and rowdyism, and the wrong kinds of excitement. In April, 1910, after a widespread campus debate on the place of football in the University, Strong urged the Board of Regents to require that the Kansas-Missouri game be played on the grounds of the two universities, like the other games, and on the Saturday before Thanksgiving. Removal of the contest to Lawrence and Columbia in alternate years would decrease its importance and thereby the importance of football generally, diminish the gambling and drinking, and cut gate receipts thus providing less money for the football program. Playing the game on Saturday would reduce the number of spectators who were neither students nor alumni. The regents agreed with Strong's suggestions, and changed the game's site and day.[32]

The next sound heard was that of grousing alumni. At first it was comparatively quiet and sub rosa, but in June, 1913, it appeared in the open in a semiofficial way. Alumni Association president Edwin C. Meservey wrote to Strong to report that at the request of an alumni committee he had polled every alumnus by mail on the question of the game's location. Of 767 replies received so far, 646 asked that it be moved back to Kansas City. Meservey asserted that playing it there had no untoward moral consequences and that the large crowds did not mean that football had become commercialized. Lawrence and Columbia were difficult to reach by train, he went on, and lacked accommodations for the crowds of alumni and other spectators who wanted to attend. Strong and the faculty owed the alumni the pleasure of watching their University team in action amid pleasant surroundings.

But the Chancellor and the University Council did not believe they owed the alumni anything at all in the way of sporting events. Although a committee of the Kansas City alumni went to Lawrence to argue with them, the Council unanimously adopted a motion offered by Olin Templin that left the Kansas-Missouri game on campus. There was some sentiment in the Council for telling the alumni to mind their own business. A committee of Frank H. Hodder, Arvin S. Olin, and Charles G. Dunlap brought in a reply stating that "the game at its finest is after all a college game for college men and women"—that is, that the desires of former students were much less important than the welfare of present students. Although this was probably the opinion of most councillors, the words were insulting; the Council struck them out.[33]

Within a year alumni opposition expanded into a general dissatisfaction with the way Strong was running the University. In December, 1914, the Chancellor began to understand just how unpopular he was. On the morning of October 23, students had held an unofficial pep rally to stir up support for the football team in the next day's game with the Agricultural College. Overcome by school spirit, a number of students coursed through Fraser Hall, invaded classrooms and broke up classes, and hurled coarse and "almost obscene" threats at teachers who objected. The Men's Student Council, which then punished disciplinary infractions, suspended three of the ringleaders for three weeks. Strong and the University Council approved the action. Probably "no one except a college administrator," Strong wrote, "appreciates the fact that football makes more trouble in university discipline than all other factors combined; that it seems to center about itself all of the sinister influences, not only of the university but of the town."[34]

The alumni did not see things that way. Punishing students for an abundance of spirit seemed self-defeating. They were even more distraught when the football team lost its last two games of the season to its chief foes: Nebraska whaled Kansas 35 to 0, and Missouri beat the Jayhawks 10 to 7. In December some fifty alumni met in the University Club in Kansas City to make the expected charges that University officers were not properly sympathetic to football. But now there were other complaints as well: that the quality of the whole University had deteriorated in the past few years; that the quality of the faculty had degenerated; that the faculty was dominating the Student Council and the *Kansan* and crushing school spirit; and that there were too many restrictions of all kinds on the Hill. Comparatively little evidence appeared to support those beliefs, said the moderate Thornton Cooke of the class of 1893, but the opposition was powerful nonetheless. The real trouble, Cooke thought, was that Strong had "failed to grip the imagination and affection of the students as they have passed through the institution." Why Strong had failed, he did not know. But the alumni did not remember their chancellor fondly.[35]

J. C. Nichols of the class of 1902, now a prosperous Kansas City realtor, was much blunter. There was, he wrote to Strong, no "close and binding feeling" between the University's leaders and its alumni, and it was not the alumni's fault. "I hear a great many people express themselves as never having been able to feel very close to you; that they have met you a number of times and had different matters arise but they have never been able to feel that they were very well acquainted with you, or that you cared very much about them. There is no denying the fact that there is a very widespread feeling at this time among several of the alumni here in Kansas City."[36]

Strong's trouble was that while he was an able, dedicated, earnest, vigorous man with high principles and great hopes for the University, he lacked the common touch. He had neither the jovial, bouncy, almost boyish manner of Francis H. Snow, nor the easy geniality of his successor, Ernest H. Lindley. Too stiff and impersonal, very much convinced that no one else's ideas about the University were as good as his own, Strong had always sought alumni support when pleading before the legislature, but seldom consulted them about policies or problems. His response to the Kansas City alumni was in character. After asserting that school spirit was excellent and denying that he had interfered with the recent disciplinary cases, he made it plain that he and not the alumni headed the University. He had always followed and always would follow the pledge he made to himself in 1902 "that I would do what seemed to my judgment and conscience necessary for the best interests of the University without fear or favor and that I would do nothing merely from the standpoint of my own advantage." The "main ideal and function of the University," Strong averred, had nothing to do with football. "My conception of the University is that the intellectual and moral standards of an institution are the vital and all important things and that other things must be secondary."[37]

As the troubled teens moved on, however, Strong found the

virus of discontent spreading among the members of the Alumni Association. Though the Association's Board of Visitors in 1915 lambasted the Board of Administration in a way that warmed Strong's heart, later visitors found that the Chancellor had committed sins of both omission and commission. In 1916 the Board of Visitors charged that University authorities were encouraging or at least permitting too many "alluring opportunities" in extracurricular affairs, causing students to neglect their academic work. A year later the visitors, led by Scott Hopkins and J. Willis Gleed, viciously assailed Strong's idea of state-service work. During their preliminary investigations the visitors had requested comments about the University from several ex-faculty members who had departed for greener academic groves. Among the respondents was Carl L. Becker, now at Minnesota, who had been at Kansas from 1902 to 1916. Becker damned the Board of Administration in the usual way, but also condemned Strong for spreading the University's resources too thinly over too many areas. Needless expansion had hurt the school. Money spent foolishly on the new Medical School, Extension Division, School of Education, and Journalism Department meant suffering for the rest of the institution. Salaries were too low, the library was pitifully inadequate, too many able men had left. As a whole the University was not as good as it had been when Becker came.[38]

Becker's analysis impressed J. Willis Gleed. The report of the Board of Visitors included his strictures on needless expansion. In the name of "state service work," the visitors said, the University's officers had saddled some departments with illegitimate functions and added other departments which had "no real connection with the work of the University as such." Only the "educational function" of the University mattered. "State service" might "tickle the legislative ear and coax a few dollars from unwilling and niggardly hands, but in the end such dollars cost the University too much. . . . 'State service' is a siren song leading to disaster." There was no justification for turning the institution into an "amusement syndicate or lyceum bureau." Except as service work grew out of teaching or was an adjunct to it, the activity should be divorced from the University and conducted by the state government itself.[39]

The report, smashing and scorning one of Frank Strong's noblest dreams, hurt him deeply .Though the visitors of 1918 praised the

Extension Division and, by implication, the idea of state-service work,[40] many alumni continued to think that the University was stretching itself beyond reasonable financial limits. And there were still other grievances. In 1918 there were alumni petty enough to accuse Strong and other officers of discriminating between alumni and nonalumni faculty members in setting salaries, of packing important University committees with nonalumni to the detriment of the alumni faculty, and of slighting prominent Kansans in selecting speakers at University affairs. "More and more," said a group of irate graduates in 1918, "the detailed management of our University is left to committees, chosen by our faculties, dominantly non-Kansan, and men who are not acquainted with Kansas people, and who manifest no desire to become so acquainted." The result was allegedly estrangement and neglect in the state at large: "In this way our best friends and best supporters are slipping away from us."[41]

Besides war weariness and alumni discontent still another factor helped Frank Strong decide to resign. As the University was returning to its peacetime work in 1919, there broke out among the faculty a dispute about the respective roles of the faculty and the administrators in setting University policy. The disagreement troubled the Chancellor. Because he refused to yield any of his powers to the leaders of the movement for what was called "faculty democracy," the argument would remain to plague both Strong's successor, Ernest H. Lindley, and the Board of Administration. War had brought the University unprecedented problems. Peace brought problems that were, alas, all too familiar.

21

Saving the University
from Democracy

*A*S President Woodrow Wilson and millions of other Americans saw it, the main goal of the United States in the World War was to make the world safe for democracy. The University's leaders agreed. But during the first six years of peace Chancellors Strong and Lindley and their supporters faced problems coming from an exactly opposite direction. Their main struggle was to keep the University safe *from* democracy. They won battles on two main fronts. In 1919 and 1920 they fought off a challenge to their administrative power from a group of disgruntled associate and full professors. From 1923 to 1925 they beat down an effort by Democratic Governor Jonathan M. Davis and his henchmen on the Board of Administration to control the University to suit themselves. Out of the second battle came a new fundamental law for the school restoring a Board of Regents to authority.

When the war ended, the University's theoretical structure was still confused. The Constitution of 1915 was in limbo between its approval by the old Board of Administration and the law of 1917 enlarging the chancellor's power. In February, 1919, Chancellor Strong recommended that the Senate expand the Committee on Revision of the University Constitution, appointed in 1917, and rename it the Commission on Reorganization of the University. He gave no hint, however, of what its duties would be. Instead he talked vaguely about "taking stock," now that peace had come, adding that the University should reflect "to some degree" the "great changes" caused by the war. The Senate expanded the original group, but by the time of Strong's resignation the new committee had done nothing.[1]

Soon afterward the argument about the faculty's role in internal administration broke out. Strong himself bore major responsibility for starting it. Discovering a growing restlessness among the faculty, in December, 1918, he suggested to the Senate that each school and the University as a whole should have a faculty budget committee. He was imprecise on the committee's functions, speaking generally of giving "justice to all interests" in the case of "conflicting interests in regard to salary schedules" in schools and departments and answering "new questions" in the University at large. At once the Senate authorized and requested each school to choose a budget committee to act on the "number of teachers in departments and the salaries to be paid." Then it voted to create a University Budget Committee, its members to be picked by the Senate from the members of the school committees. No duties were specified for the higher group.[2]

Realizing that the Senate's grant of power to the school committees conflicted with the provisions of the law of 1917 authorizing the chancellor to recommend salaries to the Board of Administration, and the Board to set them, Strong declared the Senate's act "unconstitutional."[3] The first response was a moderate essay by Professor David L. Patterson of the History Department in the April, 1919, issue of the *Graduate Magazine*. He pointed out that across the nation there was a growing movement for greater faculty power in the administration of colleges and universities. At Kansas, Patterson said, the movement was relatively advanced. For evidence he cited more frequent and vigorous faculty meetings, the fact that the Senate was now an "active legislating body," and the tendency of University committees to become elective rather than appointive. He called special attention to a budget committee of the College which during the past year had worked with Dean Templin to prepare the budget.

But Patterson reminded his readers that the movement at Kansas was not yet triumphant and stressed that it must continue. Frank Strong could be sure that the words were meant for him along with others. "No institution will keep abreast of the forward march in academic development, no institution will prosper," Patterson warned, "which does not admit members of its instructional force to at least partial participation in its administration and the formation of its policies."[4]

Other faculty members were less temperate than Patterson. They seized upon Strong's resignation as a grand opportunity to increase faculty power. After discussing the matter with the Board of Administration in the summer of 1919, Strong formally resigned on September 13. A month later the Board accepted the resignation, at the same time electing him, at his own request, professor of constitutional law in the Law School.[5] At a meeting on November 12, the Senate discussed the desirability of appointing a committee to confer with the Board about the selection of the new chancellor. Knowing what was in the wind, Strong had talked with Board secretary Wilbur N. Mason, who told the Chancellor that the Board would not appreciate the Senate's interference and would confer with Senate members at its own discretion. Strong, with high satisfaction, passed on Mason's warning to the Senate.

Only half of the senators were cowed. The boldest advocate of faculty democracy was Frank H. Hodder of the History Department. He proposed that the Senate, without the chancellor's interference, choose a "standing committee on University Policy," to consider "such questions, not directly affecting the interests of particular schools, as may from time to time be referred to it." Thus the chancellorship and everything else would be within its purview. Strong at once protested that the Senate should not try to bind his successor in any way, that it should wait to discuss with him the creation of such a committee. By a narrow margin Strong won. On November 14, the Senate defeated Hodder's motion, 46 to 44. Immediately afterward Leon N. Flint offered a weakened version, which called for the same committee but did not specify its duties. At that point some anti-Flint senator moved adjournment and his motion carried. Trying to outflank the faculty democrats, in January, 1920, with the approval of the Board of Administration, Strong prevailed upon the University Assembly—that officially powerless advisory body—to appoint a committee of fifteen to "confer" with the Board about the chancellorship. Among the members were Flint, Patterson, Frank W. Blackmar, Olin Templin, and Mervin T. Sudler—but not Hodder. Strong commended the group to the Board as an "excellent committee representing broadly the interests of the University and made up of men of sincerity and good judgment."[6]

Sincere and judicious they may have been, but nothing they did could affect the existing power structure. In the January, 1920, issue of the *Graduate Magazine* Professor C. Ferdinand Nelson of the Biochemistry Department attacked the existing system in an article entitled "Problems of Democracy in University Administration." The quality of every university, he said, depended on the quality of its faculty, which in turn was a composite of idealism, loyalty, and scholarship. Those characteristics arose from academic freedom and administrative responsibility. "So long as the faculty are considered hired men rather than responsible partners in the affairs of the University—in the important as well as less significant problems that present themselves for solution—academic freedom means little or nothing and independence must wait on administrative toleration." In the "university administration" of the day, however, faculties held responsibility only in such minor matters as student discipline or credits for work done elsewhere. "Three professors arrange for music, punch and wafers at the Commencement Ball," while "another group decorates the gymnasium for commencement exercises. A professional culinary committee all but cooks the alumni dinner. In these matters faculty participation is indeed complete." But the faculty played no role in day-to-day administration, had no share in choosing new faculty members, and as yet had no "real voice" in selecting the new chancellor. A university's mission was to be a "breeding ground for originality and advanced thought in letters, science, art, and the professions." Scholarship required "force, vitality, and independence," and they demanded internal democracy. On the answer that the Board of Administration gave to the question of the faculty's place in the University's government hung the institution's future.[7]

Two months later the *Graduate Magazine* carried an essay by Professor Orrin K. McMurry of the University of California Law School asserting that the same idea was true for all American universities.[8] Faculty democrats at Kansas took heart from McMurry's message. What was gladness in the breasts of some professors, however, was a festering sore in the bosom of College Dean Olin Templin. In April he attacked the idea of faculty democracy and slandered its proponents. Templin believed that the University existed to supply "the people" with the knowledge they desired; a faculty member, then, was a "public educator." "The ideal university," he contended, "consists of the best possible body of teachers who are getting the information they have to the people in the most direct and most economical manner." To serve the people's interests the faculty had to know them, and the information came through the governing board and the board's administrative officers. They, of course, had to have all authority within the University to make sure that the school was meeting its obligation to the people. The fact was, Templin said bluntly, that the people had "more ultimate rights involved in the administration of the university than the faculty have."

Behind the movement for faculty democracy, Templin asserted, was a theory that the "administration might be abolished, or almost so, without great loss to the institution. . . . The abolition of the university president and corps of assistants, and the substitution of the requisite number of clerks to carry on the details of the management as directed by the discretion of faculty committees, chosen by election from and by that body, is proposed." His charge was untrue, of course, but it was the basis of his argument against greater faculty control. If the faculty could successfully run the University without detriment to their "superior function" as teachers, he said, let them do it. The fact was that they could not. Not only was the administrative work far too detailed and complex for them to master, but actual experiments at greater faculty control had proved failures. Offering no evidence whatever, Templin claimed that professorial participation in appointments, promotions, and salary setting had neither improved faculty morale nor made the faculty more efficient. While the University's officers would always welcome faculty advice, outright faculty control would bring disaster upon the institution that adopted it.

True democracy, Templin asserted, was the system that now existed: it placed ultimate authority in the president's hands and then required him to keep the support of the students, faculty, governing board, and public, or resign. "The truth is that the proposed plan of complete control by the faculty is not democracy at all. It is simple socialism." Just as "socialistic administration" had failed outside the University walls, so it would fail inside. No great American university could function effectively without an "intelligent, sincere, prudent, courageous chief executive." Such a man would not be an autocrat. But even if he were, there were worse conditions. "A disposition to shrink from weighty responsibility that has been laid upon him is worse. The tyranny of the oligarchy that fatally springs out of any attempt at socialistic control is worse. The degeneracy and dilapidation that come from no administrative leadership is worse."[9]

Templin's attack was unprincipled, and two faculty members grabbed for their pens to skewer him. Professor R. D. O'Leary said that Templin was a bad logician and the next thing to a liar: since the Dean must have read the articles by Nelson and McMurry, he must have known that his charges were untrue; he had attributed to his opponents "absurd views," which they did not hold, in order to denounce them. Even worse was his dragging in the irrelevant question of socialism, one of those "bad words of the moment," to change a real issue into a false issue. In making it seem as if some faculty members had a severe case of "chancellorphobia," Templin had done the University great harm. The faculty hoped to find the new chancellor a "fair and reasonable man, a human being, a friend, and not a natural enemy, a person, not a mere academic functionary or, worse still, an autocrat looking down from lonely heights on a swarm of underlings, the head of any one of whom it may be his austere pleasure at any moment to demand." Yet he must understand that the days of autocracy were over. No president or chancellor, whatever his abilities, could do without advice from and consultation with his faculty, for the problems he faced were too huge. Nor would any kind of faculty oligarchy arise from a larger role. Indeed, there was greater danger in the present system, which allowed a few men to hold and retain authority "largely by the cultivation of one man's favor."[10]

Frank H. Hodder was just as annoyed. In a letter to the *Graduate Magazine* he pointed out that at the end of a war in which thousands of men had died to preserve democracy, a curious paradox existed in university government. In Europe, he said, the nations with the most autocratic governments had universities whose government was the most liberal and democratic. But in the United States, founded on democratic principles, a purely autocratic type of university structure was prevalent. That paradox had to be broken. "The doctrine of divine right has been driven from its last stronghold in the old world. It cannot survive in theories of university administration in the new. . . . If democracy will work anywhere it will work in university faculties composed, as they are, of exceptionally well trained men and women." Olin Templin was entirely wrong, Hodder said, in claiming that faculty democracy meant abolishing the administration. Hodder and others were simply asking administrators to share their power. It would lighten their burden, guarantee that the general interests of the group were reflected, educate the faculty, and help prevent the professors from being regarded as "hired help," an attitude which was causing many of them to desert academic life.[11]

The division over internal democracy and the chancellor's powers came close to costing the University the services of Ernest H. Lindley, whom the Board of Administration finally chose to succeed Frank Strong. During the months from October, 1919, to April, 1920, the Board reviewed dozens of candidates, who either nominated themselves or were recommended by Board members, alumni, the faculty committee, or interested citizens. By the spring of 1920 the Board was closely scrutinizing the qualifications of several men of note including Presidents Frank L. McVey of Kentucky and Raymond Hughes of Ohio's Miami University, ex-President Henry J. Waters of the Agricultural College, now editor of the Kansas City *Weekly Star*, and alumnus Edward E. Slosson, editor of the New York *Independent*. But the most attractive prospect was English professor John Erskine of Columbia University, a charming man, a fine scholar, and a beloved teacher. He had recently attracted great attention among educators through his work as head of a university in Beaune, France, run by the Army Educational Commission for American troops before they returned home. But Erskine found his resumed career as teacher and scholar more attractive than solving the problems he knew the chancellor would face, and withdrew from competition.[12]

A few days later the Board was hot on the scent of a new prospect, Ernest H. Lindley, president of the University of Idaho. His name had come from President William L. Bryan and several of Lindley's former colleagues at Indiana University, where Lindley had taught psychology and philosophy from 1893 to 1918. Upon inquiry the Board received enthusiastic reports about him from Chancellor Emeritus David Starr Jordan of Stanford, President

Henry Suzzalo of Washington, Presidents-elect Lotus D. Coffman of Minnesota and Marion L. Burton of Michigan, and others.[13] On May 30 the Board members talked with him in Denver and, liking what they saw and heard, offered him the chancellorship.

Since the Board had assured him that by law and Board decision he would have "ample authority" to "formulate and execute policy," Lindley's only doubt about accepting was the attitude of the faculty. On June 1, he visited Lawrence to discover from Chancellor Strong and the Assembly committee just how far advanced the movement for faculty democracy was. According to Strong, Lindley opposed the trend and thought that the Constitution of 1915 gave faculty groups too much authority. In a meeting lasting several hours Lindley presented his own ideas "very frankly and very decidedly." Unfortunately for his peace of mind the faculty democrats on the committee were just as frank and decided. Lindley left "somewhat depressed and undecided and dissatisfied," Strong reported to the Board, and not at all certain that he would accept.[14]

To reassure him, Strong, Olin Templin, and the Board all wrote that he need have no fears about too much faculty power. Strong asserted that most of the faculty shared Lindley's own "high ideals" for the University's development; Templin said that not more than a half-dozen faculty members held ideas "radical enough to cause any concern," and that even they would "gracefully acquiesce" in any policy once established and understood. The Board reported that the law of 1917 superseded the University Constitution, that the "sane judgment" of the faculty would approve all desirable changes in the document, and that the Board's "fullest support" would go to any new program for the "University's improved efficiency." Lindley consulted his conscience and friends for almost a week, then accepted. On June 8, the Board formally elected him. He was to receive $10,000 a year and a free residence.[15]

A tall, courtly, genial man, Lindley brought to the chancellorship the same abundant vigor—perhaps more—that Frank Strong had had in 1902, and the same determination to make the University of Kansas better than it was. Born in 1869 in Paoli, Indiana, he had moved with his parents to Bloomington. There he attended Indiana University, taking his B.A. in 1893 and M.A. in 1894. Three years later he received a Ph.D. in psychology from Clark University in Worcester, Massachusetts, which under G. Stanley Hall was one of the nation's foremost centers for the study of the new science of man. After taking his doctorate, Lindley studied for a year at the Universities of Jena, Leipzig, and Heidelberg and spent another year in postdoctoral work at Harvard. Within his field he had several special interests: the psychology of puzzles, invention, work, and leadership; the psychology of prayer; the philosophy and psychology of value; and the relation of mental hygiene to practical ethics. Though widely read and professionally knowledgeable, he had written comparatively little. His doctoral dissertation, "A Study of Puzzles with Special Reference to the Psychology of Mental Adaptation," appeared in the *American Journal of Psychology* in 1897. It was a report on the ways children learn to solve puzzles, and of the relations between puzzle-solving and the learning process. He and William L. Bryan later published a psychological study of Arthur Griffith, an arithmetical prodigy whom Lindley discovered at a teachers' institute in Warsaw, Indiana. They presented his case at a meeting of the American Psychological Association in 1899, and the next year Bryan read a paper on him at the International Congress of Psychology in London.[16]

But Ernest Lindley was always more a teacher than a researcher. During his twenty-five years at Indiana his main joy had been the classroom rather than the laboratory. His experiences there, his career as president of Idaho from 1918 to 1920, and his psychological bent combined to produce a theory of the American university that was in several respects different from those held by Chancellors Strong and Snow. Because he held similar views on particular functions and internal structure, however, he offered no proposals for fundamental change.

In his inaugural speech of 1921 Lindley's portrait of the perfect University was pragmatic: an institution adequate to the needs of the times. The modern world was a world of industrial production and organization, he said—one in which a vast amount of man's creative intelligence and imagination went to improving both the methods and the products of human industry and solving its problems. Because of the scientific revolution, the democratic revolution, and the industrial revolution, which separated the modern from the ancient world, what the Chancellor called a "new humanism" had dawned. Its main tenet was that "neither war, nor worship, nor contemplation, nor the enjoyment of leisure were the chief ends of man—but the shaping of nature through human industry to realize human ideals."

Present society, he thought, contained a "great frontier": the "zone in which modern science and the arts meet the work of the world." The task of every educational institution was to obliterate frontier barriers so that men's industries, occupations, and trades would be infused with art, knowledge, and beauty. "The conquest of the University will not be complete," he said, "until every worker shall be a thinker; every worker shall enjoy a constructive leisure; culture shall to the limit serve utility; art shall permeate industry. Ideals cannot indeed be realized until 'reals' are idealized."

When he became more precise about what he would have the University do, he was traditional. For the prosperity of American industry and the progress of American society, the school should encourage research—especially scientific research—to the maximum. The University should provide all legitimate kinds of vocational education, but had to make them meaningful by permeating them "through and through" with the "spirit of the arts and sciences." His greatest emphasis here was on broader training for business careers. Commerce had become a "learned profession," for it involved accounting, finance, salesmanship, advertising, and business administration. They drew in turn upon both the "arts and sciences which underlie the production and transportation of commodities," and the "mental and social sciences which insure fundamental satisfaction of legitimate human wants." The state of Kansas was on the eve of a great industrial era, and the University should train men to usher it in.

Besides vocational education the University should give its students a "sympathetic knowledge" of the world of industry. It should provide training for citizenship through the study of government and the practice of democracy in student organizations. It should prepare youth for the "constructive use and enjoyment of leisure." "Thanks to our Puritan ancestry," Lindley argued, "America does not know how to play. The arts of enjoyment and appreciation lag far behind the arts of production." The new humanistic leisure demanded that healthy bodies be built in play. Just as important it demanded minds enriched by the study and practice of the arts and literature, of music, painting, and sculpture.

Withal the University should continue its state-service work. In the broad sense all the University's functions served the people, but Lindley especially praised the industrial fellowships, the Geological Survey, and the institution's programs in industrial engineering, public health and sanitation, and "charities and social welfare." He promised that the University would continue its child-welfare work, and that it would join with the state's other public educational institutions to raise the quality of education.[17]

Before much improvement could occur anywhere, however, Lindley thought that the University's form of government needed changing. His original opinion of the Board of Administration is not clear. In 1925, with the legislature on the verge of replacing the Board with a new Board of Regents, the Chancellor said that he had worked from the beginning to alter the act of 1917. "The weakness of that law I knew before coming to the State," he wrote, "and sought, from the first, to get it changed." Yet in April, 1922, he had praised the Board and its work. There was nothing wrong in principle with the single Board, he said; the problem was to fill it with "high-grade" personnel. He thought that Kansas had been singularly fortunate in that respect and that prospects for the future were excellent.[18]

Even as he praised the Board, however, Lindley was collaborating in the preparation of a report that condemned the present system. In 1921 both the Chancellor and the presidents of the other state schools concluded that an independent assessment of the nature and needs of their institutions was desirable. Governor Henry J. Allen and his colleagues on the Board agreed.[19] The Board contracted with the United States Bureau of Education. Commissioner John J. Tigert chose as chairman of the investigating committee George F. Zook, a Kansas alumnus (B.A., 1906; M.A., 1907) and the Bureau's specialist in higher education, and added President Lotus D. Coffman of Minnesota and Dean Albert R. Mann of the Cornell University College of Agriculture.[20]

In light of what happened in the next two years, the most significant part of the Zook committee's analysis was the recommendation that Kansans remove their colleges and University from the control of the Board of Administration. To men familiar with previous objections to the Board the report had little new to offer. According to the committee, public institutions of higher learning were the state's "most fundamental agency for progress"; upon the proper solution of their problems and the proper determination of their policies would rest the state's "material, moral, and cultural standards" for generations to come. For best results the governing board had to include the very best men—men with "definite conceptions of the purposes of higher education and the necessary equipment and facilities to accomplish the desired ends," public-spirited men chosen on their merits alone, able to interpret the institutions and their purposes to the people. Their work should be to deal with "larger and more fundamental" problems, to lay down broad policies. Implementing them should be left to the schools' executives and faculties.

No state, the investigators said, could attract such men at the salaries its government could afford. This service appealed only to the "social instinct and to that pride that comes from performing notable public service." Although the present Board members were "good and capable men" whose work was praised at all the institutions, the system itself was bad. The law of 1917 which created it was sloppy and muddled. One part said that the Board was to "control and manage" the institutions under it; another that with the Board's advice and consent, and "under the Board," the business manager had "full authority to manage and control" them. The statute had so little precise reference to the state schools that it seemed that the legislature passing it did not have them clearly in mind: it spoke not of chancellors, presidents, professors, and instructors, but of superintendents, wardens, and other executive officers, along with clerks, officials, stewards, employees, and guards. Then there was the fallacious reasoning behind the act. No inherent relation existed, Zook and his colleagues said, between institutions of higher education and the prisons, reformatories, orphans' homes, and the State Fish Hatchery in Pratt, which the Board also supervised. Sound policy for one was not necessarily sound policy for all. Men able to deal wisely with some of the institutions were not necessarily able to solve the problems of higher education. Counting branches, moreover, the Board had twenty-seven institutions to supervise; thus the Board had no time to collect and analyze the data necessary for important policy decisions.[21]

To remedy all ills the Zook group recommended that Kansas create a separate governing board of about nine men for the five state schools. They should be prominent laymen, appointed by the governor, who would serve without pay. To guard against political meddling and guarantee continuity in policy, they should have terms of from seven to nine years. Bad experiences in other states demonstrated that neither the governor nor anyone else should be members ex-officio. The office of business manager should be kept, but his duties should be made clear and there should be competent business officers at the larger schools. If the state did not adopt the new scheme, Zook, Coffman, and Mann predicted, trouble loomed ahead.[22]

Before the Zook committee sent its final report to the Board of Administration, the members submitted it to Lindley and his chief assistant, Dean of Administration Frederick J. Kelly, for comments. Both men liked it. "The spirit of the report is most commendable," Kelly told the Chancellor. "It is constructive, scholarly, and exhibits most painstaking care both in respect to its use of facts and its forward-looking conclusions." Lindley told Zook that he was as satisfied as Kelly.[23]

To Lindley's great disappointment it proved impossible to get the report published in time for the legislature of 1923 to see it. The committee submitted it in typescript on November 25, 1922. Governor Allen's Board of Administration made no attempt to rush it into print. Allen's successor, Jonathan M. Davis, was entirely uninterested. Lindley sent him a copy, but Davis did nothing while the legislature was in session. After it rose, he told the Chancellor to see if the Bureau of Education would publish it to save Kansas the expense. Commissioner Tigert agreed, after some haggling, to issue it as a Bureau bulletin.[24]

When Davis became governor, the Zook committee's prediction of trouble started coming true. Davis was a choleric, sensitive, and crafty Democrat, determined—and naturally enough—to increase his party's weak power in state affairs. He had not run for election as an enemy of the University. Indeed, he had been a student on Mount Oread from 1890 to 1892. There he had fallen so deeply under James H. Canfield's spell that he left to join his mentor at Nebraska. His father's death in 1893 forced him to return to the family farm in Bourbon County, Kansas. Although a good student, he had not been able to return to college. In the election of 1922, in times not as prosperous as earlier years, he had run as a plain "dirt farmer" who understood the people and their needs. He promised to reduce state expenditures, lower taxes, eliminate unnecessary jobs, and make state employees put in a day's work for a day's pay.[25]

Just after the election William Allen White, who had talked with Davis at a homecoming football game, reported to Lindley that he was a "sincere man who seems interested in the University and its progress." But Davis became far too interested to suit the Chancellor. As the legislature of 1923 was preparing to meet, he was ruminating about "extra machinery" in the educational institutions that the Board of Administration should junk and "drift wood" that should be cleared away. It behooved the Chancellor to keep a weather eye on Davis. Before long he could see that a storm was near. In the spring and early summer of 1923 Davis managed to fill the Board of Administration with his own appointees. Harvey J. Penny's term expired on July 1. While the terms of E. L. Barrier and Ernest N. Underwood did not end until 1925, neither relished serving under Davis and both resigned. Replacing Penny was Albert B. Carney of Manhattan, a Democrat who had been a state legislator, school superintendent of Concordia, and president of the Concordia Normal and Business College. Barrier's and Underwood's places went to Democrat Roger M. Williams, a graduate of Baker University, now a Lawrence farmer and stockman, and Republican William P. Lambertson of Fairview, a well-to-do farmer who had attended both Ottawa University and the University of Chicago, had served several terms as a state legislator, and was Speaker of the Kansas House in 1919.[26]

At first it seemed that the new Board would be as sympathetic as the old. The members assured the educational executives of their wish to cooperate in a constructive program. Davis guaranteed Lindley that there would be no salary reductions and that the Board would not try to direct the University's internal affairs. "If he keeps to that platform," Lindley told George F. Zook, "we should get on very well." But as Lindley saw it, Davis jumped off the platform almost at once. By June the Board members were complaining that the deans were overpaid; they refused raises to those getting more than $5,000 a year. Convinced that there were too many deans and that the University was overadministered, they objected especially to Dean of Administration Frederick J. Kelly, whom Lindley had appointed in 1920. His main duties were to serve as "expert counselor" to the Chancellor, act for him in conferring with other deans, chair the school budget committees, and in general relieve Lindley of an "enormous burden of detail." Davis would later refer scornfully to Kelly as the "Dean of Deans," and thought from the start that his position was silly.[27]

The Kansas winds were blowing straws. In 1924 the tornado struck. Throughout the 1923–1924 academic year the Governor and other Democrats pestered John M. Shea, the University's superintendent of buildings and grounds, to hire party faithful as workmen. Often they urged on Shea men whom the superintendent thought entirely unfit. After Shea had turned down several Davisites, the Board determined that he had to go. Davis would later charge Shea with treating professors discourteously and using profane language when they requested his services; with "arbitrary, unfair, and partial" treatment of both actual and prospective employees; and with evading the draft in the World War. Davis's opponents claimed that the Governor was seeking support from the Ku Klux Klan, for Shea was a Roman Catholic, but Davis never suggested it. On July 23 the Board appointed H. H. Ball of Topeka to replace Shea. The members did so over Lindley's strongest protests, since Shea was an excellent superintendent, and despite the fact that the law gave chief executives of the institutions power to hire and fire.[28]

At exactly the same time, unfortunately, there occurred a more serious and more muddled affair involving Dean Mervin T. Sudler of the Medical School. On the surface and in the press it seemed that the Board had fired Sudler as summarily as it had dismissed Shea, and had thus interfered in an especially offensive way in the University's internal administration. Anti-Davis newspapers played up the alleged meddling as an attack on the school. As a result Davis suffered in the election of 1924. But the whole affair was more complex than it appeared.

Whatever Sudler's virtues, he now lacked the confidence of many Kansas physicians and of Chancellor Lindley as well. In July, 1921, the Kansas Medical Society's House of Delegates approved a report from its Committee on Medical Education accusing the Dean of not trying to promote closer relations with the Society and of not much caring whether the Medical School served the state as a whole. Beneath these charges lay the fear that Sudler lacked the administrative and leadership abilities needed to make the School a success. The position of dean, the physicians said, was a "job big enough to require the time and energy of a really big man, a man possessed of very definite qualities of leadership." That man was not Dean Sudler.[29]

For the mutual benefit of the University and the Medical Society the members proposed to Lindley a survey of the Medical School by eminent medical educators from outside the state. But the Chancellor thought a study in conjunction with the Zook inquest more practical, and he authorized a study by Dean Elias P. Lyon of the University of Minnesota Medical School. While Lyon in no way criticized Sudler, he suggested several improvements. He urged the consolidation of the School in Kansas City, said that it needed a laboratory science building at once, asked for intimate cooperation between the School and hospitals in both Kansas Citys, and recommended changes in state payment for patients, improving the Outpatient Department, and using the old hospital buildings for contagious diseases. He did point out that standards of scholarship had advanced rapidly in the past six years, and that alumni serving internships in the East, "in contact with graduates of the best schools," said that they had held their own in competition. Yet he also described the graduates as only "fairly well trained."[30]

By the time Lindley received the report in the fall of 1922, he probably wanted to replace Sudler. At any rate he distressed Sudler by refusing for months to show him the report; in May, 1923, Sudler still had not seen it.[31] And the opposition to Sudler continued to grow, with his enemies now taking their charges directly to Governor Davis. In June, 1924, Lindley gave the Dean a list of a half-dozen accusations. He had allegedly failed to win the support of Kansas physicians, had not given the staff of St. Margaret's Hospital in Kansas City, Kansas, recognition commensurate with their teaching services, and had exploited the Medical School hospital for his own gain by treating many of his private patients there. It also appeared that George E. Coghill, chairman of the School's Committee on Admissions and Advanced Standing, held only a Ph.D. and not an M.D., and was unpopular with the students besides, and that because it was unnecessary to pay salaries to men teaching clinical medicine, appropriations thus spent were wasted. Except for the charge that Sudler had used the hospital for private gain—which he denied—all were merely opinions.[32]

Opinion counted greatly, however, in deciding whether Sudler should continue as dean. In June and July, 1924, he met twice with the Board of Administration, decided that he had lost its support, and asked that he be allowed to resign as dean but to remain as head of the Department of Surgery. According to Sudler the Board agreed, and Governor Davis asked him to remain until his successor was chosen. Sudler also maintained that Lindley asked him to continue as dean at least until October, until after officials of the Rockefeller Foundation had visited the school in connection with an application for a grant. But the Board had his resignation in hand by early July. On the twelfth he left for a vacation in the East.[33]

While he was away, a series of distressing events occurred. On July 23 the Kansas City (Missouri) *Times*—the morning edition of the *Star*—published a story that the Board of Administration had removed Sudler as dean. The source of the report was said to be Board member Albert B. Carney. That afternoon the Lawrence *Journal-World* carried a more elaborate account. "Reports" had it that Lindley had refused to call for Sudler's resignation before his successor was considered and that the Board had therefore gone over the Chancellor's head in its "summary" dismissal of him. Coming at the same time that the Board fired John Shea, the alleged dismissal was tailormade for Davis's Republican opponents. The *Star* (always eager to make up the minds of Kansas voters for them), the *Journal-World*, the Wichita *Beacon*, and many other papers damned him. Davis had taken the University's management "out of the hands of the chancellor," said the *Star*, "and has made even the positions of the faculty mere political jobs." If the Sudler-Shea knavery were allowed to stand, the University was doomed, for it would bring the school to the "pawnshop of every political broker in the state." Davis's work, said the *Beacon* in an editorial which the *Journal-World* reprinted, had set Kansas higher education back by a quarter-century. It "wiped out the work of five administrations which had earnestly sought to build up a condition of merit in the educational personnel of the state institutions." Nothing in Davis's "checkered administration" had created "so definite a revulsion against him" as his forcing of politics into education.[34]

The charges were groundless, for the Board had not dismissed Sudler at all and had not, in July, even accepted his resignation. What had happened was that on July 22 some unidentified person in Lawrence had misinformed the Kansas City *Times.* Neither Albert B. Carney nor the Board ever issued a statement that Sudler had been dismissed. Chancellor Lindley publicly agreed that the Board had not dismissed Sudler over his objections.

But poor Sudler, still on vacation, began receiving newspaper clippings about his dismissal. Very much hurt, he submitted a new resignation effective at once. He sent it in at least by July 28, for on that day the Medical School faculty passed a statement of gratitude to him for his services as dean, on the "occasion of your resignation." On August 7 the Board accepted it.[35]

Whatever the truth, Sudler was no longer dean. (He was no longer a faculty member, either, for Lindley told him that the Board opposed his continuance and that it would be unwise to plead for mercy.) Anti-Davis men, moreover, had gotten in some well-placed kicks at the Governor in an election year. In the process they had made it clear that the Board of Administration offered an excellent position for political attacks on institutions of higher learning. No one knew how much the charge of meddling hurt Davis in the election. But he got only 182,861 votes to the 323,403 polled by Republican victor Ben S. Paulen.[36]

Davis as a lame duck took out on Chancellor Lindley some of his disappointment at losing. At the same time, "politically wise men of Lawrence" thought he was beginning his campaign for re-election in 1926. On December 12, Davis sent Lindley a curt letter to say that three things about the University bothered him. There had been "questions raised" about the suspensions of four men students. They had driven dates to Topeka and on the way back their car had run off the road, injuring the girls. The boys admittedly had drunk liquor before leaving Lawrence, but denied that drunkenness had caused the accident. After the appropriate deans had investigated the matter and suspended the students, one of them protested to Davis that an injustice had been done. Davis said that questions also existed about whether University authorities had followed the Board's rules on purchasing and expenditures and whether the Board's directives setting up a School of Business had been properly executed. At Davis's request Lindley conferred with the Board in Topeka, but the conference did not in any way decrease the animosity Davis had conceived for the Chancellor. On December 27, Lindley appeared for another meeting, at which the Board asked him face to face for his resignation. He refused it. The Board then dismissed him as chancellor by a vote of 3 to 1. William P. Lambertson, the Republican member, voted against the Democratic majority.[37]

When Davis tried publicly to justify the Board's action, however, he said nothing at all about the suspended students and nothing specific about Lindley's failure to follow the Board's orders. His statement to the press was a political screed, the evidence for its charges scanty. He had insisted that the Board dismiss Lindley, he said, for the good of the University and the good of the state. The Chancellor had five major deficiencies, Davis charged. He was incompetent, for he did not know his institution as he should and he constantly avoided responsibility by putting it on department heads. He was insubordinate, for he had failed to carry out the Board's orders, encouraged "false and malicious" attacks on the Governor and Board for allegedly trying to inject partisan politics into the University, and accused Davis of religious prejudice in the firing of John Shea. Lindley was also a procrastinator: he had put off "from time to time" executing the Board's orders and had failed to make "prompt and sincere efforts" to do what the Board desired. And he had engaged in intramural politics: through the appointment of new professors and the displacement of the University's "old and true friends" he had tried to build a "personal political machine within the school that would strengthen his own powers and help him in his own arbitrary control of the school and its policies." Added to everything else Lindley was aloof. Students could not get to see him personally. A mother had sought for three days to speak to him about her daughter, but could get no further than Frederick J. Kelly, the "Dean of Deans." Then there was the faculty member who tried for six months to see the Chancellor, sometimes sitting in the office for half a day at a time, "watching down town politicians come and go," and never getting an interview. "This spirit of aloofness and aristocracy," said Davis piously, "does not at all comport with the true Kansas spirit."

Toward the end of his statement Davis fired a barrage of unsub-

Governor Jonathan M. Davis. (Courtesy Kansas State Historical Society.)

stantiated accusations. He was insisting on Lindley's dismissal because

by all the showing and all that has developed, he has displayed a disposition to play a narrow, selfish, personal game, one of advantage to himself. He has schemed to control and influence those who were to appear at the recent hearings. I am informed that he has caused rumors to be circulated in the school that in case he remained there would be certain heads chopped off. He has thus created a spirit of fear, discontent and discord. He has shown a lack of broad, strong leadership. . . .

His conduct discloses a character unfit to occupy a place where the minds and hearts and souls of our young men and women are being developed, trained and instructed in the duties of citizenship—a citizenship that can only succeed and endure to that degree to which it is able to align with truth and social justice.

Davis would hold no further hearings on the matter. Lindley had to go.[38]

He went unwillingly and, as it turned out, only temporarily. Lindley returned from Topeka on December 27 in a fighting mood and immediately consulted with Lawrence attorneys Charles A. Smart and Walter G. Thiele. They convinced Judge Hugh Means of the District Court to grant a temporary restraining order against the Board until he could hold a hearing on a plea for a temporary injunction. At the hearing on January 5, 1925, Means rejected the plea. By the terms of the Moody Act appointees of the Board of Administration, replacing the Board of Regents, held office at its pleasure. Lindley's attorneys contended that the word "pleasure" should be interpreted to include sound judgment and exclude malice; they offered evidence of Davis's maliciousness. Davis's lawyers replied both that the Governor had ample reason to dismiss Lindley and that the Board's legal power to do so was clear. Judge Means decided that the discretionary act of the Board was not subject to judicial review.[39]

Frustrated at the local level, Lindley took his case to the State Supreme Court. There he sustained another defeat. Only corruption in the Board, the justices said, could prevent it from removing the chancellor at its pleasure. Otherwise there were no limits to the Board's discretionary power, certainly not prejudice or passion as Lindley had argued. Upholding Judge Means, the justices denied his right to the chancellorship.[40]

But what finally mattered was influence on incoming Governor Paulen, the new chairman of the Board of Administration. The day after Lindley's firing, the Douglas County Alumni Club, spurred on by Alumni Secretary Fred Ellsworth, sent telegrams by the dozen to alumni groups and individuals throughout Kansas to mobilize pressure. The alumni worked with impressive efficiency, holding mass meetings, signing petitions, and condemning Jonathan Davis every step of the way. It took no great perception by Paulen to see that reinstating Lindley would both win friends and discredit Davis. Two days after his inauguration Paulen met with the rest of the Board. William P. Lambertson had resigned and Paulen had appointed Mrs. Laura J. Cable in his place. Whatever the willingness of Albert B. Carney and Roger M. Williams to go along with Davis several days before, they were now properly repentant. The Board ordered Lindley's reinstatement, effective at once.[41]

Now if ever, it seemed to the Chancellor, the time had come to remove the University and the other institutions of higher learning from the Board's control. On January 2, Lindley had urged Paulen to support a new law. Many other Kansans did the same. Paulen was most responsive, asking in his message to the legislature that the schools be "separated entirely from politics, and from even the suspicion of politics" by creating a Board of Regents as the Zook committee had recommended. To make sure that the legislators responded appropriately, a number of University supporters created a lobbying group called the Citizens' Educational Council of Kansas, led by Henry Buzick of Sylvan Grove. Carroll B. Merriam of Topeka did most of the missionary work among the lawmakers, and received great assistance from Clyde W. Miller, Republican state chairman in 1924 and later Paulen's private secretary.[42]

Without Paulen's help, though, they would have failed. On February 6, 1925, the House and Senate Committees on Education introduced identical bills calling for a Board of Regents. After amendments the House passed its bill, 94 to 22. But the Senate struck out most of the House amendments, put in a few of its own, substituted the bill for the Senate measure, and then, to everyone's amazement, voted it down, 21 to 15. At that point Governor Paulen intervened, calling James W. Finley of Chanute, the Senate majority leader, into his office. Finley had voted against the bill, believing that its provisions would prevent the regents from exercising necessary control over the schools. Paulen asked him to move reconsideration of the measure, vote for it, and induce others to do the same. Finley did just that, and after a few more amendments the Senate passed the bill, 35 to 1. After the House agreed to the changes, Governor Paulen signed it on March 7.[43]

The act created a Board of Regents of nine unsalaried members appointed by the governor, who did not need the Senate's consent. Their normal terms would be four years, staggered so that in three out of every four years two regents would go out of office and the fourth year three would leave. Since the law was silent on the regents' politics, all of them might belong to one party.

They received all the powers the Board of Administration had had over the University, the Agricultural College, and the teachers colleges at Emporia, Pittsburg, and Hays. In addition the regents could remove all "executive heads, deans, professors, teachers, or other employees" at its discretion; thus the chancellor lost his power to dismiss. Despite the Zook committee's recommendation nothing in the law said that the Board should confine itself to laying down broad policies. Normally, however, the Board would meet only four times a year—in February, May, August, and November—which would make intimate supervision difficult.[44]

Knowing that many prominent Kansans were watching to see who the new regents would be, Governor Paulen chose them with care. Three of them bore a direct relation to the University. William Y. Morgan, editor of the Hutchinson *News-Herald*, belonged to the class of 1885 and had been a regent from 1907 to 1910. He had also been Jonathan M. Davis's opponent in the election of 1922. The other regents elected him chairman. Charles M. Harger, editor of the Abilene *Reflector*, had once been chairman of the Journalism Department. Charles W. Spencer, a lawyer and state senator from Sedan, had graduated from the Law School in 1903. Two other regents were agriculturalists: William J. Tod of Maple Hill, a stockman, had served as president of the Kansas Board of Agriculture and the Kansas State Livestock Association, and Bert C. Culp of Beloit, a graduate of the Emporia Normal School, was a sheep breeder and wheat farmer, and a banker and state senator as well. In 1925 Culp was chairman of the Senate Committee on Educational Institutions. The other four regents were equally prominent. Carroll B. Merriam of Topeka, who had worked hard for the new law, was a wealthy banker active in a host of civic and cultural organizations. Earle W. Evans was a Wichita lawyer, a director of several companies, and a man well known for his contributions to civic and social work. Former Governor George H. Hodges, who had demanded and signed the Board of Administration law of 1913, had yet disliked Davis and his machinations and had lobbied for the new law along with Merriam. The ninth regent was a woman, Mrs. James S. Patrick of Santanta. She was active in Republican politics, a writer of short stories and poems, and an enthusiastic clubwoman.[45]

Of the nine, two were Democrats—Spencer and Hodges—and the others Republicans. Six had attended college—Merriam, Culp, Evans, Spencer, Morgan, and Patrick. Looking at both the new law and the new Board, Chancellor Lindley and his colleagues had every reason to be optimistic. "It has been an extraordinary situation," Lindley said while the legislature was considering the new law, "and one not altogether pleasing." But with the triumph near he concluded, "It has been the biggest and most worth while fight that I have ever gotten into."[46]

22

The Material University, 1919–1929

T H E more the University changed, the more its needs remained the same. Under Ernest Lindley, as under Frank Strong, the institution was all the time laboring to make up for lost time in salaries, buildings, library books, and equipment. Like every chancellor before him Lindley held forth the vision of an ever improving, ever expanding University and begged Kansans to make that vision their own. Unfortunately his plans outran the imaginations of most citizens. At the same time the state's economy was unstable. In the early 1920s there was prosperity and optimism, but both declined after 1924. Hard upon the troubled twenties came the disastrous thirties, black with poverty and despair. It would be Lindley's misfortune to preside over the University during its history's most woeful era.

When the new Chancellor arrived in Lawrence, however, the future seemed bright. By Kansas standards the legislature of 1919 had been amazingly generous. The Board of Administration had asked about $2,692,000 for the biennium; the legislature's response was $2,034,230, the highest grant to that time. Some $600,000 would be available each year for salaries and wages, $150,000 for enlarging the power plant, and another $200,000 for a new hospital in Rosedale. While it was always risky to gamble on the future of Kansas, the war's end and the legislature's liberality were taken as harbingers of happy years.[1]

In the fall of 1919 a yeasty enthusiasm on Mount Oread bubbled

414

over into a so-called Loyalty Movement. If the Movement had a single founder, it was history professor Frank E. Melvin of the class of 1906. He saw it as an "effort of students, alumni, and faculty members to stimulate an intelligent and dynamic loyalty to the University of Kansas that will manifest itself in real college democracy. That means a good understanding and ready cooperation on the part of all members of the University in protecting the good name, and promoting the effective influence of Alma Mater as their paramount concern." For the undergraduates it meant a vindication of student government by showing that it fostered "effective self-discipline." For the alumni it meant a "closer connection with the University and fuller participation in its affairs." For the faculty it meant "support for more democracy, higher efficiency, and a stronger K.U. spirit." For everyone the slogans were to be "Not Punch, but Push," and "Put K.U. First."

Pushing K.U. loyalty was a faculty-alumni-student Loyalty Cooperating Committee with Melvin as chairman. The group was fertile in ideas to put K.U. first. It would inform people of the University's history, traditions, and ideals, sponsor rallies and ceremonies to encourage greater love for the school, and support "various undertakings which are of special value to the University or of special interest to the students." The Loyalty Movement would also "bring the conception of a greater K.U. program with specific goals to be attained each year, which eventually will mean the realization of a coherent campus plan, adequate in its facilities and beautiful in its architectural conceptions, expressing the idealism and cultural spirit of the University, and giving substance to the Great Vision of its creators and their children."[2]

In the foreground of the great vision was $1,000,000 worth of football stadium and student union. On December 12, 1919, a mass meeting in Robinson Gymnasium approved the two structures. They would both improve the University, orators said, and stand as memorials to those who fought and died in the war. To counter criticism that such structures were frivolous, an anonymous statement in the *Graduate Magazine* said that they were entirely necessary, but that the state legislature would have difficulty appreciating the fact. By increasing the alumni's comfort at football games the stadium would lessen the disgruntlement at removing the Missouri game from Kansas City; the stadium would also prove that football would not be de-emphasized. The union would provide a long needed social and recreation center and promote closer relations among students from all schools, social groups, and economic classes.[3]

A committee headed by Professor William J. Baumgartner of Zoology (K.U., 1900) talked up the Million Dollar Drive in September and October, 1920, and opened the campaign in earnest during the week after the homecoming game with Nebraska on November 13. The game seemed an omen of success, for Kansas tied the heavily favored Cornhuskers, 20 to 20; the *Graduate Magazine* asserted that the "real victory" belonged to Kansas. "A new spirit dominates the University . . . this year," said the *Kansan*—the spirit of " 'understanding loyalty.'—This University of ours has started on a new era of growth. We're going to make it the biggest and best in the Middle West. And how? Why, by every single student in the school boosting all the time, doing every thing he can to increase fellowship, to promote loyalty, to develop a sense of responsibility among students, to encourage wholesome recreation, to raise scholastic standards, and to create fair, worth-while student activities and class spirit."[4]

In the early days of the Million Dollar Drive the *Kansan* seemed correct. By the end of November students and faculty had pledged over $200,000. Outside the University there appeared to be equal enthusiasm. By May, 1921, total pledges had reached $550,000; by October they had passed $600,000; by the late fall of 1922 they were over $850,000. But the million dollars never came. When the drive petered out in 1925, pledges were slightly over $965,000. While this was hearteningly close, payments on the pledges were discouraging. Of the 2,300 installment payments to be made on May 1, 1921, only 110 were in hand by May 18. This set a pattern: by September, 1931, only $655,000 of the $965,000 had been received. Payments were then trickling in at the rate of $10,000 a year, and clearly the Million Dollar Drive had failed.[5]

Yet in the spring of 1921, with over $500,000 pledged and hopes of payment high, construction of the new stadium began with the destruction of the old. Tuesday, May 10, was Stadium Day, with classes dismissed. In the morning the men students tore down the bleachers. After a lunch served by University women there were speeches and games. Chancellor Lindley climaxed the festivities by donning overalls, grabbing a horse-drawn plow, and breaking ground for the new structure with a straight furrow across McCook Field. On the same day the directors of the new University of Kansas Memorial Corporation met for the first time. If they had had the money, they would have built the stadium then and there. Designed by La Force Bailey and Clement C. Williams of the School of Engineering after stadiums at Harvard and Princeton, it was to be U-shaped, the open end to the south, and to seat about forty thousand people. The Corporation could find only $287,000 in cash, however, which was enough to complete only parts of the west and east sides. Eighteen thousand fans packed them for the Kansas-Missouri game on Thanksgiving Day, 1921. To general delight the Jayhawks squeezed past the Tigers, 15-9.[6]

Immediately after the formal dedication on November 11, 1922, though, Nebraska whipped Kansas, 28-0. It was an augury, for zero was what the Memorial Corporation contributed to the stadium's cost in later years. Too many pledges remained unpaid; there was the union to build. The Athletic Board and spectators had to foot the bill. In 1925 the Board secured a charter for the nonprofit University of Kansas Physical Education Corporation, whose main purpose was to get money to complete the stadium, although it might also have general oversight over athletics. By floating over $350,000 in bonds, backed by prospective gate receipts, the Corporation lengthened the stadium's sides in 1925, and finished the horseshoe in 1927. The bonds were paid off only in 1947, after another gift campaign launched by Athletic Director Ernest C. Quigley and after unexpectedly good gate receipts in 1946. "Naturally I am mighty pleased to have this load off our necks," Quigley said.[7]

Progress on the student union was even less impressive. In September, 1921, Chancellor Lindley was dreaming of a magnificent building to cost about $500,000. The Chicago architectural firm of Pond and Pond, which had designed the famous student union at Michigan, drew up plans for an impressive structure north of Dyche Museum. But because the Memorial Corporation's policy was "Pay as You Build," there was no construction until 1925. And because the directors then had only about $120,000 instead of the $275,000 they had hoped to spend for the Union's first unit, what went up was merely a shell for an unfinished interior. As money appeared, the inside was completed: a basement cafeteria opened in September, 1927, for example, and the grand ballroom on the second floor was properly finished in 1934. By 1938 the Union was complete—except for the sub-basement and two-thirds of the third story, intended originally for guest rooms.

Measuring a modest 80 by 135 feet, the Union by the mid-1930s included a cafeteria, game rooms, lounges, the ballroom-banquet hall, and student-activity offices. Small and unfinished though it was, it drew a fragmented student body toward a common center, offered opportunities for recreation and relaxation of approved kinds, and, as Men's Adviser Henry Werner said in 1938, stood as a "place where all students can learn to live together."[8]

Both it and as much of the stadium as the Million Dollar Drive paid for were also symbols of the fact that the alumni were learning to live together with the chancellor. Ernest Lindley proved far more adept than Frank Strong in diplomatic relations with the alumni. The University's welfare, he constantly assured them, depended on their cooperation and support. Among the things they could do were to keep informed about the institution's condition and needs—"*Rediscover your University*," Lindley begged them— urge legislators to be generous, talk up the school to prospective students and their parents, get Kansans to visit Mount Oread, and be "actively good citizens" so as to demonstrate one of the best results of higher education. Lindley also took a giant step beyond Frank Strong by asking alumni to think of ways to improve the University and to send their ideas directly to him and other school executives.[9]

Lindley was just as solicitous privately as he was publicly. The results were gratifying. One of the livelier centers of discontent with Strong, for example, had been Ann Arbor, Michigan. University of Michigan professors Henry E. Riggs ('86), William C. Hoad ('98), and former Kansas professor Arthur G. Canfield had written and spoken of their concern about the University's deterioration under Strong to alumni throughout Kansas and the Middle West. Strong "did not seem to be able to see a Kansas alumnus," Riggs wrote, "and . . . failed miserably as an administrator simply because he did not realize the fact that the greatest asset that a university can have is a strong active enthusiastic alumni body."[10]

Instead of ignoring or merely trying to pacify vocal alumni,

Ernest Lindley made them confidants and collaborators. After Riggs wrote a public letter to a Lawrence newspaper calling for maximum alumni support for the University, Lindley invited him to Lawrence for a personal conference about the school's problems. As the meeting of the 1921 legislature drew near, Lindley asked help from the Michigan men. They responded by inviting Governor Henry J. Allen up for a visit to tell him directly of the University's wants. On a visit to Ann Arbor in 1922 Lindley captivated Riggs with his "charming personality," "ability to mix with people," and assets as a "practical psychologist." Said Riggs, "I feel that Kansas is wonderfully lucky in having him and am perfectly certain that they are going to have a fine administration from him."[11]

President Nathan T. Veatch of the Alumni Association of Greater Kansas City felt exactly the same way in 1923. After Governor Davis had appointed his new Board of Administration, the Chancellor suggested that Veatch and his fellow alumni should strive to convince the members to make Kansas "all that a modern University should be" and influence the public toward the same end. Veatch could not have been more pleased. "I am sure you do not have to be told," he wrote, "that the bunch here in Kansas City are for you, heart and soul, and are anxious to help and only need your suggestions." That was not what the Kansas City alumni had been saying to Chancellor Strong.[12]

A new vigor appeared in the Alumni Association as well. In September, 1920, Alfred G. Hill ('17) became secretary. He and the Alumni Board, led by Association President Irving Hill of Lawrence, urged all sorts of projects on the graduates. They should join the Association, imbue themselves with the "religion of higher education," and spread the word. They should contribute to pay the Chancellor's expenses as he traveled to solicit support. They should become the "Big Brothers and Sisters, or the Uncles and Aunts of promising boys and girls in the High School," encouraging them to attend the University and helping guide them through their undergradate years. In return, Hill said, "Chancellor Lindley's plans are to make the University of service to you Alumni, to feed something to you from Kansas University so that its benefits may follow you all the days of your life."[13]

When Alfred Hill resigned in 1924, the Alumni Association hired Fred Ellsworth ('22) to succeed him. Ellsworth had majored in journalism, and was an able publicist eager to win greater alumni cooperation for the University's welfare. Energetic, enthusiastic, kindly, and congenial, he continued as secretary until 1963. He did more than any other man to make the alumni feel that they remained an important part of the University even after they left Mount Oread.[14]

By 1929 the Alumni Association had some thirty-five hundred dues-paying members, in contrast to about fifteen hundred a decade before. The major means of communication with them was the *Graduate Magazine,* which in the 1920s under Hill and Ellsworth underwent an important evolution. It became more popular, less intellectual, increasingly devoted to personal news, sports, anecdotes, appeals for help and for more pride in the institution, and less devoted than in previous years to scholarly and academic matters. Although the magazine had never been given only to the intellect, it had provided a forum for the serious discussion of serious matters. In the 1920s such discussion was hard to find. Florence Finch Kelly ('81) complained in 1928 that the magazine told nothing about what the "young people" on Mount Oread "are doing with their brains," nothing about whether "ferment . . . in the educational world" was "touching our alma mater." Ellsworth replied that he was simply too busy—visiting alumni clubs, showing returning alumni around the campus, planning dedications and conventions, working with student organizations—to gather much news on the "thought of the University." The kind of information Mrs. Kelly wanted took time to obtain and report. If more alumni would join the Association and pay their dues, the *Graduate Magazine* could enlarge its staff and raise its intellectual tone. But Ellsworth also believed that the magazine's main function was not to portray the University's intellectual life. "The Graduate Magazine is a magazine of personal news about alumni," he wrote. "It features that and must stand or fall on that plank. The alumni office and magazine are organized to furnish that material." Whatever else it carried had to be "usually pretty ordinary stuff," unless Ellsworth managed to get a prepared speech by a noteworthy Kansan relating to the University. All of which meant that the alumni's understanding of the school would be inaccurate and incomplete.[15]

At the same time that Chancellor Lindley and his aides were revivifying the alumni and pressing the Million Dollar Drive, they also tried to make the University as a whole a more attractive object for private donations. One agency for getting them was the Kansas University Endowment Association. Organized in 1891 and chartered in 1893, the Association's purposes were to receive, invest, and disburse the income from gifts, which state law forbade the Board of Regents from accepting directly. During its first thirty years, however, it did little more than hold the title to McCook Field, buy the University pipe organ, and administer a $500 fund given by the Kappa Alpha Theta sorority for library books. By 1920 it had only that fund and $109.01 in cash. But in that year Olin Templin, then retiring as College dean, secured appointment as Association secretary and interested Lindley in the cause of private giving. Together they chose a new board of trustees, who resolved to begin a "systematic campaign to encourage donations of all kinds."[16]

Throughout the 1920s, however, receipts were small, mainly because the Million Dollar Drive came first. In 1927 the trustees resolved to open a campaign to be "prosecuted vigorously and with confidence and determination." But by June, 1932, the Endowment Association had principal funds of only about $19,000, which during the previous year had yielded about $1,344.[17] Yet there had been two remarkable gifts for specific purposes. One came from Association Trustee Solon E. Summerfield, a Lawrence native, a member of the class of 1899 and a graduate of the Law School in 1901 and now president of the Gotham Silk Hosiery Manufacturing Company of New York. In June, 1929, he offered $20,000 a year for the rest of his life, and a trust fund to provide that sum after his death, for scholarships for men undergraduates. Summerfield Scholars were to be chosen solely according to intellectual ability and character; there would thus be differences of financial need among them. Those who could pay part of their expenses had to do so; those with no money had all their legitimate expenses covered for four years. With the money the Association's officers found that they could select about ten new Scholars each year.[18]

Another great gift came from Mrs. Elizabeth M. Watkins. The widow of Lawrence millionaire Jabez B. Watkins, who had died in 1921, she gave the rest of her life and much of her fortune to philanthropy for both the University and the city of Lawrence. Childless herself, she made the undergraduates, especially the women, her foster children, watching over them from her mansion at the southeast corner of the campus, seeking through systematic benevolence to promote their welfare. Her direct gifts and bequests to the University ultimately reached about $2,000,000. The first of them was an entire cooperative dormitory building to house thirty-eight women. Located just north of her home, across from Fraser Hall, Watkins Hall opened in the fall of 1926. Built of brick, it had several small kitchens and dining rooms, each accommodating five or six students, who were to eat together and share the expenses. Living rooms and lounges were for all in common. Each woman paid but $27 room rent a year. The girls were, of course, under the supervision of an older house director. Watkins Hall offered opportunities to live even more cheaply to a number of coeds who had dwelled in off-campus cooperative houses; as a result all but one of them closed.[19]

Another source of continuing support was student fees. Starting in September, 1920, Kansas residents paid a $10 matriculation fee to all schools—nonresidents paid $15—and every student paid a $10 graduation fee. More important was the "incidental fee" levied on every student. It ranged from $20 to $30 a year for residents and nonresidents respectively, in the College and the Engineering, Graduate, and Education schools, up to $100 in the Clinical Department of the Medical School. When the legislatures of the 1920s proved stingy, fees inevitably rose. At the decade's end most undergraduates were paying $50 a year if they were Kansas residents and $74 if not; Kansas students in the Clinical Department were now charged $150, out-of-state students $200.[20]

Those fees considerably increased the University's income. In fiscal 1925, for example, they came to over $250,000; in 1926, over $310,000; in 1930, over $413,000. Among other things they allowed the University to supplement the legislature's appropriations for salaries and wages. Thus for fiscal 1926 the legislature appropriated $860,000, but the University spent about $1,119,000; for fiscal 1929, when the appropriation was the same, the total paid was about $1,159,000.[21]

Despite the Million Dollar Drive, gifts, and fee receipts, however, the legislature, as always, mainly determined the University's material history. During the postwar years the school suffered even more than usual from both an inadequate plant and inadequate faculty salaries. In the spring of 1923 a faculty committee reported to Chancellor Lindley that although the newer buildings were in fairly good shape, several older ones were disgusting. Fraser Hall had floors full of cracks and crevices so packed with dirt that the only way to clean them was to replace the floors entirely. The Department of Home Economics attracted hordes of rats and mice. Toilets were dirty and ill ventilated; the plumbing continually broke down. In classrooms and offices the paint was dirty and scaling, lighting and ventilation were inadequate, the heating system was "uncontrollable throughout the building." Conditions in the old Chemistry Building, now housing the Department of Journalism, were just as bad. Even in moderate weather the antiquated heating unit joined with the wretched ventilation to raise temperatures in the smaller offices to 100 degrees. The walls of the main lecture hall were dirty and cracked, and water was always leaking in; the wooden floor of the smaller lecture hall was filthy, splintered, and worn through with holes; noxious fumes collected in the basement type and linotype rooms. Since it was impossible to put the building in "acceptable hygienic condition," the committee urged that it be "dispensed with." It would be used for almost four decades more.

The third oldest building was Snow Hall, constructed in 1886 and housing the Departments of Botany, Zoology, Entomology, and Bacteriology. It was so obviously "delapidated," the faculty committee said, that no improvements could redeem it and no description of it was necessary. A replacement was needed at once. An insider's report came in 1927 from H. H. Lane, head of the Zoology Department. Snow Hall was both too small and a menace to life and limb. The piers were crumbling and settling, making gaps of up to three inches between walls and floors. The building was a firetrap in which careless use of a hotplate or bunsen burner could start a roaring blaze. In winter some rooms were unusably cold, while others warmed to 120 degrees. Rats galore bore parasites which constantly threatened an epidemic. Parasitology and bacteriology classes, which used dangerous organisms, had to share inadequate rooms with other classes, and the danger from infection was constant. Conditions in Snow Hall, Lane suggested, were probably responsible for the repeated illnesses of the faculty who worked there.[22]

The more recent structures—those of the past thirty years—varied in adequacy. Green, Haworth, and Marvin Halls were excellent in most respects, as were the several parts of the Administration Building. Blake was solid, though its ventilation was poor and its wasted space considerable. Spooner was also structurally sound, if small and outmoded. While the Chemistry Building was physically serviceable, it now lacked space for effective teaching and faculty research. Robinson Gymnasium was both too small and a fire hazard. Dyche Museum had reasonable space for exhibits, but in the basement the Anatomy Department suffered from poor lighting, worse ventilation, and private laboratories which were "indescribably uncomfortable and stuffy."[23]

At the Clinical Department of the Medical School in Rosedale there still had not appeared a large, modern, and well-equipped hospital and medical center. In 1920 the main hospital had fewer than a hundred beds, which made satisfactory training impossible. Thanks to the legislature of 1919, $200,000 was available for a new hospital. Thanks to the misplaced generosity of Simeon B. Bell, however, the present site of the Clinical Department left no room for expansion, and it took time to gather money to buy a new campus. In the meantime the 1919 appropriation remained unspent.[24]

Large plans were expected of a new chancellor, and Ernest Lindley had no small ideas. Besides the completed Administration Building and an enlarged heating plant, he told the Board of Administration, eleven new structures or additions were needed. A few were minor: a greenhouse, additions to Haworth and Marvin Halls and Fowler Shops, another unit for the electrical engineers. The others were major: a medical building for the two years' work in Lawrence; a new Rosedale hospital, requiring more than the available $200,000; a "woman's building" for home economics, physical education, and a cafeteria; "a unit" of a new library; an auditorium; a student hospital; and a building for the Music Department. Governor Allen shared the Chancellor's ideas. "At the state university," he told the legislature of 1921, "we are no better off in some respects than we were when the institution had a student body of twelve hundred, although the enrollment has now reached more than four thousand and with added room it would be much larger."[25]

The legislators of 1921 were warmly responsive. For the 1921–1923 biennium they reappropriated the unspent $200,000 for the hospital and $150,000 for the power plant, and added $150,000 more to the latter to make possible a modern facility. Minor appropriations came for a cafeteria and another engineering shop building behind Marvin. Far more significant than these, however, were grants of $250,000 each for a new library and for completing the Administration Building, and $500,000 to the Board of Administration for dormitories.[26]

In the next few years the University knew the joys of another building boomlet. In 1922 the new and enlarged heating plant made Mount Oread's indoor environment a little more pleasant. A year later the Administration Building was done. But these were routine things. Not at all routine was the University's first student dormitory, Corbin Hall, which opened in the fall of 1923 on the site of Old North College, torn down in 1919 before it crumbled of its own accord. Though the desire for dormitories and the idea of the University's responsibilities as a foster parent were decades old, Corbin Hall was the product of recent efforts by Alberta L. Corbin, the adviser for women. By 1920 she thought that the housing situation had become intolerable, and that at least 25 percent of the students had unsatisfactory rooms. "Some are living at inconvenient distances from the University; some are paying exorbitant prices for uncomfortable quarters; some have not the care and supervision they need. This last is true of freshmen girls, especially." Women's dormitories, Miss Corbin believed, would set standards for sororities, boarding houses, and the four cooperative houses, help to control prices in Lawrence, and "serve the interests of democracy" by bringing together women of different backgrounds, classes, and interests. She and many other like-minded women had lobbied successfully with the 1921 legislature.[27]

Corbin Hall housed 128 women under the supervision of a house director and a social director, both of them responsible to Agnes L. Husband, Alberta Corbin's successor. The girls had a constitution governing dormitory life and elected their own officers to enforce it. Miss Husband asserted that hall life was extremely popular; its success was an "unanswerable argument in favor of a dormitory system in our state institutions. What we need now is more of them."[28]

Like Corbin Hall the University's new library building was both long overdue and too small for the school's needs. Since $250,000 was nowhere near enough for an adequate structure, all that Lindley could do was stretch the money as far as possible and hope that

An inadequate library grows.

The library room in the University Building, about 1890, Carrie Watson behind the desk at the right rear.

The main reading room in Spooner Library, about 1900, Carrie Watson as before.

The reference room in Watson Library, about 1930, with Carrie Watson on duty.

A Watson Library reminder to the Philistines, 1940s.

future legislatures would be generous. Designed in the Collegiate Gothic style by Engineering graduate George L. Chandler, it stood west of the Journalism Building and behind Snow Hall, which produced a peculiar stylistic conglomeration. When fully in use in January, 1926, it could seat eight hundred students. This was the kind of spaciousness that Spooner had lacked, yet stack space was still at a premium. When Earl N. Manchester, appointed director of libraries in 1921, collected as many books as he could from the ten department libraries around the campus, he had on his hands over 184,000 volumes, which overflowed the stacks into nearby corridors. He was already much worried about what to do with the 8,000 volumes being received each year. But there were now carrels for faculty and graduate students, several seminar rooms, and nearly adequate space for the Cataloguing Department and for periodicals and reserved books. In response to pleas from many alumni—including William Allen White and Governor Davis—but over objections from Chancellor Lindley, the Board of Administration named the building for Carrie Watson.[29]

Meanwhile lesser structures appeared in Lawrence. Behind Marvin Hall was a new electrical engineering building, two stories high, with a dynamo laboratory and several smaller rooms for specialized equipment and work. Its completion allowed the School of Engineering to move its hydraulic engineering equipment from Fowler Shops to the old power plant structure south of Marvin. In October, 1921, a University Commons, or cafeteria, opened; it served an average of eight hundred meals a day.[30]

Had the University been able to sustain the pace of building begun in 1921, it would soon have had a most impressive physical plant. But as usual the boomlet was only temporary. In 1923 the Senate was willing to appropriate $300,000 for an auditorium, but the House Ways and Means Committee was not. Two years later both houses agreed on an auditorium appropriation of $250,000; in 1927 the University got a necessary $100,000 more. With the extra funds the regents completed the building, designated, by order of the legislature, Hoch Auditorium after ex-Governor Edward W. Hoch. Its exterior, suggested by Watson Library, was a modified form of Collegiate Gothic; the two buildings were so far apart, however, that the harmony was lost. Its interior was a large, suitably ornate theater, modeled upon Hill Auditorium at the University of

Michigan and seating some thirty-five hundred people. To the great annoyance of many faculty members it was a basketball arena as well as a theater for concerts, plays, addresses, and convocations. Lindley and his advisers laid a flat basketball floor at the front, before the stage, in order to accommodate the crowds that were overflowing the unsafe Robinson Gymnasium to watch the teams of Coach Forrest C. Allen. The aesthetically sensitive protested that the temporary chairs put on the floor for other events would be a rattling nuisance, but the Chancellor promised all precautions to keep things quiet.[31]

Only one other building rose on the Lawrence campus out of state appropriations in the 1920s. It was new Snow Hall, and it came in the nick of time. At first H. H. Lane, his colleagues in the biological sciences, and Lindley dreamed of a well-appointed replacement for the decaying older structure, to cost about $350,000. But Lindley and the regents scaled their dream down to $250,000 before appearing before the legislature of 1927, and the solons cut another $50,000 from that. (In 1929, however, the legislature granted $70,000 more for equipment and supplies.) Standing across Jayhawk Boulevard from Hoch Auditorium and reasonably complete by 1930, Snow held the Departments of Zoology, Bacteriology, Botany, and Entomology. Within the limits of money and space the members of each department had been allowed to design their own quarters. Snow was a six-story split-level structure whose first two stories were below the street-level entrance on the third. Like Hoch and Watson its architecture was modified Collegiate Gothic. A graceless tower imposed on the façade made it uglier than necessary.[32]

With the erection of new Snow, state-supported building expansion stopped for years. Chancellor Lindley, of course, refused to rest content. In 1928 he told the Board of Regents and the citizens that the library building was too small and the School of Engineering still too cramped, and that the University needed both more dormitories and a student hospital. He also wanted a medical science building, a music building, a journalism building, and either a new education building or an addition to the minuscule Oread High School. While he proposed to go slowly, however, asking money for but one or two buildings at a time, his efforts began and ended in failure. In 1929 both the Senate and the House Ways and Means Committees rejected funds for the medical science building, to which Lindley gave first priority. He would go on pleading from then until his retirement in 1939; he regularly found sympathy, but nothing more. Hard times had come again and the clouds of gloom banished until a later day the moderate optimism and moderate progress.[33]

Adding to the despair was the fact that the University's depressingly low faculty salaries had not risen much during the 1920s. Before Frank Strong left the chancellorship in 1920, he faced an angry faculty who threatened to take the salary question into their own hands. Strong had appointed a committee led by Graduate School Dean Frank W. Blackmar to investigate the University's salary structure in order to prepare a petition to the Board of Administration for higher pay. But in April, before the committee was ready to report, the University Senate passed a motion offered by Goldwin Goldsmith of the Department of Architecture calling for a campaign to urge the institution's alumni and friends to pressure the legislature into remedial action. The Senate asked the Board of Administration to let a faculty committee gather "such facts as will constitute a genuine program of public information" for the alumni and their allies. In cooperation with well-wishers of the other state schools, they would lobby in Topeka for higher salaries throughout the state's higher educational system. The Board approved the plan, provided that no information went out without the Board's approval. A week later, after Blackmar's committee reported to the University Assembly that salaries were preposterously low, the Assembly members voted to petition the Board for a 50 percent increase for everyone.[34]

And well they might. Statistics collected for the Senate by Dean of Administration Frederick J. Kelly showed conditions that, by any standards, were deplorable. Computing a University average from the average of the maximum and minimum salaries in each of the four ranks, Kelly came up with an annual figure of $2,325. He had computed similar averages for twenty other institutions, ranking in national prestige from Harvard and Columbia to the universities of Arkansas, Missouri, and Nebraska, and the Kansas State Agricultural College. He placed the University of Kansas twenty-first. While the difference between Kansas and Nebraska (average $2,369), the next highest on the list, was slight, the gaps between Kansas and Minnesota ($2,819), Washington ($2,819), Wisconsin ($3,256), or

California ($3,350) were disgraceful, and those between Kansas and Columbia ($4,312) and Harvard ($4,606), which led the list, indescribable. And if the Kansas average salary was poor, the highest salaries paid to full professors were worse. In the sixteen state universities and land-grant colleges of the North Central States almost 40 percent of the full professors received over $4,000 a year. At Kansas only three of seventy full professors (4.3 percent) got over $4,000. The most paid to any full professor was $4,500.

Kelly also asserted that the rate of salary increase was inadequate. From 1915–1916 to 1920–1921 his figures showed an average 37 percent increase in faculty wages, which compared poorly with the increases for elementary-school teachers (109 percent) and factory workers (110 percent during the war) throughout the nation. Two years later, seeking to enlighten the legislature of 1923, he also alleged that the faculty had suffered a decline in real wages from 1914–1915 to 1920–1921, but had improved its position from 1921 to 1923. Here his argument was weaker than when based on comparative salaries. Bradstreet's Index showed a 35.5 percent rise in living costs from 1914–1915 to December, 1922. During that period the average salary of Kansas faculty members went from $1,700 to $2,488, an increase of slightly over 46 percent.

In his analysis of 1920 Kelly also claimed that Kansas's inadequacies caused a high faculty turnover. Although he lacked statistics from other institutions, he pointed out that over half the Kansas faculty—20 percent of the full professors, 31.5 percent of the associate professors, almost 70 percent of the assistant professors, and over 87 percent of the instructors—were new since 1916. Kelly did not explain how many new appointments were replacements for men who had resigned, retired, or died. But since the faculty (including graduate students who taught) had increased only from 243 in 1916–1917 to 262 in 1920–1921, the turnover rate did seem excessive.[35]

Hard upon the salary statistics came figures showing that in comparison with people of other states Kansans were niggardly in their appropriations. Using statistics for 1912—the most recent available —Kelly noted the per capita wealth of Kansas was $2,652, which placed it above Minnesota ($2,582), Wisconsin ($1,875), Michigan ($1,873), and Ohio ($1,817), whose universities paid higher average salaries than Kansas. In the nation, he said, Kansas ranked tenth of the forty-eight states. It had no public debt, moreover, and its citizens spent no more on things such as cigars, cigarettes, soft drinks, and theater tickets than people in surrounding states. Further, of every 10,000 people in Kansas, 27 went to the University or the Agricultural College, a considerably higher number than in Michigan (24.4), Minnesota (22.4), or Wisconsin (19). Yet the expenditure per student at the University of Kansas for 1919–1920—not including spending for buildings, extension work, and summer school —was only $230.43, while Michigan spent $384.36, Wisconsin $459.60, and Minnesota $540. For good measure Kelly threw in statistics from 1917–1918 to show that Kansas was behind many other schools—Wisconsin, Minnesota, Iowa, Illinois, Michigan, Ohio State, and even Nebraska and Arkansas—in the dollar value of buildings per student. He concluded that Kansas could afford much more for higher education than its citizens were paying.[36]

Publicly, at least, Chancellor Lindley put his faith in that old saw of American democracy that when the people had the facts, their desire for progress would make them eager to help the University. "All that is necessary is to bring to Kansas the evidence that other states are advancing faster than she is," he said. "When she knows the facts she surely will respond." This, of course, was wishful thinking. Had he and the sympathetic Board of Administration had their way, the legislature of 1921 would have granted about $1,123,000 for salaries and wages during each of the next two fiscal years. But with the huge building requests that the Board was also making, the legislature settled on a mere $780,000 as a reasonable figure. Although this was a 31 percent increase over the $598,000 annual appropriation for fiscal 1920 and 1921, the average faculty salary increase of about 5.3 percent was much less remarkable, because the Board decided to use most of the money to enlarge the faculty.[37]

Making up for lost time was obviously going to take a long time. As the 1920s wore on, the University's officers and faculty became glummer, for successive legislatures were unwilling to grant much more than the 1921 legislature had appropriated. In December, 1922, Lindley and Dean Kelly prepared another elaborate statistical analysis concluding that the University needed some $260,000 more for salaries than it had had for the past two years. Even that impressive sum would yield only an average increase of 9.5 percent in salaries, for many new faculty and staff members were still needed. Making the Kansas salary scale equal to that of seven major universities with which Kansas competed—Wisconsin, Michigan, Illinois, Minnesota, Iowa, Oklahoma, and Nebraska—demanded an increase of 27 percent instead of 9.5. Lindley and Kelly were pleading for support from the Board of Administration as well as the legislature, and they received some much needed aid from George F. Zook and his fellow investigators. They were "frankly amazed," they said, at the poor comparative showing of both the University and the Agricultural College. In salaries Kansas was far behind "other progressive states."[38]

But Jonathan M. Davis had not won election in 1922 by promising to increase the salaries of state employees. His Board of Administration approved a request of only $993,000 a year for fiscal 1924 and 1925, and the Governor took no interest in the effort to get it. Knowing the charms of economy for the voters, the legislators approved but $860,000.[39] That sum remained a magic figure for the next six years. In 1925 the Board of Administration refused to ask for more; the new Board of Regents tried for $957,000 in 1927, but failed. By 1928 Chancellor Lindley was distraught. Admitting that increased fee receipts had raised salaries—the full professors' average salary, for example, was now $4,000 a year—he contended that salaries at other institutions had been rising even more rapidly. Thus the University's relative standing was actually declining. "Our losses"—he had provided a list of faculty members who had fled Kansas during the past year—"are beginning to assume formidable proportions and are prophetic of what will continue, unless the state checks this impoverishment by prompt measures of relief." To avert calamity the Chancellor and his colleagues asked the legislature of 1929 to raise the annual appropriation to about $1,050,000. But the lawmakers approved only $919,000 a year, an annual increase of but $60,000. There was no joy in the University. On March 15, 1929, Lindley reported to the Senate on his and the regents' failure to get more, and told the senators what they already knew: during the biennium ahead "strict economy in the budget" would be the University's watchword.[40]

The inability of the Kansas legislators and their constituents to see the University's needs through the eyes of its officers and faculty meant not only low salaries but a faculty too small to do justice to the growing student body crowding Mount Oread. In the decade between 1919–1920 and 1929–1930 the number of students rose from 4,002 in all schools to 5,766, or by almost 44 percent. But the number of faculty members rose in the same period from 256 to 259, or by about 1.1 percent. Put another way, in 1919–1920 the faculty-student ratio through the University was about 1:16. Ten years later it was about 1:22. While it was difficult to determine the ideal ratio, it was certain that things were getting worse instead of better.[41]

A growing student load, salaries that were too low, and insufficient classrooms and equipment did not necessarily mean that the University gave its students an education that was qualitatively poor. They did mean, however, that that education fell short of what University leaders thought it should be. The more the University of Kansas changed, then, the more its needs remained the same.

23

Drifting with the Tide

*A*N D the longer those needs remained the same, the less certain it was that the state could ever satisfy them. Where the 1920s had been merely disappointing, the 1930s blasted all dreams of excellence on Mount Oread. The crash of 1929, the subsequent national depression, and wretched weather sent profits, prices, and spirits plummeting. In 1929 Kansans had earned an average per capita income of $535 a year. By 1932 this had been reduced by half and by 1933 it was down to a low of $251. Although the figure rose during the rest of the 1930s, it never came within $100 of the 1929 amount. During the 1930s annual rainfall averaged four and a half inches less than in the 1920s; 1936 was the driest year in the state's meteorological history. Temperatures rose, and billowing clouds of topsoil filled the air. The Stafford *Courier* suggested that the decade would likely be remembered as the "dirty 30s." Thousands of "busted" farmers left southwestern Kansas, and many of those who remained were as depressed as the economy. Lawrence Svobida, for example, endured tenaciously on his farm in Meade County, but had not one crop for harvest between 1931 and 1937. Even the formerly ubiquitous rattlesnakes were all but extinct: he had not seen one for five years. In 1938 Svobida gave up. "With my financial resources at last exhausted and my health seriously, if not permanently impaired," he said, "I am at last ready to admit defeat and leave the dustbowl forever. With youth and ambition ground into the very dust itself, I can only drift with the tide."[1]

The state university could do no more. While it was drifting, moreover, it frequently threatened to smash against rock-ribbed Kansas anticommunism. Depression at home and the rise of fascism in Germany, Italy, and Spain produced a growing American interest in the various forms of socialism. Inevitably some Kansas students and faculty developed an incipient—and, in a few cases, a full-blown —radicalism. Just as inevitably many citizens thought that radicalism to be un-American and sought to stamp it out. A resolute stand by the University community and the common sense of most legislators spared the school the indignities of a full-scale inquisition and purge. Yet the winds of conservatism carried up the Hill the discouraging message that many citizens did not yet understand that a university was a home of the freely inquiring mind.

In 1931 and 1932 the University's supporters found that days of doom were near. Chancellor Lindley and the regents hoped to get from the legislature of 1931 an increase of about 22 percent, to $3,444,000, above the $2,814,000 two-year total awarded in 1929. "Fully aware" of the "business depression" and current high taxes, they contemplated only a "minimum of expansion" as they sought to guarantee that the present "high quality of educational work" would not deteriorate. Unfortunately for their cause, however, the regents admitted that they did not need all the money. "The University," they said, "can, of course, operate on a smaller budget." Who were the legislators to argue? With tax receipts at their lowest since 1917–1918 and every state officer from Democratic Governor Harry H. Woodring on down demanding retrenchment, the legislature retrenched. It not only denied the University all the increase it asked, but sliced off another $56,000 as well.[2]

From this low point things slid steadily downhill for the next two years. Expected state revenues failed to appear in fiscal 1932, and state officers predicted even worse conditions for 1933. In August, 1931, the regents urged school heads to try to spend far less than the legislature had granted. Board Chairman Charles M. Harger noted that underexpenditure would be a "recommendation to us" when they faced the next legislature. Later in the month Governor Woodring secured the regents' consent to a special economy drive. They reexamined the budget, cut it where they could, and constantly urged the officers and faculty to spend less. Mainly by reducing maintenance expenses in Lawrence and Rosedale the University spent some $450,000 less than the amount available from appropriations, fees, and the previous year's balance.[3]

It was not enough. After another conference with Governor Woodring, the regents decided to slash by 25 percent the expenditures for fiscal 1933. Now they included faculty salaries, untouched in 1931–1932. "I feel that teachers should, like others," Harger wrote, "bear some of the burden which every business firm feels, and be thankful that positions are held." Faculty members in Lawrence took a general 10 percent cut, those at the Medical School over 5 percent. Literally every cent counted, the regents warned. Since the cost of first-class mail rose from two to three cents an ounce in July, 1932, the schools should wherever possible use penny postcards and send several letters in one envelope. Around the University all sort of conveniences and necessities disappeared: funds for furniture, library books, and travel, even soap and paper towels from the rest rooms.[4] Throughout the years the University's leaders had contended that merely to stand still was to fall behind, that no progress was regress. What, then, was regress itself?

The legislature of 1933 would help the University find out. Chancellor Lindley and the Board had prepared modest requests designed to show their willingness to sacrifice. They would hold to the salary reductions and ask for a total other than salaries of only $560,000 for the biennium; the whole sum was about $2,337,300, down over $420,000 from the last biennial appropriation, and included no buildings. But after mingling with the lawmakers Regent Charles C. Wilson reported, "That legislature has me alarmed. It looks like they might wreck us unless there is some way to change their minds." There was no way. With the Senate Ways and Means Committee doing most of the hatchet job, the legislature chopped about $312,000 off what was allegedly needed, reducing the appropriation to some $730,000 less than that of 1931. Especially discouraging was that where the University had asked for $730,000 a year for salaries and wages in Lawrence, the legislature approved only $615,000.[5]

For the still underpaid faculty members the moment of truth had arrived. With the salaries of 1931–1932 as a base, the regents pared 15 percent off the first $1,000 or fraction thereof, 20 percent off the next $1,000, 25 percent off the third $1,000, 30 percent off the fourth, and 35 percent off each succeeding $1,000. No salaries except those of Chancellor Lindley and the presidents of the other state schools, however, could be lowered by more than 25 percent. Lindley's annual salary went from $10,000 to $7,000, Hamilton P. Cady's from $4,800 to $3,620, Frank H. Hodder's from $4,500 to $3,425, and Edwin M. Hopkins's from $3,800 to $2,960. There were no equivalent reductions, of course, in teaching loads or class sizes.[6]

In such decreases lay a grave threat to the University. Once the legislature discovered that, despite lower salary and maintenance appropriations, teachers would keep teaching and the institution keep going, it might be extremely slow to make up the reductions. To guard the school, in 1933 and 1934 Lindley started a campaign for restoration. He had to convince the Board of Regents first, however, and the Board proved unsympathetic. To Lindley's contentions that Kansas salaries were from 10 to 23 percent below the Middle Western average—a difference twice as great as that before 1930—and that living costs were again on the rise, Chairman Harger replied that the state was still poor and that there was no point in asking for what there was no chance of getting. The "basic work of the colleges is going on satisfactorily"; their faculties were "carrying on with a good morale." Lindley had warned that continuing low salaries would cost the University its better professors, but Harger was not impressed. "Even in the highest salaried days we were constantly losing good men," he said, "because the ambition of every man is to better himself or to make a change, feeling that he ought not forever to stay in one location. This has always been going on and always will—no matter what salaries we are able to pay."[7]

If Harger had a point here, it was not the one Lindley hoped the Board Chairman would make. When the regents decided to ask the legislature of 1935 for exactly the same amount appropriated for salaries in 1933, the Chancellor emphasized in his biennial report that the decision was the regents' own, not that of the University's executives. Behind the Board's back he sent the substance of a proposed editorial to the editor of the Topeka *Capital*. The faculties of the state schools had "cooperated most loyally in the economy program of the state," he wrote, but the time for relief had come. "Already handicapped by a relatively low scale," the Kansas institutions would "suffer seriously if competing institutions secure budgetary relief that is not matched in Kansas." Nothing helped. Desiring not to antagonize the lawmakers, the regents asked about

$2,112,000 for the coming two years, including $200,000 for a hospital ward for black people and a dispensary at the Medical School. The legislature reduced the amount to $2,002,000. There would be no salary increases and no buildings for the next two years.[8]

Atop Mount Oread a dream was dying. Lindley's greatest despondency came from the fact that no one outside the University seemed to care very much. The regents seemed unwilling to work as hard as they should, the legislature was unresponsive, and in 1936 the Chancellor got a horrible shock from Governor Alfred M. Landon. Visiting him on a minor item of business, Lindley suggested that all the state schools would soon be in a "difficult situation" unless they obtained financial relief. Landon's reply left him, as he said, "in a daze." For the Governor said that the University was the only state school and Lindley the only executive that had complained of inadequate funds. With a smile he suggested that Lindley had been bemoaning a lack of money for the past fifteen years, thus implying that conditions now were no worse and the need for relief no greater than they had been for some time. Equally discouraging was that Landon "could not remember," Lindley told Charles M. Harger, "that the Board of Regents was seriously worried about the situation."[9]

From Lindley's viewpoint the shortage of money yielded low-grade educations. Not only did the faculty-student ratio continue to worsen in the 1930s, but it had been necessary to hire "inexperienced teachers"; and the paltry funds allowed hiring "'fewer of these than are required to keep classes from being overcrowded.'"[10]

Overcrowded buildings and insufficient equipment also diminished the quality of a Kansas education. In 1938, supporting a proposed ten-year building program prepared for the regents, Lindley described the consequences of the "ten-year holiday" in building appropriations. The want of stack space in Watson Library meant that thirty-six thousand volumes—and the number was growing at the rate of nine thousand a year—were shelved in public corridors where they might be stolen, in a sub-basement where they deteriorated from dampness and mold, in cartons in the attic where they were unavailable, and even in one of the staff toilet rooms. Instruction and original research in the medical sciences were poorer than they should have been: there was too little classroom and laboratory space, departments were divided and scattered, certain necessary courses—x-ray and cross-section anatomy among them—could not even be offered because space and equipment were wanting. The chemical engineering work was squeezed into the basement and subbasement of Bailey Hall; the high-pressure equipment and distillation apparatus constantly threatened fire in a building neither fireproof nor modern. The School of Education suffered not only from lack of classroom, conference, and storage space, but also from the inadequate facilities of its Oread Training School. In laboratory schools, Lindley said, the "best of conditions" ought to prevail; but the Oread school was "inadequate to meet the needs in every detail." A five-room frame structure, it had no auditorium, gymnasium, or library, no rooms for music practice or group meetings, and no laboratory, conference, display, or work rooms.

And so it went. The old Chemistry Building, built in 1883, had been wretchedly suited for the Department of Journalism in 1923; it was worse now. In 1922 the School of Fine Arts had moved into the Administration Building on a strictly temporary basis. Sixteen years later it was still there, its musicians annoying both each other and half the people in the building. Across Jayhawk Boulevard stood Robinson Gymnasium, built for fourteen hundred students. To keep its programs going, it had to be used from 8:30 a.m. to nearly midnight. Dyche Museum was not even usable, for state authorities had closed it for structural repairs in 1932. While state and federal Public Works Administration funds had allowed some repairs, another $60,000 was required before the building could open again. In addition the Lawrence campus needed more dormitories and the Medical School a number of structures. All together the University required some four to five million dollars for building during the next decade.[11]

Although the state's economic system improved after the horrors of 1935 and 1936, the days of true prosperity lay far in the future. Hoping for great things, the Chancellor and regents requested of the legislature about $1,235,000, or 62 percent, more than they had received in 1935. Of the increase almost $500,000 was for salaries and wages, over $200,000 for maintenance, and $400,000 for Medical School buildings, enlarging Watson Library, and strengthening Dyche Museum. Those requests went the way of earlier ones, though not quite as far. After Governor Walter A. Huxman had vetoed $25,000 worth of physical improvements for the Medical

School, the University had about $2,653,000, $700,000 less than the $3,237,000 asked. Most disappointing, the legislature yielded only about $148,000 of the proposed half-million-dollar addition for salaries and wages.[12]

What was good enough for the legislature of 1937 was good enough for the legislature of 1939. Lindley and the regents, after their usual dickering, agreed to beg for $3,661,000, up about 38 percent from the previous grant. Thinking that the legislators might be softened by the 1938 description of the physical plant and endorse the ten-year building program, the regents asked $700,000 for a medical sciences building in Lawrence, $135,000 more for completing buildings at the Medical School, and $60,000 to restore and reopen Dyche Museum. They also sought to increase the annual sums for salaries and wages from $675,000 in Lawrence and $110,000 in Kansas City to $735,000 and $140,000 respectively. But what appeared after routine passage was an appropriation of $2,647,500 shorn of the medical sciences building and lacking over half of what was allegedly needed at the Medical School and over a third of what was needed for Dyche. Instead of an annual total of $875,000 for salaries and wages, the University would have $830,000.[13]

Although the University was changing for the worse during the 1930s, a few of the institution's friends lit candles to lighten the gloom. Individual gifts came each year in money for various purposes and books for the library.[14] From 1932 to 1941 the Endowment Association's principal investment fund rose from about $19,000 to over $112,000. While large donations were hard to come by, Mrs. Elizabeth M. Watkins did expand her program of philanthropy begun in the 1920s. Chancellor Lindley carefully cultivated her good will and nurtured her natural generosity. In the fall of 1930 she offered a student hospital, completely equipped and furnished, which officially opened on January 4, 1932. Costing $175,000, it had 46 beds and all the modern facilities, including an operating room, a pharmacy, examining rooms, a sunroom, and a kitchen. Director Ralph I. Canuteson boasted that the only university hospital in America that might surpass it was that of the University of California at Berkeley. Five years later Mrs. Watkins gave a second cooperative residence hall to house thirty-seven coeds, and followed it with a nurses' home for the hospital. When she died in 1939, she bequeathed the University $250,000 as an endowment fund for

Mrs. Elizabeth M. Watkins, with her instrument of benevolence at the ready.

Watkins and Miller halls, $175,000 for a hospital endowment, her home, "The Out Look," and 26,000 acres of farmland in southwestern Kansas. To balance Watkins and Miller halls for women, in 1940 two cooperative halls for men opened. One was Templin Hall, a fraternity house converted by an $18,000 gift from the alumni; the other Battenfeld Hall, given and furnished at a cost of some $70,000 by Mr. and Mrs. J. R. Battenfeld of Kansas City in memory of a son killed in an automobile accident.[15]

Amidst the University's general deprivation the students had great financial problems of their own. Money and jobs were scarce, and many students faced the dismal prospect of having to drop out. Both for their personal welfare and because a diminishing student body was a poor justification for larger grants from the legislature, University officers tried to find money to keep them in school. The search proved difficult. In September, 1930, Lindley urged working students with other means of support to quit their jobs in favor of the needy, but few did. A year later the Chancellor's Cabinet began a drive among faculty, and the Alumni Association solicited in Lawrence for contributions to the student loan fund. But the $10,000 raised was not enough for students wishing to borrow; many needy students, moreover, wanted to work their way through school rather than go into debt. To help the near-destitute, in January, 1933, the University began offering ten-cent meals to those who could demonstrate that they were almost penniless and had a satisfactory scholastic standing. There were few takers.[16]

The real need was more jobs. As usual some students proved ingenious in finding them. One taught contract bridge to Lawrence society women at fifty cents a lesson; another worked as night chief of police; a third prowled the heating-pipe tunnels to collect cockroaches which he sold to an entomologist in another institution for two cents apiece. Others did odd jobs for Lawrence residents or worked in local stores. Early in 1933 Men's Adviser Henry Werner and Alumni Secretary Fred Ellsworth sent over four hundred letters to faculty members and Lawrence citizens begging jobs—or even loans—for students who would have to leave school unless they secured help at once. The following fall University officers sponsored a "Keep the Student in School Week," urging everyone who had some kind of job around his home or business to give it to a student.[17]

Despite these efforts, from the 1929–1930 to the 1933–1934 academic years the University lost over five hundred students. The loss would have been still greater had not the legislature of 1933 ordered the regents to reduce the matriculation and incidental fees by 25 percent. Those who managed to stay in school did have a new seriousness and earnestness, Lindley reported in 1933. They had discovered that "our lives are governed by forces which we do not thoroughly understand"—forces that cost men the work of a lifetime, whatever their "diligence and unusual capacity, and fundamental integrity." So students were "determined to master these forces if possible. They are studying with deepened interest history, economics, social sciences and psychology." These trends, also obvious in many other parts of the country, seemed a "most hopeful augury."[18]

An even more hopeful augury, however, was the willingness of the federal government to help Kansans do what they could not do for themselves. Hopes in 1933 of getting the Reconstruction Finance Corporation to make loans to college students—$100,000 was to go to Kansas—came to nothing.[19] But later in the year Lindley began supporting a federal program to provide jobs for college students. It was originated and promoted mainly by alumnus George F. Zook, now the United States commissioner of education, and former Dean of Administration Frederick J. Kelly, now chief of the Bureau of Education's division of colleges and professional schools. The plan was that federal funds be granted to the states in order to employ college and university students at jobs in and around their schools. Zook had pressed the idea on Harry Hopkins, the New Deal's administrator of relief funds. In January, 1934, Chancellor Lindley went to Washington to solicit Franklin Roosevelt's support. Through the intercession of his son, the journalist Ernest K. Lindley, he secured an audience with the President. A few days after he returned to Lawrence the administration announced approval of the College Students Employment Project (CSEP). At the start the Federal Relief Administration allocated up to $7,000,000 for the rest of the 1933–1934 academic year for colleges and universities whose applications were approved. State relief committees were to administer the money. A number not more than 10 percent of the total enrollment as of October 15, 1933, could receive aid. Payment for work was to be between ten and twenty dollars a month.

Starting on February 15, 1934, a committee headed by Fred Ellsworth quickly found work on campus for 350 students, the University's quota. A satisfactory academic record and the need for a job to stay in school were the major requirements. Later there was formed a Committee on Policies, Projects, and Selection, chaired by Raymond Nichols, Chancellor Lindley's executive secretary. In the project's early days the emphasis was on clerical and physical labor. But in the 1934–1935 year the CSEP joined with academic departments to find jobs for majors—to make the CSEP a "practical training school for its student workers." Qualified undergraduates assisted in laboratories, aided faculty members in their research, and worked at special projects in the library. During 1933–1934, 374 students earned over $20,000 on CSEP jobs; the next year 523 students earned almost $53,000. The program, a tremendous boon to the students and the University, lasted through 1937.[20] As it was ending, the regents raised student fees to their old levels, meaning that in most schools Kansans would be paying $50 a year instead of $37.50 for incidental fees, and non-Kansans three times as much. The benefits to the University were immediate. In the 1936–1937 year, with 5,589 students in residence including those in the Summer Session, fee receipts were about $425,000. The next year, with a slightly smaller number of resident students, receipts were over $560,000.[21]

If the University community in the 1930s had had only a dollar drought and indigent students to worry about, it would have had trouble enough. But it also had to contend with a sizable number of anticommunist crusaders who, like their counterparts in other states, believed that the school was harboring, or even nourishing, un-American radicals among the students and faculty. Such beliefs, and the attacks to which they gave rise, had been common for years. On November 21, 1918, for example, Professor Frank H. Hodder of the History Department told the University Women's Forum that Germany was not the only nation that had suffered from Prussians: "In the United States, Theodore Roosevelt is a typical Prussian and a militarist in every sense of the word." After that remark appeared in the *Kansan,* the hoary veterans of the Lawrence Washington Post No. 12, Grand Army of the Republic, resolved that any history teacher capable of expressing such an idea was "unfitted to teach the youth of Kansas in our State University," and petitioned the Board of Administration to demand Hodder's resignation. Governor

Henry J. Allen said that he fully sympathized with the Civil War veterans, yet referred the matter to Chancellor Strong for investigation and recommendation. Strong shot back that he had no intention of asking Hodder to resign. Hodder had been speaking outside the classroom as a private citizen; he was, moreover, as patriotic as any Kansan alive. He was also "one of the ablest members" of the faculty who had "conferred distinction both upon the University and the State by his high qualities as a teacher and investigator." To dismiss him for exercising, "even though unwisely," his citizen's right to free speech would be "unwise and unjust and contrary to the best interests of the University and the State." In the face of Strong's counterattack and the press of other business, the Board retreated and the question died.[22]

But similar questions continued to arise. In 1922 an indignant Topekan who claimed to speak for many other Kansans said that the University should fire zoology professor Bennett M. Allen for publicly supporting the idea of biological evolution. According to Hugh C. Gresham the notion was contrary to Christianity and a hindrance to faith. Since the common people thought it worthless, Allen should stop attacking what God and the common people knew to be true about the origin of species. Lindley tried to soothe Gresham by replying that in his opinion there could be no inconsistencies between scientific truths and religious truths. Scientists as a group were "quite as reverent of the great values of life as any group of men in our civilization"; Bennett Allen himself was a good churchman. Indeed, Allen testified in an accompanying statement prepared at Lindley's request that he believed Christianity and evolution compatible in every respect and that his scientific research had "purified and intensified" his religious convictions. Writing privately to Lindley, Allen was less restrained. His attacker, he said, "shows a sweet Christian spirit that would do great credit to the devoted leaders of the Spanish Inquisition and the kindly spirits who carried out the massacres of St. Bartholomew's day. . . . This will make me strive harder to root out of my students their bigotry and to make them get some glimpse, however imperfect, of the scientific spirit which is the spirit of the age. . . ."[23]

Some faculty members delighted so much in public and classroom controversy that they courted opposition. Professor John Ise of the Economics Department, indeed, almost lusted after it. Ise was a native Kansan and University alumnus (B.Mus., 1908; B.A., 1910; LL.B., 1911) who had taken his Ph.D. at Harvard in 1914 and returned to the University as a faculty member two years later. As crusty as the Kansas sod, Ise had the self-imposed mission of shocking both students and the public from their intellectual lethargy. In 1925, for example, he insisted that President Calvin Coolidge was a "tool in the hands of the big business interests of the country," and that appreciation of that fact was indispensable to understanding Coolidge's economic policies. When Ise passed on that information to his classes and lecture audiences, many Kansas Republicans struck back. Ise ought to teach ideas that were "in accordance with those of the various business men of the state," one zealous alumnus wrote Lindley—and both Ise and Lindley should keep in mind that faculty criticism of political figures would destroy the unanimity of alumni support.

Ise continued on his independent way, however, whacking at icons left and right—mostly right—as he went. Many Kansas oilmen were outraged in 1926 when his book *The United States Oil Policy* appeared. In typical Isese he asserted that the results of private ownership and exploitation of the nation's oil pools had been disastrous: "instability in the industry, over-production, wide fluctuations in prices, with prices far too low; curtailment campaigns carried on in a generally vain effort to secure stability and reasonable prices; waste of oil by the millions of barrels, waste of capital by hundreds of millions of dollars; waste of human energy; speculation, and fraud, and extravagance, and social inequality; and finally, the development of monopoly conditions as the only means of escape from the intolerable conditions of private competition." The only remedy, Ise claimed, was state and national government control to preserve the nation's reserves, to limit production, drilling, and waste, and to encourage true monopoly, which would keep production down and prices up. William Allen White, the Emporia pundit, was so worried about the book's reception by the oilmen that he declined to review it in the *Gazette* "with any great candor." There was no point, he told the Chancellor, in contributing to an anti-Ise, anti-Lindley, or anti-University campaign. Lindley stood with Ise when the attack came. Actually he had no choice, for the Graduate School Research Committee had both sponsored *The United States Oil Policy* and approved it before publication.[24]

Some of the students were as outspoken as the faculty and as worrisome to conservative Kansans. In 1925 there appeared on campus an unofficial student newspaper called the *Dove*. It took its name from the traditional Christian symbol of peace among men, at that time expropriated by the Communists. To accentuate the *Dove*'s radicalism the editors usually printed it on pink paper (red would have made it too hard to read). Actually the *Dove* was liberal rather than radical, dedicated to a free discussion of all questions and "subject to no authority," its editors said, "except the laws of the land, the dictates of common decency and a semblance of dignity." Every student and faculty member was welcome to submit articles, whatever his viewpoint.[25] But some of its contributors were too free for men who were always worried about social radicalism in the University. Despite claims to the contrary by the "bourgeois-intelligentsia," Editor Seizo Ogino wrote in the second issue, military preparedness always led to war instead of peace. "On every university campus, we find self-satisfied fools in military dresses, marching along. Citizens' Military Training Camps are filled with other fools every summer. . . . When will they see that their steps are but to the altar of sacrifice of their own blood and lives to fill the stomachs of capitalists and jingoists?"—whom he dubbed "blood suckers and human slaughterers."

"Religion—Aw, Hell, what's the use of talking about it[?]" Steve Merrill asked in the same issue. "I can't figure out where just talk ever did much good. I'm what you call an iconoclast. I don't give a hang for all the religious doctrines and theories in this world, or any other, for that matter."[26]

On reading such outbursts, the simple-minded and the vicious charged that the *Dove* was subversively un-American. "It appears to be almost past belief that such a publication would be tolerated in any respectable school but there it is," said the Leavenworth *Times* after quoting from Ogino's and Merrill's articles. "It would be bad enough were such a paper to be put forth by a society of anarchists as an appeal to adults, but when it is circulated among immature students to poison their minds it is time to enter protest." "It appears that the university is . . . infested with people who seek to spread foreign propaganda and disloyalty—disloyalty to country and disloyalty to God," editorialized the Horton *Headlight*. "Will the people of Kansas permit the teachers of such radicalism to be educated by the state they seemingly wish to destroy?" In May, 1927, Major H. A. Palen, a crusader against radicalism in American universities, waved a few copies of the *Dove* at an audience of some three hundred people in Myers Hall and declared that their editors and writers were helping to promote communism. He and many Kansans wanted the University's officers to censor the *Dove*. But Lindley's position then was that the University lacked power over it because it was an independent newspaper published off campus. "This independent movement in the colleges is not . . . a 'red' movement directed against government," he had written in 1925, "but a general critical attitude of youth against University life as they find it."[27]

As the depression deepened and appropriations sank in the 1930s, however, Lindley showed more caution. In November, 1931, sociology professor Carroll D. Clark analyzed the "rise of modern capitalism and forms of collectivism" before the Unitarian Forum of Topeka. His most radical utterance was that all institutions of the day, both American and foreign, should be objectively scrutinized. Both he and Lindley were therefore distressed when Edwin F. Abels, editor of the Douglas County *Republican*, who had been convinced for some time that radicalism was rampant on the Hill, accused Clark of advocating socialism and being un-American. Lindley thereupon conferred with Clark and suggested that he be more careful in the future. As Clark recalled, the Chancellor urged upon him the "necessity of avoiding so far as possible engagements where one's scientific integrity is apt to be compromised through misunderstanding or misrepresentation." On May Day, 1934, Lindley tried to impress upon the University Senate the need for prudence. Press reports had said that a special committee of the Kansas Legislative Commission would investigate "radical teachings" in the state schools. "In view of evidences of a national movement tending to restrict political expression on the plea of checking radicalism," the Senate minutes read, describing Lindley's comments, "he intimated that caution in our utterance was one protection for rights of free speech and free teaching."[28]

Just how cautious the University community would have to be to satisfy everyone became apparent early in 1935 when the Lawrence Branch of the League for Industrial Democracy, a Socialist organization, sponsored a lecture series on contemporary social problems. Although the lectures were off campus, the University seemed involved in them: the *Kansan* advertised them, tickets were on sale in the Union, and Dean Paul B. Lawson of the College introduced the first speaker, Socialist Oscar Ameringer, who was to be followed by Powers Hapgood, James Yard, and J. B. Mathews. All four Socialists were described as un-American radicals in Elizabeth Dilling's anticommunist book *The Red Network*, which purported to be an authoritative handbook on subversion. Anticommunist Kansans protested. Those men were "revolutionary radicals and Communist speakers," said Walt Neibarger, publisher of the Tonganoxie *Mirror*, and some were engaged in furthering "strikes, atheism, sex freedom, disarmament and seditious academic freedom." Former Regent Charles F. Scott produced an editorial in his Iola *Register* condemning both the appearance of the four men in Lawrence and Lawson for introducing Ameringer. Many disturbed citizens complained directly to the regents, who heard them gladly. At least one regent, Chairman Harger told Lindley, was willing to fire any faculty member who presided at a meeting where un-Americans spoke. Harger's own position was that no one in the University should be associated in any way with such meetings, for involvement brought discredit and attacks on the school. "In the present state of public mind, with the radios blatting radicalism and propaganda of destruction of our national life so active," he warned, "certainly the schools should be a bulwark of safety and sane constructive policies in government."[29]

Neither Lawson nor Lindley took such criticism kindly. Lawson told Charles F. Scott to stop being silly. Advocating economic or political changes did not make a man an enemy of democracy; *The Red Network* was entirely unreliable; and there was no inconsistency between orthodox religious and political ideas and the free discussion of social issues. Lindley told Regent Harger that no one at the University had done anything wrong. Agreeing that the state university should be the "bulwark of the people," he said that an environment permitting free discussion served the people best.[30]

Regent Baillie P. Waggener of Atchison did not appear to share that view. In an address at the opening convocation in September, 1935, he condemned "socialism" (which he did not define) as a "very unpatriotic teaching." No faculty member should "teach socialism," for that would be "like an employee in a factory or in any corporation or employed in any business going out in the world and criticizing and abusing his employer." The Board of Regents, Waggener told his audience, "will be only too gratified to have any of you students report to them any such teachings if they might occur in the University of Kansas, as such teachings would be contrary to any of our ideas and very unpatriotic. . . ."

The reactions to Waggener's request were immediate and predictable. Although Lindley learned from Regents Fred M. Harris and Drew McLaughlin that Waggener did not speak for the whole Board, he wrote to Harger to warn off the Red hunters—though gently. Hoping that an "anti-red campaign would not invade Kansas," he explained that the "invitation to students to report directly to the Regents classroom experiences is certainly an innovation in university government." The *Dove* asserted that Waggener's speech showed that the whole Board of Regents agreed with the repressive policies of Adolf Hitler. A student's letter to the *Kansan* described Waggener's plea as a "definite attack on the student's right of discrimination" and a "direct affront to the intelligence and integrity of the entire university faculty; it is an insult to the student body that they be asked to organize themselves into a corps of voluntary stoolpigeons as their part in a cheap conspiracy to violate the Bill of Rights of the American constitution."[31]

In the months ahead those who wanted to find radicalism on Mount Oread found what they wanted. The League for Industrial Democracy's national secretary came to campus in November, 1935, to form a branch among the students. After her public talk a temporary committee began to consider organizing some kind of "liberal group." During the 1936-1937 academic year a chapter of the Young Communist League was organized at a meeting attended by a representative of the Communist party and some two dozen students. A year later the chapter had between fifteen and twenty members, although no University officer knew who they were. John Ise kept peppering everyone with comments critical of American pieties, and Kansans fired back. Nothing made the "farmer members" of the legislature "more antagonistic to granting liberal appropriations," said an unconsciously punning state representative, "than to hear that the tendency is toward so called 'liberalism' in state schools." There were "a lot of 'half-baked reds' " on the *Kansan* editorial board, agreed the editors of the Wellsville *Globe* and

452   THE UNIVERSITY OF KANSAS: *A History*

the Douglas County *Republican.* The Journalism Department should strictly censor them.[32]

The climax of the growing concern about radicalism in the University was a low-key affair which developed intermittently from 1937 to 1941. While it did the University no good, it did show that most Kansans were not overly troubled by an apparent red glow emanating from Mount Oread. On October 3, 1937, the *Kansan* reported the death of Don Henry, a former student, in Spain. Henry had been a first-aid man serving in the Abraham Lincoln Battalion with other Americans who were trying to crush the rebellion of Francisco Franco and his fellow Fascists against the Spanish Republic. Wounded on September 2 on the Aragon front, Don Henry died the next day.[33]

Don Henry's father was unhappy both because his son had died and because he had gone to Spain in the first place. Among the antifascists were numerous Communists, anarchists, and others on the Left. Edward Henry believed that some radical at the University had induced Don to go to Spain and had paid his way. He demanded an investigation by University authorities. According to a newspaper report Henry specifically accused Dean Lawson and John L. Hunt, secretary of the University YMCA, with inspiring Don to leave. Both men publicly denied the charge and denied that they had any Communist affiliations.[34]

The regents, knowing that a special session of the legislature was to meet early in 1938, superseded Lindley's investigation with one of their own. They formed a committee with Regent H. L. Snyder of Winfield as chairman, and Regent Ralph T. O'Neil of Topeka and ex-Regent Charles F. Scott as members.[35] In February, however, while the three were beginning their work, Representatives Donald Muir of Anthony and Clay Carper of Topeka, both Kansas Law School graduates, introduced a resolution for a committee to investigate all subversive activities in Kansas. While the committee was to range over the entire state, the House debates and newspaper publicity made it seem that the University would be the main target.

Opposition to the proposed investigation was immediate. Several students donned red shirts; someone hoisted a red flag up the flagpole atop Fraser Hall. Other students wrote open letters to the public and the legislature and organized a delegation of campus leaders to protest in Topeka. Meanwhile almost every Kansas news-

paper that took a stand opposed the investigation as childish, harmful, vicious, or unnecessary. Nothing, however, could stop the anti-
radical movement in the House, which approved the resolution 92
to 4. But after the Senate Ways and Means Committee had recommended it for passage, the upper house at first put it far down the
calendar and later struck it off.[36]

Free from investigation by the legislature, the University still
faced an inquiry by the regents' committee. After talking with officers, examining pertinent documents, and interviewing allegedly
radical students, Snyder, O'Neil, and Scott concluded that aspects of
the University environment *had* changed Don Henry's ideas. He
had come up from Dodge City a "religious boy with a normal outlook," a Boy Scout "interested in patriotic and religious activities,"
with no Communist tendencies. But he joined the YMCA, which
was—according to Chancellor Lindley—dominated by a "leftist
group," grew solicitous for the lower classes, and progressed to the
Young Communist League. During the 1936–1937 year, moreover,
the *Kansan* published numerous editorials supporting the Loyalist
(Republican) cause in Spain, and arguing that the Loyalists were
fighting the "crucial battle for democracy in Europe." "It is common knowledge," the investigators said, "of the Communist support
and participation with Spanish Loyalists." Don Henry grew interested in the Loyalist cause and Communists paid his way to Spain.

Nothing in this, the committee reported, implicated any faculty
members. None had "exceeded his authority in teaching theories of
government. Neither have we found any faculty member who is
affiliated directly with any leftist organization." There had been
and was now "some Communistic and probably some Fascist activity" in the University, but no more than in other institutions. The
1936–1937 year had seen a decline in Communist efforts compared
with the preceding two years. Mentioning no names, the committee
asserted that since its appointment "some changes have been made
at the University, eliminating certain of the personnel which we
believe will minimize un-American activities."[37]

These conclusions were not sufficient for anticommunist state
politicians determined to keep the Don Henry case open. On March
28, 1939, the Kansas House of Representatives, rebuked by the
Senate a year before, approved the appointment of a committee to
furnish material on the affair to the U.S. House of Representatives

Special Committee on Un-American Activities headed by Martin Dies of Texas. The Kansas House committee consisted of Edwin F. Abels of Lawrence, Clarence P. Oakes of Independence, who had introduced the resolution, and A. F. Cross, a farmer from Ellsworth County. In the next two years they conducted a new investigation into Communist activities on the Hill. The regents cooperated by providing all their relevant material, but Chancellor Lindley took an opposite approach. When Oakes asked about his knowledge of the Young Communist League and other subversive groups on campus, Lindley replied that he had already told the regents all he knew and that any further inquisition would not "serve the cause of good government."[38]

The Kansas House committee had better luck with his successor, Deane W. Malott. After learning that he would cooperate, Oakes asked him several questions. Was it true that Professor José Maria Osma of the Spanish Department had distributed literature and raised money for the North American Committee to Aid Spanish Democracy and the Medical Bureau to Aid Spanish Democracy? Did John Ise have any relations with the League for Industrial Democracy? Had Professor Seba Eldridge of the Sociology Department actually been state chairman of the American Civil Liberties Union in 1937? What about the ideas and activities of a number of other faculty members whose names Don Henry had written into his memo books? Malott and others faithfully checked on all the questions. Their answers offered no evidence whatever to show that there was any Communist influence in the University.[39]

Except for details about Don Henry's life at the University, the committee's report of December 30, 1939, had nothing of importance to add to the regents' report of 1938. Much of it was merely an anti-communist sermon which criticized the Board of Regents for making a "superficial inquiry," condemned those who had protested the proposed legislative investigation in 1938, and warned the citizens to be on the alert for signs of Communist machinations in the University. For the school had failed Don Henry and the committee hoped it would fail no one else. "We are proud that he was brave enough and willing to die for what he thought was a righteous cause," the committee quoted Don's mother. "But, oh, it was senseless. Our boy is gone. . . . Now we can only hope to save other K.U. boys by helping all we can to clean up things at Lawrence so that other parents may send their sons to the university without having them exposed to the same environment." The committee hoped so, too. A year later the University seemed purer. In a supplemental report of December, 1940, the committee claimed that it was "now making an outstanding contribution to the national defense effort and the students reflect a wholesome attitude toward the principles of Americanism and the American system of government. . . . In the light of what has happened, it is our belief that Kansas public opinion, the Board of Regents, and the Kansas legislature will in the future tolerate no return to the conditions which contributed to the death of Don Henry."[40]

Nevertheless, the allegations of radicalism, combined with the depression, had hurt the school. By the fall of 1937 Chancellor Lindley was much worried about the University's image in the minds of Kansans. He therefore appointed a Committee on Public Relations to investigate and make recommendations to improve publicity. The chairman was Dean Lawson of the College; its other members were Deans Frank T. Stockton of Business, Raymond A. Schwegler of Education, and Donald M. Swarthout of Fine Arts, and Harold G. Ingham, director of the Extension Division.

Their report, submitted in October, 1938, was a depressing account of sins of omission and commission, of opportunities wasted and assets unexploited. By implication at least, most of the blame had to fall on Lindley. The committee did assure Lindley that they were "in no way finding any fault whatever with your administration and your handling of the public relations of the University," and affirmed that Lindley had done a "wonderful job in representing the University . . . to the people of the state." Yet where else than upon the Chancellor and his aides was the blame to be placed? Indeed, they criticized Lindley directly for not effectively cultivating the good will of the legislature. Instead of "preaching" and presenting statistics, Lindley ought to go to the legislators "individually and personally, inform them of our problems and of the needs of *their* University, and ask their help."

But much more than legislative relations needed improving. One great cause of ill will toward the University was the *Daily Kansan*. More interested in gossip and "sensationalizing" than in representing the "whole University and its higher interests," "at present it speaks freely, but accepts no responsibility. It contains features which are distinctly obnoxious to people of culture." One professor familiar with state conditions told the committee that "practically every small town editor who takes the *Kansan* is an enemy of the University." Then, too, the University catalogues were unattractive; the University radio station, KFKU, was low in both wattage and program quality; the Alumni Association did not hold enough meetings in Kansas towns; there was little rapport between the University and the Kansas high schools. Still more, there was insufficient contact between the faculty and the people, the present Publicity Bureau was lagging in its labors, and Kansas newspapers were not getting enough information about the University's regular work.

To improve things there should be more publications, more words, a wider circulation of the *Graduate Magazine,* more press releases, more faculty speeches to various groups, more social contacts. There should be divisional and departmental bulletins; an expanded distribution of the learned publications in the *Science Bulletin,* the Humanistic Series, and the Social Science Series; more and better radio programs; more invitations to all kinds of groups to visit Mount Oread and participate in programs and conferences; an enlarged Extension Division; more state-service work. There should be guides to show visitors around the campus and up-to-date movies about the University. And University leaders should try harder to inform people in the state's smaller communities and at the "lower economic levels." To present the school to the public in a "clear and winning manner," a "high administrative officer," perhaps with the rank of assistant to the chancellor, should be made responsible for the University's public relations. Under him would be the director of the Publicity Bureau, who should be "well trained academically" so that he could appreciate the work of the several departments and schools, and should have training and ability in feature writing. Every department and major office of the University should daily report to the Bureau "all possibly desirable news. ... Such a scheme," the committee concluded, "would give the University of Kansas publicity facilities similar to other state universities in the West, and be of immense benefit."[41]

Clearly the University, now almost seventy-five years old, had failed to win the support it needed for its maximum welfare and service to society. Amid general economic hardship, to be sure, the institution's officers, faculty, and students could not hope for prosperity. But what occurred during the 1930s was, so to speak, a setback from a setback. If the University had been, before the depression struck, all or almost all that its members could have wished, the decade would have been bearable. But the predepression University was itself a disappointment to idealistic—and even realistic—men, and thus the 1930s were disastrous. When Chancellor Lindley resigned in 1939, to be replaced by Deane Malott, no one could be sure that the school would ever recover.

24

New Searches for the University's Nature

*D*EBATES with the legislature about appropriations and public arguments about radicalism on Mount Oread were, of course, controversies over the University's nature. During the 1930s the question of its proper identity appeared in other forms as well.

The first of them was an inquiry by the University Senate, originally into its own powers and organization and then into the essence of the ideal University. When Ernest Lindley became chancellor in 1920, the institution's organization was even more confused than usual, and he added to the chaos. Neither the Senate nor Chancellor Strong had resolved the contradictions between the Board of Administration law of 1917 and the Constitution of 1915. No one seemed to care. On February 7, 1922, Lindley told the senators that the Constitution was "no longer in force," and that he would shortly be recommending a "Committee on New Constitution." The Senate minutes record no reaction to these surprising statements.[1]

No Committee on New Constitution appeared. Instead there was a committee charged with the considerably less important task of codifying the Senate's often forgotten rules. It consisted of Edmund H. Hollands of Philosophy, Louis E. Sisson of English, and John A. Dent of Mechanical Engineering. In October, 1924, they produced a preliminary report suggesting a routine clarification of the rules under four heads: Senate organization and functions, academic regulations, student interests and organization, and miscellaneous. But Hollands, Sisson, and Dent then said that they intended to incorporate into their final report the part of the Constitution of 1915 dealing with the Senate's organization and powers. As if Lindley had said nothing two years before, they pointed out that since the Board of Administration had never rescinded approval of the document they assumed it was "still in force so far as public announcement to the contrary has not been made by competent authority." Although the Senate's acceptance of the preliminary report was not approval, it put the senators in a perplexing relation to the Chancellor's statement of 1922.[2]

The committee never made a final report, however, and for almost seven years the problem of the Senate's powers bothered few faculty members. While the Senate continued to meet several times a year, it was not a significant body. In 1931 another committee considered and condemned its defects. That group itself was born in confusion. A year earlier Lindley had suggested that the Senate select a committee to study its functions. U. G. Mitchell of the Mathematics Department moved to refer the matter to the committee of 1924, but no one seconded his motion. Then the Senate decided that Secretary F. Ellis Johnson should investigate and report on the duties of the earlier committee. Two months later he stated that the committee "presumed to have been appointed some years ago for a consideration of the functions of the Senate" had actually had another purpose. Lindley then explained that it was "to study the problem of Security of Tenure," which had certainly not been the understanding of Hollands, Sisson, and Dent. Yet the Senate took Lindley's word, and then agreed that he should choose a new group to study the Senate's functions. Mitchell became its chairman. Its other members were Deans Lawson of the College and Robert M. Davis of Law, and Professors William C. McNown of Civil Engineering, Frederic H. Guild of Political Science, and Frederick E. Kester of Physics.[3]

Of late, the Mitchell committee said in November, 1931, the Senate had become generally inactive, useless, and sterile. The members conceived of the 1915 Constitution as still in force and reminded the senators of their powers under it. In recent years they had acted only on minor matters such as the University calendar and advanced standing. They had done next to nothing on questions of scholarship, student life, or the control of University divisions. Far more significant, the Senate had never passed on any matter of "general university policy" before the chancellor recommended it to the Board of Regents, although the Constitution had forbidden such recommendations without Senate consent. That power was the most important one the Senate had.

Perhaps because Mitchell and his colleagues feared offending Chancellor Lindley, they did not dwell long on this point. Instead they stressed that the Senate had not been a forum for the discussion of significant questions affecting the University as a whole. Because the Constitution allowed the Senate to address the regents, chancellor, and faculties on "any educational concerns" over which it lacked direct jurisdiction, and gave it authority over all general University policy not otherwise delegated, the Senate could have fostered an "intimate discussion" of all University matters. It could be making a magnificent contribution to the University's welfare by "penetrating analysis," the exposition and consideration of varying ideas, a "rounding-out" of university-wide opinion, and "free and unfettered" debate. But the Senate had done nothing. It was "fast losing its chief value. To vote on routine matters without real debate, to listen to expositions which are undebatable," the committee said, describing the Senate's activities for the last ten years and more, "these are of little value."

Most responsible for the Senate's low estate, the committee thought, was the senators' toleration of an unwieldy committee system which hampered their proper work. In the 1931–1932 academic year there were twenty-five Senate committees. Most never reported to the Senate; both the Senate and the University as a whole were uninformed "concerning what is actually being done in the exercise of functions recognized as Senate functions." Because many of the committee chairmen and members did not regularly attend Senate meetings, moreover, it was impossible to ask them what they were doing, with the result that questions about what was happening in the University had to be put directly to the Chancellor. This was highly unsatisfactory because it forced Lindley to answer on the spot important queries which he might wish to ponder, and because the senators inevitably tended to consider his replies official and final. So the senators hesitated to ask questions that Lindley might hesitate to answer officially, and they were "greatly embarrassed" if they desired to press for an answer or information. Without committee responsibility on the Senate floor, Mitchell's group said, "freedom of debate and discussion has been noticeable, primarily by its absence."

The obvious solution was to demand committee responsibility. But Mitchell and his colleagues also suggested that certain committees, called University Committees, such as those on alumni affairs, student affairs, health and housing, Rhodes Scholarships, and other matters should be chosen by and made directly responsible to the Chancellor. Senate committees—on athletics, extension work, libraries, publications, the Summer Session, relations with other institutions, ROTC, and the like—should report directly to the parent body. The Mitchell committee also recommended the creation of a new Senate Advisory Committee. Composed of five members, none of them a member of the Chancellor's Cabinet—no deans or other administrators need apply—it was to bring before the Senate "such matters as it may consider advisable" and consider such subjects as the Senate referred to it.

These recommendations to increase the Senate's vigor were trivial, however, compared with the Mitchell committee's shearing the Senate of its greatest power under the Constitution of 1915. According to the committee, the Senate had three kinds of powers. First there were those exercised subject to veto by the chancellor or the regents: choosing the regular Senate committees, arranging the University calendar, regulating scholarship, and the like. Second was the right to address the chancellor, regents, and faculties on any question of "general concern to the University" over which the Senate lacked direct jurisdiction—such as the creation or abolition of schools, divisions, or departments; duplication of courses; and student relations. Last was the power to appoint advisory and special committees.

The second power, as the Mitchell committee described it, was the crucial one, for suddenly a real power under the Constitution became a merely advisory power. According to the Constitution the chancellor was absolutely forbidden from recommending to the regents any "general university policy, such as the establishment of new schools and divisions . . . without the consent of the Senate." "There is no record since the adoption of the constitution of any Senate action in such cases," Mitchell's group reported, "but your committee has included this in the list of advisory functions." This was disingenuous, for in the Constitution the Senate's power in such matters was not advisory: it was absolute, it was entirely clear, and it was now being removed. If the Mitchell committee was really assuming that the Constitution as it applied to the Senate's authority was still in force, its own proposal was unconstitutional.[4]

Things grew even more muddled as the Senate considered the committee's report. After generally dividing the committees into University and Senate groups,[5] on January 5, 1932, the Senate reached that part of the report dealing with its duties and functions and then, most curiously, bypassed it. Mitchell "re-stated interpretively" what his committee meant to do. His interpretation "involved asking the Chancellor to refer pertinent parts of the special report to the Board of Regents, with a view to obtaining an official statement regarding the proper functions of the Senate." Mitchell's motion to do this carried unanimously, without debate. On February 15, the Board formally approved his committee report, which apparently amended the Constitution. Whether it was actually amended was another question, for neither the Senate nor the Board mentioned the Constitution directly.[6]

Over objections by Frank H. Hodder of History and Carroll D. Clark of Sociology the Senate also approved and established an Advisory Committee. The two opponents had tried to change its name to the University Policies Committee and broaden its scope to match. To the five-man group the Senate elected Frederick E. Kester of Physics, Frederic H. Guild of Political Science, William C. McNown of Civil Engineering, Henry H. Lane of Zoology, and William Savage Johnson of English. In March, 1932, the Senate enlarged the committee to six—adding Henry C. Tracy of Anatomy —and staggered the terms.[7]

Although the Senate was now theoretically a less powerful body than the Constitution of 1915 had made it, Chancellor Lindley and many senators hoped that the changes would reawaken it. After the regents approved the Mitchell committee report, he greeted the Senate as a "new" body and urged the members to take a "new interest" in Senate affairs and show a "bigger and better" attendance at Senate meetings. In October, 1932, he went even further and gave the Senate an opportunity to investigate and discuss the University's very nature and meaning. At a special meeting on October 6, the Chancellor reported that the National Association of State Universities believed that the depression provided a challenge to the nation's universities to study various readjustments. After talking with several faculty members and administrators, Lindley had decided to suggest that the Senate choose a committee to study the University and recommend desirable changes. The Senate immediately designated the Advisory Committee as the investigating group, giving it power to add other members as necessary. In November the Advisory Committee reported that it had formed itself and a dozen other faculty members into a University Survey Committee, divided into eight subcommittees: on the University's aims and functions, University administration, curricular organization, duplications of materials of instruction, extracurricular activities, service load, faculty efficiency, and cooperation with the chancellor.[8]

During the next two years the Survey Committee met sixty-eight times to complete its work. The Senate began its debate on the committee's proposals in March, 1935, and the discussion went on until April, 1937.[9] From it emerged a document potentially of great moment, both because it went far beyond the Constitution of 1915 in its theories of education and the University's nature and because it was the only comprehensive statement of the University's nature and functions to come during the University's first century from the senior faculty members and officers as a group.

The historical development of American higher education, the Senate noted, had produced a "standard" university, usually including an undergraduate college of arts and sciences, various professional schools, and a graduate school. Their union in one institution presumed that their goals and work could not be reached or done separately. All their functions, therefore, should relate to the university idea: the college should do what was expected of a "university college," and so for the professional and graduate schools. Every state university had three "functions and objectives": to educate the state's youth, prosecute research in all fields of knowledge, and create a state "cultural center." Educating youth implied "advanced study" in the liberal arts and sciences, professional training in fields of "fundamental concern to general welfare, provided their study involves a broad foundation of theoretical knowledge," research training, and the preparation of "those who are to carry on the tradition of learning and scholarship in the various arts and sciences." Research implied continued efforts to extend the frontiers of knowledge, "maintain and advance civilization," and provide scientific resources to create "better living conditions and new wealth." As a cultural center for the state a university was to conserve the "means of knowledge" in libraries, laboratories, and museums; educate and inform beyond the campus; and interpret "knowledge in its various relations" in an "impartial, disinterested, and fearless manner."

Those ideas implied three "fundamental principles" of university education. The first was that of complete intellectual freedom: "The university is devoted to the development of the powers and activities of the free intelligence, unrestricted by any control save that of the reality—physical, cultural, or ideal—which it seeks to know." Devotion to the activities of the unrestrained intelligence, according to the second principle, was sustained by the "conviction and purpose that this free life of the mind shall make possible the best forms of human life and the unselfish service of the common good." The third principle was that one of the state university's paramount obligations was to "help the new generation meet the problems of the new age." Among the corollaries of this idea were that the "scientific attitude" should be represented in the study of social problems and that university research should serve the people "fully and well in the study of social and economic problems to the end that social activities or changes be guided by relevant knowledge."[10]

From those general principles flowed several specific ideas. Ideally the university should be free from all threats to its autonomy, prosperity, or goals. Administrators should be "subject to the faculty in respect to selection, tenure, and power." An ideal governing board would have three main functions: "to see that a genuine university, which requires to be self-governed, is provided"; to see that sufficient funds were available, without determining their internal allocation; and to protect the faculty against "attempts at interference with freedom of teaching and investigation." (The Survey Committee suggested that faculty representation on boards of regents or trustees might be desirable.) A university, too, should be relieved of "sudden variations in its financial support arising from political or other exigencies." University curricula had to be subject to "constant adjustment" in both courses offered and balance among fields of knowledge. Relatively useless subject matter and overspecialized courses should be eliminated; the "undue multiplication" of courses should be checked; the university should not offer high-school-level subjects. Universities should eliminate or regulate most severely such extracurricular activities as fraternities and sororities, athletics, and "student self-government with its political activities," for they interfered with the purposes of higher education. The faculty should be made more compatible with these purposes by being awarded "stable tenure and adequate compensation"; and means had to be found to choose new members more carefully, especially with respect to their teaching ability, and to give the faculty as a whole "some understanding of the function of education, and of university education in particular."[11]

When the Survey Committee and the Senate turned their eyes from the ideal university to the University of Kansas, they saw two major problems: the "administration of instruction" and curricular organization.[12] In theory, the Survey Committee said, the University's administration was simple. Each school had a dean; each department had a chairman or head and its faculty members. But the growth of the schools and the appearance of other agencies—the Senate, the University Assembly, the Chancellor's Cabinet, "interlocking school faculties," and numberless committees—had wildly confused things. To straighten out the powers of deans and chairmen, the Survey Committee and the Senate defined them much as the Constitution of 1915 had done. Since the Senate Advisory Committee could be considered "representative of the interests of the University as a whole," it should be consulted about the choice of both kinds of officials, and there should also be an interschool committee to be consulted about vacant deanships. To guard against deans or chairmen continuing into incompetent old age, the terms of the former were to end at age sixty-five, the latter at sixty-seven, though annual appointments beyond those ages could be made.[13]

Greater internal democracy also seemed to demand changing the budget-making process and equalizing committee work. There should be a central budget committee of three, chosen annually by the chancellor, which with appropriate deans and department chairmen and, if the chairman requested, one more member appointed by the chancellor, would be the budget committee of each department. After the budget conferences had yielded a University-wide plan, the chancellor could modify it at will before sending it to the regents. Here was more committee work for faculty members, but the Survey Committee thought faculty committees the price of University democracy. While recommending that committees be made smaller to spread the work load around, the members thought that a large number of committees "cannot be avoided without surrendering a procedure to which we are apparently committed."[14]

Democracy's twin was faculty freedom. So that "all may know that the University is committed to the support of generally approved standards" of academic freedom and tenure, the Survey Committee recommended and the Senate approved the criteria adopted by the National Association of American Colleges in 1925. No institution could restrain a teacher's freedom of investigation unless necessary to prevent "undue interference with teaching duties." Neither could there be limitations on the freedom of classroom teaching or on off-campus addresses and publications, save where the "necessity of adopting instruction to the needs of immature students" or stipulations in denominational or partisan schools limited the scope and character of instruction. No teacher might discuss in class "controversial topics" outside his own field. Outside the institution, however, teachers had the same freedom and responsibility as other citizens in writing and speaking on any and all subjects. When necessary, of course, faculty members speaking extramurally should "take pains to make it clear" that they expressed only their personal opinions, not those of their institution. Yet a teacher might be held to account for ideas expressed outside. If they raised "grave doubts concerning fitness for his position," the question should be submitted to a committee, of which he was a member.

Four main rules governed academic tenure. The "precise terms and expectations of every appointment" should be stated in writing. Termination of a temporary or short-term appointment should always be possible at the term's expiration, although at least three months' notice should be given; resigning teachers should also give ample notice. Third, termination of a permanent or long-term appointment for cause should require action by both a faculty committee and the institution's governing board, except in cases of gross immorality or treason where the charges were admitted, when "summary dismissal would naturally ensue." Where other offenses were charged and the facts were disputed, the accused was to have the right to face his accusers and be heard in his own defense. Where a man's professional competence was at stake, the testimony of other scholars, from either his own or other institutions, should always be taken. Dismissal for reasons other than immorality or treason should ordinarily come at least a year after the decision was made.

The fourth rule was of more than ordinary interest to the Kansas faculty. "Termination of permanent or long-term appointments because of financial exigencies should be sought only as a last resort, after every effort has been made to meet the need in other ways and to find for the teacher other employment in the institution. Situations which make drastic retrenchment of this sort necessary should preclude expansions of the staff at other points at the same time, except in extraordinary circumstances."[15]

If academic freedom and tenure were matters of great moment, discussion of the University generated controversy of lesser moment as well. Although the subcommittee on duplication of instruction could find no "conclusive data" on overlapping, it found evidence of duplication. Some of it was desirable—in different kinds of statistics courses for business, education, and mathematics students, for example—but much of it was not, and should be eliminated. Henceforth the Advisory Committee was to act as a committee on new courses, with appeals going to the Senate.[16]

The last part of the Survey Committee's report offered recommendations about several "extra-curricular" activities supported by state appropriations. To harmonize the institution's parts the Senate's control of general academic policies was extended to "such activities of individuals and organizations which may seriously concern the policies, reputation, and good faith of the University." The intent was to cover such agencies as museums, bureaus, surveys, and laboratories. "Nothing in this section," however, was to be "interpreted as limiting an instructor's freedom of action or speech as an individual." Although the Survey Committee and the Senate recognized the work of the Extension Division as important, they affirmed that the "first responsibility of the University is to support its residence work of instruction and research." Thus the Division should be as nearly self-supporting as was consistent with the University's "obligations and best interests." Each school should annually review its correspondence courses. Special lectures were more desirable than all-University convocations; the Alumni Association should get aid until it could become self-supporting; the YMCA and the YWCA should not be supported from the state university budget. Since the University's various publications were "essential to its proper functioning," appropriations for them, which had been curtailed, should be increased; and a committee should be appointed to study the feasibility of establishing the University of Kansas studies, to be composed of various series.[17]

Like the Senate, the Board of Regents and the legislature thought the depression decade a time for taking stock, though their concern was not only the University but the whole state system of education. In 1929 and 1930 the regents had tried to induce Dr. Arthur J. Klein, chief of the Division of Higher Education of the United States Office of Education, to make a comprehensive study of higher education in Kansas. But Klein asked too much money for himself and a considerable staff, and would not come alone. While the regents continued to be interested in someone to prepare a "comprehensive report" enabling them to decide "with all possible information at hand what changes, if any, are desirable for the greater usefulness and progress of the institutions," they could find no one to do the work.[18]

Three years later the legislature decided that the time had come for a study, although not exactly of the regents' kind. To the appropriation act of 1933 the lawmakers attached an amendment directing the Board to make or have made a survey of the institutions under their control and report to the legislature of 1935 a plan for the "unification, coordination and cooperation of said educational institutions so that duplication of effort not absolutely necessary, and all competition between said institutions, shall be eliminated, to the end that the best possible facilities for higher education may be afforded the youth of Kansas at the least possible cost to the state." In making the survey the regents were to investigate procedures in other states and consult with both informed Kansans and "expert educators" outside the state. To procure the survey and the report at the least possible cost, the legislature appropriated no money at all for them.[19]

Upon discovering that no extra money was available from University funds, in December the regents professed their "hearty accord" with the legislature's intent and then directed the heads of the five state schools to conduct the survey. Besides Lindley, then, the committee included Francis D. Farrell of the College of Agriculture, Thomas W. Butcher of Emporia, W. A. Brandenburg of Pittsburg, and Acting President C. E. Rarick of Fort Hays. They were to report especially on the advisability of "consolidations" in the five schools and the question of whether graduate work should be limited to one or two institutions. In addition they were to comment on revising courses of study to eliminate a "large number of unnecessary topics," and the possibility of ending duplication among the schools in engineering, journalism, education, and extension work. Lindley became chairman of the committee, which began its work in January, 1934. During the winter and spring the members held eleven day-long sessions in Topeka. They reported in June.[20]

To the disappointment of economizers and reformers, *A Survey of the Five State Institutions of Higher Education in Kansas* was a plea that things be kept just about as they were and that the legislature give the schools more money. After briefly reviewing their histories,[21] the *Survey* considered and quickly rejected the idea of a consolidation of two or more of them. Kansas was not unique in separating its agricultural college from its university; exactly half the states had done that. Nor did it stand alone in disconnecting its teachers colleges from both, for each state had an average of 3.7 such colleges. Data on comparative costs, moreover, were inadequate to show whether the Kansas system was inferior or superior to that of states with consolidated schools.

There were, the *Survey* admitted, legitimate arguments for consolidation: lower administrative and operating costs, improvement in teaching quality caused by the attractiveness of a larger institution to more able faculty members, and simplification of the legislature's task of appropriating money and the regents' task of determining policy. But the disadvantages were much greater. "Alumni loyalties" and local and regional attachments to particular institutions would be thwarted. Fewer Kansans would seek a higher education, for each school presently drew a large percentage of its students from within a hundred-mile radius, and they would presumably be unwilling or unable to travel farther. Consolidation would be costly because of the loss of the physical plants shut down and the great outlays for new buildings at the schools continued in operation.[22]

A better method of improvement, the committee said, was to increase coordination of work among the schools—but they had few recommendations to make. Within a "clearly defined general field" the regents should enable each school to continue developing a "distinctive individuality." In addition to the subject matter of each school's general field each should offer a "reasonably rich selection of liberalizing subjects and activities" to prepare students not only for professions and vocations but also for "satisfactory living and effective citizenship." Since quality was of first importance, each school should take care not to sacrifice its intellectual and academic development to an overemphasis on state service. Any changes made for the sake of coordination, Lindley and the presidents warned the regents, should come only gradually and with plenty of advance notice, in order to minimize "harmful disturbance of the schools and of their service to students and to the general public."[23]

The *Survey* then summarized the state of graduate instruction at the five schools and endorsed the existing system. All the schools were offering graduate study and all of them should continue to do so. Only two restrictions were in order: each institution should "promote" graduate work in fields where its "main service" lay, and should confine its work to the fields in which it was best qualified. Thus the University would be expected to cover a "wide range" of study, but exclude agriculture and home economics; and the College of Agriculture might be expected to limit itself to the scientific, agricultural, vocational, and engineering fields and related subjects. The teachers colleges should limit their graduate courses to one year—for the master's degree—and to those fields taught in the public schools that were not covered at the two larger institutions.[24]

But it was duplication at the undergraduate level that troubled Kansans most. It did not trouble the *Survey* committee. To be a college, the members said, an institution had to offer work in accepted fields such as English, mathematics, the sciences, languages, and history. But such duplication in Kansas did not mean wasted money, for the cost of instructing a given number of students in a given subject was the same whether the students were in one school or several; the size of classes could not be increased if teaching effectiveness was to stay high. Furthermore, the degree of duplication in the professional fields was desirable. In engineering—the old bugaboo that had so disturbed Frank Strong—both the University and the Agricultural College were well patronized. From 1929 to 1933 the two schools had over sixty-two hundred students. Uniting the Engineering Schools would require the same number of faculty members and a huge expense in new equipment. And a rough distribution of work already existed. Appropriately the University had courses in sanitary engineering in relation to the Medical School, in mining engineering in relation to the State Geological Survey, and in chemical, industrial, electrical, and architectural engineering in relation to "nearby industrial centers." Equally fitting, the College of Agriculture had programs in agricultural, chemical, mechanical, electrical, civil, and landscape engineering in connection with its schools of Agriculture, Home Economics, and Veterinary Medicine. Instead of consolidating the two institutions, the regents should continue efforts to coordinate their work.[25]

In journalism the situation was about the same. Both Lawrence and Manhattan had journalism departments; both were working efficiently; both were needed. The University emphasized "general journalism," while the College of Agriculture stressed "industrial journalism." Consolidation would accomplish nothing of importance.[26]

Although the school heads were harmonious on most matters, they were at odds on the work in education and teacher training. Somebody—apparently one of the teachers-college presidents—questioned the continuance of the "departments" of education in Lawrence and Manhattan. The doubts arose from the old idea that the University and the College of Agriculture had as their main objectives not the preparation of teachers but the preparation of youth for the "other professions, for business life, for the fine arts, for scientific research, and for wholesome living." Neither Chancellor Lindley nor President Farrell appreciated these comments, and the committee at last agreed that their institutions should have the education courses to qualify their students to teach. Someone also suggested that the two schools restrict their education courses to less than a major and that the University offer education courses only to juniors and seniors, but the committee as a whole would not endorse the ideas.[27]

In extension work relations among the schools were allegedly perfect. For four years the extension directors had been conferring regularly to try to end duplication and render extension work of maximum benefit to the people. Coordination had been of particular value in the important spheres of offering courses for college credit and providing general services such as visual education, lyceum work, library loans, and answers to the multitude of questions Kansans asked. A third significant program, developed of late, was adult education, especially in homemaking and agriculture. Future expansion would probably include "phases of vocational and professional education" together with noncredit courses for "cultural development," "reading courses for leisure time," training for citizenship, and similar work. Such enlargement was certain to avoid duplication and provide balanced offerings. Consolidation of all the extension work at one institution, indeed, would probably result in reduced service to the state.[28]

What should not continue, Lindley and his colleagues believed, was the present low level of legislative appropriations. Depression or no depression, the committee reminded the Board of Regents that their schools needed more money. Once again they spoke of the value of higher eductaion: it helped Kansans to understand their society, to solve its problems, to function as effective citizens of a democracy, to protect society from the evil effects of ignorance, incompetence, and rascality. Yet in 1932 only two and one-half cents of the average property tax dollar went to support the five schools. For the 1933–1934 year the legislature had granted only about $3,500,000. In 1933, by contrast, Kansans had spent almost $37,500,000 for gasoline, over $32,000,000 for life-insurance premiums, and more than $3,000,000 each for cigarettes, motor-vehicle licenses, and candy and chewing gum. The moral was plain.

The committee further pointed out that "every great depression in our history has been followed by a marked expansion of public education. It was so in 1837, in 1873, in 1893, and in 1907. People learned from bitter experience that more knowledge and more education are the only means of ultimate control of the economic and social forces of human welfare." Added to this was the fact that the "advance of machine industry" created technological unemployment, which fell most heavily on the young. "The function then of higher education," the *Survey* said, becomes not only one of preparing them better "to earn a living, but also to provide a constructive substitute for unemployment, and thus preserve the morale of a most significant portion of the new generation."[29]

In a special report to the legislature of 1935 the regents presented the committee's conclusions as their own, without mentioning the source. Assuring the legislature of their desire to eliminate all unnecessary duplication, they argued, as had the heads of the five schools, that there was no such duplication in present work. And although the Board was always interested in economy in higher education, its members claimed that the state institutions needed more money. "We should not permit ourselves to allow our educational institutions, which have been built up through the tedious work of generations, to be adversely affected by temporary economic difficulties."[30]

In addition to the problems of the University's nature and the relations that should prevail among the five state schools, still another organizational difficulty confronted the institution in the 1930s: the political complexion of the Board of Regents. During the University's first seventy-five years both Republicans and Democrats believed that the dominant political party should dominate the Board. This meant that most regents, and most members of the Board of Administration, had been Republicans. But in the 1930s Kansans elected two Democratic governors—Harry H. Woodring, who served from 1931 to 1933, and Walter A. Huxman, in office from 1937 to 1939. Both men thought Democrats more deserving of appointment as regents than Republicans; the result was frequent changes in the Board's personnel and party affiliations. In 1939 a Republican legislature and governor moved to end the political jockeying by the apparently paradoxical means of tying the Board's membership tightly to the state's party structure.

Republican Governor Ben S. Paulen in 1925 had picked a Board of Regents of seven Republicans and two Democrats.[31] Two years later the Board had one Democrat less, for George H. Hodges resigned because of ill health and Paulen put Republican Mica G. Vincent of Kansas City in his place. He was vice-president of the Federal Reserve Life Insurance Company, a state senator in 1921 and 1925, and a graduate of the Musselman Business College in Quincy, Illinois. When William J. Tod of Maple Hill died in 1928, Paulen replaced him with Republican William E. Ireland, a farmer and stockman from Yates Center who had been a state representative from 1917 to 1925. At the expiration of Tod's term later that year Ireland received a full four-year term of his own.[32]

Paulen's successor was Clyde M. Reed of Parsons, who also thought that Republicans made more able regents than Democrats. To replace Earle W. Evans and Mrs. James S. Patrick in 1929, he chose Oscar S. Stauffer and Charles C. Wilson. Stauffer, who had attended the University from 1908 to 1910, was a prominent newspaperman from Arkansas City who in 1930 would become president of Stauffer Publications, the publisher of several newspapers around the state. Wilson was a lawyer from Meade, county attorney of Meade County from 1917 to 1925, and an unsuccessful candidate for lieutenant governor in 1928. He had an LL.B. from the University of Kentucky. Reed's two appointees in 1930, replacing William Y. Morgan and Mica G. Vincent, were also Republicans. Fred M. Harris of Ottawa had taken his LL.B. at the University of Kansas in 1898, and was now a successful lawyer. From 1929 to 1933 he was also a state senator. Drew McLaughlin was editor of the Paola *Republican*. He was not a college graduate, but both his sister and his daughter were University alumnae. Reed also renewed Charles M. Harger's appointment for another four years.[33]

In 1931, however, Governor Harry H. Woodring began adding Democrats to the Board. He had the chance to make appointments to replace Carroll B. Merriam, Bert C. Culp, Charles W. Spencer, and Ireland. Lawyer Ralph T. O'Neil of Topeka, his first appointee, was a graduate of Baker University and the Harvard Law School. He became national commander of the American Legion the same year. Leslie E. Wallace, editor of the Larned *Tiller and Toiler*, was Woodring's personal secretary. His third selection was Baillie P. Waggener of Atchison, who had received both his undergraduate and law degrees from the University. He had been a state legislator in the late 1920s and Woodring's legal adviser in 1931. The fourth Democratic regent was Dudley Doolittle, who had taken an LL.B. from the University in 1903 and was now an attorney in Strong City. A Congressman from 1913 to 1919, he had also been a Democratic national committeeman since 1925.[34]

By the time that Woodring left office in 1933, then, the Board of Regents was as bipartisan as one could wish. It had five Republicans—Harger, Harris, McLaughlin, Stauffer, and Wilson—and Woodring's four Democrats. Governor Alfred M. Landon, Woodring's Republican successor, thought the Democratic minority too large. To replace Wilson, who retired in 1933, Landon picked the Republican William D. Ferguson, a graduate of Washburn University in 1910 and president of the Thomas County National Bank in Colby. Landon also reappointed Stauffer in 1933 and Harger,

Harris, and McLaughlin in 1934. The next year, in place of Leslie
E. Wallace, who resigned, the Governor chose another Republican,
Lester McCoy of Garden City, an automobile dealer, farmer, and
civic and political leader. And while Landon did reappoint Democrat Ralph T. O'Neil when his first term expired in 1935, he chose
two more Republicans to succeed Doolittle and Waggener, whose
terms ended in 1936. One was Dr. H. L. Snyder of Winfield, who
had taken his medical degree at Jefferson Medical College in Philadelphia and who sent five of his six children to the University of
Kansas. His companion was Sam R. Edwards, a College of Emporia
graduate, a former legislator, and a Blue Rapids stockman.[35]

The elections of 1936 went Democratic in Kansas as they did in
the nation at large. Expectedly, Governor Walter A. Huxman also
played politics with the Board of Regents. In his first year the terms
of Stauffer and Ferguson ended, and the vacancies went to Eurie F.
Beckner, the Democratic mayor of Colby and a graduate of the
Washburn University Law School in 1913, and John L. Bradley, a
Democratic lawyer—though not known as a strong party man—from
Wellington. Bradley had graduated from the University's Law
School in 1912.[36] In 1937 and 1938 Huxman had five more positions
to fill: Bradley resigned a few months after taking office; Edwards
died on April 1, 1938; and the terms of Harger, Harris, and
McLaughlin—Republicans all—ended on June 30. Chancellor Lindley thought he had "authentic evidence" proving that Democratic
"pie hunters" were seeking to load the Board with Democrats in
order to open jobs in the five state schools to political patronage. In
response to the Chancellor's request William Allen White urged a
sensible course on Huxman by admitting the legitimacy of Huxman's appointing Democrats to the Board but recommending that
he reject ardent aspirants for positions and refuse the advice of the
Democratic State Committee, which, White said, cared nothing for
the quality of higher education in Kansas.[37]

White offered several suggestions for regents, none of which
Huxman took. Walking his way straight down the party line, he
chose five Democrats. Bradley's unexpired term went to Clarence
G. Nevins, a well-to-do hardware dealer from Dodge City and an
alumnus of the Agricultural College. Edwards's place went to
Howard E. Payne of Olathe, whose LL.B. was from the University
in 1926; he had served as both the Olathe city attorney and as the

Johnson County attorney. The chairs of Harger, Harris, and McLaughlin were filled by Democrats Maurice L. Breidenthal of Kansas City; Leslie E. Wallace, now Huxman's private secretary, and back for a second term; and Dr. L. J. Beyer of Lyons. Breidenthal was one of Kansas City's most influential citizens. A University alumnus of 1910, he had become president of the Security National Bank, a leader in numerous civic, service, and professional organizations, and a willing worker for the University in the Endowment and Alumni Associations and on the Athletic Board. Beyer was an alumnus of the University's Medical School, where he had been president of the class of 1910.[38]

Together with the appointment of Beckner and the continuance of O'Neil, these appointments made a Board of seven Democrats and two Republicans. Now, this did not mean that the Board was planning to convert the state institutions into Democratic strongholds. But if both Democratic and Republican governors continued to pack the Board with their party cohorts, membership might become little more than a political prize, and whither responsible management then? In the work of Woodring and Huxman, moreover, lay a clear threat to Republican domination of the Board, assuming that Democratic support throughout the state continued strong.

In 1938 Kansans elected another Republican governor, Payne H. Ratner of Parsons, who urged the legislature to take the state schools out of "partisan politics. The removal of the State Board of Regents from political consideration or the creation by law of a bipartisan board," he thought, "would be a significant forward step." The legislators thought so, too. On January 26, 1939, the Senate began considering a bill directing the governor to appoint a new Board of nine "competent citizens." Five were to be members of the political party casting the highest number of votes for secretary of state in 1938—that is, Republicans; the other four were to be from the party casting the next highest number of votes—that is, Democrats. The bill also provided that in the future not more than five regents could be members of the same political party, and unlike the act of 1925 required that the Senate confirm all the appointments. On February 23, the Senate passed it, 28 (23 Republicans, 5 Democrats) to 7 (all Democrats).

The House accepted the principle of the five-four division, but tied it in the future to the highest and second-highest party votes for secretary of state at the last general election, and then passed it, 80 (Republicans) to 12 (Democrats). After the Senate accepted the change, Governor Ratner signed it on March 27. Henceforth both political independents and members of lesser parties, whatever their qualifications, need not apply for membership on the Board; henceforth no regent could be chosen solely on the basis of his interests and abilities.[39]

To the new Board went all the powers of the old, including those of appointing the executive heads of the institutions under its control, and of removing "executive heads, deans, professors, teachers or other employees" at its discretion. Like the old regents, the new ones were to serve appropriately staggered four-year terms. But besides the four colleges and the University, the new regents would have to supervise the state schools for the blind and for the deaf and dumb, the vocational school in Topeka, and Western University of Quindaro (a school for blacks), now removed from the control of the Board of Administration.[40]

Governor Ratner divided the new Board not only between Republicans and Democrats, as the law required, but also between present or former regents and Kansans without experience. From the existing Board he chose Ralph T. O'Neil, H. L. Snyder, and Lester McCoy, and to them added former regents Fred M. Harris and Drew McLaughlin. His four new appointees were Mrs. Donald Muir of Anthony, Mrs. Elizabeth Reigart of Baxter Springs, Walter T. Markham of Topeka, and Grover C. Poole of Manhattan. Mrs. Muir was one of Kansas's best known women, for she was either an officer or an active supporter of an enormous number of educational, social, cultural, patriotic, and philanthropic organizations and causes. She had taken degrees in piano in 1911 and pipe organ in 1912 from the University's School of Fine Arts. Mrs. Reigart was a Phi Beta Kappa and graduate of Smith College who had taught school in Michigan and Minnesota, and the wife of a mining engineer. Markham had just completed six years as Kansas state superintendent of public instruction; prior to that he had served a decade as superintendent of schools in Yates Center. He had an M.A. in Education from the University. Poole was an alumnus of the College of Agriculture and the owner of a three-thousand-acre farm on which he raised purebred Herefords and Rhode Island Red chickens. He, O'Neil, Markham, and Mrs. Muir were Democrats. The new Board chose Fred M. Harris as chairman and Hubert Brighton, formerly an undersecretary in Governor Ratner's office, as secretary.[41]

"For the first time in Kansas history," the Board announced shortly after its appointment, "these educational institutions have been taken out of politics and placed where they rightfully belong."[42] Another way of looking at the matter, however, suggested that the Board of Regents, with its members chosen for their political professions as well as their competence, was now so solidly entrenched in politics that the party maneuverings and partisan appointments of the past were minimized. Men would continue to play party politics with the University and other schools, but the rules of the game had changed.

At the same time that they were changing, so was the chancellor. On December 1, 1938, Ernest H. Lindley formally offered his resignation to the regents. Both his successor and the new Board would take office at about the same time in 1939. As a result, and as a result of the Second World War, the University began still another metamorphosis.

25

A New Chancellor and
Another War

CHANCELLOR Lindley's decision to resign, he told the Board of Regents, was not a sudden one. For several years he had intended to quit not later than age seventy, which he would reach in October, 1939, and he thought it would be to his successor's advantage to take office at the start of the 1939–1941 biennium. He told the University Senate a few days later that he had been contemplating resigning for "some years," but that the "existence of highly critical questions"—he meant the effects of the depression and the anticommunist investigations—"forbade stepping out in an hour of need." The regents accepted the resignation at once and gave him a year's leave of absence at a salary of $8,000; after his return he was to teach at the University at a salary of $5,000 a year. Both he and his wife were delighted at the prospect of his becoming a faculty member once again, but his hopes for the future vanished in sickness and death. On a trip around the world he fell ill in Peking, grew worse in Shanghai, and died on the Japanese ship *Asama Maru* on his way back to the United States. He was buried at sea.[1]

To produce all possible harmony in the choice of a new chancellor, the regents asked the University Senate to appoint a faculty committee to consult with them, approved an alumni committee to do the same, and asked the entire faculty for recommendations.[2] While they were gathering candidates, however, Olin Templin, executive secretary of the Endowment Association, was seeking unofficially to gain the chancellorship for the man the regents finally chose—Deane W. Malott, associate professor of business at the Harvard Graduate School of Business Administration.

An Abilene, Kansas, native born in 1898, Malott had graduated from the University of Kansas in the class of 1921 with a B.A. in economics and journalism. After taking an M.B.A. from Harvard two years later, he joined the Harvard Business School faculty as assistant professor. From 1929 to 1933 he temporarily forsook the groves of academe for those of Hawaii, becoming vice-president of the Hawaiian Pineapple Company, but returned to Harvard in 1933. By the end of 1938 he had written or cowritten four books, had three others in preparation, and had established a growing reputation as a consultant. He was a tall, handsome, affable man with splendid energy, natural gregariousness, and abundant enthusiasm. One observer thought he was "just what he looks like . . . a tall, well set up Kansan with the gleam of the distant horizon in his eye and the flame of the Kansas sun on his cheeks. He looks as much a prosperous farmer as he does a college head. He is the kind who doesn't mince words . . . he'll go far."[3]

Through Edmund P. Learned and Ralph Hower, two other Kansas alumni on the Harvard Business School faculty who were enthusiastic about the idea of Malott as chancellor, Olin Templin sought to discover how interested Malott was in the position. At the same time he suggested Malott's name to Regent Charles M. Harger. A few days later Learned reported from Cambridge that although Malott did not consider himself an active candidate, he was pleased by Templin's interest and attracted by both the opportunities and the challenges of the job. The only hitch that Learned could see—he did not say that he spoke for Malott—was that Malott's total income was almost $14,000 a year, and that he should not be asked to make too great a sacrifice to become chancellor. Along with Learned's letter came one from Hower, which praised Malott's every aspect. Thus fortified, Templin submitted Malott's name, along with the two letters, to the alumni committee, from which they quickly reached the Board of Regents. Templin also wrote several private letters on Malott's behalf to regents and alumni.[4]

Thanks to the enthusiasm that Templin's lobbying generated, the regents' screening committee, chaired by H. L. Snyder, at once began to consider Malott along with other candidates. While many members of the regents' and alumni committees thought that the chancellor's salary of $10,000 was too small to lure him back to Kansas, the Board sent Snyder in February, 1939, to the Council on Medical Education meeting in Chicago with orders to interview candidates while there. Snyder wrote Malott to make an appointment, explaining—to give him a clearer understanding of what his acceptance would mean—that the Board had no money to bring candidates to Lawrence and that the maximum salary would probably be $10,000 a year and the chancellor's residence. Such bluntness was unusual, Snyder admitted, "but I speak the Kansas language and I am quite sure you have not forgotten it, hence the directness."[5]

No native of the Sunflower State ever forgot the Kansas language, and Malott met Snyder in Chicago. Snyder returned greatly impressed with Malott; but Malott returned to Cambridge, Learned wrote, dubious about the low salary. Nevertheless when the regents offered him the chancellorship, he accepted. On April 10 he was in Topeka to confer with Governor Ratner and the Board. That day the regents accepted their committee's recommendation to hire him. He was to receive $10,500 a year and a residence, with the provision that he pay the premiums on his own retirement insurance policy so that the Board would not have to pay him a pension in his old age.[6]

In several ways Chancellor Malott differed from his predecessors. He was the first native Kansan in the position and the first University alumnus as well. He was also the first chancellor to have extensive business as well as academic experience. Of his seven predecessors—not counting Acting Chancellor William C. Spangler—one had been a psychologist, one a historian, one a scientist, three ministers, and one a teacher and soldier. Malott's selection was, in a way, public recognition of the fact that running the University required at least as much business acumen as scholarship.

But if Malott was a chancellor of a new type, his University was the same old school. On September 22, 1939, the Chancellor pledged in his inaugural address to maintain it essentially as it was. He stated, that is, that he fully approved the institution's four component parts: research, general education in the liberal arts, professional education, and the "gregarious activities of student life." A proper balance among them constituted a properly balanced University organization. Research would prevent the institution from shriveling into a "mere merchandiser of knowledge, retailing stale and obsolete wares in annual and repetitive routine." The liberal arts were the "cultural, broadening influences which go to make up a great civilization"; in maintaining them—and Malott stressed their importance for the future as well as their past glories—the University was the "sanctuary of the inner life" of Kansas, the keeper of the all-important "things of the spirit." Professional education had an important place in every American university because it had an "intellectual and ethical content requiring a high order of mental ability"—although he cautioned against stretching the word "professional" until it covered every vocation: "I hope here in Kansas," he said, "we may avoid the urge for unlimited additions of boondoggling courses in the curricula." Balanced—that is, neither understressed nor overstressed—extracurricular activities provided opportunities for "qualities of leadership and competitive excellence" to contribute to the "character of the individual."

Malott proposed three familiar objectives for the University. The first was high standards of scholarship. Next came freedom, a "quality for which the University of Kansas has always maintained an enviable reputation." Warning off zealous anticommunists, Malott explained that to its members freedom meant the liberty to "examine and to discuss, to appraise the thoughts, the theories, the practices of all that goes to make up our civilization. Either we are afraid of heresy or we are not." Third, Malott desired to preserve the University's traditions, through which "we find expression for the idealism inherent in all youth." As a result of tradition the University gave "whole-hearted support to keen athletics and to clean sportsmanship." Through them the citizens of the University community fostered loyalty to the school, "which assures the preservation of this institution for the benefit of oncoming generations."[7]

The lack of novelty in Malott's program was fortunate. In 1939 the last thing that the University needed in the outlook and plans of its chancellor was major innovations. At a time when the school was trying to shake off the depression's disasters, a suggestion of fundamental changes would have been an invitation to dissent and turmoil. Within the existing framework, moreover, there was plenty of room for experimentation in curricula, courses, methods, and ideas. Malott was asking for a revitalizing of the existing University, and that only. It was exactly what he should have asked.

"I have a feeling," he wrote in 1940, "that public relations is one of my biggest jobs, that we must constantly be at work to get the University off this Hill and out over the state, and the people of the state up on the Hill. . . . All in all, there is a good deal going on, and we need to have all of this interpreted to the people of the state."[8] The first thing to be interpreted, of course, was the University's financial need. In the summer of 1940 the Board of Regents asked for the appointment of a committee in each institution to propose a ten-year building development plan; from the institutional suggestions the regents would prepare a master plan. Information about the plans, the Board said shrewdly, should be dispensed to "various interests and organizations" around the state so that they could "assist"—that is, put pressure on the governor and legislature—in the development of an adequate program.[9]

This was no time for modesty, and from the University came an impressive proposal. It began, as such documents usually did, with lamentations for the past. Although the Medical School plant in Kansas City had grown during the 1930s (see chapter 30), the Lawrence plant had not. *"For seventeen years the classroom and laboratory facilities have not been expanded"*—new Snow Hall was merely a replacement—even though enrollment had increased by over six hundred and several new departments had appeared. "The pressure for additional space at Lawrence has become acute in the library"—Watson now had 202,000 more books than its stacks could hold—"in the medical sciences, in pharmacy, in the geological survey, in chemical engineering, in petroleum engineering, in military science, and in certain administrative offices; and is rapidly approaching an emergency in several other departments, such as education, journalism, business, chemistry, music, and art. All available space has been utilized. Offices have been divided, temporary rooms have been constructed in dark, unventilated basement corners, and even subbasements have been excavated and utilized."

Since the legislature of 1939 had rejected Ernest Lindley's medical sciences building in Lawrence, Malott gave highest priority to a mineral resources structure. To justify it, he pointed out that the state's mineral industries ranked second only to agriculture in the wealth they produced, and that the relevant departments at the University had long needed a "research center." Behind that building came, in no particular order, expansion of Watson Library; the medical sciences building; a home for the School of Fine Arts (what was temporary in 1922 was still temporary in 1940); a new training school, offices, and classrooms for the School of Education; a new gymnasium; more dormitories; the remodeling of Fowler Shops for the Journalism Department; more engineering shops; space for the School of Business. In addition the ROTC needed an armory or fieldhouse for its seven hundred students—almost double the number of two years before—who had extremely poor facilities in the east end of Fowler Shops. Malott also urged that the state replace the University's oldest building. "From time to time the State Architect has inspected Fraser Hall," he reported, "and his opinion is that the walls are in such a state that the building must be torn down and replaced in the near future."

Malott agreed with Lindley that the Medical School in Kansas City needed a new laboratory building, a new operating suite and ward unit, expansion of the nurses' home, a psychiatry unit and ward building, a medical library, two more ward structures, an addition to the old clinic, and an isolation and tuberculosis unit located on the School's main campus instead of the old site.[10]

While the Chancellor and his colleagues dreamed of the future, immediately they faced the legislature of 1941. Partly because of an upswing in the Kansas economy in the preceding two years and partly because the regents were more economical than those of 1939, they met considerable success. Lindley and the Board had sought over $3,800,000 for the 1939–1941 biennium, but the Board now asked only about $3,334,000, including $400,000 for the mineral resources building, for the next two years. This was not an "expansion budget," Malott explained, but rather a "rock-bottom appraisal" of the University's "minimum requirements." To prove it, he added that the proposed budget called for no general salary increases, and that the individual raises proposed "would leave eighty percent of the staff who were here in 1931 still receiving less than they did before the 1932 salary cuts."[11] Responding to lobbying by members of the Kansas Mineral Industries Conference, including Regent Lester McCoy, the legislature ignored the recommendations of State Budget Director Floyd Shoaf by keeping the mineral resources building in the appropriation bill. In all the University received $3,227,000.[12]

If that appropriation was cause for quiet rejoicing, two other acts delighted University partisans. For the first time the lawmakers imposed a special mill tax for buildings at the state colleges and University. Governor Ratner had pressed it on the legislature by saying that it would provide for an "orderly program to meet the future building needs of our state educational institutions. . . . Long-range planning and permanent benefits could be achieved," and the tax would end the "competitive bidding between schools for legislative attention to building needs, and . . . end the moratorium which has hampered the development of the state's educational facilities." By votes of 29 to 1 in the Senate and 75 to 44 in the House, the proceeds of a one-fourth-mill property tax would constitute the Kansas Educational Building Fund. The legislature was to appropriate the money "as needed" for building erection, equipment, and repair.[13]

Still another act, passed routinely by both houses, provided new methods for financing student unions and dormitories. It allowed the regents to lease parts of the campuses to nonprofit corporations "officered" and directed by faculty members, students, and alumni, which could borrow money to construct buildings. To pay building, equipment, and operating costs, the regents could assess fees of the students, except that union fees could not exceed $5.00 a semester. Each of the five schools of higher education under the Board was limited to indebtedness for no more than two buildings at once, and principal and interest were to be amortized within forty years. Afterward the property would belong to the state. The act meant, of course, that instead of taxing the people for unions and dormitories, the legislators were passing the cost along to the students and their parents.[14]

Despite the appropriation of 1941 it was not until 1946 that the University could use the mineral resources building solely for educational purposes. Completed in February, 1943, Lindley Hall was an L-shaped, stone-faced structure with four stories above the basement. Ultimately the Departments of Geography, Geology, Chemical and Petroleum Engineering, Mining and Metallurgical Engineering, the subdepartment of Astronomy, and the State and Federal Geological Surveys would occupy it. But with the coming of the Second World War, government priority approval for its construction depended on the University's agreeing that the finished building would be used for defense work during the conflict. Until

February, 1946, it was primarily a dormitory and mess hall for the Army Specialized Training Program and University military trainees.[15]

In its military uses Lindley Hall symbolized the whole University, whose response to the Second World War was like that to the First. Before the war, to be sure, opposition to America's military involvement in European affairs had been widespread on campus. Pacifist students had organized numerous mass meetings; many anti-war editorials had appeared in the *Kansan* and the *Dove*. On April 12, 1935, leaders of a Student Strike Against War Committee joined their counterparts throughout the nation in sponsoring an hour-long protest meeting during class time. Seven hundred students attended an orderly outdoor gathering on the lawn before Fowler Shops. Its purpose, said the Committee, was to show Americans that the student body was "declaratively against war and all the agents of war, and that it is definitely aligning itself against those evils." Similar demonstrations took place in 1936 and 1937, and in February, 1938, the *Kansan* assailed the allegedly growing spirit of militarism in the nation. Condemning the Roosevelt administration for efforts to "fan the flame of preparedness," the editors asked, "How long will it take us to understand that militarism is the denial of democracy? How long before we realize that war is the antithesis of Christianity?" To meet "militarism with militarism is to become the victim of the very thing we are supposedly attempting to destroy. For militarism has no gradations. It is always bad—whether the model is German, Japanese, or American. Always it has meant regimentation, unreasoning obedience, class consciousness, surrender of individual rights, and dictatorship—and it always will." In a student vote on public issues in September, 1939, after war had begun in Europe, 1,995 wished to keep America out of it, and only 371 wished to aid Britain and France. And a poll in May, 1940, by a student who attempted to question a cross-section of his fellows found 390 of 393 opposed to the United States declaring war on Germany "to help the democracies and for our own protection."[16]

Not all the University community, naturally, felt the same. In January, 1941, Dean Paul B. Lawson of the College in a *Kansan* article urged students to be prepared to do whatever the government thought necessary and to train themselves to "feel continuously that the blessings of our democracy and freedom are of extreme value and, therefore, worthy of any price we may be called on to pay to preserve them." Lawson was not, he said, advocating war; but he certainly was advocating intellectual and spiritual preparation for war. Unfortunately a *Kansan* printer's error had Lawson saying, after making several such points, "In one of the above am I urging that we go to war," when he had originally written, "In none of the above." Two days after his article appeared, John Crutcher, a graduate student from Hutchinson, pounded two large signs into the sod in front of Strong Hall. One read, "LAWSON! A War Monger," the other, "I don't like LAWSON and War !!!!!" After a conference with Malott, Crutcher apologized to the Dean, yet his ideas were popular.[17]

But just as Frank Strong's pacifism had died in April, 1917, the new student pacifism died on December 7, 1941, when the Japanese bombed Pearl Harbor. "Do you realize, Mr. Hirohito, just what you have done?" the *Kansan* editors asked the Emperor on December 10. "You have deliberately provoked war with the most powerful nation in the world. You have pitted your people and your scrawny resources against a nation with the greatest natural resources in the world, and the greatest determination in the world that this shall be a bitter fight to the finish. And that finish will not come until America is victorious. You can paste that in your hat, Mr. Hirohito."[18]

Although the *Kansan* had never before been the voice of the entire University, it was now. The war, Chancellor Malott said in his convocation address in the fall of 1942, was "part of civilization's struggle—the common cause of the United Nations as they plan a world in which men stand straight and walk free, free not of all human trouble, but free of the fear of despotic power, free to develop as individuals, free to conduct and shape their affairs." Malott asked each student to stretch himself "mentally, morally, and spiritually," to discover what the war meant, to meditate on the nature and value of freedom as he went from class to class, to prepare himself in new ways for a new future.[19]

But the University had more immediate and practical things to do than make students conscious of the alleged values for which their nation was fighting. The first, of course, was to preserve the vigor of the institution itself. Fearful lest the draft, enlistments, and departures for war industry cripple it, both before and after the

United States entered the war Malott urged the students to stay in school. At his request in 1942 Governor Ratner issued a statement—written by the Chancellor—arguing that continuing their education was the "most important contribution to the war effort" that young Kansans could make. Malott told their parents the same thing.

Despite such efforts enrollment fell off. Including the Summer Session the University had 5,299 students in the 1940–1941 year, but only 4,756—a reduction of over 10 percent—in 1941–1942. Enrollments fell by another 350 in 1942–1943, rose to slightly over 5,000 in 1943–1944 because of the influx of servicemen, then dropped to about 3,800 in 1944–1945.[20]

With students leaving for the armed forces, University officers had to determine, like their predecessors in 1917 and 1918, whether they would give academic credit for military service. At first Malott thought it "really a foolish thing to do as military science has nothing to do with academic credit." If the national government issued a general call to arms, he told the regents on December 11, 1941, he would let the students take final examinations in the work completed to date, with grades and credits given accordingly. The regents overruled him, however, by deciding that students leaving for the armed forces who did not wish to take a final examination covering an entire course should receive credit proportional to the time they had been in the course, calculated to the nearest half hour. The students had to be doing passing work, and the faculty would base the grade on the work done to date. At the same time the Board allowed students enrolled in courses whose completion would fulfill requirements for degrees either in June, 1941, or at the end of the Summer Session, and who had completed three-fourths of the work, to take a final examination over that material. If they passed, they would receive their degrees.[21]

As the war continued, the more complex problem appeared of what credit to give for academic work completed during military service. During the conflict the federal government sponsored over six hundred programs of college-level courses such as the Navy's V-5 program, the Area and Language Curriculum, and several officer training plans. From November, 1943, to the war's end a Senate committee headed by Guy W. Smith of Mathematics spent inordinate amounts of time with Registrar Laurence C. Woodruff trying to reach decisions and set policies. Finding that no two cases were the same and thus that no general policy would make sense, the Senate authorized Smith's group to act as an Advanced Standing Committee to give credit where credit appeared to be due.[22]

Like the officers and faculties of many other American colleges and universities in the early 1940s, those on Mount Oread wished, as Malott said, to "speed up the educational process" by beginning a trimester system to keep the University going at full speed the year round. In January, 1942, the Senate approved Malott's request to lengthen the Summer Session from eight to twelve weeks; the extra time would be gained by omitting the Easter recess and advancing commencement by a week. As the Chancellor pointed out, freshmen who entered in June, 1942, and who took the maximum amount of work could now graduate in what would normally be the middle of the junior year, which for many would mean a college degree before military service. A year later the University began a system of three semesters of sixteen weeks each beginning on July 1, November 1, and March 1. This formalized the program started the year before and also made the civilian academic year coincide with the demands of military education, which the University had undertaken on a large scale. And by a delicate squeezing of the calendar University officers managed to work in a "fall term" of five weeks from late September to the end of October for civilian students starting as freshmen in the fall. If they took the single five-hour course which they were allowed, and if they worked industriously, they could become sophomores by the following March 1, since sophomore standing required twenty hours and thirty grade points.[23]

An inevitable result of the speedup was pressure on the students. In December, 1942, there was a mass protest. To get days for the trimester starting the following July, the University Senate had shortened the Christmas vacation to a fleeting four days. On Friday morning, December 18, four hundred students, alerted by anonymous telephone calls to student living units, surged through Strong Hall to Malott's office to demand a longer vacation. The Chancellor's absence on a speaking trip checked their enthusiasm, but his return later that day sparked a "Vacation Starts Tonight" rally which climaxed in a thousand students jamming the wide hall in front of Malott's office. After argument Malott suggested the appointment of a student committee. Over the weekend student leaders apologized for the near-riot, discretion being the better part of the vacation crusade, and on Monday the Senate reconsidered its calendar. Noting that many freshmen had not been home since the semester's start, that many students had far to travel, and that several parents had telephoned to request a longer vacation, the Senate started it that evening and extended it to December 30.[24]

Another kind of educational speedup appeared in 1942 and 1943 as the University Senate allowed high-school seniors without diplomas to enroll for college work. In 1942 the Senate Committee on Examinations had before it an application for admission from a high-school student in Larned, Kansas, who had two units of entrance requirements—American history and English—to complete. In the background of a decision was one by Northwestern University to admit high-school students before graduation provided they completed a preparatory summer course. After considerable disagreement on procedures between the Committee on Examinations and Chancellor Malott, the Committee asked the student to complete a correspondence course in American history and take a special examination in English. She passed both and was admitted.[25]

If one qualified student could be admitted without a high-school diploma, why not all other qualified students? Curiously the new idea of admission by examination was a throwback to the University's early days, when students could gain admittance by either graduation from an approved high school or examinations in appropriate subjects. In December, 1942, the Committee on the University in War-Time, chaired by John W. Ashton of the English Department, recommended a system of "screen test examinations" for the possible admission of all students who had finished the junior year of high school. The following March the State Board of Education decided that the University's freshman year might also count as the senior year of high school for qualified students, and the University Senate approved the principle. Subject to similar action by the other four state schools—which was soon forthcoming—the University would grant admission to high-school students with twelve credits (instead of the usual fifteen) who stood in the upper 10 percent of their class, provided that their principal considered them qualified for college work and that they passed an aptitude test. Those new entrance opportunities remained in effect until 1947. The Senate also allowed competent high-school seniors to take up to five hours of University-level correspondence courses for college credit, and arranged for credit, upon examination, for private study and some kinds of occupational and technical experience.[26]

While speeding up the "educational process" in wartime was advantageous for many students, it also presented the University of Kansas—and every other institution that tried it—with an awkward intellectual problem. If the assertions of educational leaders were true, much of the educational process, especially in the liberal arts, was normally inefficient, hesitant, tentative. A liberal education, at least, allegedly involved considerable speculative thought, free experimentation with ideas, and dislocations of mind when teachers challenged traditional concepts. That kind of education required a certain leisure and the relative absence of artificial pressures, along with adequate faculty, library, and laboratory resources. If, as Malott had said before the conflict, the "imminence of war" was "no basis on which to plan a life,"[27] the wartime spirit of haste, acceleration, and confusion was an even less satisfactory basis. Educational speedups, the completion of academic requirements as fast as possible, made a degree even more of a commodity than it had been before, even more something to be obtained for its utilitarian value in military service or civilian life.

Along with opportunities for earlier degrees came suggestions to help students prepare for greater contributions to the war effort. Early in 1942 the University published a pamphlet called *K. U. Students and the War: Suggestions Regarding the Selection of Courses at the University of Kansas during the Present Period of Conflict and Industrial Expansion.* Moderate in tone, it advocated that undergraduates should at least consider the nation's needs as they determined their programs. Freshmen and sophomores undecided about their majors or life's work should realize that the country needed more physicians, nurses, engineers, and chemists, more physicists, accountants, and industrial managers. Men entering the armed forces or industry should be aware of mathematics, chemistry, and physics courses, and of opportunities in astronomy, civil engineering, geology, and military law. For women there were several special Red Cross courses, numerous classes in home economics, typing, and stenography, and a curriculum in occupational therapy. In cooperation with the Civil Aeronautics Administration the University offered courses in flight instruction; on another front the men were reminded of the ROTC. Both army and navy officers had emphasized that to "keep oneself physically fit at this time is a primary duty of all loyal citizens," and in the intramural sports program, physical activity courses, and a special class in Individual Gymnastics created by Forrest C. Allen, professor of physical education, were opportunities for everyone. All students should also try to understand the causes and issues of the war. There were valuable insights in courses in War Economy Problems, Recent World History, International Relations, and others. More generally, faculty from the Economics, History, Political Science, and Sociology departments were preparing a new course of evening lectures, open to the public but carrying an hour's credit for enrolled students, on "The World at War." Among the lectures would be "What Was the Matter with Versailles?" "How the War Came to Europe," "Japan, China, and the United States," and "Requirements for Victory and a Durable Peace."[28]

By the fall of 1942, however, recommendations had given way to demands. Students arriving in September found placards urging "A War Course for Every Student" across the campus, which tried to make them feel guilty for not enrolling in at least one. Chancellor Malott's convocation address told students that they "must gear" their minds to "new outlooks and new responsibilities," "must learn the meaning of this war," "must prepare" for "active participation" in world affairs during the war and after. "Every student must realize," he told the University Senate, "that he is in effect on furlough to the University for special training in the war effort." The Senate had already accepted the idea: in July, 1942, it required physical education of all men registered with selective service or in the enlisted reserve of the armed forces, and of all undergraduate women in their first year of residence. A year later the Senate required every male student in the University, except those specially excused or enrolled in an armed service program, to enroll in three hours a week of "physical conditioning."[29]

Wisely the University's leaders did not attempt to create a corps of student cadets, as the Senate had done in the First World War. Yet by contract with the federal government they enlarged the University's training of enlisted men and officers far beyond what had been done for the old Students' Army Training Corps, and they also began several voluntary courses for civilian personnel. In the early months of the conflict, that war training went smoothly enough. By

April, 1942, the School of Engineering had started a special two-year course to train skilled workers for war industries. Nearly fifty senior women enrolled in a special class in mechanical drawing, sponsored through the United States Office of Education and administered by Guy V. Keeler of the Extension Division. From June 2 to September 11, the University was to offer a pretraining program for Air Force cadets, and in the offing was University participation in the Navy's V-1 and V-7 officer training programs.[30]

But that summer a sort of semicontrolled chaos came to campus with the arrival of some five hundred Navy machinists' mates from the Great Lakes Naval Training Station, whose teaching the University had agreed to undertake. Navy authorities demanded that the group be kept together, in living quarters as well as classes. The only building large enough and safe enough for a military barracks was Strong Hall, the entire top floor and west wing of which were leased to the government. When the mates came, there was a frantic redistribution of departments, faculty, and classrooms. The Drawing and Painting Department of the School of Fine Arts found itself on the third floor of Dyche Museum, displacing the stuffed bird collection, while some of the Business School faculty held classes in a Strong Hall women's lounge. The Navy moved double-decker bunks into former classrooms, converted physiology laboratories into shower rooms and laundries, and strung clotheslines along the crest of the hill to the north of Strong Hall.

Everyone—the sailors included—bore up well under the strain, but the University was not what it used to be. Three times a day the mates marched to mess in the converted ballroom of the Union, and they also paraded to their technical courses in other buildings. On Saturdays and Sundays they were at liberty in Lawrence. Every Saturday night there was a dance for them at the Community Building, and many residents invited them to their homes. In the 1942–1943 academic year the so-called United States Naval Training School expanded to about eight hundred men, and it came to include cooks, bakers, and electricians as well as machinists' mates. Most sailors took four-month courses and then moved on to new assignments. When the Naval Training School closed in October, 1944, it had trained some three thousand men. In addition to them the University also offered special courses to almost five hundred naval engineering students, who were housed in the fraternities.[31]

If there were obvious disadvantages to having troops on Mount Oread, there were equally obvious assets. Their presence prevented a disastrous decline in enrollment statistics; payments by the national government for their education meant an increase in income as well as in the head count. Taking advantage of every opportunity, in 1943 Malott opened the University to the Navy's V-12 program. To that time the school had been participating in the V-1 and V-7 schemes. The first consisted of enlisted men taking a two-year course. Those who did poorly in it left to become apprentice seamen, a second group went into aviation training, and the third group, the V-7, were allowed another two years of undergraduate studies. After taking their degrees and passing appropriate examinations, they became engineering and deck officers. By January, 1943, the University had about three hundred students in the V-1 and V-7 programs.

The V-12 was a more flexible arrangement for training all sorts of officers, including chaplains, physicians, and aviators. Selecting qualified high-school seniors, recent high-school graduates, and enlisted men, the Navy gave them from two to twelve trimesters of college. Fortunate students could work straight through to a degree, while those called early to active duty could count their work toward degrees after the war. The V-12 students appeared on campus almost as ordinary nonmilitary students. They were free to carry elective subjects and to participate in varsity athletics, fraternities, and other extracurricular activities. Unlike the machinists' mates they roomed and ate where they would and did not disrupt the campus.[32]

Malott and other University officers had hoped to cooperate with the Army as fully as with the Navy, especially in training engineers. But in 1943 the War Manpower Commission designated the University as a center for teaching naval engineers only, and the Navy always outnumbered the Army on Mount Oread. In the summer of 1943, however, the University joined the Army Specialized Training Program, in which men who had completed basic training were sent to college for three twelve-week terms to study mathematics, the sciences, English, and other subjects appropriate to engineers. They numbered about three hundred. The University also offered a twelve-week course for several hundred soldiers in the Army's A-12 program, which preceded basic training.

Along with these larger programs went several smaller ones. During the 1942–1943 year, for example, the University operated a radio school for the Army Signal Corps, an air training group for the Marine Corps, and a number of short courses in such things as medicine, physics, chemistry, and mathematics for the Army and Navy College Training Programs. In the biennium from July 1, 1942, to June 30, 1944, the University trained over sixty-eight hundred servicemen.[33]

Like the Lawrence campus, the Medical School in Kansas City also went to war. Its curriculum was quickened by abolishing the summer vacation, which made it possible to accept a new freshman class every nine months and increase the number of graduates by a third. More important, the national government seized about 80 percent of the medical students, allowing them to stay in school and paying their expenses. By mid-1943, 85 students were preparing to become Navy physicians, and 175 were in training for the Army. The other 20 percent, including women and physically disqualified men, were reserved for the home front.[34]

In September, 1943, with between two thousand and twenty-five hundred servicemen on campus and wartime activity at its height, Malott announced that "the University of Kansas is now converted to war." Unlike Frank Strong twenty-five years before, however, Malott was much exhilarated by the fact. He saw no inconsistency between war training and civilian education. "The training of soldiers in science, of sailors in engineering, and coeds in education or music or philosophy, does not seem an incongruous thing on a university campus," he thought. "All are young people, ambitious, earnest, hard-working, unselfish,—all have in mind the fundamental objective of winning the war. But they are also hopeful of establishing a peace, based upon reality, tolerance, and logical thinking." Room had been saved, moreover, "in order that education in all the professions and disciplines, in all the liberal arts and sciences, may be preserved for the boys and girls of K.U. No department has been abandoned, no fundamental activity has been stopped."[35]

After the School of Engineering's war industries training program and the mechanical drawing course for women proved reasonably successful, the University broadened its wartime offerings for civilians. The results were not always happy. In 1942 the Hercules Powder Company established its mammoth Sunflower Ordnance

Works thirteen miles east of Lawrence. After the University had agreed to train some of its employees in chemistry classes, the company suggested a more specialized course for prospective women employees, and Professor Ray Q. Brewster began one. When only two of the twenty-four enrollees actually got jobs at Sunflower, however, Brewster dropped plans for a second course. The University had better luck training women employees as aeronautical technicians for the Boeing, North American, Beech, and Cessna companies in Wichita, for the manufacturers hired the women before they began training, paid them while they learned, and guaranteed them employment afterward. Throughout the war the Extension Division trained several thousand more war workers in correspondence courses and direct classes.[36]

But both the Extension Division and the University as a whole did more than train fighting men and war workers. The citizens at home had to be informed of the principles at stake in the conflict, both to keep their morale high and to prepare them for the postwar world. While Malott presented right ideas to the students and groups around the state, faculty members and the Extension Division did the same. Thus on the eve of war in 1941 Professor L. R. Lind of the Department of Latin and Greek asserted that the war was being fought to preserve the great principles of freedom and democracy inherited by Americans from the Graeco-Roman past. Thus did the Sociology Department in January, 1942, issue a pamphlet called *Morale and the Democratic Community*, which stressed the importance of proper attitudes in the public at large and suggested means to promote them. And various faculty members lectured to the public in the World at War course.[37]

Early in 1942 the United States Office of Information designated the University a Key Center of Information for the eastern part of Kansas. Malott established a committee headed by Extension Division Director Harold C. Ingham, which set up headquarters on the second floor of Watson Library and created a War Information Center and Civilian Morale Service. Ingham hoped that its work would provide the enlightenment necessary for victory in "our all-out struggle for the survival of democracy and the ideals of self-government." To that end the Center offered printed and mimeographed materials on almost every wartime subject (they were the modernized form of the old package libraries) for use by service and study clubs, schools, and individuals, and sent them out by the hundreds of thousands of pages. The Center also established a Victory Speakers Bureau under Professor E. C. Buehler of the Speech Department. On request from groups of Kansans the Bureau sent out advanced speech students to talk on any appropriate subject, from "War Taxes and How to Pay Them" to "The Airplane versus the Battleship," from "The Point System in Food Rationing" to "Know Your Enemies, the Japanese."[38]

To Chancellor Malott's disgust the Board of Regents thought they knew their enemies, the Japanese, far better than he and many students. During the war the regents prohibited the matriculation in all state schools of any Nisei student—that is, a student of Japanese ancestry born in the United States and therefore a citizen. Their attitude struck Malott as "un-American and dangerous," and he thought that in the "light of later years" it would seem "utterly foolish." He was right on all counts. The question arose in March, 1942, when President Robert G. Sproul of the University of California wrote the heads of numerous midwestern colleges and universities to ask if they would accept Nisei students from his institution whom the national government was planning to remove from the West Coast as part of its general removal of Japanese aliens and people of Japanese ancestry. Malott had received a similar letter from President Lee Paul Sieg of the University of Washington. The Chancellor and faculty members with whom he talked were eager to have them. There had been less trouble with Japanese students than with those of any other nationality, Malott told Board Chairman Fred M. Harris, and the new ones would be an "interesting leaven in our group." Unless there were "very valid reasons against it," the Chancellor added, "there is a question as to whether or not the University does not have a duty to bear some fair share of this problem which, somehow, the nation must solve."[39]

The regents thought otherwise. Later in March they forbade the admission of Nisei students from the West Coast, and they continued the prohibition for the war's duration. Admittedly, Malott told William Allen White, the Board was a "bit sheepish" about the decision. But the regents had found that many Kansans, especially of the older generations, were opposed to admitting the Nisei, and they had to consider as well a decree by Governor Ratner barring all Japanese from the state. Uppermost in the regents' minds was the presence of important military and industrial installations in Kansas. Malott, the *Kansan,* and another student publication, the *Gadfly,* pleaded with the Board, but to no avail. Even when Kansas Wesleyan University in Salina admitted Nisei students in 1943, and the Universities of Nebraska, Missouri, and Colorado welcomed them in 1943 and 1944, the Kansas regents refused. In September, 1944, the Board did agree to admit Nisei who had honorable discharges from the armed forces, but they would go no further.[40]

The freedom for which Kansans were fighting, then, had its limits. On the whole, however, the University fought well. The demands of war subverted the institution's normal peacetime work, made it far more of a trade school than ever before, and brought great inconvenience to faculty members whose office and classroom space contracted as their teaching duties expanded. From 1939–1940 to 1942–1943 the number of faculty members in Lawrence fell from 301 to 255,[41] and in several departments the loss of graduate assistants put a still heavier burden on the faculty who remained. The Department of Chemistry, for example—always among the best in the University—found both its part-time and full-time staff depleted; the seven faculty members and five assistant instructors who remained by the spring of 1944 were distressingly overworked. In the fall of 1942, indeed, two staff members suffered nervous breakdowns, and Hamilton P. Cady fell ill, possibly because of the extra teaching load he had to carry. In May, 1943, he died.[42]

In peacetime the University's foundation had been maximum service to society, and the school was no less an agency for social progress now. Again paralleling developments during the First World War, many students became less frivolous, and many of them determined to make the world a better place after the war. "The old 'college spirit' of goldfish swallowing and steak fries has passed," said the *Kansan* in 1944. Students generally were more serious about their studies and their futures; the women were more concerned about their sweethearts and husbands in service than about the usual campus activities; many undergraduates took example from the armed forces and concentrated on getting their work done and requirements completed. "Movements are stirring throughout the civilized world," the *Kansan* had said the year before, "movements for a better world, a freer world, an integrated world; movements toward simplification and union. The backbone of these movements is youth, for only youth has the energy, the imagination, the resilience to conceive their purpose, to believe in their goals, and to carry them through to their successful completion. . . . We may well adopt the battle cry of Hitler to our own uses. Let this be the battle cry of freedom, tolerance, union, and the international outlook: Today the United Nations; tomorrow the world!"[43]

While the University marched to war, in terms of progress toward the traditional ideal of excellence it merely marked time. In the summer of 1942, at the request of the Board of Regents, executives from the five state institutions of higher education met to discuss the requests that the regents should make of the legislature of 1943. They concluded that although the war might last through the 1943–1945 biennium, wartime conditions were no satisfactory basis for appropriations. Their schools had not only to care for the "military and industrial needs of a nation geared for a desperate war," but also to "provide decent education for the young people upon whom will depend the future of the state of Kansas, and to be ready for large new demands when the war ends." The legislature should look forward to peacetime, when thousands of veterans and dozens of returning faculty members would require more money. "Appropriations made on the basis of continued war will not take care of a return to a non-war status," while appropriations "set up on the basis of a post-war situation will care for either situation."[44]

The tradition of the Kansas legislatures, however, was not to plan realistically for the future, but either to catch up with a few of the needs of the past or to keep things about as they were. Since the spring semester of 1943 found only 3,201 students enrolled and since the federal government had pumped over $600,000 into the school in the 1942–1943 fiscal year, Malott and the regents knew that the lawmakers had no intention of looking much beyond the immediate present. They begged some $3,190,000 in regular appropriations, which included no money for academic buildings or a general salary increase, and received all but $56,000 of it.[45]

There was $69,000 more, though, to complete the Military Science Building for the campus ROTC. Originally it was to be financed mainly by the federal Works Progress Administration, which would give some $143,000 if the University raised $25,000 more and contributed some of the building materials. The Endowment Association secured the money from twenty-two alumni and friends, and construction had begun in the spring of 1941 down the hill south of Hoch Auditorium and Marvin Hall. When the WPA closed down in 1942, however, the University was left holding the unfinished structure and turned to the legislature for aid. Completed on November 1, 1943, and dedicated the next month, it was a three-story building faced with the stones of old Snow Hall—thrift and sentiment had combined to save them—complete with a rifle range, artillery storage room, and a large drillroom as well as classrooms and offices. It was said to be one of the most modern military science buildings in the Middle West.[46]

It opened during the year that the University's special wartime work was at its height. Yet that work, as everyone knew, was but prefatory to greater labors in the years of peace that lay somewhere ahead. Those early postwar years—full of striving, idealism, readjustment, and change—were exciting indeed.

26

The Beginnings of Reconstruction

IF Chancellor Malott had his way, the postwar University of Kansas would become a great center for the service of mankind, whose ideals and ideas lifted students above a narrow, self-centered individualism to new realms of international brotherhood and helpfulness. To participate in this "historic era," he told the students in his convocation address in 1943, "you must be men and women of breadth of knowledge, of liberal and enlightened intellects, aware of the sweeping forces of change and danger that beset us, and ready to lend the power of your leadership in the preservation of our way of life." Malott went on to mention several problems that needed solution: governmental paternalism and excessive taxation in the United States; winning the war and creating a just and peaceful world; and making good use of the world's tremendous technological resources. Calling on the students to "think widely, to read voraciously, to discuss endlessly, to explore, and to affirm," he reminded them of Woodrow Wilson's advice to Princeton students more than four decades before: "Do not forget, as you walk these classic places, why you are here. . . . You are here to enrich the world, and you impoverish yourself if you forget the errand."[1]

Again and again during the troubles and uncertainties of the postwar years Malott hammered away at the theme of service to the world. Scholarship itself had to have new objectives, he believed. "In the old days," he maintained, "scholarship honors went largely to the disciplined minds which absorbed and retained the accumu-

501

lated knowledge of the past, and facilely reflected that accumulation in brilliant conversation or writings." But now scholarship had to mean leadership—leadership in solving America's domestic problems, in showing that American democracy could work in a "war-torn world," in "courageously assuming our international responsibilities as a great power." If scholarship did not result in making the world happier and freer, the people braver and more thoughtful, scholarship was sterile. "The world is too sober for academic drifters," Malott warned the Kansas student body in 1950. "Education must be purposeful, creative, backed by energy." Because "man's survival depends both upon his intelligence and upon his faith," it was "the challenge of your university years to grow in the power of your faith and in the vigor of that intelligence sharpened by your teachers, by your reading, by your discussion—but more than all by your own determination to do honest, hard, continuous work to develop the latent powers of leadership which reside in each of you."[2]

As Malott knew very well, his ideas were neither novel nor unique. In the war and postwar years the same admonitions and pleas, in almost the same words, rang forth from a thousand college rostrums. Malott's notions, moreover, were but another modern form of the old concept that higher learning, especially that offered and pursued in public institutions, ought to increase the public welfare. Yet the problems of the postwar world *were* new and demanded new solutions. With unusual urgency, even for a chancellor, Malott was demanding that the University revitalize itself, make itself virtually a new school. Both before and after the war's end, he prodded the faculty to assess and then to reassess their curricula, their teaching methods, their impact upon students.[3] At the same time he told Kansans as directly as he could, always speaking the Kansas language, that unless they helped the University to their utmost ability the postwar world would pass them by.

During the years from 1945 to 1949 it sometimes seemed that no one was bypassing the University. Along with undergraduates fresh from high school, a flood of veterans threatened to drown the institution. Eager to begin or continue educations deferred by war, eager to get the money offered by the national government for educational expenses, the veterans swelled enrollments beyond all expectations. The University's largest prewar enrollment had been

5,896 in 1930–1931. But in the 1945–1946 year the enrollment (veterans in parentheses) was about 6,300 (2,239); in 1946–1947 over 10,400 (6,536); in 1947–1948 almost 10,900 (6,438); and in 1948–1949 over 11,000 (6,092).[4]

The immediate result was a sort of welcome chaos: chaos because the University suddenly had to find rooms and apartments to house the students and classrooms in which to teach them; welcome because the several thousand additional students were an excellent justification for larger appropriations and because veterans brought extra funds from the government in the form of compensatory fees over and above the regular matriculation and incidental charges. Malott, indeed, was prepared to accept every qualified student whom the University could cram in somewhere. "The University of Kansas will not turn down a single applicant for enrollment," he told the Lawrence Chamber of Commerce in June, 1946, "as long as there is a room, garret, basement, attic, cellar or warehouse left in Lawrence, that can be made into a decent place to live." He gaily pointed out that the coeds were delighted to have the swarm of veterans on campus, "but that, in turn, attracts more girls. Thus," he concluded happily, "expansion spirals upward." In his biennial report for 1946 he noted that many classes were swollen far beyond the limits of effective teaching: two introductory philosophy courses had 225 students apiece; twelve classes in introductory economics averaged 105 each; eleven beginning history courses averaged 66; eight classes in political science averaged 90. Many new teachers were needed to shrink such classes to a reasonable size. Classrooms and laboratories, Malott added, were being used from ten to fourteen hours a day. Although the University was in the process of acquiring thirteen emergency classroom buildings—ten at federal expense—they were but a temporary expedient. Buildings had been crowded before the war, he told the legislature of 1949. "The tremendous current enrollment . . . is accommodated only by severe overcrowding and the use of three quonset huts provided by the University and twelve war surplus buildings erected largely at the expense of the federal government. . . . The early replacement of these temporary facilities by modern educational buildings is urgent. Our building program cannot longer be delayed if the thousands of Kansas young people now in high school are to have adequate modern facilities when they come to K.U."[5]

But in those crowded classrooms occurred some of the liveliest intellectual activity in the University's history. Many of the ex-servicemen were more mature and more sophisticated than the ordinary undergraduates, more serious in their studies, less willing to accept traditional ideas. Many of them were also more than ordinarily eager to complete their formal educations. Collectively they applied themselves to their books and classes with welcome diligence. They stayed away in droves from University and class dances —from 1945 to 1948 the majority of dances had a net operating loss— and they disappointed the Lawrence tavern owners, too. "The most pleasurable experience I have ever had with undergraduate students . . . was teaching the 'G.I.'s' who returned from service in the '40's," said one faculty member several years later. "These men, not always well endowed intellectually, were almost invariably well-motivated, earnest and hard-working. . . . I often felt that these men, when they represented the majority of a class . . . helped make the class the ideal in teaching according to my opinion—that is, a truly intellectual interchange. Neither pushing nor pulling was required, and not infrequently I found the class was leading as well as being led." "The influence of the veteran on campus has been stimulating," Malott added. "He has been purposeful, willing to work, eager to learn, and patient under the crowded and sometimes ineffectual facilities of present-day university life."[6]

University officers did their best to find housing for all the students. Malott appointed Irvin E. Youngberg director of housing, and he scoured Lawrence for rooms. Responding to Youngberg's exhortations and to their own desires for money, Lawrence landlords jammed students in everywhere—often, Youngberg reported, at exorbitant rates. Still there was not space enough. While fraternities rented additional houses for the brothers and at least one married student built his own small house of cement blocks, the University moved men into the basement of the old Spooner Library, now the Spooner-Thayer Art Museum, into Robinson Gymnasium, and into rooms beneath the football stadium; erected a war-surplus dormitory west of the stadium; rented a few houses; and even got a church from the Lawrence congregation of the Reorganized Church of Jesus Christ of Latter Day Saints as a swap for worship rooms in University buildings.[7]

To help students the more—especially the married ones—in 1946

Malott sought and received the regents' consent to negotiate with the Army for the use of rooms and apartments at the Sunflower Ordnance Works. The dwellings had been constructed during the war for workers and their families, and were now vacant. By the end of July the University had secured quarters for some fourteen hundred students and their families, along with recreation facilities and a cafeteria, which the commandant agreed to furnish. Students rented their apartments directly from the government. Buses to Lawrence were furnished for students who lacked automobiles. Not all of the available space was occupied; the largest number housed at Sunflower at once was 971. In general the housing was excellent, for the rooms and apartments were both clean and inexpensive. But the distance from campus was a drawback, and as more rooms became available in Lawrence during the 1946–1947 year, the Sunflower students moved into town. The last of them left in February, 1947. But the University retained the privilege of using the rooms for students.[8]

Just as the students suffered from the Lawrence housing shortage, so did new faculty members. To house them, the University procured surplus buildings from the federal government and set them up on land south of the main campus—the only time in the school's first century that it provided faculty housing. The first four apartment-barracks were ready in November, 1946. Eventually there would be 186 apartments in 31 buildings. Collectively called "Sunnyside," and later occupied by married students as well as faculty families, the buildings were ugly and often of shoddy construction. Some of the floors had great cracks; many of the water pipes were above ground and froze in winter; the development attracted rat colonies. But at least there were roofs, walls, and floors, along with a sense of deprivation shared that drew the community together. Not until 1961 was the last of the Sunnyside buildings torn down.[9]

Along with the intellectual quickening, the money that the veteran students brought with them more than compensated for any problems they caused. Through the Veterans Administration the federal government paid extra fees for each returning serviceman: a veteran, Malott reported in 1948, was worth about three times as much as a nonveteran. In fiscal 1947 the University received about $819,000 in compensatory fees; the next year the amount was almost

$789,000. And for the purposes of argument, at least, the veterans were as valuable when they left as when they came. One reason Malott offered the legislature of 1949 for greatly increased appropriations was compensation for the loss of income when the veterans departed. Since the fall of 1946, he said two years later, the number of veterans had declined by 510 while total enrollment had increased by 679. "The accelerated decline of enrollment of veterans as predicted (1,500 fewer next year, 2,000 still fewer in the following year) will translate itself into tremendous loss of revenue."[10]

To help prepare for both the veterans' and the University's more general postwar needs, in late 1944 and early 1945 its officers went to the legislature with a sizable appropriations increase in mind. The legislature of 1943 had granted $3,134,000, plus another $69,000 for the Military Science Building. Now the regents asked for about $4,898,000. That sum would provide for no general salary increase, but would allow a large number of raises for the Lawrence faculty in specific cases "necessary to maintain the staff in the face of the scale being paid in competing states," and reasonable merit increases for the Medical School staff. Buildings were the major need: $200,000 to enlarge Watson Library; $150,000 to remodel Fowler Shops for the new School of Journalism; $100,000 for an engineering shop; and another $350,000 for the Medical School hospital.[11]

At first disaster loomed, for Governor Andrew F. Schoeppel and Budget Director Floyd Shoaf pruned the budget left and right, eliminating all the building requests and cutting some $306,000 from the salary and maintenance requests. The loss of the building money was not overly troublesome, for Schoeppel thought it should come from the Educational Building Fund, but the salary and maintenance reduction was painful. "As you realize," Malott wrote the Governor, "this is making an uphill situation for me, which I fear will jeopardize the future of this University for many years to come. . . . What a hole we are in!!" In the weeks ahead, however, the legislature proved eager to help the school out of the depths. Two bills for buildings and general operating costs, which together restored all the major reductions made by Schoeppel and Shoaf, sailed easily through both houses, and the Governor signed them in March. In all the University received about $4,702,000 for the coming two years.[12]

Authorization for the buildings was the first step in completing a great series of postwar capital needs of which Malott was dreaming. He believed that $10,000,000 worth of buildings was necessary, $3,325,000 for immediate needs and the rest to meet longer-range requirements. In the plans was $4,000,000 worth of dormitories and student-union additions on both campuses, money for which could be borrowed under the act of 1941; $450,000 for a fieldhouse-gymnasium; $1,210,000 to expand the Medical School hospital; $350,000 for a medical sciences building in Kansas City; $350,000 for a fine arts structure; $300,000 for new engineering shops; and almost $400,000 to expand Watson Library. Facing up to the difficult task of setting priorities, the Chancellor at last decided that the fine arts structure, whose price grew to $500,000 within a year, should come first, an $850,000 chemistry and physics building second, and a $400,000 classroom building third, to be followed by $100,000 worth of Law School library stacks. After the veterans had come and gone, Malott explained in his report in 1946, the "normal college attendance" would probably be about eleven thousand a year. Either facilities and personnel had to be increased "consistent with sound education for these increased numbers," or the University would have to limit enrollments or lower its standards. With the "backing of the people of Kansas and their legislature, Kansas can be a part of the great educational progress of tomorrow. Kansas young people deserve it; they are the state's greatest of its many natural resources."[13]

With the war over, with veterans and new students straining the University's resources at every point, Malott and the regents asked for a huge increase in salary and maintenance appropriations. Two years earlier they had received slightly over $1,127,000 a year for salaries and wages throughout the University; now they petitioned for about $2,130,000 a year. In 1945 they had gotten $462,000 a year for regular maintenance, whereas now they asked about $656,000. Including $265,000 for a new power-plant boiler and turbine which could not be paid for from the Educational Building Fund, the total reached about $6,755,000. The Budget Director allowed all but about $63,000 of it, and Governor Frank Carlson expressed Malott's own sense of urgency in his message to the lawmakers. "This state's primary concern now centers upon its veterans and its youth," he said. "By all means, let us face these problems without delay, in the sure knowledge that provision for our colleges is for the permanent good of Kansas."[14]

With such support in high places, the legislature gave the University just about all it asked. Appropriations fell short of requests by only some $73,000. In a separate action the regents sought and received from the Educational Building Fund $100,000 more for Watson Library, $190,000 for engineering shops, and $350,000 for the Medical School.[15]

Suddenly the University had entered on boom times. While tax money poured in from the citizens and the legislature, millions more came from the national government through normal and compensatory fees, and more still from the fees of nonveteran students. Not counting gifts, borrowing, or income from the Endowment Association, in fiscal 1945 the University's total income was about $4,500,000. Four years later it was over $15,000,000, with about $8,115,000 available to the Lawrence campus and about $6,950,000 to the Medical Center. Although the latter figure included a special grant to the Medical Center of over $3,860,000 for fiscal 1949, the total was still impressive—and more impressive still when compared with the $2,618,000 available in fiscal 1941, the last prewar year. Over $1,980,000 of the income for fiscal 1949 had come from the Veterans Administration, most of it in compensatory fees.[16]

Although such figures pleased Chancellor Malott and the University's other officers, the process of improving the University took longer than they hoped it would. For one thing, except for additions to Watson Library, the new Medical School facilities, and the engineering shops, there had been no appropriations for academic buildings; since the completion of Strong Hall in 1923 there had been no major classroom and laboratory additions, for new Snow Hall was a replacement and Lindley Hall was largely given over to the State Geological Survey. Facilities had deteriorated badly, Malott asserted. "We are almost literally held together with string and chewing gum, and are getting by largely with the shacks and shanties from the federal government which have added more than 10% to the classroom space on the campus." Meanwhile many of the University's "sister institutions in other states" had started "large and aggressive building programs." Although Kansas could not hope to match the University of Illinois's $62,000,000 plans or the University of California's $90,000,000 request to the state legislature, greater attention had to be given to local problems.[17]

Like his predecessors Malott tried to spur Kansans on by appealing to their state pride, to their presumptive desire to match as nearly as possible what other state universities were doing. In asking the legislature of 1949 for money for a fieldhouse in which the University could display its fine basketball teams, he urged that "we should get a start, if we are to keep in the game, in view of such progress as Kentucky's nearly completed $2,000,000 structure." In salaries, too, the University had to be competitive. "Present rates, while reflecting gains over two years ago," Malott said succinctly in his biennial report, "have not kept pace either with the cost of living or the increases granted in other states with which we compete for faculty. . . ."[18]

In 1948 and 1949 Malott managed to instill in the regents both something of his own despair about things yet undone and something of his eagerness to get a major commitment to progress from the legislature. Including money from the Educational Building Fund the appropriations of 1947 had been almost $7,894,000. Now the regents asked for the stupendous amount of $16,636,500. Salary requests for 1949–1950 were up by $1,100,000 over the previous year; for 1950–1951 they were up by still another $1,000,000. Regular maintenance appropriations for the 1947–1949 biennium had been $1,356,000; now the regents begged $2,228,000 for the two years ahead. But proportionately the greatest increase came in requests from the swelling Educational Building Fund. The total granted for 1947–1949 had been $1,142,000. The new request was $5,309,000: almost $2,000,000 for a science building, over $800,000 for a fine arts structure, $700,000 for a fieldhouse, and almost $600,000 to complete and equip the new hospital building at the Medical Center and build a small dormitory for medical students.[19]

Both the Budget Director and the legislature handled the salary and maintenance requests tenderly, and the University came out with only $124,000 less than the Board had asked. Although the building appropriations faced more opposition, the results were still heartening. The House members saw no need to help the School of Fine Arts, but both senators and representatives agreed on $1,972,000 to start the replacement for Bailey Hall and $750,000 to begin the fieldhouse. Another $90,000 went to Watson Library, $150,000 to finish the remodeling of Fowler Shops, and $335,000 to the Medical Center. The legislature also increased to ¾ mill the tax supporting the Educational Building Fund; happier times were coming.[20] In a semi-independent maneuver, moreover, Dean Franklin D. Murphy of the Medical Center and his supporters convinced the legislature that the shortage of Kansas physicians needed immediate relief. The legislature created the University of Kansas Hospitals Building Fund and gave it $3,862,500, taken from a surplus in the state retail sales tax fund.[21]

To sustain the University's material momentum, Malott and the regents sought from the legislature of 1951 over $4,500,000 more than the legislature of 1949 had awarded. The request's most notable feature was the inclusion of $497,000 a year for the Lawrence campus and $151,000 a year for the Medical School to support the faculty's "general research." In the past the University had had small sums for faculty research, but this was the first time it had suggested a specific grant from the state. The immediate reason for the request was that Malott had learned that President James A. McCain of the Kansas State College of Agriculture had asked for $295,000 in state funds to support general research in his own school, and the Chancellor knew a good opportunity when he saw it. "Never before in the history of the University have so many members of the faculty been interested in research," Malott said. While a few of them had grants from outside sources, "most investigations are being conducted by faculty members on their own on very modest scales." Outside funds were hard to get unless the University matched them dollar for dollar or promised to assume the entire cost after an initial period; and the University had not been able to get the federal grants and state appropriations that the land-grant colleges and universities received. "Support of faculty research," Malott claimed, "will repay the state many fold—in improved teaching, in recognition of the University, in placement of graduates, and in actual contributions to knowledge and human welfare."

And then there were building requests galore: $1,500,000 more for the fieldhouse, $1,200,000 for the fine arts building, $750,000 for a women's dormitory, $350,000 to enlarge Snow Hall, and some $660,000 to equip new Medical School buildings and the power plant. Impressively large though the request was, Malott described it as the "minimum needs of the University for the next biennium."[22]

W. G. Hamilton, the state budget director, had no animus against the University, for he had approved almost all its requests two years before. But a recession had ended the postwar economic boom, and now Hamilton lopped his way through the nonbuilding requests, removing over $500,000 from salaries and wages, all the research funds, $835,000 worth of state-service funds, and some $637,000 from maintenance requests. He came up with a budget of about $3,572,000 less than the University allegedly needed. The University community was appalled, but the legislature relieved its distress a little by diminishing the reduction to only $2,000,000. Where the University's leaders had hoped for $8,415,000 for salaries and wages, the legislature gave $7,312,000; of the biennial total of $1,296,000 asked for general research the lawmakers allowed only $600,000. As a result the regents decided to raise student fees, once again forcing the students and their parents to contribute money that the legislature would not grant. Out-of-state students, of course, suffered more than Kansas residents. While incidental fees for most Kansans rose by $10 a semester to either $50 or $55, depending on their school, the fees for nonresidents went up $30 to either $130 or $140. The gain to the University was about $226,000 in Lawrence and $56,000 at the Medical Center.[23]

There were disappointments in the search for building moneys, too. From the Educational Building Fund there was $1,863,000 more for the fieldhouse, a supplementary grant of $679,000 for the science building, and all the money asked for the Medical Center. But the fine arts building, the Snow Hall addition, and the dormitories fell under the ax of the Senate Ways and Means Committee.[24]

Still, the six years past had seen considerable physical growth. Chancellor Malott and the regents had started the University on the long trek from the depression of the 1920s and the 1930s toward a more prosperous era. Unsuitably, however, the two great buildings that they won from the legislature would appear only after Malott left Kansas for the presidency of Cornell University in 1951. Malott Hall, the chemistry-pharmacy-physics structure, was completed in 1954. Standing south of Haworth Hall, it was seven stories high in its central section and provided not only the space and facilities for teaching and research so severely lacking in Bailey Hall for more than twenty years but also room for the University's excellent science library. Professors Ray Q. Brewster of Chemistry and J. D. Stranathan of Physics, along with University Business Manager Joseph J. Wilson and State Architect Charles Marshall, had toured a number of institutions to the east, including M.I.T., Harvard, and the Mellon Institute in Pittsburgh, to get ideas. "The building will be planned from the inside out," Wilson said in 1949. "By that I mean that no outside dimensions will be set and the requirements fitted in later, but the rooms will be arranged and the resulting outside appearance will be a minor point." So it was, with the result that the interior was as commodious and modern as money could make it, while the exterior—squarish, plain, and faced with native stone—added nothing at all to campus beauty.

A year later an equally serviceable and architecturally nondescript fieldhouse was completed southwest of the main campus. Named for Forrest C. Allen, whose long and successful career as basketball coach would end in 1956, it was a huge barnlike structure with seats for seventeen thousand fans, along with athletic offices, exercise and practice rooms, and a dirt track. Its construction allowed the use of Hoch Auditorium exclusively for nonathletic events, as many faculty members of the 1920s had desired in the first place.[25]

Numerous smaller structures were completed or begun while Malott was chancellor, some from state appropriations, others from donations or revenue bonds. Gifts from dozens of alumni, students, faculty, and friends went to build a nondenominational chapel in 1946; gifts from Mr. and Mrs. Joseph R. Pearson and a bequest from Mrs. Grace R. Stephenson built Sellards, Pearson, and Stephenson Halls for self-supporting students in 1951. From legislative appropriations new Fowler Hall—engineering shops—was finished in 1950. In the fall of that year the regents voted to float some $1,300,000 in revenue bonds to expand the Memorial Union. Both the addition and the remodeling of Fowler Shops for the Journalism School would be finished in 1952.[26]

While buildings of all sorts were rising and being planned, Mrs. Malott and a campus planning committee led by Mrs. John H. Nelson, wife of the Graduate School dean, did their best to fulfill Chancellor James Marvin's dream of transforming the campus "from a rough common to a beautiful park." Over the years all the chancellors and many faculty members and wives, students, alumni, and friends had secured trees, shrubs, and flowers to make the campus more beautiful; the most significant piece of landscape architecture was lining Jayhawk Boulevard, the University's main street, with elm trees in 1925. But Mrs. Malott and her allies were mainly responsible for making the campus truly lovely. They induced more townspeople than ever to donate plantings; they secured twelve hundred flowering crab trees from the class of 1945 and money for flowers and trees in front of Lindley Hall from the class of 1947; they summoned the superintendent of buildings and grounds and his crews to heroic efforts. By 1951 there were flowering and shade trees, flowers, and flowering shrubs everywhere: crab, redbud, plum, forsythia, and innumerable other varieties. In the spring especially, before the summer's heat and drying winds, the campus was incredibly pretty, and one had difficulty believing that the former Hogback Ridge had once been as unattractive as its name.[27]

Starting on May 27, 1951, Mount Oread—and half of Lawrence—had a treat for the ear as well as the eye, for then the University's new carillon rang out for the first time. The fifty-three-bell Campanile, 120 feet high, and the Memorial Drive, north of Strong Hall, on which it stood, were the University's memorial to the 276 students and alumni who died in the Second World War. From 1945 to 1951 over eight thousand people had contributed about $343,000 to the new University of Kansas Memorial Association for the projects—though the legislature of 1951 had to appropriate $56,000 to finish the drive. The Campanile was a new departure in the University's history. It was the first structure that was purely a luxury, the first built merely to please people rather than to meet some pressing want. Replying in 1946 to a suggestion that a fieldhouse would be a suitable memorial, Malott said it would be entirely inappropriate. "The Stadium was built as a World War I memorial. No one thinks as he sits in it, about the sacrifice of several score of young men of this institution who lost their lives in that struggle. We have been determined this time that we would have a memorial that would be truly a memorial, and not merely use that as an excuse to fill a need at the University." There were scoffers aplenty among the townspeople and alumni, so little were they used to ornaments on the Hill, but the beauty of the frequent carillon recitals in the years ahead won many of them over.[28]

While the University's appearance was changing, a minority of faculty members were seeking, without notable success, to make changes in its structure, especially in the powers and vigor of the Senate. After the long debate on the University Survey Committee's report in the 1930s, and under the pressures of the Second World War, much of the Senate's strength was spent. A committee to reappraise its functions, appointed in January, 1940, never reported; in 1947 Malott correctly said that although the body did a considerable amount of work through committees, it was "not very aggressive as to meetings, meeting four or five times a year."[29]

The reason, of course, was that it had so little of significance to do, and that fact rankled many members of the local chapter of the American Association of University Professors, which itself had been something less than energetic since its organization in 1915. After almost two years of discussion, in February, 1949, the chapter passed and sent to the Senate an amended report from a committee on faculty participation in University government designed to give the Senate the "proper vitality" it so conspicuously lacked and rescue it from its "languishing state." There were three main proposals. First, the Senate Advisory Committee should "be regarded as having the duty of being aware of, and of considering, and of calling to the attention of the Senate for the purpose of further discussion, *all* such current major problems of policy as affect the University as a whole." Second, to restore some of the status the Senate had under the Constitution of 1915, it should be empowered to "consult and recommend on matters of general policy with regard to university schools and divisions, bureaus, museums, and publications," to establish policy "in regard to faculty personnel standards," and through an appropriate committee to "advise in the University budget-making process, and to review the university budget before submission to the Board of Regents." Third, to facilitate discussion and action, the Senate itself was to be reduced to the chancellor, two deans chosen by him, and forty-five "non-administrative" members of a new University Assembly composed of all faculty members and administrators.[30]

Partly because the AAUP members apparently were unwilling to support those proposals before the Senate,[31] they were rapidly rejected. At a meeting in November, 1949, the Advisory Committee presented the AAUP report without recommendations. The Senate thereupon approved the first part, though without the word *"all."* But then College Dean Lawson, a member of the minority, moved that the recommendation be referred to the Senate Advisory Committee for clarification. When Advisory Committee chairman Edwin O. Stene said that such a motion, being equivalent to a reconsideration, had to come from the majority, Chancellor Malott then "requested"—read "ordered"—the Committee to clarify it and report back. Then the Senate defeated the second part of the report, immediately after which it was sent back to the Advisory Committee for clarification; and the Committee also chose to reconsider the third.[32]

Since the Advisory Committee[33] was at the same time codifying the Senate's rules and regulations, it emasculated the first AAUP recommendation by putting under the Senate's advisory functions "the establishment or abolition of schools, divisions, and departments within the University and the institution of general policies regarding the operation of schools, divisions, and departments." The even more timorous Senate cut out everything after the word "University." The Advisory Committee listed as another advisory function "establishment or modification of general policy regarding standards to be applied in the selection of any faculty personnel and in the advancement or promotion of faculty personnel," but the Senate refused to approve it. No recommendation about a smaller, reconstituted Senate came from the Committee, except that the Senate consider it. After a "lively discussion" at the May meeting, the Senate voted its sense to be that "at the present time . . . there be no reorganization of its membership."[34] These decisions practically guaranteed that the senators' future meetings would be as spiritless as ever.

Chancellor Malott, however, would not have to attend many more of them. To the sorrow of the Board of Regents and many faculty members,[35] early in 1951 he decided to accept an invitation to become president of Cornell University. Knowing that the University of Kansas was at a most critical point in its development, the regents appointed both faculty-administration and alumni committees to confer with them, sifted recommendations with exceptional care, and on June 26 unanimously made a choice that was as sensible as it was foreordained: Dean Franklin D. Murphy of the Medical Center. Murphy was then only thirty-five. But as dean since 1948 he had been a marvel: an excellent administrator, a superb publicist and lobbyist with both private donors and the legislature, a man of high intellectual and cultural standards who was both a creator and an eager recipient of new ideas. Already he had won a widening national reputation for himself, and national reputation was something the University could always use more of in its chief executive.[36]

Malott left with an unusual testimonial from the Board of Regents—one as true as it was warm. The Malott years, the regents said, were "strenuous years . . . and the problems were complex. Chancellor Malott met every challenge. His was a wise guidance and able administration. . . . A truly wonderful contribution was given the University and the State by both Chancellor and Mrs. Malott. They just seemed to 'fit in.'" It was natural that Malott become a "spokesman for Kansas," the regents thought. "Over the entire area he stressed the Kansas ideals in the Kansas language. His leadership was sound. . . . Regret because of his leaving is eased as he administered in such a constructive way that during the years to come, the youth of Kansas will benefit as a result of his planning and carrying through."[37]

If *Time* magazine proved correct, Franklin D. Murphy would do even more. After praising his accomplishments as Medical Center dean, *Time* asserted, "In the last twelve years, K.U. has begun to climb from its place as a solid but unspectacular state university. Under Chancellor Murphy, it hopes to climb even faster."[38]

27

Crises at the Crossroads.

$\mathcal{F}$IVE years after Franklin Murphy became chancellor he was convinced that the University had reached the crossroads of its development. In November, 1956, he attended meetings of the Ford Foundation, the Carnegie Corporation, and the American Council on Education; he was a director of all three. Immediately on his return to Lawrence he wrote to Chairman Oscar Stauffer of the Board of Regents to say that a crisis was upon Kansas higher education. For in talking with other leaders he had learned that all the more prestigious schools were forging ahead at a great rate. "From California to the east coast and from north to south," he said, "I heard evidence that state after state has either already or will shortly substantially increase the support of their state university and/or land-grant colleges. . . ." It was absolutely necessary that Kansas gain an ever greater momentum of growth in salaries, buildings, equipment, books, and number of faculty, and, more important, continue the improvement in quality that larger resources made possible. Convinced that the University was "poised on what could be the most remarkable qualitative growth" in its history, Murphy urged the regents to do their utmost to wrest more money from the legislature. Too little money would mean that it

will fall by the wayside in the running, and what could very easily be a really glorious future for us could turn into ashes quicker than anyone realizes.

517

This is a crossroads—it is a crisis—and lack of vision, shortsightedness, political in-fighting, at the expense of adequate investment in higher education could be devastating.[1]

In offering the idea of crisis at the crossroads, Chancellor Murphy was making a thoroughly familiar—almost trite—appeal. But this time he was entirely correct. The University of the mid-1950s *was* at the crossroads; it *was* an institution in crisis. He had put the idea in a contemporary context. When put in a historical context, the crisis of the 1950s was an end of the century-old hope that Kansas would become the equal of the nation's finest and most famous schools. There was a turning-point in the 1950s—although there is no way to fix its exact date—when realistic observers knew once and for all that the University would never catch up with the institutions ahead of it in the race for quality, wealth, and renown, that the best that it could do was continue to improve itself. An ever better university it was and would be. It offered most of its students a fine education; it had on its faculty scholars of national and international repute; its physical facilities, especially its library, became increasingly adequate to its needs. Under Murphy's leadership the University of the 1950s became a far more stimulating place than ever before.

That, however, was just the trouble. Murphy and his colleagues enlarged Malott's great effort to make up for the lost time of the Second World War, the depression of the thirties and twenties, the dislocations and disappointments of the teens. Yet everything together—the University's greater prosperity, its improving quality, its growing prestige—pointed up the fact that neither the citizens of Kansas nor their legislators were willing to make the sacrifices necessary to convert the University from good to great. The institution shared as it should in the state's relative prosperity of the 1950s, but there was no great leap forward, no sudden or massive increase in faculty salaries, no great building boom. Progress was there, in other words, but like the University itself it was unspectacular.

All of which was a great disappointment to Chancellor Murphy, who to that time was the University's liveliest and most provocative —though not always best-loved—chief executive. Like his predecessors Murphy believed that the right kind of education was the most important part of the solution to the problems then plaguing mankind. And the most important problem, he said in his inaugural address in 1951, was to make sure amid the difficulties and dangers of the 1950s that man continued his progress toward higher civilization. Following the "dramatic curve" of man's ascent through recorded history, Murphy remarked, "we cannot but be filled with a sense of wonder at the magnitude of his endeavor and success. At the same time we must feel the heavy obligation this record imposes on us. Have we the skill, the imagination, and the fortitude to carry our fair share? Will our generation be recorded as one which slipped and fell, thereby setting back mankind's time table for a century or two?"

Murphy was determined that Kansas would not let mankind down. To prepare its students he would make his University a cornucopia of all good things. Realizing that intellectual growth without moral growth could produce great evil, he insisted that the school honor the ideals of Kansas's founding fathers and mothers. "The courageous men and women who founded our state," he claimed, repeating the old myth, "were moved to do so as much by moral principle as by economic opportunity"; they "infused into this actual heart of America a burning appreciation of the dignity of man." Murphy intended that the University express their idea that "no intellectual effort, however advanced it may be, can have purpose without moral and spiritual direction."

It would express that idea, moreover, within an environment of democratic freedom. In 1951 many Americans were excited by the unproven assertions of Senator Joseph R. McCarthy of Wisconsin and other demagogues that Communists or Communist sympathizers filled the national government and many universities. Their techniques were slander, innuendo, guilt by association, character assassination generally. In 1949 concern about communism in Kansas had impelled the legislature to pass a law forbidding the teaching or advocacy of the "duty, necessity, desirability or propriety of overthrowing or destroying any government in the United States by force or violence." Every public officer and employee had to sign an oath that he did not advocate such ideas or belong to any party or organization that advocated such ideas and that during his tenure he would not perform the objectionable acts. Refusal to sign the oath subjected officers and employees to immediate dismissal. Like

Malott before him Murphy accepted the oath, but warned off potential anticommunist investigators. The people of Kansas, he said,
had always "accepted and lived the dictum 'the truth shall set you
free.'" Their University must continue to practice as well as to
preach the doctrine of freedom of expression without fear of re-
prisal. "Would it not be a ghastly irony if in the process of defending ourselves against a force which denies all personal freedom, we
lost our own?" Yet Mount Oread was to be no home for communism. Arguing that men could not allow "freedom to be murdered in
the name of freedom," Murphy pledged that "any influence which
has as its avowed purpose the ultimate elimination of the personal
rights of individual people must and will be rooted out with dispatch and vigor."[2]

The world was not as Chancellor Murphy would have it, and
through the University's work he hoped to change it. "What are
the realities of 1951?" he asked. "We see a world made so small by
man's ingenuity that we are the near neighbors of all the peoples of
the globe, millions of whom are chronically hungry and ill, in spite
of untold natural wealth under their feet and who are therefore
fair game for the Communist with his glittering lies." Despite two
world wars in less than thirty years the planet was as far as ever
from a durable peace. Upon the American people had fallen the
"leadership of the free world, attended by unavoidable responsibilities"—but the Americans were still far more interested in material
things and less interested in exercising their leadership than they
should be, and too many Americans were asking the government to
do for them what they should be doing for themselves. To reduce
such moral flabbiness, the Chancellor proposed that the University
"guarantee as nearly as possible that students in all curricular fields
have, in addition to sound technical knowledge, a broad understanding of the outstanding problems faced by the world of today,"
that it make its graduates "interested citizens first, masters of their
chosen specialty next," and that it build their character and develop
both their spirit of self-reliance and their feelings of social responsibility.[3]

But the University, of course, should do more for society than
merely educate students. Faculty research, Murphy pointed out,
was indispensable to human welfare. Research scientists, for example—often called dreamy or impractical—had written the "drama of

the atom" and were now the "designers of instruments of the utmost practicality and of unbelievable potential for the health and welfare of mankind. Stop research, and the kind of human progress known to us all will die." He then praised the legislature of 1951 and the "forward-looking people of Kansas" for creating the General Research Fund. Another of the University's responsibilities was "making available numerous direct services to the state," such as those of the Geological Survey, the Bureaus of Business and Governmental Research, University Extension, and the Medical Center. They and others "almost daily contribute to the development of the physical, cultural and human resources of Kansas." Within the "limits set by its budget" the University would extend and increase them "vigorously." In rendering such services, the Chancellor said, the institution was merely repaying the people of Kansas for their support.[4]

At every opportunity during the next nine years Murphy preached that gospel. The nation's educational system, he told an audience at Bethany College in Lindsborg, Kansas, in 1953, had to relate to people's present needs and problems, which were global in their importance and their relations. Technical or professional training was never enough, for educators had to prepare youths to deal with "ideas as well as things." A concern for the liberal arts "must become paramount in our educational pattern." And the "material loaf," he added, "must be leavened with the yeast of spirituality." "The staggering fact slowly begins to emerge," he said three years later, "that we are all the near neighbors of each other— that science is forcing us to look on this globe and its inhabitants as a unity, and that in spite of cultural and physical differences we must all live together or perish in violence." In 1958 he answered protests against the University's growing emphasis on research by asserting that mankind's peace, happiness, and freedom all depended on the discovery of new knowledge. "It is ironic," he wrote Editor Whitley Austin of the Salina *Journal*—who would shortly become a regent—"that in the middle of the 20th Century and the greatest scientific revolution the world has ever seen, one must still devote a substantial amount of time in defending the needs for the highest quality of higher education and research." Every "objective and thoughtful observer" that Murphy knew or read had stated "beyond question that our economic future, our national security, our life expectancy—indeed every phase of our personal and collective destiny is tied up in research more than any other phase of human activity today."⁵

Murphy also worried about the place of the Great Plains states in the nation. Though always more a nationalist or internationalist than a regionalist, he knew—along with many other Great Plainsmen—that the states of the farther Middle West suffered in comparisons of several different kinds with the states of the East. In manpower, he told a conference on higher education in the Great Plains in 1956, the Middle West had been an "export area," sending its youthful scientists, engineers, and creative artists—intellectually excited, alive with new ideas and plans—to the "older, more established parts of the nation. This, of course, has been good," he said. "It has guaranteed that the blue has received a continuous infusion of red blood, and I have always accepted the validity of this." Yet if the Great Plains states wished to win "prominence in the twentieth century," they could not allow the drain to continue. For the twentieth century belonged to *"that area, that state, and that nation, which invests the most in the intellectual equipment to produce trained and educated people. . . ."* While the Great Plains public universities could produce men of brains in sufficient numbers, their states could not keep them unless they made themselves more attractive by expanding the area's cultural horizons and opportunities. "Music, literature, the history of our development, man's capacity to describe his environment with a brush or chisel, the collecting and utilization of basic books and manuscripts which describe man's intellectual and cultural achievements—such matters are central to this necessary and continuing cultural expansion." To be sure, there already existed fine art galleries, libraries, and symphony orchestras. But there was much more to be done in encouraging cultural activities, and it was up to the universities to do most of it.⁶

On the whole, Murphy found the regents of the 1950s moderately sympathetic with his desires for a better and more prosperous institution. It was, of course, necessary to prod them from time to time, as the letter to Oscar Stauffer showed, for they were thorough realists who knew that the legislature would permit no quantum jump forward and so never suggested it. When Murphy became chancellor in 1951, the Board consisted of Lester McCoy of Garden City, Walter Fees of Iola, Mrs. Elizabeth Haughey of Concordia, Arthur W. Hershberger of Wichita, Willis N. Kelly of Hutchinson,

Drew McLaughlin of Paola, Grover Poole of Manhattan, Dr. LaVerne B. Spake of Kansas City, and Oscar Stauffer of Topeka. That Board held together through December, 1954, and Murphy was generally pleased with it. Before the terms of Spake, Poole, and McLaughlin ended that year, he and President James A. McCain of the College of Agriculture tried to persuade outgoing Governor Edward F. Arn to reappoint them. The two men said they were "entirely satisfied" with the present Board. Arn, however, was not. His new appointees were a banker, a farmer-banker, and a politician-newspaper editor. Ray Evans, of Fairway, Kansas, was a University alumnus (1947), a former All-American football hero, and a vice-president of the Traders National Bank of Kansas City, Missouri. He would later become both president of the bank and chairman of the Board of Regents. Lawrence D. Morgan of Sherman County, a College of Agriculture alumnus, had been a ranch operator since 1940, and in 1953 had become vice-president of the Goodland State Bank. The politician-editor was McDill Boyd of Phillipsburg, editor of the Phillipsburg *Review* and publisher of several western Kansas newspapers. He had attended the College of Agriculture from 1928 to 1930, when the depression forced him to return home. In 1952 he had been state campaign director for both Dwight D. Eisenhower and Governor Arn; the next year he became Arn's executive and administrative assistant. Evans and Boyd were Republicans, Morgan a Democrat.[7]

Arn's appointments were the start of a general reorganization of the Board. When Murphy resigned in 1960, none of the regents of 1951 was left. On January 1, 1956, Clement H. Hall of Coffeyville succeeded Willis N. Kelly. Hall was a lawyer, a graduate of the University Law School in 1933, and a second cousin of Governor Fred Hall, who appointed him. When Walter Fees and Lester McCoy left the Board a year later, Harry Valentine and Claude C. Bradney, both Republicans, took their places. Valentine was a member of the University's class of 1936, editor of the Clay Center *Dispatch*, and a participant in numerous political and civic affairs. Bradney, of Columbus, had attended the College of Emporia, and was president of the Columbus Ice Company and public relations representative for the Spencer Chemical Company. He had served in the state Senate from 1929 to 1941.[8]

The next year three more oldtimers left: Stauffer, Hershberger,

and Mrs. Haughey. Appointing their successors was George Docking of Lawrence, the state's first Democratic governor since Walter
A. Huxman's term ended in 1939. Stauffer's replacement was
another Republican newspaper editor, Whitley Austin, who had
attended Emporia State College but had graduated from the University of Wisconsin. Taking the places of Hershberger and Mrs.
Haughey, both Democrats, were two more of the party faithful,
George B. Collins of Wichita and Russel R. Rust of Topeka. Collins was a Georgetown University Law School alumnus, the senior
member of a large Wichita law firm, and a man of national prominence through his cochairmanship of the National Conference of
Christians and Jews. Rust was a Topeka insurance executive who
had formerly been a state representative. The last two changes before Murphy left were the substitutions in 1959 of Charles V. Kincaid of Independence and Leon Roulier of Colby for McDill Boyd
and Lawrence D. Morgan. Kincaid, a Republican, had been state
business manager under Governor Andrew F. Schoeppel; he was
now in the war surplus property business. Roulier, a Democrat, was
a lawyer—his degree had come from the University of Nebraska—
who was past president of the Northwest Kansas Bar Association.[9]
By 1960, then, with new appointments and reappointments the
Board's five Republicans were Evans, Austin, Bradney, Valentine,
and Kincaid; its Democrats, Collins, Hall, Roulier, and Rust.

Along with Chancellor Murphy the regents of the 1950s wit-
nessed the end of one of the most important ideas in the University's
history: that, with enlightenment, Kansas citizens and their legislators would so much desire a great state university that they would
tax themselves to build it. Murphy, with the regents' approval,
began saying more frankly and more often than anyone before him
that as long as the University had to rely on the people and the
legislature, it would never become great. Because they would never
give the school enough, more private gifts were necessary.

At the end of April, 1953, officers of the Alumni and Endowment associations joined to establish the Greater University Fund
as an inducement and a means for enlarged private philanthropy.
Murphy explained the new fund-raising campaign to the alumni by
saying that although the legislature, "by tradition and by law, is
committed to provide the core of our financial support" and had
appropriated in a "most generous and enthusiastic way," it could

never do enough. "If . . . we are to do those special things that add uniqueness and distinction to high quality, we must turn to the host of friends and alumni of the University. Through them can be provided those things which traditionally are not the responsibility of the state, but without which a truly distinguished educational institution cannot exist." In the "essential search for library excellence," said an Endowment Association pamphlet in 1959, applying private giving to a specific area, "private support is of basic importance—private support by way of gifts or bequests of book collections or of funds with which to acquire books. The State of Kansas generously provides the basic budget with which to staff and operate the University Libraries as well as funds for purchasing the 'bread and butter' books of normal development. Private support alone, however, can provide the added stimulus that means excellence and distinction, over and beyond normal and routine operation." Private giving by the alumni, Murphy said in his last biennial report in 1960, would be a "crucial factor in the ultimate development of the University of Kansas."[10]

The creation of the Greater University Fund in 1953 was the start of a growing campaign for private gifts which came to a climax in 1966—the University's centennial year—with the start of a drive for some $18,400,000 for buildings, endowed chairs, research funds, and other necessities of distinction. From the start the campaign paid off. In the Greater University Fund's first year it took in about $42,000 from some sixteen hundred alumni and friends; the sum rose each year until by 1960 almost six thousand people gave a total of $243,000. Fund directors used the money for purposes as varied as buying a casting of Frederic Remington's statue "The Bronco Buster" for the art museum, purchasing the William Butler Yeats Collection for the library, and providing scholarships for secondary-school students in the University's summer science and mathematics camp. But more important than the Fund itself were the efforts of Murphy, Alumni Association Secretary Fred Ellsworth, and Executive Committee President Maurice Breidenthal and Executive Secretary Irvin E. Youngberg of the Endowment Association, the regents, and many alumni to broaden and quicken the stream of private gifts. From 1951 to 1959 the book value of the Endowment Association's assets rose from $3,835,000 to over $8,252,000. In 1952–1953 the University received gifts of $886,000; in 1959–1960 they amounted to about $1,884,000, and in the 1960s they continued to rise. In purely intellectual terms the most important private gifts were those creating endowed professorships. The program began in June, 1958, when alumnus Roy A. Roberts, publisher of the Kansas City *Star*, gave $200,000 for two equal endowments, the income from which would be added to the salaries of the professors who occupied the endowed chairs. Roberts's dream was that the University might "take its place among the handful of select institutions of higher learning" in the country, "distinguished, not for size, but for scholarship." He hoped that his two Distinguished Professorships would start a new trend by making it possible for the University to get and keep "some of the exceptional researchers and scholars of the country." With Roberts's example and Chancellor Murphy's missionary work the University gained seven more endowed professorships in the next two years.[11]

While the Chancellor and other officers sought to enlarge private philanthropy, the faculty—especially the scientists—also went beyond the legislature for research money. Starting in 1950 with the establishment of the National Science Foundation, the federal government began pouring money into research and during the 1950s private philanthropic foundations followed suit. Murphy was delighted to see that outside money come in. He was concerned, however, about the question of classified research for the government, for he thought secrecy incompatible with the long-cherished idea of free intellectual exchange among scholars. Yet since security measures were necessary in an age of cold war, he favored segregating classified research in special laboratories, so that secrecy would not infect the entire institution. At Kansas, however, the amount of classified research was always small, and never troubled the University as a whole. From 1951 to 1960 nonlegislative research funds grew from $535,000 to over $2,400,000; here again was money that Kansas citizens and legislators would never have supplied.[12]

All the while, of course, the students and their parents continued to subsidize the school. The direction of University fees was always upward. By the 1956–1957 year the incidental (that is, tuition) fee stood at $57.50 a semester for Kansas undergraduates and graduate students and $132.50 for out-of-state undergraduates. But many legislators had been hounding the regents to increase the incidental fee to help meet increased instructional costs, and the Board at last complied. Starting in the fall of 1957, most Kansas residents would pay $70 a semester instead of $57.50; the fee for most non-resident students rose to $165. With ascending fees and ascending enrollments fee receipts grew splendidly. In fiscal 1952 student academic fees brought about $1,044,000 to the Lawrence campus and $157,000 to the Medical School; in fiscal 1960 the respective amounts were $1,959,000 and $314,000.[13]

The legislature and the public, then, could never do enough for the University. In fiscal 1960, for example, total income was about $28,343,000. About $14,903,000, or 53 percent, came from state appropriations, the rest from fees, gifts, research grants, charges at the Medical Center, and the like.[14]

Murphy and his colleagues discovered, moreover, that not all of the state's politicians were eager to have the legislature do even as much as it could. In 1956 amid a severe drought Kansas voters elected Governor George Docking of Lawrence, a Democrat. Docking was no enemy of the University in general, but he certainly did not share the Chancellor's ideas about its future growth and greatness. An unseemly public argument between the two men from 1957 to 1960 slowed the University's growth and served as a reminder that Kansans were still uncertain and divided about the institution's proper character and work.

Both the drought and the Democrat arrived at exactly the wrong time. Under Deane Malott and the regents who worked with him the University had had a remarkable growth, and Murphy—who had been responsible for much of it as Medical Center dean—hoped to accelerate it. The task proved more difficult than he had hoped it would. By the time the legislature of 1953 met, the school was pinched by the loss of federal compensatory fees brought about by the veterans' departure. From $500,000 in fiscal 1952 they dropped to $196,000 in 1953 and $100,000 in 1954. Equally troublesome, enrollments had fallen from about 10,400 in 1949–1950 to about 8,200 in 1952–1953, thus cutting fee receipts. In fiscal 1952, Murphy explained to the Senate in the fall, fees of all kinds had brought the University about $1,500,000; but he expected that by 1955 they would be producing only about $1,000,000. To compensate for the losses and make a modest advance—including an average 5 percent faculty salary increase—the request for 1953–1955 came to some $17,200,000 in regular appropriations and another $2,900,000 for buildings: equipping Malott Hall, remodeling Bailey, constructing the fine arts building. The total was about $4,865,000 more than the legislature of 1951 had bestowed. It was, Murphy told a member of the House Ways and Means Committee, an "honest, unpadded" budget.[15]

Governor Arn, State Budget Director W. G. Hamilton, and the majority of legislators, however, thought it overstuffed. With reductions of several different kinds, including salaries, the University wound up with some $16,142,000 in regular operating expenses and $2,460,000 from the Educational Building Fund; the Malott Hall appropriation, at the regents' request, was raised from $500,000 to $800,000, while the legislature trimmed the $1,500,000 requested for the fine arts structure to $700,000. The rest of the money would come later. Murphy reported to the University Senate that he was "more than satisfied" with the legislature's generosity. Happily, he said, the legislators did not feel that they had been "talked into anything," and that augured well for 1955.[16]

One of the results of that appropriation, however, boded ill for some faculty members. The average increase of 5 percent for salaries and wages sought from the 1953 legislature, and which would be sought again in 1955,[17] could not mean 5 percent increase in each individual's salary. For one thing the salaries of new faculty had to come from the amount. For another, and this the more important, Murphy, the University Budget Committee, and the regents rejected the idea of a cost-of-living or annual increase for each faculty member. The University, he explained to the faculty Senate in May, 1954, was returning to a "pre-war program of budgeting," which would probably continue unless the cost of living markedly increased. Salary increases were to be "primarily meritorious" awards for good teaching, research, and state-service work.[18] Now, there was much to be said for merit increases alone. They would encourage the faculty to greater activity of higher quality, attract better men and women to the faculty and help to keep them, and reward the teacher and state-service worker along with the researcher. Yet there was also much to be said against the policy—especially that it was horribly unfair to many faculty members hired before the Second World War who had suffered from the reductions of 1932–1933. Surely fairness demanded not only that the salaries of those older faculty members be restored to prereduction levels, but also that—assuming that money was available—they be raised to the point they might have reached had the cuts never been made. The very least that Murphy and the regents should have done was to promise those older professors a regular annual increase to make up their losses and reward their sacrifices.

Enough money was not there, however, for general increases, merit increases, and hiring new faculty at higher wages. Those professors who should have received general raises continued to subsidize the University exorbitantly. In 1953, for example, at least one full professor was getting only $4,200 a year, and an associate professor was getting $3,900. Both amounts were distressingly lower than the $5,000 paid at least one instructor. At the time the Committee on the Economic Status of the Profession of the Kansas Chapter of the American Association of University Professors reported that for full professors to maintain their salary's purchasing power for 1939–1940, and share in increased national productivity since that time, required an increase of about $1,230 over their present median salary of $6,500. The corresponding amount for associate professors, whose median salary was now $5,300, was $345; but for assistant professors the amount was $20 and for instructors $40. This meant that while the University desired to raise salaries in all ranks, the emphasis of the Malott and Murphy administrations was on the newer members rather than the older.[19]

Always believing it best to be realistically modest, the regents approved a request of $9,616,000 for general operating expenses for fiscal 1956, and asked $1,000,000 more from the Educational Building Fund. (It was generally understood that the Fund would yield that amount annually for the University until 1962.)[20] The amounts were for fiscal 1956 only, for beginning in that year, according to a recent constitutional amendment, the legislature was to meet annually. But the increase of almost $1,175,000 pleased neither incoming Governor Fred Hall nor the new state budget director, James W. Bibb, who pared about $950,000 from the requests; the most significant reduction was some $629,000 in salaries and wages on the Lawrence campus and $249,000 at the Medical Center. Taking the recommendations to heart, the legislature awarded the University about $8,869,000 for the coming fiscal year. To that the lawmakers added the $1,000,000 in building funds, $750,000 of it for the music and dramatic arts building, the rest for remodeling

Bailey Hall. In fiscal 1957, $950,000 more would be available for the fine arts structure.[21]

At the first of the new budget sessions of the legislature the following year the University found it would continue to progress slowly. It received $9,580,000 in appropriations from the general revenue fund, another $100,000 for minor building additions, and $542,000 for a library building at the Medical Center, which was close to what Hall and Bibb had recommended. Had Murphy had his way, the amount would have been $165,000 larger, but that difference was slight.[22]

After six years Chancellor Murphy could take considerable pride in the University's growth. In fiscal 1957 the school had an income of about $21,650,000, in contrast to the $13,100,000 of fiscal 1952. The median salary of full professors had risen from $4,800 in 1947–1948 to $6,500 in 1952–1953 to $8,100 in 1956–1957. Since the low of 8,235 students in the 1952–1953 academic year the student body had grown to about 10,800 in 1956–1957. In 1957 the music and dramatic arts building was completed—the regents in 1960 would name it Murphy Hall—and by that time the regents were also borrowing heavily to finance several new dormitories and apartment buildings for married students. As long as the Educational Building Fund held out, other academic buildings were certainly in the offing.[23]

But Murphy also knew better than any other man how far short of perfection the University fell. During the second half of his chancellorship many of his hopes for excellence foundered on the prejudices of Governor Docking. Their dispute fed on political, intellectual, and emotional differences. Like the chancellors before him Murphy was a Republican; unlike most of his predecessors, however, he worked for the party. After Warren W. Shaw had won a bitter primary fight for the Republican gubernatorial nomination in 1956, Murphy promised to do what he could to help the party cause in November. One way to beat the Democrats, he thought, was to remind the people of the "creative, expanding and wonderful days from 1946 to 1954 when the state of Kansas and its people moved forward more than any time in the previous fifty years. Within our limitations," Murphy promised, "we shall do our bit to see that this story is told." Making the same promise to State Senator Howard M. Immel of Iola, who had worked hard for Shaw, the

Chancellor said that Kansas Democrats had no ideas of their own about how to increase the public welfare. They could not start programs for mental health, rural health, education, or highways and turnpikes, as the Republicans had done. "They can only promise to *continue*, or at most *expand*, Republican programs. This should be put to the electorate so constantly and so frequently that they cannot forget it."[24]

After Docking defeated Shaw, Murphy reminded the Governor-elect that in the last two years the state of Maine had made great progress with a Democratic governor and a Republican legislature. The people of Kansas, he opined, were "quite completely fed up with political infighting at the expense of the continued progress of our state"; the opportunity for "creative leadership" was greater than it had been for many years. "I certainly wish you well," Murphy wrote, "and pledge whatever assistance I can provide to help you create for a bigger and better Kansas."[25]

None too happy about the fact that one of his political foes was chancellor, Docking was also unenthusiastic about Murphy's vision of the University. Early gusts warned of the blasts to come. In December, 1956, and January, 1957, Docking supported Budget Director Bibb when he pruned about $1,000,000 from the University's appropriation requests. Addressing the legislature of 1957, he called for a survey of the state's entire public educational system by "experts from outside of the state who have no vested interests" to make sure that Kansas youths received an improved education. Later in January, Docking found a provision in a law of 1949 that required his consent before state funds could be used by the faculty for out-of-state travel. After directing the regents and their employees to comply with the requirement, in March he canceled two travel requests of seven made by the Anatomy Department to allow members to attend a meeting of the American Association of Anatomists in Baltimore. Only a quarter of the travel funds would have been state money; the rest was to come from federal and foundation grants. "I hate to interfere with their management," Docking said, "but it is necessary when they can't manage themselves. This department has been so inefficient that something has to be done. It is obvious that they have some money left in the budget and they want to spend it so the Legislature won't cut their appropriation." Docking denied that he was against all travel by professors, but

said, "They've got a sacred cow there called 'education' and anything is supposed to be good." It was needless to have the University so well represented at the Baltimore meeting, he believed, and
he said that the Department would lack sufficient teachers while the
seven were gone.

University spokesmen immediately struck back. Anatomy Department members denied that the trip would leave classes understaffed. Chancellor Murphy accused the Governor of ignorance of
the needs of the intellect: "In any field you cannot keep up very
long by locking yourself in a closet." The Republican Lawrence
Journal-World warned its readers to be wary of the Governor. Every
"sensible citizen" desired economy at all levels of government, but
Docking's interference might be the start of an effort to control all
the state schools for political purposes.[26]

It was not that, however, so much as an expression of ideas of
education different from those prevalent on Mount Oread. When
the Governor thought about the nature and functions of the state
schools, he thought mainly about giving undergraduates an "education" and doing so at the lowest cost consistent with quality, with
no frills or luxuries added. In September, 1957, he told the regents
that since Kansas was facing an increasing demand for higher education at a time when state revenues had leveled off, they should
review the work of the state colleges and University. A study of the
aims of higher education, Docking thought, should answer the question " 'What do we want in education?' Is our objective the end
product—the student? How well is he prepared technically? What
kind of citizen is the graduate?" It was necessary to review "all programs . . . which do not contribute directly to on-campus education." The Board should determine, for example, "what kind and
what amount of research should be paid for by the taxpayers of
Kansas," and how much extension work they should support. Putting it another way, he asked the regents to distinguish carefully
between "those things which contribute directly to higher education and those things which though desirable may represent luxuries
which the taxpayers cannot afford." The Board especially should
reconsider its institutions' policies in the operation of museums, art
galleries, and libraries to "determine what portion, if any, the general taxpayer should pay for the accumulation of art objects which,

even though desirable, may need to be sacrificed to meet the immediate demands of our children for education."

Such ideas chilled the University's officers and faculty. Obviously extension work did not contribute to "on-campus education" —it wasn't supposed to—but to suggest that there was little or no relation between research and teaching was foolish. Even worse was the suggestion that University activities, including research, that might not contribute directly and immediately to the training of students, were illegitimate or suspect.

Asked in January, 1958, about the policy differences between himself and Murphy, Docking replied, "I want the schools run on an efficient basis. It's mainly a battle between the salesman and an auditor." With that view of himself Docking said that the regents must "simplify the curriculum, reduce its size, and raise its quality" by surveying all courses to see how many could be eliminated or consolidated "so that the maximum utilization of the faculty can be obtained." To the same end they should explore the possibilities of giving students more responsibility for their own education through independent study, relieving teachers of tasks that assistants could perform as well, "adapting different class sizes to accommodate more efficiently the various objectives in learning," and using films and other devices to bring "rare and unusual teachers" before more students. To maintain quality, Docking also suggested reviewing admissions requirements to make sure that only those capable of doing college work were allowed in—which in turn would make it possible to drop remedial courses below college level—and considering a uniform grading system at all the schools.

The Governor also urged the regents to review the schools' building programs and then went on to ask some frightening questions about salaries. Though easily answerable, they bespoke an unpleasant mood. "Is the practice of budgeting a five percent increase in pay and overhead each year realistic? Does this not result in the spread in pay growing each year both in the same school and between schools? Why is there a pay differential between the large schools which give the Ph.D. degree and the smaller state schools for those teaching jobs that deal with undergraduate students only? Should not pay be based on the amount of work and the class of work done by the individual?"[27]

At that point the Murphy-Docking match really began. Its most important arena was the newspapers. After Docking had personally urged his ideas on the regents, news of his notions circulated around the University campus, leaving consternation in its train. Murphy accused the Governor of willingness to settle for mediocrity in higher education. There were those who "evidently think Kansas can afford only a mediocre university or an 'average' or 'adequate' institution," he said. "But I maintain that Kansas cannot afford not to have the best possible state institutions. Otherwise, we will lose our outstanding young men and women to other states."[28]

As the conflict continued, both men denied that there was personal animosity involved. "We disagree completely on methods of operation," Docking said at a news conference in January, 1958. "But people who think we have personal disagreements aren't sufficiently civilized to realize persons can disagree on issues without becoming emotionally involved." Murphy said that he shared the Governor's views and hoped and believed there would be no personal disagreements in the future. But since both men were forceful, blunt, and sensitive, the argument had to get personal—if, indeed, it was not personal from the start. According to A. Lewis Oswald of Hutchinson, a Democrat who broke with Docking on several issues, the Governor was out to destroy Murphy. As Oswald reported it, when he asked the Governor why, Docking shouted, "By *** because he has snubbed me. Time and again he could have invited me to university affairs, and by *** he snubbed me." As Oswald remembered it, on the eve of a press conference in February, 1957, at which Docking would ask the state schools to release to the public their out-of-state travel expenses for the past two years Docking arrived late at a dinner party at which Oswald was also a guest. The Governor came panting into the parlor, threw down his topcoat, and exclaimed, "I am going to blow hell out of that little punk tomorrow."[29]

In the spring of 1959 Murphy told the faculty Senate that the last three years had been the "most difficult in University history." That was mere hyperbole, for earlier sufferings had been incalculably greater; but it was true that things went from bad to worse. The 1957 legislature restored about $300,000 of the $1,000,000 that Docking and Bibb had excised from the regents' requests; the University received about $10,500,000 from general revenues for fiscal 1958 and $2,177,000 for buildings for the 1957–1959 biennium.

Included in the appropriation was a salaries and wages appropriation of $5,858,000 which, raised from the $4,450,000 of the present year, would permit an average increase of 10 percent for the present staff.[30] But while both the regents and the legislature, according to Murphy, had accepted the raise "as part of a necessary and desirable trend,"[31] the Governor had not. The following January he gave the legislature the substance of the ideas he had offered the regents and emphasized his dissatisfaction with even a standard 5 percent annual increase for salaries. Pointing out that the regents had had no time to revise their requests between his comments in September and the opening of the legislature, he did so for them. In his budget he proposed that for fiscal 1959 the legislature appropriate to the Board of Regents a sum equaling 5 percent of the total salary appropriations for all the state schools in the present fiscal year. The amount would be just under $950,000. With the money the regents could review the "actual salary requirements of each department of each school" and then "transfer the amount necessary for salary increases to the salaries and wages general revenue fund appropriation account of each school." The Board should eliminate "inequalities in pay between schools and within schools" and guarantee that "adequate salaries would be paid in each of the state institutions." In the year ahead, getting ready for the 1959 legislature, the regents could prepare a budget "based on an established salary policy for the entire system of state supported higher education"—that is, one that Docking liked.[32]

Neither Murphy nor the regents were happy with this scheme, partly because the 5 percent figure was low, partly because the division of the fund by the regents was sure to cause hard feelings. Murphy was also angry because in December, 1957, the Governor had barred him and the college presidents from presenting their appropriation requests at the budget hearings. "College administrators are getting to be nothing but politicians," Docking had said. "We have to change the thinking of many of our administrators." To help them adjust to his version of reality, Docking and Bibb cut $800,000 from the regents' general request of $11,330,000; but the legislature granted $11,200,000. Some $426,000 of the Governor's reduction came from salaries in Lawrence. Although the legislature restored most of it and rejected Docking's 5 percent scheme, he and Murphy were obviously moving in different directions. Docking

had refused to recommend any appropriations from the Educational
Building Fund, but the legislature gave the University $450,000 to
continue the addition to Snow Hall and build a structure to house
a nuclear reactor.[33]

Contemplating past, present, and future in his biennial report
of 1958, Murphy grew bitter. To fail to build a great state university, he said, "would represent criminal negligence as regards the
future of our children, our state and our nation." Stressing that
median faculty salaries in every rank at Kansas were below those of
all American state universities, he argued that "if we cannot *at least
reach the national median,* or indeed climb a little above it, our
pretensions for distinction at K. U. are completely without meaning." The school also needed an adequate faculty retirement program and more building funds.

If we cannot somehow correct these growing deficiencies IMMEDIATE-
LY, it will be too late. We shall be so far behind in the building of a
first-rate staff that we simply could not catch up short of dispropor-
tionately larger expenditures five or six years from now.

Somehow those of us who believe in the mission of the University
and understand the central importance of an adequate quality and quantity of higher education for the future of our state, our nation, and above
everything else, our children, must become much more militant and
vigorous in interpreting the needs of the University and insisting that
they be resolved NOW—not lavishly but adequately.[34]

While Murphy was growing bolder, the Board of Regents was
growing more like Governor Docking. In May, 1958, the Board
issued directions for preparing requests of the 1959 legislature
which showed that the members had no intention of joining Murphy's crusade for excellence. All salary increases had to be for the
"sole purpose of increasing the quality of teaching and research in
essential subjects." There were to be no increases in order to raise
general salary averages or reward "seniority or longevity." In perfect tune with Docking's ideas of efficiency and economy the regents
reminded the institutions' heads that the Board had to approve all
new courses of study before adoption. They directed the universities at Lawrence and Manhattan (the Kansas State College of Agriculture and Applied Science became Kansas State University in
1959) to coordinate their programs "to prevent duplication and for
mutual improvement with maximum economy, so that each univer-

sity may become and remain outstanding in its historic fields." And they further ordered that "diligence shall be used in eliminating any department or course or any personnel that no longer contribute substantially to superior instruction and the prime mission of the institution."[35]

Like Governor Docking and the regents, Chancellor Murphy was delighted to scrap the idea of a fixed percentage increase each year for faculty salaries; but where they thought it would result in smaller raises, the Chancellor hoped for just the opposite. University budgetmakers, he told the regents later in 1958, had calculated a salary for each faculty member by considering the quality of his teaching and research. Raises would go as high as 25 percent, he reported, but percentages were no longer relevant. There would be increases, moreover, not only to reward outstanding research and teaching, but also to compensate the "solid average or above-average performance of large numbers of our staff, without whom there would ultimately be no quality of performance or perhaps even performance itself."

To reward past performance and compete for new men, Murphy emphasized that the University needed, for the first time in its history, a funded retirement plan, such as that sponsored by the Teachers Insurance and Annuity Association. Indeed, Murphy thought it more important than a salary increase. Until 1944 the University—along with the other state schools—had had no retirement program at all. On July 1, 1944, however, following a four-year study urged by Chancellor Malott, the regents began a policy by which staff members had to retire at age seventy, and might receive a maximum retirement salary of $2,000 a year. In no case could a man's average retirement salary exceed half of his average salary for the five years preceding his seventieth birthday. Maximum allowances could go only to faculty members who had served twenty-five years or more; those who had served between ten and twenty-five years would get proportionate allowances, while those with less than ten years' service would get nothing. In 1950 the regents increased the maximum annual benefit to $2,500, but a year later they voted to reduce their payment by the amount that retirees received from their Social Security benefits. Since practically every other state university had either the TIAA program or something like it, Murphy told the regents in 1958, and since those plans were superior in every way to what the University had, Kansas was in a "position of great disadvantage not only for getting new people, but keeping the ones we have."[36]

The regents included the retirement program in their requests to the legislature of 1959, and to it added a 10 percent increase in the salary budget, the proceeds of which were to be distributed on a merit basis only. They also asked $790,000 for buildings on the Lawrence campus and $100,000 for the Medical Center. The total was about $13,100,000. After the legislature met they added a request for $900,000 more from the general revenue fund to enlarge Wahl Hall at the Medical Center, so that all the medical students could be trained in Kansas City.[37]

If George Docking had proved difficult in the previous two years, in 1959 he was insufferable. Not only did he and his budget advisers cut requests back to about where they were in the present fiscal year, but they opposed the retirement program, opposed the building program, and insulted the University. In an extraordinary interview with a *University Daily Kansan* reporter in February, 1959, Docking charged that the school was a "trouble spot" that needed "cleaning up." For twenty years the University had allegedly "run wild," free of effective control by the people it was supposed to serve. The University administration and the Republican party, he charged, were "tied up together," and perhaps for that reason he had "encountered much opposition" from the officers. Commenting on an earlier *Kansan* article comparing University salaries unfavorably with those of other state universities, the Governor commented that he was "getting awfully tired of phony statistics." Less expectedly, he also charged that the University was failing to implant correct moral values in its students. In the fall of 1958, he contended, a group of K.U. Young Republicans had demonstrated in Leavenworth at a Democratic dinner for Senator Paul Douglas of Illinois. He accused the president of the Young Republicans of "spitting in the face of a crippled Democrat." "This is about as low as you can get," Docking complained. "The lack of discipline and human dignity as evidenced by the group of Young Republicans and the incident in Leavenworth could be the fault of the instruction. . . . What is being taught in the way of ethical concepts?"

Murphy's only public comment on the outburst was that he had the "greatest confidence in the integrity and ethical standards" of the vast majority of Kansas students at the state schools. But others flayed the Governor. His "unprovoked attack . . . on the University of Kansas," said an editorial in the Topeka *Capital*, "is, we believe, one of the most intemperate comments ever made by a Kansas chief executive. He has insulted our leading institution of higher learning. He has insulted its administrators, its faculty, its students and its alumni. . . . He questioned the 'ethical conduct' of the University while he himself was debasing his own high office." The University's All Student Council demanded that Docking apologize publicly for his "irresponsible charges," while Bill Witt, president of the class of 1959, wrote to the legislature to affirm the students' pride in the University and its faculty, condemn the Governor, and urge the lawmakers to "come to our defense and right the wrongs of unjust accusations leveled at us as a collective group."[38]

Meanwhile the legislature had been mediating between the regents' budget requests and the Governor's recommendations, which were close to the appropriations of 1958. Where the regents had asked about $13,100,000 (exclusive of money for Wahl Hall) from the general revenue fund and Docking had recommended $12,238,000, the solons granted $12,600,000 and then added $900,000 more for Wahl Hall. Although the total seemed impressive, specific appropriations meant that the legislature had bowed before Docking's will. Thus where the regents had asked for about $7,236,000 for salaries and wages in Lawrence, Docking suggested $6,585,000, and the legislature granted $6,921,000, enough for about a 5 percent average increase. For general research the legislature of 1958 had given $300,000, the standard amount since 1951. The regents now asked $400,000, Docking reduced it to $304,000, and the legislators granted just that. Hoping to make the University Senate members feel better, in April Murphy reported that many legislators seemed favorable to a new retirement program, and commented on the legislature's "friendly attitude" and on "some evidence of its desire to consider further salary increases at the next session."[39]

But real peace of mind on the Hill required George Docking's departure from the governorship. That could not come until January, 1961, at the earliest, even assuming that some Republican defeated him in 1960. In the meantime the University and the regents had to face him once again in the budget session of that year. The regents at first decided to hold the amount asked for salary increases to 5 percent, then raised it to 7; there were to be no increases in operating expenditures over fiscal 1960, except to provide for the maintenance of an enlarged physical plant. But before the legislature met, the regents had approved the first part of a new $14,550,000 building program, the projected completion date for which was 1970. It was an updating of a slightly more modest plan worked out from 1951 to 1953 by a new University Planning Council headed by former Dean of the University Ellis B. Stouffer. In all there were seventeen projects. Four were needed at once, Murphy asserted: additions to Snow Hall ($750,000), a new engineering building ($1,900,000), new boiler and oil-storage facilities ($550,000), and a great addition to Watson Library for stacks, study areas, and offices. They made a neat $5,000,000 package. The next four projects, totaling $2,900,000, also bore the "label of great urgency": they were additions to the student hospital, Lindley Hall, Malott Hall, and Dyche Museum. Looking farther ahead, Murphy saw $6,650,000 more of new and remodeled buildings: a structure for University Extension; a classroom and office building for the social science departments, most of which were still in temporary military surplus buildings behind Strong Hall; the remodeling of Haworth Hall; a building for architecture, architectural engineering, and art; the replacement or remodeling of Fraser Hall; the remodeling of Marvin and Green Halls; a new structure for Buildings and Grounds; and a new biological science research building. In October, 1959, the regents accepted the first, most urgent, part of the plan. With money now available to add on to Snow Hall, they decided to ask the legislature of 1960 for $600,000 to expand the power plant and $450,000 to begin the new engineering building, hopefully to be completed in 1963.[40]

Now, 1960 was an election year, and George Docking had no intention of going before the voters as a spendthrift. "Although money is important," he said, "there are no problems in education which ingenuity and inventiveness cannot solve." To encourage the University's officers to become more ingenious and inventive, he and Budget Director Bibb bit about $1,000,000 off the regents' request of some $14,200,000. The Board appealed over their heads to the Senate Ways and Means Committee and the legislature, which restored all but $170,000 of the bite. Taking further advantage of the legislators' good will, the regents sought and got $1,450,000 more from the general revenue fund to hasten completion of the engineering building. But Docking vetoed the bill, saying that the Educational Building Fund would "adequately" care for all needs, and House support for the regents was not great enough to override the veto.[41]

Shortly after the legislature adjourned, Governor Docking rose before a Democratic convention in Great Bend to sneer at Murphy once more. The Chancellor, he said, was "receiving a salary of $22,000, plus a free house, a free car and overseas junkets paid by the federal government." "He's in South America now," Docking went on. (Murphy was in Santiago, Chile, at a meeting of the Council on Higher Education in the American Republics, of which he was co-chairman.) "I think he is getting enough. We can get plenty of others as good for less." This was a singularly offensive remark, but by that time Murphy and his supporters were replying almost in kind. After Murphy returned in March, he defended his various trips, such as those for the Carnegie Corporation, the Kress Foundation, or the federal government's Advisory Committee on Educational Exchanges, by saying that they "possibly reflect a little credit to the state." Murphy then said that a recent editorial in Regent Whitley Austin's Salina *Journal* expressed his position "much more eloquently than I myself could." Entitled "His Jealousy Is Showing," the piece charged the Governor with envying Murphy because the "chancellor's job is a far bigger one than the governor's. And the qualifications are higher. . . . So Docking, because of a personal feud, to cover his own grievous faults as an administrator, in the hopes of gaining a few votes from the envious, makes the chancellor a target because he is successful."

Murphy had received "better offers from bigger universities," Austin claimed, but had rejected them because of his "loyalty to Kansas."[42] That loyalty, however, had its limits. On March 16, 1960, Murphy announced that he would resign the following July 1 to become chancellor of the University of California at Los Angeles. His decision was the result of both the greater opportunities of the U.C.L.A. position and his own desire to escape an increasingly unpleasant environment. U.C.L.A. was the second largest of the seven campuses of the University of California: it had seventeen thousand full-time students, another ten thousand in its evening classes, and a faculty of fifteen hundred. Both its prestige and its potential for growth and quality were considerably greater than those of Kansas. So was the chancellor's salary, by $3,000, though Murphy said that he had had far more lucrative offers. "I think this is the only other educational administration position in the country I would have seriously considered over the position I now hold," he said charitably.[43]

Friends of the University reacted predictably. Whitley Austin said Murphy's resignation was a "tremendous tragedy. He's been a tremendous inspiration to the academic standards of Kansas." A gaggle of other Republican newspaper editors agreed that the resignation was a "tragedy," a "lamentable loss," a "crying shame," a "disaster to Kansas education." "A few decades hence," wrote a maudlin *Kansan* editor,

our grandchildren will come to us and say: So you graduated in 1960? Wasn't that the year Murphy left Kansas? Well, why did he leave? And what was he really like?

"He was a good man," we will answer. "There was no better man in American education. He was intelligent, cultured, understanding—a rare man indeed. He knew what was important in this crazy world. He tried to serve his fellow citizens—but even there he butted his head against a stone wall. The state of Kansas wasn't big enough to appreciate him." . . . We will never get another man as good.

On March 18, nearly four thousand students jammed into Hoch Auditorium for a protest meeting called by James Austin of Topeka, president of the student body. Many undergraduates were in an ugly and resentful mood, and there had been talk of a mass protest march on the State Capitol. Murphy urged them to react in a mature and respectful way, whereupon the inevitable petition was circulated. The several hundred signers "deeply" regretted Murphy's decision, thinking it a "great loss not only to the University of Kansas but to all of higher education." They promised to give their "continuous support to the person chosen as his successor. Nevertheless, we feel that our University has been abused. But with help we will be able to face and overcome the handicaps which have been placed upon us."[44]

Governor Docking took the resignation more calmly. He had not expected Murphy to resign, he said, but he wished him well. "I hope this is a nice promotion for him," Docking said. "I know the Brentwood area where the University is. My wife's uncle used to live there and it is a nice place. I hope he does well. I am glad to see young men get ahead. U.C.L.A. is an enormous school." Murphy, though less jocular than the Governor, also remained calm. He left Kansas, he told the student protest meeting, with "deep feeling and regret." Yet he hoped his departure would lead to a "clearing of the atmosphere," to the elimination of "political troubles." In his last biennial report to the Board of Regents—and the public—he said that if the University was to prosper as it should, "all the people of the state of Kansas" would have to help. "There must be recreated and maintained in this state a truly educational climate. This means plainly that educators in Kansas must be given the opportunity to proceed with their difficult tasks unencumbered by extraneous and traditionally unrelated matters. Politics and education simply cannot be mixed."[45]

This had long been a slogan of the University's leaders and friends. It was, of course, not true. Politics and education had to be mixed in public institutions of learning. Most of the time in Kansas they mixed easily: that is, the politicians who had ultimate power allowed the educators, sometimes by choice, sometimes by default, large freedom to run their schools as they thought best. At other times, as in the past three years, they mixed poorly. The argument between Murphy and Docking went to illustrate two things. One was that as the University's first century was ending, there was no unanimity in Kansas about the institution's purpose, character, or value. The other was that there was no general commitment by Kansas citizens and their representatives to build a state university as splendid as its leaders thought it should be.

28

The Quest for a Liberal Education: "Changes with Us Are Made Rather Slowly"

*W*HEN Chancellors Malott and Murphy—and everyone else in the University, for that matter—sought to make the institution more responsive to the needs of the modern world, one of their more difficult problems was deciding what to do with the several curricula. Shaping the curriculum of the College of Liberal Arts and Sciences was both the University's most interesting and most important effort to give its students a proper education. Interesting, because the words "liberal arts" or "liberal education" were so vague as to generate all manner of intriguing definition and debate. Important, because the College continued to be the University's largest school—it had 2,600 of the 5,900 students in 1930–1931; 3,660 of 11,800 in 1959–1960—and because only it could have pretensions of offering an education varied and flexible enough to relate to a fast-changing world.

Variety and flexibility, however, had their limits. After the adoption of the elective-major-minor system in the 1880s, all the decisions—though not all the debates—for the next eighty years about the nature of a liberal education reflected four ideas. The first two years of college were mainly for general education, which meant taking courses from selected groups and disciplines. The last two allowed some general education, but were more for professional or pre-professional training. The students' freedom to choose their courses should be wide, but never unlimited. And those courses should be of the lecture or recitation type. While those four notions were often criticized and reexamined, they seemed to the majority of College faculty members and officers to meet every test.

When the First World War ended, College students were subject to a curriculum that had prevailed, though with changes from time to time, since 1903. During the 1920s Dean Joseph G. Brandt and many faculty members were eager both to improve that curriculum and raise the quality of the College degree. Brandt, who had his Ph.D. from Wisconsin, had joined the Kansas faculty in 1916 as assistant professor of Greek and had succeeded Olin Templin in 1921. Although his was "not the most agile mind among the faculty," as Professor William Savage Johnson said at Brandt's memorial services in 1933, and although he lacked "the grace of manner or readiness of wit that give charm to some personalities," he had enormous virtues in his integrity, tolerance, modesty, and zeal. If he did not make the deanship or the College exciting, he gave painstaking and pleasant service to both, and in the process won the respect and affection of colleagues and students—especially those with problems, for Brandt was lavish with sympathy and wisdom.[1]

The Dean and faculty found it easier to raise the level of scholarship, at least on paper, than to revise the curriculum. In the early 1920s graduation demanded only a C average in merely 90 of the required 120 hours. From 1921 to 1923, however, a committee chaired by Brandt worked on the problem and at last secured approval for requiring a C average in all work. Starting with the class of 1925 every hour of D had to be balanced by an hour of A or B. The College would cling to the C average for the rest of the University's first century.[2]

Meanwhile two other committees were puzzling over the general nature of the College and its curriculum. Neither group offered much of value. In May, 1922, a committee headed by Associate Professor of English Josephine M. Burnham suggested but slight or vague means to fulfill the goals of a "liberal" education: explaining the College more clearly to prospective students, giving freshmen a general orientation course, integrating high-school and freshman-sophomore courses more closely, and seeking truly liberal results from administering the curriculum, rather than "mechanical enumeration of credits and groups."[3]

The other committee was an elected group of nine, chaired by Brandt, created to study the College curriculum. It proved unable

546   THE UNIVERSITY OF KANSAS: *A History*

to make an effective investigation. At various points its inquiry bore on "problems of the all-University type, both on and off the campus," Brandt told Chancellor Lindley in 1924, but the members did not feel free to examine them. And since the "view point of the average faculty man" proved "sharply departmental," the committee found it hard to study particular courses "from the standpoint of the University as a whole." Brandt wanted an all-University curriculum committee to examine everything: the curriculum itself, relations with high schools, standardizing underclass work in the junior colleges with that of the University, the problems of a "senior college," and the professional graduate schools.[4]

No such group appeared, however. During the rest of the decade the only major curricular change was a new foreign language requirement applying first to freshmen entering in 1926. Before the end of the junior year they had to complete at least ten hours of one foreign language. But the requirement could be met by two units of a foreign language in high school or by one unit in high school and a five-hour College course.[5]

Only after the University Survey had begun did the College faculty give its curriculum any great attention. In November, 1933, the Senate accepted Lindley's recommendation that a committee be appointed—although the University Survey Committee already had a subcommittee investigating the curriculum—to consider emphasizing the "cleavage between the Junior College and Senior College years, viewed from the standpoints of facilitating the transition to graduate work, providing early courses better suited to student needs, and effecting economies." College Dean Paul B. Lawson, an entomologist (Ph.D., Kansas, 1919) who succeeded Brandt on his death in 1933, chaired the new committee. Before its members sent their proposals to the Senate, they tried them out on the College faculty. The results were argument, confusion, and inaction. Across the nation, the Lawson committee reported in 1934, there was growing recognition that the work of the underclass years was really the "last stage of the upper or secondary period of common schooling." Junior-senior work, by contrast, was "University work" proper —that is, specialized study mainly in a particular department or school. Because many freshmen and sophomores were neither desirous nor capable of undertaking University work, there should be a division between the two periods, marked by separate institutions, curricula, and degrees. Ideally there should be a University College embracing *all* freshmen and sophomores. But since the deans and faculties of the undergraduate professional schools disliked that idea, only the College should be divided at this time. In the first two years the University College would both prepare students for more advanced work and offer a special "cultural curriculum" leading to the Associate in Arts degree for those not wishing to continue. The present upperclass years would become the School of Arts and Sciences, conferring the B.A. and B.S. degrees. One dean—presumably Lawson—would head both schools; their faculties would be all persons actually teaching in them, together with their department heads.[6]

Opposition to those proposals was immediate and telling. A committee led by Professor John H. Nelson of English urged the creation of a special curriculum leading to the A.A. degree (it said nothing, however, about a University College or separate faculties). Although the Dean said that the "whole educational world" was moving "in the direction indicated by this proposal," and although Chancellor Lindley strongly supported the idea, too many faculty members fought it. Some believed that "perhaps the University need not concern itself with those students who cannot meet our standards," others that there would be too sharp a cleavage between the two faculties. To disarm such opponents, the Nelson committee got faculty consent to bypass the main question in favor of a discussion of what the requirements would be *if* the faculty approved it. After making decisions on mundane matters of hours and credits, required and elective courses, and the like, the faculty then skittered around the main question by referring it to the College Administrative Committee for study and recommendation. There was no recommendation, however, and the subject died.[7]

Yet these discussions did lead to a reconsideration of the College curriculum and thence to changed requirements. In March, 1935, the faculty asked Dean Lawson to choose a committee to consider the revision and simplification of existing groups of courses. Lawson made Edmund H. Hollands of Philosophy chairman and selected as its other members Nelson, now associate dean of the College, Herbert B. Hungerford of Entomology, Frederick E. Kester of Physics, and Walter E. Sandelius of Political Science. They agreed on three principles: the College requirements should serve the students, rather than "departmental interests as such"; the curriculum should offer a liberal education rather than specialization, except as specialized study could be offered as part of a liberal education; and the first two years should provide a "good fundamental general education."[8]

Those ideas, combined with faculty suggestions, led to a restructuring of the group requirements, first binding on freshmen entering in the fall of 1936. There were three main divisions of courses, each subdivided into fields. In Division I, Field A included English, speech, and journalism; Field B, foreign languages. Fields A, B, and C of Division II were respectively mathematics, physical sciences, and biological sciences. In Division III Field A was history, B was economics, political science, and sociology, and C was philosophy and psychology. There was also a Division IV, whose Field A was miscellaneous work and Field B professional work. By the end of the sophomore year students had to have at least fifteen hours in each of the first three divisions, with at least five hours in each of two fields within the division. Before graduation, students had to complete at least twenty hours in each of the first three divisions.

Above these "distribution" requirements were several others. Unless excused by special examination, students had to complete five hours of English rhetoric, either an English literature or a foreign language literature course, and at least one laboratory course in the natural sciences. Those lacking foreign language training in high school or wishing to start a new language had to take ten hours of it before the senior year, while students with one high-school unit had only five hours to take; those with two units were exempt from further study if they passed a proficiency examination. There was also a "qualifying examination in the writing of English prose," to be completed by the end of the junior year. It was the result of continuing complaints—which would persist far into the future—about the students' inability to write intelligibly after finishing the English rhetoric course. Or, as Dean Lawson said, it was an effort to "substitute scholastic attainment for grades."

The major requirements stayed about the same: not less than twenty or more than forty hours in one department, with at least twelve hours in courses closed to freshmen and sophomores. Majors could take no more than sixty hours in the distribution field which included their department, and no more than twenty-five hours in one department outside the major. Graduation demanded a C average both in the major and overall; the hour requirement was now 124, of which 4 could be in physical education.

Here was conservative progress—or was it progressive conservatism? Either way, it was well within the University's traditions. "Some might think the faculty of the College of Liberal Arts and Sciences is very conservative and unduly slow in effecting curricular changes," Dean Lawson wrote for public consumption in 1936. But the faculty seemed sluggish only because it was "tremendously concerned over the maintenance of adequate standards of scholarship, and is, therefore, not likely to commit itself to untried methods which may lower standards without a thorough investigation of these methods. . . . Consequently, changes with us are made rather slowly, but they are made, nevertheless. . . ."[9]

At the time one could only hope that the new curriculum would serve the students of the future better than its immediate predecessor had served those of the past. For while the College faculty was reconsidering its curriculum, the University Survey Committee was concluding that *all* undergraduate education in the University left much to be desired. So numerous were the curricular problems and so widespread their ramifications that the committee had decided to investigate only "major aspects" and "broad principles." But even then it was obvious that the University's curricula were poorly conceived and implemented, and that only new ways of thinking and major reforms could set things right.

Failures at Kansas, the Survey Committee thought, were part of a broader national failure to educate students properly. "Many university graduates are not really literate, as is shown by their choice of books and their inability to understand what they read. Educational institutions should be concerned with the number of students who are not only not educated, but who are not really interested in the life of the mind or in continuing their cultural development. Many cannot reason accurately. Many cannot distinguish real knowledge from sham in other fields than that in which they are themselves active or trained. Many show no enlightened devotion to the common good. For such failures in the education of the individual the university is not wholly responsible; the general cultural conditions of contemporary society are largely beyond its control. But it is responsible for the activities and interests in which it seeks to engage the lives of its students, and for any substitution of lower ends or parasitic activities which it encourages or passively permits."

The University's chief means of instruction, the committee reminded the Senate, was the individual course; and degrees depended on the acquiring of credits in them. While most faculty members were so accustomed to the course system that they seldom questioned it, many critics had called it to account. Abraham Flexner, whose book *Universities: American, English, German* appeared in 1930, was the most scathing. Offered to the student in the standard "bargain-counter" curricula was "almost every imaginable article—Latin, Greek, history, science, business, journalism, domestic arts, engineering, agriculture, military training, and a miscellaneous aggregation of topics and activities that defy general characterization." Subject to certain restrictions the student nibbled at a "confusing variety of 'courses'—four months of this, six weeks of that, so many hours of this, so many hours of that, so many points here, so many there . . . until . . . at the close of four years, he has won the number of 'credits' or 'points' that entitle him to the bachelor's degree. The sort of easy rubbish which may be counted towards an A.B. degree or the so-called combined degrees passes the limits of credibility."[10]

Although the Survey Committee admitted that the course system had its assets—it was convenient to administer and expressive of faculty members' specialized interests, and it made credits easily transferable from one institution to another—the liabilities mattered more. The University's courses were "frequently artificial, arbitrary, and difficult to equate fairly." Courses tended to become "segmental and disparate, and thus shut off comprehensive views of knowledge in interrelated fields." When organized in "fixed courses," subject matter might "outgrow its natural limits," or become "out-of-date and obsolescent." A course once established "may persist beyond its usefulness because it is somebody's hobby, or for traditional reasons." Moreover, the coordination of courses into a "well rounded program of study, except where orderly sequences are arranged in the same department," was difficult.[11]

But departmentalization itself—though probably no more common at Kansas than at other American universities—produced "undesirable results in instruction." Unworthy and undignified department rivalries played major roles in shaping curricula. "Departmental insularity" helped explain why "so many students fail to grasp the interrelated aspects of all special fields of knowledge." Because departments were largely the "outgrowth of specialization in research and scholarly pursuits," they were better adapted to the specialized studies of juniors, seniors, and graduate students than to the "exploratory studies and broad general education which, presumably, should be the primary objectives" of freshmen and sophomores.[12]

The Survey Committee knew very well that educators had been bemoaning the American university curriculum for decades. To give its analysis more than ordinary force it reported the results of a study of the class of 1932. Of the 731 freshmen entering in 1928, only 212, or 28 percent, qualified for the junior class in 1930; and 80 of them did not return. In June, 1932, only 14 percent—104 students—of the original 731 were graduated. Fifty more completed their degree requirements during the next two years. Of the original 731, 530 entered directly from high school, and but about 16 percent of them received College degrees in 1932; another 6 percent, however, took degrees in the next two years, and still another 6 percent received degrees from other schools in the University. A study of the grades of the classes of 1932, 1933, and 1934 told an equally sad tale. Junior standing required a minimum of 50 hours and 60 grade points, where A counted 3 points, B, 2; C, 1; D, 0; and F, −1. At the end of their second year about 70 percent of the sophomores in each class were *in*eligible to become juniors.[13]

That fact distressed the Survey Committee. Clearly the freshmen and sophomores profited little from the introductory courses that filled their schedules. "This means, in human terms, that the University turns out two-thirds of its incoming freshmen as failures. This process has many deleterious effects. Youth should have its successes in order to develop balanced personalities. The political effects are also undoubtedly harmful to the University; there is ample reason to believe that there is through the state a good deal of smoldering antagonism to the University and its aims which result from this situation."[14]

Neither underclassmen nor upperclassmen, moreover, received from the University the "broad general education and cultural foundation necessary for effective participation in community life and for intelligent understanding of contemporary civilization."

College freshmen and sophomores found their courses aimed primarily at preparation for advanced, specialized work in a given department rather than at a "general understanding of the field of knowledge concerned or of those fields with which it is interrelated." Juniors and seniors—many of whom, the Survey Committee believed, were poorly qualified for upperclass work—suffered because the present major system did not insure a "coherent and logical concentration of work": the courses were neither flexible enough for the students' needs nor integrated enough to provide a "comprehensive mastery of a specialized area of knowledge." And then "the general level of most courses is set to the average student. Compulsory class attendance, routine course requirements, and other external formalities are emphasized at the expense of inquisitive exploration, independence of critical judgment, and originality of ideas." In the four-year undergraduate professional schools things were worse, for they offered little more than professional training and thus militated against the attainment of a "broad basis for the interpretation of knowledge or an adequate understanding of the social organization in which the profession must function." Without being specific, the Survey Committee suggested, indeed, that some of the school's activities and interests were "not of the type properly associated with university standards." If a professional school had dominant purposes that made it "function independently along narrow lines tangential to or at cross purposes with the fundamental objectives of the University," it would seem to be "out of harmony with the University spirit and aims, and best maintained as a wholly separate institution."[15]

Amid these problems students suffered the more from the want of an adequate guidance system. "The campus environment is one which precipitates mental and social difficulties that produce strain and crises in the lives of students." For help they had the advisers of men and women and of the several schools, along with department chairmen, and major and faculty advisers. All of them were doing their duties with the "utmost diligence and care," yet the "growing mass of scientific knowledge bearing on guidance functions and the various techniques of personal service are insufficiently brought into play. Guidance remains a residual function, handled by busy people who have other responsibilities that must come first." There was, moreover, no satisfactory mental-health or mental-hygiene program.[16]

Cheated children and "smoldering antagonism" in the state seemed to the Survey Committee to demand a wholesale "overhauling and reorganizing" of the underclass curriculum, and adjustments in the upperclass curriculum as well. But no one in the Senate of 1936–1937 was ready to confront those problems head on. The Survey Committee offered two possible plans for fundamental change of the freshman-sophomore curriculum, both of which the Senate refused to consider. The more radical plan called for the organization of the first two years of work in *all* the schools into a University College with its own dean and faculty. Its students would have two options. The first was a curriculum of a "broad general nature" leading to the Associate in Arts degree. It would be half survey or exploratory courses in the several general fields of knowledge; a quarter "tool" courses such as English composition and a foreign language; and a quarter electives. The second alternative provided that students desiring either a B.A. or a professional degree should complete the common first year, then enroll during the second as candidates for entrance into one of the "upper-division" schools—the professional schools, the College junior-senior years, or, later, the Graduate School. Although each school could set its own general prerequisites, the "central core" of all underclass curricula was to be "broad survey courses . . . to the end that every student receiving a degree from the University may have some breadth of culture and a knowledge of his natural and social environment."

The second plan reorganized only the College curricula into four divisions: physical sciences, biological sciences, social sciences, and humanities, with departments appropriately grouped. Each division would offer a survey course of not more than ten hours' credit, which would provide a "means of exploration of the field of knowledge represented by the Division, and . . . a basis for correlating and integrating for the student the knowledge of its special branches." Underclass candidates for both the A.A. and the B.A. would have to take all four survey courses, as well as several "tool" courses; in addition they would be offered a number of departmental and interdepartmental survey courses as electives.[17]

But the Senate rejected without debate both plans in favor of continued study of the curricula. A Senate Committee on Curriculum Organization would keep investigating the University-wide situation, while each school was to survey its own problems, try to solve them, and report to the Senate group. A Committee on Fields of Concentration was to study the College major system "with a view to submitting a plan for a more effective system of concentration." Independent study programs and comprehensive examinations were recommended for consideration to all the undergraduate schools. The Senate further directed that the University Health Service be given the services of a psychiatrist, and that the University create a Bureau of Guidance and personnel under a full-time, experienced guidance director to coordinate all guidance and advising.[18]

Once the Senate had disposed of the Survey Committee report, the faculty sank back into its customary torpor. After a year of observation Chancellor Malott determined that he himself would have to prod it into action. In October, 1940, he told the Senate members that they and their colleagues had to keep education "abreast of the new order in the present world," and urged them to reappraise their teaching objectives and methods. Endorsing several suggestions by Dean Lawson, he asked all departments to review their courses, and also told the senators that they should take a greater personal interest in student problems and develop closer contacts with the people of Kansas.[19]

Three years later, writing to the College faculty, Malott was far more specific. The war, he said, had brought all kinds of changes to the University: acceleration, new courses, new methods. They and the spirit of innovation that accompanied them gave liberal education "greater opportunity for reappraisal than it has had for a hundred years. . . . But the war will end," he warned, "and then what? Unless we give some thought to it, we shall go back exactly to things as they were": to "continuation by default," "substitution of habit for inquiry and debate," "vested interest and self-seeking departmental alignments," and "lack of realistic thinking in the search for solutions to present-day academic problems." Malott therefore proposed that the faculty examine critically some of their "fundamental educational policies and procedures so that the University of Kansas in the future may develop by the direct and thoughtful action of the

Faculty of today, accepting the ways of the past only after careful consideration of their present-day validity."

The goal of the liberal arts, Malott thought, was to give a "broad understanding of life and to prepare men and women with ability to meet life as individuals, as citizens, and, either in pre-professional training or in the various disciplines of the Liberal Arts curricula, as self-supporting members of our economic society." If that was so, then why was English composition the only course required of every student? Why weren't American history and American government required, for example, or personal hygiene ("a neglected study in most homes"), or human relations, family and social organization, and mathematics? Shouldn't the College be offering more general courses for nonmajors—in biology, say, or in home management? The latter was surely no more foreign to the goals of the liberal arts than courses in Editorial Practice or the American Indian. Why was there no interdepartmental major in American Life or American Civilization? Why wasn't the faculty more solicitous in seeking out and recommending to students "broad courses of social significance" in other schools? And the advising system, the process of selecting courses, needed to be made less confused, less hurried, more sensible.

More important, Malott also asked the faculty to search together for ways to improve their teaching. *"Why should this Faculty not be constantly discussing, in its meetings, the methods by which we present the subject matter of the various disciplines? I have never heard such a discussion in a faculty meeting anywhere. Can it be safely assumed that this should be left entirely to the individual teacher, or department? Is it a matter too sacred for academic freedom? . . . Can we give more attention to actually acquiring that contact with students, that subtle contact, both in class and out, which permits the teacher to inspire, to lead, to stimulate, as well as to tell?"* He offered his catechism not as a critic, so he said, but as "merely an expediter" who had a "very humble pride in this Faculty and the work which each of you are [sic] doing." The faculty should consider his questions during the year, and either affirm existing practices or adopt new ones "at least experimentally."[20]

Immediately after the College faculty received Malott's letter, its Committee on Curriculum and Program, chaired by Dean Lawson,[21] began a comprehensive survey of what the College should be

The varieties of University learning.

The oatmeal-cookie caper, Department of Home Economics, 1951.

The bare bones of Fine Arts, 1950s.

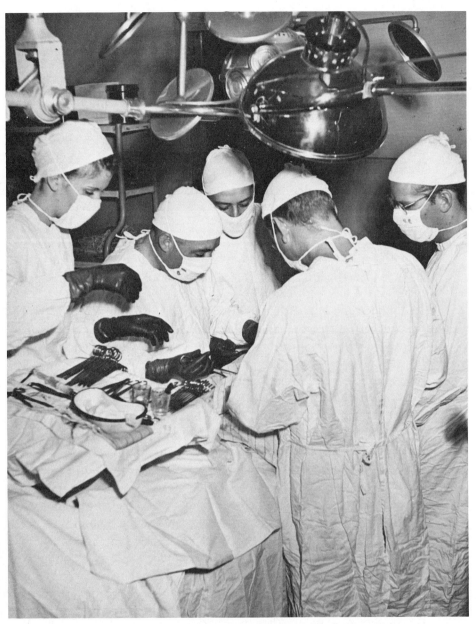

The training of a surgeon, 1950s.

doing to prepare students for lives in the postwar world. After getting suggestions from individuals and departments and studying the curricula of other colleges, the committee concluded that there was much that was good about the present program: "We are far in the vanguard of educational progress." Yet certain reforms were imperative. Throughout the American college community there was "rebellion against the elective system," as both educators and non-educators concluded that particular skills and areas of knowledge were essential to a liberal education and "intelligent citizenship." Mildly sympathetic to the criticism, the committee also believed that students in a "modern state university" had too many different interests to be served by a "too-rigid restriction of our present flexible curriculum. We do not find ourselves too enthusiastic about the combined wisdom of those who think they know just what these essential subjects are that every student must take, regardless of what kind of life he is to live or regardless of what part of the world he may live in."[22]

To keep the curriculum both rigidly flexible and flexibly rigid, the committee recommended and the faculty accepted four major underclass revisions and the creation of a new Western Civilization Program, all to start in the fall of 1945. Freshmen and sophomores would have to take ten hours of English composition and literature, and since all of them needed help in the "proper use of their voices, even in private conversation," a two-hour course in Fundamentals of Speech. Those who showed on their matriculation examinations a "serious lack of ability to handle the arithmetic of everyday life" had to take a noncredit course to get it. In line with Malott's desire that students know more about the biological sciences, they also had to pass a new three-hour general biology course and follow it with an introductory course in either botany, entomology, physiology, or zoology. All the proposals had the approval of a new Student Curricular Committee of the All Student Council.[23]

For the faculty reformers it was fortunate that the Council committee also approved the Western Civilization Program, for many faculty members did not. The proposal came originally from a special committee appointed by the Committee on Curriculum led by Walter E. Sandelius of Political Science, and including John W. Ashton of English, William Watson Davis of History, Hilden Gibson of Political Science and Sociology, R. S. Howey of Economics, and Clifford P. Osborne of Philosophy. Behind the scheme was the belief that every graduate should understand "at least the basic characteristics of the present society of which he is a part and . . . the cultural heritage of that society." The Western Civilization requirement would stress "not merely a reasonable knowledge of historical fact, but also an understanding of the significant ideas involved, and some ability, therefore, of the self-reliant student to read and to reflect on what has been read, as becomes the maturing citizens of a democracy."

Whether they wanted to or not, those maturing citizens should have to pass a comprehensive examination in Western Civilization, in most cases by the end of the sophomore year. They would prepare for it not by taking courses, but by independent reading, supplemented by general weekly lectures, attendance at which would be voluntary. The reading was to include a "fair sampling of the outstanding classics in our political, economic, and philosophical tradition together with the best of recent commentaries to make that tradition clear." Lawson's committee, however, feared that freshmen and sophomores were not ready for such responsibility, and softened the recommendation to provide for discussion groups led by senior proctors, and for a trial period of five years. When the proposal came to a vote on December 19, there occurred what one faculty member recalled as a "wordy and heated battle." Opponents argued more against the methods than the goal, asserting that the lack of a formal course contradicted in principle the English and speech requirements, that beginning students were too much academic and intellectual novices to prepare for the examination as they should, and that the examination should really be a graduation requirement. But the proposal passed. An interdepartmental committee was to administer the program. Passing the examination earned six credits for underclassmen, and four for junior and senior transfer students. Approval was for five years, after which the program would be considered for renewal.[24]

With Sandelius as chairman of the General Committee and Gibson as director of the instructional staff, the Western Civilization Program faced its first students in the fall of 1945 with a reading list whose length many of them found appalling. A knowledge of the American past and present within the context of Western Civilization, the study manual stated, would let students understand something of the mistakes of the past—especially wars and economic depressions—and foster a willingness to change outmoded ideas and institutions. So there was a text, *Civilization Past and Present*, volume II, by T. Walter Wallbank and Alastair M. Taylor; a collection of readings, the *Contemporary Civilization Source Book*, prepared for use in the college of Columbia University and containing selections running from Machiavelli to John Dewey, from Thomas More and John Calvin to Walt Whitman, Abraham Lincoln, and Franklin D. Roosevelt, and a goodly number of men in between; and seven other books, among them *The Challenge to Liberty* by Herbert Hoover, *The Pursuit of Happiness* by Herbert Agar, and Carl Becker's *How New Will the Better World Be?* A large manual with topic summaries, suggestions, and study questions completed the material.[25]

When the five-year trial period ended in 1950, the faculty heard a report from the General Committee on the program's nature, and then voted to make it a permanent requirement. Malott thought it much better than the required American history courses—filled with mere "chronological dates and facts"—adopted by many other colleges and universities. Students completing the program, he said, were better fitted for "intelligent citizenship in the nation" than they were before. It seemed good to the faculties of other schools and departments as well: in the future students in education, journalism, and chemical engineering would have to pass the examination before graduation. Although readings and administrative details changed with time, the program's character stayed the same.[26]

Other changes accompanied the major curricular reforms. Chancellor Malott never believed that the faculty was keeping up with the times,[27] but by the fall of 1947 he thought that the University was shaking itself up, the better to meet modern problems and grow toward excellence. New students were now very carefully tested to help them and their advisers; there were now reading laboratories, foreign language laboratories, and a speech clinic, and several new departments and programs in the various schools. From the ferment of rethinking would come a stiffened foreign language graduation requirement in 1948—the equivalent of ten semester hours in high school and college—and Malott's favored American Civilization program in 1949.[28]

The most significant prospective change, however, never came to pass. In May, 1948, Malott asked and got University Senate permission to appoint an eleven-member committee, with Merrill D. Clubb of English as chairman, to survey what other schools were offering in the way of a "general education" or "core curriculum" program, requiring essentially the same courses for all freshmen and sophomores. A year and a half later Clubb's group weighed in with a skeptical, irreverent, and inconclusive report. General education meant different things at different institutions, but its usual form was the "four-or-more-general-course curriculum" in which education was "handed out wrapped up in a package." Normally there were three general science courses—physical, biological, and social— and a very broad and inclusive humanities course. Clubb and his colleagues were not impressed with them. Such curricula had a "tendency toward oversimplified, indoctrinational integrations of subject-matter and an inevitable limitation to a lock-step series of works and topics to be run through." There was in them a "certain depersonalizing and de-humanizing of the learning process due to the dominance of the large formal lecture system." Curtailment of laboratory opportunities caused a "loss of what one might name almost a *tactile* sense of the materials of the sciences." A *"general-education program limited entirely to the first two years is bound to be both superficial and incomplete.* . . . One of the most serious problems of general education," the committee said, "is to restrict what at the time can in the nature of the case be no more than orientation, to a reasonable compass, *so that the student may early have time to gather solid materials for integration at the proper place,* lest the cart be eternally before the horse."

Refusing to recommend that Kansas create a general education program like those elsewhere, Clubb's committee emphasized that such education was an idea rather than a program, approved that idea, and inquired about how the University could promote it. General education was "that kind of education, or better those aspects of education, which develop students who are broadly curious and well informed in the major fields of human activity, who are normally socialized in their learning, and fully enlightened regarding the responsibilities and privileges of democratic citizenship." Its goal was a "rich and well-balanced human character over and above proficiency in individual subjects and activities." Already much was being done toward that end through the new College requirements;

through the new advanced course in general physical science, the humanities major, the coming American Civilization program, and new offerings in music and fine arts; and through support given to "general culture" and the humanities by the Engineering, Journalism, Education, Law, and Medical schools. Yet these things were "largely uncorrelated," and because of professional school and departmental segregation they influenced too few of the undergraduates.

True general education, the committee thought, would arise from a "fresher, more vibrant, more cooperative spirit among both K.U. students and K.U. teachers, rather than through a doctrinaire, made-to-order curricular system superimposed uncomfortably upon existing departments, and upon the entire undergraduate body as well." At that point the committee raised a host of possible changes for consideration—and emphasized that it recommended none of them. Among them were the four-general-course program; general science courses designed for "non-research and non-technical students"; extending the ten-hour English requirement throughout the University; supporting electives in music and art more forcefully than before; or requiring three or six hours of psychology and ethics. More broadly, the method and content of the Western Civilization Program might be extended throughout the students' eight semesters to give them twenty-four hours of "directed and self-directed study" of general education materials.

Whatever the Senate and faculty did, Clubb's committee believed they should keep several ideas in mind. The general education learning process should be "socialized" in every way possible "so that it may function outside of classes and formal study"; faculty-student barriers should be lowered and contact broadened. To promote self-education, the faculty should encourage students to audit courses, provide browsing rooms in the library and art and music rooms elsewhere, and keep students informed of lectures and concerts. But the faculty could best demonstrate the value they attached to general education by "systematically" enlarging their own "general culture," however hard it might be amid the pressures of teaching, administration, and specialized research. Time permitting, faculty members might audit or even take courses in other fields. There should be a faculty club with "adequate and comfortable meeting places," for it would encourage the faculty's "intellectual expansion" and help bring the "problems of general education to a focus."

The committee's report gave rise to considerable discussion, especially in the College, but its results for the University as a whole were slight. At its end the committee proposed that a specially appointed group study the question of general education during the ensuing year, and devise means to bring a full debate on the subject before the Senate. Had the Senate approved those recommendations, the University might have been in for exciting times. But the senators merely passed a motion asking Clubb's committee to continue its deliberations. Senate interest then petered out, and a grand opportunity for a full consideration of the nature and relations of all the University's curricula and schools slid by.[29]

During the next decade, however, there were two major innovations in the College curriculum, both the products of a new dean. Paul B. Lawson, who was scheduled to retire on July 1, 1954, died on March 30. His successor was George R. Waggoner, formerly associate dean of the College of Liberal Arts and Sciences at Indiana University. An Oklahoman, Waggoner had taken a Kansas B.A. in 1936 and an M.A. in 1939, completed work for the Ph.D. in English literature at Wisconsin in 1947, and served at Pennsylvania State College before going to Indiana. Waggoner was a happy contrast to Lawson. Lawson was the son of a Methodist missionary—he was born in Sitapur, India—and emanated both pompous piety and a certain dullness. On Sundays he served as pastor of the West Side Presbyterian Church, and he believed that students could find in Christian ethics solutions for many of their academic difficulties. On the College bulletin board appeared moralistic and Biblical messages, changed fortnightly: "Discipline is never pleasant at the time; but to those who are trained by it, it afterwards yields peace of character," for example, or, "If thou faint in the day of adversity, thy strength is small." Waggoner was neither moralistic, pompous, nor dull. Rather he was sophisticated and urbane, witty and provocative, and always interested in any idea that promised to improve liberal education.[30]

One of Waggoner's keener interests was in challenging to the maximum the College's intellectually gifted students. In the fall of 1955 the Dean gave them a new program which challenged them both quantitatively and qualitatively. A pioneer group of thirty-one Summerfield and Watkins Scholarship finalists was offered the chance to take more courses than normal, to enter upperclass courses while still freshmen and sophomores, and to enroll in honors sections of underclass courses—to seek, in short, as much intellectual stimulation as they could bear. Two years later Associate Dean Francis H. Heller pronounced the experiment a success. Members of the first group advanced rapidly, did excellent work, and even proved in their extracurricular lives that "one can be a campus leader, a socially popular individual," while carrying a heavy academic load. In 1956 and 1957 the gifted-student program was expanded: it included others than the Summerfield and Watkins finalists; more departments offered more honors sections; with a small grant from the Carnegie Corporation the College gave twenty of the best students stipends as research assistants to faculty members. All of this, Heller said, was "but a beginning in the effort to stimulate the best brains that can be brought to the Mount Oread campus." It was a double effort to produce effective leadership for the nation's future and to preserve for Kansas the "brain power of Kansas—a commodity that for many years has been considered the highest export item of the Sunflower State."[31] Unfortunately many of the gifted students went on to graduate or professional schools, and then to careers, outside the state.

Hard upon the Honors Program came a Waggoner-inspired change in the B.A. curriculum. In April, 1957, after two years' deliberations, the College Administrative Committee offered the faculty a set of exploratory suggestions to revise the distribution requirements, created mainly in 1936, and so began yet another round in the apparently endless search for the meaning and nature of a liberal education. After some two dozen faculty members had praised, questioned, and confessed themselves bemused by the proposals, the Administrative Committee took them back, clarified and sharpened them, and resubmitted them in May. After two meetings and several amendments a new clutch of requirements came forth, to apply first to students matriculating in September, 1959.[32]

Although the new program expressed the old idea of general education in the underclass years and specialized and elective education in the upper, there were notable changes. For one thing the old divisions and fields vanished. In their places appeared three areas, humanities, natural sciences and mathematics, and social sciences, each composed of "principal" courses—that is, said the 1959–1960 catalogue, courses "essential to an understanding of the conceptions and the techniques underlying the respective subject." They included such things as Introduction to the History of Art, a survey history of the United States, Main Currents of Modern Thought, offered by the Philosophy Department, General Chemistry, Introduction to Insects, and Elements of Sociology. By the end of the sophomore year students had to complete at least fourteen hours of principal courses, with at least three hours in each of the three areas. Additionally underclassmen had to take the ten hours of English composition and literature, the speech course, and at least five hours more of laboratory science principal courses. As sophomores they had to enroll in the discussion sections of the Western Civilization Program. Those lacking two years of a foreign language in high school or failing a placement examination had to take a beginning course; underclassmen who could not pass a mathematics placement examination at the level of intermediate algebra had to take an appropriate course.

For juniors and seniors the most radical change from the old curriculum was a stiffened language requirement. Ideally students were to attain "proficiency" in a foreign language, which was interpreted as a "command of the language sufficient to enable a person to live in a foreign environment without suffering unduly from a language handicap (or a comparable ability to absorb and associate concepts and ideas in one of the classical languages)." Proficiency was to be demonstrated by passing an examination. But to prevent embarrassment and get students graduated on schedule, they could be excused from the examination by completing sixteen semester hours. To broaden upperclass education, juniors and seniors had to take a fifteen-hour minor or a second major and also complete at least one course in each of four departments outside the area containing the major. The Western Civilization and English Proficiency examinations remained. Students entering in the fall of 1961 and after faced an upperclass mathematics requirement as well.[33] In the 1960s, of course, College officers and faculty members would continue to tinker with the curriculum—the most important change abolished the English Proficiency examination in 1967—but the tinkering occurred within the structure and ideas of 1957.

By such means did the faculty seek both to forward the "type of education rightly called 'liberal,' " and to lay foundations for specialized or professional training. Yet there remained a widespread feeling among the students, the administrators, and the teachers themselves that the quality of instruction was poorer than it should be. Since the 1920s there had been sporadic efforts to rate the faculty's power and prestige as teachers, but they had been informal and sometimes impolite, and thus of slight effect. In 1936, for example, the *Kansan* opened a professor-grading campaign. "Students of the University, unite!" urged the editors. "Break the ties that bind you. You have everything to gain and only grades to lose. For decades the bourgeois professors have held the bludgeon of Grades over your heads. You have been serfs in that unholy power. The grading pen has been the whip of your subjugation. Its ink has made scars on your backs. . . . Raise your thumbs to your nose in answer to the system under which you are enslaved. Retaliate in like manner and GRADE YOUR PROFESSORS!" The students were delighted to have the chance. Their favorite teacher turned out to be Junius Flagg Brown of Psychology, who scored 2.8 of a possible 3.0. Next at 2.3 came John Ise of Economics and Alfred M. Lee of Sociology. The *Kansan* editors mercifully refused to print the names of the nine faculty members who flunked, and of the many more who received low grades, but promised to notify them privately.[34]

From 1945 to 1960 students frequently graded their teachers. Now, however, they did it formally, and originally with Chancellor Malott's support. In April, 1944, a College Curriculum Committee subcommittee on the improvement of teaching urged that the faculty and administration give "sincere and careful thought" to several suggestions: more careful preparation of lectures, more frequent quizzes, smaller classes, advice to students on how to study, higher salaries generally and more specific rewards for good teaching, and the like. The following December the All Student Council decided to conduct a comprehensive survey of the faculty and their courses. Students drew up, distributed, and tallied the questionnaires, but Dean John H. Nelson of the Graduate School acted as faculty adviser. The poll came in February, 1945, and the questions were pointed enough. "Do you consider this teacher to have: A broad mastery of his subject? Ability to convey this knowledge to his students? A sympathetic appreciation of the problems and efforts of his students? A stimulating personality? None of these qualities?" ran one of them, and there was room for the students' own comments. At first the Council had planned to publish the survey's findings and to check the results against faculty salaries to see if the poorer teachers were paid more than the better. Faculty opposition killed that scheme, but the questionnaires did go to Chancellor Malott, who found them most useful. Student opinion, he discovered, corresponded closely with evaluations "which we are, of course, constantly acquiring from all sorts of sources. They afforded an opportunity for discussions which I had personally with all of those having weak ratings," and led to the "elimination of some of the ineffective members of the staff, and to promotions for others."[35]

Happily for the faculty's peace of mind this was the last time in the University's first century that student questionnaires would become officially available to their superiors. Starting in 1951 with the next survey—they continued biennially until 1959—class monitors collected the opinion sheets in class, and sealed them in envelopes. They were then stored by the registrar and returned to the faculty, still sealed, after the semester's end, when grades were in (although the questionnaires were unsigned, the students were taking no chances). The questions were mostly of the objective type. Students checked blanks from "excellent" to "very poor" on aspects of the quality of teachers and courses; they could also write in the most and least satisfactory characteristics of their instructors and what they liked and disliked most about the classes. In 1960, after some protests by both faculty and students against evaluations, and after rumors circulated that some of the sealed envelopes had been returned unsealed to faculty members, the practice ended.[36]

Meanwhile faculty members and administrators kept prodding their colleagues. In February, 1948, Malott complained to the Senate that too many faculty members gave objective examinations testing only the student's memory rather than his "power to think." A year later he told department heads that too many teachers had fallen into bad habits: using the same examinations semester after semester, giving too few examinations, coming late to class, and cutting classes without providing work for class hours. Calling on the chairmen to give "close attention to the improvement of instruction," Malott hoped that "more drastic action" than calling the faculty's attention to their faults would not be necessary. In 1951 a committee on the improvement of teaching of the local chapter of the American Association of University Professors approved the student questionnaires, and suggested that the faculty improve their examinations, try to train junior staff members in good teaching—and get the deans to help needy senior staff members—and reward good teaching with higher salaries and earlier promotions.

During the 1950s and the 1960s, however, research and publication remained the most important determinants of a faculty member's rise to affluence. To balance the research emphasis, in 1959 the senior class began offering to superior teachers its Honors for Outstanding Progressive Educators (HOPE) award of $100 and appropriate publicity, and in 1961 the University started bestowing the annual H. Bernerd Fink Award for excellence in teaching, with the prize money of $1,000 coming from Fink, a Topeka businessman.[37]

But the impact of a teacher on a student—and the impact, indeed, of the College and the University—always depended at least as much on the student as on the faculty member and the school. In 1962 Dean Waggoner reported to the College alumni the results of his poll to discover whom the graduates remembered as their finest teachers. Asked to list between three and five names, the alumni cast 6,064 votes for 1,081 faculty members from the 1890s to the 1960s. The great number of teachers suggested that the College had something—or somebody—for everyone. Along with the nominations came comments showing that while most alumni recalled their teachers fondly, others did not; if the quality of teaching arose in part from the professors' own abilities, it was also affected by the students' own characteristics. Thus Helen Fellows Wilson ('32) asserted that she was "fortunate in having some of the great teachers in every field I ever studied!" and an anonymous member of the class of 1936 claimed that he had had only one poor teacher. But an anonymous member of the class of 1938 replied that "had you asked for 'poorest' professors, I could have given you a page of names," and Reva Jean Rapp ('46) reported that "there were some teachers and courses that seemed a waste of time."[38]

Every student, in other words, had his own standards of good teaching—and those standards could change with time and graduation. Still, if statistics related to quality, by the early 1960s the University and the College were offering about as good a liberal undergraduate education as could be found in the United States. In 1961 twenty Kansas students won Woodrow Wilson fellowships for graduate study, which ranked the University sixth in the nation. At that time the University also placed its third Rhodes Scholar in three years, a record unmatched by any other state university, and Kansas students also won three of the prestigious Danforth Fellowships, the maximum number available to one institution. The victories of the next three years kept the University among the top dozen schools for receipt of Woodrow Wilson fellowships and in a class by itself for Danforth grants, and there were additional Rhodes Scholars in 1964 and 1965. Most of the award winners came out of Dean Waggoner's gifted-student program. "This University and its faculty," Chancellor W. Clarke Wescoe said with great pride in 1964, "are accumulating evidence that they can provide a superior undergraduate education—an education, indeed, that is difficult to surpass anywhere, in any kind of academic institution."[39] Although the great researcher usually received more money and other perquisites than the great teacher, the ideal of excellent teaching—confined though it was to a College curriculum as unchanging as it was changing—remained one of the school's brightest.

29

Undergraduate Professional Education

$\mathcal{E}$ACH in its own way, the undergraduate professional schools faced the same problem as the College: how to realize the ideals their officers and faculties professed. But often those schools seemed even more bedeviled than the rest of the University.

Take, for example, the School of Education. In 1915 Dean Frederick J. Kelly arrived to rescue it from two years of aimless drifting since Charles H. Johnston left for Illinois. Kelly had taken a B.A. at Nebraska in 1902 and had just received a Ph.D. from Columbia. In between he had headed state normal schools in Spearfish, South Dakota, and Emporia, Kansas. Kelly came with all the modern ideas about education as a profession, and also with a great desire to become the state's educational czar. He wished, Frank Strong told the State Board of Education, to be made the "advisory head of all the professional work in education in all the state higher institutions of learning so that the work in Education in the Normal Schools, Agricultural College and University may be correlated and unified."[1]

Unity of that sort proved impossible to get, however, and it was only a little less difficult to produce well-trained graduates. In the 1920s from 50 to 75 percent of the students who completed the requirements for state certification had had no supervised teaching experience at all, though every educator thought it desirable. The Board of Education did not demand it, but even if it had, the School could not have offered it to every graduate. The best contemporary

570

theory held that practice teaching should be done in a university laboratory or experimental school amid modern facilities and ideas, rather than in the usually stodgy public high schools. But the University laboratory was the pitiful Oread Training School, which lacked everything—space, equipment, teachers—that even a merely respectable school should have. In 1930 the pinch became acute when the Board of Education at last ruled that all candidates for certification had to have ninety clock hours of supervised practice teaching. Throughout the thirties Dean Raymond A. Schwegler pleaded for a new school. "What a hospital is to a medicine school, the training school is to a School of Education if it pretends to be more than such in name." Although Chancellor Lindley regularly endorsed the plea, he never gave the school first priority; and there were no buildings to be had from the legislature, anyway.[2]

The rest of the academic and professional training was in better shape. Until 1945 the Board of Education certified both graduates of the School of Education and graduates of other schools—except Pharmacy—who took enough education and related courses to qualify for the Teachers' Diploma. The School of Education set the requirements for both the School degree and the Teachers' Diploma, and they remained fairly constant over the years. Juniors entering the School had completed in high school and college ten to twenty hours[3] each of English, foreign languages, mathematics, biological sciences, physical sciences, and history–political science, and introductory courses in economics, sociology, psychology, speech, and American government. As education students they took from twenty-five to thirty hours of professional courses—including practice teaching when they could get it and courses in how to teach their subjects—and another twenty-five in a subject specialty: English, social sciences, physical sciences, and the like. Candidates for the Teachers' Diploma took from fifteen to twenty hours of professional education courses and completed a regular major, but they had to take in addition a minor of at least twenty hours in one of the recognized teaching fields.[4]

All the deans and faculty members knew, however, that the School's reputation depended as much on the services they rendered educators as on the certified teachers they produced. Hence there were undergraduate and graduate programs for administrators. Until 1927 the graduate degrees were the M.S. and the Ph.D.; in that year the regents approved the Master of Education degree, and a decade later the doctorate of education.[5] In 1916 the School opened a Bureau of School Service and Research to enlighten both teachers and administrators on various problems. Ten years later the Bureau began reporting many of its discoveries in the *University of Kansas Bulletin of Education*, a bimonthly that lasted until 1933 when it stopped for want of money; it revived in 1938. The *Bulletin*'s purpose was to promote "scientific education" in Kansas, which meant the adoption of every new idea and technique that would benefit the child. In the 1936–1938 biennium the School also created a curriculum laboratory in order to bring the curricula of the public schools "more nearly into harmony with current human need." In addition the faculty sponsored statewide education conferences each year, both to help educators and to increase the School's renown.[6]

As announced by Dean Schwegler in 1939, the philosophy of the School of Education was that education should prepare young people for "efficient living"—that is, for happy and fulfilling lives in a democratic society. Efficient living embraced four main goals: "radiant health"; vocational training for those who wished it; mastery of the "art of getting along with other human beings"; and making the "young learner" responsive to the "emotional values of the GOOD, the TRUE, and the BEAUTIFUL. He needs to be led to raise his eyes above the clod to the skies above," Schwegler contended, "and to discover his kinship to the cosmos of which he is a part." The School's faculty, he said—they numbered thirty-one in 1938–1939 and were teaching some 350 undergraduates—were ever alert to the latest scientific investigations and discoveries that would help to reach those objectives.[7]

Whatever the School's assets, however, Chancellor Malott thought them fewer than they should be. In 1941, upon Dean Schwegler's resignation after fifteen years, the School acquired a new dean, George Baxter Smith, who had a Columbia Ph.D. and was associate professor of education at the University of Iowa. To help him upgrade the School, late in 1944 Malott toured about seventy Kansas schools in which University graduates were teaching. On March 29, 1945, he reported his observations to the Education faculty in a whipping letter much like the one he had sent to the College faculty several months before.

"How can we attain the acknowledged leadership in the field of

education in this state?" he began. "We do not now have it. We have distinguished members on this Faculty, but we are not a distinguished school." What could be done to improve the teacher training program, its curricula, its courses, its prestige? How could the faculty guarantee that their students were *"well fitted in personality, character, and ability to become able teachers?"* Why was the faculty so neglecting the renamed (in 1941) University High School? "It is sometimes suggested that we need a new building," he said. "That to my mind places the cart before the horse. Why a new building until there is something of real significance, experimental or demonstrative, or laboratory, going on inside?" Malott also urged greater cooperation between the School and College departments, the reactivation of the sluggish Bureau of School Service, and more state-service work through Extension and teachers' institutes.[8]

Dean Smith and many of his faculty were as eager as Malott for innovation and improvement. In the next few years they made notable changes, the most important of which led to a heated dispute with the College. Starting in 1946–1947 all students seeking teacher certification had to enroll in the Education School and take its B.S. degree. As part of the new policy, moreover, Smith and his colleagues virtually closed their courses to students outside the School. College faculty members were appalled. In 1952 Dean Paul B. Lawson told Smith that the faculty of a third of the College departments, and many individuals in the rest, felt that the educators had done "everything to further the 'vested interests'" of their School without regard for "the harmony and the morale of the University faculty as a whole."[9]

That opposition meant little to either Smith or Chancellor Murphy. After the College faculty had formally asked the Senate Advisory Committee to investigate the dispute and report to the officer or group it thought best, Murphy intervened and in the process struck another blow for administrative autocracy. At a Senate meeting in May, Professor A. W. Kuchler of Geography asked about the status of the investigation. Murphy curtly replied that he had already written to the Advisory Committee to say that the matter was purely an administrative one. If after discussions "he felt that the advice of the Senate would be valuable," the Senate minutes reported, "he would ask for it." Although Dean Lawson defended the College's position, Advisory Committee Chairman Leland J. Pritchard ended discussion by saying that his group would take no further action unless the Senate so directed. Timid—as usual—before Murphy's assertiveness, the senators sat silent.[10]

Lawson continued to beg Smith to let students from other schools enroll freely in education courses, and more important, to allow concurrent registration for the B.S. in Education and a degree from another school. His pleas went for naught. Outside students continued to need Smith's approval before they could enroll in any education class, and there were no concurrent degree enrollments. And while graduates of other schools could enroll to complete the certification requirements, the catalogue discouraged them by stating, "It is probable that few such programs will be as brief as one academic year."[11]

Other significant changes came in the School's curricula and practice teaching. Starting in 1946 most education students had to fulfill the freshman-sophomore requirements of the College before admission. The minimum required number of education hours dropped from twenty-five to nineteen, including six credits for supervised teaching. Where earlier most of the academic majors and minors were in general fields including several departments— social studies, for example, rather than history—there now were majors in particular departments and disciplines. Dean Smith and his faculty also took to heart Chancellor Malott's advice to close the University High School if they could not improve it. In 1947, with the cooperation of local officials and teachers, they began sending seniors to Atchison, Topeka, and Kansas City, Kansas, for practice teaching. In the next three years schools in twelve more cities welcomed the fledgling instructors. They taught all day for six or seven weeks; in the University High School they had taught only an hour a day for a semester. In 1950 the University closed its high school forever. A year later the little building—remodeled and redecorated, but still too small and too plain—reopened as the Faculty Club.[12]

Other changes came thick and fast. In 1950 Smith announced a new Specialist in Education degree for school administrators; it required six years of university work, including one year after the master's. At the same time the School reorganized the duties of its teaching methods staff to make them more available to public schoolmen. Above all the faculty in 1950 began to coordinate its programs with a recent—and long overdue—decision of the State Board of Education to certify teachers specifically for either elementary or secondary schools. Until then the Board had certified Education graduates for both kinds. Although the School of Education had been offering correspondence and summer school classes for elementary teachers, it had no systematized curriculum for them until it devised one in 1950. And while the School was reinvigorating itself in intellectual and curricular matters, it was also preparing to occupy new and modern quarters. With Malott Hall abuilding for Chemistry, Physics, and Pharmacy, Dean Smith pleaded for Bailey Hall: "On my professional knees I am down-getting." Malott had hoped to foist off old Blake Hall on the Education School, but relented before Smith's pleas. In 1956 the remodeled Bailey was dedicated to its new uses.[13]

At the end of the First World War the School of Education was the University's only two-year professional school. It much resembled a department in the College. In 1924 the University acquired a second two-year school in the School of Business, and in 1948 still another in the School of Journalism. Both of them, too, looked more like College departments under new names than distinct schools.

The creation of the School of Business followed logically Chancellor Lindley's ideas about the modern world. Much of the modern creative intelligence—the "supreme intellectual activity of man" —he pointed out in his inaugural address in 1921, was engaged in industrial production and organization. Therefore it was very important, he thought, that the industrial world be "conquered by humanistic ideals." One way of doing so was to recognize that "commerce . . . has become a learned profession. Training for a business career, involving accounting, finance, business administration, salesmanship, advertising, levies tribute not only on all the arts and sciences which underlie the production and transportation of commodities, but also the mental and social sciences which insure fundamental satisfaction of legitimate human wants. The University aspires to train the young men of Kansas for leadership in the commerce of Kansas."[14]

Faculty members of the College Department of Economics and Commerce,[15] however, did not believe that commercial training required a separate school. The Department then had programs in banking, accounting, marketing, and insurance, as well as the regular economics major, which seemed adequate. In July, 1921, John Ise told Lindley that all Department members, past and present, opposed a school of commerce. Their reasons were probably much like Ise's own. The standards of most business schools, he thought, were "cheaper" than those of most economics departments. Good schools of commerce were costly, for they had to be staffed by successful businessmen at high salaries. Since Lawrence and Kansas had but poor facilities for studying business, moreover, the best students would go elsewhere, leaving the University with the second-raters. And the flow of graduates would undoubtedly be out of the state to Kansas City, Missouri. In all, schools of business were of little "social benefit" when compared with economics departments. "A science that devotes itself to the problem of how to get the dollar out of one man's pocket and into another's, is hardly in the same position as one which aims at the creation of new wealth."

Nevertheless Ise and his colleagues were willing to have a school of commerce if two conditions were met. One was that the Department of Economics should not be treated as a "mere appendage to the school"—its separate nature and its dignity must be retained. The more important condition was that any school established should be a first-rate institution headed by a first-rate man of "preeminent scholarship." But since Ise believed that the University lacked the money for such a school, he thought it should strengthen the business programs within the Economics Department.[16]

Although Lindley had desired a separate school in 1920, Ise's comments gave him pause. During the next two years he sought a prestigious scholar to head an expanded department rather than a separate school.[17] Finding no one, he and the Board of Administration went ahead to create a new school. They offered the deanship to Frank T. Stockton, a Johns Hopkins Ph.D. who was then dean of the College of Arts and Sciences and professor of economics at the University of South Dakota. After both Ise and Arthur J. Boynton warmly welcomed Stockton as dean and urged him to accept, he did so.[18]

During the 1920s and the 1930s the School of Business remained a disappointment to those concerned for its, and the University's, welfare. There was no money to make it first-rate, to lure prominent businessmen to Mount Oread as teachers, to construct the separate building that Stockton wanted. For the most part the School was merely an expanded economics curriculum. Entrants had to have two years of college work, including several economics courses. The curricula they found in such standard subjects as general business, finance, marketing, production, accounting, and personnel were similar to the old economics programs. Most of the specific courses were also listed in the Department. But the School could require of its students from fifty to sixty hours of professional courses, in contrast to the maximum of forty that the College allowed in one department, thus permitting, as Stockton said, a "degree of specialization not otherwise possible." Graduates received a B.S. in Business. In its second year the School began offering a Master of Business Administration.[19]

The School of Business put the Economics Department in a strange position. Financially the Department was part of the School, for the School carried its budget. A decade after the School opened, it shared twelve of its seventeen members with the Department.[20] But Stockton insisted that while the Department was the "backbone of the School of Business," it was still a "distinct organization," a "general service department" for the College and the University's other schools. "I would like to emphasize the point," he said in 1932 lest a casual observer should miss it, "that the School of Business and the Department of Economics are not identical; one is a degree-granting division while the other is an all-university teaching unit."[21]

To emphasize its separateness, swell its fame, and serve Kansas businessmen, the School engaged in extracurricular activities. Most notable were those of the Bureau of Business Research—the faculty in disguise—which reported on business problems and conditions. By 1926 the Bureau had published studies on the credit policies of Kansas retail clothiers, on employee training in Kansas department stores, and on Kansas chambers of commerce. Numerous other reports and analyses followed under the general title of *Kansas Studies in Business,* which, Stockton said in 1932, enjoyed an "excellent reputation." The Bureau also joined with state agencies to gather and analyze economic information.[22]

Whatever the School's services and assets, Chancellor Malott was at first unsympathetic to it and its dean. The divorce of business programs from the College, he thought, had led to an unhealthy increase in the number of courses and in expenses without improving teaching. Separation had actually lowered standards, Malott said in 1941, "because the Business School has aggressively attempted to attract students from the College, to set up its own rules, not always in conformity with sound practice or with existing College standards." Stockton was "interested in getting students to enroll in the Business School rather than major in economics," with the result that "the economists are dissatisfied—feel disfranchised, as it were." The School's independence also made difficult its cooperation with various College departments such as Journalism and Political Science.[23]

Eternal vigilance over the Business School seemed to be the price of excellence. When the School's faculty voted in 1941 and 1942 to give academic credit for secretarial training courses, Malott was appalled; he had opposed credit, for it cheapened the School still more.[24] When Stockton resigned in 1947, Malott thought the choice of his successor a question of "major proportions" whose implications for the University's future were great. Finding no one exactly suitable, Malott and the regents approved an interim appointment for Leonard H. Axe, professor of business law and assistant to the Chancellor. A year later the regents made his appointment permanent.[25]

Under both deans in the postwar years the School of Business expanded and improved its programs. At the war's end there were four: general business, accounting, industrial management, and secretarial; two more, in finance and marketing, were temporarily suspended. They were soon restored; the industrial management program was integrated with the School of Engineering; and curricula in supply corps (for ROTC students) and in personnel were added. In 1949 the Business School instituted a series of eight "core requirement" courses in economics for all students. Under Axe's leadership the faculty increased its emphasis on the so-called problem or case method of instruction. According to Malott, this made possible the "substitution of up-to-date materials and training" for the old lectures and textbooks and offered "experience in analyzing and thinking, so clearly needed in a day of almost universal confusion." At the same time the now listless Bureau of Business Research was reactivated, and on September 15, 1948, the School began publishing a monthly *Kansas Business Review*, which offered information on economic and business conditions in the state and went free to those requesting it.²⁶

The creation of the William Allen White School of Journalism showed that the "universal confusion" of which Malott had spoken existed on campus as well as off. White had died in 1943. As editor of the Emporia *Gazette*, pundit on world and national problems, and adviser to national leaders, he had been one of the state's chief claims to fame. Everyone—especially the faculty of the Department of Journalism—was eager to cash in on his reputation. In 1944 the regents authorized the metamorphosis of the Department into a school, though it did not open until four years later. In 1946 the William Allen White Foundation appeared. It had ex-Governor Henry J. Allen as president; a Sponsors Committee which included Herbert Hoover, Walter Lippmann, and Harvard President James B. Conant; and a General Committee on which sat, among others, *Saturday Evening Post* editor Ben Hibbs, who was an alumnus of the University (1924), Jean Hersholt, president of the Academy of Motion Picture Arts and Sciences, and Wilbur Forrest, first vice-president of the American Society of Newspaper Editors. Operating from Mount Oread, but supported by funds from the publishing, radio, and movie industries, the Foundation planned to assist the School by importing distinguished lecturers, issuing student casebooks based on actual problems in the media, and doing anything else that seemed necessary. The Foundation, Malott said at the kickoff dinner in New York on April 24, 1946, would keep alive "something of the thrift, the tolerance, the wisdom, the honesty and the energy of this great American, and of those qualities which, working in all of us, are the life-blood of what we call the American way of life."²⁷

But the new School was merely the old Department with a new name and power now to establish its own degree requirements. At the end of the Second World War the Department had two programs—advertising-business and news-editorial writing—and thirty-nine courses, most of them narrowly technical: Reporting I, Direct Mail Advertising, Advertising Campaigns, Publicizing Social Agencies, and the like. On the retirement of Leon N. Flint as chairman in 1941, Elmer F. Beth became acting chairman, and held the position for the next seven years. Although Beth and Flint, who remained a faculty member, gave their students as much professional training as possible, they continued to emphasize the importance of a liberal arts education for journalists. Students in the William Allen White School had to meet College requirements for graduation.[28]

Even so, the School's existence troubled Dean Lawson of the College. He had never cared much for the Department of Journalism anyway, for its growing number of "technical or applied courses" made it more a "semi-professional department" than part of a liberal arts curriculum. He now hoped that College students would be able to take a journalism major in the School, but receive the B.A., and lamented the tendency of all professional schools to limit their courses to their own students.

Journalism Dean Burton W. Marvin, whom the regents hired in 1948, had different ideas. A graduate of the University of Nebraska, he had taken an M.S. at Columbia in 1937, spent the next nine years on the Chicago *Daily News,* and joined the Columbia journalism faculty in 1947. Believing that journalism was as much a profession as law or medicine, Marvin opposed the enrollment of College students as majors in his field, for afterward they might try to pass as journalism graduates while lacking all the "advanced courses required to give them the rounded training necessary to prepare them for work in journalistic fields." Marvin thought, indeed, that since journalism graduates had to meet College requirements, they should receive the B.A. The news of the world, he told Malott in 1949, was "about the very fields studied in much of the liberal arts—especially the social sciences. . . . In other words, the ideal product of our School will be a specialist in applied liberal arts. He will integrate techniques and knowledge."[29]

But if granting only the B.S. was the price of keeping journalism out of the College, Marvin was glad to pay it. While willing to admit College students to many courses and even to create a journalism minor for them, he was no more disposed than Dean Smith in Education to cooperate with the College in a joint degree program. In July, 1949, Marvin, Lawson, and Malott agreed that there should be no journalism major in the College, that the Journalism School would offer only the B.S., and that the deans would jointly determine the courses that College students might take.[30] Those decisions meant that the Journalism School would remain a peculiar hybrid. As a school its requirements matched those of both the earlier department and the College itself; but those demands, now set by a separate school, were not good enough for the B.A. In size and scope, moreover, the School continued to look like a department. By 1964 it had sixteen faculty members offering forty-one courses; at commencement forty-five of its students received B.S. degrees. At the same time the Department of English in the College had forty-five members offering eighty-four undergraduate courses; fifty-six English majors received B.A.'s. The School continued to offer the news-editorial and advertising-business sequences, and to them added programs in home economics—journalism and radio-television, later radio-television-film. An interdepartmental division supervised the latter program; its requirements could be met in either the Journalism School or the College.[31]

If the University's two-year professional schools had some strange and interesting relations to the College, the four-year undergraduate schools—Engineering, Pharmacy, and Fine Arts—also offered problems for a theory of undergraduate education. Their needs and curricula raised the question of whether the University's educational goals, and the goals of the schools themselves, could be attained through programs that were narrowly conceived and narrowly implemented. The leaders of all three schools knew that their subjects had social, cultural, and ethical ramifications that needed consideration. Yet the technical demands of professional training left too little time for them.

Dean Frank O. Marvin had believed early in the twentieth century that something like an age of the engineer was dawning, in which people would recognize the engineer's peculiar ability to solve large public technical and managerial problems. His successors agreed. "This is a time of awakening to the public service character of the engineer's work," said Dean Perley F. Walker in 1921. The modern world was a scientific, material world whose great task was to improve the environment by adapting new forces to human uses. Hence the engineer's importance: "The direct trend in civilization is toward him and his point of view."[32] In 1930, with the nation sinking into the worst depression in its history, and with former engineer Herbert Hoover in the White House, Dean George C. Shaad[33] was urging the "engineering method of attack" on the country's ills. "The method can be described in a very few words: Obtain a clear conception of the result desired; learn all of the facts relative to the problem; carefully analyze these facts as determined and from them outline the work necessary to the completion of the problem, if a solution is possible; determine whether or not the solution is practical; and, finally, organize the working forces . . . to get the results." Shaad hoped that, with Hoover already using the engineering method, the voters would send more men "trained to engineering thinking" to Congress. Dean Ivan C. Crawford, Shaad's successor in 1937, accepted Shaad's definition of the method, and was equally committed to using it in government and business.[34]

To help solve social problems, engineers needed an appropriate education. In 1925 Walker told the Society for the Promotion of Engineering Education that students had to learn about "those forces which are controlling the material and social development of mankind under the modern system" so that they could interpret "engineering activities . . . in their true social significance." Chancellor Lindley, too, believed that engineers needed more than the ability to think clearly about technical problems. They had to be public spirited. "The job for the job's sake, or for mere profit, is not enough. One must see the relations of his task to the comfort and safety and service of the public. Work done with pride in service gives new power and prestige. It lifts the day's work to the level of an art—and of a religion."[35]

Now such ideas—especially when voiced by engineers—were as much efforts to increase the engineer's professional prestige as expressions of altruistic idealism. In the 1920s and 1930s engineers were still trying to convince the public that they belonged to a profession. "Engineering is a profession, not a trade," insisted a School bulletin of 1928 prepared for high-school students who were "looking forward to careers of service and distinction." Six years later Dean Shaad was warmly supporting the new Engineers' Council for Professional Development, a conference of engineering bodies formed to "enhance the professional status of the engineer" through propaganda and raising standards in engineering schools. One of the Kansas students perfectly expressed the desire for dignified professionalism which pervaded Marvin Hall. "I am an Engineer," rhapsodized R. DeWitt Jordan of the class of 1927,

> A humble worker in material things,
> An inspired builder,
> A high priest before the Altar of Progress.

My Beacon is a torch of hope
   Kindled with a faith in myself and my fellow men.
Through time eternal it has come to me, never flickering.
   May I strive to hand it on undimmed.

. . . .

I labor that other souls, yet unborn,
   May tread the earth,
Or sail the wastes of air and sea unafraid.
   Mine is the hand which sets countless wheels in motion,
Spans mighty chasms,
   Throws down the gauntlet before the elements,
I am an engineer.[36]

But the ideal of the broadly trained, public-spirited engineer was more easily voiced than realized. Chancellor Lindley thought that knowledge of "human engineering" was best gained "through study of the mental and social sciences, through history and literature." Dean Walker and his successors had other ideas. Most introductory social science courses, Walker said in 1925, were taught by younger instructors who, implicitly, could not be trusted. "In the engineering branches," however, "they meet the more mature men from whom they gain their conceptions of the engineering profession. The responsibility for guidance is thus laid upon ourselves, and there it rightly belongs." In 1940 Dean Crawford told Chancellor Malott that most faculty members thought a three-hour Principles of Sociology course desirable, but only if taught by a "mature, well-balanced individual." All courses that engineering students took outside their school, Crawford emphasized, should have "seasoned and well-balanced teachers."[37]

Until the end of the Second World War the engineering curricula made only minor concessions to the liberal arts and the social sciences. The School did continue its five-year program, which allowed students to spend a year in the College, and even encouraged it. Only a few students enrolled in it, however, which meant that formal nonengineering instruction for most students was slight. By the 1938–1939 year the civil and mechanical engineering programs allowed only five hours of nontechnical electives and the standard electrical engineering program six. The required nontechnical subjects—three or four semesters of English composition demanded of everyone, the introductory economics course asked of many—had obviously professional purposes. A student editor of the *Kansas Engineer* pointed out in 1934 that the University environment itself—the concert and lecture courses and all those library books—offered a "broader education" which was "ours for the simple taking." But there was no telling how many took.[38]

After the war, though, with Malott urging new ideas and improvement on everyone, and with national engineering leaders and societies calling for a broadened course of studies, changes came. Students in the new five-year architecture course, which began in 1947, had to take six hours of Social Sciences 15, a general survey of Western civilization. Chemical engineering students had to enroll in the discussion sections of the College Western Civilization Program. More fundamentally, starting in 1948–1949 all students except those in architecture had to complete at least eleven hours of College courses, distributed mainly among psychology, philosophy, and the social sciences. A decade later the faculty increased the requirement to thirteen hours and made it more flexible: six had to be in psychology, philosophy, or social science courses, while the rest could be in any field "such as: art, music, religion, etc."[39]

In its programs the School tried to move with the times and keep its standards high. By 1920 there were seven regular courses of study: civil, electrical, mechanical, mining, and chemical engineering, an architecture course for students showing "proficiency in architectural design," and one in architectural engineering for students "best fitted for construction." There was also an engineering and administrative science program with industrial engineering and transportation-construction options. With various interior changes—in 1924–1925, for example, an aeronautical engineering program was introduced into the mechanical engineering curriculum—these remained the School's offerings until the late 1930s.[40]

Unfortunately the School found it hard to maintain quality. Late in 1936 a committee of the Engineers' Council for Professional Development, which surveyed the School as part of a national accreditation program, found its administration poor, its limited resources overextended, its laboratory facilities in several fields inadequate, and its salary scale discouragingly low, even compared with those of schools of equal quality. There was too little coordination among the programs; too little thought had been given to course sequences; the "present small staff" offered too many courses; and there were too many specialized program options. But the School's most urgent need was a "competent dean vested with authority commensurate with his responsibility," for George C. Shaad had died the previous summer.[41]

At first Chancellor Lindley had thought of elevating a Kansas faculty member to the deanship, but talks with alumni and other engineers changed his mind. "No one is outstanding," he decided, "and there is divided opinion in the faculty as to these men." Among the E.C.P.D. investigators, however, had been Dean Ivan C. Crawford of the College of Engineering at the University of Idaho. He had much impressed the Kansas faculty and proved agreeable to accepting the job. He stayed only until 1940, when he left to head the University of Michigan Engineering School, and was succeeded by John Jay Jakosky, a Kansas B.S. (1920) in mechanical engineering, an Arizona D.Sc., and now president of his own company, International Geophysics, Inc., of Los Angeles.[42] Crawford, Jakosky, and their faculties worked hard to meet the criticisms of the accrediting agency, revamping curricula, eliminating duplications, consolidating options, vigorously pleading with the chancellor and regents for more money and equipment. The industrial engineering program vanished; a most important petroleum engineering program began in 1938–1939. After four years of steadily improving wartime service and another five of postwar expansion and modernization along with the rest of the University, Dean T. DeWitt Carr, Jakosky's successor, could report in 1950 that the E.C.P.D. had accredited nine programs, which "establishes a new record for this School."[43]

Although most engineering students concerned themselves with mundane technical problems, the School had a fine arts division as well. On the third floor of Marvin Hall the tiny Department of Architecture—it had but three faculty members, though seventy-five students, on the eve of the Second World War—worked to fulfill Dean Marvin's dream of beautifying the physical environment at the same time that the forces of nature were being mastered. The Department had begun in 1913 when Goldwin Goldsmith came to Lawrence. Formerly personal secretary to the great Stanford White of New York, Goldsmith had also been a partner in his own firm. At first at Kansas he offered only a program in architectural engineering—though he knew that architecture was "essentially a fine art," and therefore insisted that the program include both "appreciation of the esthetic nature of the subject" and "reasonable skill in expression."[44]

Starting in 1920 there were separate courses in architectural engineering and architecture. In 1922 Joseph M. Kellogg, a former Kansas student who had taken his degree at Cornell, joined the Department. A year later George M. Beal, who had just been graduated from Kansas, began a long career as a faculty member. When Goldsmith left for the University of Texas in 1928, Kellogg became chairman, and Verner F. Smith, another Kansas graduate, came as the third member. Kellogg, Beal, and Smith were a stimulating combination for the students. Kellogg's ideas were traditional; Beal was, as a former student and later colleague described him, a "radical modernist"; and Smith was more the practical builder. In the 1920s and the 1930s the Department—like its School—won no great national or international distinction. But it was noteworthy that by 1932, five years before Walter Gropius arrived at Harvard to attack the Beaux Arts traditionalism of most twentieth-century architects, Kellogg, Smith, and Beal were breaking with the tradition at Kansas.[45]

Like the University as a whole, the School of Engineering and Architecture (renamed in 1927) both improved and expanded after the Second World War. In 1944–1945 the School had fifty-two faculty members and about five hundred students, most of whom were in various navy programs. Ten years later, over eighty faculty members were teaching over sixteen hundred students. Aeronautical engineering appropriately became a full program, and from time to time others appeared: in engineering physics, geological engineering, metallurgical engineering. After years of dwelling in the increasingly cramped Marvin Hall, in 1963 the School moved into a new $1,900,000 structure to the west of Lindley.[46]

In several ways the twentieth-century development of the School of Pharmacy was much like that of the School of Engineering. So complex and technical was the subject that there was little or no room in the curriculum for anything else. "The school particularly strives," said the 1957–1958 catalogue, summing up the approach from the beginning, "to give its students such education in pharmacy and the allied sciences as will enable them to meet present and future demands of their chosen profession in an able and intelligent manner. Both the professional and the commercial sides of pharmacy are given consideration in order that students may become good businessmen as well as good pharmacists." Electives had appeared here and there in the curricula, but most of them were in the sciences. A curricular reform in 1941 restricted the nonscientific electives to a course in philosophy and one in sociology; and of the 130 hours required for the B.S. in 1957–1958, only eight were elective. Of the twenty-seven suggested courses, ten were in pharmacy and ten more were in natural sciences. Pharmacy students did have to take two semesters of English composition and literature, a speech course, and two economics courses, but all of them were intended to have professional value. Until a curricular reform took effect in the fall of 1958, the School made no important concessions to the idea that students might be something more than pharmacists.[47]

On the death of Lucius E. Sayre in 1925, L. D. Havenhill, a faculty member since 1899, became dean. He had his problems from the start. As always, the School's physical facilities were inadequate, for Pharmacy had but one classroom and one laboratory in Bailey Hall. Overcrowding, as both Sayre and Havenhill said publicly, meant poor instruction. The School also had trouble keeping students. Many left just as soon as they thought they had enough training to pass the certifying examination of the State Board of Pharmacy, which until 1934 did not require college graduation for certification. The great demand for pharmacists, Havenhill said in 1926, had forced the faculty to "use all their persuasive power to keep the students in school." Those short-term students, moreover, paid little attention to the School after they left; the faculty, in turn, paid little attention to the alumni.[48]

The obvious solution to the problem, and also to that of offering better training, was to require a longer program for all students. When Havenhill became dean, the School had programs of two, three, and four years; the first two led to the degree of pharmaceutical chemist, the last to the B.S. in Pharmacy. In 1926 Havenhill dropped the two-year program, asserting that the three-year minimum was "destined to greatly strengthen the course." The Dean also began a required weekly "Colloquy hour" at which "speakers of repute in pharmacy and related subjects" addressed the students on matters not normally covered in class. To improve alumni relations, in 1928 the School began issuing a *News Letter*.[49]

If a required three-year course was good, a required four-year course would be better. In the late twenties and early thirties there was a swing to the four-year curriculum among national leaders in pharmaceutical education; starting in the fall of 1932 only the four-year course would be recognized by the American Association of Colleges of Pharmacy. In that year Havenhill secured the regents' approval for such a course; after commencement in 1936 the School no longer offered the pharmaceutical chemist's degree. Starting June 1, 1934, moreover, a state law made graduation from a recognized pharmacy school a prerequisite for the examination to become a registered pharmacist. The University had the only such school in the state, with the result that enrollment soared from 52 in 1933–1934 to 106 in 1937–1938. Within the B.S. curriculum were three options: a commercial plan for druggists; a scientific plan for researchers, food and drug analysts, hospital pharmacists, and the like; and a premedical plan for future physicians.[50]

Despite the improvements, an inspection team from the American Council on Pharmaceutical Education reported in 1939 that the "quality of the work given is not as good as it should be because of the crowded condition. . . ."[51] To J. Allen Reese, Havenhill's successor in 1940, would go the pleasure of leading the School—with its six faculty members and 120 students—into its new laboratories and offices in Malott Hall in 1954. Reese, who would serve until 1963—in almost eighty years the School had only three deans—was a graduate and former faculty member of the Medical College of Virginia; in 1938 he had taken a Ph.D. at the University of Florida. The modern quarters and a modern outlook encouraged Reese and his faculty to introduce a new curriculum in the fall of 1958. It was a five-year program of 150 hours of which thirty might be free electives and ten had to be from a humanities-social science group. No one could take more than fifteen hours of science electives. Later the School began specifically recommending a large number of nonscientific courses, including Introduction to the History of Art, Modern French Writers, and Social Problems and American Values.[52]

More versatile than the other undergraduate professional schools was the School of Fine Arts. It not only offered professional training, but also—and more important—continued its traditions as the University's most important source of extracurricular culture. After the Board of Administration fired Dean Charles S. Skilton in 1915, the School for a time, however, proved a considerable annoyance to Chancellors Strong and Lindley. Skilton's replacement was Harold L. Butler, a fine basso who had received both a B.A. and an LL.B. from Valparaiso University in Indiana, had graduated from the Gottschalk Lyric School in Chicago in 1898, and had for the last eleven years been director of the Vocal Department at Syracuse University. He was every bit as committed and enthusiastic as Deans Skilton and Penny to strengthening and enlarging the School, and proved adept in attracting students and money. But he also proved too authoritarian for many of his faculty members, and tactless and abrupt in treating with the administration and the College faculty. From 1917 to 1919 practically open warfare raged between the College and the School of Fine Arts over whether the School would be allowed to have space in the central section of the new Administration Building. In 1917 the state architect declared Old North College unfit for human occupancy, and the School moved to a nine-room house. Both Butler and Strong had hoped to get $75,000 from the legislature of 1917 for new quarters, but the lawmakers included that amount in the $225,000 for the Administration Building and thus made a separate structure impossible. Thereupon Butler wrote and spread broadcast over the state a pamphlet stating that Fine Arts would have more than thirty classrooms and studios in the new building, which would give the University the finest Fine Arts School in the Middle West.

But many College faculty members who for years had been yearning to get out of Fraser Hall and who had no desire to dwell cheek by pianoforte with Butler and his practicing students were determined to block them. Hard upon the Dean's pamphlet came a College petition to Strong and other officials asking that Fine Arts be put in the vacated space in Fraser. Butler countered with the argument that he was mainly responsible for getting $75,000 of the total $225,000 appropriation and convinced Strong that he should have roughly a proportionate amount of space. And so on a night in the summer of 1919 with no opponents alerted to bar the way, the School moved into quarters in the basement and on the first floor. Both Strong and Butler hoped the stay would be a short one, and so had only thin partitions separating the studios. But the School would remain in Strong Hall for the next thirty-eight years.[53]

Butler, however, would remain for only the next four. Under his direction enrollments grew from 182 to 412, and the number of teachers from eleven to twenty. Starting in 1916, moreover, the faculty was put on the regular University payroll. But several of the staff liked Butler much less than Dean Skilton, and there were rumblings of intrigues. In June, 1921, Butler discovered that despite his labors his salary was not to be increased for the coming year, and he peremptorily resigned. A month later the Kansas City *Star* published a vicious attack on the School, apparently because Butler had in some way offended the *Star*'s publisher, Fred Trigg. Citing several cases of faculty members who had either resigned or been dismissed since Butler came, the *Star* charged that the School had become a "laughing stock among the musicians of the country" and that it was "not keeping pace with the University." Lindley at once began what he called a "thorough investigation . . . of Mr. Butler's standing as a musician and as an administrator," found both reasonably satisfactory, and prevailed on Butler to stay. But when the deanship at the College of Fine Arts at Syracuse was offered him in 1923, he accepted.[54]

His successor was a far more satisfactory choice. Donald M. Swarthout, a pianist, had received his training at the Balatka Musical College in Chicago and the Royal Conservatory in Leipzig, and as a pupil of Isador Philipp in Paris. Before coming to Kansas he had been for nine years associate director of music at James Millikin University in Decatur, Illinois.[55] Swarthout had both the congenial nature that Butler lacked and a remarkable genius for organization; and he surpassed all his predecessors in his desire to give the University and the state just as much music and art as they could bear. His very first year saw the formation of the Lawrence Choral Union, a five-hundred-voice, town-gown group, which presented Handel's *Messiah* in the spring of 1924; the institution of four all-musical vesper concerts, which proved enormously popular; the organization of the K.U. String Quartette and String Trio, two other immediate successes; and the inauguration of a Music Week full of concerts, recitals, and lectures. Swarthout also revitalized the men's and women's glee clubs and the University band and symphony orchestra. The opening of Hoch Auditorium in 1927, moreover, provided for the first time a suitable hall for the many concerts of the year; and larger crowds meant more money to attract better and more expensive artists and performers for the University Concert Course: pianists Myra Hess and Ignace Paderewski; the Don Cossack Chorus; violinist Jascha Heifetz; the Shan-Kar Hindu Dancers; the original New York company in *Green Pastures*; the Ballet Russe de Monte Carlo; and many others.[56]

Wherever Swarthout and his increasingly enthusiastic faculty saw an opportunity, they grabbed it. Thus in 1926 they took to the airwaves over the new (1924) University radio station, KFKU, for semiweekly musical programs. Music Week in 1928 featured a "Skilton Jubilee" to honor that long-time faculty member and eminent composer. In addition to Music Week there was an annual Fine Arts Day, which brought to campus for convocation addresses such worthies as sculptor Lorado Taft and musicologist Sigmund Spaeth. In the spring of 1935 Russell L. Wiley, University band director, organized a three-day Band Festival, at which over two thousand high-school musicians came to campus to study and play under the direction of several great bandmasters invited for the occasion, including the incomparable Edwin Franko Goldman. The following summer Wiley began a six-week Summer Music Camp for high schoolers as an experiment to see if Kansas and its region would support an annual camp modeled on the famous one at Interlochen, Michigan. The experiment was a great success, and the camp was thus continued from year to year. With Wiley giving it great publicity, the camp speedily acquired a national reputation. And after the war came the organization of the KU Opera Guild, which presented Gilbert and Sullivan's *The Gondoliers* in 1949 and Victor Herbert's *Sweethearts* in 1950.[57]

Although music came first with both Butler and Swarthout, they tried to give the visual arts and design a reasonable amount of attention through numerous exhibitions of work by faculty and students.[58] But in the visual arts the only things that could really compare with the public musical presentations were the Thayer and, to a much lesser extent, the Brynwood art collections. The Thayer collection was a great windfall for the University, not only for the objects it contained, but because it would provide a base and a building for a University collection that in the 1950s and 1960s would become outstanding. Mrs. Sally C. Thayer of Kansas City,

Missouri, was the widow of a wealthy department-store owner. Her money, her travels abroad, and her practically catholic tastes resulted in a most varied collection of objects which she gave to the University in 1917 and just before her death in 1925. There were Coptic and Byzantine textiles, Renaissance Venetian embroidery, and Chinese tapestries of the Ming period. There were Chinese ceramics and jade articles; Japanese shrines, lacquers, ivories, and swords; hundreds of Japanese prints; a large group of Korean pottery; and a collection of Presepe dolls from Italy. There were works by the American painters Winslow Homer, George Innes, J. S. Murphy, and several others. The Brynwood collection came in 1919 on more or less permanent loan from the family of Brynton M. Woodward of Lawrence. It consisted of fifty-two oils and watercolors, including works by Innes, Murphy, Lambinet, Leemputten, Edward Gay, and others. For want of a better place, the University put the collections on the third floor of Strong Hall, home of the Departments of Design and Painting. This pleased no one, Mrs. Thayer least of all. But after the construction of Watson Library freed Spooner, that medieval structure became the Spooner-Thayer Art Museum. Miss Minnie Moodie, formerly the Chancellor's secretary, became the curator.[59]

Until after the Second World War, however, the collection remained largely stable—and stodgy. But in 1948 Chancellor Malott and the University acquired John M. Maxon, an enthusiastic art historian with a Ph.D. fresh from Harvard, as museum director. Under him and his successor Edward A. Maser, who came in 1953, funds were found for a regular—though small—acquisition program and prospective donors were subtly wooed. Both the museum and the Department of Art History became most important parts of the University.[60]

On the whole, the public musical and artistic presentations of the students and faculty of the School of Fine Arts were more significant than the institution's curricula and degrees. Deans Butler and Swarthout paid them much more attention in their reports.[61] In 1923–1924, Swarthout's first year, the School's degree programs were four-year courses in piano, voice, violin, organ, and composition, leading to the degree of Bachelor of Music; a four-year course in drawing and painting, which led to the Bachelor of Painting degree; and a four-year course in design, leading to the Bachelor of

Design degree. The School was also marvelously free with non-degree options: there were four-year curricula in the above subjects which led to an "artist's certificate" for those who could not meet the scholastic requirements for degrees or who did not wish to take the small number of College requirements in the degree programs; three-year curricula leading to a "teacher's certificate"; and two-year curricula in public-school music and public-school art, the completion of which entitled one to a certificate to teach those subjects from the State Board of Education. Starting in 1930 the public-school music course led to a Bachelor of Music Education degree, and the degrees in the painting and design curricula were consolidated into the Bachelor of Fine Arts, a more professional and more apt degree.[62] The major program changes during the rest of Swarthout's deanship were the dropping of the artist's certificate work in 1940 and of the teacher's certificate eight years later and the expanding of the number of instruments in which work was offered.[63]

After twenty-seven years as dean, Swarthout retired in 1950. His successor was Thomas Gorton, who had both an M.M. and a Ph.D. from the Eastman Conservatory, and who had most recently been professor of music and director of the School of Music at Ohio University.[64] With his coming and with the opening of the great new music and dramatic arts building in 1957, the programs begun by Dean Swarthout would be greatly expanded and improved, and the University's cultural life enriched accordingly.

30

Graduate Professional Education

*W*HATEVER the quality of undergraduate education at Kansas, the attention given to it disgusted Dean Frank W. Blackmar of the Graduate School. "Just as the University is historically built from the freshman class upward," Blackmar wrote in 1920, two years before his retirement as dean, "so budgets grow from the bottom upward, and the Graduate School, which represents the highest purpose of scholarship, is neglected because of the great demands to care for the training of undergraduate students. The Graduate School should no longer be content to live upon the crumbs dropped from the freshman table," for without the research that the Graduate School supported and the degrees it granted a "full-blooded university" simply could not exist.[1]

Both Blackmar and his successor, Dean Ellis B. Stouffer, believed that Kansas had a unique opportunity to build at least the greatest graduate school in the American Southwest. There was such a need for the school, Blackmar wrote, that if the University did not develop it, "other institutions less prepared for the work" would be forced to try. Stouffer heartily agreed with the Zook committee report of 1923. "In all the Southwest," the committee thought, "there is not for many hundreds of miles an institution which has the same opportunity to develop graduate work as the University of Kansas. The State will be lacking in its opportunity to develop a graduate school comparable in importance with the State universities of Iowa, Michigan, Minnesota, Illinois, and Wisconsin, if it

594

does not encourage the university to take that portion of leadership in research and graduate study which its location places within its grasp."[2]

But the days of even regional distinction were far in the future. In the five years from 1926 to 1930 inclusive, Stouffer pointed out in the latter year, the University granted some 590 master's degrees, but only 44 Ph.D.'s. The Graduate School could not even serve the state, let alone the Southwest: "Every year large numbers of our most brilliant young men and women leave Kansas for their graduate training because the work they desire is not offered adequately in this University." A large proportion never returned, which meant that Kansas threatened to decline "educationally, economically, and every other way." The reason for the Graduate School's deficiencies, he said tritely and truly, was that the University was not paying salaries high enough to attract numerous "productive scholars, research workers, men known the nation over for their investigations."[3]

The depression decade, however, was no time to build a great graduate school. During it Stouffer could only lament the present and hope for the future. As he did so, his southwestern vision narrowed to one that was merely statewide. When he wrote to Chancellor Malott in 1941 to give his ideas about graduate study throughout the state, his emphasis was on a University graduate school for Kansans. A first-rate institution would keep Kansans in Kansas and profit the state; it would "naturally assume educational leadership in the state and raise the level of all other educational institutions. Thus students throughout the state will be benefited and the state's reputation as a good place in which to live will be enhanced."[4]

Yet even such a local school required more money than the legislature could pump in. The University had to continue to build from the undergraduate program up, rather than from the graduate program down. It had, of course, its scholars of distinction, men of ability and national or international renown who would have graced the graduate faculty of any university: James C. Malin in American history, Raymond H. Wheeler in psychology, John Ise and Jens P. Jensen in economics, Raymond C. Moore in geology, Edward H. ("Snakes") Taylor in herpetology, Herbert B. Hungerford in entomology, and many others. And the University produced some excellent Ph.D.'s who went on to distinguished careers: Malin himself, who took his degree under Frank Hodder in 1921; Cora M. Downs in bacteriology, the University's first woman Ph.D. (1924), who like Malin stayed at Kansas; Chester M. Suter (1927), an outstanding medical chemist; and others.[5]

The presence of notable scholars and the training of notable students, though, did not make a graduate school of the first rank, or even an adequate one. "When we attempt to choose those members of our faculty whose [research] work has received most recognition," College Dean Paul B. Lawson wrote in 1934, "the rather definite impression is gained that down through the years the leaders in their fields have been rather steadily leaving the University of Kansas for other institutions. Either that, or in more recent years the teaching loads have kept our best men busy, with a consequent loss in the production of research." Dean Stouffer made about the same point—though more gently—in an address to the campus chapters of Phi Beta Kappa and Sigma Xi in 1940. In the 1890s, he asserted, the University faculty reached sort of a crescendo of scholarly activity. Just before and during that decade the "flame of scholarship" that had "flickered feebly" since 1866, "burst into a brilliance which lights our path after half a century." That faculty had "little encouragement, financial or otherwise, but its accomplishments in scholarly production, and in the stream of inspired students sent forth"—for they were also excellent teachers—"form a glorious chapter in the history of this university. That faculty put *first things first.*" And so should the present faculty.[6]

For many faculty members, however, great research demanded a great library. After the First World War as before it, unfortunately, the library collections, building, and services were abysmally beneath what they should have been. Many people shared the blame: the taxpayers and legislators who never gave the University the money it needed, the regents and the chancellors who seldom and then but weakly pressed the library's wants. Yet what was the point of trying to increase Watson Library's holdings when the building itself was from the start too small to hold what books there were? Earl N. Manchester, librarian from 1921 to 1928, said just before he left that enlarging the University's mediocre collection of something over two hundred thousand volumes was less important than increasing stack, carrel, and reading space, and binding some five thousand volumes of periodicals which cluttered the whole building. Charles

M. Baker, who succeeded Manchester and served until 1952, pointed out that in 1929–1930 Kansas spent only $6.73 per student for books and periodicals, in contrast to North Carolina's $17.70, Colorado's $14.60, Michigan's $13.50, and even Missouri's $9.40. But "I cannot recommend a large increase in the book fund," he said, "until stack space is provided in which to shelve our present and future accessions."[7]

While books piled up everywhere in the 1930s, Baker campaigned, with support from the University Senate, for a westward expansion of Watson Library, as provided in the original plans. In 1934 and again in 1936 he said that without it the library was "rapidly heading into a chaotic condition that no amount of administrative skill can avert." There was no money for a new wing, however, and a storage room for fifty thousand volumes excavated in 1937–1938 beneath the basement reading room did not help much. Among other disadvantages to the chaos, Baker said, was that in the library's present state he could not appeal for gifts of valuable private collections. "It is impossible to promise any prospective donor that his gift will be given even decent, not to say dignified treatment."[8]

Like the University's other divisions, moreover, the library was always short of funds for hiring qualified personnel. In 1930 only 21 percent of the staff had both the B.A. and the year's professional training that Baker thought desirable; this contrasted poorly with such universities as Indiana (73 percent), North Carolina (51 percent), and Missouri (50 percent), whose collections were about the same size as that of Kansas. By 1940 Baker had raised the figure to 50 percent. Trained or untrained, however, the staff was poorly paid. In 1932, 1934, and 1936 Baker published figures showing that the mean salary of the University's staff ($1,360 in 1932, $1,138 in 1934) was the lowest of all the state schools—some $500 behind the College of Agriculture, which led the list. So humiliating was it that starting in 1938 either Chancellor Lindley or the regents precensored his report. "The median salary of this University library staff is $1,200 for eleven months service," Baker wrote. "How much lower this is than the median of the other Kansas state institutions, I am not permitted to state in print."[9]

Faculty dissatisfaction in the 1940s with Watson Library's holdings, personnel, and procedures culminated in 1951 in a special report by a College faculty committee to the Senate Library Committee. By then things had changed for the better: the west wing had been added in 1950; collections now totaled about four hundred thousand volumes and were growing by some twelve thousand a year; the regular library book appropriation was up to $65,000 a year from only $25,000 in 1946, and there was an "extra" fund of several thousand dollars for special purposes. But so many faculty members were so indignant about inadequacies that they chose a group of six, chaired by William H. Shoemaker of Romance Languages and Literatures to study the "possibilities of improved library services." Since the committee had Chancellor Malott's authorization to make a full study, it really functioned as an all-University group.[10]

Expectedly, the committee emphasized that the University library was not an effective research collection: "It is no secret . . . that . . . with a few notable individual exceptions, the most highly developed departments are those which least depend on the library. . . ." From 1929 to 1949, indeed, Kansas lagged behind all other Big Six schools except Oklahoma in growth. Shoemaker and his colleagues thought that an expenditure of $100,000 a year for books was a bare minimum and $150,000 better still. And at least as bothersome as the library's paucity of materials were the inadequacies of its staff. The number was too small; only seventeen of thirty-one qualified as trained; only fourteen had library degrees. It cost Kansas about $3.00 more than the national average of $4.50 to accession each volume; the ordering and cataloguing departments were far behind schedule; a general sluggishness was everywhere apparent. The library staff had been negligent in getting books rebound, notifying departments about book orders and the availability of rare and second-hand books, seeking private gifts, filling periodical gaps, and replacing lost books, and highhanded in canceling unfilled orders, eliminating uncatalogued materials, and imposing restricted classifications on books. While the library staff should stop committing these sins, the faculty should also do more for the library's welfare: "push the cause of the Library on all occasions," provide better estimates of book needs, appoint library representatives in each department, and also observe library rules. Lying at the "heart of research," the report said, the library held the "key to academic development."[11]

Chancellor Murphy could not have agreed more. If Deane

Malott had been committed to improving the library, as shown by the increase in funds and the new wing, Murphy was obsessed with the idea of library distinction. During his first year as chancellor he increased the regular library appropriation to $100,000, in the second to $150,000. Better still, when Baker resigned in 1952 Murphy secured Robert H. Vosper, then associate librarian at U.C.L.A., to succeed him. Vosper was much like Murphy himself: young (forty), aggressive, articulate, on the one hand publicity-hungry but on the other committed to excellence in quality, quantity, and service. He attacked on all fronts at once, and seemed to be everywhere at once, even barnstorming the state in 1956–1957 to explain the library's importance to alumni groups. "Frequently the audience expressed particular pride in the fact that the university thus saw fit to send a library emissary," he reported, "instead of the football film that is traditional fare at American university alumni meetings."[12]

The well-conceived library, Vosper thought, required three different kinds of materials: those for faculty and graduate research; those for undergraduate general reading; and rare materials, to be housed in the new Department of Special Collections, which deserved "special care because they are great human documents or because they illustrate the history of the art and craft of making books." With cooperation from Murphy and the Senate Library Committee, the library's holdings went from about 483,000 to about 875,000 volumes during the 1950s, which immeasurably assisted all faculty members and students. For undergraduates Vosper tried to promote a "more bookish atmosphere" by creating an open-stack Undergraduate Library in the old reserve reading room; on its shelves were several thousand "general interest books," "carefully selected from all fields of knowledge." He also set up a new-student orientation program. The result was a substantial increase in undergraduate use of the library. In 1958 Vosper reported with something of both pride and despair that student reading space was overcrowded.[13]

Vosper's and Murphy's greatest pride, however, was the expanding Department of Special Collections. "We have frankly glorified the book," Vosper said in his first report. "We don't foolishly try to emulate a Morgan Library," but since most students and faculty would never see the Morgan, they should "learn at Lawrence something of the central part books have played in the history of civilization." Both men also knew that they could use the rare book and manuscript collections to publicize the University. Among the more notable acquisitions were the Spoerri Collection of James Joyce's writings (1953), the huge Fitzpatrick Collection of books, pamphlets, and manuscripts on botany (1953), and the P. S. O'Hegarty Collection on William Butler Yeats, Lady Gregory, and the Irish theater (1955–1956). In the fall of 1957 the library sent special collections head Joseph Rubinstein abroad on the institution's first foreign book-buying tour.[14]

By the late 1950s, naturally, many faculty members were complaining that Special Collections was consuming too much money, which would have been better spent for more prosaic items that the library still lacked. But overall the better library, along with improved facilities and an expanded faculty, supported an expanded graduate program. In 1946 John H. Nelson, professor of English and assistant dean of the Graduate School, succeeded Ellis B. Stouffer as dean. During the next seventeen years, with Nelson's genial, soft-spoken guidance and encouragement, the Graduate School increased its enrollment from 637 to 2,347, the number of degrees granted from 98 to 509, and the number of departments actually training graduate students from 32 to 72.[15]

Along with the expansion, however, went several of the old problems about the Graduate School's relation to the rest of the University. So, at least, thought Dean William P. Albrecht, who left the chairmanship of the English Department to succeed Nelson in 1963. The main difficulty with the Graduate School, he told the members of the graduate faculty the next year, was that its main function was administrative: it kept records, made sure that students met the formal requirements, and recommended them for degrees. It did little to influence the quality of students through admission policy, fellowships, and the like; it did equally little to determine the graduate faculty's quality, for that faculty was still the undergraduate faculty in mufti. Albrecht thought that he and his school should have more authority, in keeping with their importance to the University at large. Graduate schools at other universities did more than his to "implement their responsibilities for the quality of graduate work," he said, and Kansas ought to catch up with them.[16]

Hard upon those comments came a shower of changes proposed by the Graduate Council and passed by the faculty, albeit with *sotto voce* grumblings about the Dean's "grab for power." Membership in the graduate faculty would henceforth require the dean's approval, as would authorization to direct doctoral dissertations. To supervise dissertations, moreover, faculty members would not only have to have the doctorate or its "clear equivalent in experience, training, and creative productivity," but would also have to have demonstrated "continuing productivity in research or other creative activity after the receipt of the degree." The eligibility of new faculty members—for the old ones were exempt—would be subject to periodic review.[17] Other notable changes were the raising of the usual admission requirement, which had been wondrously flexible in former years, to a B average, and permission to departments to substitute appropriate research skills for either or both of the then required foreign languages. Every department was informed that a thorough review of its graduate program was in order, and the Graduate Council immediately set to work examining proposed changes. And the Graduate School sought to increase the number of better students by eagerly soliciting fellowships under the National Defense Education Act and by asking for greater state appropriations for fellowships and assistantships.[18]

Like the Graduate School, the School of Medicine had a midtwentieth-century renaissance, but it had begun some fifteen years earlier in 1948 with the appointment of Franklin D. Murphy as dean. With his accession the School began a rush toward distinction far more rapid than that of the University as a whole. By the end of the University's first century, indeed, the Medical School was its most distinguished division, its greatest single claim to excellence and fame.

In dark days and bright days alike through the teens and twenties University and Medical School leaders held to a vision of an outstanding medical center. "No state in the Union has so magnificent an opportunity to build up a great medical school as Kansas has to-day," said the Board of Administraton in 1914. All it needed was money from the legislature. "Our School of Medicine," said Chancellor Strong the same year, "is probably destined to be one of the few competent schools . . . in the country. It will serve a great and expanding region and will command centers of the finest clinical material." Dean Harry R. Wahl thought that the institution could become the "medical center of the Southwest," while Dean

Elias P. Lyon of the University of Minnesota medical school, who investigated the Kansas school in conjunction with the Zook committee's inquiry in 1922, thought that it had at least a "good opportunity in medical education. . . . I believe the time is ripe for a big forward movement."[19]

Actually the time was still green. When Lyon wrote, the Medical School was constructing a $200,000 hospital on a new site in Kansas City a mile south of the old Bell Memorial Hospital and laboratories. To be completed in 1924, it was the first major addition to the hospital plant since 1911. More important was that the appropriation of the money by the legislature of 1919 finally determined that a University medical school should exist. During the teens many Kansans had continued to doubt the wisdom of a state school. Some opposed all professional education, others thought that a medical school would cost too much, still others believed that Kansas could never hope to build a school to compare with the nation's best. Frank Strong conceded the doubters nothing. When Governor Arthur Capper wrote in 1914 to say that many physicians were among the doubters and that he himself had reservations about continuing the School, Strong replied that it was indispensable to the state's welfare. "I . . . confidently expect the School of Medicine to be in twenty-five years the most important professional school in the University and that a state . . . without this agency will be seriously at a disadvantage and will then at a very great and almost prohibitive cost have to replace its school of medicine or substitute some other less efficient and more costly agency."[20]

Because a poor, static school would have soon died, the $200,000 grant was a solid vote for Strong. Yet the legislature conceded a point to men still opposed to the School's location in Kansas City-Rosedale by appointing a committee headed by Governor Allen to fix the site of the new hospital—at no cost to the state—and thereby the site of the School itself. After consulting Strong and the faculty, Allen's committee recommended keeping the School where it was. But when it proved impossible to buy land around the original site, University alumni, faculty, and friends, and Rosedale boosters put up the $65,000 for the new area to the south. With the new hospital's completion, the Medical School made still another new start.[21]

Like Abraham Flexner before him, however, Dean Lyon thought

the School had far to go. While its graduates were "fairly well trained" and the School was constantly raising its scholastic standards, the deficiencies were more important. Chief among them was still the separation of the Clinical Department in Rosedale from the Scientific Department in Lawrence, which deprived older and younger students of mutually beneficial contacts and hindered the two groups of faculty members from cooperating to teach common principles and solve common problems. "Medicine becomes more and more biochemistry and physiology, and less and less pathological anatomy. The bacteriologist, the biochemist, and the physiologist should all have their contacts with the hospital."[22]

Lyon also reported that the Medical School was underfinanced, understaffed, and underambitious. It needed more laboratories, classrooms, and hospital beds, more cooperation with hospitals in Kansas City, Missouri, stronger ties with the state's medical profession and medical society. Since the School's true goal was to produce "better human beings," it needed a "positive program of public health and preventive medicine," or "hygiene in its broadest sense. To this end the medical school should foster all forms of educational activity, both intramural and university extension which will produce doctors with ideals of public service and which will bring to the people a knowledge of the applications of science in combatting disease and supporting human efficiency." Lyon also asked for consideration of a dental school as part of the "greater medical school."[23]

Dean Harry R. Wahl, who succeeded Mervin T. Sudler in 1924, added numerous criticisms of his own. Wahl was a graduate of the University of Wisconsin who had taken his M.D. at Johns Hopkins in 1912. After teaching pathology at Western Reserve University, he had come to Kansas in 1919.[24] Modern medical education, he constantly pointed out, was dependent on physical facilities: on large hospitals for adequate supplies of clinical material, on the latest equipment for treatment, on money and ever more money for laboratories, supplies, nurses' homes, outpatient departments, social-service work, and public health. But the Medical School's "outstanding characteristic" and "bane," he said in 1926, was its "physical disintegration." Everywhere there was crampedness and decay. One significant result was that the School could not train all Kansas youths who sought to become physicians. In 1925–1926, 270

Kansans were enrolled in medical schools, but only 139 of them were at the University Medical School. The School should be graduating seventy students a year to replace Kansas doctors who died, retired, or left the state, but it had room for only forty in each class.[25]

During the next twenty years Wahl and his faculty discovered that the legislature was willing to keep the School's quality high but not to make it great. An appropriation of $300,000 in 1927 allowed the addition of 120 beds, which in turn permitted a 50 percent increase in each class of students. Wahl, of course, wanted much more; in 1930 he pointed out that the School's quality far outran its resources. It was one of only forty American medical schools "recognized by Great Britain," and it had just received a chapter of Alpha Omega Alpha, the honorary scholarship fraternity to which only the top half of the nation's schools belonged.[26] From 1936 to 1939 some $980,000 in state appropriations, federal grants, private gifts, and surplus funds from hospital charges made possible a children's pavilion, a new outpatient building connected by a corridor to the main structure, a three-story building for the segregated Negro patients, the Hixon Laboratory for Medical Research, and an addition to the power plant. But while all these structures were welcome, they did not mean that the Medical School was about to become as fine as Wahl wished. When he thought about the School's "more urgent needs," he thought of almost $2,000,000 to equip and complete the present plant and then to enlarge it with a new laboratory and operating unit, two more ward buildings, a tuberculosis unit, a psychiatric unit, and an expansion of the nurses' home. By the time he resigned the deanship in 1948, he had gotten none of them, although the legislature of 1947 gave him a going-away present of $70,000 for a psychiatric clinic.[27]

In addition to training new physicians, Wahl hoped to help older doctors keep up with medical developments. But his funds never stretched very far. In the 1927–1928 year the Medical School and the Extension Division cooperated to send Dr. Wayne A. Rupe of the Washington University (St. Louis) Medical School to twenty-seven centers around the state to offer "post-graduate courses" in pediatrics. In the next six years there were similar circuit tours by other physicians; the program lapsed in 1933, but later revived. In 1931 the School began sponsoring postgraduate clinics of a few days each in Kansas City. One day, Wahl hoped, the School would have a postgraduate training center that would keep doctors "informed from year to year of the advances in medical science."[28]

The School was also limited in the direct public services it could perform. In 1934—eight years after the Dean first called for it—there was at last enough money to start a Social Service Department. Its employees referred the unfortunate to the hospital, made sure that they followed doctors' orders, and advised them on their financial condition.[29] Wahl's great plan for educating both physicians and the public in preventive medicine had a less fortunate outcome. With the cooperation of the Kansas City, Kansas, Health Department, medical students secured valuable field experience. But the School's Department of Preventive Medicine and Hygiene never had enough money to pay a full-time professor and his assistants, much less to establish a well-conceived program. In 1937 the Department of Obstetrics joined the city and state health departments in starting a maternity center, supported by federal Social Security funds. It offered maternity care in the home and supported a mother-baby clinic. This helped, but the Medical School fell short of being a great public health center.[30]

Because the School itself fell short of adequacy in the 1930s and the 1940s, criticism of it came from outside and inside the state. In 1936 a joint inspection team from the Council on Medical Education of the American Medical Association and the Association of American Medical Colleges found faculty quality and morale both high, but severely criticized both the division of the School between Kansas City and Lawrence and the physical facilities. After the inspection Wahl reported that although the School and its training were reasonably good, they were not first-rate.[31] During the Second World War, moreover, the Medical School suffered even more than usual from shortages of teachers, nurses, labor, supplies, and equipment, and from the educational speed-up. By 1944 there existed throughout the hospital the consequences of what Dr. J. Harvey Jennett called the "neurotic and psychoneurotic attitude of the times": high blood pressure, discourtesy, snippiness, depression. Many faculty members, including leading light Logan Clendening, came to think Dean Wahl incompetent and tyrannical.[32] By the mid-1940s there was also great opposition to him in the Kansas medical profession. A committee appointed by Chancellor Malott to find a successor discovered that many physicians thought that the School offered inadequate clinical instruction, discouraged interns and students from applying at Kansas hospitals, did not utilize the "talent of Kansas physicians," and failed to cooperate with local public health officers. Other complaints were that the outpatient clinic and the hospital took patients (and therefore income and prestige) away from local physicians; that the School failed to offer "desirable post-graduate care" for Kansas physicians; and that patients with incomes higher than those that entitled them to clinic care were referred mainly to University of Kansas physicians.

The committee thought the Medical Center's "crying need" was "vigorous and visionary administration." Wahl's successor should have "youth, vision, and aggressiveness," be experienced in "academic medicine," and be familiar with both national and local medical problems. Malott himself wanted a young man skilled in "public relations and educational policy," which were his "most important jobs."[33]

The committee and Malott were exactly describing Franklin D. Murphy. The son of Dr. Franklin E. Murphy, a former faculty member, the new dean had taken his B.A. at Kansas in 1936 and, after a year as an exchange scholar at the University of Göttingen, had studied for his M.D. at the University of Pennsylvania, where he ranked first in his class on his graduation in 1941. Then came an internship and residency in internal medicine at the University hospital and two years of army duty. In 1946 Murphy began practice in Kansas City, Missouri, and became an instructor in the Kansas Medical School. When chosen dean in 1948, he was thirty-two years old.[34]

The next three years were the most stimulating and productive in the Medical School's history, for Murphy not only had awe-inspiring amounts of idealism, enthusiasm, and energy, but also knew just how to knock on the doors of opportunity. Immediately after his appointment he promised to work for everything at once: "a bigger plant, better faculty, and increased activity in research," and the "continued expansion of the school's post-graduate services to practicing doctors in Kansas and elsewhere. We want the school to serve this community and area, its health needs, on a bigger and better scale."[35]

With Malott's encouragement,[36] Murphy whirled around the

state to win support for a huge request of almost $3,900,000 to the legislature of 1949 to begin a great "rural health program." Since 1906, Murphy pointed out, the state's population had increased 25 percent while the number of doctors had decreased by 30 percent; the decline had been especially sharp in communities of fifteen hundred people or less. To correct the situation, Murphy proposed a three-pronged attack. With more money he would, first, increase the average Medical School class size from eighty to one hundred. Then he gave great publicity to a scheme to induce newly graduated physicians to settle in rural areas. In interviewing members of the class of 1948 he had discovered that many of those with a predilection for small-town life were too much in debt to invest in expensive medical equipment and that they also feared becoming "medically isolated," or unable to keep up with the latest methods. Murphy's scheme—though not original with him—called for communities to put up money for office space, examining rooms, and modern laboratory facilities. The doctor would pay office rent and amortize equipment costs from his earnings. If he left, taking his equipment with him, the town would still have the original investment and the building to attract a successor.

To help M.D.'s keep up with medical advances, Murphy's third proposal was an "in-residence program" by which physicians would return to the Medical School for several weeks at a time every three to five years. With bedside instruction, clinics, lectures, and conferences, they would have "all the opportunities formerly available only to the specialist." The School would also conduct two- or three-day refresher courses in Kansas City as well as circuit courses around the state.[37]

The key to the whole project was pressure on the legislature. Murphy proved the compleat lobbyist. Before the solons met, he had won the support of the State Board of Health, the Kansas Medical Society, the Kansas Farm Bureau, the Agricultural Council of the State Chamber of Commerce, and Governor Frank Carlson. Representative Paul R. Shanahan of Salina, the Republican floor leader, and two prominent farm leaders brought Murphy's measure into the House. After passage Governor Carlson signed it on February 19. The act created the University of Kansas Hospitals Building Fund and supplied it with $3,862,560. Together with another $460,000 granted by the federal government, the Medical Center would construct a basic science building, a service building, a wing for the study and treatment of chest diseases, and another wing for psychiatric patients. There would also be additions to the Eaton Building—the Negro ward—and the clinic building, and a doubling of the size of the nurses' home. And there was $420,000 more for equipment.[38]

Heartened by both the victory and the fame it brought, Dean Murphy rushed to implement and publicize the several parts of his program. In the fall of 1949 the class of 1953 entered as the first of the hundred-student classes. Starting in March, 1950, every senior would have to spend several weeks as an observer in the office of a rural general practitioner in a community of twenty-five hundred or less. The physicians would serve as preceptors; the students would accompany them on their rounds and participate in their examinations, diagnoses, and other work, although they would not actually practice medicine.[39]

Meanwhile the plan of settling new doctors in rural communities moved ahead. In Topeka Dr. R. M. Heilman, director of the Division of Hospital Facilities of the State Board of Health, kept a reference list of several dozen rural communities needing physicians. From January 1, 1949, through October, 1960, 67 of the 252 physicians who located in Kansas established practices in towns smaller than twenty-five hundred; many of them were lured by the rural health program. So grateful were the people of Mankato in Jewell County for Murphy's help—even though they had begun their own program—that they proclaimed November 17, 1949, "Dean Murphy Day." Governor Carlson and Dr. R. M. Owensby, the town's new physician, joined Murphy in ceremonies opening a new $12,600 clinic complete with x-ray and other modern equipment.[40]

With the building and rural health programs expanding, Murphy turned to his "continuation education" or "in-residence" scheme. Exclusive of the internship, he pointed out in 1950, 70 to 80 percent of postgraduate teaching had, at least until recently, been for specialists. Yet between 70 and 80 percent of the nation's medical care was provided by general practitioners. Murphy began to indoctrinate students with the idea that they were embarking on a forty-year educational program, that they must continue their medical education until they retired. He and his staff expanded and improved the Medical Center's refresher courses in Kansas City, and standardized the circuit courses. Teams of two doctors—usually a faculty member and a practicing physician—gave lectures and advice at eight centers. Equipped with movies, slides, and printed materials, they gave programs on such things as "Modern Advances in the Treatment of Diabetes," and "Office Procedures in Urology."[41]

Even more promising to Murphy was bringing G.P.'s back to the Medical Center for from a month to a year to brush up on phases of medicine that they found especially useful for their own practice. At first Murphy hoped to get about $950,000 for a continuation center and hospital unit at the Medical Center. Believing that the chances of procuring it from the legislature were poor, he and Malott applied to the Kress Foundation of New York, which had recently given $6,000,000 for a postgraduate medical education center at New York University. The Foundation pledged $150,000, providing that the University matched the amount, and $50,000 a year for five years to 'expand the postgraduate courses. After the Endowment Association and a number of Greater Kansas City contributors pledged the matching funds, Murphy and the regents secured more money from the legislature. As the Continuation Center appeared, however, it was joined to the student union, and there was no special hospital for the returning practitioners alone.[42]

But the additions to the Medical Center made plain that it was entering upon an era of growth and improved quality. From 1947 to 1960 the Center's operating income grew from $2,393,000 to $9,725,000. By 1960 the faculty had grown to about 530, up from about 300 in 1948. Many of the members were enthusiastic researchers as well as teachers. In 1959–1960 the Medical Center spent $1,368,000 of a University total of about $3,606,000 for organized research.[43] To solve the old problem of the relation between the teaching and the private practice of the clinical faculty members, in July, 1950, Murphy introduced his "geographical full-time" plan. All department heads, section heads, and other key teachers and researchers who were paid full-time salaries had Medical Center offices in which they could see private patients up to three afternoons per week. In return the School charged them 7 percent of their income for office overhead, and another 11 percent for the development of their departments.[44]

The new facilities and the expanded faculty immediately offered a better training for students, interns, and residents; and Deans

Murphy and W. Clarke Wescoe kept well up with the latest ideas in medical education. The five-story medicine and surgery building dedicated in November, 1949, had closed-circuit television cameras in the surgery suites to allow students in classrooms to watch the operations. In 1952 and 1953 the curriculum, which had remained largely unchanged since the 1920s, was extensively revised in order to correlate instruction in all departments, focus on the whole human being and human body rather than its parts, and decrease the amount of classroom instruction in favor of clinical and practical work. In 1962 one of the longest-standing complaints against the Medical School was lifted when the whole four years of instruction were at last consolidated in Kansas City.[45] Withal, neither Murphy nor Wescoe ever forgot that they were training men and citizens as well as physicians—although that idea was always difficult to express in the formal curriculum. "We are trying to teach our young doctors," Murphy told a physicians' conference in December, 1948, "to quit thinking that they lose their franchise to vote when they get their medical diplomas. Technical knowledge is only half the doctor's development. He must be a citizen first, a physician second," a man always concerned with the social and political consequences of scientific progress.[46]

In the meantime the Law School, which became the University's third graduate professional school, was having its ups and downs— and then ups again. It took the School only a short time to recover from forty years of stodginess and low standards under Dean James W. Green. Uncle Jimmy, Chancellor Lindley wrote in 1920, was of the "older generation in his views of legal education." After he died on November 4, 1919, there was a need to "unstiffen conditions in the Law School." During the next two years, under Acting Dean William L. Burdick, the faculty of five began to atone for Green's sins. Starting in September, 1921, the School required two years of College work—three-fourths of it of grade C or better—for admission, which brought it up to the standards of most members of the Association of American Law Schools. At the same time the College faculty voted to allow students to apply thirty hours of Law School credit toward the B.A. degree, making it possible to obtain both the B.A. and the LL.B. in six years. The Law School faculty hoped that this would encourage prospective lawyers to take an undergraduate degree, rather than leave the College after the sophomore year.

Then, too, the faculty raised slightly the grades required for graduation—now three-fourths instead of two-thirds of the ninety hours would have to be of C grade or better—and moved almost entirely to the case method of teaching.

Lindley thought the results excellent. Student and faculty morale was high; there were more students—over 250—than ever before; and there existed a "fine attitude on the part of the law alumni —a disposition in short to support a genuinely modern law school with all that that implies."[47]

Finding a genuinely modern dean willing to come to Lawrence, however, took over two years. Burdick was the logical choice, but Lindley made him University vice-president. In the summer of 1920 Lindley and the regents offered the job to Professor Paul V. McNutt of Indiana University, but he declined.[48] After fruitless searches in 1920 and 1921 Lindley at last came up with a first-rate prospect in Herschel W. Arant, a Yale B.A., M.A., and LL.B., then teaching at his alma mater. The testimonials to his teaching, scholarship, and personality, the Chancellor thought, "measure up to the best possibilities we have in mind. . . ."[49]

Arant measured up so well that Ohio State stole him away in 1928. During his tenure the School weathered the shock of sharply reduced enrollments and stabilized itself for the future. The requirement of two years of College, a new prohibition against the enrollment of College juniors for law credit (only seniors were privileged), and the higher grades required for admission combined to cut the student body from 267 at the end of the 1921–1922 academic year to 150 the following fall to 137 in 1923 to 134 in 1924, after which the number began to climb again. Better yet, in October, 1924, the School received a chapter of the Order of the Coif, the national honorary law school society. Arant thought it a great stimulus to scholarship, for only 10 percent of each graduating class was eligible, and the society's prestige was great. At the same time, however, a problem of the University as a whole continued to plague the Law School: miserably inadequate funds for both faculty salaries and the library. Arant took great pride in the favorable comments on the School's quality made by members of the State Board of Bar Examiners, but pride was not enough to keep him in Kansas.[50]

During the eight years after his departure, instability seized the Law School. Professor Philip Mechem succeeded Arant as acting dean. When he resigned in June, 1929, for another position, the School brought in Robert M. Davis, who had a Harvard B.A. and a Chicago J.D., and since 1923 had been dean of the law school at the University of Idaho. All of his qualities served him ill as dean. Naturally stiff and formal, he departed from the Uncle Jimmy Green tradition by remaining aloof from the students. With that remoteness went exceedingly high—and immediately unpopular—standards of admission and scholarship, which he persuaded the faculty to accept. From 1930 to 1932 the minimum admission requirements rose to above a C average, and Davis proved remorseless in weeding out the intellectually incompetent and the ethically deficient. And despite his announced standards of excellence, many students, alumni, and lawyers inside and outside the state apparently thought him pretty much a fraud as a teacher and scholar. At least so Herschel W. Arant, who had kept up his Kansas contacts, told Lindley in 1931. "The most disquieting statements I have heard of," Arant reported, "have come from the Supreme Court, one member characterizing the situation at the Law School as requiring immediate and drastic action."[51]

Students and alumni took that action in the 1931–1932 year. At the Kansas-Missouri Homecoming game in the fall, with the Board of Regents and Governor Harry H. Woodring in attendance, several students calling themselves a "group of loyal K.U. upperclassmen," issued a handbill attacking the Dean. The following June forty-four members of the Law School classes of 1931 and 1932 sent to Woodring and the regents petitions stating that the School's quality was declining and asking for Davis's resignation. All the Law School faculty members immediately issued a rebuttal stating—too gently— that some of the critics had "misunderstood" Davis's struggle for scholastic excellence. "He has had . . . at all times, the confidence and esteem of his associates, and they sincerely appreciate his unfailing courtesy and devotion to the cause of legal education. The faculty feels as a unit that it is a time when all friends of the school should give it their undivided loyalty and support."[52]

In 1932 Chancellor Lindley did not believe that Davis should resign or be dismissed, and the regents kept him. But anti-Davisites kept up the attack, and the Law School student body declined from 147 in 1930–1931 to 119 in 1933–1934—with a number of former students enrolling in the rival Washburn University law school in

Topeka—and the Board grew restless. Davis did not help his cause very much. In his biennial report for 1934 he pointed out that in legal education and the bar's ethical standards the "state of Kansas stands much above the average, and in some respects at the top." Yet he also said that the Law School's policy was shaped with national conditions in mind. Those conditions were an overcrowded profession and resulting widespread unethical and even criminal conduct as lawyers fought to survive. Time was, moreover, when the American lawyer was a "social philosopher" whose function was to "coordinate social and political activities." Now he was merely a "legal technician" who was incapable of dealing with the present "social disorders" or locating the "causes of the evil" and prescribing the "way of reconstruction." The way to end rascality and to restore status was to raise the standards of law schools so high that about half of the present forty thousand students would be forced out; this would be a "great public service."[53]

Chancellor Lindley and the regents always stood for high standards, of course, but there was such a thing as reaching them too soon. Davis resigned as dean under pressure in 1934, to be succeeded by William L. Burdick, first as acting dean for a year and then as dean for two more. But Burdick's heart was not in the deanship. After faculty member W. J. Brockelbank resisted efforts to lure him into the position, the faculty, Chancellor, and regents turned to another Kansas professor, Frederick J. Moreau. A graduate of the University of Wisconsin and its law school, he had practiced in Madison, taught two years at the University of Idaho, and come to Kansas in 1929. His teaching specialty was corporation law, and he was a productive scholar.[54]

Moreau's deanship lasted for twenty years, during which time the School made steady progress toward something more than adequacy. When he took office, the Kansas Supreme Court, prodded by the state Bar Association, was in the process of raising the requirements for admission to practice above those of all other states. Starting June 1, 1936, the Court had ruled in 1934, applicants for admission to the bar had to have three years of college. Even as that requirement was taking effect, the Court was demanding that after July 1, 1940, every candidate would have to have a degree showing that he had completed a college course in the "arts and sciences," and an LL.B. from an accredited law school (previously three years of reading in an attorney's office had been sufficient). With the University's College of Liberal Arts and Sciences continuing to accept the first year of Law School work as the fourth year required for the B.A., the Court's requirement could be met in six years. The faculty was delighted with the new rules. The state of Kansas, Dean Moreau said, was clearly "blessed with a progressive, forward-looking bar and an equally clear-thinking court." "This is an epoch in legal education," William L. Burdick had written in 1936, "and distinctively makes the bar in Kansas a learned profession."[55]

Moreau also hoped to make his graduates something more than learned professionals. The law, he knew, was intimately related to philosophy, economics, political science, and sociology—as the catalogues always said, "the law touches every human interest"—and future lawyers should grasp all of the law's ramifications. "Frankly, I still think we teach too many rules," he told Chancellor Lindley in 1937. "Now I do not mean that we should be less definite about law, but that we need greater understanding of fundamental thoughts. I feel that we have done too little faculty collective thinking." Moreau was keenly aware that the University of Chicago law school, urged on by University President Robert M. Hutchins, was changing its whole curriculum to enable students to pursue the law in all its aspects and relations. Moreau and his faculty, however, were far more conservative than Hutchins. Instead of major curricular changes, Moreau would arrange faculty dinners to discuss "basic books" on various subjects; invite as speakers both "leading thinkers from other departments" in the University and men "on the fringe of changing thought" from other law schools; and develop "close, friendly relations" with the country's leading law schools, whence came new ideas.[56]

Whatever individual faculty members might gain from such devices or teach in the classroom, however, the general curriculum remained a standard professional one, though it allowed for considerable flexibility. From 1920–1921 to 1932–1933 second- and third-year students had been allowed to elect their own courses—as long as they carried at least fourteen hours—after a freshman year of such subjects as contracts, criminal law, personal property, procedure, equity, and torts. Beginning in the 1933–1934 year juniors were once again subject to required courses; increasing freedom for second-year students after the Second World War brought full freedom in 1953–1954—though recommendations of courses were made.[57] In the mid-1930s the faculty added several courses in public law and, after Moreau became dean, new courses in various forms of business law, including that of oil and gas. By the mid-1950s the roster of elective courses included industrial competition, labor law, municipal corporations, and legislation. Matriculants after September 1, 1953, had to complete ninety hours instead of the previous eighty-two (the drop from a still earlier ninety in 1920–1921 had come gradually over the next fifteen years), though still with the average grade of C.[58]

By the 1950s, then, the School of Law had left behind forever the simpler (though more democratic) ideas of Uncle Jimmy Green. Arant, Davis, Burdick, and Moreau, with their faculties, had made it a solid institution with a student body of at least reasonable quality. To be sure, only a C average was still required for admission. But in 1952 the students showed their mettle by joining with the faculty to start the *University of Kansas Law Review,* a learned, well-written publication that put the old *Kansas University Lawyer* to shame. When John G. Hervey surveyed the School in 1955 for the American Bar Association's Section of Legal Education and Admission to the Bar (it was the first such survey since 1923), he found much to praise. Expectedly he noted that faculty salaries were too low and faculty members (eleven, but only eight full-time, for 169 students) too few. He also said that the faculty should be doing more scholarly research and suggested that standards of student scholarship were inadequate. But he reported that Professors Quintin Johnstone and Charles H. Oldfather, Jr., had attracted great attention as scholars, lauded the faculty as "keenly aware of the trends and things current in legal education," and praised the student body as "definitely . . . superior to what I usually encounter" and as "superior and alert." The law library was excellent. "A dignified, scholarly, professional atmosphere prevails in and about the place. . . . There is nothing marginal about this school. . . ."[59]

Speaking generally, by the end of the University's first century there was nothing marginal, either, about the University itself. Yet everything about the institution testified to the fact that there was a great distance between supermarginality and the highest quality. And here the influence of the students was considerable.

31

Students and Other Undergraduates: The Twentieth Century

*L*A T E in the summer of 1959 the Associated Women Students of the University published a handbook, designed especially for entering freshmen, titled *Wise Words for Women*. Its purposes were to answer questions about "life at K.U." and to describe the "many opportunities for self-improvement and just plain fun" on Mount Oread. There was information on the AWS, the residence halls, and various student groups. There was an appropriate emphasis on matters intellectual ("You'll find that studying, often so casually disregarded in movies, songs, and stories, is very much a part of your University life"), on extracurricular activities, and on the "social whirl" ("Certainly no college education would be complete without it!"). To explain the niceties of University etiquette there were paragraphs on general courtesy, how to introduce people, where to wait while a date bought movie tickets (in the lobby), and even on table manners at fraternity parties: "Ice cream should be eaten from the side of the spoon. . . . Small fish bones and fruit pits may be removed from the mouth by using the thumb and fore-finger."[1]

In *Wise Words for Women* the University was far more than a center for learning. It was instead an environment in which the students might hope to fulfill all sorts of diverse desires. But this, of course, was what the school had been in the nineteenth century; the most notable characteristic of student life in its second fifty years was its continuity with the past. Allowances had naturally to be made for changing local, national, and world conditions. The 1880s, for example, had had social idealism aplenty, but it was of a different sort, concerned with different problems, than the pacifism or communism of the 1930s or opposition to racial discrimination or the Vietnam war thirty years later. In the late nineteenth and early twentieth centuries many a student had worried about how and where he would fit into society after graduation. Fifty years later many a student was still worrying, but his society was remarkably different, enormously more complex, uncertain, threatening. Student sensualism remained undiminished, but the gyrations of the twist, frug, and watusi of the 1960s were not those of the shimmy, camel-walk, and toddle of the 1920s.

Whatever the apparent changes, though, the University remained all things to all students. They came to Mount Oread for all sorts of reasons, found in the institution opportunities as varied as they themselves, and kept it as cosmopolitan as their intellectual, social, and emotional backgrounds. No two students saw the University in exactly the same way, and thus it is impossible to say what experiences on the Hill meant to all of them.

Yet there was one characteristic of the University that affected most. During the twentieth century the school grew from a small provincial institution to a huge emporium of knowledge whose leaders after 1945 constantly stressed its importance to the entire world. In the 1909–1910 year the University had 2,303 students; twenty-five years later it had 4,902; in 1959–1960 there were 11,783. At the same time the student body became more variegated. Of the 3,437 students on campus in 1916–1917, for example, 91.1 percent were Kansans; 7.2 percent were from the adjacent states of Missouri, Nebraska, Oklahoma, and Colorado; 1.3 percent were from eighteen other states; and but 0.10 percent were from foreign countries. But by the fall of 1959 Kansans constituted only 72.1 percent of the students; Missourians, Nebraskans, Oklahomans, and Coloradans, 14.5 percent; those from the forty-three other states, Alaska, and Hawaii, 10.5 percent; and foreigners 2.9 percent.[2] Cosmopolitanism inevitably produced a certain confusion and splintering of the student body, for now students could know a far smaller percentage of their fellows than their predecessors had, and the old sense of continuity suffered; foreign students, moreover, often complained of unfriendly natives. But it also gave the campus a welcome multiformity.

There was also a greater maturity in the student body, caused by the changing ratios of graduate to undergraduate students. In 1909–1910 only 131 of the 2,303 students (5.7 percent) were enrolled in the Graduate School, which alone of the University's divisions required an undergraduate degree for admission. Fifty years later the Graduate School, together with the Schools of Law and Medicine, which had since raised their admission standards to require B.A.'s, had 24.4 percent of the students.[3]

At no time were the students united about the University's proper goals. The school's purpose, said a conventional *Kansan* editor in 1932, was not to provide an "accumulation of cut and dried facts," but to "teach men and women how to form habits of work, how to cooperate with fellow workers, and how to take advantage of our own capacities." But graduate student Frank McClelland had different ideas. The worth of knowledge, he believed, lay in its potential for radical social change. "Contemplation of knowledge is worthless," he wrote the same year, "without carrying that knowledge into direct and immediate action" for the redress of social wrong, and he went on to accuse most of the faculty of cowardice for refusing to use their ideas for reform.[4]

Other students joined McClelland and the *Kansan* in repudiating the idea of the intrinsic value of knowledge yet remained uninterested in their social goals. In the fall of 1944, for example, freshman Edmond Marks contended that the College curriculum was ill-designed because it required courses in so many different fields. Most College students were seeking to prepare themselves for a particular profession or occupation after graduation. The modern tendency was for undergraduates to "concentrate more and more upon one field of activity and they are not very interested in wasting their subjects"; the College should be more responsive to their needs. So said undergraduates in the University's professional schools. "Cultural knowledge," or "knowledge of the culture of the universe," was admittedly "prerequisite to the successful engineer," said *Kansas Engineer* editor Robert Kipp in 1952. But since undergraduate engineers had only limited time at their disposal, and since cultural explorations could be undertaken after graduation, the "tendency toward technical engineering education seems not only justifiable, but quite logical." Many technically trained engineers were anything but uncultivated rubes: look at Herbert Hoover,

Students at home, about 1891. The more that things change . . .

. . . the more they remain the same. Battenfeld Hall scene, 1950s.

David Sarnoff, and former United States Senator from Kansas Harry Darby.[5]

But not even the engineers were united on such ideas. Four years earlier editor Frederick G. Gartung had pointed out that the problems of engineering were social as well as technical and were of a "world wide nature." Therefore "forward looking engineering schools recognize the importance of educating students in a humanistic-social sense" by requiring "humanities courses" of them. Engineers trained in a "liberal as well as scientific atmosphere should develop the broad, unbiased point of view which is so necessary for fair evaluation of the claims of society." Proper training would help the engineer "see the problem, weigh the facts, and seek a correct solution without yielding to radical impulses."[6]

From the nature of the University to the nature of the faculty was a short step. Twentieth-century students continued the nineteenth-century practice of telling their teachers how they felt about them—and not only through questionnaires. There were two types of faculty members, the *Kansan* said in 1921. The "unpleasant, as well as small minority" included those who were "either indifferent to their own lack of efficiency, or who attempt to cover it up by bluster and ridicule," and those who had "simply forgotten that they themselves were once just as unlearned and full of mistakes as the students for whom they make life a grind and a drive." Most faculty members, however, either had a "pleasant, confidence-winning attitude that makes the work of preparing assignments a pleasure from the start," or were a "little more distant to meet, but yet . . . always reasonable, kindly and considerate." A year later the paper was hot after time-wasting professors who frittered away class time discussing irrelevant trivialities. "From day to day, the students in these courses hear lengthy talks on how the dodo bird got its name or how pie may be cut into even pieces; and from day to day, these students, who are paying hard-earned cash that they may fit themselves for positions in the world, leave the classrooms disgusted." There was a steady flow of other complaints: classes were too large and teachers too impersonal; textbook changes were too frequent and often unnecessary; too many professors gave true-false instead of essay examinations, which led to "slovenly, careless habits of thought and loose, disjointed thinking," and also to temptation, for it was always hard not to look at a neighbor's answer sheet.[7]

Bolder students occasionally attacked faculty members by name for intellectual errors. In 1937 the editors of the *Dove* assailed Dean Raymond A. Schwegler of the School of Education for alleged anti-Semitism. Schwegler had allegedly accused the Jews of being 99 percent Communists and allegedly said that there was grave danger of their gaining control of the United States. "While most of his talk sounds like the rantings of a mad man," the editors said, "there is some method in his madness. After a brief glance one seems to see the outlines of a swastika through a haze of sophism. Cool analysis condenses this fog and the Nazi emblem shows more plainly." Schwegler's ideas sounded like an "American version of *Mein Kampf*." A year later Elmer F. Engel of the German Department was under attack in the *Dove* for planning to teach and travel in Germany during the summer of 1938. Since the Nazis controlled the universities, Freda Schaeffler argued, and since only avowed Nazis had been allowed to keep their faculty positions, the Nazis must approve of Engel. His obligation, she lectured him, was to perpetuate America's "ideals of liberty and democracy, not to retard their progress by doing anything that would strengthen the slavery of fascism."[8]

Another—though lesser—form of slavery came through faculty supervision of examinations. A continuing hope of many students was to institute the honor system, by which students would pledge not to cheat on examinations and to report cases of cheating to a student committee, which would assess the penalties. Supporters of the honor system believed that it would not only end dishonesty but increase University democracy as well, for, as the *Kansan* said in 1919, every individual would have an "active part" in its working. At the time both the Men's Student Council and the Women's Student Government Association were backing it, and the University Senate had approved it, provided that 75 percent of the students voted for it in a referendum. But late in the spring only 840 students favored it, while 1,650 votes were required to institute it.[9] In the years ahead there was never enough interest or enthusiasm to change the system of faculty supervision prevalent throughout the University. Schools that tried an honor system reported different results. The Law School began one in 1922. Dean Herschel W. Arant asserted that the honor system greatly decreased dishonesty and gave the students a "proprietary feeling in the Law School, a pride in its equipment and standards," and a sense of obligation to protect its good name against the unscrupulous. Six years later the engineering students voted by a ratio of five to one to start an honor system. But the *Kansas Engineer* reported in 1929 that it was the "biggest farce connected with the curriculum of the school," for large numbers of students continued to cheat, and no one reported them. A University-wide poll of 957 students completed in 1930 revealed that eight of every nine believed that cheating was sometimes justified; and a large majority felt responsibility for no one's honesty but their own. The trouble was, said the *Kansan* in 1933, that American education put its emphasis on grades rather than true education, and that competition fostered cheating. Dishonesty would vanish only when a "new standard of education" appeared.[10]

The students' social theories varied as much as their ideas on the purposes and practices of higher education. They ranged from left through center to right, and thence to apathy. If some observers were to be believed, indeed, apathy about society's problems was the student body's outstanding characteristic. "The University of Kansas is perhaps primarily a social institution," John Ise wrote in 1925, "and that means that it has a more selfish spirit than it should have. I hear little about the spirit of service around here; while I am constantly reminded that the most important thing in the world is to make a swell social fraternity," and the next most important to discover how to make money. A decade later the editor of the *Gale*, a short-lived literary magazine, said that the campus was in the doldrums. The magazine had no central purpose or objective, he told an exasperated reader, because "any attempt to build a magazine around a set idea denouncing the hundred or so ails and ills one might think of . . . would, in the present surroundings, be simply a hurling of tinted pebbles into a static river. People hereabouts aren't easily excited mentally. They manage to keep alive enough to follow fairly well worn pathways, that's all. . . ." "Are you bored? Listless? Uninterested?" asked an editorial of 1952 in *upstream*, a student periodical dedicated to the humanities and politics. "Then you probably go to school at KU. Mount Oread, once a scene of intense rabble-rousing, seems to have lapsed into its traditional role of a country club college" with a "student body of cheerful automatons who wave banners on Saturday afternoons and get 'potted' on Saturday nights." Fifteen years later a *Kansan* editorialist was

Potter Lake in clear-water days, 1925.

apathetic about apathy itself: it was, she yawned, a "well-worn subject, and . . . a problem which can be solved by only very sensational means"—such as raising the price of beer or abolishing the brew.[11]

Despite the moans, the campus had sizable numbers of reformers. None of them, to be sure, had original ideas to offer; all borrowed from adults and from reformers on other campuses. Thus in the fall of 1919 the *Kansan* supported immigration restrictions on foreign radicals to prevent America's "flower bed of liberty" from being "trampled on and destroyed by this undesirable foreign element." Five years later the paper was mocking Kansans who wished to bar the *American Mercury* from the state because a recent issue contained an iconoclastic article on John Brown of local fame. The *Dove*, begun in 1925, continued on its irreverent way—though sporadically—until 1948. In the 1930s the student body had Marxists and Communists, and branches of the League for Industrial Democracy and the Young Communist League, which so troubled Edwin F. Abels, Clarence P. Oakes, and their allies.[12] On the whole, however, the radicals had no lasting impact on the student body. And while there was pacifism aplenty in the 1930s and widespread support for Franklin D. Roosevelt's New Deal, a study of a sample of 245 upperclassmen showed a considerable ignorance of national economic and political issues apart from war news.[13]

After the Second World War propaganda from the right became a minor feature of campus life. What passed for student conservatism was originally a reflection of a national movement conditioned by the Cold War between the United States and Russia, the hot war in Korea, the loyalty investigations of President Truman's administration, and the patriotism mongerings of Senator Joseph R. McCarthy of Wisconsin. "The 'dove of communism' is now in flight to spread the parasitic diseases of unrest and distrust into the people of our nation," Richard Tatum wrote in 1947 in a new publication called the *Eagle*. It was time that "we of this university and of this state be on guard against the common elements of this 'red menace.' " "The time has come for thinking conservatives to unite," wrote Kent Shearer in 1950. "Militant anti-radical action is needed as it has never been needed before," for the "left-wingers, locally and nationally"—they included President Truman and the Americans for Democratic Action—were on the move. "Militant conservatives must fight fire with fire. We must unite to combat this rising tide of hyper-progressivism."[14]

But militant conservatives found it an uphill struggle. The *Eagle* of 1947 soared for only two issues. When Shearer and others pushed a new *Eagle* from its nest in 1950—it was to be a "sounding board for various forms of Kansas anti-radical expression"—it plummeted into oblivion. A third *Eagle* came in 1951—though not liberal, it was at least anti-McCarthy—but after one issue its strength, too, was spent. Apparent permanence for the student conservative movement came only in the fall of 1961 with the organization of a campus chapter of the Young Americans for Freedom, a national society allegedly designed to preserve American values and institutions.[15]

Even as the YAF appeared, however, increasing numbers of Kansas students, like their counterparts throughout the country, were shifting—or drifting—leftward, though the left of the 1960s was not that of the 1930s. Throughout the sixties, moreover, the rate of shift accelerated. The public catchwords for the modern forms of ultra-liberalism or radicalism were the "new left," the "new morality," the "new student," or simply "the movement." The emphases of the "new students" were on the autonomy of the individual—upon the person as his own ethical guide, on opposition to the tyranny of traditional authority, and on a search for new means of effecting moral and social change. As a group they had lost the faith that their predecessors had had, not only in the several forms of Marxism, but in many of the institutions of American democracy itself as means of solving social problems: of the blacks and the poor, of war and peace, of indecency, cruelty, hypocrisy, and oppression. Most of the reformers had a new impatience, a contempt for gradualism, a hope—for some it was a conviction—that immediate action would produce almost immediate results. Whatever the nature of their attack on the University or on the evils of society at large, they demanded that adults treat them as autonomous persons, capable of deciding moral questions (at bottom, they knew, every question was a moral question) for themselves, capable of judging at every point what they should believe and how they should act.

The wellsprings of the new independence and the new criticism were as varied as the students themselves; they lay both within their own hearts and far afield. Some came naturally to protest and reform, prompted by their own moral urgings, and found in the University environment a freedom denied them at home or in high school to develop as moral agents. But they and others drew inspiration from the new civil-rights movement, in which students were deeply involved from the start; from the apparent dynamism, toughness, and grace of President John F. Kennedy and his New Frontiersmen, so different from the drifting bourgeois centrism of Dwight D. Eisenhower; or from Mario Savio and his fellow rebels at the University of California at Berkeley in 1964. Kennedy's assassination in 1963 shocked many of them into something approaching a comprehensive awareness of how much was still wrong with the nation. Many found inspiration in other heroes: Robert Kennedy, perhaps, or Martin Luther King, or Pope John XXIII, or Dr. Timothy Leary. For still others it was a senseless, imperialistic war in Vietnam that triggered their moral zeal; or Bob Dylan's records, which protested against everything deceitful and hurtful; or magazines, books, and plays: *Liberation* and *Ramparts*, Joseph Heller's *Catch-22*, B. F. Skinner's *Walden Two*, or Barbara Garson's *MacBird*, which in their various ways asked for a renewed appreciation of human dignity. Whatever the reasons, the new reformers looked into the abyss between ideal and reality in America and were appalled at its breadth and depth.

Although no individual or movement was typical of all the rest, many of the newer ideas appeared in a sit-in in 1965 protesting discrimination against blacks in both the University and the city of Lawrence. During the twentieth century, as during the nineteenth, University students—and some of the faculty—continued to manifest a strong racial prejudice. "What happens to the Negro student when he comes to Lawrence to enter the University?" Noel P. Gist asked in the *Dove* in 1927. "He enrolls regularly," Gist answered, "pays his matriculation fees, and enters classes to pursue his studies. But the story changes at that point in his career." During his four years he was "virtually segregated, entirely socially ostracized, discriminated against and shunned by the 'superior' whites. No wonder he believes that 'free Kansas' is a myth, a fantasy." He was barred from the swimming pool—despite the University's requirement that every student learn to swim—barred from intercollegiate athletics, barred from the glee club, the band, the orchestra, and the debating team. The ROTC rejected him, the Men's Student Council refused him membership, the University segregated him at concerts and basketball games, most Lawrence restaurants and cafés refused to serve him, local white churches and ministers greeted him with cold stares "provided, of course, he is greeted at all." Gist might have added that black girls could not live in Corbin Hall, that white coeds shunned the toilets black coeds used, that Negroes had to hold their own dances separate from those of the whites, and that no white fraternity or sorority would pledge a black. When the Memorial Union opened a new cafeteria in 1927, blacks had to sit in a special area; while the section was open to whites, the rest of the cafeteria was closed to blacks. And if most faculty members treated Negroes and whites equally in class, at least one professor—probably more—segregated them in the rear.[16]

Discrimination was the result of white student prejudices, which they learned from their parents and the larger society; the prejudices of Lawrence citizens generally; and the reluctance of Chancellors Lindley and Malott and the regents to fight them head on. Neither chancellor bore the slightest taint of prejudice; yet neither was a crusader. Most of the white students would not associate with Negroes under any circumstances, Lindley explained repeatedly to the critics of segregation and discrimination. If blacks were not segregated in the cafeteria and at concerts, he said in 1928, the cafeteria would have to close and the concerts cease from lack of patronage. He also believed that open agitation did more harm than good, that a quiet gradualism and the slow spread of good will were the best means of ending the evils. Malott agreed. "I have no antipathy whatever for the negro and have great sympathy for the plight in which they find themselves," he told Governor Schoeppel in 1943 in the midst of a propaganda campaign by the Kansas branch of the NAACP against discrimination on Mount Oread. But the Chancellor thought that "we have gone as far in non-discrimination as the people of this state are willing to accept. I propose to lie low, avoid argument, avoid public statements, and trust that we can temporize with the situation for the present."[17]

The result of temporizing good will was creeping progress toward equality. Segregation in the cafeteria died an unnoticed death in the early 1940s, though it continued for a while at the soda fountain; in 1943 the student government groups voted to admit Negroes to University dances; starting in 1947 the athletic staff decreased

THE UNIVERSITY OF KANSAS: *A History*

their opposition to blacks trying out for varsity sports. After the Second World War there was no ban on Negroes living in University residence halls, although the Housing Office required racial identification on applications and roomed blacks either together or with consenting whites. White fraternities and sororities continued to reject blacks as members, and the School of Education catered to the prejudices of local school boards by identifying students racially in advance and by sending black practice teachers only where they were welcome.[18]

But from the late forties to the early sixties the Negro rights movement on campus was concerned more with discrimination in Lawrence than with discrimination on the Hill. Thus in 1947 and 1948, when several students formed a chapter of the Committee of Racial Equality, they sought mainly to desegregate Hill cafés and restaurants and theaters downtown. On April 15, 1948, twenty-five CORE members and sympathizers held a sit-in at Brick's Cafe to force the manager to serve blacks. After three hours other students threw them out. CORE's greatest grievance against the University was the refusal of Dean of Students Laurence C. Woodruff and Chancellor Malott to allow the organization to meet in rooms on campus, on the grounds that it was not a student group but a national organization and that it was concerned mainly with "business practices in the city of Lawrence. Those are not the University's problems. . . ."[19]

Even here, however, policy changed. While students continued to condemn the practices of private businessmen—in the early 1960s the student Civil Rights Council was after barbershops and taverns for discriminating—Chancellor Murphy and several faculty members urged theater and restaurant owners to treat blacks as they did whites. After Murphy threatened in 1954 and 1955 to show first-run movies free on campus unless he got action downtown, the theater owners stopped segregating blacks and in the next few years the Eldridge Hotel restaurant and several taverns allowed Negroes to enter.[20]

Yet on campus there was no direct action against contemptible practices—not, that is, until 1965. In 1955 Murphy had boasted that campus discrimination had been "virtually eliminated" except in fraternities and sororities. It did not seem that way to students of the next decade. On March 8, 1965, the Civil Rights Council and its allies repudiated several years of moral suasion and allegedly fruitless discussions with University officers by a sit-in in the office of Chancellor W. Clarke Wescoe. Their goals were to force Wescoe to order fraternities and sororities to end discrimination; to compel the University to break all ties with discriminatory organizations; to compel the *Kansan* to refuse ads from landlords and organizations that rejected blacks. The Housing Office, they said, should screen out racist landlords; the School of Education must refuse to assign student teachers to discriminatory schools; the All Student Council must pass legislation to improve race relations. And a board of faculty, students, and administrators must be created to deal with landlords and organizations who pretended not to discriminate, but really did.

After a demonstration outside Wescoe's office in the afternoon, some 150 people crowded inside. On the whole they were both polite and orderly. Though informed that they were subject to arrest if they remained after the normal closing time of 5:00, 110 stayed on. At 5:25 the Lawrence police began arresting them and hauling them in University buses to the county jail and court, where they were charged with disturbing the peace. The University suspended them. Then each side accused the other of hindering the antidiscrimination cause. "Now these young men and women want to stop talking and start acting," Wescoe said, "but their action may well help build back up a wall other men have been working to take down stone by stone." But patience was no virtue to CRC members. "They no longer care to participate in vague discussions which only show how difficult it will be to reach a solution," a spokesman said. "They have no desire to negotiate until they stand to gain from negotiations. They will listen when they have something concrete before them. Is this such a deplorable tactic?" That night sympathizers staged a great anti-Wescoe parade that wound around Lilac Lane in front of his house and Jayhawk Boulevard, alarming the Chancellor and his family.

But the tension quickly vanished with notable gains for the CRC. Wescoe reinstated the students the day after he suspended them. On March 10, having won promises of CRC cooperation, he announced the formation of a University Human Relations Committee, chaired by Dean Woodruff, to investigate charges of racial discrimination and make recommendations. Late in March it urged

Changing forms of student protest.

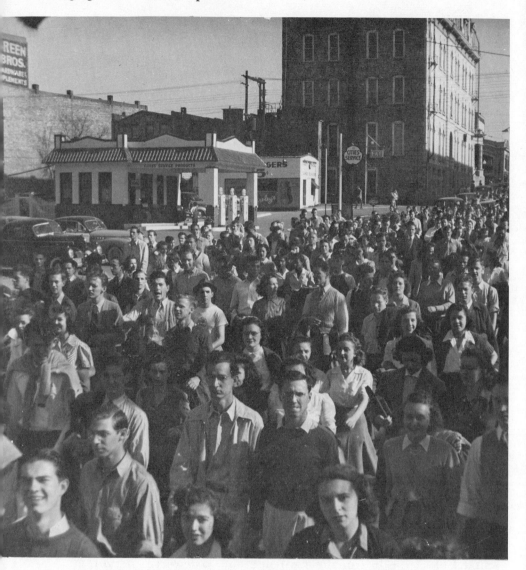

After a 20–16 KU victory over K-State on November 15, 1941, which
followed a K-State triumph over powerful Nebraska, KU students march
to demand a Monday holiday. They lost.

The sit-inners overflow the chancellor's office on March 8, 1965, in their protest against various forms of University-sanctioned racial discrimination. They won.

that all student publications reject ads for things not equally available to all students, and Wescoe signed an All Student Council bill forbidding ads by discriminatory individuals and firms. A week later he and the Human Relations Committee decreed that discriminatory landlords were to lose their listing in the University housing file. In May they affirmed the University's "present policies" prohibiting dormitory assignments on the basis of color, race, or creed. Later that month the committee recommended that the School of Education sever connections with Kansas school districts that discriminated in the hiring of both student and full-time teachers. And the following fall the regents themselves decreed that while student organizations had the right to establish "standards of membership," that right existed only "provided that all students are afforded equal opportunity to meet those standards." CRC leaders professed themselves pleased, said that all their demands had been met, and asserted that the main problem of the future would be the enforcement of the policies adopted.[21]

The sit-in was a harbinger of a new emphasis on direct confrontation, unorthodox and illegal action, and even violence as a means of reform in the later sixties and early seventies. A harbinger of change of another kind came on the evening of March 7, 1967, when by invitation student members of the College Intermediary Board visited the campus AAUP chapter to lecture the faculty on the University's proper nature and their responsibility to the students. While research and publication were valuable, two of the students said, every professor's "primary goal" should be to become an "effective teacher." It was important that "a university remember that meaningful knowledge is not simply something put in a book to be checked in and out of the library," said two others. "It is conveyed primarily by real persons in a dynamic situation." To make relations with the faculty ever more dynamic, they recommended more student power by letting students assist departments in course evaluations, curricular changes, the promotion of better teachers, and "departmental innovation" generally. "What we propose . . . is that you include students in those activities in which you are now engaged, in everything from your coffee breaks to your research, in many of your departmental activities and parties, and even in faculty business. Is it really outrageous to suggest that students might have an interest in the selection of a departmental chairman?

Or that students might have valid comments on the structure of departmental courses?" "Truly effective criticism of the University can be initiated by neither the Administration nor by the Faculty from the permanent nature of their positions," added Gary Gregg. "Only the Students, who should add a perpetual element of dynamism to the university community, can call attention to the fact that this is not the best of all possible worlds."[22]

Those ideas heralded three years of ferment which would see students admitted to a restructured University Senate and to school and department committees. If the changes were clearly the start of a new era of student-faculty relations, they also marked the end of an era of University control over the students in which the authorities played the role of substitute parents. University authorities, of course, had never tried to supervise all that the students did. While they preached the highest moral standards to the students, they left them to live their private lives in private: thus they did not prowl the country lanes looking into parked cars or patrol the fleshpots of Lawrence and Kansas City. Objectionable acts performed in private were never unobjectionable, but there was nothing that could be done about them.

Public transgressions against decency and good taste, however, were something else again, for they both influenced taxpayers and legislators and set evil precedents. In 1914, then, the University Senate formally disapproved the "vulgar and offensive language being used in University yells and songs," and asked the Men's Student Council to help check it. The next year an enraged Chancellor Strong and Senate swooped down on the editors of the *Sour Owl*, a student humor magazine, for a number of tasteless statements in an issue celebrating the May Fete. "The University," Strong said, "is entirely opposed to the publication of any vulgar, indecent or libelous matters and has always strenuously upheld the highest and purest type of student life." He would hold all students "strictly to account" for any statements that "by direction or indirection, openly or by implication could be regarded as indecent or vulgar or offensive by right minded people." In the same spirit Chancellor Lindley in 1921 issued an edict against "improper" and "indecent" dancing at University affairs and gave chaperones power to enforce it; and Chancellor Murphy in 1952 asserted his moral authority after two nights of panty raids. On May 19 and 20 the then popular male college sport of raiding women's dormitories and sororities for panties, brassieres, and other undergarments reached Mount Oread. Between five hundred and a thousand men stormed three dormitories and five sororities. "We want falsies," the lads bayed outside the Alpha Chi Omega house. There was little viciousness and only slight property damage, but one girl was struck near the eye by a thrown rock. Murphy—surrogate parent to all the students—said that he would hold every raider responsible not only for damage, but also for his "actions in an extra-legal activity. He will be responsible to me for his future as a student at the University of Kansas."[23]

But the officials were always happier when they were saving students from temptation and helping them toward happier lives than when punishing them for their transgressions. Thus there were advisers (later deans) of men, women, and students generally, along with their innumerable assistants; housemothers for the fraternities and sororities; floor counselors for the dormitories; the YMCA, YWCA, and other campus religious groups. Watkins Hospital offered psychiatric as well as regular medical care. Early in 1964, in addition, the regents banned cigarette machines and sales on all state-supported campuses. Two years later Dr. Raymond Schwegler, director of Watkins Hospital, and son of the earlier dean of the School of Education, stubbornly resisted student pressure to issue contraceptive materials to unmarried students. "I know this is old fashioned, mid-Victorian, and that the *Kansan* will cut us to ribbons," he was quoted as saying, "but I don't want to do it and my staff backs me completely. . . . Watkins will not contribute to the recreational activities of the campus."[24]

During the two decades after the Second World War the construction of several huge dormitories became the most important expression of the University's concern for the quality of the students' extracurricular lives. The "increasing accent on the modern university and college," Chancellor Malott wrote in 1946, was to provide students with a "well-rounded experience," and the "experiences of the college environment outside of the classroom and laboratory are perhaps as important in developing the character and personality, the curiosity and imagination, and energy of the future citizen, as the hours spent each day under the various professors and teachers." Kansas parents, moreover, were no longer "satisfied to

send their youngsters off to shift for themselves, relatively unsuper-
vised, in rooming houses of various and assorted types and standards,
or to the garret and basement rooms where students too often eke
out a lonely and unsatisfying existence." The University had to
provide them with opportunities for "gracious living together,"
"wholesome food, proper chaperonage," and a "better-regulated
existence."[25]

By 1946, with the University on the edge of a great enrollment
boom, the situation was tight indeed. With the regents anticipating
seven thousand students, there were only 455 dormitory rooms.
Even with the fraternities and sororities the University could house
only about 28 percent of the student body; and there was also a
housing shortage throughout Lawrence. The regents thought that
in the future there should be dormitory rooms for about five thousand students. In 1947 the legislature authorized revenue bonds to
finance construction; the federal government provided low interest
loans; and in 1955 the tax for the Kansas Educational Building Fund
was increased to one mill, with a quarter of the amount to go for
dormitories at the state schools. There were also numerous gifts for
dormitories and scholarship halls. The University's greatest bene-
factors were Mr. and Mrs. Joseph R. Pearson of Corsicana, Texas,
he a largely self-educated oil man, she an alumna of 1901. Together
they gave almost $700,000, which, supplemented by other funds,
provided two halls for self-supporting students (1952), two women's
dormitories (1955), and a men's dormitory (1959).[26]

In the fall of 1966 the University housed 4,818 of its 14,892 students—32.3 percent—in dormitories and scholarship halls; fraternities and sororities took in 2,517 (16.9 percent) more. To provide
apartments for the growing number of married students, in 1956 the
regents authorized the University to borrow $1,000,000 from the
Federal Housing and Home Finance Agency. Ten buildings with
120 apartments opened in August, 1957; another ten went up in
1959 and five more in 1962. In the fall of 1966 there were 385 students in them, along with spouses and children.[27]

The impact of dormitory life on the denizens was impossible to
assess in a general way, for the students' reactions depended as much
on their own personalities and backgrounds as on conditions they
faced. Some undergraduates rejoiced in the new environment, in
making new friends, in participating in the halls' social and athletic

activities. Others disliked sharing rooms with strangers, lamented the institutionalized lack of privacy in toilets, lounges, and cafeterias, and complained of noise, discourtesy, dirt, and unimaginative menus. Still others pointed out that large dormitories inhibited intellectual development, for one's fellow dormitory dwellers were usually not one's fellow students in class.[28]

Reactions to the University's *in loco parentis* policy also varied. Some students favored it. When Chancellor Lindley forbade indecent dancing in 1921, he had been heeding a request from all the organized women's groups, whose members were solicitous for Mount Oread's moral atmosphere. Five years later the Men's Student Council advised him to ban automobiles from campus. Lindley asked the students and their parents to keep cars at home, agreeing with the student leaders that they were unnecessary in a town as small as Lawrence, that the auto opened the way to a "more tempting social life," thus interfering with the life of the mind, and that cars were the playthings of the wealthy minority of students and therefore "out of keeping with the democratic spirit which should prevail."[29]

But to expect that most students would rejoice in moral supervision was to forget the spirit of the American adolescent. When Lindley tried to ban cars from campus in the spring of 1926, the *Sour Owl* lambasted him for his presumption. Appropriate traffic laws would relieve the apparent congestion, the editors said, and inequality of wealth was no concern of the University. Most students judged their peers by their personal—not their monetary—worth; and the edict would lead to "intolerance instead of democracy and drab uniformity instead of individuality." A more comprehensive objection to the institution's parental concern came in 1932 from Frank McClelland, who was running for election to the Men's Student Council. McClelland's platform was nothing if not inclusive:

1. To hell with the administration. The university's topheavy.
2. To hell with all the deans, especially the dean of women.
3. To hell with the state legislature. It is a bunch of ignorant yokels.
4. To hell with the Y.M.C.A., the Y.W.C.A., the W.S.G.A., the L.W.V., the R.O.T.C., and the A.A.U.W., the W.C.T.U.,—and so on for the rest of the alphabet.
5. To hell with prohibition. If elected, I promise to install a completely equipped speakeasy in the Union Building.

6. To hell with prudery. If elected I promise to decapitate all house mothers and to make the fraternities and sororities pair off and move in together. I also promise to install either a maternity ward or a birth control clinic in the hospital.

7. To hell with most of the faculty. If elected, I promise to make all faculty positions subject to the control of the students who have to take the courses involved.

To hell, in short, with all silly rules and all silly people.

Liberty *is* license—or nothing.

Vote for me and install a new era of Rabelaisian good times on the campus.

Haven't we all suffered long enough?

Yours for the campus revolution.[30]

But McClelland lost and the revolution never came. Most students who desired to reduce the University's authority and increase their own were liberals, not radicals. One of their major goals was to expand the power of the Men's Student Council and the Women's Student Government Association to set rules for student conduct and punish the violators. They were aided by the fact that the chancellors and the University Senate found supervision always onerous. Immediately after the First World War the ferment of student democracy bubbled every bit as yeastily as the ferment of faculty democracy. When the Senate in February, 1919, rejected a plea for liberalized rules permitting more student dances and allowing them to continue past midnight—then the normal closing hour—law students hung the Senate in effigy (a rag doll), and a mass meeting passed a resolution demanding greater authority in their own government. "If we are not capable of self government," it said, "then we are unfit to be citizens of this state, and this Institution is violating the purpose for which it was founded in not allowing us this right." Unless the students had their way, moreover, they threatened the "possibility of more drastic action."[31]

They had their way. After a student committee conferred with Chancellor Strong and several senators, in March the Senate created a new Committee on Student Affairs. It consisted of ten faculty members of the Senate's Student Interests Committee, and ten students. During the 1919–1920 academic year Strong, the students, and the faculty worked out a new constitution for the men. While it left ultimate power with the faculty and officers, it made the Associated Men of the University of Kansas the "responsible governing body for the men students," with power to promote and regulate their activities, under the powers granted by the chancellor, the Senate, and the Board of Administration. An elected Student Council had power to foster University traditions, control rallies and parades, supervise (with the executive council of the WSGA) student social affairs, call mass meetings to consider matters of general concern, and arbitrate all disputes between members of different schools, classes, or organizations. The Council could also investigate and punish infractions of its rules. Like the University Senate the constitution authorized the Joint Committee on Student Affairs, which was to act as a "clearing house for all questions at issue between faculties and students." After the men and the Senate approved the constitution in 1920, Strong told the Board of Administration that it represented the "best judgment and sentiment of the best judges of student government in the student body and the faculty." A year later the Senate approved a similar document for the women.[32]

Things at first went so well that in 1925 the Senate gave the Men's Student Council "full responsibility for whatever control and regulation may be necessary of the extra-curricular affairs of the men students" except regulating contracts for student rooms. Although "university representatives" retained power to punish students for major transgressions, the MSC now had authority to compel the observance of city, state, and national laws and also the "observance of the code of morals usually thought of in connection with the phrase 'Conduct becoming a gentleman.' "[33]

Yet student democracy, like American democracy itself, had its seamy side. In the 1920s and 1930s the students often seemed far more interested in winning elections for the sake of prestige and power rather than accomplishing any intelligible objective. Until the mid-1940s the dominant political group was the Society of Pachacamac, founded as a men's honor society in 1912 and supported by most of the fraternities. According to one of its opponents it won power by actually playing down the importance of student government, divining that if the Greeks did not take it seriously they would vote for fellow Greeks out of loyalty, and if the independents were apathetic they would not vote at all. Numerous opposition parties appeared, but their successes were slight and they were often subject to violent counterattack. During the campaign of 1934, for example, vandals attacked the Delta Chi, Beta Theta Pi, Acacia, and Sigma Alpha Epsilon fraternities, which led the anti-Pachacamac Oread-Jayhawk party. The houses were bombed with eggs and brown paint, and "Beat the Oreads" was painted on the Delta Chi porch.[34]

Whether or not Pachacamac was responsible, during the 1930s the students became increasingly cynical about student government. Both the Men's Student Council and the WSGA were of slight importance, and even the Joint Committee on Student Affairs grew listless. But interest in student government revived in the early 1940s when Student Council members grew convinced that Chancellor Malott and the University Senate had autocratic tendencies. On November 30, 1942, the Council noted that the Senate had arbitrarily shortened the Christmas vacation and charged University authorities with ignoring laws passed by the Council and with failing to consult with the Joint Committee on Student Affairs, the "mirror of student opinion." After appointing a committee to discover Malott's ideas about student government, the councillors resolved to resign en masse unless "some workable plan of active student participation in the government, especially in all phases of the student government of the University" appeared.[35]

The result was a flurry of student-faculty-administrative meetings from which came a new student government constitution and a pledge of student representation on University committees whose work bore upon extracurricular activities. Starting in the fall of 1943 there was a single All Student Council, of some thirty elected members. It had power to promote and regulate extracurricular activities and coordinate student activities with "programs of faculty and administrative governing bodies," and in so doing to "promote the highest interests of the University of Kansas and to cultivate loyalty to the University among its students." When the regents approved the new constitution, however, they gave the chancellor an absolute veto on all the Council's laws. Besides approving the new constitution Malott approved student representation on numerous committees such as the Athletic Board, the concert course, the extracurricular and curricular calendar committees, and the general committee on aids and awards. There was also to be a joint student-faculty committee to "consider and discuss problems of student welfare and general University interest."[36]

With the creation of the All Student Council and the end of the Second World War, student government became somewhat more important and responsible. Several organizations appeared to challenge Pachacamac: the Independent Students Association, the Progressive Student Government League, FACTS, the Allied Greeks and Independents. Although student apathy and cynicism about all of them were still abundant, in the mid-1950s Pachacamac had to go underground. In the early 1960s the two main groups were the Vox Populi and the University Party, both of which were combinations of fraternities, sororities, and dormitory groups. Whether or not they expressed different principles was not readily apparent.[37]

Despite the changes that the twentieth century brought to the University, there was no evidence to show that the general interests and desires of the student body changed very much. If campus concern about the outside world and its problems grew, most students were concerned mainly with getting their degrees and finding success and happiness beyond the campus. Many deans and professors testified that there were growing numbers of increasingly intelligent and perceptive students on campus, but the overall academic average of undergraduates for 1964–1965 was 1.46 of a possible 3.0, which was little different from the 1.44 overall average of 1938–1939.[38] As one walked the campus, one heard mostly the comments of yesteryear: about incredibly large classroom assignments; incredibly easy courses; excellent teachers, poor teachers, and teachers in between; term papers due on Friday yet not begun on Thursday; forthcoming job interviews; sex; approaching parties, games, and celebrations. Only the idiom was new.

Intellectual activity beyond the classroom continued to run through familiar channels into a great variety of special interest groups, departmental clubs, and student publications.[39] The *Kansan* continued without direct competition as the campus newspaper, its editorial views changing with the times, the editors, and sometimes for no discernible reason at all, its reportage varying from wretched to mediocre, its letters-to-the-editor columns filled with angry or pseudo-angry comments about everything imaginable. From the fall of 1914 until 1956 the campus had the assets and liabilities of a humor magazine, the *Sour Owl*, begun by the Owl

Society, a semisecret men's honor society, but later sponsored by the All Student Council. Always trembling on the edge of good taste, now and again it disappeared under administrative wrath, only to reappear with the same emphasis on satire, sex, booze, and student hedonism generally. From 1946 to 1950, with the *Sour Owl* temporarily banned, the All Student Council sponsored the *Bitter Bird.* It began with two faculty advisers who hoped to keep the humor clean. But in the spring of 1948 its editors complained that all the students wanted was dirty jokes. These, successive editors provided, with the result that the administration abolished the magazine in favor of a new *Sour Owl,* now under the supervision of the School of Journalism. After the *Bitter Bird* and the new *Sour Owl* came the vulgar *Squat* (1955–1958).[40] But by the mid-1950s the days of the campus humor magazine were numbered. Kansas students neither wanted nor were able to produce a magazine equal in quality or imagination to, say, the Harvard *Lampoon,* whose wit might have survived the years. In the morally tolerant climate of the later 1950s and the 1960s, moreover, students could find ample sexual titillation in *Playboy* and its less pretentious imitators, which were bolder and better than publications the students could produce for themselves.

During the decade after the Second World War students did issue several literary or literary-political magazines whose quality and earnestness recalled the *University Review* of the 1880s and 1890s. The best of them was *upstream,* which appeared first in February, 1949. Concerned with humanities and politics, it was intended to "contribute to this dream of an integral democracy based on the principles of human dignity and responsibility, individual freedom, and economic and social justice." Drawing upon faculty members as well as students—Walter Sandelius wrote on "The Politics of Common Sense," John Maxon on modern art, John Ise on the cultural impoverishment of a super-technological society —*upstream* surveyed the campus and the nation with passionate rationalism, and reviewed books and motion pictures with sophistication. It lasted until 1954.[41] Except for the *Kansan,* the only student publication that survived the years was the yearbook, the *Jayhawker,* first published in 1901.

Beyond intercollegiate athletics and the student government groups the two most important kinds of organized extracurricular

activities in the twentieth century were the fraternities and sororities. Both of them continued to plague and pleasure the University
as a whole. "If there were no fraternities in American colleges,"
Chancellor Strong (Psi Upsilon) wrote in 1912, "and the matter
were to come up de novo I should probably have some doubts about
the matter." While they had "great possibilities" of standing for
all the "best things in the college," the potentialities "have not by
any means been developed": liquor and sexual immorality were
rife, scholarly tendencies conspicuous by their absence, "selfishness
on the part of members that leads them to neglect the general interest of the institution" prevalent.[42]

So in general said Men's Adviser John R. Dyer in 1925 and
Chancellor Malott in 1949. Their comments gave fairly accurate pictures of fraternity and sorority life. The "chief, if not the
only, function of the American fraternity," Dyer thought, "is to
replace the homes of our students." Into the words "home" and
"fraternity" should be read "affection, encouragement, stimulation,
comradeship, food, shelter, refuge, rest, and a thousand other blessings which defy enumeration." From them should be abolished the
prevalent snobbery, politics, "social display," the "cheap publicity
during Hell Week," restricting social contacts to other Greeks, and
"kindred perversions" of "fraternity." If without question the fraternities had made sizable beneficial contributions to the University, without question they should be making more. Dyer thought
that the Oxford plan of residential colleges for all students was "in-
finitely preferable" to the fraternities and sororities but impossible
to establish under present conditions.[43]

Chancellor Malott (Beta Theta Pi) believed that fraternities and
sororities were heading for abolition from without unless they re-
formed from within. Speaking to a convention of the Alpha Chi
Omega sorority, he couched his remarks in "sorority terminology,"
but said they applied equally to the fraternities. Admitting that
sororities fostered self-government, aided moral growth, provided
leadership for the women students, gave "maximum training and
help in the gracious art of living," and offered other benefits, Malott
used most of his time to point out their failings. Intersorority competition for top ranking in such things as social prestige, athletic
prowess, and even scholarly excellence often discouraged the very
loyalty to the University as a whole that sororities were supposed to

promote. The "pressure for excellence," moreover, often became ruthless, and a "psychology develops of attaining group objectives no matter how many are trampled on in the process." Sororities tended to give "high priority to conformance—conformance in dress, in hair styling, in social participation, in taking the usual easy courses on which adequate notes exist in the chapter house files." Sorority standards were often aimed merely at "superficial success and . . . esteem," rather than at "what the sorority can do for the development of the intellect, the poise, and the character of its individual members. . . . And I have never seen a book in a sorority house," Malott said. "There may be some somewhere, but they are not in public view." (Back in 1920 William Allen White's son had bemoaned the fact that in his fraternity, Phi Delta Theta, there were only two books. One was *Tarzan of the Apes* and the other H. G. Wells's novel *Joan and Peter*, whose owner was trying to trade it for a translation of *Hannibal in the Alps*.[44]) Atop everything else sororities were far less democratic than they should be. They had too many rules and regulations. "Life by formula has been a Utopian dream since the dawn of our civilization," Malott said, "but the attempt has always ended in slavery." In general sororities were not doing nearly enough either to build their members' characters and intellects or to increase the University's quality.[45]

Yet all was not of a piece and there were changes for the better. In 1956, when there were twenty-seven social fraternities and thirteen sororities on campus, a study reported considerable variety in the fraternities' treatment of pledges as they introduced them to the meaning and life of the houses. Some imposed almost tyrannical rules while others left the pledges quite free; some made pledges virtually the equals of active members, while others made them abject inferiors; within some fraternities individuality was encouraged, while in others it was not. Taking all of them together, there was the widest possible latitude of accepted behavior, beliefs, and customs.[46]

Although cruel exclusiveness continued—Negroes and most Jews were pariahs, and most non-Greeks were shunned—and although the old emphasis on fun and games was always there, by the mid-1950s there was a greater emphasis on scholarship (or at least grades) than before and a new stress on social service. In 1952 the overall scholastic average of fraternities at Kansas ranked thirty-eighth of all fraternity systems on state university campuses. But by that time Kansas fraternity leaders were heeding a call from the National Interfraternity Conference for an elevation of averages: for the 1954–1955 year Kansas fraternities ranked fifth. A decade later fifteen of the twenty-eight fraternities exceeded the all-University scholastic average. Replacing some of the inanities of Hell Week were such things as helping the poor and neighborhood cleanups, designed to improve both society and the fraternities' public image.[47]

Yet just as a counterpoise to greater maturity and better public relations, Kansas continued throughout the twentieth century to have a chapter of Theta Nu Epsilon on campus. Banned and banned again, it always reappeared, dedicated, the *Kansan* said in 1923, to the "furtherance of debauch and . . . the gaining of questionable political ends." TNE carried on the good old traditions of fraternity fun: burning its initials into the stadium grass and painting them on every convenient wall, publishing leaflets mocking its detractors, womanizing, drinking, and gambling, defying the authorities to discover and punish the members. One onlooker recalled a Kansas Relays parade in the early 1950s in which a hired Negro led a donkey down Massachusetts Street with "TNE" painted on its side and a sign across its back saying "They're trying to ride our ass off the campus."[48] But it proved impossible to do so, and here was still another testimony to both the continuing variety and the continuing sameness of the student body and student life.

32

Intercollegiate Athletics: "What is Football to Mean at the University of Kansas?"

IN the history of intercollegiate athletics at Kansas what mattered was not whether its teams won or lost, but how the University played the games. It played them like most other large American universities: with the University community divided against itself about the place of athletics in the school, about the importance of winning at any cost, about the meaning of amateurism. The arguments were efforts to answer the question of the extent to which the institution's quality and prosperity depended upon the quality of its teams. Starting in the 1890s, students, faculty, officers, and alumni wrangled over that and related problems with at least as much heat and vigor—and often more—as the athletes displayed on the field.

Once upon a time University athletics had been touchingly innocent and the school had neither football nor basketball teams. From 1866 to 1890 students played at a variety of sports and formed a number of intercollegiate teams, but their organization was informal, often haphazard, and always amateur. There was a baseball team in 1874—but it apparently existed mainly to get its members' pictures into the yearbook. Another nine appeared in 1875, but the first intercollegiate contest of which record remained was a 23–20 victory over Washburn University of Topeka in 1880. Baseball teams were a regular feature of the 1880s, but played only a few games each year. From time to time other teams were formed. In September, 1887, Professor Arthur G. Canfield and several students formed a tennis group, which during the next seven years lost only

645

one match. Beginning in 1880 there were sporadic intramural track and field meets, but the first intercollegiate games came only in 1893, when the University defeated all comers in an open contest. While intramural rowing races started on the Kaw in 1890, the sport never aroused enough interest to produce a University eight.[1]

Until 1890 there was no group to coordinate or manage inter-collegiate sports and teams. Each team each year was in effect an ad hoc organization. Several students formed a Kansas University Athletic Association in 1884, but when only a few undergraduates joined and the Board of Regents refused to grant a requested $150, it languished. Arthur Canfield reported in 1891 that most Kansas students were apathetic about intercollegiate athletics, unlike students elsewhere, and hence the University had little to offer.[2]

Even as Canfield wrote, however, enthusiasm was on the rise. On December 13, 1889, a mass meeting of students and faculty members in the auditorium of the University Building heard Canfield and William H. Carruth extol undergraduate athletics and call for a new Athletic Association to pep things up. Alive with "University spirit," the meeting approved one, with Carruth as president and a student-faculty board of directors. The Association's first goal was to get an athletic field. Since the regents had no money, Carruth and the directors asked for student contributions to grade and drain part of the northern campus.[3] But there was a difference between cheering and giving, and the athletic entrepreneurs had to await a benefactor. He appeared in 1890 in the person of John J. McCook, a Harvard alumnus who was now general counsel and a director of the Santa Fe Railroad and thus an associate of Regent Charles S. Gleed. McCook had given the commencement address, and so warmly had the University received him—among other things he got an LL.D.—that he offered $1,500 for an athletic field. After debating locations for a year, a regents' committee persuaded ex-Governor Charles Robinson to sell half of a 12½-acre site north of the campus for the $1,500, and to donate the rest.[4]

Soon after the University opened in September, 1890, Athletic Association officers held another mass meeting to keep spirits aboil—Canfield replaced Carruth as president—and then organized a football team. After a preliminary contest against the Kansas City, Missouri, YMCA, the team played games with Baker University on November 22 and December 6. Baker wrecked the Kansas debut,

22–9, and according to umpire William H. Carruth also won the second game, 12–10. In the closing minutes, with Baker leading by that score, William J. Coleman of Kansas ran the length of the field for the apparent winning touchdown. Carruth disallowed it, claiming that Kansas had called time out before Coleman got the ball. Kansas rooters were appalled. "Whatever process of reasoning Prof. Carruth may adopt to justify his decision," the *University Courier* said, "whatever technicalities he may find to fortify him in his position, the game will always be claimed by the entire student body, and will always be remembered as a brilliant and fairly won victory."[5]

For the future of football on Mount Oread, however, what counted was not the alleged victory itself, but the reaction to it. The scene that followed Coleman's run, the *Courier* reporter said, "beggars description. Every University man went wild, hats were ruined and canes were broken. A crowd of enthusiasts piled on Coleman and then bore him off on their shoulders." That night Coleman led a great parade through Lawrence to a huge bonfire and rally, climaxed by an enthusiastic speech by Chancellor Snow, who had as much school spirit as any undergraduate. Football had come to stay. In 1891 and 1892 the University played full seasons of eight games each; its record was fourteen wins, a loss (to Baker), and a tie (with Washington University of St. Louis).[6]

The immediate popularity of football arose from several factors. It was a team sport—which gave fans a group as a whole to cheer for —yet with ample opportunity for individual heroics. In the 1890s it was a brutal and dangerous game played only by the brave (who might also be sadists or masochists). Players wore little protective equipment; there were no helmets: to protect their skulls players let their hair grow from summer to December. Games were played in halves of forty-five minutes with a ten-minute intermission; there were no substitutions except to replace men who had incapacitating injuries or who were absolutely exhausted. While the rules outlawed throttling, slugging, and tripping, observance of the rules was casual and punishment lax.[7] As had been true from time immemorial, the weak of both sexes lionized the brave, and sadistic or frustrated fans found vicarious satisfactions aplenty. Making football still more attractive was its playing in the invigorating fall season when student hearts were relatively unburdened by the weight of classes or yearnings for the summer vacation.

Most important, though, was the prevalent belief that an excellent football team bespoke an excellent university, and the knowledge that football triumphs would bring a much desired fame. Since the first intercollegiate contest between Princeton and Rutgers in 1869 the popularity of football had grown rapidly. Many of the universities that Kansas spoke of equaling one day—Harvard and Yale, Cornell and Michigan—had teams of national repute.[8] "The fact that a university supports winning athletic teams shows it to be a live and energetic institution," said the *Weekly University Courier* after the 1890 season. Winning teams advertised their colleges nationally, and "young men just to enter college are attracted to the school with the greatest reputation both for scholarship and for the maintenance of live and successful college enterprises." After the 7–0–1 football season of 1891 the *University Review* asserted that the "influence and result of our football victories can hardly be estimated. . . . It [*sic*] has advertised the University more than an outlay of a thousand dollars could have done in any other way." As long as athletics remained subordinate to intellectual matters, victories meant progress for the whole school. "Let croakers step back; we are marching on. Long live and prosper the athletics of K.S.U.!"[9]

Chancellor Snow and many faculty members agreed. But Snow also believed that when the players had good leadership from the coach, football fostered the "control, concentration of mental faculties in sudden emergencies, and the rapid exercise of intelligent will in doing the right thing at the right time and place. These are qualities which secure success in practical life, and for their development properly regulated athletic training should be promoted." Or, as team member Fred B. Gump (Law, '97) wrote: "Just a short time after our midwestern pioneers had quit chasing the buffaloes out of the back pastures, they began to send their crop of sons to the state universities; these boys were big and restless and had bred into them several generations of toughness and stamina. Some diversion had to be found to keep them from taking the college towns apart and the answer was football. Here was a sport where they could pit their strength individually and collectively, and did they love it."[10]

To improve character, control violence, and win games, Athletic Association officers sought the ideal coach. In 1891 and 1892 they found him in, of all men, Professor Edwin M. Hopkins of the English Department. While Hopkins had not played the game at Princeton, he carefully studied its tactics, stressing to his players that football was not a mass fight but a "mental and physical contest between two numerically equal manpower entities, but practically unequal in training, speed, strategy, and strength." He inspired his teams, one player remembered, with the "all-for-one, one-for-all spirit and morale, unity in action and never-quit tenacity, and a vocabulary that knew not defeat, and the slogan 'Attack with fury, defend with double fury.' "[11]

Here was strictly amateur football. Team members received no money for playing; the coach was a faculty member in an academic discipline who received no extra pay, had a perfect moral character, and won games. Unfortunately Hopkins was the last as well as the first of his breed at the University. Coaching took too much time, and he resigned after the 1892 season. Not until 1894 did the Athletic Association find a satisfactory successor. After the 1893 season Hopkins was able to recommend the Reverend Hector W. Cowan, who seemed almost too good to be true. A Princeton graduate who had been a superb tackle on the football team, he had coached his alma mater in the 1893 season; now he was a Presbyterian pastor in St. Joseph, Missouri. When Cowan proved unwilling to leave his parish unless he received full-time employment at the University, Chancellor Snow immediately suggested that in addition to coaching football he might be instructor of men's physical education, conduct the voluntary chapel services, and promote campus religious life generally. So attractive a prospect was he that when the regents proved unable to pay his $1,000 salary for 1894–1895, individual faculty members pledged $400; Lawrence citizens provided the rest. Cowan's hiring was an "immense thing for K.U.," Snow wrote a friend, "and will tend to develop the green eyes rapidly in other Kansas institutions. We must get all the bright eyes at K.U."[12]

The first University faculty member hired because of his coaching ability, Hector Cowan was also the first football coach fired because his teams lost too often. His record over three seasons was a respectable 14-7-1, but already athletic supporters were looking for a perfect season every season, and the idealism of such desires quickly turned to bitterness and insult in defeat. Many players, moreover, sniggered at Cowan as a moralistic dilettante who was ignorant of the way the game should be played. All of which greatly worried Edwin M. Hopkins. "What is football to mean at the University of Kansas?" he asked after the 1895 season. "Is it to stand for Christian manliness, courage, endurance, self-control, strength, moral as well as physical?"—in other words, what Cowan stood for. Or "does it . . . stand for brutality, for trickery; for paid players, for profanity, for betting before games and for drinking after them?"—in short, for a win-at-any-price philosophy and moral holidays. "There is no lack of evidence . . . that to some it means all and precisely this. If this is to be its meaning, then by all means Professor Cowan must go; but let us devoutly pray that football may soon follow him."[13]

Cowan went—as coach, though not immediately as physical education instructor—but football stayed. The coach in 1897 and 1898 was Dr. Wylie G. Woodruff, formerly an athlete at the University of Pennsylvania, who had 5–2 and 7–1 seasons, and beat arch-rival Missouri both years. He was an excellent publicist, the prototype of many a later coach and athletic director. "To all those parents who will be at home in fear and trembling, I want to say that football and other college sports are not to make cripples and slay the young men of the land, but . . . to make them stronger, more manly, nobler, more self-reliant, braver and men of brains, who may know how to properly honor their fathers and their mothers and respect and defend the state at whose institution they are imbibing that knowledge for which mankind has so long been in search." But after Woodruff swore at his players for a lackluster performance against the Kansas City Medical College in 1898, the University Council asked Snow to tell him that his resignation would be acceptable at the season's end.[14]

Along with the problem of successful, as well as moral, coaches came the problems of pay—both direct and indirect—for the players and of the "tramp athlete" who played each season for a different school. In 1892 the University joined with Missouri, Nebraska, and Iowa to form the Western Inter-State University Foot Ball Association. Its rules forbade pay for playing and required every player to be regularly matriculated in the school whose team he joined.[15] Yet the Athletic Association and its backers went all out to attract good players, and sometimes the ideal of amateurism suffered as a result. Extravagantly praising the University and its athletic program, the Association contacted promising high-school seniors and promised

Professor Edwin M. Hopkins,
the University's finest
football coach.

A football scene, 1898.

to help them find part-time jobs in Lawrence. In the 1895 season several Lawrence citizens raised $300, part of which went to hire help for a farm family to release a son for University football; another part apparently ended up in the pockets of three other players. And in 1899 Lawrence businessmen hired a player who was allegedly a law student but who disappeared from campus forever after the season.[16]

Distressing as such activities were, they did not mean that the University was fielding a professional or quasi-professional team. Yet they alerted Snow and his faculty to the dangers of professionalism and the need for close faculty supervision of athletics. In the early 1890s the Athletic Association constitution did not require faculty members on the board of directors, and the manager of athletics—the most important officer—was regularly a student. Although the faculty assumed greater authority, however, they did not try at any time to subject all athletics to their control, for that would have antagonized too many students, alumni, and fans. In the spring of 1894, amid suggestions that the baseball team should hire a badly needed pitcher and play only teams allowing him to hurl, the faculty reorganized the Athletic Association. Any student, faculty member, or University officer could join, and thus help elect the board of directors, but now there was to be a faculty advisory committee. By decision of the University Council the committee was to approve team schedules and also the hiring of coaches and trainers. Without the committee's permission no man not a "regular member of the University in good standing" from the start of the semester in which his team's contests were played could join a team. And, of course, no athlete could play for pay.[17]

Other regulations soon followed: athletes had to be passing their courses to play; only faculty-approved candidates could become team managers. Late in 1897 Kansas joined several other prominent midwestern universities—Michigan, Illinois, Wisconsin, and Minnesota among them—in adopting the "Chicago Conference" rules approved by a group of university leaders the year before. The rules forbade pay to athletes and tried to eliminate the tramp athlete by surrounding transfer students with several rules to insure their good faith. Every team candidate had to sign a statement that he was eligible to participate under the new rules.[18] After the firing of Wylie Woodruff the University Council itself promulgated a new Athletic

Association constitution. Of the eleven members of the board of directors two were to be the chancellor and the professor of physical training, and four more would be chosen by the University Council. This gave the faculty six of eleven seats; the other five were to be filled by the president and four men elected by the members. Now, however, the alumni as well as students and faculty could become members. The directors would appoint the general manager of athletics, the team managers, and the coaches.[19]

While the faculty worried about professionalism, many members were also concerned about football's violence. At its best football in the 1890s was rough; at its worst it was a bonebreaking, bloody battle royal. "Force was the thing," a Princeton star reminisced later, "and smashing, battering plays were depended on solely." The terrible flying wedge, the "guards back" formation, "roughing the kicker, piling up, hurdling—these were the outstanding weapons of attack and defense. . . . We were trained mainly for endurance." Although Edwin M. Hopkins told his teams never to start a dirty play, he also told them never to "permit one to go unrequited" or withhold "interest thereon." In 1894, in a typical ploy in a game with Michigan, after a Kansas back scored a touchdown a Wolverine jumped on him with both feet—yet the act went unpunished by officials. Worse still, on November 16, 1896, Burt Serf of Doane College, Nebraska, who had been knocked unconscious in an earlier game, awkwardly tackled a Kansas back on McCook Field, struck his head, and died. "The whole community and state are considerably excited in regard to the game," Snow said, "and its enemies are disposed to favor legislative action prohibiting it." But the legislature passed no law, and in the University Council Samuel W. Williston and several others who wished Kansas to forsake the game until it became safer were held scoreless. After a hot discussion the Council asked the Athletic Advisory Committee to consider means of eliminating football's dangers. But the committee could not decide what to do.[20]

Professor William H. Carruth, however—the University's greatest idealist—had perfectly clear concepts about the place of football in the school. Carruth was enthusiastic about all sports, both intramural and intercollegiate, as long as they were cleanly played by true amateurs. But during the 1890s his idealism suffered a series of shocks, and after Coach John Outland used an ineligible player with an assumed name in the 1901 season, Carruth was disgusted. Throughout the fall he kept up a steady criticism of the University's misplaced emphasis on football. On December 4, he brought before the University Council a motion that the "time and interest at present devoted to the game of football in the University of Kansas is excessive, leading to certain evils which it is the duty of the authorities to correct if possible." "I think the influence of the training tables and salaried coaches has been pernicious," Carruth argued. "The great desire to win breeds professionalism and encourages gambling, and what is of most importance, calls for risk of lives of the students." As the first step in decreasing the game's importance, he moved to require that all intercollegiate games be played on school grounds. His main objects were to get the rowdy Kansas-Missouri game out of Kansas City and to restrict gate receipts. Only four other Council members found his arguments persuasive, however. His motion lost, 13–5.[21]

More important than the motion's defeat were the profootball passions that Carruth's ideas aroused. Within the University the hottest hotbed of support for winning teams was the School of Law, led by Dean James W. Green, whom the Topeka *Capital* described as the "patron saint of K.U. football." At a student mass meeting in November law student Clyde W. Allphin flayed Carruth with passionate discourtesy. After the Council rejected Carruth's motion, the *Kansas University Lawyer,* which spoke with Saint Jimmy's voice, accused Carruth of bad faith and of hurting the University's best interests. Since those in charge of athletics were "just as honest, truthful and manly as can be found in any walk of life," anyone who attacked them "without any more cause than [Carruth] has, surely does it more for personal gratification than to advance the interests of the University. . . . This criticism, then, coming at this time when athletics in this University have reached such a state of purity that it is not even equalled by any denominational school in the state is certainly unjust and not exactly in harmony with the best interests of the University."[22]

By 1902, then, all the problems and plagues of intercollegiate football had appeared: securing winning and decent coaches, determining and enforcing amateurism and eligibility standards, seeking to eliminate brutality, arguing over the importance of the game itself. And during Chancellor Frank Strong's administration things got worse instead of better. Strong and his fellow regents got off to a good start by resolving in July, 1903, that they were "unanimously in favor of clean athletics." But the following fall officials at both Kansas and Nebraska believed that the other side had used ineligible players in their game—which Kansas won, 6–0; the result was a suspension of athletic relations. In the spring of 1904 Strong had to fire Coach Harold S. Weeks for allegedly fornicating with a freshman girl.[23] Weeks's replacement was Dr. A. R. Kennedy, a Lawrence dentist, which was all to the good since his character was of the highest, he was an excellent coach, and he stayed through the season of 1910. But a year after he arrived, University authorities had to check a group of insurgents within the Athletic Association who, in secret meeting, produced a new constitution shifting the balance of power from the faculty to the students and alumni and then tried to foist it upon the Association. Strong and the University Council disallowed it.[24]

About the only promising development of the early twentieth century was the creation of the Missouri Valley Conference in 1907. The Western Inter-State University Foot Ball Association had proved impermanent, and the Kansas College Athletic Conference, which Kansas officials had helped form in 1902,[25] too local for a University on the make for a national reputation. Even as the Athletic Board was considering a tri-state league among Kansas, Missouri, and Nebraska—which with expansion might rival the Western Intercollegiate League (Big Ten)—Athletic Director Clark W. Hetherington of Missouri was starting efforts to make the "athletic relations of the colleges of the Southwest better and stronger." After preliminary negotiations, in January, 1907, Kansas representatives joined those from Iowa, Nebraska, Missouri, and Washington University of St. Louis at a meeting in Kansas City to establish the conference. In March Kansas formally joined it.[26]

Although the conference would regulate amateurism and eligibility, it also worked to increase football's importance, for now there was a regional championship to be won. At just that time, moreover, changes in the rules of the game promised to make it more exciting and hence more popular than ever. After 18 players died and 159 more suffered serious injuries in the season of 1905, opponents of the game were in full cry for its abolition. On the invitation of Chancellor Henry M. McCracken of New York University and leaders of several other eastern schools, representatives from sixty-two colleges and universities met in December, 1905. They voted to keep the game, but change the rules; and to do the work— and also to supervise other sports—they formed the Intercollegiate Athletic Association of the United States, which in 1910 became the National Collegiate Athletic Association. In 1906 representatives of the Association joined with the American Football Rules Committee to recommend rule changes. Much of football's violence was the result of mass or gang plays; since the forward pass was illegal the ball was advanced only by running. The new rules were designed to open up the game and spread the players out. Forward passing was legalized; now there was to be a neutral zone between the teams before the center snapped the ball (previously the lines had crouched literally head to head and shoulder to shoulder); ten yards instead of five were required for a first down; and hurdling was outlawed. Other changes toward the same end followed from year to year.[27]

While it would take time for the forward pass to change the game—its great popularity dated from 1913, when Gus Dorais of Notre Dame drove Army wild—the new rules opened a new era of spectator enthusiasm. A great problem of University leaders, William H. Carruth only half-humorously told a meeting of the Kansas State Teachers Association in 1908, was "How Can Studies Be Made as Interesting as Athletics, or Can Study Be Made as Interesting as Football?" Carruth had no answers, but he kept pleading that "scholarship should be exalted to its proper place, and that physical training should not be placed above intellectual culture." Football was chief among the distractions of college life, Chancellor Strong told the student body in September, 1910, and the source of a popular belief that the "serious work of educational institutions is being neglected for ephemeral and unimportant considerations. My advice is that we be sound and reasonable in our athletics; that we see to it that they occupy their rightful, subordinate place in an institution of learning."[28]

Strong spoke only a few months after a University-wide debate about the abolition of football—the last such debate of any significance in the institution's first century. Several events in 1909 and 1910 suggested to many men, Strong and the regents among them, that football was more trouble than it was worth. First, rumors reached the Chancellor that the forbidden practice had reappeared of paying substitutes to fill in at part-time jobs held by athletes to release the players for practice and games. Then he heard that the cost of the season training table at the Eldridge Hotel would exceed the $400 authorized by the Missouri Valley Conference. W. C. Lansdon, the general manager of athletics, denied both charges, but that was to be expected. Even more distressing was that some opposing coaches had apparently used alcohol or drugs to vivify their players in games against Kansas. While the Kansas coaches would never sink to that damnable practice, it seemed an offense against clean athletics generally and the result of a growing overemphasis on winning. And there was also the annual problem of what location for the Kansas-Missouri game would best serve the University's welfare.[29]

On the Board of Regents, furthermore, sat William Allen White and J. Willis Gleed. Both had attended the University before football became the great sport, and both had watched its rise with the keenest distaste. White had long been convinced that the University was "too gross, too worldly," too little dedicated to the "spiritualization" of Kansas, by which he meant rule by men believing in "equitable laws and customs growing out of gentle Christlike hearts." Since football contributed much to the University's materialism, White would have abolished it outright if he had the power. Gleed thought that football made unthinking brutes of the players by "arousing the smashing and destroying instinct which comes down to us from our animal ancestors"—the very thing that the higher learning sought to suppress. "Inter-collegiate football puts the emphasis on the wrong place; holds up a false ideal. It exalts force; treats wisdom, truth, culture and justice with ill-concealed contempt." The "large miscellaneous audiences" which football amused and excited should seek their satisfactions in more worthy pursuits. Educational institutions had no business trying to appease their lower appetites.[30]

On January 28, 1910, Gleed moved that the Board of Regents abolish intercollegiate football until the rules were changed to the Board's approval. Of the four regents present Gleed and White supported the motion, while Strong and Scott Hopkins opposed it; the tie defeated the motion. Hopkins thereupon won approval for a more flexible resolution. Stating that the Board opposed football as it was then played, it directed Strong to invite the heads and governing boards of the Missouri Valley Conference schools to "confer upon and take permanent action in regard to the betterment of the present game." If the rules could not be satisfactorily amended, the Board desired to replace American football with English rugby. And if neither suggestion proved agreeable to conference members, the regents would abolish football.[31]

With the meeting scheduled for April 19, football backers huddled and came forth with a varied offense. A mass meeting on March 30 heard Coach Kennedy, Athletic Director James Naismith, and several excited students plead for football's retention. By April 5 football supporters had some nine hundred signatures on a petition stating that they were "radically opposed" to English rugby. There were still other profootball mass meetings on April 4 and 8, the latter meeting approving committees to visit the regents, mobilize the alumni, and solicit money for and issue propaganda.[32]

Whatever the meeting might do later in the month, Strong and the regents did win one important victory as a result of the brouhaha. Because football proponents feared what the regents might do later, on April 8 they approved transferring the Kansas-Missouri game to the campuses and playing it on the Saturday before Thanksgiving rather than on the holiday itself. Strong was delighted, and William Allen White thought that "we have got without a great struggle a great gain in this football situation."[33]

On April 19, 1910, twenty representatives from six Missouri Valley Conference schools—Kansas, Missouri, Nebraska, Drake, Iowa State, and Washington University—met to kick intercollegiate football even farther toward purity. Only five of the delegates wished to abolish football; and on the unit system of voting all six schools wished to keep the game. What troubled the leaders most was not the technical rules, which still kept football violent, but the significance of football to the students and alumni. To de-emphasize it, they abolished the training table, forbade freshmen to play varsity ball, prohibited athletic contests on Thanksgiving Day, and decided that all intercollegiate games should be played on college grounds. A committee appointed to consider the rules was also to discuss the more general questions of the time consumed by athletics, amateur standing, and schedule limitations. In order to eliminate the purely professional coach who rendered no other service than coaching, the conferees resolved that after 1910 "no athletic coaches be allowed except such as are regular members of the teaching staff employed by the governing board of the institution, for the full academic year." On April 28, the Kansas regents formally approved the new regulations.[34]

Over the next four years the regents and the Board of Administration tried to tighten their own control over athletics and to integrate them more closely with the rest of the University. Probably they would have done so in any case, but their reforming zeal was the greater because in the 1911 season the Kansas football team used an ineligible player, disguised as a Law School student, who was paid for his services. When the regents discovered the fraud, they could not have been angrier. Placing football above the University's honor, the students who had connived at the transgression were willing to see the school "held up to the scorn of the people and made the target of its enemies." "If such a group of students insists upon thus protecting football at the cost of the University's good name and at the risk of losing the University the support of Kansas people, the Board must not be blamed if it seriously considers the abolition of football."[35]

But the Board did not abolish the game. When it failed to do so, a crisis had been reached and passed, and football would remain with the University. In 1912, however, the regents imposed a new constitution on the Athletic Association, which gave power to an eleven-member board, six of whom were the chancellor and five faculty members, the other five elected students. In 1913 and 1914 intercollegiate athletics became a division of the Department of Physical Education, Professor James Naismith, who supervised physical education, and Professor W. O. Hamilton, general manager of athletics, were to govern the Department so that, the Board of Administration hoped, "there may be unity and cooperation between all its parts."[36]

From the teens to the sixties Kansas football was racked by inconsistency. The school never became a consistent national football power: Kansas was no Notre Dame, Ohio State, or Nebraska. Here and there, of course, the University produced superstars on teams that attracted national attention: Jim Bausch ('32), who doubled as a track star and won the Olympic decathlon that year; the superlative Ray Evans, who with his great team went to the Orange Bowl in 1948 (only to lose to Georgia Tech, 20–14); or Gale Sayers ('65), who in his first year with the Chicago Bears became, next to Cleveland's Jimmy Brown, the finest running back in professional football. From 1890 through the season of 1931 the overall record of the Kansas elevens was 205–107–26, which averaged out to a 6–3–1 record per ten-game season. In the same period the University had twenty different coaches, as the boosters sought the man who could win every game, year after year.[37]

Several cases from the years before 1950 illustrated the continuity of frustration arising from the continuing desire for ever victorious teams. In 1912 the regents hired Arthur St. Leger Mosse as the first of the new breed of coaches who were also to be faculty members. Mosse had captained the Kansas team in 1898, then coached and played professional football; he returned to Lawrence in 1906 as an assistant coach.[38] He proved an honest and dedicated man, but his teams were relatively inept, compiling a 9–7 record in 1912 and 1913, and losing to Nebraska, Oklahoma, and Missouri the second year. Many students and alumni determined that Mosse had to go, faculty member or not, and there were mass protest meetings and widespread charges that Mosse and his assistants were incompetent. At a meeting on December 10, Strong pleaded that Mosse be kept for at least one more year in order to teach his players his style of ball. But he convinced few undergraduates, and he had no better luck with the hardnosed Kansas City alumni. "Our whole aim," he told their secretary, "is to preserve the discipline of the University and the integrity and standards of our athletics." Coaches had to be appointed "in the same manner as are other teachers and upon the same basis of tenure." Otherwise there would be no "permanence and confidence," and it would be "impossible for us to persuade thoroughly competent and high grade men to have anything to do with our athletics and to build up permanent, thoroughgoing athletic efficiency." Most alumni and students lacked Strong's idealism, however; the 1913 season was Mosse's last.[39]

Coaches came and coaches went in the teens and twenties. Many men hoped that the construction of the stadium would symbolize the start of an era of bigtime football, but it was not to be. From 1921 through 1927 under Coaches George "Potsy" Clark and Franklin C. Cappon, the team's record against its major foes was 3–3–1 with Missouri, 0–6–1 with Nebraska (the terror of the plains), 4–2–1 against Oklahoma, and a really shameful 1–4–2 against the Agricultural College. In 1926 and 1927 Cappon's teams produced 2–6 and 3–4–1 records, sending alumni howling along the warpath once again. Losing teams, two graduates told Athletic Director Forrest C. Allen, blighted the all-important "school spirit." That "spirit of loyalty and devotion to K.U., as evidenced at the recent football games," was "surely at a very low ebb." There were disturbing rumors of intrasquad strife, of outside meddling with the team and its coaches, of Allen's willingness to sacrifice football, the "spirit-making game of the University" for the "indoor game of basketball." Whatever was wrong, the "glory of old K.U." was not what it should be.[40]

The opposition forced Cappon and his assistants to resign. In December, 1927, the Athletic Board recommended William Hargiss, then athletic director and coach at Emporia State Teachers College, to the regents as head coach. But the alumni, it appeared, were after larger game than Cappon. What many of them wanted was representation on the Athletic Board. Over the weekend of December 2–4, a committee appointed by some sixty Kansas City alumni visited Lawrence to talk with Allen, Lindley, and everyone else who could help explain the team's failings. They came away convinced that improvement demanded alumni on the Board. Lindley said that he had no objections, providing that the Missouri Valley Conference rules requiring faculty control were obeyed. There had been a substantial identity between the Athletic Board and the Physical Education Corporation, which had completed the stadium. In 1928 the Board merged into the Corporation. The thirteen directors would include seven faculty members, three alumni, two students, and Lindley. The executive committee of six, which held most of the power, was composed of two alumni, a student, a faculty member—at first W. W. Davis of the History Department, a super-fan—and Allen and Lindley.[41]

But not even the alumni could stop the football team's long—though sometimes temporarily halted—slide into darkness. During the 1930s there were poor teams, scandal, dissent, charges, counter-charges, and investigations. The University would have been much better off without a team. The decade opened with an uproar over the alleged professionalism of two players. In 1927 and 1928 Kansas had joined Nebraska, Missouri, the Kansas Agricultural College, Iowa State, and Oklahoma in forming the "Big Six" conference. Its rules, of course, forbade athletes from being paid for their efforts on the field, but reports suggested that many Kansas backers had been none too scrupulous in observing them. According to the *Dove* Lawrence businessmen "made" jobs for athletes, some of which required no work at all, and fraternities roomed and boarded athletes without charge. There was also a special Athletic Student Loan Fund to provide athletes with cash on the easiest possible terms. Although the fund was not technically illegal, other Big Six representatives thought it unethical. On their protests the University abolished it in 1930.[42]

Far more serious was the charge of athletic subsidies to Jim Bausch, fullback and star of the fine 1930 team, which lost only to Nebraska and Pennsylvania and won the Big Six championship, and to a freshman named Phil Borello. Bausch's notarized affidavit stated that after his freshman year at the municipal University of Wichita, he determined to fulfill an old desire to attend the University of Kansas. No member of the Kansas athletic staff had talked with him. But during the summer of 1928, while painting seats in the Kansas stadium, he "became acquainted" with Elmer C. Lupton, president of the Bank Savings Life Insurance Company of Topeka. Lupton offered him a job selling insurance at $75 a month, in lieu of commission, contingent upon Bausch's completing work for a B.A. at a Kansas institution chosen by Bausch, but approved by Lupton's company. Lupton offered later to allow Bausch to attend any school in Kansas, Missouri, or Oklahoma, where his company was authorized to sell insurance, but Bausch entered the University in the fall of 1928. During the next two years he sold $269,000 worth of insurance.[43]

Borello's sworn affidavit said that while he was a high-school student in Kansas City, Missouri, Judge C. A. Burney—an alumnus who had led the 1927 investigating committee—had taken him to Lawrence and commended the University to him. Burney had introduced him to both Allen and Hargiss, but neither had asked him to attend the school or offered inducements to do so. After enrolling he got a job at W. O. Hamilton's Chevrolet garage, working four hours a day for $15 a week.[44]

If both affidavits were honest, there had been no violation of Big Six rules. But when faculty representatives met in October, 1930, Professor W. A. Tarr of Missouri claimed that Bausch was

Coaches and players at practice, some sweating, some not, 1925.

Homecoming, 1931. Kansas Governor Harry H. Woodring wishes the best of luck to Kansas captain Otto Rost, as Missouri captain Frank Bittner and various officials look on. Kansas won, 14–0.

getting $125 a month and Borello more than $15 a week; that Lupton was paying nine other Kansas athletes; and that rules against paying and recruiting athletes had been violated. As George C. Shaad, the Kansas representative, pointed out, Tarr's only evidence was hearsay. Yet so convincing were his charges that the delegates voted four to one (H. H. King of the Agricultural College abstained) to excommunicate Kansas from the Big Six.[45] A month later, however, a special meeting of Big Six presidents, athletic directors, and faculty delegates met in Kansas City at Chancellor Lindley's request to smooth things over. Big Six membership, they resolved, should be restricted to schools agreeing that no athlete should receive a subsidy "either directly or indirectly, or any advance payment or guarantee of salary from any source." After the Kansas Athletic Board approved that resolution, the representatives voted in December to readmit the University. Then and in 1931 the Big Six forbade all payment and promises of payment unless for jobs performed in advance of payment, and all loans and employment to athletes which were not open equally to nonathletes. Lindley promised that Kansas would obey those rules, and an ugly situation had passed.[46]

Yet other forms of ugliness remained—all of them connected with losing football teams. The 1931 season was a disaster, for Kansas lost three of four Big Six contests—it beat only Missouri—and wound up with a 4–5 record. A year later, after Kansas scraped to victory over a weak University of Denver team and then lost to Oklahoma, the Athletic Board gave Athletic Director Allen power to do whatever he thought necessary to improve the team. Allen replaced Hargiss as coach—while keeping him as track coach—with Adrian Lindsey, a former Kansas star ('17). According to Allen the Athletic Board instructed him to be present in an advisory capacity on the practice field and in the dressing room. He was to help condition the players and build team morale, and would also be a consultant on game strategy.[47]

The new regime determined to put more emphasis on basic football: "simplification of offensive plays, harder charging lines . . . and, withal, better blocking and tackling." This also meant duller football, which was all right as long as the team won, but awful when it didn't. After a semirespectable 5–3 season in 1932 and a 5–4–1 in 1933 the team's best season during the rest of the decade was a 4–4–1 in 1935; the eleven went 1–6–1 in 1936 and 3–6 in 1938. Everyone had suggestions to make. When Kansas finally opened up its passing and lateral attack to beat St. Benedict's College of Atchison, 34–12, in 1934, Governor Landon told Lindley that people were "not concerned so much about winning as seeing an open game,—running the ends and forward passing and lateral passing."[48]

What the fans really wanted, however, was both exciting football and winning football. They got neither. The team drew poorly, the stadium was rarely filled—necessitating the refinancing of the stadium bonds in 1935[49]—and enthusiasm was at an all-time low. Then in October, 1936, Forrest Allen, always outspoken, said that Kansas school spirit was rapidly becoming a thing of the past and that it was high time the students got behind the team. Allen was foolish, replied the *Kansan* editors next day. School spirit was a spontaneous thing. If the coaches got their "archaic, obsolete ideas out of their heads," and gave the fans "real, honest-to-goodness modern football"—that is, the "new type of game, the open, tricky, fast-running, and passing game"—a "healthy, roaring school spirit" would reappear.[50]

Lindsey responded that while he favored the open game, training a green team took time. Allen criticized the *Kansan* for its opposition, the editors struck back, and by the end of the season another athletic uproar was deafening the campus. After the team's miserable record the alumni peppered the regents with anti-Allen letters, and the results of a *Kansan* poll had the students overwhelmingly in favor of firing Allen as athletic director, replacing Lindsey as coach, and doing everything within Big Six rules to improve the team's quality.[51]

During the next two years the regents worked out a new system of athletic management. After January, 1937, the immediate direction of athletics would be in the hands of a three-man committee of the Athletic Board. The position of athletic director was abolished. A more direct slap at Allen was the provision that no coach—and Allen was coach of basketball—could be an Athletic Board member. To make it easier for athletes to remain scholastically eligible, the present two-year physical education curriculum was expanded to a four-year course open to freshmen. Later the Board reinstituted the athletic directorship—now that Allen had been eliminated—and filled it with Gwin Henry, from 1923 to 1932 football coach at Missouri and now coach and athletic director at New Mexico. After the 1938 season the regents made Henry football coach as well and showed their confidence in him by making him an Athletic Board member.[52]

Ironically, while athletic boosters hoped to make the University famous for its football teams by deposing Allen as athletic director, the school achieved a far greater renown for the basketball teams that he coached. While basketball never mattered as much as football, over the years Allen's teams helped people forget some of their gridiron disappointments and gave Kansas national and even international prestige.

Kansas was not the birthplace of basketball, but it might just as well have been. Until 1956 the University's basketball program was shaped mainly by two men: Allen and Dr. James Naismith, the game's inventor. Naismith came to Lawrence in 1898 to replace Hector W. Cowan as associate professor of physical culture and chapel director. Back in 1891 as a faculty member of the International YMCA Training School in Springfield, Massachusetts, Naismith had combined aspects of several different games to create a new sport that could be played indoors during the winter,[53] and it proved as popular in Lawrence as it had in Springfield. By 1898 the game was even more exciting than it had been at the start, for dribbling had become legal and the teams were restricted to five men—Naismith had begun with nine on a side because there were eighteen in his class—and thus the game was opened up. On February 3, 1899, Naismith took his first Kansas team to Kansas City, Missouri, to play the YMCA team in the University's first regularly scheduled game—and returned embarrassed by a defeat. "K.U. undoubtedly played a more scientific game," a reporter wrote, for its team "worked the ball to the basket and then tried for a goal," while the YMCA players shot whenever they got the ball. At the half the YMCA led, 4–3. In the second half Kansas scored only one goal, while the YMCA picked up 12 points to win, 16–5. "Our goal throwing," the reporter said dryly, "was nothing phenomenal."[54]

But the Kansas goal throwing would become something phenomenal as the years passed. In the next three decades Kansas won 377 of the 549 games it played, outscoring its opponents by an average of almost 7 points a game. Naismith continued as basketball coach until 1909; W. O. Hamilton coached the team during the next decade. Then Allen replaced him and remained as coach for the next thirty-seven years. "Phog" Allen—he came by his nickname as a foghorn-voiced baseball umpire—was typical of the new type of coach in American universities, for he depended almost entirely on intercollegiate athletics for his livelihood. A native of Jamesport, Missouri, Allen had begun his basketball career in 1902 with the Modern Woodmen of America team in Independence; in that year he first met Naismith. He then played for and coached the Kansas City Athletic Club "Blue Diamonds," and with his five brothers also formed a family basketball team. In 1905 he matriculated at the University and the next year lettered in basketball.[55]

Allen's coaching career began in 1907 when Naismith laughingly told him that Baker University in Baldwin, Kansas, wanted him as coach. Naismith believed that basketball was a game to be played by amateurs rather than coached by professionals, but Allen thought otherwise and so began a remarkable career. He coached at Kansas and at Haskell Indian Institute in 1908 and 1909, becoming so busy that he never graduated from the University, took a Doctor of Osteopathy degree in 1912 at the Central College of Osteopathy in Kirksville, Missouri, coached all sports at Central Missouri State Teachers College in Warrensburg for seven years, and then succeeded W. O. Hamilton as general manager of athletics at a salary of $3,500 a year.[56]

When Allen reached the mandatory retirement age of seventy during the 1955–1956 season, he was still suiting up for daily practice, still generating controversy with his outspoken opinions, and still winning basketball games. His overall coaching record was 771 victories in 1,004 games—a 77 percent average—and he won twenty-four conference championships for the University. His finest hour came in 1952 when his team won the NCAA national championship by beating St. John's University, 80–63. Allen also wrote extensively on basketball techniques; originated changes to make the game more one of skill; helped organize the National Association of Basketball Coaches; and regularly served on the national rulesmaking committee. He was also largely responsible for getting basketball accepted as an Olympic sport, starting in 1936. Unlike Naismith, who was very much the Christian, amateur gentleman, Allen was a diamond in the rough. Usually at odds with the Amateur

Athletic Union, he once claimed that AAU stood for "asininities amplified, unfathomable." On another occasion he remarked, "The A.A.U. is a lousy, toady bunch of rats that don't even own a hurdle." But he had an enthusiastic following, and in 1954 the regents named the University's new fieldhouse for him.[57]

By that time the University of Kansas, like most other large American universities, had begun to use quasi-professional athletes on its teams. Across the nation after the Second World War, re-turning football players found their services in such high demand that various universities openly competed for them by holding out such bait as salaries, apartments, and automobiles. To end a lengthening series of scandals, especially in the Southeastern Con-ference, the NCAA in 1947 enacted the so-called sanity code, to take effect in 1948, which allowed athletes to receive money for tuition and fees, but prohibited all other subsidies. When the "sanity code" proved ineffective in preventing subsidization, in 1951 the NCAA gave up its effort to become a national regulatory agency, and threw the problem back to individual schools and conferences.[58]

At that point the Big Seven[59] formally approved a wider program of subsidies. While the reasons were obvious, certain statements about the nature of the new amateurism were inscrutable. Accord-ing to the rules, effective in June, 1951, no student who had violated the conference's rules of amateurism could participate in any inter-collegiate athletic contest. An "amateur sportsman," the rules said, "is one engaged in sports for the physical, mental, or social benefits he derives therefrom, and to whom the sport is an avocation. Any athlete who accepts or agrees to accept pay for participation in athletics does not meet this definition of an amateur." The words and the idea they carried could not have been nobler. But then the rules went on to say that member universities could give "financial aid in the form of part-time work and/or grants" to "make it pos-sible for student athletes to attend school, participate in athletics, and have adequate time for their studies." Maximum aid available to any student athlete included all payments for tuition, fees, books, and room and board at dormitory rates, and $15 a month for "inci-dentals."[60]

From a viewpoint that one might call "practical," there was something to be said for such payments: athletes who were poor found it possible to attend college; there was less of a tendency to subsidize athletes in secret; without such official subsidies the University would have been forced either to end its major sports program or to play unprestigious schools. Besides, said Dean of Students Laurence C. Woodruff in 1954, University employees should be paid decent wages. "An athlete working for his institution during the athletic season between 20 and 40 hours per week," he argued, "certainly deserves every consideration that we would give to any other student who, because of his economic condition or his personal choice, is forced to put in that amount of time outside the classroom."[61]

True enough, one could say. It was also true that now "amateurism," like the words of Humpty Dumpty in *Through the Looking Glass,* meant only what athletic managers chose it to mean. Once upon a time an amateur had been a person who received no money at all from participating in sports. Now he was a person who received no money unless it came in the proper amounts from the proper authorities. Which meant that the University of Kansas was moving with the times and doing what apparently had to be done: engaging in activities which probably made some contribution to its prosperity but had nothing at all to do with higher learning.

33

The Race Against History

*I*N the fall of 1960 the philosophy of Satchel Paige, the great base-ball pitcher and comedian, had a certain vogue on Mount Oread. When Chancellor Murphy departed for Los Angeles, he left a note with Paige's words of wisdom for W. Clarke Wescoe, which the new Chancellor incorporated into his inaugural address. After consider-ing the available subjects, Wescoe said, he had decided to talk about the future, about the "work that lies ahead of us and the work that must be done." In so choosing, he had overcome the "great temptation" to prepare a scholarly address, and had also rejected the idea of a historical analysis. "I could have used this occasion," Wescoe commented, "to remark upon the history of the University and, in particular, to delineate its substantial growth over a period of years. This temptation, too, I resisted, remembering the words of that distinguished philosopher, Satchel Paige, 'Don't look back. Some-thing may be gaining on you.' "[1]

This was good advice. To look back at the University's past from the early 1960s was to see that something unwelcome had always been running with the institution stride for stride. It was history itself. It was the history of a century's disagreements about the Uni-versity's nature and proper stature, of a constant gap between ideal and reality, goal and achievement. "We labor under the handicap all the time," Frank Strong had told the legislature of 1907, "of having to make up for lost time." Fifty years later the University's officers and faculty were still trying to escape from history's dis-

670

appointments, to outdistance a heritage of errors, missed opportunities, uncertainty, and tragedy. There had been, as Wescoe noted, a "substantial growth" of both quality and quantity, but it had never been as great as the University's friends desired. It was no wonder that the most important feature of the centennial celebration in 1966 was an "Intercentury Seminar on Man and the Future," and that during the festivities one heard far more about the potentialities of the days ahead than the glories of those behind.

Yet the past had determined the route of the future race. It would continue to wind through the misty vales of perplexity and the dark woods of confusion about the University's proper character, its legitimate functions, the most desirable relations among its parts. More unfortunate, unless there was a wholesale change in faculty and student attitudes—a second wind for a second century—there would remain a wholesale uncertainty even about how such matters should be discussed.

According to Chairman James O. Maloney of the Senate Advisory Committee the faculty's outstanding characteristic was its intellectual torpor. On October 6, 1958, he rose before the Senate to chastise his colleagues for their sluggishness. He spoke, he said, with the "deepest affection" for the University and its people, but affection made his words bitter. Across Mount Oread, he lamented, there was a "lack of concern for developing an understanding of the nature and ideals which must exist in order to form a great university. . . . When is the time," he asked, "that the University and the Senate should subject themselves to critical analysis in order to begin a serious effort to achieve greatness?" Now, he answered, for "every month or year or decade we put it off, by that much, at least, shall greatness escape us." Yet while Chancellor Murphy had been making "prodigious efforts" to bring the school excellence, the faculty had done comparatively little. Greatness would not come by accident. "It requires first of all a great deal of work and a definite vision of a goal. In addition it seems clear to me that the really great universities of the past and present have had a sense of corporate unity, both in their work and their vision." But at Kansas there was very little discussion of the "essential nature of a university. . . . It is hard to comprehend in any definite and vivid way what we are trying to do here."

The reasons were "our preoccupations, our lack of tradition, the absence of a ready model and our own ignorance—all these conspire against the initiation of a conscious effort toward greatness." Individual interests and duties—research, writing, teaching—consumed energy. The University itself had no "pervading tradition of greatness, a tradition which we might effortlessly inherit." Few Kansas faculty members had served in the "professional ranks of any of the great universities and consequently, the great majority of us possess no ready pattern as a guide. Finally, as we operate today there is no attempt on the part of the faculty either to teach or to learn a significant amount about the historical backgrounds and characteristics of the great universities of the Western World."

Those reasons also conspired to make the Senate itself a dreary, spiritless body. Thus the year before, after Chancellor Murphy had addressed it "fervently and well" on the need for foreign language proficiency among Americans, "the Senate sat stunned and mute, barely rousing itself enough to applaud. Watching this body, it seemed to [me] as if not a muscle so much as quivered—administrators, deans, associate deans, [ROTC] soldiers, professors and associate professors—all alike—all paralyzed." In the thirteen years that Maloney had been a senator, it seemed to him that the Senate had spent its "creative time in marginal activities," and he went on to recall with mordant humor that the previous spring more than "100 man hours" had gone to considering the mechanics of reenrolling a student in a course in which he had received a D.

Other reasons also might help to explain the Senate's lethargy and fribbling. Some senators might say that the separate faculties decided all important matters and that therefore there was nothing for the Senate to discuss or do. Others might suggest that faculty members had "no basic interest in the University beyond the department level," or that the Senate needed more power, or that the Senate could well be disbanded. Still others might say—and here was a really frightening idea—that the Senate was "not supposed to discuss basic issues of University education or the future of the University; and that any such discussions, if held, would destroy our 'togetherness.' "

Unfortunately Maloney had no suggestions about how the Senate might rescue itself from apathy and ignorance to consider the ingredients of greatness. He modestly said that he lacked the capacity to offer a program of action. Even if he did offer one, he said, "each of you could attack it with the sharp tools of scholarship or the blunt one of special interest and dissect or destroy it." It was up to the Senate to devise its own method and do its own work; the Advisory Committee was ready to do "as little or as much as you want done." As a conclusion Maloney offered advice both sarcastic and sincere: "Know Thyself—discover the true measure of university greatness—so that, if the fancy strikes you, you will know how to strive for it intelligently."[2]

The fancy did not strike. Many senators were as eager as Maloney to seek greatness, but the Senate as a body had no interest in the subject. There was neither debate on his address nor discernible reaction to his plea. The Senate of 1958–1959—and of the years ahead—was not the Senate of the early teens or the 1930s. Despite what everyone took to be a qualitative improvement of the faculty since the end of the Second World War, there had been a decline in the Senate of intellectual vigor, boldness, individuality, concern for the meaning of the University of Kansas and of the university in America. All the officers and many faculty members, of course, watched other institutions—to copy or improve on their experiments or profit from their mistakes or be among the first to start new programs. But watchfulness hardly amounted to a general inquiry into the proper nature of a university.

Here and there, however, from committees and individuals on and off the Hill came opinions about how Kansas might free itself from the burden of history. Yet often they merely illustrated how divided and uncertain the University community was about how to run the race against time past. Consider the old, old problem of the relative values of scholarly research and teaching undergraduates. In the fall of 1960 Chancellor Wescoe, at the unanimous request of the deans, appointed a committee to study the place of research in the University. Its chairman was William J. Argersinger, professor of chemistry, associate dean of the Graduate School, and a prodigious researcher; among the thirteen other members were several of the institution's more eminent scholars, including George L. Anderson of History, Charles D. Michener of Entomology, Edward E. Smissman of Pharmacy, and William W. Hambleton of the State Geological Survey. Their report appeared in June, 1962.[3]

It had only praise for research and the men who did it. The

modern American university, they said, was "more than books, more than buildings, more than students, teachers, administration, staff, and alumni, more than all of these. . . . A university is a community of scholars with diverse and catholic interests; it is dedicated to the extension, preservation, and dissemination of knowledge in an atmosphere of mutual respect and support, creativity, and unrestrained pursuit of scholarly interests; it offers well-defined and tangible recognition for excellence and achievement; and it fulfills its responsibilities through the combined and consistent efforts of all its parts." A university was properly dedicated to the "process and products of learning in its broadest and most complete sense," and that process had to include both the "study of what is known and the organized search for what is still to be learned." The "creative element" in the learning process was the individual scholar; the "creative portion of the entire process" was research. And research, of course, demanded publication. "There is no more certain method of creating a campus atmosphere unfavorable to research than to promote those members of the staff who consistently refuse to submit the results of their activity to the judgment of their peers in their profession."[4]

The report hedged on the relative amounts of time that faculty members should give to research and teaching. "The life of the teacher-scholar, the learner, cannot be reduced to a formula expressed in minutes, hours, or percentages. The addition of a new staff member is in a sense an act of faith that he will make the best use of his time, giving some of it to enhance his own stature as a scholar by seeking new knowledge, and giving some of it to his fellow-learners by sharing what he has learned and what he is learning with them." At another point, however, the report seemed to argue for a fifty-fifty ratio. "The University and the public must realize," the Argersinger committee said in appealing for more money, "that research (including training of researchers) is as important to the nation and the state as undergraduate teaching; the two should receive equal attention from administrators, faculty, regents, the legislature, and the people of the state."[5]

Inevitably, however, most undergraduates were ignorant about the place of faculty research in the University. Despite the belief of the Argersinger committee that the quality of undergraduate instruction depended on the quality of research,[6] few students believed it. Thus when the College Intermediary Board members explained their ideas about the University's purpose to the AAUP in 1967, they slighted research in favor of teaching. Like "clergy and doctors," Nancy Gallup and Sara Paretsky wrote in the *University Review*, university professors had chosen a public vocation: teaching. "The fulfillment of that vocation and hence of themselves as persons demands an intimate involvement with those isolated members of academia, the undergraduates. . . . Because we see the faculty as priests, we see them in living groups talking to their majors, we see their houses open to students for informal discussion, we see them eating lunch with their students while talking about directions in their fields and what role the students play in them." Scholarly research mattered little, if at all.[7]

Clearly some reconciliation or compromise between the two points of view was necessary if the University's nature and functions were to be made clear. Yet as the institution entered its second century, no general discussion or clarification of the opposing ideas had begun—or seemed likely to start.

Another problem from out of the past that received but confused discussion in the 1960s was that of open admission. The legislature of 1915 had passed a law requiring that the University and the four state colleges admit all graduates of the state's accredited high schools. For the rest of the University's first century many men thought the law and the idea of the University on which it rested equally bad. Chancellor Strong had disliked the law from the start. In 1922 the Zook committee had urged the law's repeal, pointing out that many accredited high schools failed to prepare their graduates for higher education. Four years later College Dean Joseph G. Brandt said that open admission made it difficult to maintain scholastic standards, forced the faculty to bear an "ever-increasing load of elementary instruction," and disappointed students who wrongly thought themselves ready for college work. From 10 to 12 percent of each freshman class flunked out in the fall semester, Brandt reported; he thought the rate excessive. A decade later the University Survey Committee was also disturbed about the academic mortality rate, and in 1940 the Senate asked the Board of Regents to appoint a joint committee from the five state schools to consider the question of entrance standards. But the exigencies of war prevented any effective discussion.[8]

The open-door policy had advantages as well as disadvantages, however, and thus the University community continued to be divided about it. Ever larger numbers of students were the University's best argument for more money. Denying admission to high-school graduates who failed to meet some arbitrary standard on an entrance examination, moreover, would bar some who could do satisfactory undergraduate work—students whose ability, desire, and capacity for growth were not measurable by examination or high-school grades. Then, too, as Dean of the Unversity George Baxter Smith said in 1956, the modern state university had so many majors —painting, piano, community recreation, radiation biophysics, and dozens more—that it would be practically impossible to prepare entrance examinations to test all individual talents and potentialities.[9]

After the Second World War, Smith was the University's most enthusiastic defender of open admission. The survival of a free society, he thought, depended on the "widest and fullest possible development of *all* its human resources"; this meant giving every high-school graduate the chance to see how far his own resources of mind and character would take him. The best way to discover whether a student was ready for college work was to let him in, and then dismiss him if he failed. In Kansas, Smith noted, there was a self-selection process at work. High-school graduates who were dubious about their abilities either did not go on to college or did not attend the University. About 28 percent of the freshman class of 1959 were in the upper 10 percent of their high-school class, and another 18 percent were in the second tenth; almost 80 percent were in the upper half. On the average about 40 percent of all entering freshmen never gained junior standing, which meant that the law of the survival of the fittest was at work. Smith's favorite argument, though, was the intellectual and social cost of selective admission. In the graduating classes from 1955 to 1959 there were over eleven hundred students who would not have been admitted if the cut-off point had been the 50th percentile on the widely used American Council on Education and Speed of Reading examinations. Had those students been barred, Smith said, the "loss to the state and the nation would have been 202 teachers, 176 engineers, 22 journalists, 31 lawyers, 25 medical doctors, 43 pharmacists and 482 graduates of the College of Liberal Arts and Sciences and the School of

Business who majored in areas where the supply of trained man-power is in equally short supply."[10]

Beyond Smith's argument was the question of whether a state university on the make should set its own standards or live with a law made by other men for other times. Like many another question, this one both needed and failed to get the kind of discussion it deserved. Individuals or small groups, of course, occasionally took a stand. In 1955 Chancellor Murphy told the AAUP executive committee that the University would one day have to stop trying to educate "everyone who came to its doors," and start admitting students on the basis of the results of both academic and psychological tests.[11] Chancellor Wescoe thought just the opposite. On May 14, 1963, Professor Leslie R. C. Agnew of the Medical School asked him from the Senate floor "if it would not be advisable for the Senate to look into the matter of selective admission to the University of Kansas." Wescoe replied that the Senate Advisory Committee could of course consider the matter, but added that he opposed selective admission. He mentioned the self-selection process and asserted that other universities had become "disenchanted" with selective admission because it did not take motivation into account. He did say that the legislature might wish to change the law when the state's junior colleges became better able to receive students if they were ineligible to enter the University. But he added "with some fervor," the minutes reported, "that he did not want the University of Kansas to shut its doors to any Kansas students who might wish to enter. He felt this too was a matter of academic freedom," and also that selective admission would cost the University some of its "widespread public support."

Although the Chancellor invited Agnew to respond, he also suggested that the Senate might take up the matter again at some future meeting. That suggestion, combined with his warm defense of the open door, killed open discussion.[12]

In the meetings of the Senate, indeed, open discussions of anything of consequence were nonexistent. Two strong-willed chancellors with little use for faculty democracy had no difficulty mastering the professoriate, and Chancellor Wescoe made no major effort to change things. Thus the Senate—and the faculty as a whole—paid no attention to two general surveys of higher education in Kansas in 1960 and 1962. The first was the *Comprehensive Educational Sur-*

vey of Kansas, authorized by the legislature of 1957. Preliminary studies in 1955 and 1956 by the Education Committee of the Kansas Legislative Council had shown that the state's school system was so confusedly organized and financed that many children were suffering from poor instruction, poor guidance, and inadequate facilities. A thorough study of the system by outside experts seemed desirable, and the Legislative Council decided to include institutions of higher as well as lower education. After the legislature of 1957 appropriated $75,000 for the survey, the Council contracted with Professors·of Education Otto E. Domian and Robert J. Keller of the University of Minnesota to head it. Domian would supervise the study of primary and secondary education, Keller, the study of higher education. In their investigations they and their staffs had assistance from over eighty citizens and college and university officers divided into a Citizens Advisory Committee for Elementary and Secondary Education, a similar group for higher education, and a Professional Advisory Committee for Higher Education.[13]

Keller's part of the *Comprehensive Survey* had little new to offer about the University's problems and their solutions. Assisted by A. L. Pugsley, dean of academic administration at Kansas State University, and Nathaniel H. Evers, head of the Department of Education at Washburn University of Topeka, Keller wrote a report whose most important conclusion was that more students were coming—the University was due to grow from 8,600 students in 1958 to some 18,000 by 1975. Keller's most important recommendation was that the University should prepare to serve them better by getting and spending more money. Assuming a continued high and efficient use rate, and assuming that no classrooms and laboratories were built in the years immediately ahead, the University would run out of classroom space in 1962 and laboratory space in 1963.[14] More significant, because of the University's low salaries and lack of an adequate retirement program, its faculty was less scholarly and less stable than it should be. In 1958–1959 the full-time faculty members had reported that on an average they spent about 66 percent of their time teaching, about 14 percent in research, about 4 percent in public service and the rest of their time in other duties. Even when the distribution of the part-time staff—mostly graduate students—was averaged in, the faculty spent only about 20 percent of their time in research. That "amount of research effort," Keller thought, "is far less than would be expected of a state university of this type." At Minnesota, for example, about one-third of the faculty's time went to research, and one-sixth to public service. During the previous five years, moreover, the University had lost 296 full-time faculty members; 41 percent had gone to out-of-state colleges, and another 21 percent had gone into business or industry. The loss constituted 48 percent of the 621 full-time faculty members it now had, which far exceeded the national average of about 6 percent a year.[15]

In addition to greater state appropriations for existing institutions, Keller, Pugsley, and Evers had numerous other suggestions of ways in which Kansas tax moneys could be spent. The state should study the possibility of incorporating the two municipal universities—Washburn and Wichita—into the state system under the Board of Regents. It should provide up to 40 percent of the costs of the accredited public junior colleges, then supported by people in the school districts they served. It should also study the possibility of providing state scholarships to students wishing to attend private colleges. Just where the additional money was to come from, Keller and his associates did not say. Kansans were already spending $9.43 per $1,000 of personal income for state higher education, in contrast to the $5.68 of the country as a whole, and $50.37 per $1,000 for all public education, in contrast to $40.94 for the country generally. The higher figures, however, arose from the fact that 90 percent of Kansas youth attended public schools and colleges, while only 73 percent of the country's youth did so. Kansans were thus paying at about the national average. But Keller wanted them to pay much more.[16]

Several other recommendations were more surprising. The most radical was that the legislature should grant a lump sum each year to the Board of Regents, leaving the Board free to distribute it to the schools. Accompanying that idea was the notion that the Board should carry "state-wide responsibility for all higher education and the role determination which a state system of higher education should supply in providing leadership and planning to meet the needs of the years ahead." In line with that enlarged role the regents should cooperate with the State Board of Education and the Department of Public Instruction to develop criteria for the creation and operation of the public junior colleges, and should join the

Board of Education to review at least once a year the junior colleges' "role and contributions." The quality of the regents should also be improved. Though refusing to criticize anyone directly, Keller and his colleagues urged Kansans to give such "serious attention" to the regents' appointment that it "becomes one of the highest forms of recognition which the state can provide. The status of the Regents must be held in such high repute that appointment to membership is made on a nonpartisan basis." Toward that end the prohibition of more than five regents from one political party should be repealed; and the regents should be able to hold their posts long enough to become "fully informed about matters of higher education and statesmanlike in their approach to the problems involved."[17]

On the whole the *Comprehensive Survey* pleased the Legislative Council. While it could not support either the lump-sum grant to the regents or the abolition of party representation on the Board, it did back larger appropriations, higher faculty salaries, the TIAA retirement system for faculty members, and the expanded role of the regents.[18]

In approving those recommendations, however, the Council was approving merely a program for adequacy, rather than distinction. Because Keller, Pugsley, and Evers studied all higher education in Kansas, they had little opportunity to investigate the characteristics and needs of any one institution. There was nothing in their analysis suggesting how the University—or any of the other schools under the regents' control—might rise to new levels of excellence. Despite the time spent and all the statistical analyses offered, the number and scope of the recommendations were less than they might have been. And the prose itself was routine, unexciting, not at all calculated to spur Kansans to action.

One reason for the *Comprehensive Survey*'s soberness, perhaps, was that too many Kansans—Pugsley, Evers, the Citizens Advisory Committee for Higher Education, and the Professional Advisory Committee for Higher Education—helped prepare it. In the fall of 1962 the regents received a report on higher education in the state from a group of non-Kansans which made the *Comprehensive Survey* seem even drabber. It came from a seven-member advisory panel to the Board whose chairman was Alvin C. Eurich, vice-president and director of the Ford Foundation's Fund for the Advancement of Education. Its other members were Dean Francis Keppel of the Harvard Graduate School of Education; Millicent C. McIntosh, president emerita of Barnard College; Frank H. Bowles, president of the College Entrance Examination Board; Samuel B. Gould, formerly chancellor of the University of California at Santa Barbara and now president of the Educational Broadcasting Corporation; Douglas Whitaker, vice-president of the Rockefeller Institute; and Sidney G. Tickton, the panel's secretary, who was a program associate of the Fund for the Advancement of Education.[19]

The Eurich Report, as it was generally called—the formal title was *Kansas Plans for the Next Generation*—had been conceived by the regents in 1961 in the midst of confusion and uncertainty about the future of the institutions under their control. After four years of Governor George Docking, Chancellor Murphy's resignation, and the appearance of the *Comprehensive Survey*, it was not surprising that the regents wanted a study of their own by investigators of some stature to help them prepare for the years ahead. In the spring of 1961, moreover, the legislature had passed a concurrent resolution introduced by seventy-four representatives directing the Legislative Council to make a "study, evaluation and examination" of the needs of higher education in the light of the offer of the board of regents of the University of Wichita to give their school to the state. The resolution assumed that the state would accept the offer one day, but said that before it did, an investigation of facilities, programs, and duplication of efforts was necessary. Originally the resolution had called in its title for the Council to make the study "with the professional assistance of the state institutions of higher education." Ominously the Senate struck out the phrase, the House concurred, and the Council went ahead on its own. Thereupon the regents went ahead on their own to contract for a separate study.[20]

After the regents read the Eurich Report, they described it as a "magnificent accomplishment of the greatest significance for all Kansans."[21] They were half correct: only the future could determine its significance, but it was a magnificent document, even if it did start with a statement of questionable validity. "Kansas mirrors America; its past, its hopes, and especially its dreams for the next generation," the report began. "Education is central to those aspirations and the universities are the capstones of the educational system. The future of this modern age will reflect in every way the strength of our institutions of higher learning." It sounded like Franklin Murphy, and so did the report's general criticism of higher education, which in a way summed up the University's first hundred years. "Kansas is now doing too little and the educational deficit is growing here as in the rest of the country. . . . Salaries of faculty members, increased as they have been in recent years, are still too low. Research effort is too low. And the willingness of the State to bid for university personnel of outstanding calibre and talent is too low indeed to retain people important to the State's future development. . . . To put it bluntly, the quality of higher education in Kansas, as elsewhere, adequate as it may have been in the past, falls short of standards acceptable for tomorrow and the long run future."[22]

Most of the report was recommendations by which the University could allegedly begin to assure its future as an "outstanding center for graduate and professional study" and "university-based medical, scientific and industrial research," and as an "outstanding citadel of learning in a great variety of academic and technical areas." The Eurich Report made no survey of the present scene. Higher education in Kansas had already been surveyed enough, with too few results, its authors said, and their eyes were on the future.[23]

To improve the organization and increase the efficiency of the state system, the panel urged the regents to assume greater responsibility for coordinating higher education throughout the state, to delegate part of this responsibility to a new Council of State Colleges, and to create a joint Board for State Universities Extension Services. They should seek the closest possible cooperation between public and private institutions. They should establish a panel of "highly qualified" out-of-state consultants, who with an "impartial and objective view of Kansas institutions" would inform the Board of the "most important new developments in higher education throughout the country and advise how these might be applied in Kansas." But such advisers could help the Board only so much. The regents themselves should pay more attention to their responsibilities by holding longer meetings than they had in the past in order to "discharge more fully the responsibility for leadership and co-ordination of higher education in the State, and devote more time to policy matters." Ideally they should serve nine-year terms, with only one new member appointed each year; the panel urged the legislature to make it possible.[24]

The Eurich Report's most important suggestion for coordination, however, had to do with the municipal University of Wichita. Properly handled, the institution had much to offer the students of its area. One fourth of the state's college-age youth lived within commuting distance of the school, and it had a commendable record of serving the many part-time students of the state's largest population and industrial center. Rejecting the incorporation of the institution into the state system as a third university equal to those in Lawrence and Manhattan, the panel proposed that Wichita become a State Universities Center controlled by a board representing the other two schools. Using Wichita's resources and also those of the other institutions, the Center should offer a "wide variety" of programs leading to the B.A. and B.S. degrees, to be awarded by the University of Kansas, and also offer "whatever programs are needed" at the graduate and professional levels. In addition the Center should include a technical institute to furnish "semi-professional" and "technical and sub-professional training," and establish a close liaison with the industrial and commercial firms in the region needing advanced training for their employees. In return Wichitans should give their university to the state clear of bonded indebtedness, and pledge a "substantial proportion" of the tax revenues now supporting it to scholarships for students attending any of the state schools.[25]

But while the two parent universities were begetting the State Universities Center, they should improve themselves—mainly through a renewed emphasis on research. Eurich and his colleagues agreed with the Argersinger report that research was an "inescapable responsibility of the university and an inseparable part of its total educational function." During the 1962–1963 academic year, they reported, the two universities would have about $9,300,000 from all sources for research of all kinds. This was far too little. The two should form an interuniversity research committee to stimulate activity and make recommendations for money to the legislature. They should seek more private support, expand their facilities, provide opportunities for off-campus research and advanced study for faculty members. They should arrange to publish more scholarly works, to pay travel costs to professional meetings, to create Distinguished Regents Professorships to attract and keep outstanding scholars.

Although the recommendations applied to all kinds of research, the panel was most enthusiastic about the kind that contributed to economic growth. Noting the relation between university research and industrial development around San Francisco, Los Angeles, Boston, and Pittsburgh, the panel averred that the two Kansas institutions should imitate those examples. "These three elements: strong universities, research, and economic growth, are inextricably interwoven in the fabric of a modern dynamic and developing society." The Eurich Report thus proposed an interuniversity research foundation whose board of directors would include several industrialists or professional men along with the university heads and chairman of the regents. It would encourage and manage research supported by outside sources, including the federal government.[26]

Last of the policy recommendations were those to improve professional and graduate training. To train better school teachers, all the institutions should eliminate unnecessary professional courses from their curricula and give more attention to a five-year program placing more emphasis on the liberal arts; the three state colleges should become all-purpose institutions. Practice teaching should last a full semester and come after the B.A. For other kinds of professional education the panel recommended that the regents undertake no new "educational program in professional areas not now offered," and that the schools speed up their M.A. and Ph.D. programs. Advanced graduate work should rest on the idea of a three-year M.A. for brighter students, two years of which would be the junior and senior undergraduate years. Two years beyond the M.A. should be sufficient for the Ph.D.[27]

At the heart of the Eurich Report was the question of whether Kansans could afford the improvements the panel had in mind and at the same time provide for the oncoming hordes of students. The panel thought they could. For the next five years, the report said, the highest priorities were for greater faculty salaries at all the state schools and "increased financial underpinning" for both higher education in Wichita and the public junior colleges, which the panel members thought should be put under the regents' control and given state aid. If classrooms and laboratories were used most efficiently—which meant steadily from 8:00 a.m. to 10:00 p.m. week-days and to 1:00 p.m. Saturdays, eleven months of the year—it would be possible to postpone new construction until enrollments were nearly double the present number. Thus there would be more money for both salaries and research.[28]

In a special memorandum, secretary Sidney G. Tickton estimated that by 1980 the public institutions would probably have about 117,000 full- and part-time students, in contrast to the 48,000 they had now. A larger ratio of them would be graduate and professional students whose instruction cost relatively more than that of under-graduates. By 1976, Tickton believed, the increased cost of higher education, *excluding* construction, federally financed research, and auxiliary enterprises such as dormitories and hospitals, would be about $100,000,000. He and his associates believed, however, that the money could be found. It seemed reasonable to think that by 1980 the state's population would have grown by 243,000, and that by 1976 gross personal income would have grown by $4,000,000,000. The increase of $100,000,000 was 2.5 percent of that amount; this meant that such costs would be from 1.5 to 1.75 percent of total personal income. Kansans were paying just under 1 percent now for higher education; the percentage increase that they should pay in the future was considerable. And clearly, the total increase, in-cluding buildings, was going to be much greater. Besides raising taxes, however, the panel suggested that the regents and other offi-cers be more diligent in seeking federal aid and private gifts, and that they force the students and their parents to pay higher tuition fees. Two-thirds of the country's state universities and land-grant colleges charged more than either of the Kansas universities. "Charges can be higher in Kansas," the panel said, "without seri-ously restricting educational opportunity. . . ."[29]

At the same time the panel urged the regents and citizens to stretch every dollar to the maximum by eliminating waste and duplication, and offered a number of practical proposals for doing so. But the members recognized that efficiency had its limits. Much waste arose from the failure of the institutions to cooperate in using facilities and personnel, from the duplication of courses, programs, and schools, and from the necessity of enrolling "many undergrad-uate students who have not demonstrated their capacity for high quality academic study." Yet what could be done? Each institution had its own "special interests, alumni, and local constituency," and each school and department was "naturally a special pleader for its own students, faculty, and areas of study." Further, the history of Kansas higher education had been marked by "intense but healthy competition for appropriations, status, public support, etc.," and public enthusiasm had always existed for the "wide-open-door" admissions policy for high-school graduates. The panel believed, however, that the state should educate more students in the junior colleges, where the cost per student was lower than in the four-year colleges and universities.[30]

The Eurich Report was optimistic about the future. Kansas had "great traditions that have shaped its pattern of higher education," it said. "They are deeply embedded. They furnish a firm, stable foundation on which colleges and universities will build their future. . . . Kansas, we are fully convinced from our study, is ready to move ahead vigorously. As the late eminent historian Carl Becker has so aptly said, 'With Kansas history back of him, the true Kansan feels that nothing is too much for him. . . . Kansans set their own standards, and the state becomes, as it were, an experiment station. . . . The Kansas spirit is therefore one that finds something exhilarating in the challenge of an extreme difficulty. . . . Nowhere is there more loyal devotion to such words as liberty, democracy, equality, education.' "[31]

One could only hope that the prediction proved correct. Becker himself had discovered, however, that a devotion to words and ideas did not necessarily mean a devotion to institutions, that Kansans were capable of making what he thought were foolish decisions about higher education. The Eurich Report called upon Kansans to give some real substance to the concept of "academic excellence" in both teaching and research in order to make up for lost time. "The nation needs, and Kansas needs, a reappraisal of educational policies designed to eliminate the educational deficit that has been tolerated since the end of World War II."[32] But by the 1960s the deficit was not two decades old, but ten. An accounting of that deficit, indeed—now growing enormously, now shrinking a little, now remaining about the same—was the University's history to the end of its first century. Whether a similar accounting would be the history of its second century remained to be seen.

NOTES
SOURCES
INDEX

ABBREVIATIONS

The following abbreviations are used in the notes:

BRUK	Biennial Report of the University of Kansas
JBR	Journal of the Board of Regents, MS, University Archives
KHJ	Kansas, House of Representatives Journal
KL	Kansas, Laws of the State
KSJ	Kansas, Senate Journal
MBA	Minutes of the Board of Administration, MS, University Archives
MBR	Minutes of the Board of Regents, MS, University Archives
RBA	Report of the State Board of Administration
RBR	Report of the Board of Regents
RHC	Regional History Collection, Spencer Research Library, University of Kansas
UA	University Archives, Spencer Research Library, University of Kansas
UKC	University of Kansas Catalogue

Notes

CHAPTER 1

1. *The Helianthus, (Annuus) Published from the State University of Kansas. 1889* (Lawrence, 1889), title page.

2. For this and similar expressions of the Free-State legend, see Hannah Oliver, speech on September 30, 1926, "Annual Freshman Induction Ceremony, Speeches on the History of Kansas University by Hannah Oliver, Graduate of the Class of 1874, Professor Emeritus of Latin" (MS, UA); *When You Come to K-U*, Bulletin of the University of Kansas, 23 (May 15, 1922), 56; Scott Hopkins, "Address on Behalf of the Board of Regents by Hon. Scott Hopkins," *Graduate Magazine of the University of Kansas*, 1 (November, 1902), 56; Franklin D. Murphy, *Statement by Franklin D. Murphy on the Occasion of His Inauguration as the Ninth Chancellor of the University of Kansas, September 17, 1951* (Lawrence, 1951), 3, 4.

3. Samuel A. Johnson, *The Battle Cry of Freedom: The New England Emigrant Aid Company in the Kansas Crusade* (Lawrence, 1954).

4. *Ibid.*, 17, 33; Amos A. Lawrence to Charles Robinson, November, 1854, William Lawrence, *Life of Amos A. Lawrence: With Extracts from His Diary and Correspondence* (Boston, 1888), 115–116; Frank E. Melvin to Ernest H. Lindley, October 28, 1938, UA; Frank W. Blackmar, *Higher Education in Kansas* (Washington, 1900), 17.

5. William F. Zornow, *Kansas: A History of the Jayhawk State* (Norman, 1957), 70.

6. *Journal of the Council of the Territory of Kansas, at Their First Session* (Shawnee Manual Labor School, 1855), 16; *The Statutes of the Territory of Kansas; Passed at the First Session of the Legislative Assembly, One Thousand Eight Hundred and Fifty-five* (Shawnee Manual Labor School, 1855), 931–936.

7. Lawrence *Kansas Free State*, November 26, 1855.

8. Donald G. Tewksbury, *The Founding of American Colleges and Universities before the Civil War: With Particular Reference to the Religious Influences Bearing upon the College Movement* (New York, 1932), 167, 178, 192, 195, 198–200, 202, 203.

9. Lawrence *Herald of Freedom*, December 13, 1856. See also William F. M. Arny to John W. Geary, December 8, 1856, *ibid.*, December 20, 1856.

10. *Ibid.*, January 3, 1857.

11. *Ibid.*, January 31, 1857; "The Topeka Movement," *Kansas Historical Collections*, 13 (1913–1914), 245, 246, 249.

12. *Journal of the Council of the Territory of Kansas, at Their Second Session, Begun and Held at the City of Lecompton, on the Second Monday (12th) of January, 1857* (Lecompton, 1857), 17, 241; *Journal of the House of Representatives of the Territory of Kansas, Begun and Held at the City of Lecompton, on the Second Monday (12th) of January, 1857* (Lecompton, 1857), 193; *Laws of the Territory of Kansas, Passed at the Second Session of the General Legislative Assembly, Begun and Held at*

the City of Lecompton, on the Second Monday (12th) of January, A.D. 1857 (Lecompton, 1857), 112–113.

13. Lawrence *Herald of Freedom*, June 6, 1857.

14. Daniel W. Wilder, *The Annals of Kansas* (Topeka, 1875), 143, 148.

15. *Ibid.*, 176.

16. Harry G. Larimer, comp., *Kansas Constitutional Convention: A Reprint of the Proceedings and Debates of the Convention Which Framed the Constitution of Kansas at Wyandotte in July, 1859. Also the Constitution Annotated to Date, Historical Sketches, Etc.* (Topeka, 1920), 14; G. Raymond Gaeddert, *The Birth of Kansas* (Lawrence, 1940), 68.

17. Larimer, comp., *Kansas Constitutional Convention*, 170–171.

18. *Ibid.*, 172–173.

19. *Ibid.*, 173–174.

20. *Ibid.*, 135–137.

21. *Ibid.*, 192–193.

22. Sections 2, 7, and 8 of Article VI read:

Sec. 2. The legislature shall encourage the promotion of intellectual, moral, scientific, and agricultural improvement, by establishing a uniform system of common schools, and schools of a higher grade, embracing normal, preparatory, collegiate, and university departments.

Sec. 7. Provision shall be made by law for the establishment, at some eligible and central point, of a State university, for the promotion of literature and the arts and sciences, including a normal and an agricultural department. All funds arising from the sale or rents of lands granted by the United States to the State for the support of a State university, and all other grants, donations or bequests, either by the State or by individuals, for such purpose, shall remain a perpetual fund, to be called the "university fund"; the interest of which shall be appropriated to the support of the State university.

Sec. 8. No religious sect or sects shall ever control any part of the common school or university funds of the State.

Several parts of the Wyandotte Constitution had come from other state constitutions which the delegates used freely when they wrote their own. The first part of Section 2—through the word "improvement"—came directly from the Iowa constitution of 1857. The rest of the section, except for a few changes in wording, came from the Leavenworth Constitution of 1858. Most of Section 7 was modeled after the Wisconsin constitution of 1848, except for the words setting forth the purpose of the institution and providing for a normal and an agricultural department. The concept of the university's promoting literature and the arts and sciences had appeared in the charter of the University of the Territory of Kansas granted by the Bogus Legislature in 1855. The protection of the common-school fund against control by religious sects was a natural result of the old American idea that church and state should be separate; it had appeared in the Leavenworth Constitution, and now the protection was extended to the University Fund as well. Section 9, in turn, came from the Wisconsin constitution, the only change being the substitution of the Kansas superintendent of public instruction for the Wisconsin state treasurer.

See Larimer, comp., *Kansas Constitutional Convention*, 583–584, and Rosa M. Perdue, "The Sources of the Constitution of Kansas," *ibid.*, 677, 687–688.

23. Gaeddert, *Birth of Kansas*, 116; *KHJ*, 1861, pp. 95, 112, 113, 151, 178–179.

24. *Ibid.*, 1861, pp. 271–273; Julius T. Willard, *History of the Kansas State College*

of Agriculture and Applied Science (Manhattan, 1940), 11–12; John D. Walters, *History of the Kansas State Agricultural College* (Manhattan, 1909), 18.

25. *KHJ*, 1861, pp. 274, 296, 316, 349, 354–355, 460, 494, 509–510, 539; Gaeddert, *Birth of Kansas*, 117–118; *KSJ*, 1861, pp. 287–293.

26. Amos A. Lawrence to Ephraim Nute, December 6, 21, 1856 (copies), Charles Robinson Papers, RHC.

27. Amos A. Lawrence to John Carter Brown, January 10, 1857 (copy), "Copies of Letters of Amos A. Lawrence about Kansas Affairs and to Correspondents in Kansas: From June 10, 1854, to August 10, 1861; Presented to the Kansas State Historical Society by Mrs. Sarah E. Lawrence, September 17, 1888" (typewritten MS, Kansas State Historical Society, Topeka); Charles Robinson to Sara Robinson, January 11, 1857, Charles Robinson Papers, Kansas State Historical Society; Amos A. Lawrence to Charles Robinson and Samuel C. Pomeroy, February 14, 1857, Robinson Papers, RHC.

28. Robert E. Thompson, *A History of the Presbyterian Churches in the United States* (New York, 1895), 136–137: *Private Laws of the Territory of Kansas, Passed at the Fifth Session of the Legislative Assembly; Begun at the City of Lecompton, on the 1st Monday of Jan'y, 1859, and Held and Concluded at the City of Lawrence* (Lawrence, 1859), 81–85.

29. Charles M. Correll, *A Century of Congregationalism in Kansas, 1854–1954* (Topeka, 1953), 75–76; Lawrence *Herald of Freedom*, October 18, 1859; Wilson Sterling, "Historical Sketch of the University of Kansas," Wilson Sterling, ed., *Quarter-Centennial History of the University of Kansas, 1866–1891. With Portraits of Chancellors* (Topeka, 1891), 53, 55–56; Amos A. Lawrence to Charles Robinson, November 25, 1859, and S. N. Simpson to Robinson, January 16, 1860, Robinson Papers, RHC; Lawrence to Simpson, November 9, 1858 (copy), "Copies of Letters of Amos A. Lawrence."

30. *Private Laws Passed by the Legislative Assembly of the Territory of Kansas, for the Year 1861: Commenced at the City of Lecompton January Seventh, and Adjourned to and Concluded at the City of Lawrence* (Lawrence, 1861), 29–32.

31. Gaeddert, *Birth of Kansas*, 118; H.B. 32, Legislature of 1862, "An Act to Locate the State University," including letter from Solon A. Thacher, S. N. Simpson, and others to the Legislature of the State of Kansas, January 27, 1862, and H.B. 69, Legislature of 1862, "An Act Locating the State University," Legislative Collection, Kansas State Historical Society Archives, Topeka; *KHJ*, 1862, pp. 69, 82, 97, 107, 119, 170, 237, 271, 276.

32. Gaeddert, *Birth of Kansas*, 120–121, 178–182.

33. *KSJ*, 1862, pp. 125, 127, 144, 149–150, 155, 158, 191–192.

34. *U.S. Statutes at Large*, 12: 503–504.

35. Thomas Carney, "Inaugural Message of Gov. Thomas Carney," State of Kansas, *Pub. Documents, 1863*, p. 14.

36. *KHJ*, 1863, pp. 145, 148, 162, 213, 216; *KSJ*, 1863, pp. 133, 140, 142, 158–159, 170–172; *KL*, 1863, pp. 10–12.

37. H.B. 81, Legislature of 1863, "An Act to Locate the State University," and H.B. 122, Legislature of 1863, "An Act to Locate the State University at Emporia," Legislative Collection, Kansas State Historical Society Archives; *KHJ*, 1863, pp. 82, 92, 119, 149, 162; Charles Robinson to Amos A. Lawrence, February 22, 1863 (copy), Robinson Papers, RHC.

38. "Notes on Father's Talk to Miss Minnie Moodie," January 29, 1917, in account taken down by Mrs. E. M. Owen, Lawrence, from her father, William Miller, brother of Josiah Miller, Josiah and William Miller Papers, RHC; *KHJ*, 1863, pp. 227, 237–238.

39. George L. Anderson, "Atchison and the Central Branch Country, 1865–1874," *Kansas Historical Quarterly*, 28 (Spring, 1962), 3, 10; Gaeddert, *Birth of Kansas*, 111–112, 121; Leavenworth *Daily Conservative*, February 12, March 3, 1863; C. S. Griffin, "The University of Kansas and the Years of Frustration, 1854–1864," *Kansas Historical Quarterly*, 32 (Spring, 1966), 27–29.

40. The final balloting gave credibility to the idea of a deal between the Lawrence backers and the supporters of the northern railroad line. Every one of the eleven representatives from Doniphan, Brown, Nemaha, Marshall, and Washington counties—the extreme northern tier—favored the measure; the role played by Representative Russell was obviously crucial. All except seven of the other twenty-seven affirmative votes came from the two eastern tiers of counties south of the Kansas River. The Lawrence promoters won the votes of all the representatives from Johnson County, and one of the three from Bourbon County. Beyond those, there were four votes from Leavenworth County, two from Jefferson County, and one from Osage County. The opposing votes came in part from Atchison and Leavenworth counties to the north and east of Lawrence, but mainly from the counties lying to the west and southwest, whose representatives saw no particular advantage in locating the university in Lawrence. *KHJ*, 1863, pp. 82, 92, 119, 149, 162, 213, 222–224, 230, 366.

41. *KSJ*, 1863, pp. 148–150, 170, 173–174, 191–192, 199; *KL*, 1863, pp. 115–116.

42. *KHJ*, 1863, p. 292; *KL*, 1863, pp. 93–95, 115–116.

CHAPTER 2

1. Wilson Sterling, "Historical Sketch of the University of Kansas," Wilson Sterling, ed., *Quarter-Centennial History of the University of Kansas, 1866–1891. With Portraits of Chancellors* (Topeka, 1891), 69; Julius T. Willard, *History of the Kansas State College of Agriculture and Applied Science* (Manhattan, 1940), 12; John D. Walters, "The Kansas State Agricultural College," *Kansas Historical Collections*, 7 (1901–1902), 170 n; Kansas State Superintendent of Public Instruction, *Report*, State of Kansas, *Pub. Documents, 1863*.

2. M. W. Sterling, "Early K.U. Finance," *Graduate Magazine of the University of Kansas*, 11 (April, 1913), 204–205; Frank W. Blackmar, *The Life of Charles Robinson, the First State Governor of Kansas* (Topeka, 1902), 343–344; Isaac T. Goodnow, Josiah Miller, and Simeon M. Thorp to Thomas Carney, April 30, 1863, and accompanying documents, *Report of the Commissioners Appointed to Locate Permanently the State University, with Accompanying Papers* (n.p., n.d.), 3–9.

3. Charles Robinson to Amos A. Lawrence, February 22, March 17, 1863 (copies), and R. Z. Mason to Robinson, March 30, 1863, Charles Robinson Papers, RHC; Sterling, "Historical Sketch," Sterling, ed., *Quarter-Centennial History*, 72.

4. *KHJ*, 1864, pp. 30–31, 123, 164–165; H.B. 108, Legislature of 1864, "An Act Relating to the Endowment Fund of the State University," Legislative Collection, Kansas State Historical Society Archives, Topeka; *KSJ*, 1864, p. 213; *KL*, 1864, p. 194.

5. The legislature of 1864 had ordered Charles Chadwick of Lawrence to draw up a charter bill. He relied heavily upon the charter of the University of Michigan, the leading state university of the day. Robert Taft, *The Years on Mount Oread* (Lawrence, 1955), 9–10, 192–193.

6. *KL*, 1864, pp. 195–198.

7. The apathetic five, who were replaced, were Albert H. Horton of Atchison, an attorney appointed by Governor Robinson in 1862 as judge of the Second Judicial District; Samuel A. Kingman of Brown County, an associate justice of the Kansas

Supreme Court; John H. Watson of Emporia, who had come close to being chief justice of the Supreme Court in 1862; George A. Crawford, one of Fort Scott's leading businessmen and an active Republican politician; and George A. Moore, a business-man of Leavenworth. The sixth regent, the Reverend John A. Steele, pastor of the First Presbyterian Church of Topeka, died in October, 1864. Sterling, "Historical Sketch," Sterling, ed., *Quarter-Centennial History*, 77; Topeka *Capital*, September 3, 1902, September, 10, 1904; biographical sketch of John H. Watson in D.A.R., Emporia Chapter, "Genealogical Record of Early Settler: Joseph V. Randolph" (typewritten MS, Kansas State Historical Society); *The United States Biographical Dictionary. Kansas Volume: Containing Accurately Compiled Biographical Sketches, into Which Is Woven the History of the State and Its Leading Interests* (Kansas City, Mo., 1879), 490–497; William G. Cutler, ed., *History of the State of Kansas* . . . (Chicago, 1883), 549.

8. Sterling, "Historical Sketch," Sterling, ed., *Quarter-Centennial History*, 77; Lawrence *Journal*, June 9, 1899; Lawrence *Journal and Evening Tribune*, August 12, 1895; *Kansas University Lawyer*, 2 (November 1, 1895), 22–25; *Congregational Record*, 6 (June, 1864), 61, 74; William E. Connelley, *A Standard History of Kansas and Kansans*, 5 vols. (Chicago, 1918), 4: 1885–1886; autobiographical form for the Kansas State Historical Society, written by Charles B. Lines, November, 1882, Kansas State Historical Society; *Kansas Historical Collections*, 8 (1903–1904), 509, 511.

9. Sterling, "Historical Sketch," Sterling, ed., *Quarter-Centennial History*, 77–78; *Dictionary of American Biography*, 9: 151–152; Mary Patterson Clarke, *The History of the First Methodist Church of Lawrence, Kansas* (Kansas City, Mo., 1916), 18, 25–26; Cutler, ed., *History of the State of Kansas*, 455, 615; *United States Biographical Dictionary, Kansas*, 574–579; Lawrence *Journal-World*, August 8, 1942.

10. George A. Beecher, "Address Delivered by Bishop Beecher at the Dedication of the Oliver Memorial Chapel," *Western Nebraska Churchman*, 35 (October, 1939), 2–3; David H. Robinson, "Reminiscences," Sterling, ed., *Quarter-Centennial History*, 160–162.

11. JBR, March 21, December 6, 1865.

12. R. Z. Mason to Charles Robinson, December 12, 1863, March 8, 1864, and H. L. Blood to Robinson, April 4, 1864, Charles Robinson Papers, Kansas State Historical Society; Executive Committee, Board of Regents, Minutes, August 17, November 13, 18, 1865, June 18, July 27, August 3, 1866, UA; JBR, December 6, 1865, July 17, December 6, 1866.

13. JBR, December 6, 1865, July 17, 1866; *KHJ*, 1866, pp. 45, 79, 127, 265–266, 423–424; *KSJ*, 1866, pp. 331, 341, 377, 391, 399; *KL*, 1866, p. 38.

14. JBR, July 17, December 5, 1866.

15. Abstract of title to North College grounds between Ohio, Quincy, Indiana, and Berkeley streets, June 30, 1903, UA; Ex. Comm., Bd. Regs., Minutes, March 27, June 19, 1865; JBR, March 21, July 17, 1865; Robert W. Oliver to Francis H. Snow, May 16, 1890, Robinson Papers, RHC.

16. JBR, March 21, 1865.

17. Ex. Comm., Bd. Regs., Minutes, August 24, September 8, 18, 19, November 4, December 12, 1865, March 5, August 21, 1866; JBR, December 6, 1865, July 17, 18, 1866.

18. Francis H. Snow to ?, September 13, 1866, *Graduate Magazine*, 3 (December, 1904), 83–84; Ex. Comm., Bd. Regs., Minutes, July 27, November 13, 22, 1866; JBR, December 6, 1866.

19. *Ibid.*, March 21, 1865, July 19, 1866; Ex. Comm., Bd. Regs., Minutes, August 17, 24, 1865.

20. Hannah Oliver, "David Hamilton Robinson, Professor of Latin in the University of Kansas, 1866–1895," Francis H. Snow, "Professor D. H. Robinson as He Appeared to a Colleague in the University Faculty," and Angelo C. Scott, "What a Boy Thought of Professor Robinson," *Graduate Magazine,* 5 (May, 1907), 275–279, 279–283, 284–287; Kate Stephens, *Life at Laurel Town in Anglo-Saxon Kansas* (Lawrence, 1936), 199–200; *Kansas University Weekly,* October 25, 1895.

21. Clyde K. Hyder, *Snow of Kansas: The Life of Francis Huntington Snow with Extracts from His Journals and Letters* (Lawrence, 1953), 7–95; Francis H. Snow to Charles Robinson, December 2, 1865, Robinson Papers, Kansas State Historical Society; Robinson to Snow, January 3, 1866, Robinson Papers, RHC; JBR, July 19, 1866.

22. Hyder, *Snow,* 99–195.

23. *Alumni Record of Baker University: Including an Account of the Principal Events in the First Twenty-five Years of the History of the College, with a Roster of the Trustees and the Faculty, and Their Officers* (Baldwin City, 1917), xlviii; Ex. Comm., Bd. Regs., Minutes, July 24, 1866; Francis H. Snow to ?, December 1, 1866, February 1, March 5, September 1, 1867, *Graduate Magazine,* 3 (December, 1904), 89, 90, 92–93; JBR, December 5, 1866, August 26, 1867, August 5, 1868; *Kansas Historical Collections,* 1–2 (1875–1880), 170.

24. JBR, July 19, 1866.

25. *Ibid.,* December 6, 1865, July 18, 1866; Ex. Comm., Bd. Regs., Minutes, July 24, 1866.

26. Robinson, "Reminiscences," Sterling, ed., *Quarter-Centennial History,* 159–164; Ex. Comm., Bd. Regs., Minutes, July 24, 1864.

27. Francis H. Snow to ?, September 13, 1866, *Graduate Magazine,* 3 (December, 1904), 83; Robinson "Reminiscences," Sterling, ed., *Quarter-Centennial History,* 164–165.

28. *UKC,* 1866–1867, pp. 12, 14.

29. Robert Taft, *Across the Years on Mount Oread, 1866 . . . 1941: An Informal and Pictorial History of the University of Kansas* (Lawrence, 1941), 7.

30. Topeka *Kansas State Journal,* September 20, 1866; Robinson, "Reminiscences," Sterling, ed., *Quarter-Centennial History,* 167–168.

31. Francis H. Snow to ?, January 29, February 1, 1867, *Graduate Magazine,* 3 (December, 1904), 90; Robinson, "Reminiscences," Sterling, ed., *Quarter-Centennial History,* 165–166.

32. *RBR,* 1890, p. 6; Francis H. Snow to ?, September 15, 1867, January 10, 1868, *Graduate Magazine,* 3 (December, 1904), 94, 97; Oliver, "David Hamilton Robinson," *ibid.,* 5 (May, 1907), 276.

33. Ex. Comm., Bd. Regs., Minutes, December 22, 1866; *KL,* 1867, pp. 11, 16.

34. JBR, December 4, 1867, February 12, 1868; *RBR,* 1867, pp. 5–7.

35. Francis H. Snow to ?, February 4, 29, March 7, 15, 1868, *Graduate Magazine,* 3 (December, 1904), 97–98, 100–101; Robinson, "Reminiscences," Sterling, ed., *Quarter-Centennial History,* 167–170.

36. *KHJ,* 1868, pp. 370, 690, 901, 903–905, 907, 1001, 1005–1007, 1009, 1019–1022, 1025–1028; *KSJ,* 1868, pp. 295–296, 580–582, 593–594, 600–605, 614–616, 633–635, 643, 645–648; State of Kansas, *Special Laws,* 1868, pp. 18, 19.

37. JBR, December 5, 6, 1866.

38. Of Oliver's five recommendations, four were connected with the University of Michigan: former President Henry P. Tappan and Professors Edward P. Evans of Modern Languages, James R. Boise of Greek, and Henry S. Frieze of Latin. The other was the Reverend Edward Bourns, until 1865 president of Norwich University

in Northfield, Vermont. Ex. Comm., Bd. Regs., Minutes, April 28, 1867; JBR, August 7, 8, 26, 1867.

39. Francis H. Snow to ?, November 17, 24, 1867, *Graduate Magazine,* 3 (December, 1904), 95–96; JBR, December 4, 1867.

40. Francis H. Snow to ?, December 28, 1867, March 29, 1868, *Graduate Magazine,* 3 (December, 1904), 96, 101–102.

CHAPTER 3

1. Day Otis Kellogg to Francis H. Snow, May 6, 1890, "Letters of Congratulation to Francis Huntington Snow on His Appointment as Chancellor of Kansas State University" (MSS, UA).

2. "From Mrs. Fraser's Sketch," in "John Fraser, President, University of Kansas, 1868–1874" (notebook kept by Hannah Oliver, UA); S. A. Riggs, "Recollections of John Fraser," *Graduate Magazine of the University of Kansas,* 4 (January, 1906), 117–119; George L. Anderson, ed., *A Petition Regarding the Conditions in the C. S. M. Prison at Columbia, S.C. Addressed to the Confederate Authorities by Col. John Fraser Later Second Chancellor of the University of Kansas* (Lawrence, 1962), 3–25; Wayland F. Dunaway, *History of the Pennsylvania State College* (State College, 1946), 63, 65–70.

3. Hannah Oliver, "Chancellor Fraser as His Students Knew Him," *Graduate Magazine,* 6 (May, 1908), 285; Kate Stephens, "Acts and Facts for the University," *ibid.,* 21 (February, 1923), 12; Kate Stephens, *Truths Back of the Uncle Jimmy Myth in a State University of the Middle West* (New York, 1924), 3; Kansas State Superintendent of Public Instruction, *Report,* 1878, p. 42.

4. I have compiled this list from Fraser's notes for speeches and from his reading notes in "Notes by John Fraser. Tools with Which He Worked and Chips from His Workshop" (MSS, UA).

5. Items 126, 127, 128, 139, 158, 159 in "Notes by John Fraser," vol. 1. Subsequent citations to "Notes by John Fraser" are all to items in vol. 1.

6. Items 153, 154, 155, 156, *ibid.*

7. Items 164, 165, 177, *ibid.*

8. Items 106–121, 143, 151, 172, 177, 181, *ibid.*

9. Item 181, *ibid.*

10. Lawrence *Kansas Tribune,* June 13, 16, 18, 1868; *RBR,* 1890, p. 6; JBR, March 26, 1872.

11. Kenneth A. Middleton, "Manufacturing in Lawrence, Kansas, 1854–1900" (typewritten M.B.A. thesis, University of Kansas, 1940), 26, 28, 30, 32–33; JBR, December 1, 1869; Executive Committee, Board of Regents, Minutes, December 9, 1869, UA.

12. Robert Taft, *Across the Years on Mount Oread, 1866 . . . 1941: An Informal Pictorial History of the University of Kansas* (Lawrence, 1941), 12; *KL,* 1870, pp. 54–55, 75–76; Ex. Comm., Bd. Regs., Minutes, March 10, 1870; Charles H. Landrum, "A History of the Kansas School Fund," *Kansas Historical Collections,* 12 (1911–1912), 201; Kansas State Superintendent of Public Instruction, *Report,* 1870, p. 52, 1871, p. 72; *KL,* 1871, pp. 104–105.

13. JBR, May 4, June 2, 14, July 13, December 7, 1870.

14. JBR, January 31, 1871; *RBR,* 1870, pp. 3–4; *KSJ,* 1871, pp. 437, 448–449, 490, 509, 539, 587–588, 684, 687, 1872, pp. 172, 181, 195, 304, 306–307; *KHJ,* 1871, pp. 877, 893–895, 1872, pp. 71, 81, 195, 298, 324; *KL,* 1872, p. 56.

15. Lawrence *Kansas Tribune,* December 4, 1872.

16. Fort Scott *Monitor*, n.d., in Lawrence *Kansas Tribune*, June 12, 1872; *RBR*, 1872, p. 4, 1873, pp. 3–6, 13.

17. Ex. Comm., Bd. Regs., Minutes, January 2, 1869.

18. *RBR*, 1868, pp. 3–8.

19. *KL*, 1869, p. 22; Ex. Comm., Bd. Regs., Minutes, March 20, September 22, 1869.

20. *RBR*, 1869, pp. 2–3; *KL*, 1870, p. 23.

21. *RBR*, 1870, pp. 1, 2, 3; JBR, December 7, 1870; *KHJ*, 1871, pp. 674, 677, 892; *KSJ*, 1871, pp. 660, 676–677; *KL*, 1871, pp. 51–52; David H. Robinson, "Reminiscences," Wilson Sterling, ed., *Quarter-Centennial History of the University of Kansas, 1866–1891. With Portraits of Chancellors* (Topeka, 1891), 168–169.

22. *RBR*, 1871, pp. 1–2, 1872, p. 1; *KHJ*, 1872, pp. 933, 1006; *KSJ*, 1872, pp. 604, 729–730; *KL*, 1872, pp. 88–89.

23. *UKC*, 1868–1869, p. 5; Janet Coulson, "A History of the Fine Arts School at the University of Kansas" (typewritten M.M. thesis, University of Kansas, 1940), 30.

24. Ex. Comm., Bd. Regs., Minutes, June 25, 1869; JBR, July 7, 1869; Hannah Oliver, "Miss E. P. Leonard: Professor of Modern Languages in the University of Kansas, 1869–1874," *Graduate Magazine*, 3 (April, 1905), 257–260.

25. Ex. Comm., Bd. Regs., Minutes, September 3, 1869; Lawrence *Kansas Tribune*, August 19, 1878; Frederick W. Bardwell, "Speculations in Regard to Comets' Tails" and "Discrepancies between Theory and Observation of the Moon's Motion," *Transactions of the Kansas Academy of Science*, 2 (1873), 79–86, 3 (1874), 103–105; Bardwell, *An Essay on Methods of Arithmetical Instruction* (New York, 1878), 3, 5–6, 7, 11, 13–15, 27–30, 35–36; Bardwell, *Course in Arithmetic; A Treatise in Three Parts* (New York, 1878), vii.

26. JBR, December 1, 1869, August 9, 1870; Ex. Comm., Bd. Regs., Minutes, March 10, 1870; Kate Stephens, "In Memory of Dr. Day Otis Kellogg: Sometime Professor of English Literature and History," *Graduate Magazine*, 3 (March, 1905), 212–216.

27. JBR, December 17, 1870; *RBR*, 1870, p. 2.

28. JBR, August 23, 1871; Lawrence *Kansas Tribune*, August 24, 1871; George W. Cullum, *Biographical Register of the Officers and Graduates of the U.S. Military Academy at West Point, New York, from Its Establishment March 16, 1802 to the Army Reorganization of 1866–67*, 2 vols. (New York, 1868), 2: 288.

29. JBR, July 19, September 24, 1872; Lawrence *Kansas Tribune*, October 2, 1872; Albert J. S. Molinard, "Drawing," *Kansas Educational Journal*, 9 (June, 1872), 54–56; *RBR*, 1873, pp. 31–35.

30. JBR, August 23, 1871; Edgar H. S. Bailey, Hamilton P. Cady, and Frank B. Dains, *History of the Chemistry Department of the University of Kansas,* Bulletin of the University of Kansas, 26 (February 15, 1925), 6–7; *RBR*, 1872, pp. 1–2, 1873, pp. 29–31.

31. JBR, July 19, 1872; Ex. Comm., Bd. Regs., Minutes, July 29, August 28, 1872; Kate Stephens, "The First Professor of Greek at the University," *Graduate Magazine*, 27 (December, 1928), 13; Margaret L. Habein, "Kate Stephens: A Study of Her Life and Writings" (typewritten Ph.D. thesis, University of Kansas, 1952), 14, 15, 24; A. I. Tobin, "Introduction," and Byron Caldwell Smith to Kate Stephens, March 25, 1875, A. I. Tobin, ed., *The Love-Life of Byron Caldwell Smith* (New York, 1930), vii–xi, 44; Day O. Kellogg, "Preface," "Conclusion," and Byron Caldwell Smith to ?, May 2, 1871, Day O. Kellogg, ed., *A Young Scholar's Letters* (New York, 1897), v–vi, 274–275, 276–277, 346–350; *RBR*, 1873, p. 36, 1874, p. 18.

32. Lawrence *Kansas Tribune*, June 11, 1873.

33. *UKC*, 1868–1869, pp. 15–16.

34. *Ibid.*, 1868–1869, pp. 17–18, 1870–1871, pp. 24–25.

35. Lawrence *Kansas Tribune*, June 10, 11, 12, 1873; Taft, *Across the Years*, 16–17.

CHAPTER 4

1. James C. Carey, "People, Problems, Prohibition, Politicos and Politics—1870–1890," and William Frank Zornow, "The Basis of Agrarian Unrest in Kansas," John D. Bright, ed., *Kansas: The First Century*, 4 vols. (New York, 1956), 1: 377–382, 455–475.

2. *RBR*, 1872, pp. 2–4; *KSJ*, 1873, pp. 180, 181, 202, 203, 220–224.

3. *KHJ*, 1873, pp. 689, 695, 831, 862, 1096–1097, 1098; *KSJ*, 1873, pp. 486, 488–489, 546, 580, 583–584; *KL*, 1873, pp. 55–56.

4. Julius T. Willard, *History of the Kansas State College of Agriculture and Applied Science* (Manhattan, 1940), 25, 28–30; John D. Walters, *History of the Kansas State Agricultural College* (Manhattan, 1909), 47–48.

5. *KL*, 1873, pp. 251–254.

6. Clipping from *Churchman*, March 19, 1904, "Kansas Biographical Pamphlets," vol. 6, Kansas State Historical Society, Topeka; *Kansas Historical Collections*, 7 (1901–1902), 511–512; Topeka *Capital*, February 16, 1899; Atchison *Champion*, January 17, 1880; James L. King, ed., *History of Shawnee County, Kansas and Representative Citizens* (Chicago, 1905), 324–325.

7. JBR, April 1, 2, 3, June 10, 12, 13, 1873.

8. Kansas Board of Commissioners for Public Institutions, *Report*, 1873, p. 133.

9. *Ibid.*, 1873, pp. 3–17, 58–59.

10. John Fraser, "Outline of Defence. Written for the private use of W. R. Spooner Esqr. by John Fraser, June 2d, 1874" (typewritten copy of the original manuscript in the possession of the Kansas State Historical Society), UA. I have compared the copy with the original; the copy is accurate. See also Day O. Kellogg to Kate Stephens, October 18, 1887, *Graduate Magazine of the University of Kansas*, 7 (February, 1908), 176–177. Kellogg denied that he wished to become chancellor. Kellogg to the Editor, n.d., Lawrence *Kansas Tribune*, March 18, 1874.

11. Fraser, "Outline of Defence."

12. *Ibid.*

13. David H. Robinson, Francis H. Snow, Frederick W. Bardwell, Day O. Kellogg, and Byron C. Smith to John Fraser, December 19, 1873 (copy), "Kansas University: Items in Its History" (scrapbook, UA), vol. 1.

14. Fraser, "Outline of Defence."

15. Francis H. Snow to Francis T. Ingalls, February 18, 1874 (copy), "Kansas University: Items in Its History," vol. 1.

16. JBR, March 17, 18, 19, April 14, 1874; Fraser, "Outline of Defence."

17. Lawrence *Kansas Tribune*, June 9, 11, 1874.

18. JBR, June 9, July 15, 1874; *Dictionary of American Biography*, 3: 513–514.

19. Kansas Board of Commissioners for Public Institutions, *Report*, 1874, p. 31; JBR, August 31, 1874; Robert Taft, *The Years on Mount Oread* (Lawrence, 1955), 17–18, 193–194.

20. JBR, November 19, 1874, March 8, 1875.

21. *RBR*, 1873, pp. 11–12.

22. *KHJ*, 1874, pp. 359, 364, 431, 721, 735; *KSJ*, 1874, pp. 371, 380, 381, 389, 393; *KL*, 1874, pp. 19–20.

23. *RBR*, 1873, pp. 8–9; JBR, April 14, 15, May 8, June 9, 1874; Day O. Kellogg

to Francis H. Snow, May 6, 1890, "Letters of Congratulation to Francis Huntington Snow on His Appointment as Chancellor of Kansas State University" (MSS, UA).

24. JBR, May 8, June 9, July 15, 1874; Lawrence *Kansas Tribune*, July 16, 1874.

25. JBR, June 9, 14, 1874; *Graduate Magazine*, 7 (October, 1908), 38; *ibid.*, 29 (December, 1930), 22; J. H. Long, "Frances Schlegel Carruth," *ibid.*, 7 (October, 1908), 13; ? to Erasmus Haworth, June 4, 1917, "History of the Department of Chemistry of the University of Kansas as Recorded in the University Catalogues, 1866–1917" (typewritten MS, n.d., UA), 359; *RBR*, 1874, p. 2.

26. JBR, November 18, 19, 1874, June 16, 1875; *Observer of Nature*, 2 (March 4, 1875), 4; A. I. Tobin, "Introduction," and Byron Caldwell Smith to Kate Stephens, March 25, May 5, June 12, 26, July 1, 6, 14, 1875, A. I. Tobin, ed., *The Love-Life of Byron Caldwell Smith* (New York, 1930), xi, 44, 55–56, 67–68, 71, 74, 75, 77–78.

27. *RBR*, 1874, p. 5; William C. Tenney to the Editor, November 23, 1874, Lawrence *Kansas Tribune*, November 24, 1874.

28. Kansas Board of Commissioners for Public Institutions, *Report*, 1874, pp. 27–29, 35, 38, 40–41.

29. *KHJ*, 1875, pp. 50, 111, 400, 472, 723, 744, 759, 773–774, 847–848, 852; *KSJ*, 1875, pp. 505, 541, 567, 577, 586; *KL*, 1875, pp. 24–25.

CHAPTER 5

1. Frederick Rudolph, *The American College and University: A History* (New York, 1962), 264–286.

2. *Ibid.*, 247–263.

3. *UKC*, 1874–1875, p. 3, 1875–1876, p. 3, 1876–1877, p. 3, 1877–1878, p. 3, 1878–1879, p. 3; *The United States Biographical Dictionary. Kansas Volume: Containing Accurately Compiled Biographical Sketches, into Which Is Woven the History of the State and Its Leading Interests* (Kansas City, Mo., 1879), 32–35, 603; William G. Cutler, ed., *History of the State of Kansas . . .* (Chicago, 1883), 445; *Kansas Historical Collections*, 3 (1883–1885), 252.

4. *UKC*, 1879–1880, p. 3, 1880–1881, p. 3, 1881–1882, p. 3; Hill P. Wilson, comp., *A Biographical History of Eminent Men of the State of Kansas: With Portraits Engraved Expressly for This Work* (Topeka, 1901), 359–361; *Kansas Historical Collections*, 5 (1889–1896), 114–115; *United States Biographical Dictionary. Kansas Volume*, 220–221; John P. St. John to Cora M. Downs, December 21, 1881, Kansas University Miscellaneous Collection, UA; Lawrence *Journal*, December 27, 1881; E. C. Nettles, "George Record Peck" (typewritten MS, n.d., Kansas State Historical Society, Topeka).

5. George W. Glick to Frank Bacon, January 13, 1873, Governors' Papers, and Glick to M. P. Welch, January 20, 1883, Governors' Letters, Kansas State Historical Society.

6. *UKC*, 1882–1883, p. 3; *Genealogical and Biographical Record of North-Eastern Kansas* (Chicago, 1900), 27–39; Topeka *Capital*, September 19, 1907; Wichita *Beacon*, May 27, 1887; George W. Glick to James S. Emery, February 5, 1883, and Frank A. Fitzpatrick to Glick, February 22, 1883, Governors' Letters, Kansas State Historical Society; *KSJ*, 1883, pp. 290–292, 361, 364.

7. *UKC*, 1883–1884, p. 5, 1884–1885, p. 5, 1885–1886, p. 5, 1886–1887, p. 6, 1887–1888, p. 6; *Directory of the State Government of Kansas, for the Years 1877 and 1878: Embracing the Executive, Judicial and Legislative Departments, State Charitable and Educational Institutions, and Brief Sketches of Senators, Congressmen, and Members of the Legislature* (Topeka, 1877), 74; *Portrait and Biographical Record of Dickinson,*

Saline, McPherson and Marion Counties, Kansas: Containing Biographical Sketches of Prominent and Representative Citizens, Together with Biographies of All the Governors of the State, and of the Presidents of the United States (Chicago, 1893), 596–597; Wilson, comp., *Biographical History*, 529–531; Kansas City, Mo., *Journal*, July 26, 1920.

8. Kansas Conference, Minutes, 1902, in "James Marvin. Biographical Clippings" (scrapbook, UA); Kate Stephens, *Truths Back of the Uncle Jimmy Myth in a State University of the Middle West* (New York, 1924), 8–9; Kate Stephens to Hannah Oliver, March 14, 1910, in Hannah Oliver, "The University Seal," reprint of article in *Graduate Magazine of the University of Kansas*, 10 (January, 1912), pp. 132–134, UA.

9. Lawrence *Western Home Journal*, June 17, 1875.

10. Charles G. Dunlap, "A Few Words about Dr. J. A. Lippincott," *Graduate Magazine*, 5 (February, 1907), 155–158.

11. Joshua A. Lippincott, *The State University: Its Work, and Its Place in the Public School System. Inaugural Address, Delivered in University Hall, Lawrence, Kansas, September 26, 1883* (Topeka, 1883), 12.

12. *Ibid.*, 12–13.

13. *Ibid.*, 13–16.

14. *Ibid.*, 17.

15. Francis H. Snow, *Inaugural Address, Responding to the Board of Regents*, in *Addresses Concerning the Chancellorship, the University, Higher Education* (Topeka, 1890), 27, 28–29, 35–43, 45–46.

16. Snow, *Inaugural Address*, 29–30, 33–35.

17. Rudolph, *American College*, 264–286.

18. "Man Not a Machine. Synopsis of Dr. Marvin's Address at Baker University," unidentified newspaper clipping, n.d., "James Marvin. Biographical Clippings." See also James Marvin, "Address Delivered before the Graduating Class of 1881," *Kansas Review*, 3 (September, 1881), 10–11.

19. Joshua A. Lippincott, "A Dedicatory Address," *Kansas Review*, 10 (October, 1888), 36–39.

20. George R. Peck, *Higher Education; Its Aims and Its Results. The Annual Opening Address at the University of Kansas, Lawrence, Friday, September 7, 1888— Fall Term, A.D. 1888–89* (Topeka, 1888) 7.

21. Francis H. Snow to Josie Enderton, April 16, 1892 (copy), UA.

22. Joshua A. Lippincott to D. A. Finley, July 11, 1887 (copy), UA; *Western School Journal*, 15 (January, 1889), 37; X., "Are They Doing Their Duty?" *Kansas Reivew*, 2 (December, 1880), 91.

23. Snow, *Inaugural Address*, 38. See also *RBR*, 1880, pp. 20–21; "Chancellor Marvin on Class Education," *Kansas Collegiate*, February 14, 1877; *University Courier*, February 13, 1885.

24. Marvin, "Address," *Kansas Review*, 3 (September, 1881), 11; JBR, May 14, 1885; Joshua A. Lippincott, "Address to the Seniors," *University Review*, 6 (June, 1885), 284; James H. Canfield, "Why Does the State Educate?" *University Review*, 13 (December, 1891), 94–96. See also Lyman B. Kellogg, "Does the University Pay?" *University Review*, 14 (October, 1892), 34–41.

25. *Western School Journal*, 2 (January, 1886), 40; Calvin Thomas, "James Hulme Canfield," *Columbia University Quarterly*, 11 (June, 1909), 303.

26. Canfield, "Why Does the State Educate?" *University Review*, 13 (December, 1891), 94–95.

27. James H. Canfield, "The State and Higher Education," *Western School Journal*, 2 (December, 1885), 11–12.

28. For examples, see *RBR*, 1878, p. 13, 1884, pp. 17–18, 1890, pp. 7–8; "Chancellor Marvin on Class Education," *Kansas Collegiate*, February 14, 1877; Lawrence *Journal*, December 25, 1890; Francis H. Snow to Hiram Kline, March 3, 1892 (copy), UA.

CHAPTER 6

1. Lawrence *Western Home Journal*, June 17, 1875.

2. Raymond G. Gaeddert, "A History of the Establishment of the Kansas State Government" (typewritten Ph.D. dissertation, University of Kansas, 1937), 89.

3. Carroll D. Clark and Roy L. Roberts, *People of Kansas: A Demographic and Sociological Study* (Topeka, 1936), 31.

4. Jamestown *Cloud County Kansan*, January 1, 1887.

5. Topeka *Capital-Commonwealth*, February 15, 1889.

6. Troy *Kansas Chief*, June 13, 1895.

7. George Frey, "A Century of Education in Kansas," John D. Bright, ed., *Kansas: The First Century*, 4 vols. (New York, 1956), 2: 223–224.

8. M. S. Ward, "The Relation of the Denominational College to the Public School," *Kansas Educational Journal*, 9 (February, 1873), 319–326.

9. *Western School Journal*, 24 (January, 1908), 36–37.

10. Joshua A. Lippincott to Richard Wake, November 17, 1888, Lippincott to D. A. Finley, July 11, 1887 (copies), and ? to A. D. Moffett, August 17, 1887, UA; *Western School Journal*, 15 (January, 1889), 14.

11. *Ibid.*, 15 (January, 1889), 14.

12. *University Courier*, January 20, February 6, 1883; Baldwin *Index*, 2 (December, 1882, March, 1883), 57, 112.

13. *Kansas Review*, 4 (January, February, April, 1883), 108–109, 132, 182; Leavenworth *Press*, n.d., in Lawrence *Journal*, February 1, 1883.

14. Minutes of Faculty Meetings (MS, UA), January 18, 1883.

15. *The Helianthus, (Annuus) Published from the State University of Kansas. 1889* (Lawrence, 1889), 84; James H. Canfield, *Taxation; A Plain Talk for Plain People* (New York, 1883), 1–2, 5–9, 13–16, 21–24.

16. For testimonies to Canfield's fairness see *Kansas Review*, 4 (May, 1883), 205; *University Courier*, April 6, 1888; Lawrence *Journal*, August 23, 1888. Lippincott's views are in a letter to J. M. Swank, August 21, 1888 (copy), UA.

17. Troy *Kansas Chief*, March 22, 1888; Hutchinson *News*, July 22, 1888. See also Wichita *Eagle*, July 19, 1888.

18. *KHJ*, 1889, pp. 156, 282, 317.

19. James H. Canfield to William H. Carruth, May 6, 1908, *Graduate Magazine of the University of Kansas*, 8 (January, 1910), 130–131; *Kansas Review*, 4 (May, 1883), 205; *University Courier*, April 6, 1888; *University Review*, 10 (September, 1888), 18–19; Topeka *State Journal*, August 7, 1888; Lawrence *Journal*, August 23, 1888.

20. "Chancellor Canfield," *Western School Journal*, 7 (July, 1891), 176; James H. Canfield to William H. Carruth, May 6, 1908, *Graduate Magazine*, 8 (January, 1910), 130–131.

21. Topeka *State Journal*, June 13, 19, 1883; T. H. Rudiger to George W. Glick, May 26, 1883, George W. Glick Papers, Kansas State Historical Society, Topeka; Lawrence *Journal*, June 24, 1883; Atchison *Champion*, n.d., in Lawrence *Journal*, July 23, 1882; JBR, May 9, June 5, 1883.

22. *Ibid.*, June 6, August 29, September 5, 1883.

23. Margaret L. Habein, "Kate Stephens: A Study of Her Life and Writings" (typewritten Ph.D. thesis, University of Kansas, 1952), 1, 2, 3–4, 9, 10, 11, 13, 48–49; Byron Caldwell Smith to Kate Stephens, March 25, June 26, July 14, 1875, A. I. Tobin, ed., *The Love-Life of Byron Caldwell Smith* (New York, 1930), 44, 71, 78.

24. JBR, June 3, 1878; Habein, "Kate Stephens," 35, 36; Florence Finch Kelly, *Flowing Stream: The Story of Fifty-Six Years in American Newspaper Life* (New York, 1939), 112–113.

25. Habein, "Kate Stephens," 47; Lawrence *Journal*, May 1, 1885.

26. JBR, September 11, 1882, June 6, 1883, February 4, 1884; *RBR*, 1884, pp. 36–37.

27. JBR, April 1, 1885.

28. Lawrence *Journal*, May 1, 5, 1885; St. Joseph *Herald*, n.d. in *ibid.*, May 22, 1885; Habein, "Kate Stephens," 42–43, 48–49.

29. Lawrence *Journal*, May 1, 1885; Habein, "Kate Stephens," 44.

CHAPTER 7

1. Kansas Board of Commissioners for Public Institutions, *Report*, 1873, pp. 8–11; *KL*, 1866, pp. 228–230; JBR, July 18, 19, 1866, September 7, 1875; John Fraser to Peter McVicar, January 4, 1869, Kansas State Superintendent of Public Instruction, *Report*, 1868, pp. 155–157.

2. Kansas Board of Commissioners for Public Institutions, *Report*, 1873, pp. 10–11, 1874, pp. 29–30, 32–33.

3. *KSJ*, 1875, pp. 112, 116, 383; *KHJ*, 1875, pp. 637, 816; *KL*, 1875, pp. 225–226.

4. State of Kansas, Auditor of State, *Report*, 1875, p. 96; Topeka *Commonwealth*, June 4, 1875; JBR, September 7, 1875, March 10, April 4, 1876, November 22, 1877, April 5, 1878; *RBR*, 1876, pp. 30–31.

5. *KHJ*, 1879, pp. 110, 747; *KSJ*, 1879, pp. 488, 508; *KL*, 1879, pp. 338–339.

6. JBR, April 2, 1879; *RBR*, 1880, p. 5, 1882, p. 29; *KL*, 1879, pp. 338–339; Joshua A. Lippincott to W. J. Haughawout, October 14, 1886 (copy), and Willis K. Folks to Frank Strong, July 3, 1903, UA. See also Francis H. Snow to Mary Kuhn, April 30, 1902 (copy), UA.

7. *KL*, 1876, pp. 288–289, 1877, p. 226, 1879, pp. 320, 321, 1883, p. 215. The investment and returns from the investment fund are taken from the financial accounts of the Board of Regents, which appear in the biennial reports from 1880 to 1892, and from the reports of the Kansas treasurer of state and auditor of state for the same twelve-year period.

8. A statement of fees appears in each annual catalogue.

9. *RBR*, 1876, p. 6, 1882, p. 18, 1886, pp. 18–21, 1888, pp. 32–33.

10. Carrie M. Watson, "History of the Library," Wilson Sterling, ed., *Quarter-Centennial History of the University of Kansas, 1866–1891. With Portraits of Chancellors* (Topeka, 1891), 121–124.

11. *University Courier*, n.d., separately bound; Joshua A. Lippincott to George R. Peck, February 12, 1884 (copy), and "Will and Codicil of William Brown Spooner, Who Died in Boston, Oct. 28, 1880, aged 74 years, 6 months," UA; Samuel A. Johnson, *The Battle Cry of Freedom: The New England Emigrant Aid Company in the Kansas Crusade* (Lawrence, 1954), 32; *RBR*, 1890, p. 26; JBR, November 20, 1891.

12. For examples, see JBR, November 17, 1875, November 22, 1880, November 13, 1888.

13. *RBR*, 1875, p. 138, 1876, pp. 16–17; Minutes of Faculty Meetings (MS, UA), September 30, 1884.

14. For these and similar requests, see *RBR*, 1880, pp. 38–39, 43–44, 1882, pp. 5, 18, 42, 1886, pp. 27–29.

15. *RBR*, 1878, p. 6, 1888, pp. 21–22.

16. *Ibid.*, 1886, p. 9.

17. *Ibid.*, 1884, pp. 6–8; *Some Statistics. The University of Kansas Compared with Other Institutions* (n.p., 1884), especially 1, 4.

18. Francis H. Snow to O. C. Baker, November 14, 1890 (copy), mimeographed form letter dated August 1, 1885, and Joshua A. Lippincott to W. E. Curry, July 30, 1887 (copy), UA; JBR, March 10, 1876, September 13, 1881; *RBR*, 1880, pp. 13, 28.

19. *Facts of General Interest to the People. The University of Kansas, What It Is and What It Does* (Topeka, 1885); JBR, June 9, 1880, June 6, September 11, 1882, April 1, 1885.

20. Clyde K. Hyder, *Snow of Kansas: The Life of Francis Huntington Snow with Extracts from His Journals and Letters* (Lawrence, 1953), 212.

21. University of Kansas Alumni Association Records (MS, UA), June 14, 1876, and 1877; Minutes of Faculty Meetings, November 22, December 6, 1883; *Kansas Review*, 5 (Holiday Number, 1883), 122–123; Joshua A. Lippincott to Angelo C. Scott, February 28, 1884 (copy), UA.

22. *RBR*, 1875, pp. 29–31; *KHJ*, 1876, pp. 83, 142, 194–205, 491, 1022–1023, 1063, 1076–1079, 1420–1421; *KSJ*, 1876, pp. 737–738, 739, 749; *KL*, 1876, pp. 41–42.

23. Lawrence *Kansas Tribune*, November 2, 1876.

24. *RBR*, 1876, pp. 5–6; *KHJ*, 1877, pp. 258, 280, 590, 672, 924, 1034, 1035, 1052, 1070–1071; *KSJ*, 1877, p. 684; *KL*, 1877, pp. 25–26.

25. *RBR*, 1878, pp. 5–6; *KHJ*, 1879, pp. 204, 519, 891, 928, 940, 984, 986, 1091, 1245–1246, 1252–1254; *KSJ*, 1879, pp. 610, 620, 621, 636, 648; *KL*, 1879, pp. 33–34.

26. *RBR*, 1880, p. 8; *KHJ*, 1881, pp. 123, 148, 251, 464, 486–487, 510; *KSJ*, 1881, pp. 262, 273, 292, 347, 362; *KL*, 1881, pp. 67–69.

27. *Kansas Review*, 4 (December, 1882), 76–77; JBR, April 4, November 21, 1882; *RBR*, 1882, pp. 5, 7, 27–28. Professor Patrick and Chancellor Marvin had asked the Board of Regents to request $6,000 for a new building from the legislature of 1881, but the Board had refused. *RBR*, 1880, pp. 24–25.

28. *KHJ*, 1883, pp. 89, 109, 271, 279, 731, 755, 802–803, 870, 885, 917–918; *KSJ*, 1883, pp. 610, 616, 625–626, 688, 690, 710, 721, 726–727; *KL*, 1883, pp. 7–8.

29. Frank A. Fitzpatrick to George W. Glick, May 3, 1883, George W. Glick Papers, Kansas State Historical Society, Topeka; Glick to Fitzpatrick, May 5, 1883, and Glick to James Marvin, May 5, 1883, Governors' Letters, Kansas State Historical Society; JBR, April 4, June 5, 12, November 20, 1883.

30. Edgar H. S. Bailey, "The New Chemical Laboratory," *Science*, 3 (January 11, 1884), 53–54; Edgar H. S. Bailey, Hamilton P. Cady, and Frank B. Dains, *History of the Chemistry Department of the University of Kansas*, Bulletin of the University of Kansas, 26 (February 15, 1925), 13; *RBR*, 1884, p. 14.

31. Minutes of Faculty Meetings, September 30, 1884; *RBR*, 1884, pp. 6–8, 9–10, 16; *Kansas State University* (Lawrence, 1885); *The University of Kansas, February, 1885* (Lawrence, 1885).

32. *KSJ*, 1885, pp. 163, 182, 435, 494, 499, 507–508, 552, 623, 631, 646; *KHJ*, 1885, pp. 609, 617, 618, 796, 806, 838, 1016, 1017, 1067, 1075–1076; *KL*, 1885, pp. 27–29, 80.

33. *University Courier*, March 13, 1885.

34. J. Howard Compton, "The Building of the University of Kansas" (typewritten

M.Arch. thesis, University of Kansas, 1932), 108; *RBR*, 1886, pp. 3–4, 13–14; "Snow Hall of Natural History at Lawrence, Kan.," *Science*, 10 (December 30, 1887), 314.

35. *RBR*, 1886, pp. 7–8, 9; *KSJ*, 1887, pp. 49–50, 60, 357, 413, 426, 445, 455, 460–461; *KHJ*, 1887, pp. 653, 675–676, 808, 1039; *KL*, 1887, pp. 63–65.

36. *RBR*, 1876, p. 6, 1890, pp. 9–15.

37. *Ibid.*, 1876, pp. 5, 12, 1878, pp. 6, 9, 1880, p. 15, 1882, pp. 26–27; *KL*, 1877, pp. 25–26; JBR, April 3, June 12, 1877, April 4, 1878, June 12, 1879; W. W. Newlee, "The Trees of the Campus," *Graduate Magazine of the University of Kansas*, 8 (December, 1909), 77–80; Lawrence *Kansas Tribune*, March 5, 1877; Edward Baumgartner, "K.U. Lilac Hedge Has Long History," Lawrence *Journal-World*, April 20, 1937.

38. *RBR*, 1890, p. 6; *UKC*, 1875–1876, p. 5, 1888–1889, p. 79.

39. *RBR*, 1875, pp. 28, 32–33, 1876, p. 5, 1878, p. 5, 1880, pp. 4, 12, 1882, p. 13, 1886, p. 22, 1888, p. 28; *KL*, 1876, pp. 41–42, 1877, pp. 25, 26, 1879, pp. 33, 34, 1885, p. 28.

40. *RBR*, 1884, p. 16.

41. *KL*, 1881, pp. 67, 68, 1885, p. 29; *RBR*, 1880, p. 4, 1882, p. 14, 1888, pp. 4–6, 20–21; JBR, April 27, June 8, 1886.

42. *RBR*, 1888, pp. 6–8.

43. *KHJ*, 1889, p. 46.

44. *Ibid.*, 1889, pp. 113, 173, 535–538.

45. *Ibid.*, 1889, pp. 535, 538, 750, 755, 907; Topeka *Capital-Commonwealth*, February 15, 1889.

46. Topeka *Capital*, February 20, 1914; Topeka *Capital-Commonwealth*, January 12, 1889; *KSJ*, 1889, p. 58; *University Review*, 10 (January, 1889), 147; JBR, June 4, 1878; William H. Carruth, "A Needed Change," *Kansas Review*, 2 (November, 1880), 61–63.

47. *KSJ*, 1889, pp. 172, 315, 330, 339, 601, 619–620, 679; *KHJ*, 1889, pp. 451, 465, 467, 517, 742, 755, 814, 860, 904, 990, 1007.

48. *KSJ*, 1889, pp. 623, 642, 667, 756–757, 784–785, 847–848; *KL*, 1889, pp. 397–398.

49. *Ibid.*, 1889, pp. 392–396.

CHAPTER 8

1. Lawrence *Western Home Journal*, June 17, 1875; Joshua A. Lippincott, *The State University: Its Work, and Its Place in the Public School System. Inaugural Address, Delivered in University Hall, Lawrence, Kansas, September 26, 1883* (Topeka, 1883), 15.

2. *RBR*, 1878, pp. 7–9.

3. Carl F. Lindberg, "Dominant Factors in the Development of Public Education in Kansas" (typewritten Ph.D. thesis, University of Kansas, 1933), 93, 94–95; Clyde L. King, "The Kansas School System—Its History and Tendencies," *Kansas Historical Collections*, 11 (1909–1910), 441–442.

4. An act of 1876 required arithmetic to be taught in all the high schools, but there the idea of a common curriculum stopped. Lindberg, "Dominant Factors," 93.

5. Frederick Rudolph, *The American College and University: A History* (New York, 1962), 282–284.

6. Minutes of Faculty Meetings (MS, UA), January 25, 1872, October 3, November 21, 28, 1873, February 5, 1874; JBR, June 13, 1873; *RBR*, 1873, p. 15, 1876, pp. 4–5, 14; *UKC*, 1876–1877, pp. 36, 36a–36b, 39–41, 1882–1883, pp. 67–68, 1885–1886, pp. 77–78.

7. *Ibid.*, 1876–1877, p. 41, 1882–1883, p. 68; Kansas State Superintendent of Public Instruction, *Report*, 1883–1884, pp. 27–29; Minutes of Faculty Meetings, October 18, 1883, March 14, 20, April 3, 1884, April 14, 1885.

8. *Ibid.*, March 1, 22, 29, 1883, January 5, October 19, 1888; JBR, April 4, 1883, October 1, 1884, August 14, 15, 1888; *RBR*, 1888, pp. 17–18; *KL*, 1889, p. 395.

9. Minutes of Faculty Meetings, January 5, 1888; William H. Carruth, Francis H. Snow, and Ephraim Miller, *Relations of the University to the High Schools of the State. A Report* (Lawrence, 1888).

10. Minutes of Faculty Meetings, March 8, May 17, June 1, September 13, December 21, 1888, January 10, March 21, April 2, October 1, 1889; *UKC*, 1888–1889, pp. 45–46.

11. *Ibid.*, 1885–1886, pp. 77–78; *UKC*, Supplemental, Fall, 1890, pp. 23, 30; Francis H. Snow, *Inaugural Address, Responding to the Board of Regents*, in *Addresses Concerning the Chancellorship, the University, Higher Education* (Topeka, 1890), 39–40; Minutes of Faculty Meetings, April 15, 1890; JBR, May 6, 1890.

12. *RBR*, 1890, p. 40, 1892, pp. 17–18.

13. Minutes of Faculty Meetings, October 28, November 11, 1880, April 7, May 5, 1881, April 27, 1882, March 14, 1884; JBR, November 23, 1880, April 7, 1881, May 9, 1883; *RBR*, 1882, pp. 6–7, 1890, pp. 26–27.

14. *UKC*, 1876–1877, pp. 25–29.

15. *Ibid.*, 1876–1877, pp. 29–32; Minutes of Faculty Meetings, February 12, May 27, 1873.

16. *Kansas Review*, 1 (December, 1879), 45–46.

17. Rudolph, *American College*, 287–306.

18. Minutes of Faculty Meetings, December 18, 1879, February 5, 12, March 4, 1880; JBR, April 8, 1880; *RBR*, 1882, p. 20.

19. Minutes of Faculty Meetings, September 13, 29, December 2, 1886, January 25, February 3, 11, 1887; R. Freeman Butts, *The College Charts Its Course: Historical Conceptions and Current Proposals* (New York, 1939), 198–200.

20. There were ten groups specified for minor studies: biology; chemistry, mineralogy, and pharmacy; physics, astronomy, and engineering; mathematics; philosophy and didactics; history and political science; Greek and Latin; German, French, and Spanish; English; and music. The extradepartmental minor had to be in an entirely different group from the major. Thus a student majoring in Spanish could not minor in German.

The major-minor requirements left juniors and seniors with a free course each semester. Each of the four courses, the faculty decreed, had to be chosen from a different group, and none of the groups could be that which included the major or the minor. *UKC*, 1886–1887, pp. 47–51.

21. *RBR*, 1888, pp. 11–13.

22. Rudolph, *American College*, 221–240.

23. JBR, July 18, 19, 1866, December 1, 1869, July 19, 1872, June 16, 1875.

24. *Ibid.*, March 10, 11, 1876; Lawrence *Western Home Journal*, April 6, 1876.

25. JBR, September 8, 1876, March 9, 1877, November 20, 1879, May 24, 1880, June 7, 1881; *RBR*, 1878, p. 23, 1880, p. 22; "P. C. Williams," *Western School Journal*, 23 (May, 1907), 120–121; Clifford H. Nowlin, *My First Ninety Years: A Schoolmaster's Story of His Life and Times* (Kansas City, Mo., 1955), 52.

26. *UKC*, 1875–1876, pp. 30–32, 1876–1877, pp. 33–34.

27. JBR, April 3, 1879; *UKC*, 1878–1879, pp. 40–42, 1883–1884, pp. 41–42; Minutes of Faculty Meetings, January 26, February 9, 1882; *RBR*, 1882, p. 44.

28. *Ibid.*, 1884, pp. 9, 10, 1886, pp. 22, 26, 1888, p. 28; *KL*, 1885, pp. 28–29; JBR, April 1, 1885, November 13, 1888; *UKC*, 1884–1885, pp. 46–47.

29. JBR, November 16, 1876, April 3, June 13, 1877, June 4, 5, August 20, 1878; *RBR*, 1878, p. 13; Kate Stephens, "Judge Nelson Timothy Stephens," *Kansas Historical Collections*, 14 (1915–1918), 23, 24, 26, 27, 41, 43.

30. *Who Was Who in America*, 1: 481; Stephens, "Judge Nelson Timothy Stephens," *Kansas Historical Collections*, 14 (1915–1918), 41, 43–47.

31. *RBR*, 1880, pp. 8, 50–51, 1882, pp. 7, 14, 1884, pp. 10, 17, 19, 21, 25, 45–46, 1890, p. 6; *UKC*, 1881–1882, p. 4; *KL*, 1881, p. 68, 1883, pp. 7, 8, 1885, pp. 28, 29; JBR, April 1, 1885; University of Kansas Department of Law, *Catalogue*, 1884–1885, p. 18, 1890–1891, p. 5 n.

32. *Ibid.*, 1884–1885, pp. 17–18, 1889–1890, pp. 10–11.

33. *UKC*, 1878–1879, pp. 44–45, 1884–1885, pp. 49–50; *RBR*, 1890, p. 6.

34. *Ibid.*, 1880, p. 24; Minutes of Faculty Meetings, March 25, 1880; JBR, April 8, 1880.

35. *RBR*, 1880 pp. 8, 24; *KL*, 1881, pp. 67–69, 1885, pp. 247–253; JBR, June 8, September 13, 1881.

36. *Ibid.*, June 8, October 27, December 15, 1885, January 22, February 10, 11, March 22, 1886; *RBR*, 1886, p. 13; L. D. Havenhill, "An Appreciation of Dean Sayre," *Graduate Magazine of the University of Kansas*, 24 (October, 1925), 8–9.

37. *UKC*, 1885–1886, pp. 57–61; *RBR*, 1890, p. 6; JBR, August 14, 1888, April 10, 1890.

38. *UKC*, 1876–1877, pp. 29–30; *Who Was Who in America*, 1: 784–785; JBR, September 12, 1882.

39. Minutes of Faculty Meetings, April 19, 26, 1883; JBR, May 8, 1883; *UKC*, 1882–1883, p. 43.

40. *Ibid.*, 1884–1885, p. 45; *RBR*, 1884, p. 39.

41. *RBR*, 1888, p. 11; *UKC*, 1886–1887, pp. 69–71; JBR, April 1, 1887.

42. *UKC*, 1875–1876, p. 5, 1879–1880, p. 49; Janet Coulson, "A History of the Fine Arts School at the University of Kansas" (typewritten M.M. thesis, University of Kansas, 1940), 32; JBR, November 16, 1876, March 8, November 21, 23, 1877, August 21, 1878, June 11, 1879; *RBR*, 1876, p. 10, 1878, p. 10.

43. MacDonald received $250 a year more for providing and directing music at the chapel services. JBR, August 29, 1883, April 8, June 3, 1884, January 27, 1885.

44. Boston *Musical Herald*, September, 1889, in *University Kansan*, September 20, 1889; Coulson, "History of the Fine Arts School," 40–41, 43, 63–68.

45. *UKC*, 1884–1885, pp. 51–53, 1885–1886, pp. 52–54; Coulson, "History of the Fine Arts School," 52–53; *RBR*, 1890, pp. 6, 38.

46. *UKC*, 1876–1877, p. 5, 1877–1878, p. 5, 1878–1879, p. 5; *UKC*, Supplemental, Fall, 1890, p. 6; JBR, October 27, 1885; *RBR*, 1890, p. 6.

CHAPTER 9

1. James H. Canfield, "Recollections," *Graduate Magazine of the University of Kansas*, 3 (February, 1905), 168.

2. *UKC*, 1875–1876, p. 5, 1891–1892, pp. 6–8; *RBR*, 1892, p. 9.

3. Minutes of Faculty Meetings (MS, UA), February 14, March 5, 21, May 2, 1878, May 20, 1880, November 1, 1881, February 28, 1884.

4. *RBR*, 1880, pp. 39–44, 46–47, 1882, p. 42.

5. "History of the Department of Chemistry of the University of Kansas as

Recorded in the University Catalogues, 1886–1917" (typewritten MS, n.d., UA), 56–59; *RBR*, 1886, p. 31.

6. *UKC*, 1875–1876, p. 5.

7. *RBR*, 1880, pp. 47–49, 1882, pp. 42–43; *UKC*, 1882–1883, p. 4.

8. *RBR*, 1876, p. 19, 1880, pp. 33–34, 1882, p. 32, 1884, p. 27, 1886, pp. 29–30, 1890, p. 36; JBR, June 6, 1883, June 3, 1884, March 17, 1889; *UKC*, Supplemental, Fall, 1890, p. 5.

9. *RBR*, 1880, pp. 43–44, 1882, pp. 3–4, 38, 1884, pp. 33–34, 35; JBR, September 12, 1881, May 1, 1889; *Graduate Magazine*, 16 (January, 1918), 111; David L. Patterson, "F. W. Blackmar, Friendly Leader, Goes," *ibid.*, 29 (April, 1931), 7; Herbert Baxter Adams to ?, n.d., *University Courier*, May 10, 1889.

10. JBR, June 10, 1879, June 30, 1882, June 5, 1883, April 1, 1887; *RBR*, 1882, pp. 37–38, 1884, p. 38.

11. JBR, June 8, July 27, September 9, 1886, June 6, 1887, June 4, 1889, April 10, 1890; *RBR*, 1886, p. 12; Chester Woodward, "Dunlap's Life a Career of True Culture," *Graduate Magazine*, 35 (December, 1936), 10.

12. *RBR*, 1880, p. 32.

13. *UKC*, 1886–1887, p. 56; JBR, April 10, 11, May 6, 1890; *Graduate Magazine*, 41 (March–April, 1943), 4; *Olin Templin: In Remembrance* (Lawrence, 1943).

14. Clyde K. Hyder, *Snow of Kansas: The Life of Francis Huntington Snow with Extracts from His Journals and Letters* (Lawrence, 1953), 93–195, 269–273; Samuel W. Williston, "Francis H. Snow, the Man and the Scientist," *Graduate Magazine*, 7 (January, 1909), 131–134; *Topeka Mail and Kansas Breeze*, October 26, 1895.

15. James H. Canfield to Lewis L. Dyche, October 17, 1892, and Dyche to Canfield, October 29, 1892, Lewis L. Dyche Papers, UA; Lewis L. Dyche Diaries (typewritten copies, UA), July 4, 1895; Lewis L. Dyche, "The Red Crossbill *(Loxia Curvirostra Stricklandi)* in Kansas," *Auk*, 3 (April, 1886), 258–261; "The Golden Eagle," *Transactions of the Kansas Academy of Science*, 19 (1903–1904), 179–181; "The Puma or American Lion," *ibid.*, 19 (1903–1904), 160–163; "Notes on Three Species of Gophers Found at Lawrence, Kas.," *ibid.*, 12 (1889), part 1, pp. 29–31; "Food Habits of the Common Garden Mole," *ibid.*, 18 (1901–1902), 183–186; "Notes on the Food Habits of California Sea Lions," *ibid.*, 18 (1901–1902), 179–182. Also, "Department of Systematic Zoology," Dyche Papers; posters headed "Tell Your Kindred!" "Dashing Kansan!" and "The Greatest Hunter on the Continent—in Costume," and unidentified newspaper clipping, October 2, 1913, "Lewis Lindsay Dyche" (scrapbook, UA); *RBR*, 1894, p. 3; Frank Strong, "Lewis Lindsay Dyche," Frank Strong Papers, UA.

16. Edgar H. S. Bailey, "His Life as a Chemist," "History of the Department of Chemistry," 356–357.

17. Edgar H. S. Bailey, Hamilton P. Cady, and Frank B. Dains, *History of the Chemistry Department of the University of Kansas,* Bulletin of the University of Kansas, 26 (February 15, 1925), 13, 15.

18. *RBR*, 1884, p. 41; Bailey, Cady, and Dains, *History of the Chemistry Department*, 15–18; and the following publications by Bailey: "On the Composition of Some Culinary Utensils," *Transactions of the Kansas Academy of Science*, 9 (1883–1884), 29–30; "On the Newly-Discovered Salt Beds in Ellsworth County, Kansas," *ibid.*, 11 (1887), 8–10; "Some Kansas Mineral Waters," *ibid.*, 12 (1889), 25–29; "What Constitutes a Good Soil," Kansas State Board of Agriculture, *Fifth Biennial Report*, 1885–1886, part 2, pp. 181–184; "The Manufacture of Canned Goods," Kansas State Board of Agriculture, *Report*, 1887, pp. 91–93; "Composition and Evaporative Power of Kansas Coals," Kansas State Board of Agriculture, *Sixth Biennial Report*, 1887–1888, part 2,

pp. 157–163; "Preservatives in Food Products," *Bulletin of Pharmacy,* 10 (October, 1896), 437–438; "Importance of Raising the Standard of Purity in Drugs and Chemicals," *Pharmaceutical Era,* 32 (July 28, 1904), 83–84; *Some Simple Kitchen Tests to Detect the Adulteration of Foods,* 2nd ed. (Topeka, 1908).

19. W. C. Stevens, "Reminiscences," *The Fiftieth Anniversary of the Founding of the Kansas Chapters of Phi Beta Kappa and Sigma Xi, 1890–1940* (Lawrence, 1940), 68–69; *RBR,* 1884, p. 43. Also, Edward L. Nichols, "On the Destruction of the Passivity of Iron in Nitric Acid by Magnetization," *Transactions of the Kansas Academy of Science,* 10 (1885–1886), 13–19; "On Black and White," *ibid.,* 10 (1885–1886), 37–44; "A Spectro-photometric Analysis of the Color of the Sky," *Proceedings of the American Association for the Advancement of Science,* 34 (August, 1885), 78–79; "On the Chemical Behavior of Iron in the Magnetic Field," *ibid.,* 34 (August, 1885), 79–80; "On the Chemical Behavior of Iron in the Magnetic Field," *American Journal of Science,* ser. 3, vol. 31 (April, 1886), 272–283; "On the Duration of Color Impressions upon the Retina," *ibid.,* ser. 3, vol. 28 (October, 1884), 243–252.

20. M. E. Rice, "The Life of Professor Lucien I. Blake, Founder of the Department of Electrical Engineering," *Kansas Engineer,* 16 (October, 1930), 5–6; Mary B. Blake, "Lucien Ira Blake" (typewritten MS, n.d., UA); Lucien I. Blake, "An Inexpensive, Adjustable Condenser for High Potentials," *Electrical World,* 28 (November 7, 1896), 556.

21. James H. Canfield, *The Use and Abuse of Our Forests* (Manhattan, 1882); *Taxation; A Plain Talk for Plain People* (New York, 1883); *Local Government in Kansas,* rev. ed. (Philadelphia, 1889); *History and Government of Kansas* (Philadelphia, 1894), 47 and *passim.*

22. David L. Patterson, "F. W. Blackmar," *Graduate Magazine,* 29 (April, 1931), 7–8. Also, Frank W. Blackmar, "Spanish Colonization in the Southwest," *Johns Hopkins University Studies in Historical and Political Science,* 8th ser., vol. 4 (April, 1890), 121–193; *Spanish Institutions of the Southwest* (Baltimore, 1891); "A Chapter in the Life of Charles Robinson, the First Governor of Kansas," American Historical Association, *Annual Report,* 1894, pp. 213–226; *The Life of Charles Robinson, the First State Governor of Kansas* (Topeka, 1902); *The Story of Human Progress: A Brief History of Civilization* (Leavenworth, 1896), 374–375 and *passim.*

23. Frank W. Blackmar, *The Study of History and Sociology* (Topeka, 1890), 9, 18–19, and "Important Features in the Study of History and Sociology," *University Review,* 15 (October, 1893), 27–33.

24. *RBR,* 1873, pp. 21–22, 1878, pp. 18–19; *Kansas State University, Lawrence. Political Science* (n.p., n.d.).

25. *University Review,* 11 (October, 1889), 57; *Seminary Notes,* 1 (October, 1891), 1; *ibid.,* 1 (May, 1892), 11; *ibid.,* 1–2 (October, 1891–April, 1893), *passim.*

26. JBR, April 9, 1880, June 30, 1882, and William H. Carruth, ed., *Wallenstein* (New York, 1894); "Fate and Guilt in Schiller's *Die Braut von Messina,*" *Publications of the Modern Language Association of America,* 17 (1902), 105–124; "The Relation of Hauff's *Lichtenstein* to Scott's *Waverley,*" *ibid.,* 18 (1903), 513–525; "Lessing's Treatment of the Story of the Ring, and Its Teaching," *ibid.,* 16 (1901), 107–116; "The Religion of Friedrich Schiller," *ibid.,* 19 (1904), 496–582; "The Niebelungenlied," *Poet Lore,* 17 (Spring, 1906), 119–123.

27. William H. Carruth and Franklin G. Adams, *Woman Suffrage in Kansas; An Account of the Municipal Elections in Kansas in 1887* (Topeka, 1888), and the following by Carruth: "Dialect Word List.—No. 2," *Kansas University Quarterly,* 1 (January, 1893), 137–142; "New England in Kansas," *New England Magazine,* 16 (March, 1897),

3–21; "The New England Emigrant Aid Company as an Investment Society," *Kansas Historical Collections*, 6 (1900), 90–96; "Kansas in Literature, Part I: Poetry," and "Kansas in Literature, Part II: Prose," *Twentieth Century Classics and School Readings*, 1 (January, February, 1900).

28. William H. Carruth, "The Problems of the School, the Hope of the State," *Unity*, January 1, 1903, pp. 285–286, and Carruth, *Each in His Own Tongue and Other Poems* (New York, 1908), 2–3.

29. Charles L. Edson, *"The Great American Ass": An Autobiography* (New York, 1926), 121; William H. Carruth to Charles F. Scott, March 23, 1899, "William Herbert Carruth: Clippings" (scrapbook, UA).

30. Arthur Graves Canfield, "Wings," *Lotus*, 1 (January 15, 1896), 101, *French Lyrics* (New York, 1899), and "The Love of Literature and the Writer's Responsibility," *Kansas University Quarterly*, 7 (July, 1898), 41–45, 51–54; William H. Carruth, "Farewell to a Modest Scholar (Arthur Graves Canfield)," in Carruth, *Each in His Own Tongue*, 106–107.

31. JBR, September 12, 1881, November 21, 1883; *Graduate Magazine*, 16 (January, 1918), 111; *Dictionary of American Biography*, 17: 480–481; *RBR*, 1882, pp. 45–46, 1884, pp. 37–38.

32. Samuel Eliot Morison, ed., *The Development of Harvard University since the Inauguration of President Eliot: 1869–1929* (Cambridge, 1930), 91; *Historical Register of Harvard University, 1636–1936* (Cambridge, 1937), 319; JBR, June 4, 1889; Arthur Richmond Marsh, "Introduction," in Arthur Richmond Marsh, ed., *Sunflowers; Poems Written by Various Hands in the State University of Kansas* (Lawrence, 1888), 5–20.

33. *RBR*, 1890, p. 37.

34. *Kansas University Quarterly*, 1 (1892–1893), 6 (January, 1897); Ellis B. Stouffer, "Development of Scholarship at the University of Kansas," *Graduate Magazine*, 39 (January, 1941), 22–23. During the 1890s, the faculty members wrote over four hundred books and articles. Robert Taft, *The Years on Mount Oread* (Lawrence, 1955), 45.

35. Francis H. Snow, *Inaugural Address, Responding to the Board of Regents*, in *Addresses Concerning the Chancellorship, the University, Higher Education* (Topeka, 1890), 45–46.

36. *RBR*, 1878, pp. 21–23; Florence Finch Kelly, *Flowing Stream: The Story of Fifty-six Years in American Newspaper Life* (New York, 1939), 112; J. Willis Gleed, "James H. Canfield" (MS, UA); William Allen White, *The Autobiography of William Allen White* (New York, 1946), 144.

37. Kelly, *Flowing Stream*, 112–113; *RBR*, 1873, pp. 21–22, 1878, pp. 18–19, 1882, p. 33, 1884, p. 30; Woodward, "Dunlap's Life," *Graduate Magazine*, 35 (December, 1936), 10; *RBR*, 1888, pp. 10–11; William Allen White to Mrs. W. T. Beck, June 3, 1930, "Charles Graham Dunlap" (scrapbook, UA).

38. Stevens, "Reminiscences," *Fiftieth Anniversary of the Founding of . . . Phi Beta Kappa and Sigma Xi*, 68; *RBR*, 1882, p. 35; Minna Marvin Wilcox, "In Memory of Professor Miller," Charles F. Scott, comp., *The Class of 1881, Kansas State University: History of the Class, with Biographies of Its Members and a Report of Its Fiftieth Anniversary* (n.p., 1931), 41–44.

39. *Fiftieth Anniversary of the Founding of . . . Phi Beta Kappa and Sigma Xi*, 18–20.

40. *Ibid.*, 47–48; Edgar H. S. Bailey, "The Founding of the Iota Chapter of the Sigma Xi" (typewritten MS, 1923, UA).

41. Snow, *Inaugural Address*, 28.

CHAPTER 10

1. Frank Strong to John Francis, January 26, 1903 (copy), UA.

2. Joshua A. Lippincott to Charles S. Gleed, February 28, 1889, Topeka *Capital-Commonwealth*, March 6, 1889; Lippincott to Mr. Scott, March 20, 1889 (copy), UA.

3. JBR, May 1, 1889; *University Courier*, May 3, 1889; ? to "My Dear Mitchell," October 2, 1889 (copy), UA; Arthur Graves Canfield, *Forty Years After: Anniversary Address Kansas Alpha Chapter Phi Beta Kappa, Together with Other Addresses and Articles in Connection with the Celebration of the Founding of the Chapter* (Lawrence, 1930), 26–27; *Dictionary of American Biography*, 22: 663–664.

4. Topeka *Capital*, May 10, June 16, July 21, 24, August 4, 1889, April 8, 1890; *Western School Journal*, 5 (August, 1889), 196, and 6 (February, 1890), 50–51.

5. Arthur Graves Canfield, *Forty Years After*, 6; Charles S. Gleed, *Introductory Address for the Board of Regents*, in *Addresses Concerning the Chancellorship, the University, Higher Education* (Topeka, 1890), 7–8; *University Kansan*, January 17, 1890.

6. JBR, October 8, 1889, March 12, April 11, 1890; Topeka *Capital*, March 12, 16, 1890; Lyman U. Humphrey to Francis H. Snow, April 3, 1890, and Robert W. Oliver to Snow, April 8, 1890, "Letters of Congratulation to Francis Huntington Snow on His Appointment as Chancellor of Kansas State University" (MSS, UA).

7. F. H. Clark to Francis H. Snow, April 15, 1890, and Charles F. Thwing to Snow, May 1, 1890, "Letters of Congratulation."

8. Francis H. Snow, *Inaugural Address, Responding to the Board of Regents*, in *Addresses Concerning the Chancellorship*, 33, 44–46.

9. *Western School Journal*, 7 (April, 1891), 119; Francis H. Snow to D. J. Fair, August 7, 1894 (copy), UA; Snow, "A Good Education," Francis Huntington Snow Correspondence, 1892–1899, UA.

10. JBR, November 13, 1888.

11. Topeka *Capital-Commonwealth*, January 11, 12, 1889.

12. *KSJ*, 1889, pp. 58, 83, 172, 315, 330, 339, 601, 619–620, 679; *KHJ*, 1889, pp. 451, 465, 467, 517, 742, 755, 814, 860, 904, 990, 1007.

13. *KL*, 1889, pp. 392–396.

14. Joshua A. Lippincott to the Committee on By-Laws, n.d. [March, 1889], UA.

15. *UKC*, 1888–1889, p. 6, 1890–1891, p. 5, 1891–1892, p. 5; Kansas City, Mo., *Journal*, October 22, 1902; *Handbook of the Kansas Legislature*, 1903 (Topeka, 1903), 60; *Portrait and Biographical Album of Washington, Clay and Riley Counties, Kansas . . .* (Chicago, 1890), 448–449.

16. Joel Moody, *Annual Opening Address. Delivered at the University of Kansas, Lawrence, Friday, September 13, 1889* (Topeka, 1889), 6–8.

17. In the catalogue of 1889–1890, published in 1890, the divisions of the University, previously called "departments," were called "schools," except for the Department of Science, Literature, and the Arts (the College), which retained its old name. The Journal of the Board of Regents contains no formal authorization of the changed names; the formal creation of the separate schools in the years to come meant that the changed wording of 1890 was insignificant. See *RBR*, 1884, p. 39, 1888, p. 3, 1890, p. 36; JBR, May 7, June 11, 1890, April 3, June 8, 1891; Janet Coulson, "A History of the Fine Arts School at the University of Kansas" (typewritten M.M. thesis, University of Kansas, 1940), 78; Minutes of Faculty Meetings (MS, UA), March 30, 1891.

18. JBR, January 6, 1893.

19. Minutes of Faculty Meetings, May 31, 1892; Francis H. Snow to the President of Cornell University, February 5, 1892, Snow to Henry W. Rogers, February 18, 1892,

Snow to E. Benjamin Andrews and Charles K. Adams, February 19, 1892, Snow to
O. M. Fernold, R. H. Jesse, James B. Angell, T. J. Burrill, and Cyrus Northrup,
February 20, 1892, and Snow to James H. Canfield, February 22, 1892 (all copies), UA.

20. JBR, January 6, 1893, October 24, 1895.

21. *Ibid.*, January 5, 1893.

22. Minutes of Faculty Meetings, May 7, 10, 1875, May 5, 1887, November 21,
1893; JBR, June 12, 1876.

23. Frederick Rudolph, *The American College and University: A History* (New
York, 1962), 269–275, 335; Minutes of Faculty Meetings, June 5, November 21, 1893;
University Council Minutes (MS, UA), February 22, 1894.

24. *Ibid.*, March 8, 1894; JBR, April 13, 1894.

25. University Council Minutes, October 29, 1894, June 3, 1895; Henry B. Newson,
"The University Loses Professor Emch," *Kansas University Weekly*, January 30, 1897.
For information about Emch's later career I am indebted to Professor G. Baley Price
of the Department of Mathematics at the University of Kansas, who gave me access
to his manuscript "History of the Department of Mathematics, 1866–1970."

26. University Council Minutes, January 2, March 22, May 21, 1897; JBR, April
9, 1897.

27. *UKC*, 1897–1898, pp. 89–91, 1899–1900, p. 64.

28. *Ibid.*, 1933–1934, endsheet.

29. *University Review*, 9 (May, 1888), 222–223; *RBR*, 1888, pp. 19–20.

30. *Ibid.*, 1890, pp. 41–42; Francis H. Snow to Joel Moody, November 20, 1890
(copy), UA.

31. *RBR*, 1890, p. 28; Francis H. Snow to John Troutman, July 23, 1894, and
Snow to C. W. Marston, July 23, 1894 (copies), UA.

32. Fred B. McKinnon to Francis H. Snow, August 25, 1894, and Lucius E. Sayre
to Flavel B. Tiffany, August 25, 1894 (copies), Snow Correspondence, 1892–1899;
JBR, October 11, 1894, April 21, 1905.

33. Francis H. Snow to Charles F. Scott, September 12, 1894 (copy), UA.

34. Francis H. Snow to W. C. Boteler, September 19, 1894, and Snow to John
Sullivan, February 20, March 2, 1895, and Snow to L. H. Rose, January 26, 1895
(copies), UA; Topeka *Capital*, February 7, 12, 15, 1895.

35. Francis H. Snow to John Sullivan, March 2, 1895 (copy), UA; *UKC*, 1899–1900,
pp. 113–114; Minutes of Faculty Meetings, April 11, 1900; JBR, April 13, June 6,
July 27, October 10, 1900; *RBR*, 1900, pp. 14–15.

CHAPTER 11

1. Francis H. Snow to "My Dear Carter," March 20, 1897 (copy), Francis Huntington Snow Correspondence, 1892–1899, UA; Raymond Curtis Miller, "The Background of Populism in Kansas," *Mississippi Valley Historical Review*, 11 (March,
1925), 469–489; Richard Sheridan, *Economic Development in South Central Kansas,
Part Ia: An Economic History, 1500–1900* (Lawrence, 1956), 232–246.

2. Topeka *Capital*, January 8, March 14, 1891; *KSJ*, 1891, pp. 28, 213, 224, 284,
353, 359; *KHJ*, 1891, pp. 514, 517, 519, 643, 838; *KL*, 1891, p. 81; Francis H. Snow to
Max Winkler, March 24, 1891 (copy), UA.

3. *RBR*, 1892, pp. 6, 8–9, 20–22.

4. William F. Zornow, *Kansas: A History of the Jayhawk State* (Norman, 1957),
201–202; *KSJ*, 1893, pp. 111, 128, 135, 143, 158, 190, 191, 284, 285, 298–299, 319, 743, 744,

809, 812, 815; *KHJ*, 1893, pp. 321–322, 326, 327, 351, 359, 368, 390, 419–420, 480, 509, 527, 531, 625–626, 710, 711; *KL*, 1893, pp. 15, 16, 234; JBR, January 31, 1893.

5. Francis H. Snow to Benjamin I. Wheeler, November 8, 1893 (copy), UA.

6. *Courier Review*, October 18, 1894; *Kansas University Weekly*, September 13, 1895; *RBR*, 1894, p. 17. The chancellor's residence, a large Victorian house, stood just east of the library, down the hill.

7. Although the extra expense seemed worth it at the time, the iron nails and sash weights precluded ideal conditions, and the later introduction of the movable coil galvanometer, which was not disturbed by the presence of iron, made the expense superfluous. Untitled MS address in "Buildings of the University of Kansas" (scrapbooks, UA), vol. 1.

8. *RBR*, 1894, pp. 25–26; *Students Journal*, January 18, February 1, 1895.

9. Francis H. Snow to J. P. Sams, February 6, 1895 (copy), UA; *KL*, 1895, pp. 37–38, 373–374; *KSJ*, 1895, pp. 138, 151, 205, 225, 312, 361; *KHJ*, 1895, pp. 304, 342, 1243.

10. Francis H. Snow to W. A. Harris, November 29, 1892, and Snow to Arvin S. Olin, March 6, 1893 (copies), Snow Correspondence, 1892–1899; W. W. Admire, comp., *Admire's Political and Legislative Hand-Book for Kansas. 1891. With Maps* (Topeka, 1891), 446–447.

11. *KSJ*, 1893, p. 484; Sara Mullin Baldwin and Robert Morton Baldwin, eds., *Illustriana Kansas: Biographical Sketches of Kansas Men and Women of Achievement Who Have Been Awarded Life Membership in Kansas Illustriana Society* (Hebron, 1933), 1007.

12. Lawrence *Jeffersonian*, March 29, May 17, 1894.

13. Lawrence *Jeffersonian Gazette*, December 13, 1900; *Kansas Historical Collections*, 7 (1901–1902), 218 n; Francis H. Snow to D. A. Valentine, May 28, 1894, and Snow to C. R. Mitchell, May 29, 1894 (copies), Snow Correspondence, 1892–1899; JBR, June 4, 5, 1894.

14. Francis H. Snow to E. N. Morrill, January 26, 1895 (copy), UA; Charles F. Scott, comp., *The Class of 1881, Kansas State University: History of the Class, with Biographies of Its Members and a Report of Its Fiftieth Anniversary* (n.p., 1931), 20.

15. Francis H. Snow to Frank G. Crowell, February 12, 1895 (copy), UA; Hill P. Wilson, comp., *A Biographical History of Eminent Men of the State of Kansas: With Portraits Engraved Expressly for This Work* (Topeka, 1901), 67, 565.

16. *University Review*, 16 (April, 1895), 6; Francis H. Snow to William Rogers, May 25, 1895, Snow to William Bishop, December 8, 1895, and Snow to Charles F. Scott, January 14, 1896 (copies), Snow Correspondence, 1892–1899; Kansas State Historical Society, *Twenty-seventh Biennial Report*, 1931, p. 62.

17. Francis H. Snow to George L. Raymond, November 9, 1896, Snow to E. C. Little, November 9, 1896, and Snow to "My Dear Kellogg," November 19, 1896 (copies), Snow Correspondence, 1892–1899; *RBR*, 1896, pp. 10–13, 15–21.

18. *Ibid.*, 13, 21–23.

19. *Ibid.*, 13, 23–24.

20. *Ibid.*, 11–12.

21. *KHJ*, 1896, pp. 11–12.

22. Topeka *Capital*, January 23, 28, 1897; *KHJ*, 1897, pp. 58, 84, 173, 209, 257, 268.

23. Topeka *Capital*, February 19, 20, 21, 1897; *KSJ*, 1897, pp. 265, 276, 549.

24. *KHJ*, 1897, pp. 912, 934, 1037, 1076–1077, 1207, 1211, 1236, 1239; *KL*, 1897, pp. 91–94.

25. Francis H. Snow to Charles F. Scott, February 24, 1897, and Snow to "My Dear

Carter," March 20, 1897 (copies), Snow Correspondence, 1892–1899; *KHJ*, 1897, pp. 418, 424, 619.

26. Francis H. Snow to Fred B. McKinnon, March 22, 1897 (copy), Snow Correspondence, 1892–1899; *KSJ*, 1897, pp. 998, 1000, 1004; *KHJ*, 1897, pp. 1068, 1069, 1166, 1217, 1219–1220.

27. *KSJ*, 1897, pp. 405, 422, 444, 505, 514, 702–703; Topeka *Capital*, February 16, 1897.

28. JBR, March 22, 26, April 19, 20, 27, 1898; Francis H. Snow to F. G. Crowell, April 21, 1898, and Snow to Charles F. Scott, April 21, 1898 (copies), Snow Correspondence, 1892–1899; *RBR*, 1898, pp. 5, 14–15; *UKC*, 1900–1901, p. 22; JBR, May 5, 1899.

29. *Ibid.*, December 9, 1898; *RBR*, 1898, pp. 3–5, 8.

30. *KHJ*, 1899, pp. 64, 95, 480, 777, 819; *KSJ*, 1899, pp. 562, 599, 824, 912; *KL*, 1899, pp. 99–100; Francis H. Snow to Charles F. Scott, March 19, 1899 (copy), Snow Correspondence, 1892–1899.

31. Topeka *Capital*, February 1, 1899; *KHJ*, 1899, pp. 64, 95, 480, 777, 818–819, 1321, 1389, 1408, 1418, 1441, 1482; *KSJ*, 1899, pp. 562, 618, 823, 911–912, 1020, 1025, 1036, 1063, 1085; *KL*, 1899, pp. 98–99.

32. Edgar H. S. Bailey, "The New Chemical Laboratory of the University of Kansas," *Science*, n.s., 12 (December 28, 1900), 997–1001.

33. *RBR*, 1900, pp. 15–16; *KL*, 1901, p. 129.

34. JBR, November 8, 1900; *RBR*, 1900, pp. 3–4, 8, 10–12, 17–18; *KSJ*, 1901, pp. 112, 135, 337, 512, 587; *KHJ*, 1901, pp. 816, 818, 844, 1059, 1152, 1259; *KL*, 1901, p. 129; Compton, "Building of the University of Kansas," 132–134.

CHAPTER 12

1. *UKC*, 1933–1934, endsheet.

2. *Ibid.*, endsheet.

3. *RBR*, 1890, p. 9.

4. *Ibid.*, 1869, p. 1, 1876, p. 2, 1882, p. 24.

5. *Ibid.*, 1890, pp. 7, 8; *University News-Bulletin*, 8 (November 20, 1906), 2–3.

6. Florence Finch Kelly, *Flowing Stream: The Story of Fifty-six Years in American Newspaper Life* (New York, 1939), 104, 105; Agnes Emery, *Reminiscences of Early Lawrence* (Lawrence, 1954), 48–49, 51; *Kansas Collegiate*, October 4, 1878.

7. *Kansas Review*, 3 (February, 1882), 133–134; *University Kansan*, November 1, 1889; *University Courier*, March 23, 1888; *University Review*, 13 (April, 1892), 227–228.

8. *Kansas University Weekly*, May 15, 22, 1896.

9. *Ibid.*, February 14, 1896.

10. *Oread Gazette*, January 24, 1873.

11. *Kansas Collegiate*, January 30, 1879; *University Courier*, December 6, 1882, November 28, 1884; *University Review*, 7 (October, 1885, March, 1886), 47, 160; *ibid.*, 8 (January, May, 1887), 116–117, 205; *ibid.*, 11 (December, 1889, January, 1890), 115–116, 146; and *ibid.*, 15 (May, 1894), 163–164; *Kansas University Weekly*, November 2, 1901.

12. Constitution, bylaws, and list of members, and minutes of meetings of November 8, 1867, February 14, 21, March 13, 27, May 8, 27, November 27, 1868, March 12, 1869, February 25, March 4, 1870, March 31, April 7, 24, May 5, 12, June 2, November 24, December 8, 15, 1871, Secretary's Records of the Acropolis Society (MS, UA).

13. Arthur G. Canfield, "Student Life at K.S.U.," Wilson Sterling, ed., *Quarter-*

Centennial History of the University of Kansas, 1866–1891. With Portraits of Chancellors (Topeka, 1891), 146; minutes of meetings of January 7, 21, 28, 1870, and
constitution and bylaws of the Orophilian Society, Secretary's Records of the
Acropolis Society; *The Kansas Kikkabe. Published Annually by the Kansas Kikkabe
Company, 1882* (Lawrence, 1882), 44; Minutes of Faculty Meetings (MS, UA), April
17, 24, 1875; *Observer of Nature*, 2 (March 4, 1875); *Kansas Review*, 2 (October,
1880), 47.

14. Canfield, "Student Life at K.S.U.," Sterling, ed., *Quarter-Centennial History*,
134, 135–138; Grant W. Harrington, "When Nu Was New—1884–1910," Grant W.
Harrington, Burton P. Sears, Solon W. Smith, and the History Committee of Nu
Chapter, *Sigma Nu at Kansas University* (Lawrence, 1956), 12–14, 20.

15. *Kansas Kikkabe*, 45–46; *Observer of Nature*, April 1, May 26, 1874, March 4,
24, May 5, June 4, 1875; *Kansas Collegiate*, October 26, 1875.

16. Canfield, "Student Life at K.S.U.," Sterling, ed., *Quarter-Centennial History*,
149–150; *Kansas Kikkabe*, 46; *The Kansas Cyclone. Published Annually by E. F.
Caldwell. 1883* (Lawrence, 1883), 54–55, 56; *Kansas Review*, 3 (April, 1882), 181–182.

17. Canfield, "Student Life at K.S.U.," Sterling, ed., *Quarter-Centennial History*,
147–148; *The Helianthus, (Annuus) Published from the State University of Kansas.
1889* (Lawrence, 1889), 70; *The K K*, 1 (February 19, 1910), 5.

18. Minutes of meetings of November 22, 29, 1867, May 22, 1868, Secretary's
Records of the Acropolis Society; *Oread Gazette*, 2 (April 5, 1872–January 24, 1873).

19. Except as otherwise indicated, I have relied for information on the student
publications on four articles by Wilson Sterling, all entitled "Student Journalism in
the University of Kansas," *Graduate Magazine of the University of Kansas*, 4 (March,
April, May, 1906), 197–210, 233–248, 283–295, and 5 (March, 1907), 195–206. Also,
Observer of Nature, 1 (April 1, 29, 1874) and 2 (March 4, 1875); *Kansas Collegiate*,
October 26, 1875.

20. *University Pastime*, 1 (September 16, 1878), 1.

21. *Kansas Review*, 1 (November, 1879), 1–24; *University Courier*, November 7,
1884.

22. University Council Minutes (MS, UA), February 8, 1895, June 12, 1902; *Kansas
University Weekly*, June 3, 1895, January 14, 1899.

23. *Kansan*, September 17, 1904, May 7, 1908, April 9, 1912.

24. *Lotus*, 1 (November 1, 1895); *Automobile*, 1–2 (February, 1901–March, 1902);
Jayhawk Quill, 1 (March, 1902), 22, 23, 24.

25. *Kansas University Lawyer*, 1 (March 21, 1895), 1.

26. *UKC*, 1867–1868, pp. 16, 17, 24, 1869–1870, p. 28, 1870–1871, p. 31, 1873–1874,
p. 28.

27. *Ibid.*, 1877–1878, pp. 56–57.

28. Lawrence *Journal*, March 3, 1886; Minutes of Faculty Meetings, March 6,
1884; James H. Canfield, "Not New, but Old," *Western School Journal*, 1 (February,
1885), 10–11.

29. E. Miller, "Some Memories," *Graduate Magazine*, 3 (January, 1905), 129–130;
"Cadmus," "More Reminiscences," *ibid.*, 6 (March, 1908), 198; Canfield, "Student Life
at K.S.U.," Sterling, ed., *Quarter-Centennial History*, 140–141; *University Review*, 7
(October, 1885), 47; *Kansas University Weekly*, February 13, 1897, November 23, 1901.

30. M. A. Barber, "The Boarding Clubs of the University," *Graduate Magazine*,
4 (March, 1906), 210–217; Francis H. Snow to B. J. Barnett, January 14, 1891 (copy),
UA; Kelly, *Flowing Stream*, 101; William Allen White, *The Autobiography of William
Allen White* (New York, 1946), 136, 141; Clifford H. Nowlin, *My First Ninety Years:*

A Schoolmaster's Story of His Life and Times (Kansas City, Mo., 1955), 49–50; Charles L. Edson, *"The Great American Ass": An Autobiography* (New York, 1926), 113.

31. Kelly, *Flowing Stream*, 103; Ephraim D. Adams, "College Expenses," *Seminary Notes*, 1 (May, 1892), 189–190.

32. Larry M. Peace, "Colored Students and Graduates of the University of Kansas," *Graduate Magazine*, 7 (May, 1909), 293–303; *University Courier*, February 12, 1886.

33. Edith DeMoss to Dr. and Mrs. J. A. DeMoss, January 27, 1906, UA; *University Courier*, March 26, 1884; "An '86er" to the Editor, n.d., *Graduate Magazine*, 7 (January, 1909), 147.

34. *Kansas Kikkabe*, 28–30, 42; *The '14 Jayhawker: A Tour on Mount Oread with the Seniors* (Lawrence, n.d.), 297–361; *UKC*, 1933–1934, endsheet; Harrington, "When Nu Was New," Harrington and others, *Sigma Nu at Kansas University*, 29–30, 31, 50.

35. Festus Foster, "The Other Side," *Kansas Review*, 3 (March, 1882), 152–153; *University Courier*, November 7, 1884; *University Review*, 9 (October, 1887), 42; Charles S. Griffin, "Proportion of Fraternity Members," *ibid.*, 14 (January, 1893), 146–149.

36. *Kansas Review*, 3 (February, 1882), 132; *University Courier*, March 26, 1884; *University Review*, 9 (April, 1888), 195; Thornton Cooke, "The Proportion of Fraternity Members," *ibid.*, 14 (November, 1892), 82–84.

37. Minutes of Faculty Meetings, October 17, 1878, October 9, 1879, September 14, October 8, 1880, February 16, 1892; *Kansas Review*, 5 (December, 1883), 98; Kelly, *Flowing Stream*, 115–116; Annie B. Banks, Florence E. Parrott, and May Hotchkiss Spencer to members of the Correspondence League, May 8, 1894 (form letter), "The Women's League of the University of Kansas, Organized in 1892" (MSS, UA); Canfield, "Student Life at K.S.U.," Sterling, ed., *Quarter-Centennial History*, 152–154; *University Review*, 11 (December, 1889), 120; W. E. Hazen to Frank Strong, August 14, 1903, UA.

38. *Kansas Review*, 1 (November, 1879), 14; Kate Stephens, "Judge Nelson Timothy Stephens," *Kansas Historical Collections*, 14 (1918), 38–40; D. H. Robinson, "Reminiscences," Sterling, ed., *Quarter-Centennial History*, 175–177.

39. Minutes of Faculty Meetings, December 2, 1879, January 15, 19, 20, 22, April 15, 1880.

40. White, *Autobiography*, 168; *University Review*, 13 (January, 1892), 138–140; Francis H. Snow to D. E. Bunch, April 21, 1892, and Snow to Frank P. MacLennan, March 10, 16, 1894 (copies), UA; Snow to William Crotty, May 25, 1895, and F. O. Marvin to Snow, May 25, 1895 (copies), Francis Huntington Snow Correspondence, 1892–1899, UA.

41. William M. Curry to the Editor, n.d., *Graduate Magazine*, 32 (November, 1933), 4; William H. H. Piatt and others, "Some Memory Recitals after 50 Years of Things Athletic and Otherwise, '91 to '96, of the 'Gay '90s' at K.U." (typewritten MS, n.d., UA), 24; Edson, *"Great American Ass,"* 120; University Council Minutes, April 1, 1902; *Kansas University Weekly*, May 7, 1904; "University of Kansas Activities" (scrapbooks, UA), vol. 1.

42. *RBR*, 1886, pp. 5–6; Joshua A. Lippincott to A. G. Otis, March 4, 1887, Lippincott to Alla W. Foster, October 29, 1888, and Francis H. Snow to Girald Wilson, September 24, 1890 (copies), UA; JBR, June 6, 1887; contents of "The Women's League of the University of Kansas."

43. Frank Strong, "To the Freshmen of 1904" (typewritten MS, 1904, UA); Strong, *The Responsibility of the University Man: Opening Address to the Students of the University of Kansas, September 15, 1905* (Lawrence, 1905), 11–12; *Religious Activities*

at the University of Kansas (Lawrence, 1910); Young Men's Christian Association, University of Kansas, *Character-Service: A Record of the Work of the Past Year, with a Statement of the Present Situation and Some Suggestions for the Future* (Lawrence, 1912).

44. *Kansan*, September 23, 1905; Frank Strong to Charles S. Gleed, September 22, 1905 (copy), UA.

45. *The Jayhawker, 1908* (n.p., n.d.).

46. Frank Strong to James E. Boyle, September 6, 1906, Strong to "Members of the Sorority," November 24, 1906, and Strong to Charles F. Scott, October 10, 1907 (copies), UA; *University Courier*, September 20, 1894; *Kansan*, April 3, 13, September 28, 1907.

47. *Ibid.*, October 12, 19, November 20, December 18, 1907, January 27, February 1, 3, 1910; *Jayhawker, 1908*; H. G. Luther, Paul M. Lobaugh, and others to Frank Strong, November 23, 1908, Strong to "My Dear Sir," November 28, 1908 (copy), and Strong to Edwin H. Barbour, April 7, 1909 (copy), UA; JBR, June 18, 1909, March 17, 1910.

48. *Kansan*, March 7, April 1, 4, May 12, 19, 1908.

49. *Ibid.*, April 17, 29, May 18, 1909.

50. *Ibid.*, May 13, 1909.

51. JBR, July 15, 1909, October 6, 1911; *RBR*, 1912, p. 17; Frank R. Whitzel to the Editor, December 10, 1910, *Graduate Magazine*, 9 (January, 1911), 138–140.

52. Frank Strong to Charles S. Huffman, January 30, 1909 (copy), UA; *The K K*, 1 (March 9, 1910), 6, 7; JBR, April 26, October 5, 1911; University Council Minutes, March 23, 1911.

CHAPTER 13

1. Francis H. Snow to Richard Foster, February 7, 1890 (copy), and Snow to the Regents of the University of Kansas, May 20, 1901, UA; JBR, November 8, 1900, February 28, June 4, 1901.

2. Topeka *Capital*, August 6, 1901; Lawrence *Journal*, March 12, 1902; Francis H. Snow to Vernon L. Kellogg, April 20, 1899 (copy), Francis Huntington Snow Correspondence, 1892–1899, UA.

3. Oran T. Hester to W. C. Spangler, October 1, 1901, and Arthur G. Canfield to Spangler, October 2, 1901, UA.

4. Topeka *Capital*, June 4, July 31, August 8, 1901, March 13, 1902; Charles F. Thwing to W. C. Spangler, August 7, 1901, Thomas M. Potter to Spangler, August 16, 1901, J. W. Forney to Spangler, August 17, 1901, February 14, 1902, Scott Hopkins to Spangler, August 30, September 9, 1901, James H. Canfield to Spangler, September 4, 5, 1901, and E. R. Moses to Spangler, December 16, 1901, UA.

5. Andrew W. Phillips to W. C. Spangler, March 14, 1902 (copy), Frank Strong Papers, UA; Scott Hopkins to Spangler, March 31, April 2, 1902, UA.

6. Thomas M. Potter to W. C. Spangler, April 8, 1902, UA; JBR, April 26, 1902; Lawrence *Journal*, April 27, 1902; Henry D. Sheldon, *History of University of Oregon* (Portland, 1940), 110–118; Scott Hopkins to Frank Strong, April 28, 1902, Strong Papers.

7. *Commemoration of Dr. Frank Strong, Former Chancellor and Professor of Law, University of Kansas* (Lawrence, n.d.), vii–viii; Frank Strong, "A Forgotten Danger to the New England Colonies," American Historical Association, *Annual Report*, 1898, pp. 77–94; Strong, "The Causes of Cromwell's West Indian Expedition," *American Historical Review*, 4 (January, 1899), 228–245; Strong, *Benjamin Franklin: A Char-*

acter Sketch (Chicago, 1898); untitled bibliography, Strong Papers; Strong and Joseph Schafer, *The Government of the American People* (New York, 1902).

8. William H. Carruth to Frank Strong, June 26, 1902, and Scott Hopkins to Carruth, n.d. [1902], UA; "Inauguration of Dr. Frank Strong as Chancellor of the University of Kansas, October 16, 17, 18, 1902," *Graduate Magazine of the University of Kansas*, 1 (November, 1902), 36–43.

9. *Ibid.*, 59–64.

10. *Ibid.*, 64–65.

11. *Ibid.*, 65–66, 73–74.

12. *Ibid.*, 66–67, 70–72.

13. *Ibid.*, 67–71, 72–73, 74.

14. Frank Strong, untitled typewritten statement, in "Frank Strong, Ph.D., LL.D., 1859–1934, Chancellor of the University, 1902–1920, Professor of Law, 1920–1934" (scrapbooks, UA), vol. 2.

15. Frank Strong to C. S. Finch, October 23, 1902, and Strong to T. T. Kelly, February 20, 1904 (copies), UA; *University News-Bulletin*, 1 (October 1, 1899), 4 (December 1, 1902), 5 (November 1, 1903), 6 (November 15, 1904); and compare the catalogue of 1900–1901 with that of 1906–1907.

16. See Olin Templin, "To the Alumni," *Graduate Magazine*, 1 (October, 1902), 32; "The Alumni Association," *ibid.*, 3 (February, 1905), 180–182; and Leon N. Flint, "The New Plan and What It Means," *ibid.*, 4 (October, 1905), 24–25.

17. University Council Minutes (MS, UA), October 3, 1907; Leon N. Flint, William Higginson, William U. Moore, S. L. Whitcomb, and Robert K. Duncan to Frank Strong, January 16, 1908, UA.

18. Frank Strong to Ed. Howe, September 22, 1903 (copy), UA; E. M. Hopkins, "The Present Course in Journalism," *Graduate Magazine*, 2 (November, 1903), 43–46; *ibid.*, 2 (February, 1904), 187–188; *Kansan*, September 8, October 11, 1905; JBR, October 26, 1909.

19. William Allen White to Frank Strong, December 29, 1910, Strong to White, December 31, 1910 (copy), Strong to C. M. Harger, June 23, 1911 (copy), Minnie S. Moodie to Leon S. Cambern, August 12, 1911 (copy), and Merle Thorpe to Frank Strong, November 12, 1912, UA; JBR, October 5, 23, 1911.

20. See *Kansas University Weekly*, January 25, 1902; R. Bullimore to Frank Strong, March 18, 1905, Thomas A. Parker to Francis A. Wilber, and G. B. Buikstra to Strong, September 14, 1909, UA.

21. *Western School Journal*, 24 (January, 1908), 36–37; Frank Strong to N. J. Morrison, December 5, 1904, and Strong to L. H. Murlin, November 25, 1904 (copies), UA.

22. L. H. Murlin to Frank Strong, December 1, 1904, J. D. S. Riggs to Strong, December 8, 1904, and Edward Frantz to Strong, December 24, 1904, UA.

23. Frank Strong to Mark Bailey, Jr., October 5, 1903, Strong to N. J. Morrison, December 5, 1904, and Strong to Arthur W. Jones, June 27, 1908 (copies), UA.

24. *Western School Journal*, 24 (January, 1908), 37; Minutes of Faculty Meetings (MS, UA), January 10, 1907; University Council Minutes, February 7, 1907, October 8, 1908, January 8, 1909, June 5, 1911, May 13, 1913; University Senate Minutes (MS, UA), June 4, 1914; Frank Strong to "My Dear Sir," October 24, 1907, and Strong to E. D. Crites, November 1, 1907 (copies), UA.

25. William F. Zornow, *Kansas: A History of the Jayhawk State* (Norman, 1957), 270–271.

26. *KHJ*, 1901, pp. 797, 824; *UKC*, 1899–1900, p. 7, 1900–1901, p. 7; *Kansas His-*

torical Collections, 7 (1901–1902), 465–466; clipping from *Kansas Farmer,* January 17, 1894, in "Kansas: Biographical Scrapbook" (Kansas State Historical Society, Topeka), vol. P-3.

27. *UKC,* 1901–1902, p. 7, 1902–1903, p. 7, 1903–1904, p. 13, 1904–1905, p. 13; Topeka *Capital,* March 6, 1903; William E. Connelley, *A Standard History of Kansas and Kansans,* 5 vols. (Chicago, 1918), 4: 2111, and *History of Kansas, State and People: Kansas at the First Quarter Post of the Twentieth Century,* 5 vols. (Chicago, 1928), 3: 1218; Lawrence *Journal-World,* July 7, 1911; *KSJ,* 1905, p. 673; William Allen White to E. W. Hoch, March 7, 1905, Walter Johnson, ed., *Selected Letters of William Allen White, 1899–1943* (New York, 1947), 66; William Allen White to Frank Strong, November 30, 1912, Strong Papers.

28. *UKC,* 1906–1907, p. 15; *Who Was Who in America,* 1: 461; Hill P. Wilson, comp., *A Biographical History of Eminent Men of the State of Kansas, with Portraits Engraved Expressly for This Work* (Topeka, 1901), pp. 93–94; Kansas State Historical Society, *History of Kansas Newspapers: A History of the Newspapers and Magazines Published in Kansas from the Organization of Kansas Territory, 1854, to January 1, 1916 . . .* (Topeka, 1916), 51–52; *KSJ,* 1909, pp. 519, 568; "Kansas Senators and Representatives: Territorial and State, 1855–1958, Alphabetical List" (typewritten MS, 1958), Kansas State Historical Society, 8; Bank Commissioners of the State of Kansas, *Tenth Biennial Report,* 1910, p. 120; Connelley, *Standard History of Kansas,* 4: 1266.

29. *UKC,* 1910–1911, p. viii; Topeka *Capital,* January 29, 1923; Sara Mullin Baldwin and Robert Morton Baldwin, eds, *Illustriana Kansas: Biographical Sketches of Kansas Men and Women of Achievement Who Have Been Awarded Life Membership in Kansas Illustriana Society* (Hebron, 1933), 366; Kansas City, Mo., *Times,* March 19, 1934.

30. Frank Strong to Albert Henley, January 22, 1903, Strong to T. A. Noftzger, January 23, 1903, and Strong to John Francis, January 26, 1903 (copies), UA; *KSJ,* 1903, pp. 278, 314, 332–333.

31. Frank Strong to Cyrus Leland, September 23, 1902, January 22, 27, 1903 (copies), and Leland to Strong, September 30, 1902, January 24, 1903, UA.

32. *Kansas University Weekly,* February 7, 1903.

33. *KHJ,* 1903, pp. 645, 646, 667, 1042, 1043, 1048, 1568, 1592; *KSJ,* 1903, pp. 830, 838, 911, 934; *KL,* 1903, pp. 104–105.

34. *RBR,* 1904, p. 5.

35. Frank Strong to Cyrus Leland, March 13, 1903 (copy), UA.

36. *RBR,* 1904, pp. 5–11, 12.

37. Zornow, *Kansas,* 210; *KSJ,* 1905, pp. 45, 56, 545, 580, 614; *KHJ,* 1905, pp. 887, 911, 934; *KL,* 1905, pp. 50–52; C. C. Coleman to Frank Strong, September 3, 8, 17, 1903, UA; Strong to Coleman, September 16, 1903, and Strong to J. Willis Gleed, March 4, 1905 (copies), UA.

38. *RBR,* 1906, pp. 5–14, 37.

39. Frank Strong to Harold T. Chase, December 1, 1906 (copy), UA; *KHJ,* 1905, p. 21, 1907, pp. 37–38, 445, 458, 850, 869; *KSJ,* 1907, pp. 78, 85, 233, 257; *KL,* 1907, pp. 43–44.

40. Strong had first suggested the idea of a tax in his inaugural address. Strong, "Relation of Educational Development," *Graduate Magazine,* 1 (November, 1902), 67; *RBR,* 1908, pp. 16, 18–20. The idea had attracted support, of course, long before he became chancellor.

41. *Ibid.,* 1908, pp. 4–5, 30–31, 36. *Kansan,* February 13, 1909; form letter signed by Edward E. Brown, March 2, 1909, UA.

42. *KSJ*, 1909, pp. 40, 44, 402, 403–404, 411, 435, 436; *KHJ*, 1909, pp. 687, 719, 863, 890, 973, 986; *KL*, 1909, pp. 88–89.

43. *RBR*, 1910, p. 30; State of Kansas, Auditor of State, *Report*, 1910–1911, pp. xxvi–xxvii; Frank Strong, *What the University of Kansas Ought to Stand For: Opening Address to the Students of the University of Kansas, September 25, 1910* (Lawrence, 1910), 3–4.

44. *KHJ*, 1911, pp. 67, 82, 616, 647, 648, 671, 829–830, 869, 937–938, 1043; *KSJ*, 1911, pp. 642, 659, 696, 722–723, 837; *KL*, 1911, pp. 51–53.

45. *RBR*, 1904, p. 15, 1912, pp. 33–34; *Graduate Magazine*, 9 (March, 1911), 219–221.

46. On the complicated negotiations with Frank B. Lawrence, see Frank Strong to Lawrence, November 4, 1902, October 28, November 30, 1903, October 15, 26, 1904 (copies); Lawrence to Strong, November 13, 1902, November 23, 1903, October 8, 25, December 3, 1904; Strong to Sara T. D. Robinson, October 22, 1903 (copy); Mrs. Robinson to Strong, October 27, 1903; Strong to Thomas M. Potter, October 28, 1903, September 20, 27, 1904 (copies); statement signed by Frank Strong, October 28, 1904 (copy), all in UA. Also JBR, November 22, 1904, March 22, 1907, and *KL*, 1905, pp. 52–53. On the other land acquisitions, see J. Howard Compton, "The Building of the University of Kansas" (typewritten M.Arch. thesis, University of Kansas, 1932), 47, 85, and Lawrence *Daily Journal and Evening Tribune*, August 24, 1894.

47. JBR, April 8, May 3, 4, 1904; Compton, "Building of the University of Kansas," 136–137; *UKC*, 1905–1906, pp. 43–44; James W. Green, "The History of the Law School," *Kansas Lawyer*, 12 (November, 1905), 6.

48. *UKC*, 1905–1906, facing p. 32; George E. Kessler to Frank Strong, September 12, 1905, UA; JBR, May 11, June 30, September 15, 1905.

49. JBR, April 29, 1905; Sara T. D. Robinson to Frank Strong, April 29, 1905, UA; Compton, "Building of the University of Kansas," 140–143.

50. *UKC*, 1909–1910, p. 41, 1910–1911, pp. 41–42; Compton, "Building of the University of Kansas," 145–146, 148; "Marvin Hall" (typewritten MS, n.d.), in "University of Kansas School of Engineering and Architecture, Lawrence, Items in Its History" (scrapbooks, UA), vol. 3; JBR, January 28, 1910.

51. McArdle was also to deliver at least ten lectures in 1910 and 1911 in the School of Engineering. *RBR*, 1910, p. 27; William Allen White to Walter R. Stubbs, January 29, 1911 (copy), UA; JBR, January 28, 1910; Compton, "Building of the University of Kansas," 154–156.

52. Frank Strong to James N. Nation, July 17, 1910 (copy), Nation to Strong, July 9, 1910, and Edward E. Brown to Strong, July 12, 1910, UA; *RBR*, 1910, pp. 26–28; *KL*, 1911, pp. 50–51; Compton, "Building of the University of Kansas," 157–161; Robert Taft, *Across the Years on Mount Oread, 1866 . . . 1941: An Informal and Pictorial History of the University of Kansas* (Lawrence, 1941), 101.

53. Frank Strong to Mrs. Helen E. Moses, February 3, 1904 (copy), Mrs. Moses to Strong, February 9, 1904, and Strong to Charles F. Scott, September 27, 1904 (copy), UA; Kansas City, Mo., *Star*, November 3, 1906.

54. *UKC*, 1933–1934, endsheet.

CHAPTER 14

1. *RBR*, 1910, p. 13.

2. Frank Strong to All Instructors in the University of Kansas, March 22, 1910 (copy), UA.

3. Frank T. Stockton, *The Pioneer Years of University Extension at the University*

of Kansas (Lawrence, 1956), 4–5; *List of Lectures Offered to Kansas Communities by the Faculty of the University of Kansas* (Lawrence, n.d.).

4. Merle E. Curti and Vernon Carstensen, *The University of Wisconsin: A History, 1848–1925,* 2 vols. (Madison, 1949), 1: 717–719; Stockton, *Pioneer Years of University Extension,* 7–8.

5. *Ibid.,* 5; Vernon L. Kellogg to William Beer, August 20, 1891, and Francis H. Snow to Charles W. Moore, August 29, 1891 (copies), UA.

6. Francis H. Snow to John Sullivan, September 25, 1891 (copy), UA; Stockton, *Pioneer Years of University Extension,* 9–10, 11, 12, 13; *RBR,* 1892, p. 12.

7. Minutes of Faculty Meetings (MS, UA), September 27, October 2, 1891; JBR, October 16, 1891.

8. *RBR,* 1892, pp. 12–13.

9. Stockton, *Pioneer Years of University Extension,* 17–18, 20–22, 26, 35–39; *RBR,* 1894, pp. 15–17; JBR, December 5, 1893, February 8, 1894, April 9, June 8, 1897, March 17, 1898; Francis H. Snow to Charles F. Scott, February 8, 1896 (copy), Francis Huntington Snow Correspondence, 1892–1899, UA; Topeka *Capital,* February 20, 1897.

10. Stockton, *Pioneer Years of University Extension,* 25, 29–30; University Council Minutes (MS, UA), May 23, June 7, October 3, 1907.

11. Edwin M. Hopkins to Frank Strong, October 12, 1908, UA; *RBR,* 1908, pp. 6–7, 21–22.

12. William Allen White to Frank Strong, December 29, 1908, Strong to White, December 30, 1908 (copy), Strong to C. R. Van Hise, December 31, 1908 (copy), and Robert K. Duncan to Strong, January 5, 9 (2 letters), 19, 1909, UA.

13. Stockton, *Pioneer Years of University Extension,* 32.

14. Frank T. Stockton, *The University of Kansas Launches and Tests an Extension Division: 1909–1922* (Lawrence, 1957), 7, 8–9, 23–27, 38; Minutes of Faculty Meetings, December 2, 1909, April 25, 1910.

15. Frank T. Stockton, *Forty Years of Correspondence Study at the University of Kansas, 1909–1949* (Lawrence, 1951), 8–10, 17–23, 28, 30–31.

16. Stockton, *University of Kansas Launches and Tests an Extension Division,* 38–44.

17. *Ibid.,* 44–46.

18. *Ibid.,* 47–49.

19. *Ibid.,* 54–63.

20. *Ibid.,* 10–22, 50–54.

21. Stockton, *Pioneer Years of University Extension,* 30; *University Review,* 15 (September, 1893), 15; JBR, December 26, 1896; Francis H. Snow to J. P. Sams, April 1, 1897, and Snow to William Rogers, April 1, 1897 (copy), Snow Correspondence, 1892–1899; Minutes of Faculty Meetings, March 25, 1901.

22. Frank Strong to Frank G. Crowell, January 17, 1903, and William H. Carruth to Strong, July 22, 1903 (copies), UA; JBR, January 30, February 27, April 14, June 9, 1903; University Council Minutes, February 9, 1903; *Graduate Magazine of the University of Kansas,* 1 (March, 1903), 236–239.

23. *RBR,* 1904, p. 3, 1906, p. 22; JBR, September 15, 1903; Minutes of Faculty Meetings, November 2, 1905.

24. Clyde K. Hyder, *Snow of Kansas: The Life of Francis Huntington Snow with Extracts from His Journals and Letters* (Lawrence, 1953), 191–193; Francis H. Snow to J. N. Ward, June 27, 1894 (copy), UA.

25. JBR, July 15, October 26, 1909; Frank Strong to Henry J. Waters, January 21, 1910 (copy), UA; *Graduate Magazine,* 9 (January, 1911), 145–147.

26. *KL*, 1864, pp. 109–111, 1865, pp. 89–90; Hyder, *Snow*, 123; JBR, August 19, 1878.

27. *KL*, 1889, p. 395; Edgar H. S. Bailey, "Doctor Samuel Wendell Williston," *Graduate Magazine*, 17 (November, 1918), 35–37; Francis H. Snow, *Inaugural Address, Responding to the Board of Regents*, in *Addresses Concerning the Chancellorship, the University, Higher Education* (Topeka, 1890), 44; Charles F. Scott, comp., *The Class of 1881, Kansas State University: History of the Class, with Biographies of Its Members and a Report of Its Fiftieth Anniversary* (n.p., 1931), 16; Francis H. Snow to Erasmus Haworth, May 11, 16, 1892 (copies), UA.

28. Francis H. Snow to J. W. Powell, February 2, 1894, Snow to Charles F. Scott, February 3, 1894, and Erasmus Haworth to M. A. Low, March 23, 1894 (copies), UA; *RBR*, 1894, pp. 22–23, 1896, p. 9; JBR, March 28, 1895; *KL*, 1897, pp. 94–95.

29. Robert K. Duncan to Frank Strong, January 19, 1909, UA.

30. Table, "Statistics of State Universities and Other Institutions of Higher Education Partially Supported by the State," UA.

31. *KL*, 1905, pp. 789–790; William W. Hinkley, "A History of the Kansas State Board of Health" (typewritten M.A. thesis, University of Kansas, 1937), 49–50; Edgar H. S. Bailey, Hamilton P. Cady, and Frank B. Dains, *History of the Chemistry Department of the University of Kansas*, Bulletin of the University of Kansas, 26 (February 15, 1925), 33; Samuel J. Crumbine to Frank Strong, March 12, 1907, December 1, 1909, and Strong to Crumbine, November 30, 1909 (copy), UA; Lester B. Kappelman, "The Organization and Functions of the Kansas State Board of Health" (typewritten M.A. thesis, University of Kansas, 1947), 67–68.

32. M. O. Leighton to Samuel J. Crumbine, July 27, 1906 (copy), Crumbine to Frank Strong, July 30, 1906, Strong to Crumbine, August 31, 1906 (copy), and Strong to E. W. Hoch, September 6, 1906 (copy), UA; Bailey, Cady, and Dains, *History of the Chemistry Department*, 30.

33. *Ibid.*, 32–33; Robert Kennedy Duncan, *The Chemistry of Commerce* (New York, 1907), especially 3–4, 8–9; Duncan, "Temporary Industrial Fellowships," *North American Review*, 185 (May 3, 1907), 56–57, 62; Duncan, "On Industrial Fellowships," *Journal of Industrial and Engineering Chemistry*, 1 (August, 1909), 600–601, 603.

34. *Announcement of Industrial Fellowship Number Seven Offered by the University of Kansas, March 8, 1909* (Lawrence, 1909); Robert Kennedy Duncan, "On Certain Problems Connected with the Present-Day Relation between Chemistry and Manufacture in America," *Journal of Industrial and Engineering Chemistry*, 3 (March, 1911), 181–182; JBR, October 23, 1911; Bailey, Cady, and Dains, *History of the Chemistry Department*, 32–33, 58–59.

35. University of Kansas Engineering Experiment Station, *Engineering Bulletin*, no. 1 (November, 1909), inside front cover; George C. Shaad, "The Organization and Work of the Engineering Experiment Station of the University of Kansas," *ibid.*, no. 4, part 1 (October, 1913), 10–23.

36. "Some Notes on the State Service Work Done by the University of Kansas," Frank Strong Papers, UA; Samuel J. Hunter, "Department of Entomology of the University of Kansas: Historical Account," *Kansas University Science Bulletin*, 8 (July, 1913), 37–38; Frank Strong to Walter R. Stubbs, November 30, 1909 (copy), UA; *RBR*, 1912, pp. 5–16.

37. *Dictionary of American Biography*, 21: 677–678; William Allen White to Frank Strong, December 29, 1908, and Strong to White, December 30, 1908 (copy), UA; *KHJ*, 1909, p. 39, 1911, pp. 12, 20; Walter R. Stubbs to Frank Strong, October 16, 1909, Strong and the Board of Regents to Stubbs, October 26, 1909 (copy), and Strong to Stubbs, November 10, 1909 (copy), UA; JBR, October 26, November 10, 1909.

38. Rodney A. Elward to Walter R. Stubbs, October 23, 1911, and Frank Strong to Stubbs, October 31, 1911 (copies), UA.

39. Stockton, *University of Kansas Launches and Tests an Extension Division*, 64–65; JBR, October 23, 1911; Frank Strong to Members of the Board of Regents, November 1, 1911 (copy), UA.

40. J. C. Ruppenthal to William H. Carruth, February 8, 1908, Frank Strong to W. Y. Morgan, October 10, 1908 (copy), J. N. Dolley to Strong, January 27, 1909, UA; *KL*, 1909, p. 41; *RBR*, 1912, p. 15.

41. Arthur H. Bayse to Frank Strong, October 25, 1912, and Strong to Bayse, October 29, 1912 (copy), UA.

42. *KHJ*, 1913, pp. 16–17.

43. Frank Strong, "Address before the University Faculty Assembly, September 23, 1914," Strong Papers.

CHAPTER 15

1. John Sullivan to Frank Strong, October 7, 1902, January 25, 30, 1904, UA.

2. JBR, December 7, 1903, April 8, 1904; Frank Strong, James W. Green, and A. C. Mitchell to the Board of Regents, n.d. [1904], UA; Strong to S. S. Glasscock, December 7, 1904, Strong to Charles W. Barnes, May 13, 1905, Strong to J. C. McClintock, January 20, 1905, Strong to Clyde Miller, January 20, 1905, Strong to "My Dear Sir," February 1, 1905, and Strong to E. W. Hoch, February 4, 1905 (copies), UA.

3. *KHJ*, 1905, pp. 271, 285, 390, 473, 611, 612; *KL*, 1905, pp. 656–657.

4. Frank Strong to L. H. Rose, May 25, 1905, Strong to E. M. Hetherington, April 13, 25, 1905, and Strong to "Dear Sir," June 19, 1905 (copies), UA; JBR, April 21, June 30, 1905; *UKC*, 1933–1934, endsheet.

5. Frank Strong to L. H. Rose, May 25, June 3, November 9, 23, 1905 (copies), H. W. Yates, B. T. Sharp, George Rushton, and others to Strong, May 31, 1905, Rose to Strong, June 8, November 11, December 11, 1905, UA; JBR, November 3, 1905.

6. *Ibid.*, June 6, 1905; *Graduate Magazine of the University of Kansas*, 1 (October 2, 1902), 8, 9; George H. Hoxie to Frank Strong, May 18, 1906, and Strong to Hoxie, May 17, 21, 1906 (copies), UA.

7. JBR, November 3, 1905, February 2, November 30, 1906, January 2, 1907; *UKC*, 1905–1906, pp. 329–333; *RBR*, 1906, pp. 17–19.

8. George H. Hoxie to Frank Strong, October 14, December 12, 1907, UA; George H. Hoxie, "The School of Medicine," *Graduate Magazine*, 6 (February, 1908), 153–164; Abraham Flexner, *Medical Education in the United States and Canada: A Report to the Carnegie Foundation for the Advancement of Teaching* (New York, 1910), 226, 228.

9. *RBR*, 1908, pp. 33–34; *KL*, 1909, p. 88.

10. George H. Hoxie to Frank Strong, November 8, 1909, May 31, 1910, Louie J. Beyer to Strong, June 6, 1910, Strong to C. L. Brokaw, June 10, 1910 (copy), and Oliver D. Walker to Strong, August 13, 1910, UA; "Proceedings of the Forty-fourth Annual Meeting of the Kansas Medical Society, Held at Topeka, May 4–6, 1910," *Journal of the Kansas Medical Society*, 10 (August, 1910), 281–285.

11. JBR, December 9, 1910.

12. Frank Strong to "My Dear Doctor," December 10, 1910 (copy), William B. Sutton to Frank Strong, January 24, 25, 1911, Strong to J. Willis Gleed, February 3, 1911 (copy), Samuel J. Crumbine to Strong, February 6, 1911, Strong to O. D. Walker, February 7, 1911 (copy), Mervin T. Sudler to Strong, February 13, 1911, E. C.

Wickersham to the Committee of Ways and Means, House of Representatives, February 13, 1911 (copy), and Strong to Wickersham, March 21, 1911 (copy), UA; JBR, December 9, 1910, January 5, 1911; State of Kansas, Auditor of State, *Report*, 1909–1910, p. xxvii.

13. *KSJ*, 1911, pp. 45, 56, 521; *KHJ*, 1911, pp. 66–67, 82, 512; Frank Strong to E. C. Wickersham, March 21, 1911 (copy), UA; JBR, March 13, 15, 28, April 26, 1911; *RBR*, 1912, p. 18.

14. W. H. Mainwaring to Mervin T. Sudler, June 2, 1911, H. E. Robertson to Sudler, n.d. [1911], J. H. Hewitt to Sudler, July 18, 1911, Charles P. Emerson to Sudler, July 27, 1911, H. B. Forbes to Sudler, August 1, 1911, Cyrus W. Field to Sudler, August 2, 1911, Joseph H. Piatt to Sudler, August 3, 1911, and Sudler to Frank Strong, December 11, 1911, UA.

15. Mervin T. Sudler to Frank Strong, May 28, 1913, UA.

16. *KL*, 1893, pp. 217–220; *RBR*, 1894, pp. 10–11; *Who Was Who in America*, 1: 914; unidentified newspaper clippings in "Arvin Solomon Olin and Harry Conrad Thurnau" (scrapbook, UA); Minutes of Faculty Meetings (MS, UA), September 11, 1893, March 27, June 9, 1896; *UKC*, 1896–1897, pp. 48–49, 1899–1900, p. 168.

17. Topeka *Capital*, February 9, 1899; *KL*, 1899, pp. 365–367; Minutes of Faculty Meetings, March 13, April 10, 1899, March 25, April 15, 1901; *UKC*, 1901–1902, p. 39.

18. Frank Strong to J. Willis Gleed, July 18, 1908 (copy), UA; *RBR*, 1908, pp. 78–79.

19. H. H. Foster to Frank Strong, March 6, 1909, and Henrietta V. Race to Strong, April 16, 1909, enclosing identical letters from F. M. Spencer, D. L. McEachron, L. H. Murlin, Frank E. Mossman, E. Stanley, S. S. Kingsbury, and S. E. Prince, UA.

20. Minutes of Faculty Meetings, April 22, 1909; Arvin S. Olin to Frank Strong, April 23, 1909, UA.

21. Frank Strong to Arvin S. Olin, May 3, 17, 1909, and Strong to A. Ross Hill, May 12, 1909 (copies), Charles H. Johnston to Frank Strong, March 21, 1910, Strong to J. Willis Gleed, March 26, 1910 (copy), Strong to Johnston, March 26, 1910 (copy), and unsigned typewritten statement, n.d. (copy), UA; JBR, July 15, 1909, April 18, 1910.

22. *UKC*, 1910–1911, pp. 369, 374–376, 1911–1912, p. 352.

23. *Ibid.*, 1910–1911, p. 372, 1911–1912, pp. 355–358; Charles H. Johnston to Frank Strong, November 2, 1911, UA.

24. *UKC*, 1911–1912, p. 360.

25. *Kansan*, May 14, 1913; *Western School Journal*, 29 (August, 1913), 196; Frank Strong to Arvin S. Olin, June 5, 1913 (copy), Olin to Strong, June 9, 1913, April 21, 23, 1914, Edward T. Hackney to Strong, April 25, 1914, Strong to W. H. Carruth, April 5, 1915 (copy), and Strong to Hackney, May 25, 1915 (copy), UA; MBA, July 2, 1913.

26. Fred B. McKinnon to Thomas E. Smiley, July 5, 1895, and Frank Strong to Ed. Howe, September 22, 1903 (copies), UA; E. M. Hopkins, "The Present Course in Journalism," *Graduate Magazine*, 2 (November, 1903), 43–46.

27. *UKC*, 1903–1904, pp. 93–94; *Graduate Magazine*, 2 (February, 1904), 187–188; *ibid.*, 4 (October, 1905), 18–24; *Kansan*, September 8, October 11, 1905.

28. JBR, October 26, 1909; *UKC*, 1909–1910, pp. 175–176, 1911–1912, pp. 163–166.

29. Frank Strong, "The Relation of Educational Development to the Problems before the University of Kansas," *Graduate Magazine*, 1 (November, 1902), 71; Frank Strong to Andrew S. Draper, October 14, 1902 (copy), UA; Minutes of Faculty Meetings, March 18, 1904; JBR, April 8, 1904; *UKC*, 1903–1904, pp. 90–93.

30. *RBR*, 1904, p. 4; *UKC*, 1903–1904, p. 90.

31. *Ibid.*, 1909–1910, pp. 201–204.

32. Form letter, unsigned, March 2, 1904, and Frank Strong to Mrs. Kedzie Jones,

June 12, 1905 (copy), UA; Minutes of Faculty Meetings, March 21, 1904; Viola J. Anderson, *The First Fifty Years, 1910–1960: The Department of Home Economics, The University of Kansas* (Lawrence, 1964), 103 n.1.

33. *Ibid.*, 4, 104 n.5; *RBR*, 1908, p. 80.

34. Anderson, *First Fifty Years*, 5–7, 105 nn.21, 23.

CHAPTER 16

1. JBR, April 8, 1893; Francis H. Snow to James W. Green, March 17, 1894 (copy), UA.

2. James W. Green, "The History and Future Policy of the School of Law," *Graduate Magazine of the University of Kansas*, 4 (November, 1905), 58–59.

3. Francis H. Snow to William McDonald, October 13, 1891 (copy), UA; University of Kansas School of Law, *Catalogue*, 1889–1890, pp. 10–11, 1890–1891, p. 10, 1895–1896, p. 9, 1896–1897, pp. 9–10, 1897–1898, pp. 9–10.

4. William Burdick, "The Study of the Law," *Kansas Lawyer*, 10 (January, 1904), 3–4; untitled article by Frank Strong, *ibid.*, 11 (November, 1904), 1; School of Law, *Catalogue*, 1911–1912, p. 12, 1924–1925, p. 7; University of Kansas, *Twenty-eighth Biennial Report*, 1920, p. 25.

5. James W. Green, "The History of the Law School," *Kansas Lawyer*, 12 (November, 1905), 10.

6. *Ibid.*, 10; *UKC*, 1903–1904, p. 211.

7. *Ibid.*, 1933–1934, endsheet, 1914–1915, pp. 10, 11; *RBR*, 1892, p. 10; *Kansas: A Cyclopedia of State History, Embracing Events, Institutions, Industries, Counties, Cities, Towns, Prominent Persons, Etc.*, 4 vols. (Chicago, 1912), 3, pt. 1: 196; "Dr. Wm. L. Burdick," *Kansas Lawyer*, 6 (September, 1899), 2; and the following works by Burdick: *The Elements of the Law of Sale of Personal Property* (Chicago, 1901), *Handbook of the Law of Real Property* (St. Paul, 1914), *Illustrative Cases on the Law of Real Property: A Companion Book to Burdick on Real Property* (St. Paul, 1914), *The Law of Crime*, 3 vols. (New York, 1946), and *The Principles of Roman Law and Their Relation to Modern Law* (Rochester, 1938); "Wm. E. Higgins," *Kansas Lawyer*, 6 (September, 1899), 2.

8. Green, "History of the Law School," *Kansas Lawyer*, 12 (November, 1905), 7; *RBR*, 1880, p. 50; School of Law, *Catalogue*, 1884–1885, pp. 18–19, 1904–1905, p. 27; untitled article by Frank Strong, *Kansas Lawyer*, 10 (November, 1904), 2.

9. *RBR*, 1884, pp. 45–46, 1882, p. 47.

10. *KSJ*, 1879, pp. 135, 197, 265, 365, 385, 494, 1881, pp. 106, 108, 144, 187–188, 194–195, 201, 1883, pp. 58, 72, 89, 133, 146, 154, 1885, pp. 367, 370, 392, 432; *KHJ*, 1881, pp. 211, 241, 365, 376, 430, 621, 713, 1883, pp. 229, 249, 260, 292, 1885, pp. 202, 230, 260, 357, 375–376, 397; JBR, September 30, 1884; *KL*, 1897, p. 217.

11. Frank O. Marvin, "The Artistic Element in Engineering," *Proceedings of the American Association for the Advancement of Science*, 45 (1896), 85–87.

12. Don C. Little, "Dean Marvin as His Sister Tells of Him," *Kansas Engineer*, 11 (January, 1926), 21–22; Marvin, "Artistic Element in Engineering," *Proceedings of the American Association for the Advancement of Science*, 45 (1896), 85–96.

13. Frank O. Marvin, "The Cultural Value of Engineering Education," *Science*, n.s., 14 (July 26, 1901), 121–126.

14. W. C. Hoad, "Dean Marvin as a Friend," R. A. Rutledge, "Dean Marvin as an Associate of Young Men," and W. S. Kinnear to Erasmus Haworth, June 3, 1915, in *Dedication of the Memorial Portrait Bust of Dean Frank Olin Marvin, Marvin*

Hall, University of Kansas, June 8, 1915 (Lawrence, n.d.); *UKC,* 1904–1905, p. 189, 1891–1892, pp. 104–110, 1893–1894, pp. 68–72; *University Courier,* March 8, 1894.

15. JBR, June 3, 1895.

16. *RBR,* 1898, pp. 12–13, 1900, pp. 13–14.

17. JBR, January 18, February 7, 1912; *UKC,* 1913–1914, p. 216.

18. *Ibid.,* 1912–1913, p. 202, 1913–1914, p. 204, 1914–1915, pp. 178–179.

19. *Ibid.,* 1933–1934, endsheet, 1898–1899, pp. 83–84, 1912–1913, pp. 200–201.

20. *Ibid.,* 1911–1912, p. 11, 1912–1913, p. 13; Lawrence *Journal-World,* July 5, 1962; William C. Hoad to Frank Strong, January 16, 1913, UA; *Kansan,* February 16, 1934, March 13, 1938, July 2, 1948; Lawrence *Journal-World,* March 18, 1938, April 23, June 3, 1941; C. M. Young, *Kansas Coal: Occurrence and Production,* University of Kansas Engineering Experiment Station, Engineering Bulletin, no. 13 (March, 1925); Young, *Natural Gas,* 2 vols. (Lawrence, 1934); *Graduate Magazine,* 41 (December, 1942), 15.

21. *Ibid.,* 26 (November, 1927), 8; Perley F. Walker, *Industrial Development in Kansas,* University of Kansas Engineering Experiment Station, Engineering Bulletin, no. 12 (June, 1922), and "The Public Service Aspects of Engineering Education," *Journal of Engineering Education,* 15 (July, 1924), 32–41.

22. See the remarks made by C. M. Young, Raymond C. Moore, and Olin Templin, at the Haworth Memorial Meeting, February 23, 1933 (typewritten MS, UA); Erasmus Haworth and others, *The University Geological Survey of Kansas,* 9 vols. (Topeka, 1896–1908), 1: 8, 5: 4, and *passim.*

23. Janet Coulson, "A History of the Fine Arts School at the University of Kansas" (typewritten M.M. thesis, University of Kansas, 1940), 75–76, 116–118.

24. *Ibid.,* 93–104, 133–136; *UKC,* 1894–1895, pp. 56–57, 1899–1900, pp. 77–78, 1900–1901, pp. 105–106, 1907–1908, pp. 292–294, 1914–1915, pp. 245–247.

25. Coulson, "History of the Fine Arts School," 98–99.

26. JBR, June 11, 1890; Frank Strong to Charles W. Eliot, May 1, 1903 (copy), UA; Coulson, "History of the Fine Arts School," 83, 86; *RBR,* 1892, p. 11.

27. Coulson, "History of the Fine Arts School," 130; *Kansan,* February 9, 1915; Frank Strong to Charles S. Skilton, January 14, 1915 (copy), UA.

28. Coulson, "History of the Fine Arts School," 86–88, 124–127.

29. *UKC,* 1893–1894, p. 8, 1898–1899, p. 61 n, 1903–1904, p. 19; Florence L. Snow, "Art among Us," unidentified clipping in "Items about Faculty Members of the University of Kansas" (scrapbooks, UA), vol. 1; *Graduate Magazine,* 31 (October, 1932), 12; *Gazette,* May 28, 1940.

30. *UKC,* 1933–1934, endsheet; *Alumni Catalogue,* Bulletin of the University of Kansas, 15 (February 1, 1914), 38, 106–107.

31. Coulson, "History of the Fine Arts School," 79–80, 93, 105–115.

32. *Ibid.,* 121, 136–152.

33. *UKC,* 1933–1934, endsheet.

34. "L. D. Havenhill, 1870–1950," University of Kansas School of Pharmacy, *News Letter,* 3 (April, 1950), 1–2; Lawrence *Journal-World,* September 24, 1934; *UKC,* 1912–1913, p. 15; *Kansan,* December 10, 1948.

35. *UKC,* 1885–1886, pp. 57–61, 1893–1894, pp. 60–61, 1895–1896, p. 70, 1899–1900, pp. 105, 107–108, 1906–1907, p. 315, 1912–1913, p. 306.

36. *Ibid.,* 1907–1908, p. 327, 1908–1909, p. 270.

37. *Ibid.,* 1933–1934, endsheet; Frank W. Blackmar to the Board of Regents, October 2, 1911, and Blackmar to Frank Strong, n.d. [1902], UA.

38. Frank W. Blackmar to the Board of Regents, October 2, 1911, UA.

39. *KL*, 1905, p. 649.

40. *RBR*, 1894, p. 17; Frank Egbert Bryant, "Some Deficiencies in the University Library," *Graduate Magazine*, 5 (April, 1907), 236–246; University Senate Minutes (MS, UA), October 5, 1915; Frank Strong to Edward T. Hackney, October 22, 1915 (copy), UA; Frank H. Hodder to Ernest H. Lindley, September 19, 1920, Survey of Departments (MS, UA).

41. Carrie M. Watson, "History of the Library," Wilson Sterling, ed., *Quarter-Centennial History of the University of Kansas, 1866–1891. With Portraits of Chancellors* (Topeka, 1891), 126–128; Jonathan M. Davis to Ernest H. Lindley, May 31, 1923, and William Allen White to Lindley, May 20, 1924, UA.

42. University Council Minutes (MS, UA), March 28, 1895, September 8, 10, 1896, June 9, 1898, June 6, 1901; statement signed by William H. Carruth and E. M. Hopkins, between pp. 108 and 109 of *ibid.*, vol. 1; list of committees for the year 1900–1901, on p. 111 of *ibid.*, vol. 1.

43. Frank H. Hodder to Ernest H. Lindley, September 19, 1920, Survey of Departments; Frank Strong to Carrie M. Watson, May 17, 1909, May 27, 1919, Strong to P. L. Windsor, February 4, 1910, Strong to Edward T. Hackney, January 15, February 5, 1916 (all copies), UA; *The Constitution of the University of Kansas* (Lawrence, 1915), 15.

CHAPTER 17

1. Frank Strong to Ephraim Miller, April 7, August 20, 31, 1903, Strong to Scott Hopkins, July 23, 1903 (copies), and Miller to Strong, August 27, 1903, UA; JBR, October 21, 1903.

2. *UKC*, 1891–1892, pp. 65–69, 1892–1893, pp. 23–24; Minutes of Faculty Meetings (MS, UA), November 21, December 12, 1892.

3. *Ibid.*, 1891–1892, pp. 69–70; Minutes of Faculty Meetings, September 27, November 22, 1894.

4. *Kansas University Weekly*, February 26, 1898; Minutes of Faculty Meetings, February 14, 21, March 14, 1898.

5. Frank Strong to Arthur T. Hadley, September 27, 1902 (copy), UA; Minutes of Faculty Meetings, March 30, April 13, 1903; *UKC*, 1902–1903, pp. 77–78, 1903–1904, pp. 88–89.

6. Minutes of Faculty Meetings, May 26, 1903.

7. R. Freeman Butts, *The College Charts Its Course: Historical Conceptions and Current Proposals* (New York, 1939), 243–246.

8. Minutes of Faculty Meetings, February 13, March 11, 12, 13, April 9, May 26, 1908, February 5, April 21, May 19, 1914; *UKC*, 1908–1909, pp. 94–95, 1914–1915, pp. 12–13.

9. *UKC*, 1892–1893, pp. 17–22.

10. *RBR*, 1894, p. 14, 1898, pp. 13–14, 1900, pp. 12–13; Francis H. Snow to W. B. Hall, September 24, 1894, and Snow to S. M. Cook, December 15, 1896 (copies), UA; JBR, October 1, 1898.

11. Frank Strong to William H. Johnson, April 22, 1903 (copy), UA; *Western School Journal*, 26 (March, 1910), 93–94; *RBR*, 1904, p. 2; Minutes of Faculty Meetings, March 30, 1903, March 30, 1909; *UKC*, 1908–1909, pp. 77, 89, 1912–1913, pp. 113, 123.

12. Corwin E. Waterson, "The Operation of the Barnes High School Law in Kansas" (typewritten M.S. thesis, University of Kansas, 1929), 13–14, 20, 75; *KL*, 1905, pp. 658–660; Frank Strong, "To the Citizens of Kansas," n.d. [1905] (copy), UA.

13. *KL*, 1915, pp. 380–382; *Western School Journal*, 29 (December, 1912), 20, and 30 (March, 1914), 94–95; "A Declaration of Principles," "The Five Resolutions of the Educational Council," and "Standardizing the High Schools," *Kansas Teacher*, 1 (May, 1914); D. A. Ellsworth, "The Reorganization and Program of the Kansas State Teachers' Association," *ibid.*, 1 (October, 1914); "A Summary of School Legislation Enacted by the Legislature of 1915," *ibid.*, 1 (April, 1915); Kansas State Superintendent of Public Instruction, *Nineteenth Biennial Report*, 1913–1914, pp. 49–51, and *Twentieth Biennial Report*, 1915–1916, p. 10.

14. Frank Strong to S. M. Brewster, March 24, April ?, 1915 (copies), and Brewster to Strong, April 1, 1915, UA.

15. JBR, January 5, 1893; Frank Strong to W. E. Blackburn, March 31, 1908 (copy), UA.

16. Olin Templin to Frank Strong, March 30, 1909, UA; JBR, April 1, 1909; Minutes of Faculty Meetings, April 8, 1909.

17. Minutes of Faculty Meetings, October 25, 1909, April 25, 1910.

18. JBR, April 1, 1909; Frank Strong to Charles R. Van Hise, October 27, 1910 (copy), UA.

19. Olin Templin to Frank Strong, July 1, 1912, Joshua A. Lippincott to J. H. Drummond, December 15, 1886 (copy), and Francis H. Snow to James B. Angell, March 29, 1897 (copy), UA; *KL*, 1897, pp. 91–92; JBR, June 9, 1903, June 18, 1909, July 3, 1912; MBA, May 2, 1913.

20. William H. Carruth to Frank Strong, n.d., [1913], and note by Strong, n.d. [1913], UA; *Kansan*, March 5, 1913.

21. Frank Strong to Calvin H. Crouch, October 12, 1908 (copy), note by Strong, n.d. [1913], Robert M. Ogden to J. Willis Gleed, November 18, 1916, and Clarence E. McClung to Strong, January 10, 1913, UA; *Kansan*, March 5, 1913.

22. Edward C. Franklin to William S. Franklin, November 5, 1907, UA.

23. *Dictionary of American Biography*, 20: 310–311; Francis H. Snow, *Inaugural Address, Responding to the Board of Regents*, in *Addresses Concerning the Chancellorship, the University, Higher Education* (Topeka, 1890), 44; W. C. Stevens, "Reminiscences," *The Fiftieth Anniversary of the Founding of the Kansas Chapters of Phi Beta Kappa and Sigma Xi* (Lawrence, 1940), 70–71; E. H. S. Bailey, "Doctor Samuel Wendell Williston," *Graduate Magazine of the University of Kansas*, 17 (November, 1918), 35–37.

24. Edgar H. S. Bailey, Hamilton P. Cady, and Frank B. Dains, *History of the Chemistry Department of the University of Kansas*, Bulletin of the University of Kansas, 26 (February 15, 1925), 19–21; *RBR*, 1888, p. 15; JBR, May 1, 1889; Hamilton P. Cady, "Edward Curtis Franklin, the Chemist" (typewritten MS, 1944, UA), 1–7; and the following works by Edward C. Franklin: *On the Action of Ortho- and Meta-diazo-benzene-sulphonic Acids on Methyl and Ethyl Alcohol with Some Observations on the Action of Nitric Acid on Certain Alkoxy-benzene-sulphon-amides* (Baltimore, 1894), "Determination of the Molecular Rise in the Boiling-Point of Liquid Ammonia," *American Journal of Chemistry*, 20 (December, 1898), 837–853, "Liquid Ammonia as a Solvent," *American Chemical Journal*, 20 (December, 1898), 820–836, "Some Properties of Liquid Ammonia," *ibid.*, 21 (January, 1899), 8–14, and "The Electrical Conductivity of Liquid Ammonia Solutions," *ibid.*, 23 (April, 1900), 277–313.

25. Bailey, Cady, and Dains, *History of the Chemistry Department*, 25–26; A. W. Davidson, "H. P. Cady, Great Scientist, Teacher," *Graduate Magazine*, 42 (November, 1943), 4–5, 17; Robert Taft, *Fifty Years in Bailey Chemical Laboratory at the Univer-*

sity of Kansas (Lawrence, 1950), 31; *Kansan,* December 11, 1909; Kansas City, Mo., *Star,* September 22, 1963.

26. Bailey, Cady, and Dains, *History of the Chemistry Department,* 30, 34–35; Taft, *Fifty Years in Bailey Chemical Laboratory,* 9, 21, 31; *Graduate Magazine,* 46 (January, 1948), 12; *UKC,* 1926–1927, p. 9; *Kansan,* March 3, 1935, April 14, 1936; Lawrence *Journal-World,* March 18, 1938; Earl Farley, "Frank Burnett Dains, Friend of the Library," *Books and Libraries at the University of Kansas,* 1 (May, 1954), 4–5.

27. Edward C. Franklin to William S. Franklin, November 5, 1907, William S. Franklin to Frank Strong, November 15, 1907, and Strong to A. G. Webster, May 10, 1909 (copy), UA; Kansas City, Mo., *Journal Post,* January 20, 1929; *Kansan,* February 5, 1941, April 1, 1954; *UKC,* 1910–1911, p. 111.

28. Charles G. Dunlap, "Henry Byron Newson," *Graduate Magazine,* 8 (April, 1910), 237–241; Henry B. Newson, "Unicursal Curves by Method of Inversion," *Kansas University Quarterly,* 1 (October, 1892), 47–69, "Types of Projective Transformations in the Plane and in Space," *ibid.,* 6 (April, 1897), 63–69, "Continuous Groups of Circular Transformations," *American Mathematical Society,* 4 (December, 1897), 107–121, *Theory of Collineations* (Topeka, 1911), v–x and *passim; University News-Bulletin,* 3 (October 1, 1901).

29. *Graduate Magazine,* 40 (January, 1942), 21, and 34 (March, 1936), 10–11; Lawrence *Journal-World,* February 15, 1936; *Kansan,* October 10, 1949.

30. Vernon L. Kellogg, "Some Notes on the Mallophaga," *Transactions of the Kansas Academy of Science,* 12 (1889), pt. 1, pp. 46–48, "Notes on the Elementary Comparative External Anatomy of Insects," and "Insect Notes," *ibid.,* 13 (1891–1892), 111–112, 112–115, "Notes on Melitera Dentata Grote," *Kansas University Quarterly,* 1 (July, 1892), 39–41, "Two Grain Insects," University of Kansas Department of Entomology, *Bulletin,* February, 1892, pp. 3–9, and Vernon L. Kellogg and Francis H. Snow, "The Horn Fly of Cattle (*Haematobia Serrata* R. Desv.)," *ibid.,* May, 1893, pp. 3–7.

31. *UKC,* 1890–1891, p. 51; Kansas City, Mo., *Times,* February 26, 1937, November 13, 1948; Kansas City, Mo., *Star,* October 2, 1955; *Kansan,* November 23, 1929, May 16, 1940; Lawrence *Journal-World,* January 30, 1937, October 3, 1955, January 3, 1962; Clyde K. Hyder, *Snow of Kansas: The Life of Francis Huntington Snow with Extracts from His Journals and Letters* (Lawrence, 1953), 194, 263; William C. Stevens, *Plant Anatomy from the Standpoint of the Development and Functions of the Tissues and Handbook of Micro-Technic* (Philadelphia, 1907), and *Kansas Wild Flowers* (Lawrence, 1948).

32. Kansas City, Mo., *Times,* January 17, 1953; Kansas City, Mo., *Star,* May 26, 1946, June 18, 1953; *Kansan,* January 25, November 22, 1938, May 16, 1940; Lawrence *Journal-World,* February 12, 1945; Hyder, *Snow of Kansas,* 262–264; Marshall A. Barber, *A Malariologist in Many Lands* (Lawrence, 1946).

33. *Graduate Magazine,* 45 (January, 1947), 20; Samuel J. Hunter, "Department of Entomology of the University of Kansas—Historical Account," *Kansas University Science Bulletin,* 8 (July, 1913), 3–9, 53–55.

34. Wyman R. Green, "Clarence Erwin McClung, Teacher and Searcher," *Bios,* 6 (December, 1935), 343–347, 358–363, 369–370; D. H. Wenrich, "Clarence Erwin McClung," *Journal of Morphology,* 66 (May, 1940), 636–642, 663–673.

35. James C. Malin, "Frank Heywood Hodder, 1860–1935," *Kansas Historical Quarterly,* 5 (May, 1936), 115–121; Frank H. Hodder, "The Genesis of the Kansas-Nebraska Act," *Proceedings of the State Historical Society of Wisconsin,* 1912, pp. 69–86, "The Railroad Background of the Kansas-Nebraska Act," *Mississippi Valley*

Historical Review, 12 (June, 1925), 3–22, "Some Phases of the Dred Scott Case," *ibid.*, 16 (June, 1929), 3–22, "The Authorship of the Compromise of 1850," *ibid.*, 22 (March, 1936), 525–536.

36. JBR, June 18, 1891; Ephraim D. Adams, "European Relations," *Seminary Notes*, 2 (October, 1892), 11–17, "The Control of the Purse in the United States Government," *Kansas University Quarterly*, 2 (April, 1894), 175–232, "The Partition of Africa—a Review," *ibid.*, 8 (October, 1899), ser. B, 1–17, "The French Republic," *Arena*, 22 (December, 1899), 703–712, *Great Britain and the American Civil War*, 2 vols. (London, 1925); *American Historical Review*, 36 (October, 1930), 216.

37. *Graduate Magazine*, 1 (October, 1902), 8–9; *American Historical Review*, 52 (April, 1947), 648–650; *Who's Who in America*, 33: 49; Hartley Simpson, "Wallace Notestein," in William A. Aiken and Basil Duke Henning, eds., *Conflict in Stuart England: Essays in Honour of Wallace Notestein* (New York, 1960), 9–12, and the Notestein bibliography in *ibid.*, 258–263.

38. Frank H. Hodder to Frank Strong, April 3, 13, 14, 1908, and Strong to Hodder, April 9, 1908 (copy), UA; *Kansan*, February 14, 1916; Charlotte Watkins Smith, *Carl Becker: On History and the Climate of Opinion* (Ithaca, 1956), 16–18, 25–27; Burleigh T. Wilkins, *Carl Becker: A Biographical Study in American Intellectual History* (Cambridge, 1961), 69–72; James C. Malin to Burleigh T. Wilkins, August 25, 1956 (copy), and Malin to C. S. Griffin, May 8, 1962, in possession of author; Carl Becker, "Detachment and the Writing of History," *Atlantic Monthly*, 106 (October, 1910), 524–536, and "Some Aspects of the Influence of Social Problems and Ideas upon the Study of History," *Publications of the American Sociological Society*, 7 (June, 1913), 73–107.

39. Frank Strong to C. C. Crawford, June 17, 1907 (copy), UA; *Graduate Magazine*, 6 (October, 1907), 17–18; *ibid.*, 9 (October, 1910), 24; and *ibid.*, 38 (September, 1939), 20–21; Kansas City, Mo., *Times*, January 7, 1936; *Kansan*, January 19, 1936; *Summer Session Kansan*, June 11, 1954; *University of Kansas Newsletter*, 41 (May 16, 1942); *University of Kansas Alumni Magazine*, 52 (June, 1954), 34; Lawrence *Journal-World*, January 3, 1962; William W. Davis, *The Civil War and Reconstruction in Florida* (New York, 1913).

40. Ambrose Saricks, *A Bibliography of the Frank E. Melvin Collection of Pamphlets of the French Revolution in the University of Kansas Libraries*, 2 vols. (Lawrence, 1961), 1: ix–x; *American Historical Review*, 55 (July, 1950), 1040–1041; *Kansan*, March 20, 21, 1950; *Graduate Magazine*, 48 (March, 1950), 18.

41. Frank Strong to W. H. P. Faunce, April 18, 1904 (copy), UA; *Graduate Magazine*, 3 (October, 1904), 25–26; *Kansan*, December 12, 1906; John E. Boodin, "William James as I Knew Him, II," *Personalist*, 23 (Summer, 1942), 289, and *Truth and Reality: An Introduction to the Theory of Knowledge* (New York, 1911).

42. Boodin, "William James, III," *Personalist*, 23 (Autumn, 1942), 405–406; John E. Boodin to Frank Strong, August 5, 1911, Strong to Boodin, July 6, September 13, 1912 (copies), and Roy Stockwell to Scott Hopkins, August 15, 1912 (copy), UA; George O. Foster to Frank Strong, July 18, 1912 (2 letters), Frank Strong Papers, UA; JBR, July 5, September 19, 1912; MBA, June 9, 1913.

43. Mary A. Grant, Winnie D. Lowrance, Austin M. Lashbrook, and Oliver Phillips, Jr., *The History of the Wilcox Museum and of the Department of Classics and Classical Archaeology at the University of Kansas, 1866–1966* (Lawrence, 1966), 1–4, 11–20; "Professor Wilcox" (typewritten MS, n.d., UA).

44. RBR, 1892, p. 10; V. L. Kellogg to A. G. Canfield, July 16, 1892 (copy), UA; "University of Kansas: History of the Class of '92, Elmer F. Engel" (typewritten MS,

n.d., UA); *University News-Bulletin*, 7 (May 15, 1906); Olin Templin, "In Memory of Alberta Corbin . . ." *Graduate Magazine*, 39 (March–April, 1941), 13–14; *UKC*, 1918–1919, p. 6; *Kansan*, March 18, 1941.

45. Chester Woodward, "Dunlap's Life a Career of True Culture," *Graduate Magazine*, 35 (December, 1936), 10; William Allen White to Mrs. W. T. Beck, June 3, 1930, and Charles G. Dunlap, "Thanksgiving Day Sermon," November 25, 1914, in "Charles Graham Dunlap" (scrapbook, UA).

46. Marvin Goebel, "He Came on Trial and Remains after 50 Years of Service," *Graduate Magazine*, 38 (December, 1939), 2, 21–23; Edwin M. Hopkins, "Character and Opinions of William Langland, as Shown in 'The Vision of William Concerning Piers the Plowman,'" *Kansas University Quarterly*, 2 (April, 1894), 229–288; "Who Wrote Piers Plowman?" *ibid.*, 7 (April, 1898), ser. B, 1–26, *Circular Touching the Requirements in English for Admission to the University of Kansas* (Lawrence, 1895), and "Abstract of Report of the Committee on Elementary School English," National Education Association of the United States, *Addresses and Proceedings of the Fifty-ninth Annual Meeting*, 1921, pp. 440–442; Kansas City, Mo., *Star*, November 9, 1913; Anna Keaton to Alberta Cooper, August 26, 1926, in "Edwin Mortimer Hopkins" (scrapbook, UA).

47. Hyder, *Snow of Kansas*, 267; *Graduate Magazine*, 34 (May, 1936), 8; Ben Hibbs, "Poetry in His Heart," and Marvin Creager, "Same Spirit Through Life," *ibid.*, 34 (June, 1936), 18–19, 19–20.

48. E. M. Hopkins, "Professor Frank Egbert Bryant," *ibid.*, 9 (February, 1911), 169–175; F. H. H., "Selden Lincoln Whitcomb—'He Spurred to Greater Effort,'" *ibid.*, 29 (November, 1930), 9–10; untitled article by Theodore M. O'Leary, *ibid.*, 50 (October, 1951), 34.

49. Frank H. Hodder to Frank Strong, November 21, 1914, UA.

50. *American Political Science Review*, 44 (September, 1950), 736–738; *Who's Who in America*, 26: 766; *Who's Who in American Education*, 13: 324; Kansas City, Mo., *Times*, March 12, 1937; Kansas City, Mo., *Star*, January 27, March 14, 1937; Kansas City, Mo., *Journal Post*, March 16, 1937; Lawrence *Journal-World*, October 28, 1944, May 8, 1950, January 3, 1962.

51. *UKC*, 1890–1891, p. 56, 1904–1905, pp. 145–146, 1908–1909, pp. 156–158, 1909–1910, p. 15, 1913–1914, p. 17, 1914–1915, pp. 53–56, 1915–1916, p. 19.

52. *Ibid.*, 1889–1890, pp. 53–54, 1890–1891, p. 57, 1891–1892, p. 79, 1892–1893, p. 32, 1893–1894, p. 36, 1896–1897, p. 40, 1897–1898, p. 41, 1899–1900, pp. 128–129.

53. D. L. Patterson, "Arthur Jerome Boynton—the Man," *Graduate Magazine*, 26 (May, 1928), 8–10; *Kansan*, March 3, 1910.

54. JBR, June 16, 1911; Frank W. Blackmar to Frank Strong, June 10, 1910, and Strong to Arthur T. Hadley and others, June 22, 1911 (copy), UA; *American Economic Review*, 39 (June, 1949), 742–750; *Who's Who in America*, 24: 1643; *Directory of American Scholars* (Lancaster, 1942), 575; Lawrence *Journal-World*, September 28, 1938, November 15, 1940.

55. Frank W. Blackmar to Frank Strong, May 22, 1912, April 17, 1913, and Olin Templin to Strong, April 22, 1913, UA; *UKC*, 1915–1916, p. 8.

CHAPTER 18

1. Frank Strong to Arthur T. Hadley, January 3, 1913 (copy), William Allen White to Strong, February 23, March 8, 1913, Strong to White, December 8, 1913 (copy), Strong to Anson Phelps Stokes, January 10, 1914 (copy), J. R. Jewell to

Strong, September 25, 1913, Strong to Jewell, September 29, 1913 (copy), Strong to Ernest D. Burton, January 12, 1914 (copy), Strong to Frank W. Padelford, January 12, 1914 (copy), Strong to Charles F. Scott, January 8, 1914 (copy), Frank Strong Papers, UA.

2. Kansas State Superintendent of Public Instruction, *Report,* 1869, pp. 45–50.

3. *KHJ,* 1872, pp. 193, 201, 1876, pp. 199–202, 1066, 1089, 1425, 1901, pp. 21–22; *KSJ,* 1901, pp. 94–95, 119, 315.

4. Frank Strong, "The Relation of Educational Development to the Problems before the University of Kansas," *Graduate Magazine of the University of Kansas,* 1 (November, 1902), 68–71; Frank Strong to Edward W. Hoch, October 2, 1905, and Strong to David R. Boyd, December 15, 1905 (copies), UA.

5. *KHJ,* 1905, p. 25, 1907, p. 52; William H. Carruth to the Editor, n.d., *Graduate Magazine,* 5 (March, 1907), 212–217; *KSJ,* 1907, pp. 363, 370; John A. Edwards to Frank Strong, February 22, 1907, and Strong to A. C. Mitchell, February 16, 1907, Strong to Clyde Miller, February 16, 1907, and Strong to H. B. Miller, February 16, 1907 (copies), UA.

6. Kansas State Agricultural College, *Catalogue,* 1906–1907, pp. 41–45; Frank Strong to Garrett Droppers, January 12, 1905, Strong to E. T. Fairchild, November 28, 1906, Strong to E. R. Nichols, November 28, 1906, and Strong to C. I. Martin, January 24, 1907 (copies), UA; *Industrialist,* 33 (November 24, 1906), 104.

7. Frank Strong to Charles S. Gleed, October 25, 1907 (copy), UA.

8. U.S., Congress, House, H.R. 9230, 60th Cong., 1st sess., "A Bill to Establish Engineering Experiment Stations at Land-Grant Colleges" (copy), UA; Edward Bartow to Frank Strong, January 17, 1908, Strong to Charles F. Scott, January 14, 27, 1908 (copies), James B. Angell to Strong, February 8, 1908, George W. MacLean to Strong, February 12, 29, 1908, Strong to Oscar J. Craig, February 15, 1908 (copy), Strong to Charles R. Van Hise, February 15, 1908 (copy), Strong to William B. McKinley, February 24, 1908 (copy), UA; JBR, February 27, March 18, 1908.

9. "Engineering Experiment Stations at the Land Grant Colleges," *Industrialist,* 34 (February 29, 1908), 328–330.

10. Edward W. Hoch to Frank Strong, April 11, 1908, and Strong to J. Willis Gleed, July 18, 1908 (copy), UA; Kansas State Normal School, Emporia, *Catalogue,* 1905–1906, p. 216; Hoch to W. R. Stubbs, January 11, 1909, with accompanying Exhibit A, Governor Walter Roscoe Stubbs Papers, Kansas State Historical Society, Topeka.

11. E. W. Hoch to W. R. Stubbs, January 11, 1909, with accompanying Exhibits A, B, C, D, E, and F, Stubbs Papers.

12. *Industrialist,* 34 (April 25, 1908), 451, 460; Frank Strong to E. W. Hoch, April 29, 1908, Strong to Harold Chase, May 6, 1908, Strong to Frank MacLennan, May 7, 1908, and Strong to Charles S. Gleed, May 14, 1908 (copies), UA.

13. Frank Strong to E. T. Fairchild, May 14, 1908 (copy), UA; J. D. Walters, "Retrospect," *Industrialist,* 34 (June 13, 1908), 566–567; A. M. Story, "Engineering Legally a Department of the Kansas State Agricultural College," *Industrialist,* 35 (October 10, 1908), 19–28.

14. Frank Strong to "My Dear Sir," December 18, 1908 (copy), UA.

15. *RBR,* 1908, pp. 38–49, 55–59.

16. *Ibid.,* 50–55.

17. *Ibid.,* 59–64, 66–76.

18. *Ibid.,* 71–73.

19. *Ibid.,* 76–78.

20. *Ibid.*, 78–83.

21. *Ibid.*, 93–94.

22. *Ibid.*, 93, 96–98; Frank Strong to W. E. Blackburn, March 31, 1908, and Strong to E. T. Fairchild, April 1, 1908 (copies), UA.

23. *RBR*, 1908, pp. 93, 94–96, 98–100.

24. Frank Strong to Harold Chase, November 16, 1908 (copy), Strong to Charles S. Gleed, November 16, 1908 (copy), Chase to Strong, November 18, 1908, and William Y. Morgan to Strong, November 19, 1908, UA.

25. Frank Strong to Fred S. Jackson, December 24, 31, 1908, January 5, 1909 (copies), Jackson to Strong, January 5, 9, 1909, Strong to Clyde Miller, December 31, 1908 (copy), Strong to J. Willis Gleed, December 31, 1908 (copy), Strong to J. W. Burke, December 28, 1908 (copy), and Strong to C. S. Huffman, January 19, 1909 (copy), UA.

26. Frank Strong to "My Dear Sir," December 18, 1908 (copy), A. C. Mitchell to Strong, December 21, 1908, William Allen White to Strong, December 21, 1908, and Strong to S. W. Williston, January 9, 1909 (copy), UA.

27. Topeka *Capital*, January 21, 22, February 1, 2, 1909; *KHJ*, 1909, pp. 136, 140; *KSJ*, 1909, pp. 69, 82; C. A. Kimball, F. E. Balmer, and E. N. Rodell to "Dear Sir," January 28, 1909 (copy), UA; "Take Them as They Come and Set Them Going" and "A Visit by the Lawmakers," *Industrialist*, 35 (January 30, 1909), 211–220, 233–235.

28. William H. Carruth to Harold Chase, February 3, 4, 1909 (copies), UA; *Kansan*, February 13, 1909.

29. *KHJ*, 1909, p. 448.

30. Julius T. Willard, *History of the Kansas State College of Agriculture and Applied Science* (Manhattan, 1940), 170, 175; *Industrialist*, 36 (October 2, 1909), 3–6.

31. *Ibid.*, 36 (November 27, 1909), 103–104; Frank Strong to Henry J. Waters, March 1, 1910 (copy), UA.

32. Frank Strong to Henry J. Waters, October 19, November 18, 1909, June 27, 1910 (copies), and Waters to Strong, October 21, November 19, 1909, June 28, July 16, 1910, UA; JBR, June 24, 1910.

33. *KHJ*, 1911, p. 64; *Kansan*, March 14, 1911.

34. Frank Strong to John P. Curran, February 11, 1911, UA; Topeka *Capital*, January 31, 1911; Lawrence *Journal-World*, March 3, 1911.

35. *KHJ*, 1911, pp. 82–83, 256, 667–668, 691, 716–717; *KSJ*, 1911, pp. 93, 105, 520, 578, 698, 703, 704, 777–779.

36. *Graduate Magazine*, 9 (May, 1911), 307–312; Topeka *Capital*, March 15, 1911.

37. Walter R. Stubbs to Frank Strong, J. H. Hill, and Henry J. Waters, March 13, 1911, UA; Topeka *Capital*, March 15, 1911.

38. Stubbs also appointed a special committee to study the question of a permanent mill tax to support the three institutions. It consisted of Rodney A. Elward of the University, William E. Blackburn of the Agricultural College, and John E. Bayer of the Normal School. *Graduate Magazine*, 9 (April, 1911), 265–266.

39. Frank Strong to Charles S. Gleed, April 20, 1911, Strong to William Y. Morgan, May 10, 1911, Strong to William Allen White, May 29, 1911 (copies), and Strong to Scott Hopkins, May 15, 1911 (draft), UA; Strong to Scott Hopkins, March 29, 1912 (copy), Strong Papers; William Allen White to William H. Carruth, April 18, 1911, Walter Johnson, ed., *Selected Letters of William Allen White, 1899–1943* (New York, 1947), 118.

40. *The Organization, Government and Results in the State Educational Institutions of Kansas Presented by the Commission of Higher Education through the Com-*

mittee on Coordination, Respectfully Addressed to the Governor of the State of Kansas, the Members of the Kansas Legislature, and the Taxpayers of the State (Manhattan, 1913), 1–8.

41. *KHJ*, 1913, p. 16.

42. *Ibid.*, 168, 169, 204, 206–207, 217, 246, 268–271; *KSJ*, 1913, pp. 217, 230, 240; Frank Strong to W. E. Blackburn, February 3, 1913 (copy), UA.

43. *KL*, 1913, pp. 469–473.

44. Frank Strong to George H. Hodges, February 7, 1913 (copy), UA.

45. George H. Hodges to Frank Strong, February 13, 1913, UA.

46. W. W. Reno and R. J. Hopkins, eds., *The Kansas Blue Book: Containing the Portraits and Biographical Sketches of the Members of the Legislature of 1897* (Topeka, 1897), 88; biography of Cora G. Lewis in "Biographies" (typewritten MS, Kansas State Historical Society).

47. Frank Strong to George H. Hodges, March 8, 1913 (copy), and William Y. Morgan to Strong, March 22, 1913, UA.

CHAPTER 19

1. JBR, July 3, 1912; MBA, May 2, 1913.

2. Olin Templin to Frank Strong, May 9, 1913, and Strong to Edward T. Hackney, May 9, 15, 1913, and Strong to William H. Carruth, May 26, 1913 (copies), UA.

3. MBA, April 11, 1914.

4. Frank Strong to William H. Carruth, September 6, 1913 (copy), UA; *RBA*, 1914, p. 6.

5. Frank Strong to Edward T. Hackney, December 9, 1913, and Strong to William H. Carruth, September 6, 1913 (copies), UA; Frank T. Stockton, *The University of Kansas Launches and Tests an Extension Division, 1909–1922* (Lawrence, 1957), 55.

6. *Graduate Magazine of the University of Kansas*, 12 (October, 1913), 19–20; MBA, October 3, 17, 1913.

7. *Kansan*, January 22, 1914; Frank Strong to Edward T. Hackney, December 19, 1913 (copy), UA.

8. Frank Strong to Edward T. Hackney, February 21, March 23, 1914 (copies), UA; *Graduate Magazine*, 13 (June, 1915), 285–286.

9. Frank Strong to Charles F. Scott, May 21, 1914 (copy), UA.

10. *RBA*, 1914, pp. 5, 14; Edward T. Hackney, "An Inventory," *Graduate Magazine*, 12 (March, 1914), 305–308.

11. *RBA*, 1914, pp. 5, 6, 10, 11–12.

12. *Ibid.*, 1914, pp. 5–6, 7–8, 13, 27–28.

13. *Graduate Magazine*, 11 (June, 1913), 273–274.

14. *Ibid.*, 12 (June, 1914), 431–432.

15. Charles F. Scott to Frank Strong, May 21, 1915, and typewritten statement, n.d., Frank Strong Papers, UA.

16. *Graduate Magazine*, 13 (June, 1915), 279–283.

17. *Ibid.*, 279, 283.

18. *Ibid.*, 283–287.

19. *Ibid.*, 288–289.

20. *Ibid.*, 289–290.

21. *UKC*, 1933–1934, endsheet.

22. JBR, June 5, 1901; University Council Minutes (MS, UA), June 7, October 3, 1907, June 12, 1908; Frank Strong to W. E. Blackburn, March 31, 1908 (copy), UA.

23. Frank Strong to the Deans of the University, June 3, 1910 (copy), UA; *RBR*, 1910, pp. 31–32.

24. Minutes of Faculty Meetings (MS, UA), September 21, November 22, 1911; University Council Minutes, November 15, 22, December 12, 1911.

25. In the spring of 1912 Hoad and McClung resigned from the faculty and Dean Marvin began a leave of absence. Their replacements were Perley F. Walker and George C. Shaad of the School of Engineering, and Frederick E. Kester of Physics. University Council Minutes, January 9, September 25, 1912.

26. University Council Minutes, January 20, April 28, 1913; MBA, May 2, 1913. As approved by the Council, the Constitution everywhere referred to the University's governing board as the Board of Regents. Because of the change of 1913, and the fact that the Constitution went into effect only in 1915, I have used Board of Administration instead.

27. University Council Minutes, January 20, 1913; *The Constitution of the University of Kansas* (Lawrence, 1915), 7.

28. *Ibid.*, 7–8; University Council Minutes, January 27, 1913.

29. Frank Strong to the University Council, February 3, 1913 (copy), UA; University Council Minutes, February 3, 11, 1913; *Constitution*, 7–8.

30. University Council Minutes, February 11, 1913; *Constitution*, 8.

31. University Council Minutes, February 25, 1913; *Constitution*, 8.

32. *Ibid.*, 9; University Council Minutes, February 11, 25, March 27, 1913.

33. University Council Minutes, February 25, 1913; *Constitution*, 9–10.

34. University Council Minutes, February 27, 1913; *Constitution*, 10–11.

35. University Council Minutes, March 5, 25, 27, 1913; *Constitution*, 11–12.

36. University Council Minutes, April 21, 1913; *Constitution*, 12.

37. *Ibid.*, 12–13.

38. *Ibid.*, 13.

39. *Constitution*, 12; University Council Minutes, April 28, 1913.

40. *Constitution*, 17; University Council Minutes, April 28, 1913.

41. *Constitution*, 17–18; University Council Minutes, April 28, 1913.

42. *Constitution*, 18.

43. University Council Minutes, April 28, 1913, March 3, 1914; MBA, May 2, 1913, May 11–14, 1914; University Senate Minutes (MS, UA), April 7, May 5, 20, 1914; *Constitution*, 5.

44. *KHJ*, 1915, pp. 22–23; W. P. Lambertson and E. L. Burton, *Partial Report of the Efficiency and Economy Committee of Kansas* (Topeka, 1916), 2, 6–7; *Report of the Efficiency and Economy Committee on the Educational Institutions of Kansas* (Topeka, 1917?), 1–2.

45. *KHJ*, 1917, pp. 188, 207, 262, 304, 322, 406–409, 414–415, 499, 510–511, 580; *KSJ*, 1917, pp. 300, 311, 325–326, 352, 357; *KL*, 1917, pp. 427–435.

46. Frank Strong to Arthur Capper, February 26, 1917 (copy), UA. See also Capper to Strong, February 27, 1917, UA.

47. *UKC*, 1917–1918, p. 3; *Official Record of the Fifteenth and Ninety-ninth Annual Session of the Kansas Conference of the Methodist Church, Independence, Kansas, June 2–7, 1953* (Council Grove, 1953), 326; William E. Connelley, *History of Kansas, State and People: Kansas at the First Quarter Post of the Twentieth Century*, 5 vols. (Chicago, 1928), 5: 2300; Topeka *Capital*, January 29, 1923.

48. Frank Strong to the University Senate, September 29, 1917 (copy), UA; University Senate Minutes, October 2, November 6, 1917.

CHAPTER 20

1. Frank Strong, "Administrations of the University of Kansas, 1866–1920," *Inauguration of Ernest Hiram Lindley as Chancellor of the University of Kansas* (Lawrence, 1921), 18–19.

2. Frank Strong to the Board of Administration, October 8, 1918 (copy), UA.

3. Frank Strong to George R. Parkin, September 25, 1914, Strong to Arthur Capper, November 3, 1915, October 7, 1916, Strong to Joseph Taggart, February 21, 1916, Strong to Julius Kahn, May 11, 1916, Strong to William C. Hoad, November 19, 1915, and Strong to Charles R. Van Hise, September 28, 1916 (copies), UA; Frank Strong "Address before the University Faculty Assembly, September 23, 1914," and "Address to the Students at the Opening of the University," September, 1915, Frank Strong Papers, UA.

4. Frank Strong, "The University of Kansas and the War," July 3, 1917, Strong Papers.

5. University Senate Minutes (MS, UA), April 17, 1917, March 5, April 2, 1918; *Kansan*, April 8, 1917; Strong, "University of Kansas and the War," Strong Papers; Strong, "Mobilization at the University," *Graduate Magazine of the University of Kansas*, 15 (May, 1917), 235; Minutes of Faculty Meetings (MS, UA), December 10, 1917.

6. Frank Strong, "University of Kansas and the War," Strong Papers; Strong, *Biennial Report of the University of Kansas, Lawrence, Kansas, for the Two Years Ending June 30, 1918*, in *RBA*, 1919, p. 9; Strong to Martha G. Fain, October 11, 1917 (copy), UA.

7. Strong, "Mobilization," *Graduate Magazine*, 15 (May, 1917), 236–237.

8. University Senate Minutes, October 2, 1917.

9. *Ibid.*, October 17, 1917; Frank Strong to E. M. Briggs, October 29, 1917 (copy), UA; *Graduate Magazine*, 16 (December, 1917), 81–82.

10. *Ibid.*, 16 (December, 1917), 82; *Kansan*, November 13, 1917, January 7, 1918.

11. University Senate Minutes, January 10, 11, February 8, 19, May 7, 13, 1918.

12. *Graduate Magazine*, 16 (November, December, 1917), 46, 82.

13. *Catalogue of the Public Documents of the Sixty-fifth Congress and of All the Departments of the Government of the United States for the Period from July 1, 1917 to June 30, 1919* (Washington, 1925), 2389; *United States Statutes at Large*, 40: 957.

14. *Graduate Magazine*, 17 (October, 1918), 16–17; University Senate Minutes, September 11, 17, 1918.

15. *UKC*, 1918–1919, pp. 60–62; *Graduate Magazine*, 17 (October, 1918), 16.

16. Frank Strong to H. G. Elledge, April 8, 1919, and Strong to the Board of Administration, October 24, 1918 (copies), UA; *Kansan*, October 8, 1918; *Graduate Magazine*, 17 (November, 1918), 45.

17. Frank Strong to H. J. Haskell, July 13, 1917, Strong to Charles S. Gleed, July 14, 1917, Strong to A. A. Potter, January 9, 1919 (copies), James A. Kimball to Strong, December 2, 1918, and Strong to Kimball, December 17, 1919 (copy), UA; State of Kansas, *Biennial Report of the Auditor of State*, 1916, pp. 81, 82, 1918, pp. 47, 49, 1920, pp. 34–35, 48–49.

18. University Senate Minutes, December 3, 19, 1918, February 17, 1919; *Kansan*, December 13, 1918; MBA, February 22, 1919.

19. *UKC*, 1919–1920, pp. 401–407.

20. "War Service, the University Extension Division, the University of Kansas, July 1, 1917–May 1, 1918" (typewritten MS), UA.

21. Frank Strong to F. B. Dains, November 16, 1917 (copy), UA; *Graduate Magazine*, 16 (February, 1918), 145, 146.

22. *Ibid.*, 16 (February, April, 1918), 145–146, 207; Minutes of Faculty Meetings, January 24, April 16, May 21, June 1, December 17, 1918.

23. *Graduate Magazine*, 16 (April, 1918), 207–208.

24. *Ibid.*, 16 (November, 1917), 46; *Kansan*, January 7, 14, 1918; University Senate Minutes, May 7, 28, 1918.

25. *Graduate Magazine*, 16 (December, 1917), 81–82; Strong, "University of Kansas and the War," Strong Papers; Strong to F. A. Vanderlip, June 12, 1918, Strong to Benjamin H. Gordon, December 11, 1917, and Strong to L. Amee Brown, February 15, 1918 (copies), UA.

26. Statement signed by Frank Strong, October 5, 1917, and Strong to Irving Fisher, April 30, 1917 (copy), UA; Olin Templin to Charles Curtis, May 7, 1917, in "Olin Templin, A.B. '86, A.M., M.S. '90" (scrapbook, UA); *Kansan*, April 18, May 8, 17, 1917.

27. A. W. Davidson, "H. P. Cady, Great Scientist, Teacher," *Graduate Magazine*, 42 (November, 1943), 5; "Big War Discovery Made at K.U.," News service from the Department of Journalism of the University of Kansas, n.d., UA.

28. Frank Strong, "To the Alumni and Former Students of the University of Kansas," May 15, 1918, Strong Papers; "The War Record of the University of Kansas," *University of Kansas News Bulletin*, 19 (August 1, 1918), 2, 3–4.

29. Strong, "To the Alumni and Former Students," Strong Papers; Strong, *Biennial Report . . . June 30, 1918*, in *RBA*, 1919, pp. 8–9.

30. *Kansan*, April 10, 1918.

31. Frank Strong to the Board of Administration, July 12, 1917 (copy), UA; Strong, "Administrations of the University of Kansas," *Inauguration of Ernest Hiram Lindley*, 18–19.

32. Frank Strong to the Board of Regents, April 13, 1910 (copy), UA; JBR, April 18, 1910.

33. University Council Minutes (MS, UA), June 3, 4, 7, 13, 23, 1913.

34. *Kansan*, October 23, 26, November 6, 9, 1914; Frank Strong to Frank Mac-Lennan, November 30, 1914 (copy), UA.

35. *Kansan*, December 3, 1914; Thornton Cooke to Frank Strong, December 10, 1914, Strong Papers.

36. J. C. Nichols to Frank Strong, December 8, 1914, Strong Papers.

37. Frank Strong to J. C. Nichols, Strong to Edwin C. Meservey, and Strong to Henry Schott, all dated December 5, 1914 (copies), UA.

38. *Graduate Magazine*, 14 (June, 1916), 281; J. Willis Gleed to H. A. Millis, R. M. Ogden, Carl Becker, and W. H. Twenhofel, October 26, 1916 (copy), and Carl Becker to J. Willis Gleed, November 20, 1916, J. Willis Gleed Papers, RHC.

39. J. Willis Gleed to Carl Becker, November 27, 1916 (copy), *ibid.*; *Graduate Magazine*, 16 (October, 1917), 23–24.

40. *Ibid.*, 16 (June, 1918), 298–299.

41. "A Study of the Conditions in the University of Kansas, May, 1918" (typewritten MS), UA.

CHAPTER 21

1. University Senate Minutes (MS, UA), January 7, February 4, 1919.

2. *Ibid.*, December 3, 1918.

3. *Ibid.*, April 1, 1919.

4. David L. Patterson, "Growth of Democracy in University and College Administration," *Graduate Magazine of the University of Kansas,* 17 (April, 1919), 195–201.

5. Frank Strong to William Allen White, July 15, 1919 (copy), White to Strong, July 17, 1919, White to Wilbur N. Mason, December 22, 1919 (copy), Frank Strong Papers, UA; MBA, October 13, 1919, January 22, 1920; Strong to the Board of Administration, November 17, 1919 (copy), UA.

6. Frank Strong to Wilbur N. Mason, November 17, 1919 (copy), Mason to Strong, November 18, 1919, and Strong to the Board of Administration, January 17, 1920 (copy), UA; University Senate Minutes, November 12, 14, 1919, and Frank Strong to the Board of Administration, January 17, 1920 (copy), UA.

7. C. Ferdinand Nelson, "Problems of Democracy in University Administration," *Graduate Magazine,* 18 (January, 1920), 89–93.

8. Orrin K. McMurry, "A Californian on College Democracy," *ibid.,* 18 (March, 1920), 155–161.

9. Olin Templin, "The Chancellor to Be," *ibid.,* 18 (April, 1920), 187–191.

10. R. D. O'Leary, "Once More: The Chancellor to Be," *ibid.,* 18 (May, 1920), 217–221.

11. Frank H. Hodder to the Editor, *ibid.,* 18 (May, 1920), 221–224. See also Edmund H. Hollands to the Editor, *ibid.,* 18 (May, 1920), 224–225.

12. On a trip through the East in April, 1920, Board of Administration members Wilbur N. Mason and E. L. Barrier made what Erskine took to be an offer of the chancellorship, which Erskine declined. *Kansan,* March 22, 1920; Topeka *Capital,* April 17, 1920; John Erskine, *The Memory of Certain Persons* (Philadelphia, 1947), 115–116, 189–190, 193, 258–337, 341; Erskine, *My Life as a Teacher* (Philadelphia, 1948), 17, 18. I have not discovered, however, a formal vote or decision by the Board of Administration to offer him the chancellorship. It is possible that Mason and Barrier only asked him if he would accept if an offer was made.

13. *Commemoration of Ernest Hiram Lindley: Chancellor, 1920–1939, Chancellor Emeritus, 1939–1940, the University of Kansas* (Lawrence, 1940), 2–3; Henry Suzzallo to Ernest H. Lindley, May 25, 1920 (telegram), E. L. Holton to E. L. Barrier, May 21, 1920 (copy), and William L. Bryan to Ernest H. Lindley, May 25, 1920 (telegram), in possession of Dr. Stanley B. Lindley, Salisbury, North Carolina.

14. Wilbur N. Mason to Ernest H. Lindley, May 21, 25, 26, 31 (telegrams), and Strong to Lindley, June 2, 1920, in possession of Dr. Stanley B. Lindley; Frank Strong to the Board of Administration, June 2, 1920 (copy), UA.

15. Frank Strong to Ernest H. Lindley, June 2, 1920, Olin Templin to Lindley, June 2, 1920, and Wilbur N. Mason to Lindley, June 7 (telegram), 8, 1920, in possession of Dr. Stanley B. Lindley; MBA, June 8, 1920.

16. Margaret Lynn, "Ernest Hiram Lindley," *Commemoration of Ernest Hiram Lindley,* vii–viii; Robert M. Yerkes to Ernest H. Lindley, with enclosures, March 17, 1921, UA; Lindley, "A Study of Puzzles with Special Reference to the Psychology of Mental Adaptation," *American Journal of Psychology,* 8 (1897), 431–493, especially 482–483; William Lowe Bryan and Ernest Hiram Lindley, "Learning a Life Occupation: Arthur Griffith, Arithmetical Prodigy," in William Bryan, Ernest Hiram Lindley, and Noble Harter, "On the Psychology of Learning a Life Occupation," *Indiana University Publications,* Science Series, no. 11 (1941).

17. Ernest H. Lindley, "The University and the Vocations of Men," *Inauguration of Ernest Hiram Lindley as Chancellor of the University of Kansas* (Lawrence, 1921), 27–39.

18. Ernest H. Lindley to R. J. H. DeLoach, February 9, 1925, and Lindley to H. W. London, April 4, 1922 (copies), UA.

19. In addition to Allen the Board members were E. L. Barrier, a Eureka stockman and Republican legislator; Harvey J. Penny of Hays, a wealthy landowner and active Republican; and Ernest Underwood, a Republican farmer from Atchison. *Who's Who in the Kansas Legislature: Session 1931* (Great Bend, 1931), 9–10; Topeka *Capital*, March 2, 1919.

20. In addition John C. Christensen, purchasing agent of the University of Michigan, made a separate study of the Board of Administration's financial operations as they related to the institutions of higher learning, and Dean Elias P. Lyon of the University of Minnesota Medical School conducted an independent investigation of the Medical School at Kansas. George F. Zook, Lotus D. Coffman, and A. R. Mann, *Report of a Survey of the State Institutions of Higher Learning in Kansas,* Department of the Interior, Bureau of Education, Bulletin, 1923, no. 40 (Washington, 1923), vii–viii.

21. *Ibid.,* 22–23, 24, 25–29.

22. *Ibid.,* 22–23, 27, 29.

23. George F. Zook to Ernest H. Lindley, October 6, 1922, Frederick J. Kelly to Lindley, October 16, 1922 (copy), and Lindley to Zook, October 16, 1922 (copy), UA.

24. Zook, Coffman, and Mann, *Report of a Survey,* v, vi; Ernest H. Lindley to George F. Zook, May 17, 1923 (copy), UA.

25. Here I have benefited from Roger W. Corley, "Jonathan M. Davis: Farmer in the State House" (typewritten M.A. thesis, Kansas State University, 1962).

26. Ernest H. Lindley to William Allen White, November 17, 1922 (copy), and White to Lindley, January 2, 1923, UA; *KHJ*, 1923, pp. 9–24; *UKC*, 1923–1924, p. 9; Albert B. Carney, autobiographical form for the *Kansas Blue Book* of 1911, Kansas State Historical Society, Topeka; Kansas City, Mo., *Star*, April 8, 1923; Harold C. Place, ed., *Kansas Year Book, 1937–1938* (Topeka, 1938), 18.

27. Ernest H. Lindley to George F. Zook, May 17, 1923, and Lindley to William Allen White, June 14, 1923 (copies), UA.

28. The draft-evasion charge was made originally in October, 1923, by members of the Eli Ferrell Dorsey Post of the American Legion in Lawrence. On the basis of evidence supplied by Legionnaires in Wichita, and without hearing Shea's side of the case, the Dorsey Post publicly accused him of evading the provisions of the wartime draft law and publicly asked Davis to remove him. John M. Shea to Ernest H. Lindley, December 31, 1924, notarized statement signed by Shea, December 31, 1924, and J. H. Sawtell to Lindley, July 28, 1924, UA; *Kansan*, October 24, 1923; Fred Ellsworth, "The Hectic Birth of the Board of Regents, Part I: Who's Running the Show?" *University of Kansas Alumni Magazine,* 62 (January, 1964), 6; Kansas City, Mo., *Star*, July 24, 1924; MBA, July 23, 1924.

29. C. C. Nesselrode to Harvey J. Penny, July 3, 1922 (copy), with enclosed copy of Nesselrode to the Kansas Medical Society, n.d., UA.

30. Zook, Coffman, and Mann, *Report of a Survey,* 133–140.

31. Lindley's excuse was that the original typewritten report had gone for study first to William Allen White and then to Governor Davis, and thus was not available in Lawrence. But this did not explain why Lindley did not show it to Sudler as soon as he received it, or why he did not have a copy typed for Sudler's use. George F. Zook to Ernest H. Lindley, May 12, 1923, and Lindley to Zook, May 17, 1923 (copy), UA.

32. Mervin T. Sudler, *Concerning the Summary Dismissal of a Member of the Faculty of the School of Medicine, the University of Kansas* (Lawrence, 1924), 4–5.

33. *Ibid.*, 5–6.

34. Kansas City, Mo., *Times*, July 23, 1924; Lawrence *Journal-World*, July 23, 30, 1924; Kansas City, Mo., *Star*, July 24, 29, 30, 1924; Wichita *Beacon*, July 25, 26, 29, 1924.

35. A. B. Carney to Ernest H. Lindley, July 31, 1924, UA; Sudler, *Concerning the Summary Dismissal*, 5, 37–38; Kansas City, Mo., *Post*, August 8, 1924; Lawrence *Journal-World*, August 8, 1924. Faced with these contradictory statements, the *Star* changed its story in a peculiar way. It was true that Sudler had offered to resign, the newspaper said lamely. But his resignation was in the Chancellor's hands, and the Board did not know it. Or if the Board had known, it concealed the fact well, for its first statement spoke of the retirement as dismissal. Thus the Board had removed Sudler without knowing, or without appearing to know, that it could have his resignation. Actually, of course, the Board had made no statement, Carney denied making the statement that he allegedly made, and Carney had specifically mentioned the retirement when interviewed on July 23. Kansas City, Mo., *Star*, August 9, 1924.

36. Ernest H. Lindley to Mervin T. Sudler, August 13, 1924 (telegram), in Sudler, *Concerning the Summary Dismissal*, 36; William F. Zornow, *Kansas: A History of the Jayhawk State* (Norman, 1957), 239. William Allen White, the candidate of an anti–Ku Klux Klan faction in the Republican party, won slightly under 150,000 votes.

37. Kansas City, Mo., *Star*, December 28, 29, 30, 1924; Jonathan M. Davis to Ernest H. Lindley, December 12, 1924, and Lindley to Davis, December 16, 1924 (copy), UA; MBA, December 27, 1924; Kansas City, Mo., *Times*, January 14, 1925; Abilene *Reflector*, January 1, 1925.

38. Jonathan M. Davis to Ernest H. Lindley, with enclosure, December 27, 1924, UA; Davis, *To the People of Kansas* (n.p., 1924).

39. Means also agreed with the defense attorneys that his District Court had no jurisdiction anyway, for Lindley's action was in effect a suit against the state of Kansas in the absence of any legal authorization for bringing one. Ellsworth, "Hectic Birth, Part I," *Alumni Magazine*, 62 (January, 1964), 4–5, 6; Kansas City, Mo., *Star*, December 28, 1924; Lawrence *Journal-World*, January 5, 1925.

40. Copy of decision in *E. H. Lindley, Appellant* v. *Jonathan M. Davis, et al., Appellees*, UA.

41. On the Lindley reinstatement campaign, see the contents of "Chancellor Ernest H. Lindley versus Governor Jonathan M. Davis, 1924–1925" (scrapbook, UA), and the several hundred letters on the matter in UA. Also, MBA, January 13, 1925.

42. Kansas City, Mo., *Star*, January 3, 1925; *KHJ*, 1925, pp. 9–10; Ellsworth, "Hectic Birth, Part II: Let's Take Another Vote," *Alumni Magazine*, 62 (February, 1964), 6–7.

43. *KHJ*, 1925, pp. 124, 131, 229, 235, 248–249, 253, 368, 369, 417; *KSJ*, 1925, pp. 112, 124, 199, 210, 217, 222, 223, 229, 243–244, 269, 284, 317–318, 320; Ellsworth, "Hectic Birth, Part II," *Alumni Magazine*, 62 (February, 1964), 6–7.

44. *KL*, 1925, pp. 337–339.

45. *Graduate Magazine*, 23 (May, 1925), 9–11; William E. Connelley, *History of Kansas, State and People: Kansas at the First Quarter Post of the Twentieth Century*, 5 vols. (Chicago, 1928), 4: 1869–1870.

46. Ernest H. Lindley to R. J. H. DeLoach, February 9, 1925 (copy), UA.

CHAPTER 22

1. *RBA*, 1918, pp. 31, 42; *BRUK*, 1918, pp. 13–14, 15; Frank Strong to Lacey M. Simpson, February 8, 1919 (copy), UA; *KL*, 1919, pp. 54–55.

2. *Graduate Magazine of the University of Kansas*, 18 (December, 1919), 79–80; *Kansan*, December 15, 1919.

3. *Ibid.*, December 12, 1919; *Graduate Magazine*, 18 (December, 1919), 80, and 19 (December, 1920), 5; untitled pamphlet in "Buildings of the University of Kansas" (scrapbooks, UA), vol. 1.

4. *Graduate Magazine*, 19 (December, 1920), 5, 7, 13; *Kansan*, October 6, 1920.

5. *Ibid.*, November 15, 1920, May 18, 1921; *Graduate Magazine*, 19 (December, 1920), 5, 7; *ibid.*, 19 (May, 1921), 3; *ibid.*, 20 (October, 1921), 5; *ibid.*, 21 (November, 1922), 10; *ibid.*, 23 (November, 1924), 5; J. Howard Compton, "The Building of the University of Kansas" (typewritten M.Arch. thesis, University of Kansas, 1932), 201.

6. *Kansan*, May 11, 1921; *Graduate Magazine*, 19 (May, 1921), 9, and 20 (October, 1921), 3–4; Compton, "Building of the University of Kansas," 167, 170; *BRUK*, 1928, p. 70; *University of Kansas Scores in Major Sports, 1886–1932: Football, Basketball, Baseball, Track* (Lawrence, 1932), 3.

7. *Ibid.*, 3; copy of the charter of the University of Kansas Physical Education Corporation, July 16, 1925, UA; Physical Education Corporation Minutes (MS, UA), January 10, 19, 1927; *BRUK*, 1928, p. 70; Compton, "Building of the University of Kansas," 168–170; Lawrence *Journal-World*, September 7, 1944, March 27, 1947.

8. Ernest H. Lindley to Pond Brothers, September 20, 1921 (copy), UA; Compton, "Building of the University of Kansas," 197–201; George C. Shaad, "The Memorial Union Building," *Graduate Magazine*, 23 (June, 1925), 9–10; *ibid.*, 24 (October, 1925), 7; *ibid.*, 25 (September, 1926), 9; *ibid.*, 26 (October, 1927), 14; *ibid.*, 32 (January, 1934), 7–8; Henry Werner, "The Growth of the Kansas Memorial Union" (typewritten MS, 1938, UA).

9. Ernest H. Lindley, "Rediscover Your University," *Graduate Magazine*, 19 (October, 1920), 5.

10. Henry E. Riggs to Glen Miller, July 2, 1920, Riggs to James M. Challis, July 4, 1920, and Riggs to William Allen White, October 16, 1920 (copies), UA.

11. Ernest H. Lindley to Henry E. Riggs, September 6, 1920, Lindley to William C. Hoad, December 13, 22, 1920, Hoad to Lindley, December 20, 1920, and Riggs to Luther Thomas, April 1, 1922 (copies), UA.

12. Ernest H. Lindley to N. T. Veatch, Jr., May 17, 28, 1923 (copies), and Veatch to Lindley, May 24, 1923, UA.

13. Alfred G. Hill to Allen S. Wilber, April 7, 1921 (copy), UA.

14. *Graduate Magazine*, 23 (October, 1924), 15; Lawrence *Journal-World*, January 11, 1965.

15. *Graduate Magazine*, 17 (June, 1919), frontispiece; *ibid.*, 26 (May, 1928), 3; *ibid.*, 27 (June, 1929), frontispiece; and *ibid.*, 17–27 (April, 1919–June, 1929), *passim*.

16. *Ibid.*, 3 (November, 1904), 67–68, and 19 (November, 1920), 12; Kansas University Endowment Association, Minutes, October 31, 1891, January 14, 1898, October 6, 1904, April 25, 1908, July 29, October 2, 1920, June 7, 1927, copies of charters dated July 27, 1923 (original charter filed October 31, 1891), and January 11, 1893, Kansas University Endowment Association Archives, University of Kansas; Frank Strong to J. Willis Gleed, April 29, 1920 (copy), UA.

17. "Statement of Receipts and Disbursements, June 4, 1931 to June 3, 1932," p. 12, Endowment Association Archives.

18. *Summerfield Scholarships, University of Kansas* (Lawrence, n.d.), 3, 6–11; MBR, August 15, 1929; *The Administration of the Summerfield Scholarships* (Lawrence, n.d.).

19. On Mrs. Watkins and her benefactions, see Allan G. Bogue, *Money at Interest: The Farm Mortgage on the Middle Border* (Ithaca, 1955), 79, 204; Robert Taft, *The Years on Mount Oread* (Lawrence, 1955), 150; *University of Kansas Alumni Magazine,* 50 (November, 1951), 6–7, 10; Kansas City, Mo., *Star,* February 24, 1935, June 1, 5, 1939; Kansas City, Mo., *Times,* June 6, 8, 1939; Lawrence *Journal-World,* June 1, 1939, December 17, 1949, June 16, 1958; "Watkins Gifts to Lawrence, Kansas and to the University of Kansas" (scrapbooks, UA); *BRUK,* 1926, pp. 22–23.

20. The University fees are listed in the annual catalogues. See also MBA, May 20, 26, 1925; MBR, March 25, 1927.

21. *BRUK,* 1926, pp. 13–17, 1928, pp. 18–20, 1930, pp. 14–17.

22. C. I. Reed to Ernest H. Lindley, May 31, 1923, with enclosed committee report, and H. H. Lane to Lindley, March 9, 1927, UA.

23. C. I. Reed to Ernest H. Lindley, May 31, 1923, with enclosed committee report, UA.

24. *BRUK,* 1924, p. 51.

25. *Ibid.,* 1920, p. 59; *KHJ,* 1921, p. 20.

26. *KL,* 1921, pp. 61, 67–68.

27. Compton, "Building of the University of Kansas," 157–161; *BRUK,* 1920, pp. 49–50; Topeka *Capital,* January 2, 21, 1921; Silas Porter to George Kruk, January 24, 1921, UA.

28. *BRUK,* 1924, pp. 18–19.

29. William W. Bishop to Ernest H. Lindley, March 31, 1921, Ray L. Gamble to the Board of Administration, May 31, 1922, Jonathan M. Davis to Ernest H. Lindley, May 31, 1923, Lindley to Davis, June 1, 1923 (copy), and William Allen White to Lindley, May 20, 1924, UA; Earl N. Manchester, "The New Watson Library Building," *Graduate Magazine,* 24 (April, 1926), 3–6; *BRUK,* 1926, pp. 62–63; George L. Chandler, "The New Kansas University Library," *Kansas Engineer,* 9 (January, 1924), 9–10.

30. George C. Shaad, "The Kansas University Electrical Engineering Laboratories," and Ralph Nichols, "The Kansas University Hydraulics Laboratory," *Kansas Engineer,* 11 (March, 1925), 11–13, 13–15; *BRUK,* 1922, p. 60; *Graduate Magazine,* 20 (November, 1921), 3–4.

31. *KSJ,* 1923, pp. 195–196, 202, 210, 356, 369, 400, 419; *KHJ,* 1923, pp. 255, 263, 331, 333, 343, 362, 403–404, 406, 482, 608–609; *KL,* 1923, pp. 54–55, 1925, p. 28, 1927, p. 59; Compton, "Building of the University of Kansas," 189–190.

32. *Ibid.,* 78–80, 204–206; *KL,* 1927, p. 59, 1929, p. 79; H. B. Hungerford, "New Snow Hall Takes Its Place on the Campus," *Graduate Magazine,* 28 (March, 1930), 7–9.

33. *BRUK,* 1928, pp. 10–12.

34. *Kansan,* January 14, April 22, 1920; University Senate Minutes (MS, UA), April 6, 1920; MBA, April 14, 1920.

35. "Salaries at the University of Kansas," *University of Kansas News Letter,* 20 (December, 1920); "Salaries at the University of Kansas," *ibid.,* 23 (December, 1922); *UKC,* 1933–1934, endsheet.

36. "What Kansas Has; What She Pays," *University of Kansas News Letter,* 20 (January, 1921).

37. "Salaries at the University of Kansas," *ibid.,* 20 (December, 1920), 1; "What Kansas Has," *ibid.,* 20 (January, 1921), 1; *RBA,* 1920, pp. xxxi, 14; *KSJ,* 1921, pp. 347, 351, 380, 391, 474, 526, 557; *KHJ,* 1921, pp. 463–464, 467, 502, 503, 529–530, 531, 532,

534–535, 569, 571; *KL*, 1921, pp. 60–61; "Salaries at the University of Kansas," *University of Kansas News Letter*, 23 (December, 1922), 1; *UKC*, 1933–1934, endsheet.

38. "Salaries at the University of Kansas," *University of Kansas News Letter*, 23 (December, 1922); George F. Zook, Lotus D. Coffman, and A. R. Mann, *Report of a Survey of the State Institutions of Higher Learning in Kansas*, Department of the Interior, Bureau of Education, Bulletin, 1923, no. 40 (Washington, 1923), 114–117.

39. *RBA*, 1922, p. 6; *KSJ*, 1923, pp. 195–196, 202, 210, 356, 369, 400, 419; *KHJ*, 1923, pp. 255, 263, 331, 333, 343, 362, 403, 406; *KL*, 1923, p. 54.

40. State of Kansas, Board of Administration, Business Manager, *Fourth Biennial Report*, 1924, p. 8; State of Kansas, Director of the Budget, *The Kansas Budget for the Biennium Beginning July 1, 1927*, p. 130; *BRUK*, 1928, pp. 7–9, 13; *KL*, 1929, p. 79; University Senate Minutes, March 15, 1929.

41. *UKC*, 1933–1934, endsheet.

CHAPTER 23

1. William F. Zornow, *Kansas: A History of the Jayhawk State* (Norman, 1957), 271, 273, 277; Fred L. Parrish, "Kansas Agriculture after 1930," John D. Bright, ed., *Kansas: The First Century*, 2 vols. (New York, 1956), 2: 141, 142, 149; University of Kansas Center for Regional Studies, *Kansas Statistical Abstract 1965* (Lawrence, 1966), 26; Stafford *Courier*, n.d. in "Kansas Dust Storms" (scrapbook, RHC); United States, Department of Commerce, Weather Bureau, *Climatological Data*, Kansas Section, 54, no. 13 (1940), 97; State of Kansas, Board of Agriculture, *Biennial Report*, 1935–1936, p. 9; Lawrence Svobida, *An Empire of Dust* (Caldwell, 1940), especially 171, 185.

2. *KL*, 1929, p. 79, 1931, pp. 78–79; *BRUK*, 1930, pp. 8–9, 13; *KSJ*, 1931, pp. 204, 206, 217, 378; *KHJ*, 1931, pp. 344, 348, 477, 509, 514, 659.

3. Charles M. Harger to Heads of Institutions, August 5, 1931, Harry H. Woodring to Ernest H. Lindley, August 8, 1931, and Harger to Lindley, August 8, 1931, UA; MBR, August 19, 1931; *BRUK*, 1932, pp. 14–15.

4. Charles M. Harger to Ernest H. Lindley, March 17, 1932, and Harger to Heads of Institutions, June 27, 1932 (copy), UA; "How the Appropriations Reductions Were Met" (typewritten MS, n.d., UA); *BRUK*, 1932, p. 7.

5. *Ibid.*, 1932, pp. 76–78; State of Kansas, Budget Director, *Kansas State Budget for the Biennium, 1934–35*, pp. 209, 213; Charles C. Wilson to Ernest H. Lindley, January 25, 1933, UA; *KSJ*, 1933, pp. 339, 340, 383–384, 390, 537, 554, 566, 592, 594, 603; *KHJ*, 1933, pp. 468–469, 471, 570, 630, 660, 694, 704, 706–707; *KL*, 1933, pp. 66–67.

6. MBR, May 6, 1933; Raymond Nichols, "How the University Budget Is Made," *Graduate Magazine of the University of Kansas*, 31 (April, 1933), 7; "University of Kansas, Analysis of Regular Payroll, 1931–'32 & 1933–'34" (typewritten MS, n.d., copy, UA).

7. Ernest H. Lindley, "Chancellor's Report," 1934 (typewritten MS), Lindley to Charles M. Harger, February 2, 1935 (copy), and Harger to Lindley, February 12, 1935, UA.

8. Lindley, "Chancellor's Report," 1934, and Lindley to Charles Sessions, February 12, 1935 (copy), UA; *BRUK*, 1936, pp. 14–15; State of Kansas, Budget Director, *Kansas State Budget for the Biennium, 1936–37*, pp. 109, 111; *KSJ*, 1935, pp. 343, 351, 390, 394–396, 511, 522; *KHJ*, 1935, pp. 478, 498, 555, 581, 585, 596; *KL*, 1935, pp. 66–67.

9. Ernest H. Lindley to Charles M. Harger, April 15, 1936 (copy), UA.

10. *BRUK*, 1936, pp. 14–22.

11. *Ibid.*, 1938, pp. 21–25.

12. *Ibid.*, 1936, pp. 15–24; State of Kansas, Budget Director, *Kansas State Budget for the Biennium 1938–39*, pp. 143, 147; *KSJ*, 1937, pp. 402–403, 415, 488, 531, 603, 664–665; *KHJ*, 1937, pp. 611–612, 650, 681, 683, 696, 706, 779; *KL*, 1937, pp. 66–67, 80.

13. *BRUK*, 1938, pp. 12, 16–21; *KSJ*, 1939, pp. 435, 449, 473, 480, 485, 586, 588–589, 598, 646, 647–648; *KHJ*, 1939, pp. 638–639, 644, 716, 720, 745–746, 752, 754, 784, 804; *KL*, 1939, pp. 55–56.

14. For examples, see *BRUK*, 1936, pp. 9–10, 1938, pp. 9–10, and 1940, pp. 7–8.

15. Kansas University Endowment Association, "Statement of Receipts and Disbursements, June 4, 1931 to June 3, 1932," and "Statement of Receipts and Disbursements, June 6, 1940 to June 4, 1941," Kansas University Endowment Association Archives, University of Kansas; F. A. Russell, "Beauty and Efficiency Are Results of Careful Study in Building," *Graduate Magazine*, 30 (February, 1932), 10–13; *Lawrence Journal-World*, December 25, 28, 1931; *Kansan*, March 27, 1931; "Watkins Gifts to Lawrence, Kansas and to the University of Kansas" (scrapbooks, UA); *BRUK*, 1940, p. 8.

16. *Kansan*, September 17, 1930, January 22, February 15, 1933; Ernest H. Lindley to the faculty and staff, September 12, 1931 (copy), in "Kansas University, Student Loan Fund" (scrapbook, UA); *Graduate Magazine*, 30 (October, 1931), 3, and 30 (November, 1931), 7.

17. *Kansan*, February 10, October 11, 1933.

18. *BRUK*, 1934, p. 12; *KL*, 1933, p. 69; *MBR*, May 6, 1933; Ernest H. Lindley to Earle W. Evans, October 31, 1933 (copy), UA.

19. Ernest H. Lindley to Charles M. Harger, September 19, 1933, and Lindley to C. B. Merriam, September 23, 1933 (copies), UA.

20. Ernest H. Lindley to J. B. Penfold, January 25, 1935 (copy), "A Brief of the CSEP at the University of Kansas, 1934–'35," and folder, "NYA—1936–37," UA; Kansas City, Mo., *Star*, January 14, 1934; Kansas City, Mo., *Times*, January 20, 1934; *Graduate Magazine*, 32 (February, 1934), cover-1.

21. MBR, May 28, 1937; *BRUK*, 1938, pp. 36–39.

22. Copy of resolution of the Washington Post, signed by Theo. Gardner and S. J. Churchill, January 18, 1919, Henry J. Allen to James A. Kimball, January 22, 1919 (copy), and Wilbur N. Mason to Frank Strong, December 23, 1919, Strong to the Board of Administration, February 11, 27, 1919 (copies), and Wilbur N. Mason to Frank Strong, February 24, 1919, UA.

23. Hugh C. Gresham to Ernest H. Lindley, March 27, April 12, 1922, Lindley to Gresham, April 8, 1922 (copy), and Bennet M. Allen to Lindley, April 8, May 20, 1922, UA.

24. John Ise to Ernest H. Lindley, May 6, 1925, William Allen White to Lindley, October 27, 1926, and Lindley to White, November 1, 1926, UA; John Ise, *The United States Oil Policy* (New Haven, 1926), 274, 488–527, and *passim*.

25. *Dove*, March 30, 1925.

26. For these and similar remarks, see *ibid.*, April 29, 1925, May 19, 1926, April 12, May 18, November 22, 1927.

27. Leavenworth *Times*, May 21, 1925; Horton *Headlight*, May 26, 1925; *Kansan*, May 24, 25, 1927; ? to Ernest F. McCue, August 24, 1927, and Ernest H. Lindley to A. F. Williams, June 19, 1925 (copies), UA.

28. Carroll D. Clark to Ernest H. Lindley, November 16, 1931, UA; *Kansan*, October 16, 1930; University Senate Minutes (MS, UA), May 1, 1934.

29. Walt Neibarger to Ernest H. Lindley, January 17, 1935, Paul B. Lawson to Charles F. Scott, January 29, 1935 (copy), and Charles M. Harger to Lindley, January 31, 1935, UA.

30. Paul B. Lawson to Charles F. Scott, January 29, 1935, and Ernest H. Lindley to Charles M. Harger, February 2, 1935 (copy), UA.

31. Ernest H. Lindley to Charles M. Harger, September 26, 1935 (copy), UA; *Dove*, September 25, 1935; *Kansan*, September 24, 1935. See also Topeka *Capital*, September 24, 1935.

32. *Kansan*, November 5, 1935; Henry Werner to Ernest H. Lindley, May 18, 1938, J. A. Searcy to Lindley, November 30, 1936, UA; *Douglas County Republican*, March 18, 1937.

33. *Kansan*, October 3, 1937.

34. Hunt asserted that Don Henry's decision to leave for Spain had come after a visit in Kansas City with friends whom Hunt did not know and that both he and his wife had tried to dissuade Don from leaving Kansas. *Ibid.*, October 5, 6, 1937.

35. Ernest H. Lindley to H. L. Snyder, November 4, 1937 (copy), UA; *Graduate Magazine*, 36 (February, 1938), 5.

36. *Ibid.*, 36 (February, 1938), 5; Kansas City, Mo., *Journal-Post*, February 22, 1938; *Kansan*, February 20, 23, 24, 25, 27, March 2, 1938.

37. *Dove*, March 14, 1938; MBR, June 4, October 29, November 10, 1938; *KHJ*, 1941, pp. 803–807.

38. *KHJ*, 1941, pp. 802–803; MBR, April 10, 1939; Clarence P. Oakes to Ernest H. Lindley, June 19, 1939, and Lindley to Oakes, June 27, 1939 (copy), UA.

39. Clarence P. Oakes to Deane W. Malott, December 2, 13, 1939, and Malott to Oakes, December 7, 15, 16, 1939 (copies), UA.

40. *KHJ*, 1941, pp. 796–808.

41. The report of the Committee on Public Relations is with Paul B. Lawson to Ernest H. Lindley, October 13, 1938, UA.

CHAPTER 24

1. University Senate Minutes (MS, UA), February 7, 1922.

2. *Ibid.*, October 6, 1924.

3. *Ibid.*, March 4, May 6, 1930, November 3, December 1, 1931; U. G. Mitchell and others, "Report of Committee on Functions of the University Senate" (MS, n.d., copy), UA.

4. *Ibid.*

5. As finally settled in April and May, 1932, there were twelve University committees, appointed as Chancellor Lindley might direct. They dealt with alumni interests, assignment of quarters, commencement, museums, freshman week, health and housing, the Memorial Union, Rhodes Scholarships, Summerfield Scholarships, student interests, the student loan fund, and vocational guidance. In addition to the Advisory Committee and the Committee on Committees, the Senate also had twelve: on athletics, convocations, student eligibility for nonathletic activities, examinations, forensics, honors and prizes, libraries, publications and printing, relations with other educational institutions, the ROTC, University Extension work, and the Summer Session. University Senate Minutes, December 1, 1931, March 1, April 5, May 3, 1932.

6. *Ibid.*, January 5, March 1, 1932; MBR, February 15, 1932.

7. *Ibid.*, December 1, 1931, January 5, March 1, 1932.

8. *Ibid.*, March 1, 1932. The original members of the University Survey Committee were Professors Laurel E. Anderson of Voice, Thomas E. Atkinson of Law, Carroll D. Clark of Sociology, Domenico Gagliardo of Economics, Frederic H. Guild of Political Science, F. E. Kester of Physics, J. O. Jones of Applied Mechanics, William

Savage Johnson of English, Edmund H. Hollands of Philosophy, H. H. Lane of Zoology, William C. McNown of Civil Engineering, U. G. Mitchell of Mathematics, B. A. Nash of Education, A. L. Owen of Spanish, and O. O. Stoland of Physiology; Dean Ellis B. Stouffer of the Graduate School; and Associate Professor A. H. Turney of Education. Owen and Atkinson left the committee during the 1932–1933 year. William Savage Johnson, chairman of the Senate Advisory Committee, served as chairman of the University Survey Committee during its first nine meetings; then he asked to be relieved and U. G. Mitchell succeeded him. After discussion, both the committee on service load and the faculty efficiency committee decided to make no recommendations. *Ibid.*, October 6, November 8, 1932; "Report of the University Survey Committee, Submitted to the University Senate, December 8, 1936" (typewritten MS, UA), iv–v.

9. *Ibid.*, v; University Senate Minutes, January 8, March 5, 1935, April 6, 1937.

10. *Ibid.*, April 2, 1935; "Report of the . . . Survey Committee," 1–2.

11. *Ibid.*, 3–5; University Senate Minutes, April 2, 1935.

12. For the Survey Committee's judgments on curricular matters, see chapter 28.

13. "Report of the . . . Survey Committee," 19–20, 23–24; University Senate Minutes, May 7, 20, 1935.

14. Previously, the budget committee had consisted of Dean Ellis B. Stouffer of the Graduate School, as chairman, and Raymond Nichols, executive secretary to the chancellor, as secretary. The other members were the deans and department heads concerned in any particular conference. After the committee had made its decisions, the budget went to the chancellor for "further consideration and minor adjustment," and then to the regents. Raymond Nichols, "How the University Budget Is Made," *Graduate Magazine of the University of Kansas*, 31 (April, 1933), 7; "Report of the . . . Survey Committee," 21–22; University Senate Minutes, May 7, 1935.

15. *Ibid.*, May 20, 1935; "Report of the . . . Survey Committee," 22–23.

16. *Ibid.*, hand-numbered pp. 55–60; University Senate Minutes, May 20, 1935.

17. *Ibid.*, January 12, April 6, 1937; "Report of the . . . Survey Committee," 59–60.

18. MBR, November 7, 1929, January 4, June 6, 1930.

19. *KHJ*, 1933, p. 570; *KL*, 1933, p. 71.

20. MBR, June 19, August 21, December 27, 1933; *A Survey of the Five State Institutions of Higher Education in Kansas: A Confidential Report to the State Board of Regents*, June 30, 1934 (n.p., 1934), 27. On March 5, 1931, a state law changed the name of the Kansas State Agricultural College to the Kansas State College of Agriculture and Applied Science. *Thirty-fourth Biennial Report of the Kansas State College of Agriculture and Applied Science* (Topeka, 1932), p. 28.

21. *A Survey of the Five State Institutions*, 32–34.

22. *Ibid.*, 35–40.

23. *Ibid.*, 40–43.

24. *Ibid.*, 43–54.

25. *Ibid.*, 55–57, 58–60.

26. *Ibid.*, 61–62.

27. *Ibid.*, 63–64.

28. *Ibid.*, 65–67.

29. *Ibid.*, 28–31, 68–72, 101–111.

30. State of Kansas, Board of Regents, *Report of the Board of Regents on the State Educational Institutions* (Topeka, 1934), 5–6, 13, and *passim*.

31. The membership of the Board may be found in the biennial reports of the Board of Regents.

32. William E. Connelley, *History of Kansas, State and People: Kansas at the First Quarter Post of the Twentieth Century*, 5 vols. (Chicago, 1928), 3: 1224–1225; Sara Mullin Baldwin and Robert Morton Baldwin, eds., *Illustriana Kansas: Biographical Sketches of Kansas Men and Women of Achievement Who Have Been Awarded Life Membership in Kansas Illustriana Society* (Hebron, 1933), 579.

33. John D. Bright, ed., *Kansas: The First Century*, 4 vols. (New York, 1956), 3: 29, 30; Baldwin and Baldwin, eds., *Illustriana Kansas*, 1231; *Graduate Magazine*, 29 (October, 1930), 24; *ibid.*, 37 (May, 1939), 4; Kansas City, Mo., *Star*, February 3, 1935.

34. Baldwin and Baldwin, eds., *Illustriana Kansas*, 332, 884, 1186; *RBR*, 1932, p. 11; Bright, ed., *Kansas*, 3: 141–142; *Graduate Magazine*, 37 (September, 1938), 15; *ibid.*, 37 (May, 1939), 4; Kansas City Mo., *Star*, November 15, 1957.

35. Bright, ed., *Kansas*, 3: 128; *RBR*, 1934, p. 5, 1936, p. 5, 1938, p. 5; *Graduate Magazine*, 37 (May, 1939), 4–5; *Who's Who in the Kansas Legislature: Session 1929* (Great Bend, 1929), 65; "Kansas Senators and Representatives: Territorial and State, 1855–1958, Alphabetical List" (typewritten notebook, Kansas State Historical Society, Topeka), 39.

36. *RBR*, 1938, p. 5; *Graduate Magazine*, 36 (October, 1937), 16; *ibid.*, 37 (May, 1939), 4–5; Topeka *Capital*, June 28, 1938; Lawrence *Journal-World*, April 7, 1938.

37. *RBR*, 1938, p. 5; Ernest H. Lindley to William Allen White, January 11, 1938 (copy), White to Lindley, January 13, 1938, and White to Walter Huxman, January 14, 1938 (copy), UA.

38. George Mack, Jr., ed., *The 1933 Kansas Legislative Blue Book* (Lawrence, 1933), 70; *Who's Who in the Kansas Legislature, Session 1931* (Great Bend, 1931), 88–89; *Democratic State Handbook: Distributed by the Democratic State Committee* (n.p., 1932), 13; *Graduate Magazine*, 37 (September, 1938), 15; Topeka *Capital*, June 29, 1938.

39. *KHJ*, 1939, pp. 13, 118, 123, 311, 322, 384, 415, 578, 582, 609, 610, 640, 644–645, 651, 652; *KSJ*, 1939, pp. 98, 103, 219, 246, 256–257, 269, 271, 449, 458, 469, 494–495, 516, 529.

40. *KL*, 1939, pp. 551–554.

41. To provide for the four-year staggered terms of the future, the terms of Harris and McCoy expired December 31, 1940; those of O'Neil, Mrs. Muir, and Markham, December 31, 1941; those of McLaughlin, Poole, and Mrs. Reigart, December 31, 1942; that of Snyder, December 31, 1943. When O'Neil and Snyder died in 1940, Governor Ratner appointed Oscar S. Stauffer and Willis N. Kelly respectively to fill the unexpired terms. Kelly, a Democrat, was a graduate of the Agricultural College in the class of 1921 and was now both mayor of Hutchinson and vice-president in charge of production of the William Kelly Milling Company. *Graduate Magazine*, 37 (May, 1939), 4–5; *ibid.*, 39 (December, 1940), 15; Baldwin and Baldwin, eds., *Illustriana Kansas*, 842–843; *RBR*, 1940, pp. 2, 6; Topeka *Capital*, April 21, 1951. Because of reappointments there were but four new regents during the 1940s. They were Elizabeth Stephens Haughey (K.U., 1910), a Democrat of Concordia, appointed in 1941 to succeed Mrs. Muir; Jerry E. Driscoll (K.U. Law, 1906), a Democratic lawyer and large landholder from Russell, appointed in 1943 succeeding Walter Markham; Dr. LaVerne B. Spake, a Republican, a prominent eye, ear, and throat specialist of Kansas City, appointed in 1943 to succeed Mrs. Reigart; and Walter Fees, a Republican oilman from Iola who joined the Board in 1950 after the death of Fred M. Harris. *RBR*, 1940, p. 2, 1942, p. 3, 1944, pp. 3, 5, 1946, p. 3, 1948, p. 3, 1950, pp. 4, 5; *Graduate Magazine*, 40 (February, 1942), 10; *ibid.*, 40 (March–April, 1942), 6; *ibid.*, 41 (February, 1943), 5; *ibid.*, 42 (November, 1943), 18; *ibid.*, 44 (December, 1945), 14; To-

peka *Journal*, August 23, 1950; Kansas City, Mo., *Times*, August 24, 1950; Topeka *Capital*, April 21, 1951.

42. Kansas City, Mo., *Times*, May 19, 1939.

CHAPTER 25

1. Ernest H. Lindley to the Board of Regents, December 1, 1938 (copy), UA; MBR, December 5, 1938; University Senate Minutes (MS, UA), December 6, 1938; Margaret Lynn, "Ernest Hiram Lindley," *Commemoration of Ernest Hiram Lindley: Chancellor, 1920–1939, Chancellor Emeritus, 1939–1940, the University of Kansas* (Lawrence, n.d.), x; Alfred, N.Y., *Sun*, January 16, 1941.

2. University Senate Minutes, December 9, 1938; unidentified clipping in "Deane Waldo Malott, Chancellor of the University of Kansas" (scrapbook, UA).

3. "Deane W. Mallott," with Edmund P. Learned to Olin Templin, December 27, 1938, "Letters about the Appointment of Deane W. Malott to the Chancellorship of the University of Kansas, from Olin Templin, Edmund Learned, Charles M. Harger, Ralph M. Hower, Frank L. Carson, H. L. Snyder" (MSS, UA); Chanute *Tribune*, March 21, 1940.

4. Olin Templin to Edmund P. Learned, December 5, 16, 1938, January 5, 1939 (copies), Templin to Charles M. Harger, December 16, 1938, January 5, 1939 (copies), Learned to Templin, December 12, 27, 1938, Ralph Hower to Templin, December 27, 1938, Templin to Frank L. Carson, January 5, 1939 (copy), and Templin to H. L. Snyder, January 7, 1939 (copy), "Letters about the Appointment of Deane W. Malott."

5. According to a member of the alumni committee, in late January, 1939, four candidates besides Malott were being seriously considered: Herschel W. Arant, former dean of the University's Law School and then dean at Ohio State; Will French, a Kansas alumnus then professor of education in the Columbia University Teachers College; Law Professor Clarence M. Updegraff, a distinguished scholar at the State University of Iowa; and President Thurston J. Davies of Colorado College. H. L. Snyder to Olin Templin, January 21, 1939, and Frank L. Carson to Templin, February 16, 1939, *ibid.*; MBR, January 31, February 23, 1939; H. L. Snyder to Deane W. Malott, February 2, 1939, UA.

6. Edmund P. Learned to Olin Templin, March 2, 1939, "Letters about the Appointment of Deane W. Malott"; Kansas City, Mo., *Star*, April 10, 1939, MBR, April 10, 1939.

7. Lawrence *Journal-World*, September 22, 1939.

8. Deane W. Malott to K. Wayne Davidson, April 11, 1940 (copy), UA.

9. MBR, August 2, 1940.

10. "University of Kansas, A Survey of Building Needs, November, 1940" (copy), UA.

11. William F. Zornow, *Kansas: A History of the Jayhawk State* (Norman, 1957), 294; *BRUK*, 1940, pp. 11–17.

12. State of Kansas, Director of the Budget, *Kansas State Budget for the Biennium 1942–43*, pp. 137, 139; Lawrence *Journal-World*, December 11, 1940; *KSJ*, 1941, pp. 367, 374, 431, 437, 563, 564, 600, 601, 630; *KHJ*, 1941, pp. 576, 577, 658, 707, 708, 710–711, 719, 743–744; *KL*, 1941, p. 74.

13. Of the money appropriated for the mineral resources building, $71,500 for furniture and equipment would come from the new fund, and so would another $12,000 needed to dig a service tunnel to it. *KHJ*, 1941, pp. 16, 390, 391, 426, 453, 464,

468; *KSJ*, 1941, pp. 87, 92, 131, 155–156, 203, 208, 223, 244, 251, 275, 287, 297, 303, 310–311, 356, 370, 376; *KL*, 1941, pp. 74, 698–699.

14. *KHJ*, 1941, pp. 66, 72, 134, 161, 196, 289, 294, 299, 304; *KSJ*, 1941, pp. 240, 247, 291, 441, 450; *KL*, 1941, pp. 598–601.

15. Leigh A. Wellborn, "The Building of the University of Kansas—1931 to 1951" (typewritten B.S. thesis, University of Kansas, 1951), 8–9; *Graduate Magazine of the University of Kansas*, 41 (November, 1942), 6; Lawrence *Journal-World*, April 10, November 25, 1941, July 2, 1943, January 25, 1946; *Kansan*, July 20, 1943.

16. *Kansan*, April 7, 10, 14, 1935, April 23, 1936, April 23, 1937, February 8, 1938, September 28, 1939, May 26, 1940.

17. *Ibid.*, January 26, 28, February 5, 1941; Kansas City, Mo., *Times*, January 31, 1941.

18. *Ibid.*, December 10, 1941.

19. Lawrence *Journal-World*, September 22, 1942.

20. *Kansan*, October 16, 17, 29, 1940, May 27, 1941; Payne Ratner to Deane W. Malott, August 27, 1942, Malott to Ratner, August 28, 1942 (copy), and Malott to Parents of K.U. Students, November 23, 1942 (copy), UA; *BRUK*, 1942, p. 17, 1944, p. 20, 1946, pp. 19–20.

21. Deane W. Malott to Fred M. Harris, December 11, 1941, and Raymond Nichols to Members of the Faculty, December 17, 1941 (copies), UA; MBR, January 16, 1942.

22. University Senate Minutes, November 23, 1943, January 1, 1945.

23. *Ibid.*, January 6, 1942; *K.U. Students and the War: Suggestions Regarding the Selection of Courses at the University of Kansas during the Present Period of Conflict and Industrial Expansion* (Lawrence, 1942), 3; *Kansan*, January 16, 1942; *BRUK*, 1944, p. 5; *From the K.U. News Bureau*, July 7, 1943.

24. Lawrence *Journal-World*, December 18, 22, 1942.

25. James C. Malin to Raymond Nichols, May 26, 1942 (copy), Ruth Kenney to Malin, June 5, 1942, Malin to Kenney, June 9, 1942 (copy), Malin to Deane W. Malott, June 20, 1942 (copy), Malin to R. V. Phinney, July 14, 1942 (copy), in possession of author.

26. J. W. Ashton to Deane W. Malott, December 7, 1942, UA; University Senate Minutes, March 19, 1943; *UKC*, 1944–1945, pp. 14–15, 1946–1947, p. 14; Kansas City, Mo., *Star*, March 24, 1943; *Kansan*, March 28, May 7, 1943.

27. *Ibid.*, May 27, 1941.

28. *K.U. Students and the War.*

29. *From the K.U. News Bureau*, September, 1942; Lawrence *Journal-World*, September 21, October 7, 1942; University Senate Minutes July 24, 1942, May 7, 1943.

30. *Graduate Magazine*, 40 (March–April, 1942), 10.

31. Deane W. Malott to Frank L. McVey, August 17, 1942 (copy), UA; Lawrence *Journal-World*, September 17, 1942; *Graduate Magazine*, 41 (September, 1942), 7; *ibid.*, 41 (January, 1943), 6; *ibid.*, 41 (February, 1943), 5; *Kansas Engineer*, 28 (January, 1943), 5–7; *Kansan*, May 31, 1944; Topeka *Capital*, May 10, 1943.

32. *Graduate Magazine*, 40 (March–April, 1942), 10; *ibid.*, 41 (January, 1943), 6; *Kansan*, March 7, 1943.

33. *Graduate Magazine*, 41 (January, 1943), 6; *ibid.*, 41 (February, 1943), 5; *ibid.*, 42 (September, 1943), 14–15; *Jayhawker* (November, 1943), 30; Kansas City, Mo., *Times*, August 10, 1943; *Kansan*, July 30, August 13, 1943; Lawrence *Journal-World*, August 20, 1943.

34. H. R. Wahl, "Annual Report to the Chancellor on the School of Medicine, 1942–1943" (typewritten MS, n.d.), UA.

35. *Graduate Magazine*, 42 (September, 1943), 7.

36. Robert Taft, *Fifty Years in Bailey Chemical Laboratory at the University of Kansas* (Lawrence, 1950), 23; *From the K.U. News Bureau*, December, 1942, January 18, May, 1943; *BRUK*, 1944, p. 5.

37. L. R. Lind, "The Humanities and National Defense," *University Newsletter*, November 8, 1941; "Morale and the Democratic Community," *ibid.*, January 3, 1942.

38. Deane W. Malott to Charles M. Baker, March 17, 1942, UA; *Kansan*, April 21, 1942; *The War Information Center and Civilian Morale Service, University of Kansas, Lawrence, Kansas* (Lawrence, n.d.); *From the K.U. News Bureau*, February, 1943.

39. Robert G. Sproul to Deane W. Malott, March 13, 1942, Malott to Sproul, March 17, 1942 (copy), and Malott to Fred M. Harris, March 17, 1942 (copy), UA.

40. The problem was complicated by the fact that no one was sure just which federal agency was authorized to declare that the Nisei might relocate in a particular area. A Department of Relocation, headed by Milton Eisenhower, was approving certain areas, but elsewhere army and navy officers were prohibiting the Nisei from schools with service training programs; and at still other places the FBI was involved. When the regents inquired in 1942 about the admission of Nisei students to the schools under their control, the FBI was noncommittal; but the FBI did approve the Nisei's admission to Kansas Wesleyan University. "Memorandum of Mr. Brighton's Visit of March 26" [1942], signed by Raymond Nichols (copy), Deane W. Malott to William Allen White, October 15, 28, 1942 (copies), and Malott to Harry C. Herman, February 22, 1945 (copy), UA; *Kansan*, January 3, February 7, 1943, April 11, September 26, 1944; *Gadfly*, November 11, 1943.

41. *BRUK*, 1942, p. 22.

42. Taft, *Fifty Years*, 23–24; *BRUK*, 1942, p. 6.

43. *Kansan*, February 4, 1943, March 24, 1944. See also *Gadfly*, November 11, 1943.

44. "Report to the Board of Regents on the Meeting of Heads of the Five Institutions of Higher Learning, August 6, 1942, as Amended August 26, 1942" (copy), UA.

45. *BRUK*, 1942, pp. 12–16, 22, and 1944, p. 22; Deane W. Malott to E. A. Briles, February 1, 1943 (copy), UA; State of Kansas, Director of the Budget, *Kansas State Budget for the Biennium 1944–45*, pp. 161, 165; *KSJ*, 1943, pp. 161, 164, 171, 176, 252; *KHJ*, 1943, pp. 207, 209, 278–279, 285, 288, 296, 301; *KL*, 1943, pp. 86–87.

46. *BRUK*, 1942, p. 7; *Reception Formally Opening the New Military Science Building of the University of Kansas* (Lawrence, 1943); *KL*, 1943, p. 95.

CHAPTER 26

1. Deane W. Malott, address at opening convocation, September 28, 1943 (MS, copy), in "Deane Waldo Malott, Chancellor of the University of Kansas" (scrapbook, UA).

2. For these and similar statements, see the following works by Malott: "The Place of the Scholar in This Turbulent World" (address at the Scholarship Convocation, Missouri State Teachers College, Warrensburg, Missouri, May 12, 1948, MS, copy), "Adventures in Chaos" (address before the National Grain and Feed Dealers Association Convention, Chicago, Illinois, October 1, 1948, MS, copy), and "The World on Your Doorstep" (commencement address, University of Minnesota, July 21, 1949, mimeographed), all in "Deane Waldo Malott, Chancellor of the University of Kansas, Addresses," UA; and *Eighty-fifth Annual Opening Convocation of the University of*

Kansas: Address by Deane W. Malott, Chancellor, Monday Morning, September Eighteenth, Nineteen Hundred Fifty (Lawrence, 1950), 3–7.

3. See chapters 28 and 29.

4. *BRUK*, 1946, p. 20, 1948, p. 31, 1950, p. 29.

5. Lawrence *Journal-World*, June 7, 1946; *BRUK*, 1946, pp. 15–16, 1948, p. 25.

6. College Faculty Minutes (MS, College of Liberal Arts and Sciences, University of Kansas), March 18, 1958; Kansas City, Mo., *Times*, June 4, 1948.

7. Irvin E. Youngberg to Deane W. Malott, November 5, 1946, and Malott to Andrew F. Schoeppel, January 28, 1946 (copy), UA; *Kansan*, September 30, 1947; Kansas City, Mo., *Star*, July 18, 1946; MBR, June 13–14, 1946.

8. *Ibid.*, June 13–14, 1946; Deane W. Malott to H. W. Thomas, July 11, 1946 (copy), and Irvin E. Youngberg to Malott, November 5, 1946, UA; Lawrence *Journal-World*, July 30, 1946, February 20, 1947; Kansas City, Mo., *Star*, May 23, 1948.

9. Deane W. Malott to H. W. Thomas, July 11, 1946 (copy), and Irvin E. Youngberg to Malott, November 5, 1946, UA; Kansas City, Mo., *Star*, July 18, 1946; Taft, *Years on Mount Oread*, 172.

10. *BRUK*, 1946, p. 27, 1948, pp. 23, 24.

11. *BRUK*, 1944, pp. 11–19; State of Kansas, Director of the Budget, *Kansas State Budget for the Biennium, 1946–47*, pp. 175, 179.

12. *Ibid.*, 175, 179; Deane W. Malott to Andrew F. Schoeppel, January 27, 1945 (copy), UA; *KSJ*, 1945, pp. 136, 143, 149, 152, 178, 183, 189, 191, 203, 208, 219, 223; *KHJ*, 1945, pp. 9, 11–12, 142, 144, 188, 189, 194, 197, 200, 209, 211; *KL*, 1945, pp. 89–90, 96–97.

13. "University of Kansas Post-War Capital Needs," n.d., and Deane W. Malott to Hubert Brighton, October 19, 1946 (copy), UA; *BRUK*, 1946, pp. 6–7.

14. *Ibid.*, 1946, pp. 14–18; State of Kansas, Department of the Budget, *Kansas State Budget for the Biennium, 1948–49*, pp. 175, 179; *KHJ*, 1947, pp. 10, 13–14.

15. *RBR*, 1946, p. 11; *KSJ*, 1947, pp. 212, 218, 229, 234, 274, 276, 336; *KHJ*, 1947, pp. 300, 302, 314, 330, 336, 340; *KL*, 1947, pp. 105–106, 113.

16. *BRUK*, 1942, pp. 18–19, 1946, pp. 23–25, 1950, pp. 31–33.

17. Deane W. Malott to Walter Fees, February 22, 1949, and Malott to Willis N. Kelly, September 17, 1947 (copies), UA.

18. *BRUK*, 1948, pp. 23, 29.

19. *Ibid.*, 1948, pp. 22–29; State of Kansas, Department of the Budget, *Kansas State Budget for the Biennium 1950–1951*, pp. 169, 173. The name of the Kansas City medical complex was changed from the Medical School to the Medical Center in 1947.

20. *KSJ*, 1949, pp. 170, 175, 183, 198, 205, 207, 208–209, 216, 220, 275, 279, 302, 307; *KHJ*, 1949, pp. 184, 188, 199, 202, 278, 281, 321, 338, 339, 345, 347, 361; *KL*, 1949, pp. 45–46, 105–106, 114, 120, 753; *Kansan*, April 1, 1949; Lawrence *Journal-World*, April 4, 1949.

21. *KL*, 1949, pp. 116–118.

22. Henry L. Snyder, "Twenty Years of the General Research Fund," *Research*, June, 1971, pp. 2–3; *BRUK*, 1950, pp. 20–27; State of Kansas, Department of the Budget, *Kansas State Budget for the Biennium 1952–53*, pp. 169, 173.

23. *Ibid.*, 169, 173; *KSJ*, 1951, pp. 272–273, 282, 289–290, 311; *KHJ*, 1951, pp. 335, 338, 343, 350–351; *KL*, 1951, pp. 104–105. The fees in the College, the Graduate School, and the Schools of Education, Engineering, and Fine Arts rose from $50 to $60 for residents and from $100 to $130 for nonresidents; those in the Schools of Business, Journalism, Law, and Pharmacy went from $55 to $65 for residents and from $110 to $140 for nonresidents. In the School of Medicine the fees varied with the year;

matriculating resident students found their fees increased from $160 to $180 a semester, while the fees of matriculating nonresidents went up from $310 to $360. The increases for juniors and seniors were from $100 to $150 per quarter for residents, and from $200 to $300 per quarter for nonresidents. *UKC*, 1950–1951, General Information, 24; *ibid.*, 1951–1952, General Information, 24; MBR, March 16, 1951; *BRUK*, 1952, pp. 22, 23, 25, 26.

24. *KSJ*, 1951, pp. 71, 77, 115, 118, 215, 224, 236, 240, 288, 311; *KHJ*, 1951, pp. 93, 97, 119, 127, 134–136, 309, 314, 316, 329, 334–335; *KL*, 1951, pp. 113, 115. It should be noted that on October 20, 1950, the Board of Regents authorized the University to use $1,136,000 of accumulated savings from war programs for a number of special repair and building projects. But the 1951 legislature captured the entire amount and then authorized specific projects totaling $631,000, thus forcing the University to make a contribution to the General Revenue Fund of $505,000. Raymond Nichols to the University Press of Kansas, July 17, 1972, copy in possession of author.

25. Lawrence *Journal-World*, October 10, 1949; J. D. Stranathan and R. Q. Brewster, "K.U. Science Building Provides Class and Research Facilities," Kansas City, Mo., *Star*, August 8, 1954; *Graduate Magazine*, 53 (January, 1955), 5–7.

26. "KU Today," *University of Kansas Newsletter*, 65 (August 28, 1965), 5; Deane W. Malott to Andrew F. Schoeppel, March 30, 1946 (copy), UA; MBR, October 20, 1950.

27. Kansas City, Mo., *Times*, May 24, 1951.

28. *The Bells of Mount Oread: University of Kansas World War II Campanile and Driveway* (Lawrence, 1951); *KL*, 1951, p. 105; Deane W. Malott to W. W. Fuller, October 15, 1946 (copy), UA.

29. University Senate Minutes, December 5, 1939, January 9, April 2, 1940; Deane W. Malott to C. I. Reed, March 3, 1947 (copy), UA.

30. Mattie Crumrine, A. W. Davidson, and F. E. Kester, "Faculty Participation in the Government of the University of Kansas: A Committee Report to the Executive Committee of the University of Kansas Chapter of the American Association of University Professors, April 3, 1947" (mimeographed); Minutes of AAUP Chapter Meeting, May 24, October 23, 1947, January 23, 1948, February 23, 1949; Edwin O. Stene to the Executive Committee of the Kansas Chapter, American Association of University Professors, n.d., all in American Association of University Professors, University of Kansas Chapter, Papers, UA. Also "Faculty Participation in the Government of the University of Kansas," n.d., UA.

31. See Dewitt Dearborn, James W. Drury, J. O. Maloney, Rufus H. Thompson, and Marston M. McCluggage, "Faculty Participation in the Government of the University of Kansas, January 26, 1951" (mimeographed), UA.

32. University Senate Minutes, November 1, 1949.

33. In addition to Chairman Stene the committee members were E. E. Bayles, George M. Beal, A. W. Davidson, J. O. Jones, and L. J. Pritchard.

34. University Senate Minutes, November 9, 1948, October 11, 1949, March 14, May 24, 1950.

35. See Leland J. Pritchard, J. Eldon Fields, W. D. Paden, and others to Deane W. Malott, January 22, 1951 (copy), AAUP Papers.

36. *Kansan*, February 8, 1951; Lawrence *Journal-World*, February 15, July 2, 1951; MBR, February 15, June 26, 1951; University Senate Minutes, April 12, 1951. On Murphy's earlier career, see chapter 30.

37. MBR, September 17, 1951.

38. *Time*, 58 (July 16, 1951), 84–85.

CHAPTER 27

1. Franklin D. Murphy to Oscar Stauffer, November 23, 1956 (copy), UA.

2. *General Statutes of Kansas (Annotated) 1949* (Topeka, 1950), 819; Franklin D. Murphy, *Statement by Franklin D. Murphy on the Occasion of His Inauguration as the Ninth Chancellor of the University of Kansas, September 17, 1951* (n.p., 1951), 3–5, 9–10.

3. *Ibid.*, 6–7.

4. *Ibid.*, 8, 9–10.

5. Franklin D. Murphy, *Education for What?* in *Education for What? by Franklin D. Murphy, Chancellor, University of Kansas, and Education in the Shadow of the Church by Robert A. L. Mortvedt, President, Bethany College: Addresses Delivered at the Inauguration of Dr. Mortvedt as President of Bethany College, November 12, 1953* (Lindsborg, 1953), 1–6; Kansas City, Mo., *Star*, April 11, 1956; Murphy to the Editor of the Salina *Journal*, n.d., in Lawrence *Journal-World*, December 11, 1958.

6. Franklin D. Murphy, "The Problem of Cultural Leadership in the Great Plains," Paul G. Ruggiers, ed., *Cultural Leadership in the Great Plains: A Report of the Great Plains Conference on Higher Education Held at the University of Oklahoma* (Norman, 1956), 4–16.

7. Franklin D. Murphy to James A. McCain, December 2, 1954 (copy), UA; Topeka *Journal*, August 29, 1953, December 27, 1954; Topeka *Capital*, December 31, 1954; Wichita *Morning Eagle*, February 6, 1960; *University of Kansas Alumni Magazine*, 53 (February, 1955), 22; *ibid.*, 58 (January, 1960), 15; and *ibid.*, 61 (May, 1963), 12.

8. *Ibid.*, 54 (January, 1956), 10; *ibid.*, 55 (January, 1957), 10.

9. Topeka *Journal*, December 14, 1957; Topeka *Capital*, December 20, 1957; *Alumni Magazine*, 56 (January, 1958), 10; *ibid.*, 57 (January, 1959), 20; John D. Bright, ed., *Kansas: The First Century*, 4 vols. (New York, 1956), 3: 110–111.

10. Franklin D. Murphy to "Dear Alumnus," *University Newsletter*, 52 (May 23, 1953); *Private Support for Books and Libraries at the University of Kansas* (Lawrence, 1958), 3–4; Kansas City, Mo., *Star*, March 23, 1958; *BRUK*, 1960, pp. 695–696.

11. Letter from Maurice E. Barker, June 1, 1954, *Preliminary Report on the Charter Year of the Greater University Fund* (mimeographed, Lawrence, 1954), 2; Greater University Fund, University of Kansas, *Annual Report*, 1953–1954, pp. 3, 6, 7, 1954–1955, pp. 2, 6, 1955–1956, pp. 5–6, 1956–1957, pp. 6–8, 1959–1960, pp. 3, 4; *BRUK*, 1960, pp. 695–696, 698; Roy A. Roberts to Franklin D. Murphy, n.d., *Alumni Magazine*, 56 (June, 1958), 9.

12. Franklin D. Murphy, "National Security and New Knowledge," American Council on Education, Committee on Institutional Research Policy, *Sponsored Research Policy of Colleges and Universities* (Washington, D.C., 1954), 50–54; *BRUK*, 1960, p. 695.

13. MBR, December 14, 1956; *BRUK*, 1952, pp. 22–24, 1960, pp. 705–706.

14. *Ibid.*, 1960, pp. 705, 706.

15. *Ibid.*, 1956, p. 5, 1952, pp. 15–18, 26, 1954, pp. 21, 24; University Senate Minutes (MS, UA), November 18, 1952; Franklin D. Murphy to Howard Bentley, March 18, 1953 (copy), UA.

16. State of Kansas, Department of the Budget, *Kansas State Budget for the Biennium, 1954–55*, pp. 161, 165; Franklin D. Murphy to Howard Bentley, March 18, 1953 (copy), UA; *KSJ*, 1953, pp. 212, 220, 232, 241; *KHJ*, 1953, pp. 346, 347, 391, 393, 394; *KL*, 1953, pp. 51–52, 71; University Senate Minutes, April 14, 1953.

17. MBR, September 23–24, 1954.

18. University Senate Minutes, May 24, 1954.

19. American Association of University Professors, University of Kansas Chapter, "Report of the Committee on the Economic Status of the Profession, January 30, 1953," UA.

20. University Senate Minutes, April 14, 1953.

21. State of Kansas, Department of Administration, Budget Division, *Governor's Budget Report for the Fiscal Year 1956*, pp. 204–212; *KHJ*, 1955, p. 47; *KL*, 1955, pp. 65–67, 75.

22. State of Kansas, Department of Administration, Budget Division, *Governor's Budget Report for the Fiscal Year 1957*, pp. 220–232; *KL*, 1956, pp. 37, 82–84, 91–92; *BRUK*, 1954, p. 13.

23. *Ibid.*, 1952, pp. 25, 27, 1954, p. 18, 1958, pp. 11, 20, 22, 24; AAUP, University of Kansas Chapter, "Report of the Committee on the Economic Status of the Profession, January 30, 1953," UA; MBR, August 20, October 15, 1954, September 23, 1955, March 30, September 21, 1956.

24. Franklin D. Murphy to Warren W. Shaw, August 8, 1956, and Murphy to Howard M. Immel, August 9, 1956 (copies), UA.

25. Franklin D. Murphy to George Docking, November 8, 1956 (copy), UA.

26. Franklin D. Murphy to George Docking, December 18, 1956 (copy), Docking to the Board of Regents, January 25, 1957 (copy), Roy Shapiro to the Board of Regents, January 28, 1957 (copy), Hubert Brighton to Murphy, January 30, 1957, and Murphy to Brighton, February 12, 1957 (copy), UA; State of Kansas, Department of Administration, Budget Division, *Governor's Budget Report for the Fiscal Year 1958*, pp. 247–262; *KHJ*, 1957, p. 26; Lawrence *Journal-World*, February 12, March 20, 21, 1957; Kansas City, Mo., *Star*, March 21, 1957; *Kansan*, March 21, 1957.

27. Lawrence *Journal-World*, January 17, 1958; George Docking to the Board of Regents, September 26, 1957 (copy), UA.

28. Lawrence *Journal-World*, January 17, 1958.

29. A. Lewis Oswald, "The Squeaking of the Steps" and "The Premeditated Villainy," in *Romancer*, 13 (October, 1960), 29, 39–44.

30. *BRUK*, 1956, pp. 10–16; State of Kansas, Department of Administration, Budget Division, *Governor's Budget Report for the Fiscal Year 1958*, pp. 247–262; *KSJ*, 1957, pp. 256, 279, 288–289, 346, 362, 368–369, 376; *KHJ*, 1957, pp. 380, 381, 398–399, 422, 436, 440, 469–470, 483–484; *KL*, 1957, pp. 106–107, 116–117.

31. University Senate Minutes, May 7, 1957.

32. *KSJ*, 1958, pp. 8–9.

33. Lawrence *Journal-World*, January 17, 1958; State of Kansas, Department of Administration, Budget Division, *Governor's Budget Report for the Fiscal Year Ending June 30, 1959*, pp. 37, 257–268; *KL*, 1958, pp. 109–110, 120.

34. *BRUK*, 1958, pp. 10–13.

35. MBR, May 22–23, 1958.

36. Franklin D. Murphy to McDill Boyd, June 4, 1958 (copy), UA; MBR, January 12, 1940, May 31, 1941, June 11, 1943, April 23, 1948, January 17, November 17, 1950, September 17, 1951.

37. University Senate Minutes, October 6, 1958; State of Kansas, Department of Administration, Budget Division, *Governor's Budget Report for the Fiscal Year 1960*, pp. 292–315.

38. *Kansan*, February 20, 23, 1959; Topeka *Capital*, February 21, 22, 25, 1959; Lawrence *Journal-World*, February 21, 1959; Wichita *Beacon*, March 4, 1959.

39. State of Kansas, Department of Administration, Budget Division, *Governor's*

Budget Report for the Fiscal Year 1960, pp. 292–315; *BRUK*, 1958, pp. 14–15, 17; University Senate Minutes, April 7, May 5, 1959; *KL*, 1959, pp. 106–108, 116, 120.

40. MBR, April 23, 24, September 18, October 9, 1959; University Senate Minutes, May 5, November 10, 1959; Franklin D. Murphy to E. B. Stouffer, September 14, 1951 (copy), UA; Lawrence *Journal-World*, September 27, 1952; *BRUK*, 1954, p. 12, 1958, pp. 7–9.

41. Topeka *Capital*, February 28, 1960; State of Kansas, Department of Administration, Budget Division, *Governor's Budget Report for the Fiscal Year 1961*, pp. 308, 326–328, 330, 334–335; *KL*, 1960, pp. 105, 113–115; *KSJ*, 1960, p. 85; *KHJ*, 1960, pp. 98–99.

42. Lawrence *Journal-World*, March 8, 1960.

43. "A Release of the University of California Office of Public Information, on Thursday, March 17, 1960," in "The Resignation of Chancellor Franklin D. Murphy" (scrapbook, UA); Lawrence *Journal-World*, March 17, 1960; Kansas City, Mo., *Times*, March 18, 1960; *Kansan*, March 18, 1960.

44. Kansas City, Mo., *Times*, March 17, 1960; *Kansan*, March 17, 19, 1960; Lawrence *Journal-World*, March 17, 1960; Manhattan *Mercury*, March 18, 1960; El Dorado *Times*, March 18, 1960; Norton *Telegram*, March 18, 1960; Wichita *Beacon*, March 18, 1960; "Petition to Be Signed by the Students of the University of Kansas: Murphy and Higher Education," March 18, 1960, in "Franklin David Murphy, M.D., Chancellor of the University of Kansas, 1951–1960" (scrapbook, UA), vol. 2.

45. Kansas City, Mo., *Times*, March 17, 19, 1960; Topeka *Capital*, March 19, 1960; *BRUK*, 1960, p. 701.

CHAPTER 28

1. Remarks at the Memorial Services for Dean Brandt, in College Faculty Minutes (MS, College of Liberal Arts and Sciences, University of Kansas), November 21, 1933.

2. *Ibid.*, September 20, October 18, 1921, March 21, December 8, 1922, January 16, April 17, 1923. Starting with the class of 1927, the requirement was 120 grade points for the 120 hours where A=3, B=2, and C=1. *Ibid.*, May 19, October 20, 1925.

3. *Ibid.*, January 17, May 16, 1922.

4. J. G. Brandt to E. H. Lindley, July 7, 1924, UA.

5. College Faculty Minutes, January 19, February 26, 1926; *BRUK*, 1926, pp. 35–36.

6. University Senate Minutes (MS, UA), November 14, 1933; *Kansan*, November 28, 1922; *BRUK*, 1934, p. 34; Paul B. Lawson and others to the College of Liberal Arts and Sciences, April 17, 1934 (copy), with the report to the University Senate (copy), UA; College Faculty Minutes, April 17, 1934.

7. *Ibid.*, April 24, May 2, 23, June 9, December 18, 1934, January 29, February 19, 27, April 1, 1935.

8. *Ibid.*, March 19, April 1, 16, December 17, 1935.

9. *Ibid.*, December 17, 1935, January 21, February 18, 25, March 17, April 21, 1936; *BRUK*, 1936, pp. 43–44; *UKC*, 1936–1937, pp. 56–59.

10. "Report of the University Survey Committee, Submitted to the University Senate, December 8, 1936" (typewritten MS, UA), 13.

11. *Ibid.*, 25–27; Abraham Flexner, *Universities: American, English, German* (New York, 1930), 53–54.

12. "Report of the . . . Survey Committee," 27–29.

13. *Ibid.*, 29–41, 62–65.

14. *Ibid.*, 41.

15. *Ibid.*, 41–42, 43–45.

16. *Ibid.*, 45.

17. *Ibid.*, 50–53.

18. *Ibid.*, 45–47, 49–50, 67–75; University Senate Minutes, December 8, 1936.

19. *Ibid.*, October 1, 1940; Paul B. Lawson, "Improve College with Revised Requirements," *Graduate Magazine of the University of Kansas*, 40 (September, 1941), 9.

20. Deane W. Malott, "To the College Faculty, presented by Deane W. Malott, November 17, 1943" (mimeographed), in "Deane Waldo Malott, Chancellor of the University of Kansas" (scrapbook, UA).

21. The other members were Viola J. Anderson of Home Economics, John W. Ashton of English, Ray Q. Brewster of Chemistry, Beulah M. Morrison of Psychology, Walter E. Sandelius of Political Science, and Gilbert Ulmer of Mathematics, who was also assistant dean of the College. College Faculty Minutes, November 21, 1944.

22. *Ibid.*, November 21, 1944. For aspects of the national movement, see Frederick Rudolph, *The American College and University: A History* (New York, 1962), 455–456, and R. Freeman Butts, *The College Charts Its Course: Historical Conceptions and Current Proposals* (New York, 1939), 397–416.

23. College Faculty Minutes, November 21, December 12, 19, 1944; *Kansan*, December 5, 13, 1944.

24. The requirement demanded passage by the end of the sophomore year for students entering as freshmen or sophomores, as long as the student had been in school for two semesters. Students transferring as juniors or seniors took it before they graduated. College Faculty Minutes, December 12, 1944; Robert Taft, *The Years on Mount Oread* (Lawrence, 1955), 171; *Kansan*, December 20, 1944; Lawrence *Journal-World*, June 14, 1945; *Graduate Magazine*, 43 (December, 1944), 4; *UKC*, 1944–1945, General Information, 63.

25. *Manual for the Study of Western Civilization* (Lawrence, 1945), especially 2, 3–4, 7–8, 9–10.

26. College Faculty Minutes, April 18, 1950; Deane W. Malott to John Collyer, March 28, 1947, Malott to Alf Landon, September 17, 1947, and Malott to J. R. Garrison, September 1, 1950 (copies), UA; *UKC*, 1959–1960, Announcement of Courses, 307.

27. See the summary of his remarks to the College faculty in College Faculty Minutes, January 21, 1947.

28. Deane W. Malott to Alf Landon, September 17, 1947 (copy), UA; College Faculty Minutes, January 20, February 17, 24, 1948, May 17, June 4, 1949.

29. University Senate Minutes, May 11, 1948, November 8, 1949; Merrill D. Clubb to Deane W. Malott, September 29, 1949, UA.

30. *BRUK*, 1954, p. 6; MBR, February 26, 1954; *UKC*, 1957–1958, Announcement of Courses, 26; *University Newsletter*, 47 (November 1, 1947).

31. Francis H. Heller, "Experiment in Brain Power," *Graduate Magazine*, 56 (September, 1957), 8–9, 22–23.

32. College Faculty Minutes, September 20, December 13, 1955, May 22, December 18, 1956, April 16, May 14, 21, 1957.

33. *UKC*, 1959–1960, pp. 63–66.

34. *Kansan*, May 17, 1922, April 7, 1925, April 15, 24, 1936.

35. Beulah M. Morrison and others to the College Committee on Curriculum, April 20, 1944, and Deane W. Malott to Henry J. Haskell, March 29, 1949 (copies), UA; College Faculty Minutes, May 9, June 16, 1944; *Kansan*, December 6, 1944, February 8, 12, 13, April 3, 1945.

36. *Ibid.*, May 15, December 6, 1951, January 21, 22, February 10, 12, 23, 24, 25, March 1, 1960; *Campus Affairs Committee, Student Opinionnaire on Instruction*, 1953, in "Kansas University: Items in Its History" (scrapbook, UA), v. 15.

37. University Senate Minutes, February 10, 1948; Deane W. Malott to Heads of Departments, n.d., but either 1949 or 1950 (copy), UA; Henry P. Smith and others, "The Improvement of Teaching at the University of Kansas," April 24, 1951 (mimeographed), American Association of University Professors, University of Kansas Chapter, Papers, UA; *Kansan*, May 12, 21, 1959; W. Clarke Wescoe, *The State of the University*, 1961, pp. 10–11.

38. George R. Waggoner, *Our Finest College Teachers, 1890–1960: Third Annual Report of the College of Liberal Arts & Sciences, The University of Kansas* (Lawrence, 1962), 3, 5, 6, 7, 8, 9, 10, 11, 13, 14, 16.

39. Wescoe, *State of the University*, 1961, p. 8, 1962, p. 7, 1963, pp. 7–8, 1964, p. 7, 1965, p. 5.

CHAPTER 29

1. MBA, September 17, 1915; *UKC*, 1915–1916, Sec. I, 14, and School of Education, 5; Frank Strong to E. T. Hackney, September 8, 1915 (copy), UA.

2. *BRUK*, 1922, pp. 46–47, 1926, p. 42, 1930, pp. 45, 46, 47, 1932, p. 38, 1938, p. 83; School of Education Administrative Committee Minutes, May 3, 1930, and School of Education Faculty Minutes, May 10, 1930, School of Education, University of Kansas.

3. A unit of high-school work equaled five hours.

4. *UKC*, 1916–1917, pp. 321, 323; *ibid.*, 1919–1920, pp. 337–340; *ibid.*, 1940–1941, General Information, 92–93, 95–96.

5. *Ibid.*, 1915–1916, School of Education, 8, 1916–1917, p. 322; MBR, February 5, 1927, October 30, 1937; School of Education Faculty Minutes, December 1, 1936, February 16, 1937; *University of Kansas Bulletin of Education*, 4 (March, 1938), 59.

6. MBA, February 17, 1916; "Ten Years of Research and Service in the University of Kansas Bureau of School Service and Research, 1920–1930," *University of Kansas Bulletin of Education*, 3 (October, 1930), 3–36; R. A. S., "Editorial Statement," *ibid.*, 1 (December, 1926), 12; F. P. O., "Editorial Comment," *ibid.*, 1 (February, 1927), 13; P. A. W., "Suggestions for 'Bridging the Gap,'" *ibid.*, 1 (February, 1928), 17–19; and Carl B. Althaus and others, "Introductory Statement," *ibid.*, 4 (March, 1938), 3; *BRUK*, 1930, p. 48, 1938, pp. 82–83, 84; "The State Curriculum Program," *University of Kansas Bulletin of Education*, 4 (February, 1940), 71–72.

7. Raymond A. Schwegler, "Pros and Cons in Educational Thought," *ibid.*, 4 (April, 1939), 28–31; *UKC*, 1938–1939, Announcement of Courses, 41, and Roster of Faculty, Students, and Graduates, 103.

8. Deane W. Malott, "Memorandum to School of Education Faculty," March 29, 1945 (copy), UA; School of Education Faculty Minutes, January 2, March 29, 1945.

9. Karl D. Edwards, "Experimental Needs of Student Teachers at the University of Kansas," *University of Kansas Bulletin of Education*, 6 (February, 1952), 26; Paul B. Lawson to George B. Smith, September 2, 1952 (copy), UA.

10. University Senate Minutes (MS, UA), May 6, 1952.

11. Paul B. Lawson to George B. Smith, September 2, 1952 (copy), UA; *UKC*, 1950–1951, General Information, 80, 1958–1959, General Information, 86, 88.

12. *Ibid.*, 1944–1945, General Information, 81–83, 1946–1947, General Information, 75–89; Edwards, "Experimental Needs of Student Teachers," 25–28; Lawrence *Journal-World*, May 16, 17, 1951.

13. Edwards, "Experimental Needs of Student Teachers," 26; Kansas City, Mo., *Times*, February 1, 1950; Kansas City, Mo., *Star*, March 5, 1950; *UKC*, 1950–1951, General Information, 100–102; George B. Smith to Deane W. Malott, August 1, 1949, UA; *Dedication Program, University of Kansas School of Education* (Lawrence, 1956). In 1952 Smith, who had become dean of the University, was succeeded as dean of the School of Education by Kenneth E. Anderson.

14. Ernest H. Lindley, "The University and the Vocations of Men," *Inauguration of Ernest Hiram Lindley as Chancellor of the University of Kansas*, Bulletin of the University of Kansas, 23 (January 15, 1922), 29–30, 32–35.

15. The Department of Economics had been renamed in November, 1920. Department of Economics Minutes, November 20, 1920, University of Kansas.

16. *UKC*, 1920–1921, Description of Courses, 21–25; John Ise to Ernest H. Lindley, July 18, 1921, UA. Under the date of February 9, 1922, however, the following statement appears in the Department of Economics Minutes: "With regard to the prospects of an enlarged Department of Economics or a School of Commerce as an outgrowth of the present department investigation seems to show that such a move need not undermine standards of scholarship and especially so if the head of such a school represents and respects scholarly attainments. Prof. Ise reported favorably on the School of Commerce."

17. *BRUK*, 1920, p. 59; Frank T. Stockton, *Four Chapters in the History of the School of Business* (Lawrence, 1964), 5; Ernest H. Lindley to L. E. Young, February 14, 1922, and Lindley to Edward Bok, April 5, 1923 (copies), UA.

18. *UKC*, 1925–1926, p. 288; Frank T. Stockton to J. A. Boynton, June 10, 1924, and Stockton to John Ise, June 11, 1924 (copies), Box 4, Frank T. Stockton Papers, UA; *Graduate Magazine of the University of Kansas*, 23 (October, 1924), 12.

19. Frank T. Stockton to Ernest H. Lindley, November 7, 1924, UA; *UKC*, 1924–1925, pp. 53–57, 1925–1926, p. 41, 1926–1927, pp. 57–60, 1939–1940, General Information, 77–80; Frank T. Stockton, "The New School of Business," *Graduate Magazine*, 23 (February, 1925), 6; *BRUK*, 1926, p. 38.

20. *UKC*, 1934–1935, Announcement of Courses, 34–39. In 1934–1935 there were 225 students enrolled in the Business School. Five years later there were over 350. But now only six of the seventeen members were shared. *Ibid.*, 1934–1935, endsheet, 1939–1940, Announcement of Courses, 36–42, and Roster of Faculty, Students, and Graduates, 103.

21. Frank T. Stockton, "The Evolution of Teaching of Economics at K.U.," *Graduate Magazine*, 30 (April, 1932), 14.

22. *BRUK*, 1926, pp. 39–40, 1928, pp. 41–42, 1932, pp. 34–35.

23. Deane W. Malott to C. A. Dykstra, December 9, 1941 (copy), UA.

24. School of Business Minutes, May 8, 1941, School of Business, University of Kansas; Deane W. Malott to Frank T. Stockton, November 11, 1942 (copy), and Stockton to Malott, November 12, 1942, UA.

25. Deane W. Malott to Willis N. Kelly, June 28, 1947 (copy), UA; School of Business Minutes, June 2, 1947, MBR, January 9, 1948.

26. *UKC*, 1944–1945, General Information, 78–80, 1946–1947, General Information, 67–71, 1949–1950, General Information, 72; School of Business Minutes, February 14, 15, 1949; *BRUK*, 1950, p. 7; School of Business, Biennial Report, 1946, 1948, 1950, UA; *Kansas Business Review*, 1 (September 15, 1948), 2.

27. MBR, June 9, 1944; School of Journalism, Biennial Report, 1950, UA; *"Freedom of Expression": Texts of Speeches Delivered April 24, 1946, New York City, at the William Allen White Foundation Dinner, by Senator Arthur Capper, Chancellor*

Deane W. Malott, Frank E. Tripp, A. D. Willard, Jr., Francis S. Harmon, General Dwight D. Eisenhower (n.p., n.d.), 4–6.

28. *UKC*, 1944–1945, Announcement of Courses, 138–142, 1949–1950, General Information, 130; Elmer F. Beth to author, October 15, 1965.

29. Burton W. Marvin, "Biographical Material for Mr. Oscar S. Stauffer, publisher, Topeka State Journal," April 21, 1948, Deane W. Malott to Drew McLaughlin, May 3, 1948 (copy), and Marvin to Malott, May 26, 1949, UA.

30. Deane W. Malott to Burton W. Marvin, July 30, 1949 (copy), UA.

31. *UKC*, 1950–1951, General Information, 138, 1955–1956, General Information, 168–169, 1957–1958, General Information, 145, 175–176, 1964–1965, School of Journalism, 10–16, College, 62, 64–68; *The Ninety-second Annual Commencement, the University of Kansas, June 1, 1964* (Lawrence, 1964), 5–8, 9.

32. Perley F. Walker, "Notes from the Dean's Office," *Kansas Engineer*, 6 (January 20, 1920), 20; *ibid.*, 7 (June, 1921), 44–45; *ibid.*, 9 (May, 1923), 21–22; Walker, "The Public Service Aspects of Engineering Education," *ibid.*, 11 (March, 1925), 15–19.

33. Shaad had succeeded Walker after he committed suicide in October, 1927.

34. George C. Shaad, "Dean's Office Notes," *Kansas Engineer*, 15 (January, 1930), 17, 30; *ibid.*, 17 (March, 1931), 13–14; *ibid.*, 18 (January, 1933), 9, 13; Ivan C. Crawford, "Notes from the Dean's Office," *ibid.*, 24 (January, 1939), 9–10.

35. Walker, "Public Service Aspects of Engineering Education," 18; Ernest H. Lindley, "A Word from Chancellor Lindley," *Kansas Engineer*, 6 (September, 1920), 20.

36. See Walker, "Notes from the Dean's Office," *ibid.*, 7 (June, 1921), 44–45; *Engineering: Its Scope, Opportunities and System of Training*, Engineering Bulletin No. 15, Bulletin of the University of Kansas, 29 (February 1, 1928), especially 3, 5; George C. Shaad, "Dean's Office Notes," *Kansas Engineer*, 20 (March, 1934), 12; R. De-Witt Jordan, "The Engineer," unidentified clipping in "University of Kansas School of Engineering and Architecture, Lawrence, Items in Its History" (scrapbooks, UA), vol. 2.

37. Lindley, "A Word from Chancellor Lindley," 20; Walker, "Public Service Aspects of Engineering Education," 18; Ivan C. Crawford to Deane W. Malott, May 21, 1940, UA.

38. *UKC*, 1920–1921, General Information, 39, 41–49, 1923–1924, p. 51, 1938–1939, General Information, 89–103; W. R. C., "Liberal Education," *Kansas Engineer*, 19 (January, 1934), 11.

39. *UKC*, 1946–1947, General Information, 97–98, 1948–1949, General Information, 101, 1959–1960, General Information, 113.

40. *Ibid.*, 1919–1920, pp. 193–194, 1920–1921, General Information, 41–48, 1923–1924, p. 61, 1924–1925, p. 66.

41. A. A. Potter to Ernest H. Lindley, December 29, 1936, and Karl T. Compton to Lindley, January 11, 1937, UA. For earlier and similar criticisms from the State Education Department of New York and the American Institute of Chemical Engineers, two important accrediting agencies before the E.C.P.D., see George C. Shaad to Lindley, October 15, 1934, UA.

42. Ernest H. Lindley to E. B. Black, March 6, April 23, 1937 (copies), "The Professional Career of John Jay Jakosky," signed by W. C. McNown, June 13, 1940 (copy), and George P. Burns to Deane W. Malott, July 5, 1940, UA; Jesse Gamber, "Ivan C. Crawford—Our New Dean," *Kansas Engineer*, 23 (October, 1937), 3–4.

43. Albert B. Newman to Deane W. Malott, November 20, 1940 (copy), Ivan C. Crawford to Malott, December 12, 1940, F. A. Russell to A. A. Potter, May 1, 1937

(copy), and School of Engineering, Biennial Report, 1950, UA; *UKC*, 1938–1939, General Information, 102.

44. W. Eugene George, "Goldwin Goldsmith, Chairman, 1913–1928," *University of Kansas Alumni Magazine*, 61 (March, 1963), 10; *UKC*, 1913–1914, p. 216, 1919–1920, p. 194.

45. Robert Guenter, "Genesis: The First Fifty Years," Curtis Besinger, "Joseph M. Kellogg, Chairman, 1928–1945," and Besinger, "George Beal, Chairman, 1947–1962," *Alumni Magazine*, 61 (March, 1963), 6, 10–11.

46. *UKC*, 1944–1945, Announcement of Courses, 86–110, 1954–1955, Announcement of Courses, 126–153, 1962–1964, School of Engineering, 6; *BRUK*, 1946, p. 20, 1956, p. 17; Besinger, "George Beal," 11.

47. *UKC*, 1920–1921, General Information, 67–69, 1939–1940, General Information, 140–141, 1941–1942, General Information, 149–150, 1957–1958, General Information, 163, 165–166.

48. *BRUK*, 1924, p. 56, 1926, p. 60; School of Pharmacy, *News Letter*, 1 (Summer, 1928), 1.

49. *UKC*, 1926–1927, pp. 109–111; *BRUK*, 1926, p. 60; School of Pharmacy, *News Letter*, 1 (Summer, 1928), 1–2; *ibid.*, 1 (November, 1931), 6.

50. *BRUK*, 1930, p. 68, 1932, p. 58, 1934, p. 65, 1938, p. 113; MBR, June 2, 1932; *UKC*, 1932–1933, General Information, 118–120.

51. C. B. Jordan and A. G. Du Mez, "Copy of Report of Inspection Committee," May 10, 1939, L. D. Havenhill to Deane W. Malott, November 1, 1939, and Malott to Du Mez, November 6, 1939 (copy), UA.

52. *Graduate Magazine*, 39 (September, 1940), 11; *UKC*, 1957–1958, General Information, 166, 1959–1960, General Information, 173, 1964–1965, School of Pharmacy, 8–10, 15.

53. *Ibid.*, 1920–1921, Officers of Instruction, 10; Janet Coulson, "A History of the Fine Arts School at the University of Kansas" (typewritten M.M. thesis, University of Kansas, 1940), 153–154, 155–158, 165–168; *Kansan*, March 29, 1917; Harold L. Butler to Ernest H. Lindley, June 14, 1921, in possession of Dr. Stanley B. Lindley, Salisbury, North Carolina.

54. *Ibid.*, J. C. McCanles to Ernest H. Lindley, July 3, 1920, in possession of Dr. Stanley B. Lindley; Kansas City, Mo., *Star*, July 31, 1921; Lindley to Mrs. W. B. Thayer, August 15, 1921, and Lindley to William Allen White, October 17, 1921 (copies), UA; *Kansan*, May 21, 1923.

55. *UKC*, 1923–1924, p. 264.

56. *BRUK*, 1924, pp. 43–44, 1926, pp. 48–49, 1928, p. 51, 1932, pp. 43–44, 1934, pp. 44–45, 1936, pp. 54–55, 1938, pp. 89–90.

57. *Ibid.*, 1928, p. 51, 1930, p. 54, 1932, p. 45, 1936, pp. 55–56, 1938, p. 91. For the continuation of these and similar activities in the 1940s and 1950s, see School of Fine Arts, Biennial Report, 1948, 1950, 1952, 1954, UA.

58. For examples, see *BRUK*, 1924, p. 43, 1928, p. 52, 1938, pp. 91–92.

59. MBA, June 2, 1917, January 3, 1924; *UKC*, 1919–1920, pp. 249–250; *BRUK*, 1920, p. 23; *Dedication of the Thayer Collection of Art in the Spooner-Thayer Art Museum, University of Kansas, May 1, 1928* (n.p., n.d.); Harold L. Butler to Ernest H. Lindley, November 2, 1921, Lindley to Edwin P. Sample, January 3, 1925 (telegram, copy), and W. A. Griffith to Lindley, January 9, 1925 (copy), UA; MBR, December 8, 1926.

60. See John M. Maxon to Deane W. Malott, June 25, 1948, UA; Art Museum, Biennial Report, 1954, UA.

61. For examples, see *BRUK*, 1920, pp. 21–23, 1928, pp. 50–54, 1936, pp. 54–60.

62. *UKC*, 1923–1924, pp. 63–75, 1929–1930, General Information, 82; *BRUK*, 1930, p. 53.

63. *UKC*, 1938–1939, General Information, 104, 1939–1940, General Information, 108, 1946–1947, General Information, 107, 1947–1948, General Information, 110.

64. *Ibid.*, 1950–1951, Announcement of Courses, 13.

CHAPTER 30

1. *BRUK*, 1920, pp. 15–17.

2. *Ibid.*, 1920, p. 16; George F. Zook, Lotus D. Coffman, and A. R. Mann, *Report of a Survey of the State Institutions of Higher Learning in Kansas*, Department of the Interior, Bureau of Education, Bulletin, 1923, no. 40 (Washington, 1923), 104.

3. *BRUK*, 1930, pp. 28–30.

4. E. B. Stouffer to Deane W. Malott, January 10, 1941 (copy), UA.

5. See Paul B. Lawson to Raymond Nichols, October 27, 1934, UA; *Kansan*, May 29, 1924; *Graduate Magazine of the University of Kansas*, 46 (March–April, 1948), 12.

6. Paul B. Lawson to Raymond Nichols, October 27, 1934, UA; Ellis B. Stouffer, "Development of Scholarship at the University of Kansas," *Graduate Magazine*, 39 (January, 1941), 9, and the typescript of the address, pp. 13, 23–24, UA.

7. Earl N. Manchester to Ernest H. Lindley, June 29, 1921, UA; *BRUK*, 1928, pp. 66, 69; *Graduate Magazine*, 27 (October, 1928), 26; University of Kansas Library, *Biennial Report*, 1930, pp. 2–4.

8. *Ibid.*, 1932, p. 3; *BRUK*, 1934, pp. 68–69, 1936, pp. 86–88, 1938, pp. 57–58; University Senate Minutes (MS, UA), January 8, 1935.

9. University of Kansas Library, *Biennial Report*, 1930, p. 3, 1940, p. 3; *BRUK*, 1932, p. 62, 1934, p. 69, 1936, p. 88, 1938, p. 59.

10. University of Kansas, College of Liberal Arts and Sciences, "Report of the Special Committee on the Library," March 20, 1951 (copy), UA. The other members of the committee were Max Dresden of Physics, Francis H. Heller of Political Science, R. S. Howey of Economics, James E. Seaver of History, and J. L. Wortham of English.

11. *Ibid.*

12. *BRUK*, 1952, p. 8; Robert H. Vosper to Franklin D. Murphy, March 4, 1952, and Murphy to Vosper, April 8, 1952 (copy), UA; University of Kansas Libraries, *Annual Report*, 1957, p. 1.

13. University of Kansas Libraries, *Biennial Report*, 1954, pp. 1–2, 8–9, 22, *Annual Report*, 1956, pp. 2–3, 8–9, 1957, pp. 3–4, 1958, pp. 3–4, 1961, p. 14; Robert Vosper, "The New Look in Libraries," *Graduate Magazine*, 53 (March, 1955), 10.

14. University of Kansas Libraries, *Biennial Report*, 1954, p. 9, *Annual Report*, 1956, pp. 1–2, 1958, pp. 7–8; *Books and Libraries at the University of Kansas*, 1 (November, 1953), 3–4, 4–5, and no. 18 (May, 1958), 2–4; Franklin D. Murphy to Whitley Austin, December 1, 1954 (copy), UA.

15. *BRUK*, 1948, pp. 31, 32; *Annual Report of the Director of Admissions and Registrar for 1962–1963*, pp. 3, 37; "Graduate School Enrollments by Departmental Majors" (MS, Graduate School, University of Kansas).

16. Graduate Faculty Minutes (MS, Graduate School), April 30, 1964; *The Graduate School, 1961–1962*, Bulletin of the University of Kansas, 61 (December, 1960), 7.

17. Graduate Faculty Minutes, April 30, 1964.

18. *Ibid.*, May 21, December 17, 1964, April 16, November 11, 1965; Graduate

Council Minutes (MS, Graduate School), October 6, 1965; *The University of Kansas Graduate School Catalog*, 1966–1967, p. 5.

19. *RBA*, 1914, pp. 21–22; Frank Strong to Leroy Hughbanks, November 28, 1914 (copy), UA; *BRUK*, 1926, p. 54; E. P. Lyon, "Report on the Medical School of the University of Kansas," Zook, Coffman, and Mann, *Report of a Survey*, 140.

20. Frank Strong to Leroy Hughbanks, November 28, 1914 (copy), Strong to Arthur Capper, April 2, November 3, 1915 (copies), Strong to E. T. Hackney, April 16, 1915 (copy), and Capper to Strong, October 26, 1915, UA.

21. *KL*, 1919, p. 55; Frank Strong to James A. Kimball, January 16, 1919 (copy), Strong to R. L. Gamble, May 17, 1919 (copy), Strong to Henry J. Allen, June 2, 1919 (copy), Allen to Strong, June 17, 1919, Strong to E. E. Mullaney, October 28, 1919 (copy), Mullaney to Strong, October 31, 1919, Strong to General Education Board, November 3, 1919 (copy), UA; George H. Bowles, "Raised $33,000 for Medical Site," *Graduate Magazine*, 19 (October, 1920), 7–8.

22. Lyon, "Report on the Medical School," Zook, Coffman, and Mann, *Report of a Survey*, 134–136.

23. *Ibid.*, 133–134, 136–140.

24. *Catalogue of the University of Kansas, The School of Medicine*, 1949, p. 10.

25. *BRUK*, 1926, pp. 53–59.

26. *Ibid.*, 1930, pp. 60, 62, 64–65.

27. *Ibid.*, 1936, pp. 70–71, 1938, pp. 100–101; H. R. Wahl to Ralph T. O'Neil, August 5, 1938 (copy), and MS headed "Federal Grants (to June 30, 1939)," UA; *KL*, 1947, p. 106.

28. *BRUK*, 1928, pp. 72, 77, 1936, pp. 103–104, 1938, pp. 102–103.

29. Leonard V. Peterson, "A Study of 130 Cases to Determine How the Doctor Uses the Social Service Department at the Kansas University Medical Center, Kansas City, Kansas" (typewritten Master of Social Work thesis, University of Kansas, 1951), 5, 9–10, 34, 36; *BRUK*, 1938, p. 107.

30. *BRUK*, 1936, p. 74, 1938, pp. 104, 106–107.

31. *Ibid.*, 1936, pp. 72–73, 1938, pp. 102, 104.

32. H. R. Wahl, "Annual Report to the Chancellor on the School of Medicine, 1942–1943," University of Kansas Hospitals, Department Heads Meeting, Minutes, September 11, 1944, and Logan Clendening to Deane W. Malott, December 8, 1944, UA.

33. Paul W. Schafer to Deane W. Malott, September 30, 1947, and Malott to Claude Dixon, September 11, 1947 (copy), UA.

34. MBR, February 20, 1948; Lawrence *Journal-World*, September 2, 1951; Kansas City, Mo., *Star*, September 2, 1951.

35. *Ibid.*, February 23, 1948.

36. See *BRUK*, 1948, pp. 9–10.

37. Kansas City, Mo., *Star*, September 24, 1948.

38. *Ibid.*, September 24, 1948, January 18, February 17, 24, 1949; Topeka *State Journal*, January 20, 1949; Lawrence *Journal-World*, January 26, 27, February 25, 1949; *KL*, 1949, pp. 116–118; Kansas City, Kans., *Kansan*, January 22, 1950.

39. Kansas City, Mo., *Star*, November 21, 1949, November 4, 1950; Franklin D. Murphy to Edward H. Hashinger and Mahlon H. Delp, August 28, 1951, and School of Medicine Curriculum Committee Minutes, April 28, 1949 (copies), UA.

40. On the workings of the cooperative program, see Milwaukee *Journal*, May 15, 1949; *Jewell County Record*, Supplement, November 17, 1949; Gypsum *Advocate*, April 26, 1950; Kansas City, Mo., *Star*, November 4, 1950; Kansas City, Mo., *Times*, May 1, 1951.

41. Franklin D. Murphy, "The Concept of Continuation Education in Medicine," *California Medicine*, 74 (February, 1951), 89–91.

42. Franklin D. Murphy to Deane W. Malott, April 8, 1950, Murphy to Fred Harris, April 8, 1950 (copy), and "Plan for Continuation Study Center, University of Kansas Medical Center, Kansas City, Kansas" (copy), UA; Kansas City, Mo., *Star*, July 23, 1950, November 12, 1952.

43. *Catalogue of the School of Medicine,* Bulletin of the University of Kansas, 50 (March 1, 1949), 7–18, and 61 (May 1, 1960), 70–81; *BRUK*, 1948, p. 35, 1960, pp. 706–707.

44. MBR, September 23, 1955, November 9, 1956; Franklin D. Murphy to Hubert Brighton, October 9, 1951 (copy), UA.

45. Thomas N. Bonner, *The Kansas Doctor: A Century of Pioneering* (Lawrence, 1959), 272; University of Kansas, School of Medicine, *Catalogue*, 1953–1954, pp. 41–42, 1955–1956, p. 26; University of Kansas, School of Medicine, *Information for Applicants*, 1962–1963, p. 7.

46. Clipping from the Emporia *Gazette*, December ?, 1948, in "Franklin D. Murphy, M.D." (scrapbook, UA).

47. Ernest H. Lindley to John W. Cravens, August 6, 1920, and Lindley to Arthur L. Corbin, April 4, 1922 (copies), UA; *BRUK*, 1920, p. 25, 1922, pp. 36, 37.

48. Ernest H. Lindley to Paul V. McNutt, August 5, 1920 (telegram, copy), Lindley to John W. Cravens, August 6, 1920 (copy), and McNutt to Lindley, August 12, 1920 (telegram), UA.

49. Ernest H. Lindley to M. L. Burton, August 21, 1920, Lindley to Herbert S. Hadley, March 31, 1921, Lindley to James Patterson McBaine, May 2, 1921, Lindley to Herschel W. Arant, April 4, 1922, Lindley to Arthur L. Corbin, April 4, 1922, Lindley to J. C. Nichols, April 28, 1922 (copies), and Arant to Lindley, April 26, 1922, UA; *UKC*, 1923–1924, p. 257.

50. *BRUK*, 1922, pp. 35–39, 1924, pp. 46–50, 1926, pp. 51–53, 1928, pp. 54–56.

51. *Ibid.*, 1930, p. 57, 1934, pp. 49–50; Ernest H. Lindley to Herschel W. Arant, December 7, 21, 1931 (copies), and Arant to Lindley, December 11, 1931.

52. *Kansan*, November 20, 22, 23, 1931, June 28, 1932; Lawrence *Journal-World*, June 27, 1932. Part of the difficulties involved the refusal of Law School and University officers to rehire Associate Professor R. F. Payne and Professor Raymond J. Heilman when their appointments, described as "temporary," ended in 1930 and 1931 respectively. Both Davis and Chancellor Lindley thought them incompetent, but the law students apparently disagreed. *Kansan*, November 23, 1931; *BRUK*, 1930, p. 57, 1932, p. 48; Ernest H. Lindley to Herschel W. Arant, December 21, 1931 (copy), UA.

53. *BRUK*, 1932, p. 16, 1934, pp. 21, 48–50; *Douglas County Republican*, October 6, 1932.

54. Charles Harger to "Roy," n.d., Dudley Doolittle to Ernest H. Lindley, April 16, 1935, Lindley to Ralph T. O'Neil, March 6, 1937 (copy), Lindley to Frederick J. Moreau, April 3, 1937 (copy), Moreau to Lindley, April 12, 1937, UA; MBR, June 30, 1934; *BRUK*, 1936, p. 60, 1938, p. 94.

55. In 1938 the Court had required that after July 1, 1943, candidates for admission to the bar had to have a college degree before they began the study of law. But because of opposition that rule was not implemented. On June 1, 1960, it at last went into effect, as the result of a decision of December 3, 1954. School of Law, *Annual Catalogue*, 1937–1939, pp. 5–6, 1939–1941, p. 7; *UKC*, 1940–1941, General Information, 132, and 1955–1956, General Information, 143; *BRUK*, 1936, pp. 64–65.

56. Frederick J. Moreau to Ernest H. Lindley, April 12, 1937, UA; *UKC*, 1939–1940, General Information, 126, 1952–1953, General Information, 144.

57. *Ibid.*, 1920–1921, Section I, 64, 1932–1933, General Information, 104, 106, 1933–1934, General information, 108, 111, 1953–1954, General Information, 110.

58. *BRUK*, 1936, pp. 62–63, 1938, pp. 96–97; *UKC*, 1920–1921, Section I, 63, 1921–1922, General Information, 62, 1924–1925, General Information, 92, 1934–1935, General Information, 138, and 1953–1954, General Information, 109.

59. *Ibid.*, 1952–1953, General Information, 147; John G. Hervey to Frederick J. Moreau, October 12, 1955 (copy), with Hervey to Franklin D. Murphy, October 12, 1955 (copy), UA.

CHAPTER 31

1. *Wise Words for Women: Official Handbook for Women of the University of Kansas* (Lawrence, 1959).

2. *UKC*, 1933–1934, endsheet; *BRUK*, 1918, p. 5, 1936, pp. 29, 31, 1960, p. 703; James K. Hitt, *Annual Report of the Director of Admissions and Registrar for 1959–60* (Lawrence, 1960), 14–17, 23.

3. *UKC*, 1933–1934, endsheet; *BRUK*, 1960, p. 703.

4. *Kansan*, April 28, May 3, 1932.

5. *Ibid.*, September 21, 1944; *Kansas Engineer*, 36 (January, 1952), 4. See also *ibid.*, 38 (November, 1954), 2, 4.

6. *Ibid.*, 32 (March, 1948), 3.

7. *Kansan*, March 30, 1924, October 30, 1925, October 8, 1931.

8. *Dove*, May 10, 1937, April 22, 1938.

9. *Kansan*, January 28, May 20, 21, June 3, 4, 1919; University Senate Minutes (MS, UA), May 14, 1919.

10. *BRUK*, 1924, p. 49; *Kansan*, May 26, 1926, May 25, 1933; *Kansas Engineer*, 13 (January, 1928), 20–21; *ibid.*, 14 (March, 1928), 21; *ibid,*, 15 (March, 1929), 20; F. P. O'Brien, "What Students Say about College Instruction and Instructors," *University of Kansas Bulletin of Education*, 2 (April, 1930), 23–24; untitled circular sent by the University Veterans Organization, March 1, 1955, in "University of Kansas Activities" (scrapbooks, UA), v. 18.

11. *Dove*, September 11, 1925; *Gale*, 1 (1934), 28; *upstream*, 5 (October, 1952), 2; *Kansan*, February 17, 1967.

12. *Ibid.*, October 20, 1919, May 9, 1924; *Dove*, March 30, 1925–March 10, 1948.

13. *Kansan*, September 27, October 18, 1933, February 14, 15, May 8, 1934, January 14, 1937; Richard K. La Ban, "The Front Page and Upperclassmen in the University of Kansas" (typewritten M.A. thesis, University of Kansas, 1940), especially 98–107.

14. *Eagle*, April 22, May 28, 1947, January 5, 1950.

15. *Ibid.*, April, 1951 (?); *Kansan*, October 12, 1961.

16. On the varieties of Negro segregation, see *Dove*, April 19, 1925, February 15, 1926, March 21, 1927; Marcet Haldeman-Julius, "What the Negro Students Endure in Kansas," *Haldeman-Julius Monthly*, 7 (January, 1928), 5–16, 147–159; Ernest H. Lindley to William Y. Morgan, October 5, 1927, Lindley to W. E. B. Du Bois, December 11, 1930, and Deane W. Malott to Andrew Schoeppel, March 19, 1943 (copies), UA.

17. Ernest H. Lindley to "My dear Mr. Herman," May 11, 1928, Lindley to W. E. B. Du Bois, December 11, 1930, and Deane W. Malott to Andrew Schoeppel, March 19, 1943 (copies), UA.

18. Deane W. Malott to Andrew Schoeppel, March 19, 1943 (copy), UA; *Kansan*, April 9, 1943, April 30, 1946, January 17, May 16, 19, 20, 1947, May 21, 1965.

19. *Ibid.*, September 17, 24, 1947, February 27, April 21, 1948; Committee on Racial Equality, *Report of Direct Action against Racial Discrimination at a Cafe Near the Campus of the University of Kansas, Lawrence, April 15, 1948* (Lawrence, 1948); Beth Bell, Robert Stewart, and others to Deane W. Malott, September 18, 1947, UA.

20. *Kansan*, May 12, 13, 14, 16, 1952, March 8, 1957; Franklin D. Murphy to J. D. King, February 28, 1952 (copy), UA; "Notes on a Meeting between Chancellor Franklin Murphy and the Executive Committee of the American Association of University Professors, University of Kansas Chapter, March 19, 1955, by E. Jackson Baur," American Association of University Professors, University of Kansas Chapter, Papers, UA.

21. *Kansan*, March 8, 9, 10, 11, 16, 17, 23, 26, April 1, May 4, 5, 21, 26, September 29, October 6, 1965.

22. "A Modest Proposal: Teaching," and Gary Gregg, "The Nature of the University: Facile Myths and Harsh Realities," *University Review*, 3 (March, 1967), 8–11, 2.

23. University Senate Minutes, November 3, 1914; Frank Strong to the Faculty and Students of the University of Kansas, May 31, 1915 (copy), UA; *Kansan*, February 4, 1921; Lawrence *Journal-World*, May 21, 1952.

24. *Kansan*, February 11, March 9, 17, 18, 1964, November 4, 1966.

25. Deane W. Malott to Alf M. Landon, July 15, 1946 (copy), UA.

26. Deane W. Malott to Andrew F. Schoeppel, January 28, 1946 (copy), and report adopted by the Board of Regents, June 14, 1946, with Malott to Alf M. Landon, July 15, 1946 (copy), UA; *KL*, 1947, pp. 772–777, 1949, p. 753, 1955, pp. 761–763; *U.S. Statutes at Large*, 64: 77–78; Fred Ellsworth, "The J. R. Pearson Story," *University of Kansas Alumni Magazine*, 54 (November, 1955), 8–9; Lawrence *Journal-World*, April 17, 1956.

27. MBR, March 30, 1956, December 18, 1959; Lawrence *Journal-World*, August 21, 1957, December 18, 1959; Topeka *Capital*, August 25, 1957; Kansas City, Mo., *Star*, September 28, 1959; *Kansan*, May 14, 1962.

28. See Douglas Mackey, "The Large Residence Halls: Instant Stonehenge," *University Review*, 3 (March, 1967), 5.

29. Mary Olsen, Helen Olson, and others to Ernest H. Lindley, December ?, 1920, and Lindley to the Students of the University of Kansas and Their Parents, August 30, 1926 (copy), UA.

30. *Sour Owl*, April 16, 1926; *Dove*, April 12, 1932.

31. University Senate Minutes, February 4, 1919; *Kansan*, April 22, 1932, February 19, 20, 1919.

32. University Senate Minutes, October 4, December 12, 1919, February 3, March 2, 1920, April 5, 1921; Frank Strong to the Board of Administration, March 31, 1920 (copy), UA; *The Constitution of the Men's Student Council, University of Kansas, Revised March 11, 1920* (Lawrence, 1920).

33. University Senate Minutes, April 7, 1925; *Constitution of the Associated Men of the University of Kansas* (Lawrence, 1928).

34. William W. Adams, "Student Political Leadership at Kansas University" (typewritten M.A. thesis, University of Kansas, 1954), 92, 94, 99, 143–144; *Kansan*, April 11, 1934.

35. *Ibid.*, December 1, 1942.

36. *Ibid.*, December 10, 13, 1942, March 28, 30, 1943; Raymond Nichols to Deane W. Malott, February 24, 1943, UA; MBR, October 9, 1943.

37. Adams, "Student Political Leadership," 94–96; *Independent Kan-Do*, October, 1945–May 7, 1947; *The Jayhawker, 1960*, 291.

38. "Grades for 1937–1938," January 3, 1939, UA; "KU Today," *University of Kansas Newsletter*, 65 (August 28, 1965), 5.

39. See Will W. Willoughby, "A Study of the Extra-Curricular Activities of Senior Students in the University of Kansas" (typewritten MS, June 1, 1931, UA).

40. *Sour Owl*, 4–37 (March 16, 1917–Confidential Issue, 1956); *Bitter Bird*, 1–5 (April, 1946–Spring, 1950), especially 1 (April, 1946), 4, and 3 (Spring, 1948), 14–15; *Kansan*, May 1, 1950; *Squat*, 1–11 (1955–1958).

41. *upstream*, 1–6 (February, 1949–April-May, 1954).

42. Frank Strong to Guy Potter Benton, October 4, 1912, and Strong to George Banta, November 17, 1913 (copies), UA.

43. *Dove*, April 29, 1925.

44. William Allen White, *The Autobiography of William Allen White* (New York, 1946), 595.

45. Clipping from *Banta's Greek Exchange*, July 1949, pp. 173–175, in "Deane Waldo Malott, Chancellor of the University of Kansas" (scrapbook, UA).

46. William R. Butler, "An Analytical Study of Factors Associated with Scholastic Achievement in High and Low Achieving Fraternities" (typewritten Ed.D. thesis, University of Kansas, 1956), especially 84–85, 87–89, 94, 96–99, 109–114, 126–131, 137–139, 149–152, 191–192.

47. *Ibid.*, 2; Vincent Meyer, ed., *Fraternities at K.U.* (Lawrence, 1959), 9–10; "KU Today," *University of Kansas Newsletter*, 65 (August 28, 1965), 5. The sororities had better scholastic averages than the fraternities. In 1962–1963 twelve of the thirteen sororities exceeded the all-University average of 1.47; the all-sorority average was 1.81. By contrast only eight of twenty-seven fraternities surpassed the all-University average, and the all-fraternity average was 1.46. *Annual Report of the Director of Admissions and Registrar for 1962–1963, the University of Kansas* (Lawrence, 1963), 37–40.

48. Theta Nu Epsilon to Ernest H. Lindley, January 17, 1922, UA; *Kansan*, February 23, 1923, September 22, 1952; Leonard F. Parkinson to author, February. 1961.

CHAPTER 32

1. Arthur G. Canfield, "Student Life in K.S.U.," Wilson Sterling, ed., *Quarter-Centennial History of the University of Kansas, 1866–1891. With Portraits of Chancellors* (Topeka, 1891), 152–154; *Announcement and By-Laws of the Athletic Association of the University of Kansas* (Lawrence, 1894), 3–4, 7–8; *The Kansas Kikkabe. Published Annually by the Kansas Kikkabe Company* (Lawrence, 1882), 64; *The Helianthus (Annuus) Published from the State University of Kansas. 1889* (Lawrence, 1889), 77–78.

2. *University Courier*, March 26, 1884; *Kansas Review*, 5 (March, 1884), 202; *Announcement and By-Laws of the Athletic Association*, 4–5; JBR, April 8, 1884; Canfield, "Student Life," Sterling, ed., *Quarter-Centennial History*, 152–153, 157.

3. Minutes of Faculty Meetings (MS, UA), December 11, 1889; *University Review*, 11 (December, 1889), 123; *University Kansan*, December 20, 1889.

4. Charles S. Gleed, "Colonel John J. McCook, LL.D.," *University Review*, 12 (June, 1891), 195–197; RBR, 1890, p. 39; J. Howard Compton, "The Building of the University of Kansas" (typewritten M.Arch. thesis, University of Kansas, 1932), 33;

JBR, April 3, October 16, 1891; Francis H. Snow to Charles Robinson, September 26, 1891 (copy), UA.

5. *University Review*, 12 (October, 1890), 58; *Announcement and By-Laws of the Athletic Association*, 7–8; *University Courier*, December 12, 1890.

6. *Ibid.*, December 12, 1890; *University Review*, 12 (January, 1891); William H. H. Piatt and others, "Some Memory Recitals after 50 Years of Things Athletic and Otherwise, '91, to '96, of the 'Gay '90s' at K.U." (typewritten MS, n.d., UA), 1, 61.

7. *Ibid.*, 2–3, 81.

8. Frederick Rudolph, *The American College and University: A History* (New York, 1962), 373–374.

9. *Weekly University Courier*, January 17, 1891; *University Review*, 13 (November, 1891, January, 1892), 75–76, 140.

10. Francis H. Snow to E. A. Clark, February 2, 1892 (copy), UA; *RBR*, 1894, p. 9; Piatt and others, "Some Memory Recitals," 118.

11. *Ibid.*, 61.

12. Francis H. Snow to Hector W. Cowan, January 23, 1894, and Snow to Vernon L. Kellogg, January 30, 1894 (copies), UA; Minutes of Faculty Meetings, January 29, 1894.

13. *Kansas University Weekly*, December 13, 1895.

14. *Ibid.*, August 2, 1897, October 25, 1898; University Council Minutes (MS, UA), October 25, 1898.

15. *Weekly University Courier*, January 29, 1892.

16. R. K. Moody to C. I. Sayre, July 11, 1893, and Moody to S. S. Owen, August 29, 1894 (copies), UA; University Council Minutes, February 3, 1896; *Kansan*, February 17, 1906.

17. *Announcement and By-Laws of the Athletic Association*, 18–23; University Council Minutes, April 5, 9, June 2, 1894.

18. *Ibid.*, February 21, 1895, January 9, February 3, 6, 1896, December 10, 1897.

19. *Ibid.*, December 1, 1898, January 4, 11, April 6, 1899, October 4, 1900; *Kansas University Weekly*, January 14, May 6, 1899.

20. Allison Danzig, *The History of American Football: Its Great Teams, Players, and Coaches* (Englewood Cliffs, 1956), 21–29; Piatt and others, "Some Memory Recitals," 61; Francis H. Snow to A. H. Dooley, December 31, 1894, Snow to Caspar Whitney, December 4, 1896, and Snow to A. S. Draper, January 16, 1897 (copies), UA; Snow to Vernon L. Kellogg, November 19, 1896 (copy), Francis Huntington Snow Correspondence, 1892–1899, UA; University Council Minutes, November 19, 1896.

21. Topeka *Capital*, October 18, November 29, December 5, 7, 1901; *Kansas University Lawyer*, 8 (November, 1901), 6; University Council Minutes, December 4, 1901.

22. Topeka *Capital*, February 17, 1901; *Kansas Lawyer*, 8 (November, 1901), 6, and 8 (December, 1901), 4.

23. JBR, July 21, 1903; Frank Strong to Thaddeus L. Bolton, November 20, 1903 (copy), Bolton to Strong, December 7, 1903, Strong to Harold S. Weeks, March 21, April 4, 12, 1904 (copies), and Weeks to Strong, April 2, 8, 1904 (copies), UA.

24. *Kansan*, May 20, 1905; JBR, September 15, 1905.

25. ? to the President of Washburn College, January 23, 1901 (copy), UA; University Council Minutes, April 3, 4, 1901; *Topeka Conference Athletic Rules: Adopted February, 1902 by the Kansas College Athletic Conference.—Revised January 10, 1903.—Revised February 6, 1905* (n.p., n.d.).

26. Athletic Board of the University of Kansas, Minutes of Meetings, 1905–1913 (MS, UA), November 13, 1905, May 14, 26, 1906; Frank Strong to E. Benjamin An-

drews, September 18, 1906 (copy), Strong to R. H. Jesse, September 19, 1906 (copy), Clark W. Hetherington to Strong, March 2, December 20, 1906, UA; University Council Minutes, February 28, March 21, 1907. Iowa, Missouri, Kansas, and Washington were the charter members. Nebraska had representatives at the Kansas City meeting, but was not a charter member. Along with Iowa State College and Drake University, Nebraska was elected to membership.

27. Danzig, *History of American Football*, 29–42; Edwin E. Slosson to Frank Strong, December 29, 1905, UA.

28. *Western School Journal*, 25 (January, 1909), 44; Frank Strong, *What the University of Kansas Ought to Stand For: Opening Address to the Students of the University of Kansas, September 25, 1910* (Lawrence, 1910), 5–6.

29. Frank Strong to W. C. Lansdon, November 16, 1909 (copy), Lansdon to Strong, November 19, 1909, and Strong to H. E. Bruce, December 4, 1909 (copy), UA.

30. William Allen White to Scott Hopkins, June 7, 1907, Walter Johnson, ed., *Selected Letters of William Allen White, 1899–1943* (New York, 1947), 83–85; Walter Johnson, *William Allen White's America* (New York, 1947), 216; J. Willis Gleed, "Inter-Collegiate Football," n.d., but 1911 or earlier, J. Willis Gleed Papers, RHC.

31. JBR, January 28, 1910.

32. *Kansan*, March 31, April 5, 9, 1910; Athletic Board Minutes, April 4, 1910; *Kansas University Lawyer*, 16 (April, 1910), 296.

33. *Kansan*, April 9, 1910; Frank Strong to the Board of Regents, April 13, 1910 (copy), UA; JBR, April 18, 1910; William Allen White to Frank Strong, April 14, 1910, Johnson, ed., *Selected Letters of William Allen White*, 109–110.

34. JBR, April 28, 1910.

35. Athletic Board Minutes, December 13, 19, 1911; JBR, January 18, February 6, March 20, June 4, 1912; Frank Strong to Arthur Mosse, June 14, 1912 (copy), UA.

36. JBR, July 3, 1912; Frank Strong, "The Control and Management of Athletics," November 10, 1913, Frank Strong Papers, UA; Frank Strong to James Naismith, February 20, 1914 (copy), UA.

37. *University of Kansas Scores in Major Sports, 1886–1932: Football, Basketball, Baseball, Track* (Lawrence, 1932), 6; *Graduate Magazine of the University of Kansas*, 37 (January, 1939), 11.

38. Kansas City, Mo., *Star*, January 18, 1956; Lawrence *Journal-World*, January 12, 1956.

39. *Kansan*, December 1, 10, 1913; Frank Strong to Charles P. Woodbury, December 19, 1913 (copy), UA.

40. E. M. Boddington and O. Q. Claflin, Jr., to Forrest C. Allen n.d., *Kansan*, October 21, 1927.

41. *Ibid.*, November 28, December 4, 10, 13, 1927, November 2, 1928; Athletic Board Minutes, December 13, 1927; Physical Education Corporation Minutes (MS, UA), May 29, 1928.

42. *Dove*, November 21, 1919; notarized statement signed by W. W. Davis, November 6, 1930, UA.

43. Notarized statement signed by James Bausch, November 14, 1930, UA.

44. Notarized statement signed by Phil Borello, November 15, 1930, UA.

45. "A Statement Covering the Athletic Situation in the 'Big Six' Conference as Viewed by George C. Shaad, Faculty Representative of the University of Kansas," signed by Shaad, November 15, 1930, and Minutes of the Meeting of the Faculty Representatives of the Missouri Valley Intercollegiate Athletic Association, Held at Columbia, Missouri, October 24, 1930, signed by S. W. Reeves, UA.

46. Conference of the Governing Heads, Faculty Representatives, and Athletic Directors of the Missouri Valley Intercollegiate Athletic Association, signed by T. N. Metcalf, November 28, 1930, and George C. Shaad to Members of the Athletic Staff at the University of Kansas, December 13, 1930 (copies), UA; *Kansan*, October 24, 26, 27, 29, November 3, 10, 16, December 1, 2, 3, 4, 5, 7, 1930, March 27, 1931; Lawrence *Journal-World*, October 29, November 17, 1930; Kansas City, Mo., *Times*, November 29, 1930; Kansas City, Mo., *Star*, December 6, 1930.

47. *Graduate Magazine*, 31 (October, 1932), 7.

48. *Ibid.*, 31 (October, 1932), 7; Alf M. Landon to Ernest H. Lindley, October 18, 1934, UA.

49. MBR, November 27, 1935.

50. *Kansan*, October 6, 7, 8, 1936.

51. *Ibid.*, October 9, 14, December 1, 2, 1936; MBR, December 9, 1936; John R. Malone to Ernest H. Lindley, December 19, 1936, with results of questionnaire, UA; *Graduate Magazine*, 35 (December, 1936), 8.

52. MBR, December 9, 28, 1936, January 2, March 1, 8, April 7, 1937, December 5, 21, 1938; *Kansan*, April 8, 1937, December 4, 8, 1938.

53. JBR, June 7, 1898; Jack G. Hammig, "A Historical Sketch of Doctor James Naismith" (typewritten M.S. thesis, University of Kansas, 1962), 1–3; James Naismith, *Basketball: Its Origins and Development* (New York, 1941), 32–57.

54. *Kansas University Weekly*, February 4, 1899.

55. *University of Kansas Scores in Major Sports*, 8–13; *University of Kansas Basketball Records, Lawrence, Kansas, U.S.A., March 27, 1936: Invention of the Game, Kansas Personalities; the "Rock-Chalk" Yell, Scores, 1899–1936* (Lawrence, 1936), 7–9; *Kansan*, March 29, 1950; *Graduate Magazine*, 34 (December, 1935), 5; *ibid.*, 40 (February, 1942), 7; Forrest C. Allen, *Coach "Phog" Allen's Sports Stories for You and Youth* (Lawrence, 1947), 161, 175; Kansas City, Mo., *Star*, November 22, 1931; *Jayhawker, 1908*, page unnumbered.

56. Allen, *Coach "Phog" Allen's Sports Stories*, 175; Kansas City, Mo., *Star*, November 22, 1931; *UKC*, 1919–1920, p. 14; *Graduate Magazine*, 40 (February, 1942), 7; W. O. Hamilton to Frank Strong, June 5, 1919, ? to Strong, August 23, 1919, and Strong to the Board of Administration, September 5, 1919 (copy), UA; MBA, September 19, 1919.

57. *Kansan*, February 17, November 9, 1956; Kansas City, Mo., *Times*, March 29, 1951, March 15, April 3, 1956; Lawrence *Journal-World*, May 11, 1946, March 30, 1956, November 7, 1957, May 10, 1966; Sports News Service, *Basketball at the University of Kansas*, 1956–57, p. 4; Kansas City, Mo., *Star*, April 3, 1956; Allen, *Better Basketball: Technique, Tactics and Tales* (New York, 1937), and *My Basketball Bible* (Kansas City, Mo., 1924).

58. *Time*, 48 (October 14, 1946), 66; New York *Times*, January 7, 9, 1947, January 11, 1948, January 15, 1950, January 12, 13, 14, 1951.

59. The Missouri Valley Intercollegiate Athletic Association, better known as the Big Six, had been organized officially on May 19, 1928. The original members were Kansas, Missouri, Nebraska, the Kansas Agricultural College, Iowa State, and Oklahoma. With the addition of Colorado the Big Six became the Big Seven on December 1, 1947; on June 1, 1957, with the addition of Oklahoma State, the Big Seven became the Big Eight. *The Big Eight Conference Football Record Book 1964* (Kansas City, Mo., 1964), 9.

60. Missouri Valley Intercollegiate Athletic Association, *Rules and Regulations Governing Athletics*, 1951, pp. 12–13. In 1952 the NCAA refused to disapprove the

athletic subsidies adopted by the several conferences. New York *Times*, January 11, 12, 13, 1952.

61. Quoted in James K. Hitt, "The Sixth Annual Principal-Freshman Conference at the University of Kansas," *University of Kansas Bulletin of Education*, 9 (February, 1955), 40.

CHAPTER 33

1. W. Clarke Wescoe, *Chancellor's Inaugural Address, September 19, 1960* (Lawrence, 1960), 1.

2. University Senate Minutes (MS, UA), October 6, 1958, Professor Maloney has very kindly allowed me to see and use the address that he delivered.

3. University Senate Minutes, October 4, 1960; William J. Argersinger, Jr., and others, "The Place of Research in the University: Report of an Ad Hoc Committee, June, 1962" (mimeographed, in possession of author), 71.

4. *Ibid.*, 1–8, 16–17.

5. *Ibid.*, 19, 50.

6. *Ibid.*, 4, 5. In January, 1964, the Senate debated the relation between teaching and research, but reached no conclusion. The debate arose from a report by the Committee on Instructional Staff Time Allocation in Areas of Research, Teaching and Other Duties. University Senate Minutes, January 7, 1964.

7. Nancy Gallup and Sara Paretsky, "Associated Women Sycophants or Frailty, Thy Name Is the Women's Program," *University Review*, 3 (March, 1967), 3–4.

8. George F. Zook, Lotus D. Coffman, and A. R. Mann, *Report of a Survey of the State Institutions of Higher Learning in Kansas*, Department of the Interior, Bureau of Education, Bulletin, 1923, no. 40 (Washington, 1923), 30–33; *BRUK*, 1926, p. 33; University Senate Minutes, May 7, 1940.

9. George B. Smith, "Who Would Be Eliminated? A Study of Selective Admission to College," *Kansas Studies in Education*, 7 (December, 1956), 5–6.

10. *Ibid.*, 1–28; George B. Smith, "Who Would Be Eliminated?" in *The Coming Crisis in the Selection of Students for College Entrance* (Washington, 1960), 29–37.

11. "Notes on a Meeting between Chancellor Franklin Murphy and the Executive Committee of the American Association of University Professors, University of Kansas Chapter, March 29, 1955, by E. Jackson Baur" (copy), American Association of University Professors, University of Kansas Chapter, Papers, UA.

12. University Senate Minutes, May 14, 1963.

13. Otto E. Domian and others, *Comprehensive Educational Survey of Kansas Prepared for Kansas Legislative Council, Topeka, Kansas, March, 1960*, 5 vols. (Topeka, 1960), 1: iii–vi, 1–10.

14. *Ibid.*, 3: 75, 123.

15. *Ibid.*, 3: 195–198, 200–202, 5: 180.

16. *Ibid.*, 3: 213, 218, 219, 1: 44, 46.

17. *Ibid.*, 3: 211, 212–218.

18. *Report on the Educational Survey as Submitted to the 1961 Legislature by the Kansas Legislative Council* (Topeka, 1960), 22–28.

19. MBR, September 23, 1961, January 15, July 20, 1962; Alvin E. Eurich and others, *Kansas Plans for the Next Generation: A Report on Higher Education in Kansas to the Board of Regents by a Panel of Advisors* (Topeka, 1962), page headed "Members of the Panel." The panel had the assistance of twelve consultants, among them Chancellor Herman B Wells of Indiana University, Vice-President John

Elmendorf of Brown University, and Paul Woodring, editor of the Education Supplement of the *Saturday Review*.

20. *KHJ*, 1961, pp. 208–209, 330, 406; *KSJ*, 1961, pp. 313, 339.
21. MBR, November 9, 1962.
22. Eurich and others, *Kansas Plans*, 1, 5.
23. *Ibid.*, 7.
24. *Ibid.*, 8–9.
25. *Ibid.*, 9–10, 26–29.
26. *Ibid.*, 30–34.
27. *Ibid.*, 35–39.
28. *Ibid.*, 12, 17–21.
29. *Ibid.*, 43–54, 19.
30. *Ibid.*, 22–24.
31. *Ibid.*, 41.
32. *Ibid.*, 4, 5.

A Note on the Sources

Except for a few items—particularly the minutes of the faculty meetings of the several schools and some personal papers—all of the major sources, both published and unpublished, for this history are now (1973) in the University Archives in the Kenneth E. Spencer Research Library at the University of Kansas in Lawrence. It is there that everyone interested in the material that I have used, or in reading further into the University's history, must begin his investigations. In the years from 1960 to 1966, however, when I completed most of my research, the minutes of the Board of Regents, the Board of Administration, and the University Council and Senate were in a closet in the chancellor's office, and most of the manuscripts of that office—a collection of something over two hundred thousand letters—along with many other records were stored casually in cartons and cabinets in a vault underneath Strong Hall. Although they were roughly classified by subject and year, the letters and records were in no sense a well-arranged archive, and thus proved most difficult and time-consuming to use. To make rechecking possible, my research assistants and I worked out a crude index-identification system for each item.

Because John M. Nugent, the University Archivist, and his staff are now in the process of arranging and classifying those materials—and many others formerly scattered around the University—my own system would prove of little use to the reader. Hence I have identified unpublished materials in the University Archives only according to their authors, recipients, titles, dates, and the like, followed by a simple UA to indicate their general location. While this brief reference is far from ideal, everyone interested in locating any items that I have used will find that with the remarkable assistance and enthusiasm of Mr. Nugent and his staff, all things are retrievable. The physical facilities of the Archives, moreover—like those of the rest of the Spencer Research Library—are truly splendid. In every respect the Archives are a delight, and I encourage every reader to visit them.

Except where otherwise credited, the photographs in this book are from the University Archives, which contain thousands of other pictures as well. There are two superb and amusing pictorial histories (now out of print) of the University by Robert A. Taft: *Across the Years on Mount Oread* (Lawrence, 1941) and *The Years on Mount Oread* (Lawrence, 1955). Among KU aficionados they should be much more widely known than they are.

Index

social sciences: development of, at K.U., 325
social sciences building, 236, 540
Social Science Series, 456
social service: and university ideal, 73. *See also* state-service work
Social Service Department, 605
societies and clubs, 202–3, 208
Society for the Promotion of Engineering Education, 289, 582
Sociology, Department of: development of, 326–27; war-related courses in, 380; its *Morale and the Democratic Community*, 496
Sociology and Economics, Department of, 280–81
Sociology and Political Economy, Department of, 326
sororities: origins of, at K.U., 202; growth of, 210–11; student government movement in, 216; Strong's attitude toward, 216–17; regulation of, suggested, 465; racial discrimination in, 628, 629, 632; in twentieth century, 642–44; scholastic averages in, 764 n.47; mentioned, 635
Sour Owl, 633, 636, 640–41
South Carolina, University of, 13
South Dakota, 331, 344
Southwick, Clarence T., 206
Spaeth, Sigmund, 591
Spake, LaVerne B., regent, 523, 745 n.41
Spangler, William C., regent, 162, 169, 185, 221, 231, 481
speech clinic, 560
Spencer, Charles W., regent, 412, 474
Spoerri Collection, 600
Sponsler, Alfred L., 343
Spooner, William B., 105–6, 181
Spooner Library: completed, 182–83; reception at, 223; conditions in, 301, 424; mentioned, 380, 428. *See also* Spooner-Thayer Art Museum
Spooner-Thayer Art Museum, 504, 592
Spotts, Ralph, 261
Spring, Rev. Leverett W., 146, 156, 157
Sproul, Robert G., 497
Squat, 641
stadium: needed, 236; movement for, 415–16; construction of, 416–17; students housed beneath, 504; as World War I memorial, 513
Stadium Day, 416–17
Stafford *Courier*, 435
Stanley, William E., governor: speech by, 223; his regent appointments, 231; urges single constitution, 330

Stanton, John F.: designs Law Building, 238; designs engineering buildings, 239
Starrett, Rev. William A., regent, 31
State Board of Bar Examiners, 611
State Board of Education: and teacher certification, 273; curriculum requirements of, 275; takes over accrediting, 309; membership of, 309; admissions policy decision by, 490; certification of, 570, 571, 575, 593; mentioned, 679–80
State Board of Health: and state water survey, 257; Medical School cooperates with, 271; and influenza epidemic, 377; and 1949 legislative campaign, 607; mentioned, 256
State Board of Pharmacy, 587
state capital, 18, 19, 21
State Chamber of Commerce, Agricultural Council, 607
State Commission of Higher Education: formed, 343; function of, 343–44
State Editorial Association, 229
State Geological Survey: as state service, 252; and K.U. engineering offering, 471; in Lindley Hall, 485, 508; mentioned, 521
state geologist, 254
State Library, 261
State Medical Society. *See* Kansas Medical Society
State Normal School at Emporia. *See* Emporia, Kansas State Teachers College of
State Penitentiary, 18, 368
state-service work: Strong's ideas on, 243–44, 255; the Wisconsin Idea of, 255–56; research and consulting, 256–59; Stubbs's attitude toward, 259–60; role of, 261–62; and division of state schools, 336; as ideal university goal, 353–54, 388–89; Lindley's support for, 399–400; needed, 456; overemphasis on, to be avoided, 470; funds for, cut, 511; of Education School, 573; of Business School, 577; mentioned, 220
State Service Work, Division of, 363
State Supreme Court, 181, 187, 410
State Teachers Association. *See* Kansas State Teachers Association
State Universities Center (Wichita), 683
Stauffer, Oscar S.: appointed regent, 474, 745 n.41; mentioned, 475, 517, 522, 523, 524
Steele, Rev. John A., regent, 692–93 n.7
Stene, Edwin O., 515
Stephens, Kate: and Byron Caldwell Smith, 56, 97; joins faculty, 56; dis-